PR 5238 .P3
Packer, Lona Mosk.
Christina Rossetti

CHRISTINA ROSSETTI
del. SEPTEMBER 1866

LONA MOSK PACKER

CHRISTINA ROSSETTI

[redacted]
3506
B R529p

UNIVERSITY OF CALIFORNIA PRESS
BERKELEY AND LOS ANGELES
1963

PR
5238
.P3

University of California Press
Berkeley and Los Angeles, California

Cambridge University Press
Cambridge, England

© 1963 by The Regents of the University of California
Library of Congress Catalog Card Number: 63-21221
Printed in the United States of America

To Bertha W. Mosk

PREFACE

One of the few great women poets of the nineteenth century writing in the English language, Christina Rossetti has up to the present remained a vague and enigmatic figure. The sense of mystery enshrouding her is due partly to her own reserve and partly to the fact that there has been written thus far no satisfactory biography of her. She has come down to us interpreted solely by her brother and editor, William Michael Rossetti, whose views have been accepted uncritically by all Christina's biographers, including Mackenzie Bell, author of the first "official" biography (1898), the source of subsequent works about her.

Since Christina's centenary celebration in 1930, which produced biographies by Mary F. Sandars, Dorothy Stuart, and Eleanor W. Thomas, only two full-length studies have been published. One is Marya Zaturenska's biography (1949). The other, Margaret Sawtell's biographical study (1955), is chiefly focused upon Christina's religious development as revealed in her poetry. But these and other writers have relied exclusively upon printed material, principally the publications of Bell and W. M. Rossetti. Although the latter wrote no book-length life of his sister, his brief biographical sketch in the "Memoir" to his edition of her *Poetical Works* (1904) and his chapter about her in his autobiographical *Some Reminiscences,* as well as the comments and information regarding her scattered throughout his works, constitute the source upon which her biographers have drawn.

A need, then, exists for a fresh biography with more rigorous standards, one based upon original research, which utilizes modern scholarly techniques and insights but which at the same time aims at readability and sustained narrative interest. This biography attempts to meet such a need. Although it does not presume to say the last word about Christina, it is fully documented and uses much unpublished material not heretofore available to previous biographers.

When some years ago I began the study of Christina Rossetti, I became increasingly aware, as I read, of the discrepancy between her inner world, of which we get glimpses in her poetry, and the existing biographical

assumptions about her. Nevertheless I accepted and shared the prevailing views until the day I came upon the poem *Parting After Parting* and William Michael's comments about it in a note (see my text, pp. 122-123). This clue led to further investigation, and eventually I was brought to the realization that the traditional pattern required careful scrutiny, with error by no means ruled out. It was, then, the poet herself who first pointed the way to the new interpretation of her life presented in the following pages.

According to the traditional biographical line, Christina refused for religious reasons to marry the two men who loved her, James Collinson, Pre-Raphaelite painter, who proposed when she was eighteen, and the scholarly Charles Bagot Cayley, who made his offer when she was thirty-six. But she wrote her most impassioned love poetry during the intervening years of her womanhood. It is unlikely that a poet as subjective as Christina would conceive this poetry in an emotional vacuum; consequently, we can only surmise that it was addressed to someone who does not appear on the record.

The evidence I have uncovered points to the name of William Bell Scott, painter, poet, and intimate friend of Christina's two brothers. There is a very good reason why his name did not appear on the record in the capacity of a lover: he was married. But, although Christina's lifelong friendship with Scott is a recognized fact, needing no substantiation, its emotional intensity has been overlooked by previous biographers. My own interpretation of this friendship as a love relationship may be regarded as a tentative hypothesis, but one which solves many of the existing biographical problems and provides a clue to the puzzle of Christina's elusive personality. In my view, the conflict engendered by her "predilection" (William Rossetti's word) for Scott not only affected her creative capacity, leaving a deep mark on her poetry, but crucially shaped her life, developed her character, and finally made her into the woman she eventually became.

Although the factual events of daily life are herein given the necessary emphasis, my concern with what William Rossetti has called the "deeper internal currents" of his sister's life is what chiefly distinguishes my biography from its predecessors, for it is in these subterranean depths that the source and mainspring of Christina's poetic energy may be found.

Such an exploration into the intimate structure of another human personality, particularly one so complex and delicately organized as that of a poet, is an audacious though a rewarding adventure: one learns to proceed with caution and humbleness toward a truth which unlike the truths of science is seldom factual, seldom supported by clearly documented evidence, and never conclusive. In advancing my hypothesis, which I believe approximates the truth, I have supported it by a detailed and carefully constructed edifice of indirect evidence in the hope that

when the small pieces of the puzzle are all fitted together, the total design, like that in mosaic work, will be revealed. For this and other reasons, I have not considered it necessary to qualify every statement made in the course of my narrative or to supply documentary "proof" for every speculation hazarded.

A word more remains to be said about the value of biography to the general reader. It is a truism that a life fully lived and valiantly confronted has a quality of universal significance for all who still have a life to live. Although the sequence of circumstances within each individual time pattern may differ, the basic human problems in a life are perennial. To set them forth and show how the more gifted among us have faced them is, as I see it, the biographer's main business.

But this is not all. The aesthetic requirements of the genre oblige the biographer to treat his subject with the imaginative perception and the discipline of the literary artist. Like the latter, he must select freely, structure and arrange his material, emphasizing this and subordinating that according to his responsible judgment, in order to give the final product the aesthetic integrity we expect of any work of art. As a work of art, then, a biography should present a complete life, finished and lived, through which, despite the accidental events and irrational impulses which provide its texture, a shaping design of some sort can be perceived.

In 1883, believing Theodore Watts-Dunton was going to undertake the life of Dante Gabriel—which he never did—Christina told him that when he touched "on painful subjects . . . or any other point, our only desire will be that the simple truth shall be told with that tenderness which you certainly will not separate from it."

I have tried to follow her wish in this respect and to write the story of her own life with truth and with tenderness.

L. M. P.

March, 1963

ACKNOWLEDGMENTS

Gratitude is a commonplace in acknowledgments, but it is with a real sense of pleasure that I offer here the slight recompense within my power for the encouragement and cordial assistance given me by both friends and strangers in Europe and America. Although at times I have also been tempted to add anti-acknowledgments, should I have done so, the list, fortunately, would have been short. I am thankful to state that many more people helped than hindered me, and the work owes much to their kindness.

First, let me salute with affection and gratitude the Rossetti family, to whose generous sympathy I am greatly indebted. Though it is true that this work could not have been written without their active aid, it is in no sense an "official" biography. Even when their views did not coincide with mine, they offered no interference. For the positions taken, I alone am responsible. I am nonetheless deeply obligated to Christina's relatives, both as a family and as individuals.

I owe particular thanks to Christina's nieces, Mrs. Helen Rossetti Angeli and the late Signora Olivia Rossetti Agresti of Rome, for receiving me graciously when I came to them, a stranger, for giving me the benefit of their personal recollections of their aunt, and finally, for placing at my disposal family documents and correspondence. I wish to thank for friendship and hospitality as well as invaluable assistance Mr. and Mrs. Harold Rossetti, Mr. and Mrs. Roderick O'Connor, Mrs. Imogene Rossetti Dennis, and Mr. and Mrs. Oliver Rossetti. To this list I would like to add a name not belonging to the Rossetti family, that of Miss Evelyn Courtney-Boyd of Penkill Castle.

I want to express my special appreciation for the unfailing support and consistent encouragement given me by Jack Adamson, Dean of the College of Letters and Science at the University of Utah. I am likewise grateful for aid to the Rev. William Y. Kingston of Christ Church, Albany Street, London, who kindly gave me access to the church archives; to William F. Fredeman for valuable advice and suggestions; to Sally Allen for patient and efficient secretarial assistance; and to the follow-

ing persons: A. M. Allchin, E. E. Bissell, Iris Bonham, Bradford Booth, C. L. Cline, the late Sir Sidney Cockerell, Grace Coltman, Richard Curll, Joseph Dellon, Mr. and Mrs. John Dickinson, Harold Folland, Philip Gerber, David Gould, Eileen Grady, David Bonnell Green, E. L. Griggs, Margot Hahn, Derek Hudson, Virginia B. Jacobsen, Kenneth Johnson, Hugh Kenner, Eugene le Mire, Naomi Lewis, Lady Rosalie Mander, Morgan Odell, James E. Packer, Count Goffredo Polidori, Sarah Robertson, Karen Russell, A. H. Verstage, Milton Voigt, Louis Zucker, and many others.

For help in translating Christina Rossetti's series of Italian love poems I am particularly indebted to Charles Speroni, and for additional assistance to Donald Heiney, Sylvana Beroni, Dino Galvani, and Andrée M. Barnett.

Librarians everywhere deserve both my gratitude and my admiration. Among those to whom I am obliged are R. W. Hunt, Keeper of Western Manuscripts at the Bodleian, and his staff; Miss M. L. Hoyle and staff of the Department of Manuscripts, and the staff of the North Room, at the British Museum; S. E. Overal, Borough Librarian of Walthamstow, London; E. Jeffcott of the Highgate Library, London; the late L. K. Kirkpatrick of the University of Utah Library; Foster M. Palmer of the Harvard College Library; Stephen T. Riley, Director of the Massachusetts Historical Society; Elizabeth Fry and staff at the Huntington Library, San Marino, Calif.; and Ann Bowden and staff (particularly Clara Sitter) of the Humanities Research Center, University of Texas. I also wish to thank W. A. Taylor, Borough Librarian, Saint Pancras Public Libraries, London, and M. Price and staff of its Euston Road Branch; the Boston and Los Angeles Public Libraries; and the libraries at the Universities of California, London, Texas, and Utah particularly.

I am grateful to the firm of Macmillan & Co., London, for giving me permission to use the unpublished correspondence in their archives, and to Lovat Dickson and Timothy Farmiloe for special assistance in making it available to me. I am likewise grateful to the Pennsylvania Historical Society, the Wilmington Society of the Fine Arts, Delaware, and the Manuscript Committee of the Humanities Research Center at the University of Texas, for permitting me to reproduce material from their collections. I wish to thank *Notes & Queries, The Times Literary Supplement, Time & Tide, The University of Toronto Quarterly, Victorian Studies, The Western Humanities Review,* and the editors of *Collier's Encyclopedia* for granting permission to reprint material which originally appeared in their publications. I desire also to express thanks to Cecil Y. Lang and the Yale University Press for permitting me to reproduce letters from *The Swinburne Letters* and to Mrs. Janet Camp Troxell and the Harvard University Press for permission to reprint letters from *The Three Rossettis.*

Finally I am happy to acknowledge my deep indebtedness to the American Philosophical Society and the American Council of Learned Societies for the generous grants which made possible my two years of study in Europe and subsequently, and to the University of Utah Research Fund for assistance which enabled me to bring my work to a conclusion. I should further like to express my appreciation to Lucie E. N. Dobbie, Executive Editor of the University of California Press, for encouragement and valuable suggestions, and to Grace Wilson Buzaljko, also of the University of California Press, for editorial advice.

L. M. P.

A WORD TO THE READER

Unless otherwise indicated, it may be assumed that the place of publication is London and that the manuscripts cited are holograph. Most of the unpublished poems and deleted stanzas from published poems quoted in my text are from Christina's seventeen manuscript notebooks (1842–1866), of which nine are in the Bodleian Library, Oxford, seven in the Ashley Library at the British Museum, and one in the possession of Christina's grandniece, Mrs. Imogene Rossetti Dennis. The only existing reproduction of the MS text is Miss G. M. Hatton's unpublished edition of the early poems (B. Litt. thesis, St. Hilda's, Oxford, February 16, 1955). With a few exceptions—to be noted herein—the unpublished poems in the notebooks are listed in Appendix B to the *Poetical Works of Christina Georgina Rossetti, with Memoir and Notes,* ed. W. M. Rossetti (1904). Unless stated otherwise, all quotations from Christina's published poetry are drawn from this source—cited as *Works.*

In reproducing the poetry for the purpose of biography my practice has been to follow whenever possible the original punctuation, diction, and word order in the MS notebooks and holograph MSS. Later revisions, whether made by Christina herself or by William in editing her work, often fail to have the impact or to convey the freshness of the original. In some instances a change in punctuation alters not only the rhythm but even the meaning of a poem. (See my article, "Christina Rossetti's *Songs in a Cornfield:* A Misprint Uncorrected," *Notes & Queries* [March, 1962], n.s. 9:97–100.)

Indented quotations from unpublished sources, whether poems or letters, are set off by asterisks. But no asterisks are used when such unpublished material is woven into the text of the narrative, for in such instances it is impractical to isolate the unpublished from the published material.

In letters, words overscored in the original are indicated by pointed brackets.

Since completing this work, I have published some of the material herein cited as unpublished, generally in learned journals. The manu-

script letters in the Macmillan archives, which I quote in my text and notes, have now been published as a complete group (Dante Gabriel's and William Michael's letters as well as Christina's) under the title *The Rossetti-Macmillan Letters,* University of California Press (1963). They are occasionally referred to in my notes, particularly when I believe the reader would want fuller information than is provided therein.

Exact dating of the poetry after the last of the notebooks (1866) is not always possible, though in some cases an approximate date can be given. In coördinating the events and the later poetry, I have in general endeavored to remain within the broad chronological grouping of Christina's verse, following William Rossetti's editorial principle of dating the poems after 1866 by their publication in new collections. But with the precise dates so vague, I did not find it advisable to restrict myself to the kind of chronological organization which was feasible with the carefully dated poems in the notebooks. For example, a poem marked by William "Before 1893" means that it appeared in print in the 1893 *Verses,* but it may have been written at any time during the 1870's or the 1880's. Likewise, the poems William dates "Before 1882" could have been written between the publication of *Prince's Progress* (1866) and *A Pageant* (1881). In general, however, those he marks "Before 1886" would include new poems written after *A Pageant* but before the publication of *Time Flies* (1885), and those he dates "Before 1893" would have been composed after 1885 but before publication of the *Verses.* The problem becomes increasingly complex when we realize that early poems frequently appear for the first time in late volumes and stanzas from youthful poems are occasionally transposed to those with a later dateline. Consequently I have felt free to dip into the body of Christina's verse for the last twenty-eight years of her life without binding myself to conjectural dates which in most instances could serve no useful purpose.

CONTENTS

ILLUSTRATIONS

Crayon portrait of William Bell Scott by Dante Gabriel Rossetti, 1852. Courtesy of Miss Evelyn Courtney-Boyd. Photograph by John H. Murray, Girvan.

Manuscript pages from Christina's notebooks: *A Nightmare* (September 12, 1857), *Goodbye* (June 15, 1858), and fragments. Ashley MS 1364. Courtesy of the Trustees of the British Museum.

Manuscript pages from Christina's notebooks: two *Sing-Song* poems (1870) and excerpts from *Look on This Picture* (July 12, 1856). Ashley MS 1371. Courtesy of the Trustees of the British Museum.

Self-portrait of William Bell Scott, 1868. Copyright: The National Galleries of Scotland. Photograph by Annan, Glasgow.

William Michael Rossetti photographed by Julia Margaret Cameron. Courtesy of Mrs. Helen Rossetti Angeli.

Penkill Castle near Girvan, Ayrshire. Courtesy of Miss Evelyn Courtney-Boyd. Photograph by John H. Murray, Girvan.

Christina Rossetti, 1863. Courtesy of Mrs. Helen Rossetti Angeli.

Christina, Maria, Frances, and Dante Gabriel Rossetti in the garden of 16 Cheyne Walk, photographed by Lewis Carroll, 1863. Courtesy of Mrs. Helen Rossetti Angeli.

Chalk portrait of Christina by Dante Gabriel Rossetti, 1877. Courtesy of Mrs. Helen Rossetti Angeli. Photograph by B. J. Harris, Oxford.

❋ PRELUDE ❋

"WOOD, HAY, STUBBLE"

1830 AND ANTECEDENTS

With his usual romantic exuberance Gabriele Rossetti announced to his sister-in-law the birth of his youngest child, Christina Georgina, in London, on December 5, 1830:

> You have now another niece, born at the due time, last Sunday night, at ten minutes past three. Her mother suffered a little, and now lies nursing the dear pledge, who, to judge by her appetite, could not be doing better. She is considered to be the very picture of Maria, but more beautiful. She is fairer, and looks, with that round face of hers, like a little moon risen at the full.[1]

Many years later as a grown woman, Christina scribbled on the margin the reproachful comment, "How could my dear Father give such a report? Dearest Mamma had a fearful time with me. CGR." A difficult birth was the prelude to a difficult life; and as Christina took over the responsibility from the mother who had introduced her into the world with suffering, she was to know what it was to have an equally "fearful time" with herself.

The youngest of Rossetti's family of four children, of which the first three were Maria Francesca born in 1827 (the "Maria" of Rossetti's letter), Dante Gabriel in 1828, and William Michael in 1829, Christina in her early years was invariably described in metaphorical language by her father, himself a poet by temperament and profession. At a year and a half she was "our skittish little Christina with those rosy cheeks and sparkling eyes . . . walking all alone about the garden, like a little butterfly among the flowers." At three she was "that angelic little demon of a Christina." At six she and Dante Gabriel were "two storms," in contrast to the "two calms" that were Maria and William.

When she was two years old her inherent tendency to rebel, marked even at that tender age, provided her father with an apt analogy for a political comment. Speaking of the opposition of the House of Lords to the 1832 Reform Bill, Rossetti wrote to a correspondent, "They will make all the outcry and all the resistance that Christina is wont to make

when you force her teeth, medicine-glass in hand; but what is the end of the performance? Christina gulps the medicine." During much of her life she was to resist and to rebel, only to gulp the medicine in the end.

The Rossetti family was the important element in Christina's youth. She grew up in the midst of this large Anglo-Italian family, in a patriarchal nest padded by the nourishing love of extraordinary parents, and warmed by a host of maternal relatives, including a grandfather who privately printed her youthful poems when she was seventeen. Although she was greatly attached to this maternal grandfather, Gaetano Polidori, it was her maternal grandmother, the former Anna Louise Pierce, whom she was generally supposed to resemble. Rossetti himself was struck more than once by the similarity of Christina's "bright, bright eyes" to those of her grandmother; and upon one occasion he expressed the pious hope that she would resemble her grandmother in her "severe virtue" as well. This may have been his politer way of describing what old Polidori bluntly called his wife's "strong and warlike spirit." This spirit, along with the bright eyes and the severe virtue, was Christina's heritage from her grandmother.

In her youth Anna Louise Pierce had been a prim and elegant governess with strict Church of England principles. Her father, a conservative Tory of the old school, was deeply shocked when she conceived a romantic attachment for the Tuscan Gaetano Polidori, a foreigner and a Roman Catholic to boot, a man who after leading an adventurous life as a youth (at one time he was secretary to Count Alfieri, and was in Paris during the fall of the Bastille), came to London and earned a modest living by giving Italian lessons. He belonged, however, to an illustrious and ancient Italian family which since the twelfth century had played a leading role in the history of Orvieto.[2] Among the many distinguished members of the family prominent in Church affairs was Caterina, a sixteenth-century nun who won fame both as a poet and as a religious reformer, being entrusted by Pope Julius III to reorganize and reform the Convent of St. Tomas in Perugia.

Contrary to expectations, the marriage of Gaetano and Anna Louise was successful. Polidori, a vigorous and solid man of immense vitality, prospered; and soon he was able to settle his family at Holmer Green, his country cottage in Buckinghamshire, where during his leisure hours he pursued tastes that ran to literature and Florentine wood carving. After bearing Polidori eight children, four boys and four girls, Anna Louise retired from the duties of domesticity and, conveniently becoming an invalid, took to her bed, from which she did not emerge the remainder of her long life. Nevertheless, from her invalid chamber she efficiently directed the education of her four girls, Eliza, Margaret, Charlotte, and Frances Lavinia, training the last three to become governesses, as she her-

self had been. Eliza was the housekeeper for the family. It was Frances Lavinia who was to become Christina's mother.

Except for Frances and her brother John, the Polidori children (who grew into the aunts and uncles of Christina's childhood) were in no way remarkable. But Dr. John Polidori, Byron's young traveling physician, was a sensational phenomenon in that sober family. Handsome, dashing, brilliant, and dissolute, he led a wild and dissipated life which at the age of twenty-six brought him to a suicide's grave. Although Gaetano Polidori refused to allow his disgraced son's name to be mentioned in his household, Frances secretly cherished the memory of her favorite brother, and when she became the mistress of her own home, she hung John's portrait in the place of honor on the front parlor wall.[3]

Frances Lavinia was twenty-five when she married Gabriele Rossetti, a man some seventeen years her senior. In her bloom she must have been extremely pretty, for she retained her good looks into advanced age. As a young woman, Christina resembled her. Recalling to her father the lovely April of his wife's prime, Christina appeared to him as "her mother's very self in duplicate."

Of the four Polidori daughters, Frances was the only one who had in large measure old Polidori's love for learning and poetry, and his dry wit. In family circles she was known as "a quizz," someone with a satiric appreciation of human foibles, and the ability to express it mordantly. Trained early for the profession of governess, she possessed all the necessary accomplishments and more. She knew French and Italian as well as she did English. The only accomplishment she lacked was the art of dancing, and that was because Polidori disapproved of it as a frivolous pursuit.

At the time Rossetti made her an offer, Frances was also being courted by a Colonel MacGregor, the brother of her employer. Although all her life she was noted for her common sense, she did not display this quality in her choice of a husband. A streak of John Polidori's romanticism must have led her to prefer to the respectable and wealthy Colonel the impoverished Italian political exile, a man who although famed in his own country was unknown in England, and had little but future prospects to offer a young woman. But as Frances was fond of remarking, she had always had "a passion for intellect," and as a young woman had been ambitious to have a husband and children "distinguished for intellect." Once that ambition was gratified, she began to wish for more common sense and less intellect in the family.

II

She might well have been dazzled by Rossetti's romantic past as well as attracted by his intellect and magnetism. This quality of personal

magnetism was undoubtedly responsible for Rossetti's brilliant success as a poet-patriot early in life. The first powerful personage to notice the obscure but gifted son of an Abruzzi blacksmith was the Marchese del Vasto, the great feudal nobleman of the Italian province of Rossetti's birth, who had the youth educated at Naples. During the first quarter of the nineteenth century Rossetti, then a promising young poet and an improviser of considerable ability, flourished in the midst of the murderous political embroilments of Neapolitan life. This was no mean accomplishment in tact, a quality which Christina also possessed, for his position depended to a large extent upon political patronage. Despite the rapid shifts in power, from the Bourbons to the Bonapartes, to the Republicans, and back again to the Bourbons, Rossetti kept himself afloat, first as a librettist to the San Carlo Opera Company, then as Curator of Bronzes and Marbles at the Museum at Naples.

But it was his Republican enthusiasm that brought about his downfall. Concealed during his early years when he was a member of the Carbonari, a secret conspiratorial society with European ramifications, later it was openly proclaimed by him. During the July Revolution of 1820, his improvised ode to liberty, the *Sei pur bella,* became the triumphant theme song of the Constitutionalists. It brought Rossetti both fame as a national poet and political power as a leading member of the newly formed government. With the restoration of the Bourbons to the throne of Naples in 1821, Rossetti was exiled to Malta, from which he fled in 1824 to England.

Even in misfortune Rossetti was always able to attract influential persons who delighted in helping him. His renown as an Italian patriot-poet had in Naples brought him the friendship of a British admiral and his wife, who helped him to escape to Malta. Three years later they transported him from Malta to England in the flagship of the British navy. His gift for improvisation, soon the talk of Malta, secured for him another powerful ally in the person of Coleridge's friend, John Hookham Frere. Together with Charles Lyell, father of the famed geologist and likewise an admirer of Rossetti, Frere made liberal contributions to the support of the Rossetti family throughout Christina's youth.

For practical purposes, London put an end to Rossetti's years of active political life. For the next quarter of a century he was to devote himself to the scholarly pursuits of teaching and writing. Thanks to his influential connections, he was soon able to establish himself as a teacher of Italian in London, and when King's College opened in 1832, he was given the post of Professor of Italian. The remuneration was slight, but the prestige and security were considerable, and so long as his health lasted he was never in want of private pupils whose fees supplemented his meager salary.

His scholarly work on Dante, of which the publication was frequently financed by Frere and Lyell, proved on the whole to be a stupendous blind alley. It was his early interest in Freemasonry which led to the years of abstruse and esoteric research about Dante that absorbed him the remainder of his life. Nominally a Roman Catholic, in practice Rossetti dissented from Catholic doctrine, and, said his son William Michael, "wrote ponderous volumes to prove that Dante, Petrarch and other great writers, were in reality anti-Christians." It is an ironic comment upon Rossetti's work that after his death his wife burned every copy she could find of his *Amor Platonica,* the most anti-Christian of all his tomes.

III

At the time of her marriage, however, Frances Lavinia must have been convinced that she was marrying a conventional Roman Catholic, for two marriage ceremonies were performed, the one by a priest, the other by an Anglican minister. With her mother's example before her, Frances could not have been greatly disturbed by the divergence of her husband's religious views from her own. And the Polidori pattern was apparently bequeathed to Gabriele Rossetti's family, for the two boys, Dante Gabriel and William Michael, like their grandfather and father before them, became irreligious in later years, whereas the two girls, Christina and Maria, remained devout Church of England members throughout their lives. In 1874 Maria, the religious enthusiast of the family, joined an Anglican sisterhood.

In such a heterodox environment, Frances Rossetti serenely gave her children a Protestant religious education at home, teaching them the Catechism, reading to them from the Bible (particularly Revelation, a book that was to influence so strongly Christina's work), and quoting upon occasion Jeremy Taylor, her favorite author. It was William Rossetti's belief that his mother assumed "the absolute and divine truth of everything to be found in the Old and New Testament," and he thought Christina shared her assumption. He told Mackenzie Bell, Christina's first biographer, that she "owed *everything* in the way of early substantial instruction to our mother." Whether throughout her life Christina read the Bible for its literal as well as its symbolic truth remains an open question. Close study of her religious verse and devotional prose, as well as her unpublished comments about Genesis and Exodus, leads to the supposition that her reading of Scriptures was neither exclusively literal nor solely symbolic, but like the great work itself included both approaches.

As a young wife and mother, Frances Rossetti was a devout but not a bigoted member of the evangelical branch of the Church. But by 1840, with the accelerating momentum of the Oxford Movement, which reached

its peak the following year with the publication of Newman's celebrated Tract 90, Frances and her sisters (the Aunts Charlotte, Eliza, and Margaret) began to gravitate toward the Tractarians, attracted by the new Anglo-Catholicism which made available the beautiful rites and ceremonies, the choral music and the forms of the Catholic Church without what appeared to Frances to be its disadvantages, of which one was Mariolatry. With her mother and aunts, Christina attended in her youth St. Katherine's Church in Regent's Park. It was after 1843 that the Rossetti women began going to Christ Church, Albany Street, noted at the time for the incendiary sermons of the Reverend William Dodsworth, one of the chief preachers of the Oxford Movement, a man closely associated with both Newman and Pusey.

Indeed, from the opening of the new church, which was built in 1837, Dr. Pusey was a prominent figure in its development, and it was undoubtedly due to his influence that Dodsworth, then "deep in the study of prophecy," was appointed Perpetual Curate, as the vicar was then called. Not only did Pusey take the pulpit himself upon occasion, but he also brought in as guest preachers such distinguished churchmen as Dr. Manning, Dr. Hook, and Bishop Blomfield of London. We learn from Canon H. W. Burrows, the second incumbent, that in Dodsworth's time "a remarkable spirit of reverence" characterized the fashionable congregation, which in addition to peers, deans, and canons included literary figures such as Mrs. Oliphant, F. T. Palgrave, and Sara Coleridge.[4]

It was, however, Dodsworth himself, then according to Burrows "the most powerful spiritual influence in that part of London," who gave the impressive services their distinctive High Church character. Even Dante Gabriel, much less susceptible to the religious influence than his two sisters, records in two early poems, the first addressed to Maria, the second to Christina, the atmosphere of reverent sanctity that pervaded Christ Church and gave it a special quality. Both poems are joined under the title *The Church-Porch:*

I

Sister, first shake we off the dust we have
Upon our feet, lest it defile the stones
Inscriptured, covering their sacred bones
Who lie i' the aisles which keep the names they gave,
Their trust abiding round them in the grave;
Whom painters paint for visible orisons,
And to whom sculptors pray in stone and bronze;
Their voices echo still like a spent wave.
Without here, the church-bells are but a tune,
And on the carven church-door this hot noon
Lays all its heavy sunshine here without:
But having entered in, we shall find there
Silence, and sudden dimness, and deep prayer,
And faces of crowned angels all about.

II

Sister, arise, we have no more to sing
Or say: the priest abideth as is meet,
To minister. Rise up out of thy seat,
Though peradventure 'tis an irksome thing
To cross again the threshold of our king,
Where his doors stand against the evil street
And let each step increase upon our feet
The dust we shook from them at entering.
Must we of very sooth go hence? The air,
Whose heat outside makes mist that can be seen,
Is very clear and cool where we have been;
The priest abideth ministering, lo,
As he for service, why not we for prayer?
It is so bidden, sister, let us go.

Here Dodsworth held daily services, celebrated Communion on every saint's day as well as on Sundays, and expounded Tractarian doctrine, which, although it was sometimes beyond the comprehension of his listeners, nevertheless held them spellbound. No wonder that *The Edinburgh Review,* looking back in January, 1874, characterized the Christ Church of Christina's childhood as "a principal centre of High Church religionism in the metropolis." According to this journal, "There was a flavour of combined learning and piety, and of literary and artistic refinement, in the representatives of Tractarianism which enlisted floating sympathies; and hence besides the 'thorough-going Puseyites,' there existed an eclectic following in and around Albany Street, composed of various elements. In some cases [the Rossettis are an example] it was the old wine of Evangelicalism settling itself into new High Church bottles; in others, literary affinities fastening on congenial forms of historic or aesthetic sentiment."

It was, then, this exhilarating environment of the Tractarian Renascence, an avant-garde movement accepted alike by the Regent's Park worthies and the Albany Street literati, which had its brief but exciting day during the formative years of Christina's childhood. She acknowledged in a poem of 1890 her indebtedness to Cardinal Newman, the Oxford Movement's great originator, and in a letter of 1881 her admiration for its outstanding poet, Isaac Williams. Although she never professed herself an admirer of Keble, there is extant a curiously hand-illustrated volume of his *Christian Year* (1837 ed.) belonging to Maria, which has for each poem a pencil drawing in the margin by Christina.

If the Tractarian background to Christina's education was provided by Frances Rossetti's religious interests, the Italian environment which complemented it was contributed by Rossetti's political connections and, even more, by his predominantly Latin temperament. Although he did not interfere with Christina's religious upbringing, which throughout her life was to exert a unifying influence upon her personality, he was

responsible for those contrapuntal dissonances that gave her harmonies their deeper note. Not only did she resemble her gifted father in poetic ability and temperament (traditionally Southern Italian in its fire and ardor), but she also borrowed from him some of his characteristic Latin attitudes, sometimes at variance with English conventionality.

After her visit to Italy in 1865, Christina herself recognized the extent to which her cultural heritage shaped the conflicting elements in her personality. In her poem *Italia io ti Saluto,* written upon her departure from Italy, she contrasted the "sweet South" of her origin with the austere North of her upbringing:

> Where I was born, bred, look to die;
> Come back to do my day's work in its day,
> Play out my play—
> Amen, amen, say I.

❋ 1 ❋

GREEN WOOD

1834–1847

As a small girl, Christina was reputed to have been both spirited and lazy. She early showed an original turn of mind and a piquant and sprightly wit. Grandfather Polidori, who doted upon her, frequently remarked that she would have more wit or spirit than any of the others (*"Avrà più spirito di tutti"*). She was noticeably precocious in a family in which precocity was taken for granted. Before she was six, she astonished a feminine visitor by the aptness with which she, "a baby," used what the visitor called "a dictionary-word." She invented her first story when she was still too young to write. Dictated to her mother, it was an Arabian Nights tale she called "The Dervise." Her first poem was also dictated:

Cecilia never went to school
Without her gladiator.

Not a very promising performance, to be sure, but, as William has pointed out, the meter is correct. He tells us that there was not a time that the Rossetti children, knowing what a verse was, did not also know and feel what a correct verse was. He accounted for it by the fact that they were accustomed to hearing the elder Rossetti recite aloud his own poetry "with perfect articulation and emphasis."

The young Rossettis, Maria excepted, were handsome as well as precocious. Pretty and passionate little Christina ("and very pretty some people considered her in those days," says William) had hazel eyes, bright bronze hair which later turned the rich, dark brown hue of her mother's, and a clear, fresh, dark complexion. Once she was past infancy, her face lost the baby roundness which at her birth had suggested to her father "a little moon risen at the full," and became a delicate oval. A water-color miniature by Filippo Pistrucci, from which William Bell Scott did the etching so frequently reproduced, shows Christina at the age of eight as an oval-faced little girl with full cheeks, large, solemn, intelligent eyes, a sweet but stubborn mouth, and straight hair parted in the middle and

drawn back over a fine brow and a beautiful forehead. The image is one of a willful but lovable little girl.

"To have a temper of her own was perhaps her right," William said of her; "to be amiable and affectionate along with it was certainly her endowment." He admitted that she was given to temper tantrums and was "hardly less passionate than Gabriel." We hear of her at the age of four clamoring noisily for her "share of the cakes." It is true that no matter how self-abnegating she may have become in womanhood, as a child she was firm about getting her share of whatever sweets life offered. For those who like R. D. Waller conceive of Christina as passive, timid, and self-effacing, it is well to recall what she thought of herself as a child.[1] When she was a woman past fifty she told William Sharp that she had been "the ill-tempered one in the family," and she observed to Lucy Rossetti, William's wife, that "it is such a triumph for ME to attain to philosophic calm that, even if that subdued temper is applied by me without common sense, *color che sanno* may still congratulate me on some sort of improvement. Ask William, who knew me in my early stormy days; he could a tale unfold."

William refused to unfold the tale, but part of it is related by his daughter, Helen Rossetti Angeli, Christina's niece. As a small girl, Helen tells us, she was "naughty in some way and gave vent to an outburst of unseemly temper. Aunt Christina remonstrated with me in her urbane manner. I was calmed and subdued, and tears of rage had given way to tears of contrition, when my Aunt, exhorting me to self-control, said to me, 'You must not imagine, my dear girl, that your Aunt was always the calm and sedate person you now behold. I, too, had a very passionate temper; but I learnt to control it. On one occasion, being rebuked by my dear Mother for some fault, I seized upon a pair of scissors, and ripped up my arm to vent my wrath. I have learnt since to control my feelings—and no doubt you will!' "

The struggle to subdue that temper and to conquer the imperious clamor of the senses in a temperament naturally passionate or "stormy" was to be the chief endeavor of Christina Rossetti's life. In a long, rigorous, exhausting warfare of attrition, she tried to teach herself that simple yet most complex of all childhood lessons: the voluntary surrender of her share of the cakes. At twenty-six she was to write:

Not to be first: how hard to learn
That lifelong lesson of the past.

But at the age of four that task was still ahead of her. As the youngest and "the most 'fractious' " of the children, she was both pampered and teased, both protected and patronized by the other three. As the youngest too, she naturally occupied "the lowest place," and William, her "chief chum" during childhood, frequently acted as a buffer between her and the two eldest, who were "inclined at times to treat her *de haut en*

bas." She told Sir Edmund Gosse in 1884 that "I, as the least and last of the group, may remind you that besides the clever and cultivated parents who headed us all, I in particular beheld far ahead of myself the clever sister and two clever brothers who were a little (though but a little) my seniors. And as to acquirements," she added modestly, "I lagged out of all proportion behind them, and have never overtaken them to this day."

We cannot doubt, however, that the youngest Rossetti, who had inherited her grandmother's "warlike spirit," learned at an early age that she would have to assert her rights within the fraternal circle, possibly even fight for them upon occasion. It could not have been long before her bright, if immature, intelligence discovered that Gabriel, or "Gubby," as Maria called him, obtained his own way by frightening displays of temper, and she must have emulated him.

Although she was able to gratify her impulses in this unseemly fashion, she soon observed that her temper tantrums were highly displeasing to the beloved mother she admired from infancy to the end of her life. If she could secure some minor triumphs over her brothers and sister by being "fractious" and difficult, at the same time she lost more than she gained in her mother's disapproval of her ungoverned outbursts (we can imagine how greatly shocked Frances Rossetti must have been by the scissors-ripping incident), and this undoubtedly created for her a typical childhood conflict. In order to preserve a partially formed personality, she would feel obliged to defend herself from the encroachments upon it by the older children. But in order to win her mother's approval, even more necessary in the formation of personality, she would be equally obliged to discipline herself, to control and curb those fierce flashes of temper which distressed her mother.

"To a child of this uneasy, wayward disposition," wrote Geoffrey Rossetti in 1930, one "who was at the same time fond of her parents and pained to hurt them, there must have been much to worry and perplex. Even in her early years she may have known what it was to repress her feelings for the love of her mother, just as at a later time she repressed other inclinations for her love and sense of duty towards God."

If, as has been said, Dante Gabriel was the battleground upon which his mother fought an inconclusive but lifelong engagement with the world, Christina was no less a battlefield upon which her mother's moral discipline contended with the inherently tumultuous Rossetti strain for dominance of her spirit. It was Frances Rossetti's maternal task, as she conceived it, to tame and subdue in her two most gifted children some of the more dangerous characteristics transmitted by the Rossetti genes.[2]

II

She could not have had much early success with Dante Gabriel, whom William described as the fiery and dictatorial "leopard-cub" of his childhood. From the first, Gabriel established himself as the master (although

not the bully) of the two younger children. Maria, or "Maggie," whom the little ones regarded as "an inspiriting Muse in a pinafore," was quite capable of defying Gabriel, and did so upon occasion. But to small Christina and William, he was "a familiar but fiery spirit," whom it was not prudent to oppose. In mischief "he counted for all, and Maria for nothing."

Although Gabriel was considered to be the most gifted, the most brilliant and beautiful of the four children, Christina came next. She could not have been very old before becoming aware that she was regarded by the family as almost as beautiful, almost as talented, and, by all but Polidori, almost as clever as Gabriel—but not quite. This family attitude complicated for her the hard problem of learning "how not to be first."

Maria created a difficulty of a different sort for her. If as a child Maria had "a strong spice of jealousy in her nature," as William asserts, it is not surprising, for her looks were always being compared disadvantageously to Christina's. One time when an Italian acquaintance complimented Rossetti on Maria's appearance, she said afterwards, "Papa, I don't believe what that gentleman said. Christina is much prettier than I, everybody says so." But if with her Italian looks (she had a dark complexion, coarse black curls, and large black eyes), she was regarded as homely, she was nonetheless lively, enthusiastic, and clever. "The thinking child, without any inventive turn," was William's appraisal of her.

Unfortunately, her creative inferiority to Christina, obvious from the first, grew more apparent as the girls matured. All her life Christina tried to make it up to Maria, to console her beloved sister for the inequality of their gifts. In 1865 she did "some of the subordinate work" for a book Maria was writing, so that her sister too could get into print. "I have a great fancy for her name endorsing a book," Christina told Gabriel, "as we three have all got to that stage, so I work with a certain enthusiasm." In Christina's writing she always referred to Maria with admiring reverence. She threw a halo around Maria's head and created the legend of her saintliness that has come down to posterity. It was her way of compensating Maria for losing in the childhood competition with her more gifted sister and brothers.

William presented no problems, either to Christina or to himself. Equable and demure, he described himself as the typical good little boy. He was not "noisy nor plaguey nor volcanic," as Christina and Gabriel frequently were. And if he was not as high-spirited as they, neither was he so easily depressed. As early as 1834 he appears in the role he was destined to play throughout his life, that of Christina's "brother of brothers." Her chum and protector in youth, her admirer and adviser in later years, after her death William became her biographer and editor.

Although we have his assurance that his parents treated all four children with complete impartiality, he was at the same time willing to admit

that his father "had a certain predilection for Gabriel," and his mother for him. William was Frances Rossetti's

> Clever little Willie wee,
> Bright-eyed, blue-eyed little fellow,

as Christina was to recall him so many years later in her *Sing-Song*. Nevertheless, we must believe him when he emphatically declares that no one of the children "ever felt, or was led to feel, any sense of unfairness in family life," and that the abilities of all four were equally recognized and fostered.

The harmonious relationship existing between the parents was responsible for much of the peaceful security of Christina's early life. Apparently they never quarreled, either privately or before the children. Once Rossetti said about his wife that "at the touch of her industrious hands order ever flourishes about me." Another time when Frances was ill, Rossetti wrote her, "I never knew how much I loved you until now that you are not well. You have never seemed so precious, so necessary to my existence. . . . I love above all your lovely soul, and ten years of possession . . . have only shown me its worth more clearly."

No wonder Christina thought of home as "a nest love-hidden from ills." Although home meant both the Charlotte Street houses, first No. 38 and later No. 50 (now 110 Hallam Street), one was very like the other, and home in either was the center around which Christina's young life revolved. William tells us that the little Rossettis were inseparable during their childhood: "Wherever one was, there the other was—and that was almost always at home." In many ways the home life of the Rossetti children was ideal. Isolated from confusing contact with the world, even from other children, protected by the security assured them by their parents' warm love, petted by admiring relatives, and soundly educated by a mother who had been a professional teacher, they grew up like plants in a sheltered spot in the garden.

III

The girls had no schooling other than their mother gave them. Before they could read for themselves, Frances read to them, supplementing the religious works so much to her taste (the Bible, St. Augustine, *Pilgrim's Progress*) with edifying pedagogical novels, such as Day's *Sanford and Merton* or Maria Edgeworth's stories for children. All these they heartily detested. What they enjoyed were tales of fantasy and imagination. After *The Arabian Nights,* Keightley's collection of fairy tales was "one of the leading delights" of Christina's childhood.

Later the young Rossettis had their own adventures in reading. Although in Polidori's well-selected library they could find the works of the English classics (among them Sir Walter Scott was their favorite for a

time), in the way of children they preferred upon occasion the less reputable literature they discovered on their Uncle Philip's bookshelves. He was one of the maternal uncles who remaining unmarried still lived at the Polidori home. We learn from William that the children often "flitted to Philip's small apartment, and battened on *The Newgate Calendar,* Hone's *Every-Day Book,* and a collection of stories, verse and prose, about ghosts, demons, and the like, called *Legends of Terror.*" They also enjoyed the Gothic romances of Monk Lewis; and in adolescence Christina discovered for herself Ann Radcliffe and, with her brothers, Charles Robert Maturin. It was in Hone's three-volume popular miscellany (1825) that Christina at nine discovered Keats, whose name Hone spelled Keates, and whom he called "one of the sweetest of our modern poets." She, and not Gabriel or Holman Hunt, was the first "Pre-Raphaelite" to appreciate Keats. The poem which caught her fancy, though in an abridged and mutilated form, was *The Eve of St. Agnes.*

Rossetti's own bookshelves were filled with what he called his *libri mistici,* those esoteric volumes which fed his Dante studies, tomes that Christina and the other children sedulously avoided. They had the idea that everything read by their father was tedious and boring. For this reason, none of them was tempted to take up one of Dante's books to see "what it read like." The *Convito* in particular appeared to the children as something to be dreaded and fled from. "Dante Alighieri was a sort of banshee in the Charlotte Street houses," said William, "his shriek audible even to familiarity, but the message of it not scrutinized."

As Christina grew older, she recovered from the notion that Dante, as Rossetti's special possession, was a noxious feature of adult life. Later, as a matter of course, all four Rossettis were—in Christina's words—"sucked into the Dantesque vortex." Although she herself was to write several prose studies of Dante, more important is the pervasive Dantean influence on her poetry, an influence recognizable both in her conceptions and the poetic techniques she used to express them. The Dantean imagery and symbolism for the Dantean religious ideas may be found throughout her work.

Dante, however, was only part of the larger Italian influence which helped to mold Christina's personality. We have seen that her father was responsible for the marked Italian background and atmosphere in the home. As might be expected from Rossetti's colorful past, the Charlotte Street house became a hotbed of Italian post-Carbonari radicalism. It appeared to be a magnet for the artistic and literary Italian political exiles who emigrated to London, and in Frances Rossetti's orderly front parlor drank tea and cursed that "hell-hound," Metternich, and that "traitor" to the Republican cause, Louis Philippe of France.

William paints a vivid picture of those cosmopolitan evenings of Christina's youth. He draws back the curtain upon his father

The King's Library

> and three or four foreigners engaged in animated talk on the affairs of Europe, from the point of view of patriotic aspiration . . . with frequent and fervent recitations of poetry intervening; my mother quiet but interested, and sometimes taking her mild womanly part in the conversation; and we four children . . . drinking it all in as a sort of necessary atmosphere of the daily life, yet with our own little interests and occupations as well—reading, coloring prints, looking into illustrated books, nursing a cat, or whatever came uppermost.

The children understood all that was said, for since their infancy they had been able to follow a conversation in Italian as well as in English.

Outside the home, the children's diversions were limited to walks with their mother to Regent's Park (where on the way she would point out the leading architectural features of the Nash Regency buildings fronting the park), visits to the Zoo, and occasionally to the various galleries and exhibitions of the day.

Except for her summers at her grandfather's cottage in the country, these excursions to Regent's Park provided Christina, a London-bred child, with her sole opportunity to observe nature. That the park, then recently opened and still a wild wooded area, exerted a marked influence upon the development of her poetic imagination is evident from the dream about it she had as a small girl. The dream is related by William Sharp, to whom it was told by Gabriel. She was walking in Regent's Park at dawn, and, just as the sun rose, suddenly she saw a wave of yellow light sweep out from the trees. She realized that "the wave" was a multitude of canaries. They rose in their thousands, circled in a gleaming mass, then scattered in every direction. In her dream she knew that all the canaries of London had met in Regent's Park at dawn and were now returning to their cages. Psychologically the dream tells us a good deal about the little girl's attitude toward her own urban environment and herself as part of it, and even hints in the canary symbolism at an awareness of her poetic vocation.

But the city as such also had advantages to offer an imaginative child, and as well as nature could stimulate the image-making faculty of the poet. One of the most vivid impressions of Christina's childhood was of Madam Tussaud's waxwork exhibition, which was within easy walking distance of Charlotte Street. She felt shy, she tells us, upon first seeing the gorgeous assembly so "brilliant with costumes, complexions, and historical effigies." Not the real people present, but "the distinguished waxen crowd" abashed her, confirming her in a later view that "things seen are as that waxwork, things unseen as those real people."

Perhaps this impression was responsible for the 1847 *The Dead City,* a poem which also pictures a gorgeous assembly, though not of wax, but of stone. Human feasters at a banquet have been turned to stone at the most characteristic moment of their lives. The stone banqueters produce upon the youthful observer who wanders into their midst much the same

effect that the "distinguished waxen crowd" did upon Christina herself.

Summers the Rossetti children spent at Holmer Green, Polidori's cottage in Buckinghamshire. "This little cottage," Christina tells us, "was my familiar haunt; its grounds were my inexhaustible delight." To the end of her life she never forgot the country pleasures she enjoyed there. "If any one thing schooled me in the direction of poetry," she confided to Gosse, "it was perhaps the delightful idle liberty to prowl all alone about my grandfather's cottage-grounds some thirty miles from London, entailing in my childhood a long stage coach journey. The grounds were quite small, and on the simplest scale—but in those days to me they were vast, varied, and worth exploring."

Perhaps it was in the surrounding orchards that she first saw those "sun-red apples," the nectarines, peaches, and ripe plums which with other luscious fruit are idealized in *The Dead City* and glorified even more munificently in *Goblin Market*. At Holmer Green too she first made acquaintance with the small animals that are such a conspicuous feature of her major poems, the frogs, toads, mice, rabbits, squirrels, and pigeons that invariably compose her earthly paradise.

One day during their summer rambles about the fields and meadows, she and Maria found "a certain wild strawberry growing on a hedgerow bank." Day after day, the two little girls returned to watch it ripen. "I do not know which of us was to have had it at the last," Christina relates, "or whether we were to have halved it. As it was we watched, and as it turned out we watched in vain: for a snail or some such marauder must have forestalled us at a happy moment. One fatal day we found it half-eaten, and good for nothing."

Another time, in the grounds of Holmer Green, "perhaps in the orchard, I lighted upon a dead mouse. The dead mouse moved my sympathy: I took him up, buried him comfortably in a mossy bed and bore the spot in mind. Returning a day or two later, I removed the moss coverlet, and looked . . . a black insect emerged. I fled in horror, and for long years ensuing I never mentioned this ghastly adventure to anyone."

But the logical connection between these two incidents did not escape Christina. The youthful mind would not fail to draw the obvious conclusion: why exercise a prudent self-restraint if in the end the strawberry will be devoured by snails and the once-living flesh given to the worms. It was only in the otherworldliness of religious faith that she could find refuge from this kind of pessimistic naturalism, which nonetheless haunted her the remainder of her life.

IV

When Polidori sold Holmer Green in 1839 and moved to London, Christina's summers in the country came to an end. "After those charming holidays ended, " she tells us, "I remained pent up in London till I was a

great girl of fourteen, when delight reawakened at the sight of primroses in a railing cutting—a prelude to many lovely country sights." But in exchange for the deprivation, her grandfather's new residence near Regent's Park Canal, within walking distance of Charlotte Street, offered other advantages, not the least of which was the private printing press Polidori installed in the shed behind the garden. Here he published Christina's *Verses* of 1847.

She had been writing poetry for some five years now. It was in 1842 that she first began to write down and to date her poems in a notebook. On the flyleaf of the first of the seventeen black notebooks in which until 1866 she kept her poetry, her mother wrote, "These verses are truly and literally by my little daughter, who scrupulously rejected all assistance in her rhyming efforts, under the impression that in that case they would not be her own."

But as might be expected, the contents of the 1847 volume do not altogether justify Christina's youthful claim to originality. As early exercises in verse, they are on the whole derivative. Not only are the Italian poets Dante, Tasso, and Metastasio evident, but she herself explicitly acknowledged her indebtedness to Herbert, Crabbe, Blake, and Tennyson. She admitted that *Charity,* written when she was fourteen, was an imitation of Herbert's *Vertue.* A footnote attached to *The Last Words of Sir Eustace Grey* (printed in the Polidori book but not reproduced in the *Works*) advises the reader to "see Crabbe." Gabriel considered *Mother and Child* Blakean, and she marked *Sleep, sleep* (unpublished but extant in the MS notebook) "from Blake." She called *The Lotus Eaters,* with the subtitle, "Ulysses to Penelope," an "echo from Tennyson."

Furthermore, the 1847 volume shows her experimenting with traditional literary forms, the ballad, the sonnet, the hymn, and going for her material to the great traditional storehouses of literature: the Bible, hagiographies, folk and fairy tale collections, and of course *The Arabian Nights,* which had fired her imagination before she could write.

At fourteen she was studying with close attention a book of religious poetry called *The Sacred Harp,* and her marginal notes indicate that she read the poems in this anthology with more enthusiasm than critical discernment. Selected poems by Heber won her highest praise. His *Funeral Hymn* she marked, "Beautiful really," and poems with titles such as *A Prayer to Jesus, The Meekness of Christ, Missionary Hymn,* and *Burial Anthem* "very beautiful," "beautiful," or "most beautiful." She admired Cowper and Byron with more reserve, grading the former's *Light Shining Out of Darkness* "very good," and *The Destruction of Sennacherib* "very fine." What is evident, however, is that the young girl studied this anthology as she would have a textbook, and its poems provided her with models for the writing of religious verse.[3] She even borrowed with modifications some of the titles. Like all young poets, she learned from her

predecessors, and close inspection of her early poetry corrects the popular assumption that she was uninfluenced by literary tradition.

Poetic production during these years was further stimulated by the literary activity of her brothers and sister. Like the Brontës, the four Rossettis coöperated in literary ventures, of which the first was a weekly family journal called *The Hodge Podge* and the second another "periodical" entitled *The Illustrated Scrapbook,* a successor to what Gabriel called "the fallen *Hodge Podge.*" He originally conceived *The Blessed Damozel* for one or the other of these two family journals. Christina at thirteen contributed to the *Hodge Podge* two "poetic effusions," *Rosalind* and *Corydon's Resolution,* which Gabriel pronounced "very good," but which William, looking back from an adult altitude, thought "indisputably bad." Both were tactfully omitted by Polidori from the 1847 privately printed *Verses.*

What has been called "the morbid strain" in Christina's poetry first appears in the Polidori volume.[4] Commencing toward the end of 1844 with *Earth and Heaven,* and persisting into 1847 and later, this tendency rises to a climax in 1846. Complaints of mutability and corruptibility are mingled in these poems with the fervently expressed desire for death. Death is regarded as rest, as deliverance from "life's tainted joys," and "life's strange riot." Death was continually upon Christina's mind these years; mortality occupied her thoughts; her "mortuary pieces," as they have been called, followed one upon the other in appalling succession.

Equally marked was the young girl's pessimistic attitude toward life, as conspicuous in this poetry as her persisting awareness of death. On earth she professed to find all "dreariness and dearth." Although she generalized in high-sounding phrases about the woes of humanity, she was chiefly interested in the woes of the individual, particularly that special woe she described as "the darkness of the mind," as

the heart that's crushed and sinking;
From the brain grown blank with thinking;
From the spirit sorrow drinking.

What could have been the cause of such early pessimism? It is true that much of Christina's infatuation with death can be attributed to her romantic heritage. Certainly those verses William wisely omitted from the collected *Poems,* such as *Sappho, The Ruined Cross, Sir Eustace Grey,* and *Life Out of Death,* are extreme examples of eighteenth-century lachrymose sentimentality, and *Night and Death* (included in the *Works*) is a typical "graveyard piece." Coleridge, Shelley, and Keats added to this cumulative alluvia, but more directly evident are the sensational deposits left by the Gothic romances of Ann Radcliffe, Monk Lewis, and particularly Maturin, whose novel *The Women* inspired two of Christina's 1847 poems, and his *Melmoth the Wanderer* two others. "When Gabriel, Chris-

tina, and I were young," William told Mackenzie Bell, "we used to read Maturin's novels over and over again, and they took great hold of our imaginations."

Despite the macabre melancholy, humor is not absent from Christina's early poetry, that playful attitude which remained with her throughout life. As pronounced an aspect of her personality as the pessimism, it appears in *The Death of a Cat,* in which she calls upon the nine Muses to

> Come and mourn with tuneful breath
> Each one for a separate death,

in *The Chinaman,* a witty bit of nonsense written when she was twelve to compete with William, whose school assignment was to compose some verses on the subject of the Anglo-Chinese Opium War of 1842, and in these unpublished *Lines Given with a Penwiper,* written in 1847 and probably inspired by the sight of her father's nightly labors at his Dantean scholarship:

> *I have compassion on the carpeting,
> And on your back I have compassion too.
> The splendid Brussels web is suffering
> In the dimmed lustre of each glowing hue;
> And you the everlasting altering
> Of your position with strange aches must rue.
> Behold, I come the carpet to preserve,
> And save your spine from a continual curve.* [5]

V

In 1843 Rossetti became seriously ill. The doctors diagnosed his case as one of persistent bronchitis, but it is very likely that he had consumption. Although he lingered on for some eleven years, he never recovered his health. Incipient blindness also threatened, and he did lose the use of one eye temporarily. As a result of these troubles, he was forced to give up his position at King's College, and to relinquish many of his private pupils.

Gloom settled over the Rossetti household, and what William described as "a real tussle for the means of existence" began. Although the family's struggle against poverty continued with fluctuations until 1853, William considered the family fortunes to be "at their worst in 1844," the year the strain of so-called morbidity first appeared in Christina's verse. During this time Rossetti's earnings, which had been "sensibly dwindling," finally became "wholly extinct."

In such an emergency Frances Rossetti, whose mind and spirit were quite equal to the responsibility of family leadership that now devolved upon her, organized her forces energetically for the battle ahead. Christina was of course too young to work. Gabriel, destined from the first for the career of an artist, was a resource not to be tapped until absolutely

necessary. There remained William, now fifteen, and Maria, seventeen, and Frances decided that these two must help to earn the family living. The chief support of the family was undertaken by Frances herself. She turned again to teaching, her former occupation, and eked out a meager livelihood by giving French and Italian lessons outside the home. In the 1850's she started several day schools, one in the Mornington Crescent section of London, and, after that failed, another at Frome-Selwood in Somerset. In both these projects she was assisted by Christina, who was expected to follow the feminine family vocation and become a governess.

One of Rossetti's English admirers secured for William a position with the Board of Excise as a government clerk. Frances's sister, Charlotte Polidori, who was employed by the Marchioness of Bath first as a governess and later as a companion, used her influential connections to get Maria placed as a governess in the family of the Reverend Lord Charles Thynne. But Maria was far from happy in her new position. In 1846 she wrote home that she was anticipating with pleasure the day of her return to the "*bel nido natio,*" where she would like to remain always. For one thing, she could not find the religious atmosphere in the Thynne establishment congenial: as a High Church clergyman, the Reverend Thynne belonged to the Catholic wing of the Tractarian party, and shortly after Maria was employed in his family he joined the exodus to Rome. For another thing, Maria had to cope with children who were refractory and undisciplined. "I hope you told Lady Charles," Gabriel wrote to his mother, "that poor Maggy is not to be bullied and badgered out of her life by a lot of beastly brats; and that Lady C. fully understands the same, and has already provided the said Maggy with a bamboo."

Doubtless Maria's life at the Thynnes' must have impressed Christina as thoroughly disagreeable. The thought of being separated from her adored mother, of living in a stranger's family, and one, moreover, which could turn Catholic overnight, must have discouraged the young girl, who knew that she also was being prepared for the profession of governess. The threatening alternatives of bullying (via the bamboo) or being bullied surely appalled her. Observing the lives of the members of her own family, then, the sick and ailing father, the worried, overburdened mother, the unhappy sister, Christina must have concluded at this time that her own prospects on this earth were not of the brightest.

We have seen that the pessimistic streak first colored the texture of her poetry in 1844, the "worst" year in the history of the Rossetti family. In 1845 her health broke down. Except for the usual childhood diseases, she had been sturdy enough as a child. She now became delicate. No one seemed to know exactly what was the matter with her. Various physicians were called in before Dr. Charles J. Hare, under whose care she remained from 1845 to 1850.

Dr. Hare's medical description of her at the age of fifteen, when she

started ailing, is of interest for the light it sheds upon her physical development: "Fully the middle stature; appears older than she really is—15; hair brown; complexion brunette; but she is now pale (anaemic). Conformation good." This is not too informative, but it is the only part of her total medical history which Dr. Hare made available to Mackenzie Bell for the latter's biography of Christina. Aside from anemia, a not unusual nineteenth-century ailment, Christina's complaints were mysterious and indefinite. William, however, sheds some light upon his sister's condition in writing that "anyone who did not understand that Christina was an almost constant often a sadly-smitten invalid, seeing at times the countenance of Death very close to her own, would form an extremely incorrect notion of her corporal, and thus in some sense of her spiritual condition . . . As an invalid, she had courage, patience, even cheerfulness. I have heard her dwell upon the satisfaction—such as it is—of being ill, and interdicted from active exertion and the following out of one's own faculties." The last sentence is the significant one. In his plain way William is stating what today is regarded as the basis of some neurotic illnesses, the "satisfaction . . . of being ill."

What kind of satisfaction could Christina have derived from her youthful ailments? In a letter written some years later, she herself tells us. The letter, dated November 13, 1855, is headed H.H., which William interprets as Hampstead Heath, where Christina had a temporary position as governess:

> MY DEAR WILLIAM
>
> I hope you are glad to know that I am very comfortable in my exile; but at any rate I know I am rejoiced to feel that my health does really unfit me for miscellaneous governessing *en permanence*. For instance yesterday I indulged in Breakfast in bed, having been very unwell the day previous: now I am very tolerable again, but do not feel particularly to be depended upon. . . .
>
> I hear my young charges just come in from their walk: so in haste believe me with love to Mama and Maria. . . .

William's note to this revealing letter is even more illuminating. "It is clear," he explains, "she was engaged in some sort of tuition, not of a fully defined kind, and that she rejoiced (quite characteristically) in finding her health not strong enough for regular engagements of like description; and this was, I think, the very last attempt that she made at anything of this sort."

Writing to her publisher Alexander Macmillan, in 1877, she admitted, "I am not very robust, nor do I expect to become so; but I am well content with the privileges and immunities which attach to semi-invalidism." And in a letter of 1884 to Swinburne, she said quite frankly, "I myself feel like an escaped Governess, for had I only learnt my lessons properly at the proper age I too might have taught some one something,—and doubtless I should have had to do so." [6]

VI

It is clear that in 1845 the problem was how to escape with honor "governessing *en permanence*." Christina must have felt troubled and uneasy at the family's assumption that she, like Maria, would as a matter of course become a governess. Not only was Maria's lot a demonstration that the life of a governess could be unpleasant, but Christina would have had her own reasons for avoiding it. For one thing, the duties of instruction could keep her so busy that she would not find sufficient time to write poetry. For another, such employment would mean leaving the warmth and comfort of the home nest and the loving affection of her mother. And yet there was no reason why she any more than Maria should be spared the necessity of wage earning. To refuse to become a governess would be to shirk her share of the family responsibility.

The example of her father might have provided a way out for her. As an invalid, he was obliged to stay permanently at home instead of going out to fight the world. As an invalid, he was also entitled to Frances Rossetti's care and constant attention. The youthful Christina must have seen quite clearly, if unconsciously, that no matter how much her father suffered, at the same time he enjoyed certain advantages of the kind she craved for herself.

We can understand better now the sort of satisfaction she found in her adolescent illnesses. It is not surprising that emulating her father she herself became a kind of invalid and thereby won, in addition to more of her mother's attention, the "privileges and immunities" so necessary for the production of poetry.

Although she had gained a point, the young girl could not have been happy in the position in which she now found herself. The brothers were no longer at home: Gabriel was busy with his studies at art school, and William with his duties at the Excise Office. Maria lived away from home. Even Frances Rossetti, rushed and harassed in dividing her time between nursing and teaching duties, could have found little opportunity to be a companion to Christina. For the first time in the girl's life, she found herself almost entirely isolated, with only her sick father for company.

In his depressed state Rossetti was not the most cheerful society. William tells us that "in all those years, the threatened blindness of my father, followed by various forms of illness, including paralytic shocks and enfeeblement, saddened our thoughts far more than did the material straits of our position." Even more closely than the others of the family, Christina was forced to witness Rossetti's decline. The spectacle of his physical decay was constantly before her eyes. She did not need to go to the Bible or even back to her childhood memory of the dead mouse in the Holmer Green garden for a perpetual reminder of the dissolution of the flesh.

To make matters worse, from 1843 on, Rossetti was always expressing

the wish for death. Now that his health was broken down, he felt that his usefulness was over and that he no longer had a part in life to play. "Often left lonely and unhappy at home," writes Waller, he considered himself a burden to his family, "and longed for death to end the bitterness of life."

Is it any wonder, then, that Christina's mind dwelt so persistently upon ideas of death, decay, and mutability, and that her poetry reflects the dark mood of hopelessness the conditions of her life suggested to her? Change was the chief enemy. Lost forever were the security and happiness of her pleasant childhood, when she was part of a large, warm, cheerful, and loving family circle that both protected and stimulated her. Change had come, and it had destroyed the well-being and the stability of her childhood. Perhaps that is the reason Christina's poetry, mature as well as youthful, cries out against transience, change, mutability. It cannot be coincidental that the mutability theme appears for the first time in 1846, and that

> in the flowers she saw decay,
> And saw decay in every tree;
> And change was written on the sun,
> And change upon the sea.

VII

Although such a somber attitude, caused partially by family circumstances and partially by the romantic nature of her reading, was bound to color Christina's view of human existence, at the same time she was beginning to show a lively interest in a subject more appropriate to her years. It was in 1846, while she was turning out her dark little dirges, that she also began to think and write about love. A pair of related poems written at this time reflects both her new interest in sex and her uncertain state of mind regarding it. In *Love Attacked* she weighs and balances the advantages against the disadvantages of falling in love. Granted that "Love is more sweet than flowers," it is even more perishable. Love may be "bright as hope, seductive as music," but

> like an inundation
> It leaves behind
> An utter desolation
> Of heart and mind.

What, then, Christina asks, ought a young girl to do in order to avoid getting hurt?

> In answer to my crying,
> Sounds like incense
> Rose from the earth, replying
> 'Indifference.'

But this answer she rejects in *Love Defended,* written two days later:

Who extols a wilderness?
Who hath praised indifference?
Foolish one, thy words are sweet,
But devoid of sense.

We may be sure this was an attitude that Frances Rossetti, advocate of common sense, would have approved. In concluding her poem, Christina reflects that "the face of heaven and earth in all their beauty" (she means love)

Surely are a recompense
For a little pain.

This brave affirmation is repeated in another 1847 verse, which opens with the assertion that "Love is all happiness, love is all beauty," and finishes with the even more enthusiastic declaration that "Love kindles endless glory." In the unpublished stanzas she writes,

*And shall love cease? Ask thine own heart, O Woman,
Thy heart that beats restlessly on for ever!
All earthly things shall pass away and human,
But Love's divine: annihilated never,
It binds and nought shall sever.

Oh! it is Love makes the world habitable,
Love is a foretaste of our promised Heaven;
Though sometimes robed in white, sometimes in sable,
It still is Love, and still some joy is given,
Although the heart be riven.

And who would give Love's joy to 'scape its paining?
Yea, who would lose its sorrow and its gladness?
Then let us hear its griefs without complaining:—
This only earthly passion is not madness,
Nor leads to dearth and sadness.*

This kind of verse might create the impression that the tree was growing straight, but such was not the case. The fresh and vigorous new growth was destined to be twisted into distorted shapes by the harsh gales that blew away Christina's youth. We have already seen that in *Love Attacked* she displayed some suspicion of love, and this ambivalence was to become more marked the older she grew.

Dorothy Stuart has called attention to the early emergence of what she designates "the broken betrothal *motif*" in Christina's poetry long before experience could justify it, and she points out that "eight of the English poems in the Polidori book deal with the subject of love frustrated either by perfidy or death." This is not so remarkable as it might appear, for such subjects are traditional in balladry and romance, the kind of

literature Christina had been reading throughout her adolescence. More curious is the young girl's hostility toward and rejection of love before she had experienced it. In *The Dream,* one of the eight 1847 poems cited by Miss Stuart, Christina states her conviction that love is impossible of full realization in this life; it is "a very dream of dreams." In *A Novice,* another 1847 poem, she goes even further in pointing out the illusionary nature of love. As a cherished illusion, love is dangerous in its very power to exhilarate and quicken:

> Yea it is as a poison-cup
> That holds one quick fire draught within;
> For when the life seems to begin
> The slow death looketh up.

The problem initially raised in *Love Attacked* is again posed in this poem. In treating a nun's choice between love and the cloister, Christina proposes the renunciation of love and the subsequent withdrawal into solitude as the antidote for the poison-cup. This was an expedient she was frequently to fall back upon throughout her life. And although in part the solution was extremely congenial to her, she could never totally accept it: another side of her nature resisted it stubbornly, and continued to struggle for fulfillment in love, no matter what suffering it might bring.

Two tendencies, then, had already shown themselves by the time she reached seventeen. On the one hand was her positive and healthy acceptance of the function of womanhood and her full anticipation of the joy potential in the sexual relationship. On the other, was her fear and dark foreboding of the suffering caused by what André Gide once called the wild darkness of the passions.

❁ 2 ❁

DRY TINDER

1847–1850

Not only did 1847 mark Christina's debut as a poet, but it also defined her transition from adolescence to young womanhood. It is not always that a line of demarcation can be drawn so sharply between the close of one period in a life and the opening of another. Although it may be purely fortuitous that in the year 1847 the record turns up the names of the three men who were to be important in her life, the circumstance distinguishes the period of the opening phase of her womanhood.

Her relationship with two of these three men has been well established. James Collinson and Charles Bagot Cayley are reputed to be the two lovers of Christina's emotional history. It is notable that she married neither. Although she might have made Cayley's acquaintance in 1847 when he came to Charlotte Street for private Italian lessons from the elder Rossetti, no friendship developed from these casual meetings, and the relationship remained dormant for the next fourteen years. Christina's only mention of him until 1861 occurs in the family diary at the time of her father's death in 1854.

If she did not actually meet James Collinson at church, it was there she first saw him. By 1847 Mrs. Rossetti and her sisters had already been attending services at Christ Church, Albany Street, for some four years, and they were well-known members of Dodsworth's congregation. It was not long before Mrs. Rossetti noticed that one of the more pious among the regular worshipers at the Sunday morning services was a small, plump, thick-necked young man with an intelligent face and a modest, retiring air. After services she and her sisters commented to each other about the stranger's "heedful and devout bearing." Later they found out that he was James Collinson, twenty-two years old, a painter from Nottingham, who had come to London to study art on the small but adequate allowance given him by his father, a bookseller. Collinson was an enthusiastic follower of Newman and Pusey, and it was no doubt the increasingly Catholic features of Dodsworth's services that brought him to Christ Church.

Was he aware of the admiring interest he aroused in the mature women sitting in the Rossetti pew? If so, he must have hoped it was shared by the lovely girl who always accompanied them, the girl whose clear-cut, delicate profile, pale cheeks, and strange dark hazel eyes, so full of power and feeling, must have provoked his curiosity and aroused his admiration. Her air of enigmatic if well-bred reserve could have told him nothing. William Rossetti thought that Collinson fell in love with Christina soon after he was introduced to her early in 1848, but he was probably attracted to her at church months before that; and he may have even schemed for a way to get the coveted introduction.

She was no doubt aware of his growing interest. A young girl in the first bloom of her beauty is generally not unconscious of a man's admiring glances. Moreover, the poems she was writing at this time indicate in a mounting sequence of intensity her growing desire for love. If in 1846 she was skittish in her advances and retreats, in her circling about the center without ever alighting upon it, by 1847 the core was exerting its magnetic attraction, and she was hovering irresistibly closer.

Although as a whole, the verses of November and December have the same tone of dark pessimism as some of the earlier poems, a new alloy has appeared in her melodious monotone of complaint. In *Song* of November 7, for instance, the cause of the speaker's dejection is the unfulfilled longing for love:

> The stream moaneth as it floweth,
> The wind sigheth as it bloweth,
> Leaves are falling, Autumn goeth,
> Winter cometh back again;
> And the air is very chilly,
> And the country rough and hilly,
> And I shiver in the rain.
> Who will help me? Who will love me?

In *Repining* of December, a ballad about a girl who, longing for love, is finally wooed and spirited away by a demon lover, we perceive again the complementary notes of loneliness and desire:

> She sat always through the long day
> Spinning the weary thread away;
> And ever said in undertone,
> 'Come, that I be no more alone.' . . .
>
> Day followed day and still she sighed
> For love, and was not satisfied.

The lover she has been waiting for comes, alights in a halo of glory, and, as she has dreamed, takes her away with him. But instead of fulfilling the rich promise of life, he shows her only death in its various forms.

In this ballad, then, the same two conflicting tendencies we have al-

ready observed reappear. On the one hand, love is suggested as a remedy for loneliness; on the other, it is shown again (but in different guise) as the "poison-cup," bringing death and devastation in its wake.

In *Lady Montrevor,* one of the Maturin pieces (February, 1848), Christina declared that "I do not look for love that is a dream," but in a poem written not more than a week later, she confessed with passion that "I thirst for love, love is mine only need." Her dilemma is revealed with even more direct frankness in the autobiographical *Three Stages:*

> I looked for that which is not, nor can be,
> And hope deferred made my heart sick in truth:
> But years must pass before a hope of youth
> Is resigned utterly.
>
> I watched and waited with a steadfast will:
> And though the object seemed to flee away
> That I so longed for, ever day by day
> I watched and waited still.
>
> Sometimes I said: 'This thing shall be no more;
> My expectation wearies and shall cease;
> I will resign it now and be at peace:'
> Yet never gave it o'er.
>
> Sometimes I said: 'It is an empty name
> I long for; to a name why should I give
> The peace of all the days I have to live?'
> Yet gave it all the same.
>
> Alas thou foolish one! alike unfit
> For healthy joy and salutary pain;
> Thou knowest the chase useless, and again
> Turnest to follow it.

Three Stages is one of the earliest of Christina's linked poems, which in general consist of two or more poems written at different times and joined under one title. Although these linked poems have been neglected by Christina's biographers, who either have failed to perceive their importance as clues to her inner life, or have read them as single units, with their contextual significance disregarded, they are important emotional landmarks in what William has called his sister's "hushed life-drama."

That Christina herself wished them to be read in their linked form, not as individual poems, is apparent from the reply she gave to a correspondent who in 1883 had requested permission to reprint her verses in an anthology:

> *I do not mind what piece you select, subject only to your taking any piece in question *in its entirety;* and my wish includes your *not* choosing an independent poem which forms part of a series or group,—not (for instance) one . . . of 'Passing Away' or one Sonnet of 'Monna

Innominata.' Such compound work has a connection (very often) which is of interest to the author, and which an editor gains nothing by discarding.* [1]

Although it is true that she allowed the first poem of *Three Stages* to be published separately in *The Germ,* 1850 was too early for her to have formulated the principle which guided her later in life. The second and third poems of *Three Stages* were not published in her lifetime. "Not that she thought them below the mark," William explains, "but because of their intimate personal character." [2]

All three poems deal with the theme of love. The three stages are the levels reached successively in a young woman's pursuit of love. As we have seen, Christina's other poems of the period likewise show that she was thinking about love, weighing her chances for sexual happiness, confessing her great desire for love while at the same time expressing her fear of its overpowering force. If at fifteen Christina was mature for her age, as her physician said, by eighteen she was physically ripe for love. All that was needed was the opportunity.

II

With the formation of the celebrated Pre-Raphaelite Brotherhood in the summer of 1848, the opportunity was not long in presenting itself. Collinson must have succeeded in making the acquaintance of the Rossetti brothers some time earlier, for by that summer he was already accepted by them as a well-liked comrade. It was the PRB, however, which brought him into Christina's ken.

The Pre-Raphaelite movement is, in Graham Hough's words, "a well-documented affair." [3] Although later in life Gabriel Rossetti scoffed at it as "the visionary vanities of half-a-dozen boys," its overwhelming influence upon Victorian art and literature is generally acknowledged. Through the mediums of painting and poetry it held in solution a number of the principal ingredients of the age.

Archaic medievalism and scientific naturalism were the two chief tributaries which fed the mainstream of Pre-Raphaelitism. For the first Gabriel was primarily responsible. The innovations of the Nazarene or Early Christian school of German painters, headed by Cornelius and Overbeck in Rome, came to him through the instruction of his first self-selected teacher, Ford Madox Brown. In Brown's atelier Gabriel was brought in touch with their work.

Nothing could have been more congenial to him, for at the time he was spending his days at the British Museum translating the courtly love poetry of Dante's little-known contemporaries and studying the original manuscript of Blake's designs and poems. Furthermore, old Polidori's hobby of working in Florentine mosaics and wood carving had early ac-

customed his grandson to the Florentine tradition in art. Finally, the Nazarene attitude of serious devoutness was also a familiar part of his background, for it was, in slightly different vestments, the same stern impulse of spiritual regeneration with which the Tractarians of his boyhood had clothed the Anglican pietism of his mother and sisters.

The second element, scientific naturalism, was contributed by Holman Hunt and John Millais. Strongly influenced by the first two volumes of Ruskin's *Modern Painters,* the new naturalism aimed at "a just representation of natural objects in a scientific spirit." The early work of the two young artists was characterized by a close observation of nature and fidelity to fact in painting it, by a scrupulous precision of detail, by elaborate "invention," as they called their literary-narrative symbolism, and by experimentation with the problem of the distribution of light, which resulted in their rejection of the conventional, academic method of treating it.

The name Pre-Raphaelite was a tag casually wished upon them by a fellow student at the Academy, who, amused at their stringent criticism of Raphael's *Transfiguration,* observed, "Then you must be painting in the way they did before Raphael." What the two young men were rebelling against was not so much Raphael's art as the crystallization of his methods by later followers into a rigid technique based upon doctrinaire principles which stifled freshness and originality in the new generation of painters.

A modest beginning was made one August evening in 1848 at Millais' house, where the young men had gathered to inspect and admire Lasinio's engravings of the Campo Santo designs at Pisa. The prints fired the imagination of the young artists; and although they were aware of "the immature perspective" and the lack of individualizing focus in Benozzo Gozzoli's designs, they admired his "attentive observation of inexhaustible Nature," and his "quaint charm of invention."

When the Pre-Raphaelite Brotherhood was organized a short time later, it consisted of seven young men, only four of them painters. These were Rossetti, Hunt, Millais, and James Collinson, who had been brought in by the Rossetti brothers. Of the remaining three members of the Brotherhood, Thomas Woolner was a sculptor, F. G. Stephens an art critic, and William Rossetti a civil servant with literary and artistic interests. Of them all, the only one who did not later achieve a position of distinction was Collinson.

And yet at the inception of the PRB he seemed among the most promising of the young men. He specialized in domestic and religious subjects; like Gabriel, he wrote verse, sometimes treating the same theme in the two different art mediums of poetry and painting. Both Gabriel and William thought highly of his abilities. But if the Rossetti brothers were enthusiastic about him, Millais, who recognized that in breaking with

traditional art and seeking a return to nature the PRB would have a fight upon its hands, was much less so. "Collinson'll certainly make a stalwart leader of a forlorn hope, won't he?" Millais commented ironically to Hunt shortly after the formation of the Brotherhood. Hunt replied that the Rossettis were much attached to the "forlorn-hoper," and he himself liked "the meek little chap," and found his new picture, *Charity Boy,* not at all bad.

By August, 1848, the romance between Christina and Collinson was well under way. That month she was in Brighton with her mother and grandfather. From London Gabriel wrote enthusiastic letters about Collinson, who was "a born stunner," and whose newest poem, *The Child Jesus,* was "a very first-rate affair." From her brother's chatty letters Christina learned that Collinson was spending his holiday at the Isle of Wight, "whither I did *not* go with him," and that he was intending to leave soon for Herne Bay. The impression emerges from these letters that Collinson was in love with Christina, and had engaged Gabriel's assistance in courting her.

III

When she returned to London in September, Collinson, still encouraged in his suit by Gabriel, proposed. His proposal was ill-timed, for, shortly before making Christina an offer, he had ceased attending Christ Church and had become a Roman Catholic. Christina promptly refused him. "Her first instinct," Waller observes shrewdly, "was evidently one of retreat." The religious reason for her refusal was good enough; no one questioned it. But perhaps her instinct for retreat was more deeply rooted. The "meek little chap" might not have impressed her as "a born stunner." To a girl who passionately "thirsted" for the kind of romantic, stormy love symbolized by the demon lover, Collinson may not have had much appeal.

Despite her refusal, he still presented himself as a wooer that autumn. We have William's word for it that the painter was very much in love, "as well he might be," said William with some asperity, "for in breeding and tone of mind, not to speak of actual genius or advantages of person, she was markedly his superior." Collinson reconsidered his religious affiliation, decided that he really could be Church of England after all, went back to attending services at Christ Church, Albany Street (where he could look at Christina Sunday mornings), and renewed his suit. She accepted him in mid-autumn and they became engaged.

In discussing his sister's engagement, William admitted that she was not actually in love with Collinson when she became engaged to him, not at least "in any such sense as that she would, before knowing him to be enamoured of her, have wished him to become so." The self-conscious phrasing of this statement, cautious to the point of deviousness, deserves

notice. Subsequently William spoke out with less reserve. Collinson, he said, was "not the sort of man to excite ardent emotions of friendship." From all that is known about him, we may conclude that he was even less the sort of man to excite an emotion much more ardent than that of friendship.

Why, then, did Christina engage herself to him?

Part of his attraction for her was lent him by the Brotherhood, which cloaked him with the glamour and the romance lacking in his own personality. In the days of its inception, the Brotherhood was the exhilarating essence of youth and art. "As soon as the P.R.B. was formed," says William, "it became a focus of boundless companionship, pleasant and touching to recall." Viewing this time of his youth in the mellow light of memory, he writes:

> We were really like brothers, continually together and confiding to one another all experiences . . . for every P.R.B. to drink a cup or two of tea or coffee, or a glass of beer, in the company of other P.R.B.s . . . was a heart-relished luxury, the equal of which the flow of long years has not often presented, I take it, to any one of us. Those were the great days of youth; and each man in the company, even if he did not project great things of his own, revelled in poetry or sunned himself in art.

Obviously this was an all-male coterie, with no place in it for a girl, even a highly gifted girl. And yet the masculine stir and excitement generated by the society of seven good-looking and talented young men could not help exerting an attraction for a girl of Christina's temperament; and, as a matter of fact, she did take a lively interest in the PRB and its affairs. However, in 1848 she was not "the Queen of the Pre-Raphaelites," as she has been called, much less Gosse's "High Priestess of Pre-Raphaelitism," or Swinburne's "Jael who led our hosts to victory." In 1848 she was merely a sprightly girl of eighteen, who was accustomed to enjoying the brilliant and amusing company of her brothers and sharing their literary interests, and who was unwilling to relinquish these familiar and harmless pleasures. It was almost inevitable that she should have chosen a fiancé from among the promising young men who were on terms of fraternal intimacy with her brothers.

And yet her eagerness to participate in the PRB excitement cannot wholly explain her decision to accept Collinson's second offer. True, her brothers favored him and urged her to reconsider when he proposed again. They presented Collinson to the young girl as almost a brother himself, practically a member of the family, for the Rossettis always looked upon their intimate friends as a kind of enlargement of the family circle. But even that was not sufficient to persuade a woman as capable of making up her own mind as Christina was, even at eighteen.

More than anything else, what weighed the scales in Collinson's favor

was her realization that no other career but marriage was open to her. She knew that she was an economic burden to her family. Among themselves Frances, Maria, and William were supporting her. The only alternative to marriage for a Victorian girl was the profession of governess, and we have seen that this alternative was repugnant to her. What, then, was left but marriage?

Also, she liked Collinson even if she did not love him in the way she might have wished. He was an artist, a poet, and, perhaps more important for her, a deeply religious man. Despite his religious vacillation, she felt that at core he was an earnest Christian, and she was confident that this quality alone could provide a felicitous foundation for a solid marriage.

There was general rejoicing in the family at the news of Christina's engagement. William, now more intimate than ever with Christina's fiancé, promptly visited the Collinson family at their Pleaseley Hill residence. There he received from Christina arch, bantering, self-consciously clever letters meant for Collinson's as well as her brother's eyes. "You probably not only *profusely banqueted,* but surfeited your victims with my poetry," she wrote coquettishly, "but in this you may not have been the sole culprit."

IV

It is during the period of their engagement that we hear a great deal about a personality trait of Collinson's that must have been something of a trial to his fiancée. If William, who liked him, freely admitted that he was not the man to arouse in his friends great warmth of affection, the other Pre-Raphaelite brothers were even more outspoken in their criticism. Collinson, said Holman Hunt, was "an amiable fellow-student, painstaking in all his drawings . . . but in his own person tame and sleepy." Whether the brothers held their monthly meetings at Collinson's studio or elsewhere, he invariably "fell asleep at the beginning, and had to be waked up at the conclusion of a noisy evening." He could rarely see the humor of anything, and "although he sometimes laughed in a lachrymose manner . . . I fear our attempts to enliven him were but futile."

Except for Collinson, all the Brothers were fond of taking long walks together in the country on moonlit nights, sometimes returning only in time to see dawn and sunrise over London from Hampstead Heath. Such escapades, intoxicating to the others, were an ordeal to poor Collinson, who hated to miss his night's sleep and tried his best to get excused from the midnight excursions, but to no avail; the others insisted upon dragging him along with them. Only he, of all the seven, was not appreciative of the "moonlit and moon-shaded heath" which Hunt describes so vividly in his account of one of these nocturnal expeditions.

Arriving at a little bridge over a dwindled stream, the young men saw

"the haloed moon casting spoke-like shadows of the trees" round about them. Tramping on, they came to a small village and seated themselves on the pedestal of the village pump. "Our conversation was at first exclusively for our own benefit, but in the end we set up a lusty shout with a view to waking Collinson for the homeward journey. It was a great hurrah; at the same instant we saw a candle lighted on the first-floor window of each cottage in the little hamlet, and twenty or thirty night-capped heads were thrust out simultaneously at the surrounding casements." Walking home in the dawnlight, singing, joking, and laughing, the Brothers were obliged to support poor Collinson, who dozing on his feet leaned on one or another of them and had to be half-carried home.

Another time Hunt said of Collinson, "In his personal life the painter seemed less awake than ever; he repined daily as he sat at breakfast on the terribly bad night he had had, yawning as he sipped his tea. If I went into his studio at noon he was asleep over the fire, while a hulking model was idly earning his shilling an hour all the same, and as the home remittances had ceased, it seemed that bankruptcy must be coming on like an armed man."

This is a description of Collinson at the time he was engaged to be married. Such a worshiper of Somnus, lacking in both wit and humor, could hardly have had much appeal for a high-spirited girl. In Christina's estimation one of the most deadly of the seven deadly sins, and the one from which she prayed daily to be delivered, was the sin of sloth. Although in her poetry she expressed a ceaseless longing for rest—possibly a symptom of anemia—she looked upon it as an ideal to be achieved only in the grave. Life, as she conceived it, was a race to be run, a hill to be climbed, a fiery ordeal to be surmounted. To live this life took, as she knew, strength, courage, endurance, and, above all, energy. "Sloth precludes energy," she wrote; "sloth may accompany a great many amiable tempers and skin-deep charms, but sloth runs no race. And a race is the one thing set before us."

During her engagement she must have fought a losing battle to keep her fiancé awake, wincing at times at the good-natured jeers of his brother Pre-Raphaelites, themselves so lusty and vigorous. In speaking of the young PRB warriors who were arming themselves for the struggle ahead, William describes Gabriel as "defiant," Hunt as "tough," and Millais as combative, "all eagerness for the fray, 'longing to be at 'em,' and to show his mettle." Only Christina's future husband was not on his mettle.

Hunt's account of Christina at this time does not suggest a flourishing engagement. He shows her to us not with her future husband, but *en famille.* In the accounts of contemporaries and in her own letters, she and Collinson never appear together. Despite their engagement, apparently they did not see much of one another. Upon the occasion described by Hunt, he was a dinner guest at the Rossettis' before a regular

PRB meeting, and one would naturally expect to find Collinson present; but if he was there, Hunt does not speak of him.

Influenced by the fact that Christina had posed for Gabriel as the model for Mary Virgin in his first successful Pre-Raphaelite painting, *The Girlhood of Mary Virgin,* Hunt saw "Miss Christina" as "exactly the pure and docile-hearted damsel that her brother portrayed God's Virgin pre-elect to be." But despite the calm and placid appearance she presented to her world—a façade which misled them all, even Gabriel, into assuming that it reflected an inner state—in actuality the tinder was dry and crackling, the faggots heaped and highly inflammable.

V

Christina's visit to Collinson's family at Pleaseley Hill in August, 1849, did not help matters. Her lack of enthusiasm for her fiancé's relatives, so clearly revealed in her letters, indicates that her discontent with her engagement was in an advanced state by then, and that the infection, spreading below the surface for some ten months, had reached a head.

This was the summer that *The Germ,* the PRB literary journal conceived by Gabriel, had its inception. It started as "a project for a monthly sixpenny magazine for which four or five of us would write and one make an etching, each subscribing a guinea, and thus becoming a proprietor," said William. As it originally existed in Gabriel's mind, the periodical was on a more lavish scale another successor to "the fallen *Hodge-Podge.*"

That summer Woolner introduced his Brothers to Coventry Patmore, already a poet of assured reputation, at whose house they met Tennyson, Browning, William Allingham, Carlyle, and others. "These Pre-Raphaelites they talk of," commented Carlyle, "are said to copy the thing as it is, or invent it as they believe it must have been: now there's some sense and hearty sincerity in this. It's the only way of doing anything fit to be seen."

At Patmore's house there were earnest debates about whether Tennyson or Browning would be *"the* man" twenty years hence; and the young men listened deferentially to Patmore's very definite views about English poetry. "The present race of poets," he told them, were "highly self-conscious" compared to their predecessors, the Romantics, "but yet not sufficiently so for the only system now possible—the psychological." He singled out Christina's religious verse for praise, particularly her *Vanity of Vanities,* and found Gabriel's poems remarkable for their capacity to suggest the quality of painting. He approved the prospectus for the new magazine and agreed to contribute poems, provided his name was withheld.

Organizing the journal and getting it launched was a stimulating challenge to the Rossetti men. William, who was appointed editor, wrote

to Christina at Pleaseley Hill and asked for contributions. She replied that although she was looking forward to the appearance of the first issue and had no doubt that it would be clever, she wished to be excused from joining the staff because it included "a rabid Chartist." This was William North, an obscure novelist who not long afterwards severed his connection with the magazine. One wonders what Christina had against Chartism. Possibly in this as in other matters she was influenced by her mother's basic conservatism.

Her correspondence with William during her Pleaseley Hill visit hints that she was having a dull time of it. One of the oddest features of her engagement is that during this visit to his family Collinson himself was not present, "not even for a day," as William dryly remarks.

"Though my visit here is very tolerable," she conceded, "the postman is quite an event in my existence. Her other "sol-ace," she punned, was Sol, the Collinsons' dog.

Furthermore, she missed the shared literary activity she was accustomed to in her own family. Not only did she and her brothers enjoy the same poems, such as Barham's *As I lay a-thinkynge,* a copy of which she requested while she was at Pleaseley Hill, but they played together the literary game of *bout-rimé* sonnets, a diversion which stimulated and developed Christina's dexterity in verse writing, and which she sorely missed at Pleaseley Hill. One of the participants would give the rhyme-endings, and the other two would, said William, "knock off the sonnet thereto as fast as possible." Christina herself worked rapidly at this exercise. One *bout-rimé* sonnet which appears in the collected *Works* was written in five minutes, another in nine. For her, "ten to twelve minutes was counted a long spell."

Of course this kind of literary frolic was not to be found at Pleaseley Hill, where "the talk of beaus" was "perpetual." Although Christina admitted that fewer jokes had been made at her expense than she had expected, and of these Collinson's sister Mary was "entirely innocent," on the whole, "local converse" wearied her. "Yet this advantage it possesses," she added ironically, "I cannot join in it; so may, during its continuance, abandon myself to my own meditations."

News of the Brotherhood "or anything else," she said, would be "thankfully received." She could not have been more bored: "In my desperation, I knit lace with a perseverance completely foreign to my nature. Yesterday I made a dirt-pudding in the garden, wherein to plant some slips of currant. The unbusiness-like manner in which the process was gone through affords every prospect of complete failure. Ah Will! If you were here we would write *bout-rimé* sonnets and be subdued together." Obviously she did not relish the prospect of being subdued for life by the overpowering philistinism of the Collinson family.

Her cry from the heart brought an immediate response from William,

who not only promptly sent her the Barham poem for consolation, but also enclosed rhyme endings for a *bout-rimé* sonnet, which she wrote and returned to him by the next post. Earlier she had said that she rather liked Mary Collinson, who, although not at all affectionate, seemed "real"; but in her letter of September 8 she was less enthusiastic. "I had mentioned to Mary the sweet prettiness of *As I lay a-thinkynge*," she told William, "but she does not appreciate it; at least not as we do."

In another of the Pleaseley Hill letters (August 31) she barely managed to conceal by a tone of light irony her feeling of alienation from Collinson's relatives. "Mary desires me to kindly remember, or something of the sort, 'us' to you." About the prospect of meeting Charles, Collinson's brother, she commented, "Mary prophecies my being a favorite with C.C. on account of my unalterable self-possession. Fancy the inflated state in which I shall re-enter London, should this flattering preference result from my visit."

These letters can hardly be interpreted as an engaged girl's expression of enthusiastic affection for the family she is about to enter; rather, they suggest that Christina was provoked and exasperated at being placed in a false position, that she was trying to make the best of it, but not succeeding.

The eruption was not long in coming. By the middle of September she was back again in London and writing to William, who was on the Isle of Wight, "My correspondence with Mary Collinson has come to an end by her desire. Do not imagine we have been quarreling; not at all; but she seems to think her brother's affairs so unpromising as to render our continuing to write to each other not very pleasant. Does this not sound extraordinary? We are all very much surprised."

Collinson's affairs were not only "unpromising" but downright disastrous, as his letter to Stephens written later that autumn clearly demonstrates:

*Dear Stephens

I received your kind note last evening. I was coming down to you being penniless; but the weather turning out so very heavy and threatening I [illegible] my watch for £1 instead and returned home. Thank you most sincerely for your kind offers of assistance. Come here this evening if possible; but if you cannot, do not trouble yourself to write —Invite a lot of us to your place as soon as you have an evening disengaged and believe me ever

Your grateful and affectionate P.R.B. brother
James Collinson

Tuesday morning* [4]

Although this state of her brother's affairs undoubtedly inspired Mary Collinson's move, the Collinson family seemed to have taken no more warmly to Christina than she to them. Instead of being depressed by the

circumstance, which should have represented a serious threat to her emotional life, she appeared more relieved than otherwise. She plunged cheerfully into PRB business, and, acting as Gabriel's secretary, communicated to William the business details connected with the launching of *The Germ,* the name finally settled upon after a succession of titles such as *The Scroll* and *The Seed* had been rejected.

During the autumn Christina was Gabriel's model as well as his secretary, sitting to him for the head of the Virgin in his second Pre-Raphaelite oil, the *Ecce Ancilla Domini*—"the blessed white eyesore" and "the blessed white daub," he called it. He himself, besides painting, writing the poetic masterpiece *My Sister's Sleep* (or rewriting it), and "wasting" several days at the Museum, "reading up all manner of old romaunts, to pitch upon stunning words for poetry," still found time, before leaving for Paris with Hunt in September, to arrange with the firm of Aylott and Jones for publication of *The Germ.* From Paris he wrote that with some exceptions, everything at the Louvre was "filthy slosh," and that he had not seen six pretty faces on the boulevards of Paris.

In conspicuous contrast to her Pleaseley Hill correspondence, the letters Christina wrote that autumn are notable for their tone of vivacious contentment. Although on September 26 she mentions Collinson's new picture, *The Saint's Tragedy,* she says little about the man himself. "Whether he will be at the Heimann's tomorrow I know not. Mamma sends love," is the way she concludes the letter to William.

VI

On the last day of 1849 the ill-starred *Germ* was finally in the hands of the printer. The first number (January, 1850) contained Christina's *Dreamland* and *An End,* Gabriel's *My Sister's Sleep* and his prose fiction tale *Hand and Soul* (which on December 21 he stayed up all night to finish), Woolner's *My Beautiful Lady,* Patmore's *Seasons,* and William's introductory sonnet printed on the cover [5] and his review of Clough's *Bothie of Toper-na-Vuolich.* It was he too who drew up the statement of aims:

> An attempt will be made, both intrinsically and by review, to claim for Poetry that place to which its present development in the literature of this country so emphatically entitles it.
>
> The endeavor held in view throughout the writings on Art will be to encourage and enforce an entire adherence to the simplicity of nature; and also to direct attention, as an auxiliary medium, to the comparatively few works which Art has yet produced in this spirit. . . .

In addition to the PRB's, the other men connected with *The Germ* were Ford Madox Brown, Cave Thomas, Walter Deverell, the sculptor Hancock, and the brothers Tupper, who financed and published the last two issues. All the contributions in the first issue were unsigned, but

in the subsequent three issues signatures were used. For Christina, Gabriel invented the pen name of Ellen Alleyn. Some thirty years later the American publishers Dodd, Mead, and Company wrote to William inquiring what had ever become of that interesting poet Ellen Alleyn, who wrote such remarkable verse.

It was in the second number (Feb., 1850) that Christina published the first poem of *Three Stages* under the title *A Pause of Thought.* Three of her poems appeared in this issue. The other two were *Song* ("O roses for the flush of youth") and *A Testimony,* which Patmore praised for being "in the style which should be adopted in hymns . . . to make them good." Patmore himself was represented by *Stars and Moon.* This number, the most distinguished of the four that appeared, also contained Gabriel's *The Blessed Damozel,* that "first-rate affair" of Collinson's, *The Child Jesus,* and *Morning Sleep,* a long blank verse poem by William Bell Scott, which the young editor thought "so gloriously fine that it must absolutely come into No. 2. . . ."

But the magazine was struggling hard for existence, and the PRB's, discouraged by limited sales, accumulating bills, and other financial liabilities, were "unanimously of the opinion" that it would not reach another number. Nevertheless, under a new title, *Art and Poetry,* it managed to see the light in March but skipped April. Several of the long poems promised for the third and fourth numbers were withdrawn, and William, hard pressed to fill up space, dug out what he called his sister's "old thing," *Repining.* Although he considered it hardly "up to the mark," it was at least "long enough and in narrative form." The March issue also contained Christina's *Sweet Death.*

The fourth and last issue came out in May, and then the magazine died of inanition. Nothing of Christina's appeared in the May number. The journal's collapse was facetiously celebrated by a PRB dirge which began,

> Bring leaves of yew to intertwine
> With 'leaves' that evermore are dead,

a pronouncement that proved inaccurate, for that "curious old book," as Christina was to call it many years later, came to possess a literary and historical interest out of all proportion to its short span of life.

It was during the spring that the expected attack by the British art world was unleashed in all its fury. The previous spring (1849) both Hunt and Millais had exhibited at the Academy, Hunt his *Rienzi* and Millais his *Lorenzo and Isabella.* Gabriel had shown his oil *The Girlhood of Mary Virgin* at the so-called "Free" Exhibition near Hyde Park corner. Although all three artists had signed their work with the PRB initials ("Please Ring Bell" to the uninformed world), these initials had caused no comment and aroused very little interest. The pictures were

on the whole well received, Gabriel's *Girlhood* being warmly praised by *The Athenæum* for its invention, design, and "great sensibility." It was not until 1850, when Gabriel let out the secret of the initials and it became understood that they signified an organized movement of rebellion against traditional art, that the storm broke.

Millais' *The Carpenter's Shop* (later called *Christ in the House of His Parents)* became "the signal for a perfect crusade against the P.R.B.," William wrote in the journal which as secretary he kept for the Brotherhood. "The mystic letters, with their signification, have appeared in all kinds of papers; first, I believe, in a letter, *Town Talk and Table Talk,* in the *Illustrated News.* . . . But the designation is now so notorious that all concealment is at an end. In all the papers—*The Times, The Examiner, The Daily News,* even to Dickens' *Household Words,* where a leader was devoted to the P.R.B., and devoted them to the infernal gods—the attack on Millais has been most virulent and audacious." [6]

The Pre-Raphaelites were undoubtedly the fashionable topic of conversation that season. Stigmatized by the press as "pestilent heretics," cut in the streets and hissed at the Academy by their fellow students, Hunt and Millais were the chief targets of the savage assault, but Gabriel too came in for his share. *The Athenæum,* formerly friendly to his work, now condemned his *Ecce Ancilla* as "an unintelligent imitation of the mere technicalities of old art."

It was not until the following spring, when Ruskin came to the defense of the beleaguered Brotherhood with his two famous letters to *The Times* ("there has been nothing in art so earnest or so complete since the days of Albert Dürer"), that the movement as such gained widespread acceptance and respectability. But by then it had already begun to disintegrate as a cohesive society of brothers.

Christina's engagement, which had come into existence with the formation of the PRB, now came to an end with its dissolution, more precisely with the expiration of *The Germ* in the spring of 1850. It was hastened by the religious crisis of the fifties, the second great wave of Tractarian capitulation to Rome. Despite Christina's indifference to public issues, the two significant currents of the age inevitably drew her into the mainstream of English Victorian life. They were the rebellion against a stale traditionalism in art and the religious controversy, which, started by the Tractarians, eventually led to fundamental reforms within the Church of England. These issues reached her, however, not through intellectual but through emotional channels. The Pre-Raphaelite and Oxford Movements, far-reaching in their effect upon the national life, touched Christina only at the nerve centers of her personal relationships.

Again Collinson, tottering between Anglicanism and Catholicism, changed coats. During the height of the excitement of 1850 about the famous Gorham case, which ripped apart the very fabric of the English

Church, many prominent Anglican churchmen went over to Rome. Collinson must have listened enthralled to Dodsworth's fiery denunciations from the pulpit of Christ Church, as he castigated the Judicial Committee of the Privy Council for deciding that Gorham in defiance of his own Bishop could teach or not teach, as he chose, the doctrine of Baptismal Regeneration of Infants and still remain within the Church. Even today those sermons delivered with impassioned eloquence flame to life from the dusty page.[7] For Dodsworth the issue had become once again the great and ancient conflict between Church and State left unsolved by the Reformation. On January 27 he preached a sermon on "The Things of Caesar and the Things of God, a discourse . . . with especial reference to the claim of the State to exercise power over the Church in decisions of Doctrine." On March 10 he took as his text, "A house divided against itself." Both Pusey and Keble were distressed by the militance of their colleague. "What shall I do," Dr. Pusey wailed in a letter to Keble, "if Dodsworth continues this sort of sermon?"

The parish was deeply shaken. What these responsible leaders had feared soon came to pass. "Many of the congregation," wrote Canon Burrows in his history of Christ Church, Albany Street, "discerning the tendency of Mr. Dodsworth's mind, had already ceased to attend the Church" before his formal resignation the last day of 1850. Collinson was among those who drew the logical consequence for themselves from the preacher's eloquent rhetoric, and about May or June of 1850 he preceded his pastor to Rome. "I am doing what I can for the good cause (Popery)," he confided to Stephens, "and I am sure that you like your interesting friend in Germ No. 4[?] can have no objection to give an old lady a lift in spite of her very red cloak, which gets terribly sprinkled with mud just now."

For Christina this was the end. "As she had only accepted Collinson's suit on the understanding of his being an English Churchman, so, when he declared himself a Catholic, she revoked her troth," said William decorously: "this she did with deep sorrow and reluctance, and only at the bidding of a supposed duty." But in the light of all that had occurred, we may assume that duty had never looked more delectable to Christina.

Shortly after the engagement was broken, Collinson, who was assumed by the PRB's "to be deep in hibernation," suddenly awakened and sent in his formal resignation to the Brotherhood. As a sincere Catholic, he said, he felt that he could not "assist in spreading the artistic doctrines of those who are not." Although he would always reverence and idolize the Pre-Raphaelite painters, he was convinced that he would be "dishonouring God's Holy Saints" were he to continue to be a member of the group. In a postscript he said, "Please do not attempt to change my mind." No one did.

"Goodbye to a man that has had fine capabilities in him never allowed

fair play by himself!" William exclaimed a few years later when he heard that Collinson intended to relinquish art and enter a Jesuit college as "a working brother."

According to William the breaking of Christina's engagement left a lasting "blight . . . on her heart and spirit." He attributed her despondency, conspicuous that fall, to the aftereffects of this unhappy affair, and to support this view he related the incident of her fainting when she ran across Collinson one day by chance in Regent's Park. Granting it is not unlikely that she felt a natural perturbation at seeing the man who, had events transpired differently, would have been at that very moment her husband, the fainting proves nothing at all except that she was momentarily upset. In the nineteenth century, when fainting was fashionable, women fainted for a variety of reasons, as well as for no reason at all.

Although she continued to show interest in Collinson after the engagement was broken,[8] it is possible that the engagement itself rather than its termination was responsible for the "blight." If she was unusually dejected in the autumn of 1850, it was probably due to an entirely different set of circumstances, in which Collinson and the broken engagement played merely a subordinate part.

Had no other motive existed as a potent reason for breaking the engagement, it is doubtful whether in any case she would have brought herself to marry Collinson. As it was, her obvious reluctance to go through with the marriage was reinforced by the powerful pull exerted by a counterattraction. In the interval a new and complicating element had entered her life and entangled its threads, drawing the knot of her engagement tighter, so tight that at times it must have resembled a noose.

It was in December of 1847 that she met for the first time William Bell Scott, the most important of the three men with whom she was emotionally involved. Of the three, it was Scott, a man for whom she admittedly showed "great predilection," who was to play the leading role in the "hushed" drama of her life.

❀ 3 ❀

"FIRST SPARKS"

1847–1850

None of Christina's biographers or critics has been able to account for the passionate love poetry written between her known love affairs, after the Collinson fiasco, which ended in 1850, and before Charles Bagot Cayley's courtship, which did not begin until 1862 or thereabouts. And yet the major part of her love poetry falls within that period of her young womanhood, in the twelve years between the ages of twenty and thirty-two. It would be remarkable if the hidden emotional springs which fed her poetry could have remained unreplenished for twelve parched years, sustained only by the memory of the thoroughly unsatisfactory relationship with Collinson. Besides, these were the years—her blooming time as a woman—when she was dropping enigmatic hints about an unknown love situation, not to be explained by any of the known emotional facts of her life. And yet it was during these twelve years that her friendship with William Bell Scott (which has gone unnoticed despite William Rossetti's comment upon it in his "Memoir" to the *Works*) developed and flourished.

Most of what is generally known about Scott originates in his own *Autobiographical Notes,* posthumously published in 1892. This was Scott's second autobiography. The first, which he started in 1852 and completed in 1854, was burned in 1877 when he began the *Notes*. But a few scattered pages of the earlier journal, which escaped the flames, are still extant.[1] These pages shed additional, sometimes very illuminating light upon Scott's personality and early emotional commitments.

He was born near Edinburgh, the son of a prosperous printer, engraver, and landscape painter, who was an ardent admirer of Blake. The elder Scott brought up his four children (two of whom died in childhood) on Blake, Robert Blair, and Edward Young. As a small boy, Scott was greatly attached to his mother, and he could not understand why she would have wanted to marry his father. This traditional antagonism to

the head of the family, which psychologists have taught us is quite normal in a young lad, deepened into bitter hatred when one day Scott's father humiliated him in the presence of friends by laughing at his inability to translate a simple Latin phrase. He ran upstairs, shut himself in his bedroom, took down his Bible, and swore on it a solemn oath that, when he grew to be old enough and strong enough, he would be the death of his father.

We can trace the source of this death wish in a dream Scott considered important enough to write down in his 1854 journal. Anticipating Freud, Scott observed that dreams were worth preserving, for "undoubtedly they throw a light on character; the psychology has [as] much to do with them as the physiology of the dreamer." He then relates the following dream about his father:

> *There were a great many people and a great many forms I cannot describe moving vertically in a strange and rapid manner: they seemed to come straight down to the ground and then up through the roof again, and these I understood to be souls. I knew that I was in my old bedroom at home, and several persons about. Among others my father who appeared nearly alone. His peculiar way of looking about him, his spectacles and his [illegible] were all vividly observed by me. When he came close to the bed with a knife in his hand and apparently in explanation to some one said, 'We will see at once how high *he* can go,' I felt great oppression and the dream disappeared.*

His older brother, David Scott, a painter of great distinction, was the genius of the family. And although Scott had shown himself so sensitive to his father's male superiority, he seemed to feel neither jealousy of nor hostility toward David. On the contrary, he loved and even worshiped his brother, at times "crossing this side idolatry." Yet his attitude had a certain ambivalence, for after David's death, Scott alluded to his brother as his "tyrant and his bully."

A passage from the 1854 journal suggests a disturbed and moody adolescence, and shows Scott again unable to live up to the superego expectations instilled in him by his father:

> *Indeed I cannot understand the despondent wretchedness that took possession of me then. I must have been nearly eighteen—an age that ought to be elastic and fearless—to which the painful fancies or outcast humilities ought to be altogether foreign. It must have been nervous debility. On returning to [illegible] I was so anxious to be home again, that I started off to walk on Sunday morning, the rain pouring and not a break in the clouds. The fourteen miles I had to travel was over moorland without road; after struggling on for many hours I became faint and ready [to] give up in the next pool when I again found the road and the shepherd's cottage, with the fire in the middle of the floor, almost the only one I ever saw, where I found shelter and a bed for the night.*

As a youth Scott wrote poetry, pretentious, pompous religio-didactic verse modeled on *Night Thoughts* and *The Grave*. It was Professor John Wilson (Christopher North) of *Blackwood's* who first told him to write from experience, not invention; and Sir Walter Scott, by whom he was acknowledged as one of the clan, who advised him to write in rhyme, not blank verse, and to imitate Thomson, not Milton.

Drifting about the convivial Edinburgh of the early 1830's, Scott led the semi-intellectual, semi-bohemian life of an artist and fledgling man of letters. He made sudden friendships, notable for their fervent intensity, lived intimately and affectionately with his friends, associated with prostitutes (his poem *Rosabel* was inspired by a girl he picked up on an Edinburgh street), and, prompted by his admiration of De Quincey, then an Edinburgh "character," upon one occasion at least, tried opium.

Trained in his father's workshop as an etcher and engraver, Scott soon turned to painting. He went to London in 1837, and in 1842 entered the cartoon competition for the frescoes which were to decorate the new Houses of Parliament. Although he failed to win even an honorable mention, his work brought him to the attention of the National Board of Trade, which offered him the head mastership of the newly organized Government School of Design at Newcastle-on-Tyne. Taking leave of his London friends, among whom were Leigh Hunt and George Henry Lewes, Scott departed from London shortly thereafter, and went to Newcastle.

It was his poetry which was responsible for his friendship with the Rossettis. One day in the autumn of 1847 Gabriel Rossetti was browsing through one of the "little" literary magazines of the day when he came upon two poems by an unknown writer which seemed to him "so beautiful and original" that in his excitement he could think of nothing else for days. One of these poems was *Rosabel*. Gabriel became obsessed by the desire to know what else this remarkable new poet had written, and where his poems were to be found. No one seemed to know. Gabriel almost gave up the quest, but in November he found the scent again. As he expressed it, he "fell in with a most inadequate paragraph in the *Art Union Journal* that informed him of the publication of a new poem, *The Year of the World*, by William Bell Scott. In his delight at discovering his man, he lost no time in getting hold of the poem and "fell upon it like a vulture."

He found it to be an ambitious work. It was a long allegorical epic, tracing the progressive development of humanity from the golden age of Genesis to some future golden age when through scientific knowledge Man will have subjugated nature and conquered death. The work showed the strong influence of *Prometheus Unbound*, which at a time when Shelley's masterpiece went unappreciated, Scott considered one of the great poems of nineteenth-century literature.

The Year of the World, said its author, was his "first and last important act of literary enthusiasm." Brought out during the summer of 1847, the poem was "printed, published, and still-born." Carlyle ignored the copy Scott sent him. Emerson, more interested, sought out its author some years later during his European tour. But a certain M'Liver, a newspaper editor who rented a house Scott owned in Edinburgh, gave his landlord's literary effort rough treatment in his periodical. Reviewing the poem, M'Liver wrote:

> After considering over this book and trying to gain some clue to it, we have come to the conclusion that it has no possible elucidation, but that it has been the result of some fortuitous circumstances: an immense quantity of sounding lines and sentences have been thrown together higgledy-piggledy—made *pie* of, in short, and then printed in such confounded order as chance produced.

Scott tried to be amused by this criticism, but actually he smarted from his tenant's jibes, and when toward the end of November he received a letter from an unknown admirer praising his poem in extravagant terms, he was greatly pleased at being appreciated after the "insulting notice" from Mr. M'Liver. The letter was addressed from 50 Charlotte Street, Portland Place, and it was signed Gabriel Dante Rossetti. "A finer, more dignitous [*sic*], a more deeply thoughtful production, a work that is more truly a *work*—has seldom, indeed, shed its light upon me," Scott read. "To me I can truly say that it revealed 'some depth unknown, some inner life unlived.' "

This "generously enthusiastic letter" was, as may be imagined, an important event in Scott's life. Already in his mid-thirties, Scott feared more than anything else the blight of obscurity; and now he learned he was not ignored after all: among the new generation of artists and poets now growing into manhood, he was singled out for homage. Fame, that winged immortal, came to him creeping instead of on wings, but she came. Needless to say, Scott answered the letter immediately, and a few days later received a bundle of manuscripts containing Rossetti's own poems. Opening the packet eagerly, what was Scott's "wonder and perplexity" when he found *The Blessed Damozel, My Sister's Sleep,* "and other admirable poems marshalled under the title of *Songs of the Art-Catholic.*" What amazed Scott was the unknown youth's genius; what perplexed him was the reference to Catholicism. He wondered if "somehow or other the Oxford tractarianism just then distracting weak intellects had possibly already undermined that of this wonderfully gifted boy! I looked forward with anxiety to meeting him."

II

The meeting took place during the Christmas holidays of 1847. Scott was in London on business, and he lost no time in calling at Charlotte

Street. His correspondent was not at home, but the elder Rossetti and Christina were; and Scott never forgot his first glimpse of her:

> I entered the small front parlour or dining room of the house, and found an old gentleman sitting by the fire in a great chair, the table drawn close to his chair, with a thick manuscript book open before him, and the largest snuff-box I ever saw beside it conveniently open. He had a black cap on his head furnished with a great peak or shade for the eyes, so that I saw his face only partially.
>
> By the window was a high narrow reading-desk at which stood writing a slight girl with a serious regular profile, dark against the pallid wintry light without. This most interesting to me of the two inmates turned on my entrance, made the most formal and graceful curtsey, and resumed her writing, and the old gentleman signed to a chair for my sitting down, and explained that his son was now painting in the studio he and a young friend had taken together. . . . As the short day was already spent, I could not go there at once. The old gentleman's pronunciation of English was very Italian, and though I did not know that both of them—he and his daughter—were probably at that moment writing poetry of some sort and might wish me far enough, I left very soon.
>
> The girl was Christina, who had already at seventeen written, like her brother, some admirable lyrics, nearly all overshaded with melancholy. Melancholy I call it, but perhaps the right word would be pious sentiment. At least in her mind piety and sadness went together, and have done so all her life.[2]

That Scott was attracted to the slight, pale, reserved girl, "the most interesting . . . of the two inmates," is quite evident from this description written almost half a century later. In it Scott uses the guarded and cautious language of an old man speaking of one of the great literary figures of his age. But at the time of meeting Christina he was thirty-six, a man in his prime, and susceptible to youth and beauty. He was following an adventure in London, and the girl in the wintry twilight, with her unusual beauty and haunting charm, with her courteous self-possession and her preoccupation with her own pursuit, lent a romantic flavor to his adventure. The boy, her brother, had already whetted Scott's curiosity; the girl must have aroused it even more.

What, if anything, did this first meeting mean to Christina? The man she saw that December afternoon was, according to William, "handsome and highly impressive looking . . . of good stature, bony and well-developed but rather thin frame; pondering and somewhat melancholy air, and deliberate, low-toned utterance." He had thick brown hair, bushy black eyebrows, and very pale, clear blue eyes, of the kind "sometimes called cold and steely."

Holman Hunt's first impression of Scott was equally favorable. He found "the visitor from the North both handsome and interesting." He was then "a man of about thirty-five; in height . . . five feet ten, with brown hair flowing, although not long." When he talked to a new friend,

"his regard . . . was singularly penetrating and deliberate, while his speech was entertainingly syllabic and naïve, so that all the mischief that might be imagined in his Mephistophelean expression was dissipated in a breath." Hunt attributed the diabolical effect, or "arch-fiend expression," as he called it, to "the angle formed by his eyebrows which from their parting centre ascended sharply, and ere they deflected shot off a handsome tuft, some of the hairs of which curled downwards like young moustaches." This was the man Hunt was to call affectionately, "the Northern Vitruvius of latter days."

Other friends who knew Scott at this time of his life were likewise enthusiastic about him. George Henry Lewes called him "the grave and high-minded Scott," a man who "led a lonely life but led it like a noble soul." To see him, to know him, Lewes added fervently, "was an influence not forgotten." It was Lewes who bestowed upon him the nickname of Duns Scotus, which remained with him throughout his life. Industrious and energetic, ambitious for fame, restless in the pursuit of knowledge, Scott struck his circle of friends as the very incarnation of the medieval philosopher.

It can easily be seen that he was an attractive man, and many women thought so. Ford Madox Brown once remarked that women in general, and his own wife in particular, were "enchanted" by Scott. Whether at seventeen Christina was likewise "enchanted" can be only surmised, but it is likely. In one of the two poems she addressed to him, she admitted that the admiration she had felt for him before she was twenty was "predilect still" at fifty.

Upon first meeting the Northerner, said William, the Rossettis, "female as well as male"—and the point is unnecessarily made—"took very warmly indeed to Scott, and found him not only attractive, but even fascinating." Since Christina happened to have been the only female member of her family present when Scott first called, it could hardly have been Mrs. Rossetti or Maria whom he fascinated.

In Scott's *Notes* he commented that, although he saw no more of the Rossettis for nearly a year, the meeting with them marked "the beginning of a new interest in life" for him, and even made him "almost regret having left London." Was it Rossetti's younger sister, more than the others, who gave his life that "new interest," and was she the one he most regretted leaving? Young, lovely, gifted, she herself as well as her "admirable lyrics" made a profound impression upon the susceptible Scotsman. Partial as he was to pretty women, he had never before met a beautiful girl who was also an accomplished poet, and the combination must have struck him as ideal. During the year that elapsed before he saw her again, he might have spent much time thinking about her and looking forward to another encounter. In his 1852–1854 journal occurs this

description of an unidentified woman who had Christina's hazel eyes and well-formed forehead:

> *But is she not a fearful as well as a loveable creation of God? Cold as that icy water . . . are those hazel eyes and that perfect forehead. Loveable? rather sacred and terrible is she without knowing it. . . .*

Did she regret the parting which followed so soon upon the flash of attraction during the first meeting? Presumably she too might have devoted spare hours to that idle daydreaming which is so often the prelude to love.

Some five weeks later she wrote *Three Stages I,* in which she describes her pursuit of the fleeing object I have identified as love and in which she alludes to the heartsickness resulting from "hope deferred." Although this may have been only the expression of those vague love-longings characteristic of young girls mature enough for marriage, she might also have been "watching and waiting"—her own words—for another glimpse of the man who had entered her life, only to vanish again so quickly. To the young author of *Repining,* which was written in December, 1847, the date of Scott's first appearance, he might well have borne a startling resemblance to the demon lover of ballad legendry, even to the "arch-fiend" expression of his remarkable eyebrows.

But when he failed to return, she probably forgot him, as young girls will. His image may have remained with her only as a possible embodiment of those undefined and passionate wish-fantasies at the semiconscious level. He had undoubtedly struck a spark, but the time had not yet come to kindle a fire. In the meantime she had the PRB and Collinson, to whom she had become engaged in the autumn of 1848, some ten months after Scott's first visit.

Although he did not return to London before the year had elapsed, he was intermittently corresponding with the Rossetti brothers. His second visit took place in the winter of 1848–1849. It was probably at this time that he saw the Pre-Raphaelite paintings of Gabriel and Hunt at the latter's studio which aroused and startled him. At first he thought they were painting in the manner of the Dutch realists, but soon he realized that their work was more in the nature of an imitation of photography: a fly was actually painted into the foreground of Hunt's picture. Rossetti's canvas, *The Girlhood of Mary Virgin,* was quite in the mood and tone of his *Songs of the Art-Catholic.* Scott was pleasantly surprised to recognize in the slender, delicate, pale, and virginal figure presented in profile the charming girl who wrote poetry over the high desk at Charlotte Street. The "wonderfully gifted boy" had used his pretty sister for his model of the Virgin, and the appropriateness of it held a piquant appeal for Scott.

III

It was in December, 1848, approximately at the time of Scott's second visit to London, that Christina wrote her celebrated lyric, *When I am Dead, My Dearest:*

When I am dead, my dearest,
Sing no sad songs for me;
Plant thou no roses at my head,
Nor shady cypress tree:
Be the green grass above me
With showers and dewdrops wet:
And if thou wilt, remember,
And if thou wilt, forget.

I shall not see the shadows,
I shall not feel the rain;
I shall not hear the nightingale
Sing on as if in pain:
And dreaming through the twilight
That doth not rise nor set,
Haply I may remember,
And haply may forget.[3]

Although some writers have attributed this poem to Collinson's inspiration, it is an odd lyric to be written by a girl presumably in the first flush of triumphant love. Even if one rejects the biographical reference, one would still be obliged to consider the lyric in the context of the other productions of the period.

This exquisite dirge for a life which, although it had hardly begun, appeared to Christina as already concluded was followed on January 7 (1849) by *Symbols*. By then Scott had left for Newcastle to resume his teaching and administrative duties. The theme of *Symbols* is that the potentialities for life and for beauty in life are often cruelly unfulfilled: the rosebud fails to blossom, the speckled eggs fail to hatch. The speaker feels a surge of anger against this waste in nature, but in the end disciplines her rebelliousness by the reminder of divine justice.

Frustration again appears as the theme in a poem of January 23, *Have Patience,* which begins with the lines,

The goblets are all broken,
The pleasant wine is spilt,
The songs cease,

and continues (with a glance at Byron) in the lines,

Fill high and deep! But how,
The goblets are all broken.

This poem was followed on February 6 by another of Christina's distinguished lyrics in which she treats again the theme of a promising youth unfulfilled:

> O roses for the flush of youth,
> And laurels for the perfect prime!
> But pluck an ivy branch for me
> Grown old before my time.
>
> O violets for the grave of youth,
> And bay for those dead in their prime;
> Give me the withered leaves I chose
> Before in the old time.[4]

The poems which follow in the spring and summer, *The Last Complaint* (unpublished), *An End* and *Dreamland* (which appeared in *The Germ*), *After Death, Rest, Looking Forward, Life Hidden, Remember,* all have a similar tone of mournful sadness and resignation, and suggest that Christina might have regretted some unfulfilled possibility in her own life. Assuredly, there was "a blight upon her heart and mind" long before her engagement was broken. Was it caused by the realization that she had made a dreadful mistake, that she had bound herself to one man too soon, and hence made impossible a rich and satisfying relationship which might have fulfilled her dream of sexual happiness?

It may have been at the home of Dr. John Epps, Scott's friend and frequently his host in London, that Christina met Scott again during the holiday season of 1848–49, for it was he who introduced the Rossettis to Dr. Epps and his wife, and the Rossetti girls became frequent callers at their house next door to the British Museum. If not at the Epps', Christina would have had ample opportunity to meet Scott elsewhere, for he soon made himself an integral part of the Rossetti circle, and he himself would doubtless have provided the opportunity for meeting Gabriel's pretty sister again. And even if by then she was engaged, we cannot imagine Scott not exerting himself to fascinate a girl he admired. We have seen that none of his friends was unresponsive to the charm of his personality, a charm Hunt found both diabolical and naïve. Energetic, vital, and exciting, Scott presented a dramatic contrast to the tame and drowsy Collinson. Despite the fact that she was an engaged girl, Christina, as well as the others, must have responded to "the singularly penetrating and deliberate gaze" of the magnetic blue eyes under their bushy black Mephistophelean brows.

"From this day to this,"—Scott is referring to his first visit to Charlotte Street—"Rossetti . . . Christina and Maria, his sisters, and William his brother . . . have all been very dear and near to me." We cannot doubt that he regarded the Rossetti men, who were often "like brothers" to him,

with deep affection, but no evidence exists (other than the routine exchange of family calls and dinner invitations) of a relationship at any time with Maria, who, not being pretty, was unlikely to interest him. It is possible that he mentioned Maria in this passage only for the purpose of propriety, and that his inclusion of the Rossetti sisters in his declaration of fondness is a hint that Christina was the one he considered "very dear and near" to him.

If Collinson had previously had the status of a brother of her brothers, Scott had the same advantage to an even greater degree. And whereas the Rossettis' bond of brotherhood with Collinson was, as we have seen, of brief duration, their fraternal relations with Scott continued throughout their lives. Much more than Collinson, Scott soon became a warm and intimate family friend. In this way he possessed the attractions of both strangeness and familiarity, a combination which could have had an irresistible charm for a reserved nature such as Christina's.

IV

The persistent theme of regret for the unfulfilled hopes of youth should therefore be regarded not as the product of poetic reverie, but of a concrete life situation. Too late the potentiality for an ideal relationship had unfolded before Christina's eyes. Materializing in the flesh, the romantic demon lover of her fantasy revealed himself in his human capacity as an active, warm, virile, and energetic man in whom she must have sensed a nature as passionate as her own. For such a man, her youth and beauty would have existed to some purpose. On Collinson, who fell asleep, they were wasted.

But in the spring of 1849 she was still engaged to Collinson. At this juncture her situation would have looked alarmingly complicated. Nothing in her experience could have prepared her for the moral light in which she would now have seen herself. In her eyes a betrothal was a serious pledge, only a degree less binding than the marriage vow itself. It could have been painful enough to acknowledge to herself that she felt no great love for the man to whom she had given such a pledge. But so long as she had been ready to undertake the responsibility of wifehood, she had nothing for which to reproach herself. However, the second meeting with Scott in the winter of 1848–1849 could have aroused in her the apprehension that not only did she fail to love her fiancé as she ought, but she was actually able to feel the stir of attraction toward another man.

A number of the 1849 poems, such as *One Certainty, A Testimony, A Christmas Carol, For Advent,* show a freshened interest in religious subjects. To turn to her religion when the pressure of living became too threatening was a solution that throughout her life Christina found the most satisfying. Yet its rigors were not to be denied. Hard spiritual work

was required to obtain even the minimal amount of satisfaction in this way, a way so stern and exacting.

An easier escape from crushing tensions was the old familiar, adolescent expedient of illness. The last time Christina's health had given her family cause for anxiety was in 1845, the year she had faced initially the threat of earning her livelihood as a governess. A governess, however, could leave an unsatisfactory position; for a wife, there was no escape.

Therefore in the spring of 1849 her health "gave rise to serious anxiety." By June she was so sick that she could not even write down her own poems. *Rest* and *Looking Forward* are in her mother's handwriting, and *A Testimony* in Maria's. Other than William's brief report of this illness, no record of it exists. One is unable to say what was the matter with Christina. Possibly struggling to solve her conflict and seeing no way out, she simply surrendered, and sank into apathy and invalidism as a passive protest against a situation she was unable to control.

In view of the menace to her health, the poems she wrote that April are of particular interest. Of the four bearing the April, 1849, dateline, the two familiar anthology pieces, *Dreamland* and *After Death,* display the usual note of immature self-pity. The latter is an externalization of a wish-dream common to young girls, that of punishing the indifferent lover by their death. In this poem an older man, who condescendingly calls the deceased "Poor child," shows his repentance by weeping once she is gone:

> He did not love me living; but once dead
> He pitied me. . . .

Two Pursuits and the second poem of *Three Stages* show a more realistic approach to her problem. The former, a sonnet, may have been inspired by a scene in Shelley's *Prometheus Unbound,* which we have noted was a favorite with Scott and a model for his own *Year of the World.* In Christina's poem the speaker, like the Asia of Shelley's poetic drama, is led on by an unembodied summons:

> A Voice said, 'Follow, follow': and I rose
> And followed far into the dreamy night.

The "Voice," a mysterious Shelleyan abstraction, leads the speaker to "where bluest water flows" (an image presumably intended to symbolize sexual happiness), but will not let her drink. The poet then dramatizes the tension in her own situation by introducing a second "Voice," which likewise directs the speaker to "Follow, follow"; and in this summons she recognizes the saving Christian call.

A pursuit had also been the subject of *Three Stages I* of February, 1848. Now in the second poem of the linked series, written April 18, 1849,

we learn the result of such a pursuit. The subtitle to this poem, which was published posthumously, is "The End of the First Part":

My happy happy dream is finished with,
My dream in which alone I lived so long.
My heart slept—woe is me, it wakeneth;
Was weak—I thought it strong.

O weary wakening from a life-true dream!
O pleasant dream from which I wake in pain!

So far, this may be read as the disappointment of a girl who has been disillusioned about her fiancé, though it may be assumed that her future husband would have had some share in her "happy happy dream." But the next three stanzas challenge such an interpretation. Borrowing Tennysonian imagery from *The Palace of Art,* in this poem too personal to be published in her lifetime, Christina wrote:

I must pull down my palace that I built,
Dig up the pleasure-gardens of my soul;
Must change my laughter to sad tears for guilt,
My freedom to control.

Now all the cherished secrets of my heart,—
Now all my hidden hopes are turned to sin.
Part of my life is dead, part sick, and part
Is all on fire within.

This is one of Christina's earliest references in her lyric poetry to guilt and sin. Of all the poems she wrote during the period of her engagement this is the hardest to interpret if one assumes, as her biographers have done, that she was happily enjoying the courtship of a man whose wife she soon would be. But on this assumption, how may the fact be explained that she would permit neither this nor the third of the *Three Stages* poems to be published?

It is obvious that the subjective palace and pleasure-gardens, the cherished secrets, and the hidden hopes had little to do with the anticipated union with Collinson. Why would an engaged girl deem it necessary to hide hopes of happiness in matrimony? and, more important, what kind of buried and cherished secrets could she carry in her heart?

An omitted stanza from *Seeking Rest,* which treats the same theme, alludes to a hidden emotional life unshared with mother and sister, those closest to her:

*But evermore I kept my joy
Hidden in mine own heart;—
I could not show them my life's life:—
So now I bear the smart
Of disappointment; and I strive
To hide it with vain art.*

V

Another linked poem of the period, which likewise hovers about the related themes of guilt and sin, is *Three Nuns,* composed between February, 1849, and May, 1850. Although Christina's attitude in this poem is uniquely her own, her choice of a subject may be attributed to an important development in her immediate environment.

This was the time during which the first Anglican sisterhood since the sixteenth century was taking root and flourishing a few doors north of Christ Church, at No. 17 Park Village West. Founded and directed by Dr. Pusey, who chose the Albany Street church as the scene of a novel experiment which he had discussed as early as 1838 with Tractarian leaders, the religious community of women caused amazement and consternation even in a parish as radical as Dodsworth's. "The special vocation of a Sister," wrote Pusey's biographer, "the character involved and the claims of such a character, were altogether unknown. . . . That young ladies [of good families] should shrink from society, and entertain thoughts of a vow of celibacy in the face of an eligible marriage was almost inconceivable." [5]

One can understand the excitement such an experiment would have generated among the young women of the parish, particularly serious-minded girls such as Christina and Maria. Miss Langston, the Mother Superior of the Park Village Sisterhood, and Miss Sellon, founder and Superior of the Devonport Sisterhood (which communities later amalgamated), were not the only attractive young women who impelled by religious enthusiasm left family, friends, suitors to devote themselves to the austerities and discipline of the monastic life. That the early Sisters, who soon made themselves felt as a force in the parish, exerted a powerful attraction for the Rossetti girls is apparent. A quarter of a century later Maria actually joined the All Saints' Sisterhood in Margaret Street. We have seen that, although Christina was drawn to the conventual life, she recognized that it was not for her. "I might have been a hermit," she once told William's daughter Olive, "but not a nun." Instead, throughout her life she wrote poems about nuns.

Three Nuns, written in the form of a dramatic monologue, deals with the emotional experience of three different women who have taken the veil, the first a poet, the second a girl who has renounced the man she still loves, the third a genuine religious. The second poem of the linked series was the first to be written. Dated February 12, 1849, it was written approximately at the time Christina was composing her short lyrics expressing regret for a youth unfulfilled. The speaker is an engaged girl who in renouncing her lover suffers from an inexplicable feeling of guilt:

> I loved him; yes, where was the sin?
> I loved him with my heart and soul;

But I pressed forward to no goal,
There was no prize I strove to win.
Show me my sin that I may see:
Throw the first stone, thou Pharisee.

I loved him, but I never sought
That he should know that I was fair.
I prayed for him; was my sin prayer?
I sacrificed, he never bought;
He nothing gave, he nothing took;
We never bartered look for look.

This sounds less like the description of an engaged girl's relations with her fiancé than it does a defense against a charge. After all, a girl can hardly say about her fiancé, "He nothing gave, he nothing took," for an engaged man has certainly given something in the interests of his engagement—his liberty, if nothing else. This nun, arguing with herself the question of her own guilt, seems to be resting her defense upon the fact that no overt acts of love have occurred between her and the man she loves. Neither, she suggests, has made a sexual move. But no move can be more definite or more concrete than the announcement of betrothal, as Christina well knew. The conclusion emerges that this nun could not have been renouncing a fiancé, but a stranger, a man who had never spoken to her of love.

But for complete understanding, the three linked poems need to be considered in their setting. Christina originally made them an integral part of her 1850 prose fiction story *Maude,* thus giving them a multimirror frame similar to the one in Gide's *Les Faux Monnayeurs.* A series of reflected images hides the autobiographical reference. As *Three Nuns* appears in *Maude,* it is a poem written by the heroine, who like her creator is also a young poet. When someone in the story asks Maude if she had any originals in life for the trio of nuns, she replies defensively, "The first Nun [the poet] no one can suspect of being myself, partly because my hair is far from yellow and I do not wear curls, partly because I never did anything half so good as profess." She is equally evasive about the second nun. Although admitting that the original was Mary, an engaged girl in their circle, she hastens to explain that it is not Mary as she is, but Mary as she might become, should she renounce her lover. "The third is Magdalen, of course," she grants readily of the fictional character who in the story does join a religious order.

All this admittedly is crude and unsuccessful fumbling on the part of an inexperienced fiction writer for what Henry James once called the trick "of covering one's tracks." In reality all three nuns are Christina herself. The trio roughly represents the three sides of her nature, the poetic, the erotic, and the religious. All her life she was to reveal one of these three

facets of her personality in her poetry, often all simultaneously, and sometimes in warring conflict.

VI

In William's preface to *Maude,* he admits that the piece is thinly veiled autobiography. "It appears to me that my sister's main object in delineating Maude," he writes, "was to exhibit what she regarded as defects in her own character, and in her attitude towards her social circle and her religious obligations. Maude's weak health—even her designing the pattern of a sofa-pillow might apply to Christina herself."

What, then, one asks, were the character flaws Christina detected in herself and sought to project through her analysis of her heroine? William supplies the answer. Speaking of Maude, he says,

> The worst harm she appears to have done is, that when she had written a good poem, she felt it to be good. She was also guilty of the grave sin of preferring to forego the receiving of the eucharist when she supposed herself to be unworthy of it; and further, of attending musical services at St. Andrew's Church . . . instead of invariably frequenting her parish church.

In the following sonnet Christina not only reproaches herself for vanity, but further expresses the appeal, both religious and aesthetic, which the services at St. Andrew's had for her:

> I listen to the holy antheming
> That riseth in thy walls continually,
> What while the organ pealeth solemnly,
> And white-robed men and boys stand up to sing,
> I ask myself with a sad questioning,
> 'What lovest thou here?' and my heart answers me:
> 'Within the shadows of this sanctuary
> To watch and pray is a most blessed thing.'
> 'To watch and pray, false heart? it is not so:
> Vanity enters with thee, and thy love
> Soars not to heaven but grovelleth below.
> Vanity keepeth guard lest good should reach
> Thy hardness; not the echoes from above
> Can rule thy stubborn feelings or can teach.' [6]

But of the three charges that the author of *Maude* prefers against her young heroine, the most serious, and the one upon which the tenuous plot turns, is Maude's unworthiness to take Communion. Why Maude, a sinless maiden, feels herself unable to receive the Eucharist is not at all explained in the narrative. She merely tells her cousin that she will not go to Communion because she does not want to profane holy things. "I have gone over and over again, thinking I should come right in time, and I do not come right; I will go no more."

What this suggests is that Maude was suffering from a conviction of guilt which in her opinion kept her from participating in the sacrament in the fullest religious sense. She alone among all the girls of her circle, including Sister Magdalen, the most strictly religious of them all, suffers from such scruples. Why would this innocent and stainless young girl be so morbidly sensitive about taking the sacrament?

If we were criticizing the prose fiction piece as literature, we would be obliged to point out that it falls apart on this very issue, the lack of motivation for Maude's decision. But our concern is with the work as autobiography, and there it supplies a rich treasure of reference. The author of *Maude* and *Three Stages* guards well her "cherished secrets," refusing even the disguise of fiction for fear of betraying them. What she does reveal is the complicating intricacy of their connection with her religious life. She seems to be saying that the young soul oppressed by guilt is denied the final, the only, consolation so long as she clings to the pleasure inherent in her guilt, the pleasure that is its sweet coating.

Although we know that *Three Nuns,* which Christina called her "dreary poem," was started in February, 1849, and finished in the spring of 1850, we have no such definite date for *Maude*. All we know is that it was written some time toward or during 1850, that it was "lying perdu in a drawer" awaiting revision in 1851, and that it was not published until 1897, some three years after Christina's death. Regarded as spiritual autobiography, the short novel would seem to have been written after rather than before the break with Collinson.

But if this is so, why would the religious issue of guilt and sin have been raised so sharply in the work? We might assume that once Christina was free of the restrictions imposed upon her by the engagement, what William called "the blight on her heart and spirit" might have lifted. She had achieved her objective of ridding herself of Collinson and his family; the way would then have been open for a more satisfying union. Why, then, does *Maude* show an even more pessimistic dramatization of Christina's situation than her poetic treatment of it? Was William right? Did a secret grief connected with Collinson gnaw at her soul?

In order to answer this question, let us pass briefly in review the chronological sequence of events, as reconstructed in the preceding pages. In December of 1847 Christina first met Scott. In the autumn of 1848 she became engaged to Collinson. The following winter, 1848–1849, she met Scott again. In the spring of 1849 the effect of the ensuing conflict showed itself in illness. One may say that, negatively speaking, this was her first effort to solve her problem.

In August and September of 1849 the visit to Pleaseley Hill took place. This resulted in an estrangement from Collinson's family, which showed itself in the cessation of correspondence between Collinson's sister and Christina. If we are satisfied that unconsciously or semiconsciously she

sought to drive a wedge between herself and Collinson, this may be regarded as her second attempt at a solution. In May or June of 1850 the weight was lifted of itself when Collinson, breaking the assumed terms of their engagement, became a Catholic, and the religious disagreement at last freed Christina.

But we have seen that William observed that, four or five months after the breaking of the engagement, his sister suffered so conspicuously from some hidden trouble that he was forced to conclude she was still grieving over Collinson. William insists that it was Collinson who "struck a staggering blow at Christina Rossetti's peace of mind on the very threshold of womanly life, and a blow from which she did not fully recover for years."

That a blow was struck, that it was a staggering blow, is true. The only question is, who struck it? If any evidence exists, and none does, to point to the fact that Christina was deeply in love with Collinson, an opinion such as William's could reasonably be held. But he admits that before the engagement she was not very much in love with Collinson; from what we know of the engagement itself, it is unlikely that she would have become more enamoured after accepting him. It is obvious that any "staggering blow" requires force behind it. When it is inflicted in the sphere of sexual relations, the force must be emotional. Only a man capable of arousing and stirring Christina's emotions at their deepest level could have been responsible for an emotional blow serious enough to dislocate her "womanly life" for years. Collinson could not have been that man.

But if the man was Scott, and if by 1850 he was in love with Christina, as she with him, why, then, did he deal her the heavy blow that caused her suffering of such intensity that it was clearly perceptible to her brother? Or, to express it differently, what could have happened that autumn to have laid Christina so low?

VII

What the record shows is that William Rossetti paid Scott a first visit at Newcastle in September, 1850. At Scott's house William found himself in the sort of intellectual atmosphere he relished, "the talk being of art, poetry, and speculative outlooks in religion and politics." During this visit William learned a great deal about their new friend, for Scott invariably "imparted his thoughts freely and in an interesting way." In his company, William tells us, "one was never at a loss for some topic of conversation," such as must often have been the case in Collinson's company.

Scott at Newcastle proved to be a different man from the Scott of the London visits. If William had expected to be entertained in bachelor's quarters, he was due for a surprise. "We had not hitherto known distinctly

whether Scott was a married man or a bachelor," he acknowledges. But in 1850, "I found him to be married."

Mrs. Scott, the former Letitia Norquoy, was a sprightly and scatter-brained little woman who shopped around for a religion much as she would for a becoming hat or gown. Not much is known about Scott's marriage. Rumor had it that during their engagement Miss Norquoy contracted an illness which resulted in her incapacity for marriage. The story went that she offered to free Scott from the engagement, but that he gallantly refused, and they were married.[7] "Being about to take the most imprudent step in life" was how he referred to his approaching nuptials in retrospect. At any rate, Mrs. Scott made no demands upon her husband, and theirs appears to have been a marriage in name only.

When William came home from Newcastle, he told the family that a Mrs. Scott existed. It is not easy to understand how the Rossettis could have known Scott for some two and a half years without learning about his marriage. But then they saw him rarely, only during visits to London; and throughout his life he conducted himself more or less as an unmarried man. The shock to Christina must have been a serious one. The title of the one published poem she wrote between the autumn of 1850 and the spring of 1851 speaks for itself. It is *Dirge*.

It was of course not Scott's fault that he was married, although it may have been reprehensible of him to have hidden it from Christina, particularly if he sensed her growing interest in him. To do him justice, perhaps he did nothing consciously to conceal his marriage from the Rossettis. Christina was an engaged girl by the second time he saw her, and, although still strongly attracted to her, he would have been justified in feeling that a man has no real obligation to let another man's fiancée know he is not available for purposes of love. On the other hand, as Scott's later career proved, he at no time allowed his marriage to be an obstacle to his relationships with other women. If he was in love with Christina by 1850 or dangerously close to it, or even if he was only flirting—the preliminary to love—he would have felt a natural reluctance to mention a circumstance that would have been sure to cut the forming but still fragile bond between them.

But if she had entertained hopes that her newly won freedom would induce Scott to court her in a way that had been hitherto impossible, her expectation must have been crushed when she heard from William that Scott himself was not free. Her disappointment was sufficiently perceptible to give William the impression that she had received "a staggering blow." [8] And if this is so, she must have been considerably committed by the autumn of 1850.

There was good reason for her dejection. At twenty her prospects for a satisfying emotional life were distinctly unpromising. Before having reached that ripe age, she had already managed to engage herself to a

man she was not in love with, and, having plighted her troth to him, had been further mortified to realize that she could feel desire for another man. After the painful ordeal of breaking the engagement, normally she could have anticipated a natural development of the more attractive relationship. Instead, she learned that all the while their underground romance had been spreading strong roots, the man had been married and hence inaccessible. What had flourished with such fertility had to be killed. The rich bloom of life was not to show itself; the deeply harmonious chord was not to be sounded, the sketch not to be completed with the loving brush strokes of fulfilling detail.

If, as an engaged girl, Christina had felt guilty about flirting with Scott, what could her feelings have been after her discovery of his marriage?

No wonder, considering her strict Victorian upbringing, that the theme of guilt and sin dominates her poetry of the period and that she portrayed her young heroine Maude as unable, through a conviction of unworthiness, to take the holy sacrament of the Eucharist. Many years later, as an experienced woman, Christina was to observe that "sin of its own nature . . . like the upas tree emits a poisonous influence; like the gourd it puts forth rapidity of growth; it is like the letting out of water or the first sparks of a conflagration."

❋ 4 ❋

"A LIFE RE-QUICKENING FLAME"

1851–1854

The love affair, which had been building up so slowly, seems to have reached a tentative peak in May, 1852, and an initial climax in 1854, again in the month of May. It was during these years when Christina was writing some of her early impassioned love poetry that Scott was also writing his own love poems addressed to the unidentified "Mignon." At the same time, he was confiding his emotional history to the 1854 journal.

In his *Autobiographical Notes* Scott tells us that he began the earlier journal shortly after the death of his mother in July, 1852. While she was dying, he sat by her bedside, holding her hand until "the dear face was quieted forever." After the funeral, he walked about the streets of Edinburgh with a feeling of homelessness. As the incidents of his childhood rushed back to him in a disassociated pattern of jumbled puzzle-pieces, he recalled with detached wonder the childish passion that had centered around his infantile attachment to his mother, and his consequent antagonism toward his father. All that was over now; and at forty he felt himself "to be an aged man."

We cannot doubt that the death of Scott's mother was a crucial event that divided his life in half. During the days that he was wandering aimlessly about Edinburgh, the old solid floes were breaking up, detaching themselves from the main block and floating free, eventually to melt under the seasonal heat of his rationalism. Profoundly significant is the fact that he looked upon his mother's death as a kind of rebirth for him. Following his initial grief at his loss and his plunge back into the past, "the feeling changed; I was dead and re-born into a more self-centered and freer existence." As he describes the experience, "I woke up, returned to myself, threw off much, as a dog shakes itself on coming out of water, and began to breathe more freely." We should keep Scott's words in mind when we come to examine Christina's long poem of 1865, *Prince's Progress,* for the allegory in it is suggestive of Scott's curious experience. In

Christina's poem the hero is released from the spell cast upon him by an old alchemist only when the latter dies. The death of the old man, who controls the precious potion of life, frees the Prince for his journey toward love and his waiting bride, much as the death of Scott's mother, which signified the breaking of that infantile attachment, freed him for love and life.

The record of such a journey comprised the major portion of Scott's "big book," as he called the 1854 journal, written, as he says, when he was "unable to see what was fit and what was unfit for possible preservation." In the prologue to the *Notes* he tells us,

> I have beside me a volume of 400 pages or more, written twenty-five years ago. . . . This I now conclude must be destroyed; but before it disappears in the roaring flames of the great chimney . . . I must make some selections, thus availing myself of the distincter memory of middle life. Perhaps it is not worth while to do even this. I am writing in 1877. The big book was finished in May 1854. Still I shall try again. To destroy it altogether would be like consigning some part of myself to a premature grave. Yet I must destroy it. . . .

What did this early record of Scott's life contain which in 1877 convinced him it was dangerous to preserve? We know from what fragments still remain of the old journal that he had in places confided to its pages emotional experiences of an intimate nature and that these confidences concerned a woman. "Reading again these old papers," he acknowledged, "has frightened me out of revelations and making confessionals of notebooks."

He burned the more damaging of the revelations, but the fragments that escaped the flames give some clue to the whole. Love he describes as "a giddy dance of nature round the terminal idol, a *rabies* of mad incantations and gymnastics lunacy round and round the voracious idol." Continuing in this extravagant vein, he writes,

> *Sometimes the fascinated worshipper flies far off with self-accusations of unworthiness and handscart [*sic*] into the air, sometimes he leaps blindly with unshod feet into the sea of glass [1] that parts him from his God, and which crashes into pieces beneath his impulse and rends the flesh from his bones. . . . Sometimes he hides himself from the world and will not look it in the face lest it see the secrets of his heart in his conscious eyes. . . .*

Another passage, with its page burned around the edges, is incomprehensible unless we read it symbolically:

> *And so it vanishes; the white cloud with its pestilent lightening bursts, and only a loathesome sense of inexperience and folly is left. Loathesome at first and only in appearance, for she, like the Bride of St. Francis, with the ashen hair and the unwashed feet and hollow heart, shall assist to keep him unsullied.*

In his second autobiography Scott explains the reason he has limited his aim in this work to describing merely "some of the scenery" of his life. "To write one's mental history is too difficult as well as too dreadful," he admits. "We live surrounded by so many deceptive coverings, that a sincere attempt at self-portraiture in writing is like walking into the streets naked, and is only likely to frighten one's neighbors." What would have appeared so frightening to Scott's decorous Victorian neighbors was the sight of what he called "the devil, lying *perdu* within each of us."

Despite his strenuous disavowal of any attempt at self-portraiture in the *Notes,* he gives us in his "Prologue" a vivid sketch of himself as he was in the 1850's. "Introspection was my curse. Action was hated by me; I was an absentee, a somnabule, and gave myself much to subjects no one else cared for. I had thus a private interest apart from success, and was indeed possessed of a mystery, as it were." This tantalizing aura of mystery, this impression of a secret life hidden from the world, accounts at least in part for the fascination Scott possessed for women. "Untiring industry I certainly had," he goes on, "but it was only to meet the necessities of the hour. That accomplished, I fell back upon my secret speculations in an ocean of regrets and tobacco smoke; and on my poetry, which shared in all the peculiarities of my nature."

Undoubtedly Scott considered himself profound, a deep thinker, and something of a genius; moreover, he successfully imposed this opinion of himself upon others. Certainly if William and Gabriel Rossetti accepted it—and they did—would a susceptible young woman in her early twenties with a similar temperament and similar interests have been more likely to reject it?

II

Scott seems to have been in London both in the spring and in the autumn of 1851. Although he is vague about dates (as he himself frankly admits in the *Notes*), it was probably in the spring of that year that he saw Christina at Ford Madox Brown's experimental drawing school for artisans in Camden Town.[2] As a government official of the National Schools of Design, he was interested in Brown's innovations in workers' education; and when he visited the class at Camden Town, he found to his surprise "Christina Rossetti among the pupils who were not copying casts or beautiful objects of any kind, but drawing from wood-shavings picked up from a joiner's yard."

She was now twenty-one and lovely. Never startling or arresting, her beauty was of the subdued and delicate kind, which, if it was likely to remain unnoticed at first sight, began to grow upon the beholder at the second or third glance. At this age she was slender and well-built, with brown glossy hair, a smooth, glowing, dark complexion, olive-tinted, and bright "richly-hazelled grey eyes." Her nose, straight and shapely, none-

theless had a slight tilt, and her chin was rather longer and more pointed than would be required by a strict standard of beauty. But such irregularities more frequently enhance than mar the beauty of a charming woman.

Even at this early age she was "a marked personality" in her circle, as the artist John R. Clayton said of her. Seeing her with the family at church services, Clayton recalled that, although she spoke but seldom, what she said was generally memorable. What made it so was her "fitful power and energy in conversation." Such, then, was the young woman Scott saw copying pieces of carpenter's shavings in Brown's drawing class at Camden Town.

He would certainly have wanted to see her again. And the poems she wrote immediately following his departure suggest that there were meetings between the two. If we are inclined to wonder why she would have consented to see him after the shock occasioned by the discovery of his marriage, we should remember that she was still very young, with all the resilence and the willfulness of youth. At twenty-one the recovery from even "a staggering blow" is rapid, particularly when the same hand that has dealt the blow is there to repair the damage with tender concern. And at twenty-one a young woman who was once a passionate and self-willed little girl is generally only too ready to do combat to obtain her pleasures, and might even be willing to compromise to get them.

Christina herself has described her poetry as "prevalently in a subjective vein"; and it is well to keep her statement in mind when studying her poetry, for even her narrative poems, her ballads, and her dramatic monologues are subjective. Whether she is writing in the first person or the third, whether her speaker is a man or a woman, the personal reference is seldom lacking. Sometimes she writes about herself as object, and her narrator is a sympathetic observer; other times she takes the point of view of a lover, as in *A Dream* of May 14, in which it is the man, not the woman, who regrets a lovers' parting:

*Oh for my love, my only love.
Oh for my lost love far away!—
Oh that the grass were green above
Her head or mine this weary day:—

She lies down in a foreign land
And in a foreign land doth rise.
I cannot hold her by the hand,
I cannot read her speaking eyes
That turned mere spoken words to lies.

This is the bough she leaned upon
And watched the rose deep western sky,
For the last sun rays almost gone:

I did not hear the wind pass by,
Nor stream; I only heard her sigh.

I saw the tears that did not fall.
I saw the blush upon her cheek.
The trembling hand so white and small:
She did not speak, I could not speak.
Oh that strong love should make us weak.

Therefore we parted as we met,
She on her way, and I on mine.
I think her tender heart was set
On holier things and more Divine:—
We parted thus and gave no sign.

Oh that the grass were green above
Her head or mine; so I could pray
In certain faith for her my love,
Unchanging, all the night and day:
Most near although most far away.*

Though the speaker is masculine, the emotion is the woman's, and all we need to do is to change the gender of the pronoun in places in order to remove the disguise.

Three Enemies, written a month later, is in the form of a dialogue. Organized around the theological concept of the Flesh, the World, and the Devil, it dramatizes the temptations which beset a young novice at living. Each of the three enemies, personified as a seductive lover, offers in turn his special enticements to the feminine speaker who struggles against them.

The work suggests that Christina regarded herself as being under the stress of temptation. This is the most marked if not the earliest appearance of the temptation theme which was to run through so much of her poetry. In a late prose work she observed that "World, flesh, devil comprise all sources and varieties of my temptation." But, she qualified, "the world in itself is neither harmful, ensnaring, nor polluting." It becomes all this "as the passive agent, passive vehicle . . . of the devil, man's outside tempter, or of the flesh, man's inside tempter." In other words, the theological idea of the threefold temptation is reduced to subject and object in the ever-continuing warfare of the sexes.

III

That summer while Christina was spending her holiday with her Aunt Charlotte Polidori at Longleat, the seat of the Marchioness of Bath, William again visited Scott at Newcastle. Christina took a lively interest in this visit, and just before William left on July 28, she wrote, "When next you see them, you may remember me not only to Mrs., but also to Mr. Scott. Is Mr. Scott a good judge in art? Of course, if not, his opinion

may still occasionally be right." Her letter of August 23 is even more restrained, but still expresses a guarded curiosity about Scott and his domestic life. "Will you remember Mamma, Maria, and self, cordially to Mr. and Mrs. Scott? How do you all get on, and what do you do?—also how was your present liked?"

At Longleat she wrote the sonnet *A Fair World Though Fallen,* the only poem she turned out between June and December. It is a reply to the arguments advanced by the "outside tempter." Apparently the *diable* has been using the appeal of reason (an ancient weapon) to convince the speaker that her religion is harmful to her. In a quietly conversational tone, as though a familiar if controversial discussion is being resumed, she writes:

> You tell me that the world is fair, in spite
> Of the Old Fall; and that I should not turn
> So to the grave, and let my spirit yearn
> After the quiet of the long last night.

In view of Scott's skepticism and his opinion that Christina's lyrics were "over-shaded with melancholy or pious sentiment," it is not implausible that he would try to bring her out of what he considered the dark shadow of religion into the clear sunlight of his own Scottish rationalism.

In her reply to the argument she points out all the unanswerable problems imposed by life—not least those of undeserved human suffering—and concludes that any danger of religious introspection might well be overbalanced by the greater hazard of worldliness:

> For, though I failed to choose the better part,
> Were it a less unutterable woe
> If we should come to love this world too much?

The record discloses that about this time Scott's own position became undermined. Possibly while he was trying to win over Christina to his skepticism, she was making serious inroads upon his agnosticism. In an emotional relationship in which neither of the two contributing partners emerges unaltered from the flash and shock of contact, what frequently takes place is a fusion of personalities in which there is a temporary exchange of positions in the interests of binding Eros more strongly.

It was during these years, between 1851 and 1854, that Scott, for the first time since his boyhood, began to reconsider the question of his religious belief. "Anyone having peculiar views of or pretensions to religious character was welcome to me then," he tells us. The two related problems over which he pondered were immortality and faith. Was there in reality, he asked himself, "a conscious power above the laws of nature?" Such soul probings and spiritual searches, although they were typical of the times, suggest a growing uncertainty about his own materialistic convictions.

But the shakier his ground, the more tenaciously he would have clung to the nexus of ideas he had assembled for himself so laboriously throughout his maturity. We can imagine him defending his convictions against Christina's serene depth of faith, asserting (as he does in the *Notes*) that "such a childish idea as the value of 'unity of faith' the tractarians maunder about has an effect upon me like that of a red rag upon a bull." And if she would have refused to rise to the controversy, remaining before him quiet, with lowered eyelids, he might have charged to the attack, remarking with an inflection of irony intended to hurt her, "This anxiety about immortality is in a way contrary to nature and is strongest in those whose mothers have been their sole teachers." [3]

IV

Scott's arrival in London in May was the first of three such visits during 1852. It was in the spring that he saw for the first time Gabriel Rossetti's sweetheart, Lizzie Siddal, the beautiful red-haired model whom Walter Deverell, a fellow-artist, had discovered as a milliner's apprentice in a back shop in Cranbourne Alley. Arriving in London, Scott went promptly to Rossetti's studio, and was told that the painter was living temporarily at a friend's cottage in Hampstead Road. Deverell and Rossetti had taken a studio together at 17 Red Lion Square; but before renting it to them the landlord had stipulated that "the models were to be kept under some gentlemanly restraint, as some artists sacrifice the dignity of art to the baseness of passion." However that may be, from Red Lion Square Scott went out to Hampstead Road, then on the wooded outskirts of London, to look for Rossetti. In the garden of the cottage, he tells us,

> . . . was a painting-room or study, covered with ivy, approached by outside wooden steps. I walked up to see him in the cool of the evening; the servants directed me up these steps, and I found myself in the romantic dusk of the apartment face to face with Rossetti and a lady whom I did not recognise, and could scarcely see. He did not introduce her; she rose to go. I made a little bow, which she did not acknowledge; and she left. This was Miss Siddal.

If anything further had been required to create the mood and setting for a secret love affair, it was the romantic atmosphere of passion and intrigue in the violet dusk of the garden studio that spring evening. These were the years Scott was writing his group of "Mignon" poems, which appeared in the volume of poetry he published in 1854. In the one called *May* he describes the renascent effect of spring upon a man in love, who finding himself confined to the metropolis during the month of May, longs for freedom and for love:

> May is with us and I am pent
> In the city's huge recess,

But prison-bars nor walls of stone
Can shut out spring's caress. . . .

Open the window, let the breeze
About these brown books play,
And hark the caged bird opposite
Knows very well it is May.

The portrait is that of a bookish man restricted to his study, but stirred by the life of the senses, which is the promise of spring:

Yes, 'tis summer, the feast is spread,
The wine is poured out free.
Mignon! I could desire no more,
If I but drank with thee!

"Mignon," the girl addressed, is identified in his mind with the month of May. In another poem of the same group she is called "Lady-girl, Mignon, May!" These private and endearing nicknames suggest a mature lover's conception of his beloved as a fresh young woman in the late spring of her blossoming, in other words a young woman of twenty-two or twenty-three.

After lamenting that Mignon is unavailable, perhaps "housed with some dull guest," he expresses the longing to have her with him to respond to the ecstasy of a season which is hard to enjoy alone:

But while the mavis sings i' the bough
And the cowslip dots the mead,
If we together heard his song,
'Twere a marvellous May indeed.

Other poems in the "Mignon" group, written before 1854, also treat the circumstances surrounding a concealed love affair. There are *A Watchman's Song* with its theme of courtly love, its reference to secret meetings and to lovers' separations lasting a year or more, and the Coleridgean *Rhyme to the Departing Year,* in which the lover likewise complains of a year-long separation. Although he has not seen his beloved "these ten months past," he reflects (as the lamps light the Strand and the bells of St. Paul's ring out) that even in absence she has been to his imagination "a deep, rich, wide and sensuous heaven."

Another of the "Mignon" poems, entitled *Lines Sent with Spenser's "Faery Queen,"* seems to have been written about the time Christina was doing some research about Spenser for Dr. A. B. Grosart's editions of Spenser's works. Her assignment, said Grosart, was "to trace the Italian poets in Spenser." Although nothing came of her share in the project, Grosart received from her "two pages of notebook with a few Dante and Boccaccio references taken, I think, from Todd's Spenser, with two of (possibly) her own. . . ."[4]

The speaker in Scott's poem has found a rare copy of *The Faerie Queene,* which he presents with his poem to his "Lady Loved":

> Henceforth take, while I, thy knight,
> Offer upon bended knee
> This treasure-house of poesy.

Thus an early edition of *The Faerie Queene* would have been not only a graceful and timely gift, but one especially to be cherished by a girl, herself a poet, who at the time had a particular reason for being interested in the poet's poet.

In the concluding poem of the "Mignon" series, we learn that

> Eros is the great master, and his law
> It is we follow.

As a labor of love, the work is dedicated to Mignon, and therefore

> With the name of love
> It shall be sanctified, and unto thee,
> Hopefullest friend! do I now send it.

V

As *Three Enemies* followed Scott's London visit in the spring of 1851, so another of Christina's religious poems, the powerfully wrought *A Bruised Reed He Shall Not Break,* succeeded his visit of May, 1852. The problem in this poem is similar to that faced by the young heroine of *Maude:* the religious consciousness oppressed by its inability to feel repentance or contrition. The sinner still loves her sin; the pleasure-seeker is unable to forego her pleasure; the spiritual aspirant, still captive to the flesh, is enamoured of her bonds. Having neither the will nor the wish to be released from such shackles, all she can do is bow her head and wait. Arthur Symons has said that to read these poems of Christina's was like eavesdropping on "a dialogue of the soul with God":

> I will accept thy will to do and be,
> Thy hatred and intolerance of sin,
> Thy will at least to love, that burns within
> And thirsteth after Me:
>
> So will I render fruitful, blessing still,
> The germs and small beginnings in thy heart,
> Because thy will cleaves to the better part,—
> Alas, I cannot will.
>
> Dost not thou will, poor soul? Yet I receive
> The inner unseen longings of the soul,
> I guide them turning towards Me; I control
> And charm hearts till they grieve;
> If thou desire, it yet shall come to pass,

That thou but wish indeed to choose My love;
For I have power in earth and heaven above—
I cannot wish, alas!

What, neither choose nor wish to choose? and yet
I still must strive to win thee and constrain:
For thee I hung upon the cross in pain,
How then can I forget?
If thou as yet dost neither love nor hate
Nor choose nor wish,—resign thyself, be still,
Till I infuse love, hatred, longing, will—
I do not deprecate.[5]

That October Scott went to Paris, stopping over in London both on his way to France and upon his return. It must have been during the first visit that he looked in on Holman Hunt at the latter's Chelsea studio. Hunt was working on the sketches for his celebrated *Light of the World* (now at St. Paul's), and, hoping to catch Christina's "sweetness and gravity of expression" for the Saviour's face, he had her sit to him for the head of Christ. Though Scott was greatly interested in seeing the progress of Hunt's work, he may also have been hoping to get a glimpse of Hunt's model, who was always decorously chaperoned by her mother during the sittings.

"He would fly to the end of the earth to be away from her, but he would return before he was halfway to be near her," reads an entry in his first journal. Although each of their encounters, which seemed to occur with all the shock of a fresh impact, apparently left Christina more tormented and troubled than before, she, no more than he, appeared willing to relinquish them. A sonnet she wrote October 24 after his departure for France pictures her despair at being unable to give up the fruitless "chase" of *Three Stages I:*

'I thought your search was over.'—'So I thought.'
'But you are seeking still.'—'Yes, even so:
Still seeking in mine own despite below
That which in heaven alone is found unsought:
Still spending for that thing which is not bought.'—

'Then chase no more this shifting empty show.'—
'Amen: so bid a drowning man forego
The straw he clutches: will he be so taught?'

Not only does this sonnet show a continuity with *Three Stages,* but its sestet anticipates in theme the later *Convent Threshold* and *From House to Home,* both products of 1858. It begins,

I must unlearn the pleasant ways I went:
Must learn another hope, another love,
And sigh indeed for home in banishment.

If we read "home" as earthly love and "banishment" as divine love, we are forced to conclude that the twenty-two-year-old girl was hardly ready for the religious dedication to which she aspired.

In any event she was not going to find it easy to "unlearn the pleasant ways" of love, for upon Scott's return from the Continent, he became the Rossettis' house guest. "We have had Scott staying with us some days lately," William wrote Stephens toward the end of November.[6] Under the circumstances, with Scott in her own home and temptation powerfully present, Christina would have found it not only hard but practically impossible to carry out her resolve.

An autumnal mood of sorrow and desolation settled down upon her shortly after Scott left for Newcastle. To be deprived of the beloved's presence after enjoying it is a grief well known to lovers, whose solitude appears all the bleaker in comparison to the joys they have known; but added to the burden in Christina's case would have been the humiliating torment of acknowledging a love that could flourish only in darkness and secrecy. Such an attitude of despair appears in a poem of December 23, the first of two pieces entitled *The Heart Knows Its Own Bitterness.* The first stanza reads in manuscript:

*Weep, for none shall know
Why sick at heart thou weepest;
Wake and weep, for none shall guess
In thy loneliness
Why thou thy vigil keepest.*

The later version, revised for publication, is as follows:

Weep, sick and lonely,
Bow thy heart to tears,
For none shall guess the secret
Of thy grief and fears.

Christina of course knew better than to confide her "cherished secret" to the pages of an autobiographical journal, but seemingly she no less than Scott was haunted by it.

VI

As the winter darkened and deepened, she sank into an even gloomier frame of mind. Such verse as the following, written February 8, would have provided her mother with some cause for anxiety and even alarm:

*I wish that I were dying,
Deep-drowsing without pain:
I wish that I were lying
Below the wind and rain
Never to rise again.* . . .

Cold as the cold Decembers,
Past as the days that set:
While only one remembers
And all the rest forget,
But one remembers yet.

The last stanza was lifted for the 1884 poem, *One Seaside Grave,* supposedly written to commemorate the death of Charles Bagot Cayley, but it appears in the notebook under the 1853 dateline.

In the spring Christina and her parents moved to Frome-Selwood in Somerset, leaving William and Maria to "live in solitary asceticism"—as William put it—in rooms over the shop of Mr. Burcham, a chemist in Albany Street. In after years Christina and William disputed about the precise date of the move, she insisting it was after April 27, and he maintaining it was earlier in the month. The date must have been important to her, for she was dying when she argued about its accuracy.

Although Frome-Selwood was near Longleat, where Aunt Charlotte Polidori lived with her Marchioness of Bath, she had been there a good many years before Frances Rossetti found that a sufficient reason for leaving London. The reason usually given is that she moved to Frome in order to start a day school, with Christina as her assistant. But why would she select for this purpose a small, dull, country town with so little to recommend it?[7] And why would she install the inexperienced Christina as her assistant rather than Maria, now a professional governess with years of experience? The move surely could not have been intended to benefit the elder Rossetti, still an invalid, who if anything was growing worse instead of better, and who might have been expected to obtain more competent medical care in London than in a small provincial town. Furthermore, this was the only time throughout her long life that Frances Rossetti left London for more than a holiday trip.

"Christina was anything but happy at Frome," William informs us. Gabriel tried to cheer her up by long, chatty letters in which he discussed her poems according to Pre-Raphaelite principles, lecturing her in brotherly fashion about their vague dreaminess ("I wish you would try any rendering either of narrative or sentiment from real abundant Nature, which presents much more variety, even in any one of its phases, than all such 'dreamings' "), and giving her news about their London friends: Allingham's recent arrival in town, Hunt's projected trip to the Holy Land, Millais' election to the Academy (" 'So now the whole Round Table is dissolved' "), and poor Walter Deverell's mortal illness. He also gave her news of Christ Church, Albany Street, and its incumbent, Mr. Burrows, who became vicar in 1850 after Dodsworth's conversion, and who was to become one of Christina's life-long friends:

> Sunday night Maria and I went to see Mr. Borrows [*sic*] after attending service at his church. I liked him very well, but he rather reminded

me of Patmore in manner. The decorations at Christ Church are very poor—four gilt Corinthian capitals; item, one pulpit-cloth with seven white stars, etc., etc.

Although at Frome Christina took up drawing, possibly to occupy her mind, art, as Gabriel ironically observed, interfered with her "legitimate exercise of anguish," which he was astute enough to detect behind her "almost stereotyped smile." Obviously she was trying to make the best of a dreary situation, but with what William called "the educational drudgery" of her mother's day school, the domestic burden of a father growing daily more feeble, and the lack of any youthful companionship, her life must have been bleak indeed. Furthermore, at Frome her chances of occasionally seeing Scott were so slight as to be almost nonexistent.

It is therefore not surprising to find the theme of lovers' separation, conspicuous in Scott's 1854 "Mignon" pieces, appearing with some frequency in the love poetry of the Frome period. Like the temptation theme, it too recurs throughout the years. In addition to *Two Parted,* we find it in later poems such as *Parting After Parting, Meeting, Together Once, Goodbye in Fear,* and a great many others. It is dramatized in Christina's two important poems of 1858, *Convent Threshold* and *From House to Home;* it haunts her sonnet sequence, the *Monna Innominata,* and her group of Italian poems, the *Il Rosseggiar dell' Oriente;* and it inspires a number of her ballads, which have a more traditional claim upon it. From the prevalence of this theme and her preoccupation with it, one would think that the aspect of love which impressed her the most was the loss consequent upon the parting from the beloved. Throughout her love poetry the lover comes and goes, appears and disappears and reappears again, very much as Scott did in her own life.

Her year at Frome was highly productive, perhaps as a result of her provincial isolation. In addition to *Two Parted,* she wrote other love poems, not all of them published, a great many devotional pieces such as *The Eleventh Hour, Sleep at Sea, Easter Even, The Bourne,* the exquisite *Whitsun Eve,* with its virtuoso treatment of white imagery, and, surprisingly, some humorous verse as well.

The two most interesting love poems of the spring are *What?* and *A Pause*. In the first, although love is not named, it is celebrated in a series of rapidly shifting similes. It is "strengthening as secret manna," "dear as a dying cadence," "gay as a cowslip meadow" (an image which strikes an echo from Scott's *May:* "the cowslips dot the mead"), "pleasant as the budding tree," and so on. Yet the old ambivalence and distrust reappear. Love is

> A bitter dream to wake from,
> But oh how pleasant while we dream!
> A poisoned fount to take from,
> But oh how sweet the stream!

A Pause was written June 10. In the octave of this sonnet Christina entwines her familiar themes of love and death in the plaintive, restrained, sweetly melancholy manner of *When I am Dead, My Dearest, Remember, After Death,* and others of the earlier poems. But with the transition to the sestet the tone abruptly shifts to one of emotional realism, and the whole poem suddenly becomes charged with fresh energy:

They made the chamber sweet with flowers and leaves
And the bed sweet with flowers on which I lay;
While my soul, love-bound, loitered on its way.
I did not hear the birds about the eaves,
Nor hear the reapers talk among the sheaves:
Only my soul kept watch from day to day,
My thirsty soul kept watch for one away:—
Perhaps he loves, I thought, remembers, grieves.
At length there came the step upon the stair,
Upon the lock the old familiar hand:
Then first my spirit seemed to scent the air
Of Paradise; then first the tardy sand
Of time ran golden; and I felt my hair
Put on a glory, and my soul expand.

Toward the end of summer she wrote a long poem of twenty stanzas called *Annie,* the whole unpublished, though five stanzas of it were extracted for the printed version called *A Harvest.*[8] Whereas the latter is more impressive as poetry, some of the unpublished stanzas are more helpful in understanding the poet:

*It's not for earthly bread, Annie,
And it's not for earthly wine,
And it's not for all thou art, Annie,
Nor for any gift of thine:
It's for other food, and other love
And other gifts I pine.

I long all night and day, Annie,
In this glorious month of June,
Tho' the roses are all blossoming
And the birds are all in tune:
I dream and long all night, Annie,
Beneath the tender moon. . . .

I am sick for love, and moan
Like a solitary dove:
Love is deep as hell, Annie,
And as high as heaven above;
There's nothing in all the world, Annie,
That can compete with love.*

VII

As the year passed, the strain of separation produced love's hazard and occupational disease, doubt. Absence was a curtain hiding the loved face, dissolving its features into blank vagueness. Was he thinking of her? Did he love her, or had he perhaps forgotten? No answer. Silence. By September she was writing,

> *All night I dream you love me well,
> All day I dream that you are cold:
> Which is the dream? ah, who can tell,
> Ah would that it were told.
>
> So I should know my certain doom.
> Know all the gladness or the pain;
> So pass into the dreamless tomb,
> Or never doubt again.*

And yet despite the conditions of her life at Frome—and they could not have been more dismal—the "morbidity" conspicuous in her earlier verse is missing in the numerous poems she wrote that year. A new note of stoicism in place of the monodic wail of adolescent self-pity appears in *Our Heaven* of January: [9]

> Our heaven must be within ourselves,
> Our only heaven the work of faith,
> Thro' all the race of life that shelves
> Downwards to death.
>
> *The calm blue heaven is built too far,
> We cannot reach to hold it fast;
> We cannot touch a single star
> From first to last.
>
> Our powers are strait to compass heaven,
> Our strength is weak to scale the sky;
> There's not one day of all the seven
> That can bring it nigh.
>
> Our heaven must be within our heart,
> Unchangeable for night and day;
> Our heaven must be the better part
> Not taken away.*

She even wrote humorous verse, such as the playful *Charon* ("In my cottage near the Styx") which William said "tickled . . . Maria uncommonly," and Gabriel said "brought to light a neatly-paved thoroughfare between Maggie's ears" whenever it was mentioned. Her brothers and sister were also amused by what she called her "remarkable doggerel," *The P.R.B.*, by the verse portraits of Gabriel and William, and an odd little quatrain she called *Epitaph:*

*A slave yet wearing on my head a crown,
A captive from whose eyes no tears ran down,
Bound with no chain, compelled to do no work,
I fell a victim to the jealous Turk.*

The P.R.B. is a swan song for the Brotherhood. With Woolner now searching for gold in Australia, Hunt "yearning for the land of Cheops," D. G. Rossetti shunning "the vulgar optic" (refusing to exhibit his pictures publicly), and "the great Millais" basking in "academic opulence," Christina rightly concludes that "The P.R.B. is in its decadence." William's activities as an art critic are wittily summarized in the urbane couplet:

William Rossetti, calm and solemn
Cuts up his brethren by the column.

He is described in *Portraits* with equal economy, if less satire:

An easy length of limb,
Dark eyes and features from the South,
A short-legged meditative pipe
Set in a supercilious mouth.

Unfortunately, Gabriel destroyed the stanza containing his verbal portrait, but we learn from the concluding stanza that Christina's brothers were "unlike and yet how much the same."

Taken as a group, then, rather than singly, the poems of that year show a sustained tone of confidence, conveying the impression of a spirit constantly recharged and renewed by the consciousness that the world, if not Frome, still contained that familiar step and that familiar hand, of a spirit strengthened by the "secret manna" for which in youth there is no substitute. Christina's well-guarded secret could sustain and strengthen as well as oppress her.

Although she could not communicate with Scott directly, she heard news of him through Gabriel, who paid him a visit at Newcastle in June. Complaining that Newcastle was unstimulating intellectually, Gabriel described it as "a dreary place" and "a beastly place." For entertainment, Gabriel baited Scott about his deceased brother David, Scott's idol, and composed Scott's Newcastle epitaph:

Here lies Duns Scotus
Who died of lotus.

But although Gabriel was a trying guest, Scott became very fond of him during this visit; and it was the beginning of that strange and complicated friendship between the two men which has given rise to so much controversial comment, a friendship which was to leave a deep mark on Christina's own life.

VIII

During the year the Rossettis were at Frome both Christina's grandparents died, her grandmother in April and Polidori in December. Christina was deeply affected by her grandfather's death, for a strong bond existed between them, and it was in his memory that she wrote in February the long poem from which she published two stanzas as *The Bourne.* Like *Roses for the Flush of Youth,* this poem has been praised for its "economy of statement."

With the death of her mother, Frances Rossetti came into a small inheritance, thus relieving her mind and easing the financial strain on the family. William received a promotion and an increase in salary, and thereupon insisted on the family's returning to London, so that he could, as he expressed it, provide for his father's closing days and relieve his mother and Christina "from toiling and moiling unremuneratively at a semi-vitalized school." When the elder Rossetti heard about this prospect, he let out an exuberant "Hurrah!" a sentiment Christina must have echoed.

And so at last the dismal exile at Frome-Selwood came to an end, and by Lady Day, March 25, Christina and her parents had returned to London and were settled in the new house at 45 Upper Albany Street that William had rented for them. Situated a few doors north of Christ Church, it subsequently became No. 166 Albany Street and in 1959 was demolished to make way for the new parish school.

The elder Rossetti had little chance to enjoy his reëstablishment in the metropolis, for the following month he was stricken, and Dr. Hare pronounced him "in a highly dangerous state." Gabriel, who had recently been "discovered" by Ruskin, was sent for at Denmark Hill, where he was dining *en famille* with the Ruskins; and the Rossetti sons and daughters gathered around their father's bedside.

While Rossetti lay dying, the family kept a diary notebook as a record of his last days on earth, a custom which, initiated at that time, persisted throughout the years as each in turn departed. Christina's only entry for 1854 was to the effect that her father's former pupil, Charles Bagot Cayley, had called to inquire about his professor. "Mr. Cayley called twice at the very last," she wrote, "and waited, but did not see my father, much endearing himself to us." By the 25th of April the elder Rossetti was "clearly sinking," and several days later he died, with the cry in Italian upon his lips, "Ah God, help me Thou."

A fortnight after her father's death Christina wrote the burial anthem she called *Ye Have Forgotten the Exhortation,* from Hebrews 12:5. Liturgical in form, it concluded with the lines,

> O Lord, my heart is broken for my sin:
> Yet hasten Thine own day

And come away.
Is not time full? Oh put the sickle in,
O Lord, begin!

But the time was not yet ripe for the chastening.

The burial anthem was written May 10. On May 14 Scott was once again in London. On May 19, only nine days after the composition of the burial anthem, Christina wrote *Dream-Love,* one of her tenderest love lyrics and one which expresses with delicate simplicity the ideality of a girl's first ecstatic response to love:

Young love lies sleeping
In May-time of the year,
Among the lilies,
Lapped in the tender light:
White lambs come grazing,
White doves come building there;
And round about him
The May-bushes are white. . . .

Young love lies dreaming;
But who shall tell the dream?
A perfect sunlight
On rustling forest tips;
Or perfect moonlight
Upon a rippling stream;
Or perfect silence,
Or song of cherished lips. . . .

Young love lies dreaming
Till summer days are gone,—
Dreaming and drowsing
Away to perfect sleep:
He sees the beauty
Sun hath not looked upon,
And tastes the fountain
Unutterably deep.

The repeated use of "perfect" (a modifier generally avoided in poetry) should be noted, for it helps to define the poet's attitude toward love as a condition of blissful rapture, the most intense form of human happiness attainable.[10] In this poem, significantly, the fountain is unpoisoned.

Scott's 1854 *A Dream of Love* reads like a companion piece to *Dream-Love.* The similarity is not only one of title and year of composition, but even more of tone and content. Both poems have the same tone of lyrical ecstasy. And Scott like Christina takes for his material the dream-like, enchanting quality of love in a Maytime setting.

Cast in the traditional form of a dream allegory, Scott's poem nevertheless begins with a lover's decidedly realistic question,

I had a dream more pleasant than the truth,
And pliant as 'twas pleasant,—*must* it be
Only a dream?

In a romantic and exotic garden the dreamer finds his ideal woman, his "gardened love" and "goddess-girl." She is his "gardened love" because like Christina, she is fond of small animals, of birds and insects, and encourages their proximity:

Her hand, which held some sweet, the insects thronged,
And lighted on her hair.[11]

She is his goddess-girl because of her power to move men by her poetry. She transports the enraptured soul of her lover "into a sphered realm of everlasting melancholy" (we recall Scott's description of Christina's lyrics as "overshaded with melancholy"). Carried away by his emotions, the dreamer exclaims rapturously if somewhat incoherently,

—O Lady thou art beautiful; and now
The dark hair of thy song doth shade its eyes,
The eye-lid of thy music droops.

After more of this sort of impassioned rhapsodizing, in which the speaker praises his beloved's poetic genius as well as her beauty, *A Dream of Love* concludes with the following singular tribute:

—O Lady thou art wondrous fair and good!
The earth is filled, oh! filled with gracious things!
Slowly again to life descends thy strain,
An odour as of rose-leaves seems to fall
Upon me, and a pearly light: again
It scales the arc of higher heaven, alas!
Art thou not over me as is a God,
O Lady, with thy lute? and I will faint
Utterly into death: oh intermit
The binding of thy linked power, oh cease,
And let me drink a silence short and deep,
Then die into the Life that thou dost live.

The rose-leaf image in the fourth line foreshadows a late poem (1882) Scott addressed to Christina called *Rose-Leaves* (see below, p. 342).

IX

But if *Dream-Love* and Scott's poem express lyrically the rapturous and sublime excitement of love's discovery, the two poems Christina wrote on the 27th of June, as well as the third and last poem of *Three Stages,* completed a month later, display her characteristic distrust and fear of

love, still regarded as the heady draught with the bitter poison concealed in its dregs.

Her sonnet *The World* discloses her apprehensions. William Rossetti insisted upon a theological interpretation of this forceful sonnet, but the violence of the imagery and the explosive passion pervading it (which nonetheless is held in restraint by the strict requirement of the sonnet form) indicates that the poem derives its emotional energy from a personal problem rather than theological doctrine. Borrowing for her sonnet Dante's Protean figure of the horrid hag who could at will assume the shape of a lovely siren, Christina personifies the world as a Pre-Raphaelite charmer by day and a Walpurgis witch by night: [12]

> By day she woos me, soft, exceeding fair:
> But all night as the moon so changeth she;
> Loathesome and foul with hideous leprosy,
> And subtle serpents gliding in her hair.
> By day she woos me to the outer air,
> Ripe fruits, sweet flowers, and full satiety:
> But thro' the night a beast she grins at me,
> A very monster void of love and prayer.
> By day she stands a lie: by night she stands
> In all the naked horror of the truth,
> With pushing horns and clawed and clutching hands.
> Is this a friend indeed, that I should sell
> My soul to her, give her my life and youth,
> Till my feet, cloven too, take hold on hell?

Guesses, an unpublished poem which follows in the notebook, was written the same day, and it indicates which way the scales were dipping:

> *Was it a chance that made her pause
> One moment at the opened door,
> Pale where she stood so flushed before
> As one a spirit overawed:—
>
> Was it a chance that made her turn
> Once toward the window passing by,
> One moment with a shrinking eye
> Wherein her spirit seemed to yearn:—
> Or did her soul then first discern
> How long and rough the pathway is
> That leads us home from vanities,
> And how it will be good to die?
>
> There was a hill she had to pass;
> And while I watched her up the hill
> She stooped one moment hurrying still,
> But left a rose upon the grass:
> Was it mere idleness:—or was
> Herself with her own self at strife
> Till while she chose the better life
> She felt this life has power to kill?

Perhaps she did it carelessly.
Perhaps it was an idle thought;
Or else it was the grace unbought,
A pledge to all eternity:
I know not yet how this may be;
But I shall know when face to face
In Paradise we find a place
And love with love that endeth not.*

On July 25 she wrote the last poem of the *Three Stages* series, copying out the first two carefully from previous notebooks and adding the third, in which she reviews and summarizes experience. In the first poem of the linked group (1848) she had described the fruitless pursuit of love; in the second (1849) she described her painful awakening from a "happy happy dream"; now in the third—entitled *Restive* in manuscript—she analyzes the new and fresh reawakening to love.

William has told us that this and the second poem of the linked group were published posthumously, and in editing his sister's poetry he deleted some interesting stanzas from *Three Stages III*. The unpublished stanzas, decidedly good in themselves, give all three poems of the series a new and hitherto missing coherence, and are, moreover, a valuable addition to our knowledge of the poet at this time of her life:

I thought to deal the death-stroke at a blow
To give all, once for all, but nevermore;—
Then sit to hear the low waves fret the shore,
Or watch the silent snow . . .

'Oh rest,' I thought, 'in silence and the dark;
Oh rest, if nothing else, from head to feet:
Though I may see no more the poppied wheat,
Or sunny soaring lark.

*Rest out of sight, forgotten, and how cold
To hope and dear delights of buried youth;
Rest in the darkness, which indeed is truth
Until the earth was old.

Night came upon the noontide of my day,
Frost killed my buds fresh opening to the sun;—
Now I will leap no more, nor pant, nor run,
But plod along the way.

My joys are hidden from my sight—amen,
If mine eyes weep not, who should weep for these:—
Yet when the axe shall smite all pleasant trees,
What will it matter then?—*

'So will I labour, but will not rejoice;
Will do and bear, but will not hope again;

Gone dull alike to pulse of quick pain,
And pleasure's counterpoise':

I said so in my heart; and so I thought
My life would lapse, a tedious monotone.
I thought to shut myself, and dwell alone
Unseeking and unsought.

The long monotonous year in Frome-Selwood preceding her father's death would have left Christina in such a mood of bleak resignation. But Scott's arrival in London in May, reminding her that she was still young and desirable and that love was still alive on a fresh-growing, springtime earth, could have brought about the resurgence of dormant feeling:

But first I tired, and then my care grew slack;
Till my heart dreamed, and may be wandered too:—
I felt the sunshine glow again, and knew
The swallow on its track;

All birds awoke to building in the leaves,
All buds awoke to fulness and sweet scent;
Ah, too, my heart woke unawares, intent
On fruitful harvest sheaves.

Full pulse of life, that I had deemed was dead,
Full throb of youth, that I had deemed at rest,—

But at the very peak of elation comes the romantic break, the dull thud of a sudden drop, as the old suspicious distrust of love shows itself once more:

Alas, I cannot build myself a nest,
I cannot crown my head

With royal purple blossoms for the feast,
Nor flush with laughter, nor exult in song;—
These joys may drift, as time now drifts along,
And cease, as once they ceased.

This poem offers another interesting instance of the resemblance between Christina's diction and Scott's during the 1850's. However, his conventional metaphors become in her work fresh, clear, concentrated poetic images. The "golden crown" and "purple flush," which appear in his *A Dream of Love,* are fused in her poem into a crown of royal purple blossoms; and the flush is thriftily worked into the more vivid and concise phrase, "Nor flush with laughter."

X

With the exception of her August poem, *Long Looked For,* a tale of unhappy love related by a dying lover, Christina wrote only one poem

between July and December, an interval of almost six months. *Listening* of October would seem to differ from almost all her other love poems in that it celebrates the contented happiness of a woman courted by the man she loves:

She listened like a cushat dove
That listens to its mate alone:
She listened like a cushat dove
That loves but only one.

Not fair as men would reckon fair,
Nor noble as they count the line:
Only as graceful as a bough,
And tendrils of the vine:
Only as noble as sweet Eve
Your ancestress and mine.

And downcast were her dovelike eyes
And downcast was her tender cheek;
Her pulses fluttered like a dove
To hear him speak.

We might surmise from a reading of this poem that after July she had ceased to struggle and had settled down to enjoy the ripe fruit and the sweet flowers offered in such abundance, permitting the beasts and monsters of her night images to sink quietly into the quicksands of the unconscious. But nothing could be more mistaken.

In manuscript *Listening* is an entirely different poem, suggesting an altogether different train of events. It even has another title, *Two Choices,* one which hints at the content. As written in the notebook the poem consists of seven instead of three stanzas. The first part includes the three published stanzas reproduced above and two other omitted stanzas, of which one reads:

*She listened like a cushat dove
That never dreamed of life alone;
She listened with the same heart-joy
To love's dear monotone.*

At the end of the fifth stanza we come upon the word "Stop," but not in Christina's handwriting, after which follow the last two stanzas, crossed out:

*He chose what I had feared to choose
(Ah, which was wiser, I or he?)—
He chose a love-warm priceless heart,
And I a cold bare dignity.

He chose a life like stainless spring
That buds to summer's perfect glow;
I chose a tedious dignity

As cold as cold as snow:
He chose a garden of delights
Where still refreshing waters flow;
I chose a barren wilderness
Whose buds died years ago.*

Since *Listening* was published for the first time posthumously in the 1896 *New Poems* edited by William, no one but he could have been responsible for carving out of one poem an entirely different one, different in tone, rhythm, and diction as well as content. Christina's poem, as she originally wrote it, pictures a woman happy in love making a renunciatory choice, whereupon her lover likewise, or perhaps subsequently, makes his choice.

As poetry, the omitted stanzas are superior to those William published. But—and this may account for his motive in altering the poem so drastically—these stanzas display an aspect of the poet wholly absent from the published version. In place of the sweetly sexless, modestly fluttering Victorian maiden portrayed in *Listening,* we have in *Two Choices* a complicated, intense, passionate, and tormented woman, who still in the full tide of her youth feels compelled to give up joys for which she "thirsts," a woman who, putting the shackles on her own wrists, leads herself, her own jailer, behind the self-imposed bars, from which she peers out only to watch others pluck the flowers, taste the fruit, and refresh themselves in the bluest of life-giving waters.

❋ 5 ❋

"FEEDING MINE OWN FIRE"

1854–1856

On December 2, three days before her birthday, Christina wrote *Dead Before Death*. We have seen that the prevailing tone of the poetry which preceded and led up to *Two Choices* conveys the impression that, although she was at strife with herself, she was at the same time obtaining some satisfaction from her love: the figure of the cushat dove cooing with the conscious assurance of love given and returned hints at it. But the poems that follow have an entirely different emotional texture. Not one but two choices were made; and the December sonnet strikes the new note, one of stark and desolate, of violent, grief. For the next two years most of the subsequent pieces shade off from that mood:

> Ah changed and cold, how changed and very cold
> With stiffened smiling lips and cold calm eyes!
> Changed, yet the same; much knowing, little wise,—
> *This* was the promise of the days of old!
> Grown hard and stubborn in the ancient mould,
> Grown rigid in the sham of life-long lies:
> We hoped for better things as years would rise,
> But it is over as a tale once told.

The sestet of this sonnet is like the lament of a funeral dirge, in which the key word *lost*, repeated six times, creates the effect of the tolling of a belfry bell:

> All fallen the blossom that no fruitage bore,
> All lost the present and the future time,
> All lost, all lost, the lapse that went before:
> So lost till death shut-to the opened door,
> So lost from chime to everlasting chime,
> So cold and lost for ever ever more.

"I am unable to say," commented William Rossetti, "what gave rise to this very intense and denunciatory outpouring . . . written three days before the authoress completed her twenty-fourth year. Possibly, it may be

regarded as an address to herself—not indeed as she was, or even supposed herself to be, but as she might become if 'Amor Mundi' were to supersede the aspiration after divine grace."

Despite William's urbane attempt to guide the reader of this sonnet, which Gabriel considered even "a little sensational *for her*," to an acceptable and conventional interpretation of it, this poem and others of the period suggest that "the aspiration after divine grace" occupied very little of Christina's thoughts at the time, and the loss of love a great deal. A poem of 1855, *O Unforgotten,* sums up the burden of her perennial complaint these years:

> An unforgotten load of love,
> A load of grief all griefs above
> A blank blank nest without its dove.

II

What, then, had happened? Had Scott, formerly so eager and ardent, suddenly lost interest in the girl he had been pursuing for six years? Had he, as *Two Choices* seems to tell us, found another "garden of delights"? In order to answer these questions, we must go back to the autumn of 1854 and follow Scott's movements.

Early in October the publishing house of Smith and Elder brought out his volume of verse, *Poems by a Painter*. He immediately sent copies to everyone of importance in the world of art and letters, including Carlyle, who, misreading the title as "Poems by a Printer," at once (said Gabriel) "wrote off . . . to the imaginary printer to tell him to stick to his types and give up his metaphors." Carlyle further advised Scott to *do* rather than to speak or sing.

Furious, Scott wrote back to Carlyle, "Of all the men in the world, I appear to myself precisely the last whom it is necessary to remind that what a man *does* is more important than what he says or sings. . . . The habit of *doing* has become so natural to me that the smallest interval of time is filled by work—if not for others, then for myself. . . ." Furthermore, Scott concluded haughtily, his volume of poetry should be regarded as "*something done,* not merely said or sung, but for the most part experienced, and in some part felt to the marrow of my life."

Upon discovering his error, Carlyle had the grace to be embarrassed. Smoothing his fellow-countryman's ruffled feathers in terms Scott could take as flattering, coming from a man of his standing, Carlyle wrote, "On discovering that the Printer was a Painter, and hearing that *you* had published a volume of poems, I at once found my 'Idle Apprentice' converted into a grave, earnest man, of mature mastership . . . an earnest fellow-labourer in the vineyard, whom I once saw here."

But the reviewers did not deal so tenderly with Scott's feelings. *The Manchester Guardian* found his poems "harsh and inharmonious . . .

verse only to the eye." *The Spectator,* pronouncing them the product of a man with "a gloomy temper" and "a cynical and sour spirit," considered the volume "remarkable for the intellectual vigour it displays, and the little result that vigour produces." *The Nonconformist* observed that "as the subjects are often faulty, so the tone is frequently painful." And thus the reviews went, *The Athenæum* chiming in with this choice morsel of critical acumen: "They are the work of a man of middle age, they are pervaded by a medieval feeling, and treat of medieval subjects." Thoroughly alarmed, Scott determined to "work the oracle" (the charge he leveled at Gabriel in 1870), and he implored William Rossetti to write a favorable notice for Mackay's *Illustrated News.*

Despite the adverse reviews, however, Scott acquired some prestige as the result of his publication. In Newcastle *The Northern Examiner,* which was running a series of articles called "Public Men of the North," featured him in the twelfth of its series:

> We saw, two evenings ago, a somewhat tall gentleman in Collingham Street. His countenance was sallow and thoughtful. His features were regular, and illumined when we accosted him, with a gentle smile. His reply to a question put to him was slow and drawling. His manner altogether was placid and philosophical in the extreme. . . . He was on his way to the school of design in Westgate Street, and the gentleman we have described was Mr. William Bell Scott, the painter and poet.

A second mark of recognition was an invitation to Wallington Hall, a great house in Northumberland, where Scott's volumes of poems had met with a more genial reception than either Carlyle or the reviewers had given them. Sir Walter Trevelyan, master of Wallington Hall, whose ancestral name appeared in the Domesday Book, was a geologist and naturalist of note. His wife, who was much younger than he, was the intimate friend of Ruskin and Swinburne. She herself was both an aspiring painter and a generous patron of the arts. She had already heard of Scott through a mutual friend in Edinburgh, and shortly after receiving a complimentary copy of *Poems by a Painter,* she invited Scott to Wallington Hall for a visit.

Scott promptly accepted the invitation. Upon his arrival he found that Sir Walter was away on business. The lady of the house, however, made him welcome, and it was not long before Scott was congratulating himself upon the opportunity of having her alone for a few days, "Sir Walter being so difficult to become acquainted with." Apparently Lady Trevelyan, the "Pauline" of Scott's *Notes,* presented no such difficulties.

Scott describes her as a charming, vivacious woman, small in stature but regal and commanding. Her eyes were hazel, the color of Christina's, but there the resemblance ceased. Her gaze, sharp and penetrating, "saw through one," said Scott. She was, he added warmly, a woman "intensely

amusing and interesting to the men she liked," of whom Scott was one. His opinion of her charm is confirmed by her nephew, George Otto Trevelyan, who said that no friend of hers, man or woman, "could ever have enough of her company." Trevelyan attributed her "singular and unique charm" to her "ever-flowing spring of the most delicious humour."

Scott's account of their first meeting, guarded as it is, would seem to indicate that he and Pauline were attracted to one another immediately:

> It was a long drive at that time after alighting from the railway at Morpeth. About midday, as I approached the house, the door was opened, and there stepped out a little woman as light as a feather and as quick as a kitten, habited for gardening in a broad straw hat and gauntlet gloves, with a basket on her arm, visibly the mistress of the place. The face was one that would be charming to some and distasteful to others, and might . . . be called rather plain or rather handsome, as the observer was sympathetic or otherwise. In a very few minutes the verdict would be understood and confirmed by the lady, whose penetration made her a little feared.

From the start Scott was one of the more sympathetic observers, who found Lady Trevelyan handsome rather than otherwise. With this verdict understood,

> Lady Trevelyan said she was going to look at her own garden and asked whether I would accompany her . . . I went with her and in half an hour we were old friends; she had asked many questions, and received the directest and truest answers. . . . She showed that she liked my plain speech and recognised it to be genuine and unconventional, and in her own way felt grateful and pleased. Walking from one spot to another, she made me acquainted with various picturesque features and little nooks she had sketched, with the bulrushes and water-lilies. I rowed her across one of the artificial ponds before we returned and entered the house.

At this point Scott draws a decorous curtain over the further development of their friendship. One can only guess at the precise nature of it. That the friendship was an intimate one goes without saying. Scott frequently stayed at Wallington Hall for weeks at a time. In his *Notes* he freely admitted that he was very fond of Lady Trevelyan. In one place he referred to her as his "never-to-be-forgotten . . . angel." In another he reproduced a verse of hers, so "that my pages may possess something by her."

From his dislike of the other men in Pauline's life, it is fairly evident that he, for his part, felt more than friendship. Although he respected Sir Walter and maintained bland and courteous relations with him, Scott thought that Pauline's husband was self-centered and deficient in humor and imagination. Of Swinburne and Ruskin, Scott was even more critical. He ridiculed the youthful Swinburne for his vanity and "Gallomania,"

and considered it his duty to counteract Ruskin's "overpowering influence" in matters of modern painting, particularly his predilection for Turner.

One does not know how Lady Trevelyan felt about Scott. She obviously liked to surround herself with brilliant and entertaining men. That Scott was also handsome could not have been disadvantageous in her eyes. In love with him or not, as a woman of the world she knew how to handle him. Although she teased and amused him, she could show her kitten's claws upon occasion. Apparently she kept him zestfully and agreeably irritated, stroking and at the same time ruffling his ego. Scott said that "always amiable and often complimentary to strangers, towards me she had the appearance of severity, rating me for pride, for ignorance of the world, for conceit." Once her niece protested that she was "more cruel to Mr. Scott than to anyone else." But far from resenting such "cruelty," Scott understood it in the way it was meant, as a token of feminine preference, and he was both pleased and flattered by it. "She was a true woman," he pronounced, "but without vanity," adding with unnecessary caution, "and very likely without the passion of love."

III

It could not have taken Christina long to discover Scott's new friendship. Through her brothers she probably learned of his attachment soon after it was formed. It was certainly no secret. William met the Trevelyans not long after Scott did. And shortly following upon Scott's first visit, commissions for pictures began to flow from Wallington into the Chelsea studios of Scott's friends, chiefly Gabriel Rossetti. Scott himself alludes to the water color he advised Lady Trevelyan to commission from Gabriel, and the latter speaks of exhibiting Lady Trevelyan's drawing. The autobiographical relevance of Christina's *Two Choices* now becomes apparent. Once the first choice had been made, the second followed in short order. And if Christina had in October doubted the wisdom of her brave choice, by December she was feeling all the agonies of the amputation.

The poem she wrote on December 18, a few weeks after *Dead Before Death,* gives us a glimpse of that anguish. *Echo* is in Dorothy Stuart's opinion "one of the most interesting of her shorter lyrics, but likewise one of the hardest to interpret in the light of her personal history." Like several of Christina's other "shorter lyrics," this one is much longer in manuscript, and the omitted stanzas shed a much greater illumination on her personal history:

> Come to me in the silence of the night,
> Come in the speaking silence of a dream,
> Come with soft-rounded cheeks and eyes as bright
> As sunlight on a stream;

Come back in tears,
O memory, hope, love of finished years.

*Come with the voice whose musical low tone
My heart still hears tho' it must hear no more;
Come to me in my weakness left alone:
Come back, not as before
In smiles but pale;
But soft with love that loves without avail.

Dearer than daylight on an unknown sea;
Or an oasis in a far desert place,
Dearer than hope and life, come back to me;
Full of a tender grace,
Not changed except
For trace of weary tears thou too hast wept.

Come back that I may gaze my soul away
And from thy presence pass into my rest;
My soul as a tired bird at close of day
Pants toward the accustomed nest;
Come back, come back,
Set my life free that faints upon the rack.*

Oh dream how sweet, too sweet, too bitter sweet;
Whose wakening should have been in paradise
Where souls brimfull of love abide and meet;
Where thirsting longing eyes
Watch the slow door
That opening, letting in, lets out no more.

Yet come to me in dreams, that I may live
My very life again tho' cold in death;
Come back to me in dreams, that I may give
Pulse for pulse, breath for breath;
Speak low, lean low,
As long ago, my love, how long ago.

*So may I dream to death, the languid lull
Of death, unnoticed, trenching on my sleep,
Sealing the sentence change cannot annul;
No vigils more to keep,
No deaths to die,
Only to watch for thee as days go by.*

"It certainly seems," Miss Stuart puzzles, "as if an influence was now at work which sent the blood with a new and fuller music through her ere-while languid pulses." But the chords had been resounding long before, and, as the title of the lyric suggests, it was their echo that reverberated in this verse.

In *Zara,* an unpublished sonnet of January 18, the same subject is treated in much the same way:

*I dreamed that loving me he would love on
Thro' life and death into eternity:
I dreamed that love would be and be and be
As surely as the sun shines that once shone.
Now even that my dream is killed and gone,
It sometimes even now returns to me;
Not what it was, but half being memory,
And half the pain that wears my cheek so wan.
O bitter pain, what drug will lull the pain?
O lying memory, when shall I forget?
For why should I remember him in vain
Who hath forgotten and rejoiceth still?
Oh bitter memory, while my heart is set
On love that gnaws and gnaws and cannot kill.*

IV

The February, 1924, issue of *The Parish Magazine* of Christ Church, Albany Street, has a note to the effect that during 1854 Christina Rossetti visited on Robert Street for the church. This was, and remains, one of the depressed areas leading off Albany Street. But this limited social work in the parish was not sufficiently satisfying, and toward the end of the year she volunteered to join Florence Nightingale's expedition of nurses to Scutari.

The outbreak of patriotic enthusiasm which kindled the nation at the beginning of the Crimean War had a local center in Christ Church and the St. Saviour's Sisterhood connected with it; and the excitement radiated out from this focal point into the neighborhood. The Mother Superior herself was placed in charge of a combined corps of nurses, which in addition to the nuns (both those of Christ Church and of the Devonport Sisterhood, which later absorbed the earlier community) included "other ladies of the congregation, such as Eliza Polidori." Since the applicants were carefully screened, to be selected for service at the front was considered a great honor, and it may be taken for granted that Christina was not the only sheltered young woman of the parish who aspired to it.

Although she undoubtedly caught the contagion from the general excitement, and had in addition the example of her Aunt Eliza, who was shortly leaving for Scutari as a supervising nurse, Christina was possibly prompted by some deeper motive, one more intimately related to her inner life. If there were young Englishmen like the hero of Tennyson's *Maud,* who volunteered for military service in the expectation of solving emotional problems through heroic and bloody action on the Crimean front, there were undoubtedly also young women who hoped to anesthetize emotional pain by self-abnegating service to the wounded and dying.

Christina's application was refused because of her youth, and so this

avenue of escape was cut off. Next we hear of her in January attending a gay masquerade party at the Seddons' house. Madox Brown tells us that she appeared in "Syrian dress." By seeking distraction in social life was she trying to demonstrate to herself—or Scott—that his desertion left her unmoved? Or did she actually hope to replace an emotional by a social life?

Whatever her motive, she must have soon realized that the battlefield assigned to her was internal, not external, that neither bloodletting on Crimean soil nor the mildly narcotizing excitement of London drawing rooms could take the place of the spiritual work facing her. In the natural tendency to shirk such austere labor, she fell back upon a familiar resource of her youth, and was ill again from March to July.

Whether she wrote the powerful and curious *My Dream* of March 9 before her illness, we have no way of knowing. In examining this unusual work the first thing to observe is that Christina wrote in the margin of the manuscript, "not a real dream." Seemingly one of those dark fantasies of the imaginative unconscious, the common soil for both poetry and dreams, this poem indicates if it does not reveal the extent and the depth of Christina's emotional disturbance, which cannot reasonably be disassociated from her illness, whatever its symptoms may have been.

William attached considerable significance to *My Dream,* for he devoted almost a page to discussing it in his note to the poems. "If anything were needed to show the exceptional turn of mind of Christina Rossetti, the freakishness which flecked the extreme and almost excessive seriousness of her thought—the present poem might serve for the purpose. But as it was not a real dream, and she chose nevertheless to give it verbal form, one seeks for a meaning in it. I, for one, cannot find any that bears development."

Today we do not feel obliged to look for "meaning" in a poem which is in itself an aesthetic experience. Without questioning the nature of such experience, we can, however, investigate its relevance to the poet's inner life.

> Hear now a curious dream I dreamed last night,
> Each word whereof is weighed and sifted truth,

is the opening statement. We may ask why Christina insists upon the element of truth in a fictitious invention. We know, of course, that truth does not necessarily have to be factual. Religious truth, for instance, rests not upon fact but upon revelation. Scientific truth sometimes depends more upon mathematical formula than upon observed evidence. We can, therefore, assume that a "weighed and sifted truth" need not be interpreted literally. "Scrupulous Christians need special self-sifting," Christina wrote in her miscellany, *Time Flies* (1885). Could not a sifted truth be the kind of truth which is sifted from the chaff of actuality, one valid

only in the emotional and spiritual spheres, a truth originating not in fact, but at that deeper level of mingled consciousness and unconsciousness from which the poet, as well as the dreamer, draws his materials?

Very briefly, in this poem a ferocious, savage, sensual crocodile, monarch of all the other crocodiles, which he devours in a particularly vivid and repulsive way, grows fat in satiety. "Prudent" though he may be, at the conclusion of the poem the monarch crocodile becomes alarmed by the approach of a heavenly white ship with avenging sails; and he wrings his hands and sheds appropriate tears.

Gabriel borrowed the name of "the prudent crocodile" to bestow upon William Morris, whose wife he is said to have loved. Christina, however, could not have had Morris in mind as the model for her crocodile, for emotionally he was not at the center but on the distant periphery of her life. It is more likely that Scott was the prototype for the magnificent beast, one of Christina's few great characterizations. The distinguishing qualities of the monarch crocodile are his majesty and his lawlessness:

> Each crocodile was girt with massive gold
> And polished stones that with their wearers grew:
> But one there was who waxed beyond the rest,
> Wore kinglier girdle and a kingly crown
> Whilst crowns and orbs and sceptres starred his breast.
> All gleamed compact and green with scale on scale,
> But special burnishment adorned his mail
> And special terror weighed his frown.

The regal monster derives his power and his kingly prerogative from the beauty and terror with which he is invested; and beauty inspires terror only in a love relationship. The reverent dread of the beloved, an emotional state well known to the lover, has been given memorable and striking literary expression by both Plato and Shelley. In the *Phaedrus* the predatory lover becomes tamed and purified by the divine terror when he beholds the flashing beauty of the beloved, the earthly image of heavenly beauty. In *Epipsychidion* Shelley compresses the same philosophical concept into the terse lines, "Thou Wonder, and Thou Beauty, and Thou Terror!"

Now we have been told by William that Plato and Shelley were two of Christina's favorite writers. "Among the very great authors, none (making allowance for Dante) seemed to appeal to her more than Plato: she read his *Dialogues* over and over again, with ever renewed or augmented zest"; and "among modern English poets, I should say that Shelley, or perhaps Coleridge, stood highest in her esteem." And so once again we see Christina making creative use of literary tradition.

The "special burnishment" and the "special terror" may be interpreted, then, as the kind of royalty with which a beloved man is invested by the woman who loves him. The crown symbolism (cf. *Three Stages III*)

further supports this interpretation of the crocodile symbol as erotic in origin and conception.

Such a royal lover was to remain as a feature of Christina's mature verse, reappearing in many of her poems, notably in *Prince's Progress* and *Maiden Song.* That Scott actually did present a kind of majestic mien to the world is apparent from contemporary references to him. W. Minto, who edited his *Notes,* thought that in old age Scott resembled a Renaissance cardinal; and both Swinburne and Lady Trevelyan called him at different times "a sea-king."

Lawlessness, the second aspect of the crocodile's personality, is emphasized in the following stanza. Feeling himself above the law, the royal beast devours at will his fellow crocodiles:

> An execrable appetite arose,
> He battened on them, crunched, and sucked them in.
> He knew no law, he feared no binding law,
> But ground them with inexorable jaw.
> The luscious fat distilled upon his chin,
> Exuded from his nostrils and his eyes,
> While still like hungry death he fed his maw;
> Till, every minor crocodile being dead
> And buried too, himself gorged to the full,
> He slept with breath oppressed and unstrung claws.

Read symbolically, the lines reveal their sexual significance, for what Christina is doing here is substituting one sort of sensuous appetite for another, a common form of displacement in dreams. In a later ballad [1] she boldly uses gastro-metabolic imagery of this sort to describe a love relationship:

> Yet I loved him not for his loving,
> While I played with his love and truth,
> Not loving him for his loving,
> Wasting his joy, wasting his youth.
>
> I ate his life as a banquet,
> I drank his life as new wine,
> I fattened upon his leanness,
> Mine to flourish, and his to pine.

The seeds of sexual hostility that sprouted into such wild growth in *My Dream* were already present in *The World* (see p. 81). The ambivalence was there, even before Scott's dereliction. If we accept the sensual crocodile as a symbolic representation of Scott, must we then regard it as a purely subjective distortion, an outlet for bruised and injured feelings? Or is there any truth in the implication that Scott acknowledged no restrictions of law and that he followed his own appetites, with no moral restraint of any kind?

Writing about him in *Three Rossettis,* Janet Camp Troxell points

out that one of his characteristics was his freedom from the ethical obligations governing others. His "marked moral rigidity," she tells us, "gave way at times." She then relates the incident of Scott's theft at a dealer's shop of a picture he coveted. The scandalous incident was well-known to the Rossetti brothers. Hiding Scott's identity, William said that instead of purchasing the picture, which was one missing in a series Scott owned, "he actually stole the missing print and walked off with it, though his means were amply sufficient for bidding for the lot." Another time Scott calmly and coolly regretted that he had once failed to steal from the Carlisle cathedral some pieces of splendid brocade he needed for a picture he was painting. "Perhaps I should have stolen them," were his exact words.[2]

If we follow the line of thought suggested by *Two Choices,* Christina would logically have had no cause to reproach Scott for his interest in another woman, but the emotions are seldom directed by logic. Deprived of love and astonished at the haste with which he had apparently replaced her, she found refuge in a hostility from which she had never been altogether free. It is likely that she understood the nature of the relationship between Scott and Pauline Trevelyan no better than we do. Yet what concerns us is not the event in its actuality, but Christina's interpretation of it for the purpose of poetry. *My Dream* is another of the poems which like *The World* derives its compelling energy from the emotional conflict to which it in turn gives artistic form.

But to get back to the poem: in the succeeding stanzas the powerful appeal of the earthly lover, simultaneously loved and hated, is counteracted by the attraction of the Divine Lover, who proves to be the stronger of the two:

> O marvel passing strange which next I saw!
> In sleep he dwindled to the common size,
> And all the empire faded from his coat.

This dwindling in majesty significantly heralds the approach of the winged vessel, "subtle as flame," which displays its supernatural power by taming the waters without force. This "avenging ghost," as Christina calls the scriptural ship, humbles, diminishes, and finally banishes the earthly lover. The poem concludes,

> What can it mean? you ask. I answer not
> For meaning, but myself must echo, What?
> And tell it as I saw it on the spot.

V

Assuredly, one of the more curious aspects of this poem is Christina's attitude toward it. Although she called it *My Dream,* she took pains to point out that it was not a real dream, at the same time emphasizing that "Each word whereof is weighed and sifted truth." According to the

ending, she wished to discourage explication. Nevertheless, the poem itself teases and invites an exploration into its deeper psychological stratum.

In *Commonplace,* a work of prose fiction written in 1870, Christina also treats the subject of a fictitious dream. Her heroine, fighting to free herself from an unkind love, is haunted by "monstrous" nightmares of the past:

> By day . . . she could forbid her thoughts to shape themselves, even mentally, into words, although no effort could banish the vague, dull sorrow which was all that might remain to her now of remembrance. But by night, when sleep paralyzed self-restraint, then her dreams were haunted by distorted spectres of the past; never alluring or endearing—for this she was thankful—but sometimes monstrous, and always impossible to escape from. Night after night she would awake from such dreams, struggling and sobbing, with less and less conscious strength to resume daily warfare.

This description gives us a clue to the kind of distortions which might have appeared in Christina's own dreams. And as a matter of interest, she has recorded one such dream. It occurred in 1855, the year she composed *My Dream,* and she considered it important enough to write down. This time she took care to assert that it was a real, and not a fictitious or invented, dream:

> Night, but clear with grey light. Part of a church in the background with the cloudside towards the spectator. In the churchyard many good sheep with good innocent expressions: one especially heavenly. Amid them with a full face a Satan-like goat lying with a kingly look and horns. Three white longish-haired dogs in front, confused with the sheep, though somewhat smaller than they; one with a flattering face, a second with a head almost entirely turned away, but what one sees of the face, sensual and abominable.

"This real dream," said Christina, "left me with an impression it was my duty to paint the above subject as a picture—contingent duty, perhaps. Of course I never became competent." [3]

As a crosscut of the complex content of Christina's unconscious mind at work, one could ask for nothing better. Even her feeling of obligation to translate the materials of the dream into an art form is significant. It does not require much psychological astuteness to understand that of the good innocent sheep, the one with the "especially heavenly" expression is the dreamer, and that the satanic and kingly goat is a blood relation to the royal crocodile, another imaginative variant of the demon lover, possibly a symbolic representation of the man whose "arch-fiend" expression appeared to Holman Hunt as his distinguishing characteristic. The goat of course has always been a traditional sex symbol in mythology. The three white dogs are obviously women, or perhaps a trinity of women. We have already observed that Christina often wrote about women in contrasting groups of three, such as *Three Nuns,* and later *A*

Triad, Maiden Song, and *Songs in a Cornfield.* Probably the small dog with the flattering face and the other with averted head who looked "sensual and abominable" were one and the same woman. In the poet's febrile imagination they might have represented the rival whose face was indeed unknown to her, and hence "turned away," but whom she secretly pictured as possessing the attractions of both flattery and sensuality.

It is easy to understand that the faculty responsible for Christina's real as well as her fictitious dreams was the powerful, image-evoking imagination of the poet, operative not only in night dreams, but perpetually alive and sensitive to experience. A simple visit many years later with her niece Olivia to the aquarium in Brighton, during which, Olivia reports, her Aunt Christina "watched the octopus for hours," resulted in the following description:

> One single small octopus in an aquarium is all I have seen. It had a fascination for me. Inert as it often appeared, it bred and tickled a perpetual suspense: will it do something? will it emerge from the background of its watery den? I have seen it swallow its live prey in an eyewink, change from a stony colour to an appalling lividness, elongate unequal feelers and set them flickering like a flame, sit still with an air of immemorial old age amongst the lifeless refuse of its once living meals. I had to remind myself that this vivid figure of wickedness was not in truth itself wickedness.

In this passage we see again the poet's active imagination at work extracting rich juices from an ordinary experience of everyday life.

VI

After *My Dream* Christina wrote a few other poems in March, including one on the 26th marked "written in illness," and then the curtain drops, and we hear very little of her either in life or literature for the next six months. But perhaps at this time occurred the slight incident she described in *Time Flies.* Feeling depressed and anxious, she walked in the Botanical Gardens of Regent's Park. After a time she sat down on a bench by "a certain ornamental water." She sat "so long and so quietly," she tells us, "that a wild garden creature or two made its appearance: a water rat, perhaps, or a water-haunting bird." To become in this way part of the natural surroundings "pleased" and "gratified" her, and the consciousness of this "small secret fount of pleasure" had a restorative value for her.

In July she was in Hastings. Some correspondence between Gabriel and Ford Madox Brown in September and a brief entry in Brown's diary establish the fact that she returned to London and was a house guest of the Browns during the week of September 23.

These were the years that Gabriel was in love with Lizzie Siddal, whom he affectionately called "Guggums," a woman Christina found it difficult to like. "There is a coldness between her and Gabriel," Brown observed, "because she and Guggums do not agree. She works at worsted ever and talks sparingly." [4] Silently plying her needles at the Browns', she could not have failed to contrast the external bleakness of her own life with the golden richness of Miss Siddal's. Not only was "Guggums" beloved by Gabriel and admired by his circle, but she was also absurdly exalted as a great artist by Brown and Ruskin. The latter called her a "noble, glorious creature," and settled £150 a year on her so that she could develop her talent without financial harassment. As yet, Christina had received but slight recognition as a poet, and had met with total frustration as a woman.

In addition to acting as a combination of Medici patron and fairy godfather to Gabriel and his Lizzie, Ruskin in the 1850's also appears in the incongruous role of Maria Rossetti's admirer. His attentions were evidently not meant seriously, although Maria thought they were, and Christina was to observe in *Time Flies* [5] that "one of the most genuine Christians I ever knew, once took lightly the dying out of a brief acquaintance which had engaged her warm heart, on the ground that such mere tastes and glimpses of congenial intercourse on earth waited for their development in heaven." But if Christina admired her elder, plainer sister's plucky attitude, clearly she could not emulate it; and she must have found discouraging the need to await in heaven the development of that congenial intercourse on earth for which she longed.

In October she broke another poetic silence with a poem as terrible in its way and as dramatic as *Dead Before Death* and *My Dream.* This was the strangely bleak and lurid sonnet *Cobwebs,* in which the mood of despair is expressed symbolically by the portrait of a static landscape, one as appallingly blank, dreary, and lifeless as a planet of the New Astronomy and perhaps only equaled by the terrifying landscape in Browning's *Childe Roland:*

It is a land with neither night nor day,
Nor heat nor cold, nor any wind nor rain,
Nor hills nor valleys; but one even plain
Stretches through long unbroken miles away,
While through the sluggish air a twilight grey
Broodeth: no moons nor seasons wax and wane,
No ebb and flow are there along the main,
No bud-time, no leaf-falling, there for aye:—
No ripples on the sea, no shifting sand,
No beat of wings to stir the stagnant space:
No pulse of life through all the loveless land
And loveless sea; no trace of days before,
No guarded home, no toil-won resting place,
No future hope, no fear for ever more.

For the remainder of the year and into the spring of the following year, the prevailing theme of Christina's poetry is the loss of love. "What Happened to Me" is the original "too significant title"—the words are William's—of *Shut Out,* the first of the 1856 poems. Mourning the loss of

My garden, mine, beneath the sky
Pied with all flowers bedewed and green,

the speaker complains that she is "shut out" by a cold, hard wall. "A shadowless spirit . . . blank and unchanging like the grave," a denizen from the arid land of *Cobwebs,* guards the garden door and hears in implacable silence the speaker's plea to be given "one small twig" or "some buds to cheer my outcast state." His answer has the finality of action unqualified by words:

The spirit was silent; but he took
Mortar and stone to build a wall;
He left no loophole great or small
Through which my straining eyes might look.

So now I sit here quite alone
Blinded by tears; nor grieve for that,
For nought is left worth looking at
Since my delightful land is gone.

From the tone of this and other poems of the period, one gets the impression that Christina made little effort to reconcile herself to her loss. The finality of termination is the theme of *Amen,* each of its three stanzas beginning with a restatement of the theme: "It is over / It is finished / It suffices." *A Martyr* opens with a statement of the same theme:

It is over the horrible pain,
All is over the struggle and doubt.

Acme, a sonnet of May 9, suggests that, although the end is not yet in sight, there are occasional lulls in the battle. The most persistent pain lets up periodically. The mind refuses to dwell ceaselessly, without moments of relief, upon the source of its suffering. But with subtle psychological insight the poet understands that the relief is no more lasting than the pain, and that a brief surcease from anguish only increases its intensity:

Sleep, unforgotten sorrow, sleep awhile:
Make even awhile as though I might forget;
Let the wound staunch thy tedious fingers fret,
Till once again I look abroad and smile,
Warmed in the sunlight: let no tears defile
My path: O sorrow, slumber, slumber yet
A moment, rouse not yet the smouldering pile.
So shalt thou wake again with added strength,
O unforgotten sorrow, stir again

The slackening fire, refine the lulling pain
To quickened torture and a subtler edge.
The wrung cord snaps at last: beneath the wedge
The toughest oak groans long but rends at last.

VII

A complete reversal of attitude appears in *A Bed of Forget-Me-Nots* of June 17. Exultantly proclaiming her faith in love, Christina here expresses with an exuberant romanticism almost Wordsworthian her trust in "the passion of the instinctive pulse":

Is Love so prone to change and rot
We are fain to rear Forget-me-not
By measure in a garden-plot? . . .

Love is not taught in learning's school,
Love is not parcelled out by rule:
Hath curb or call an answer got?—
So free must be Forget-me-not.
Give me the flame no dampness dulls,
The passion of the instinctive pulse,
Love steadfast as a fixèd star,
Tender as doves with nestlings are,
More large than time, more strong than death:
This all creation travails of—
She groans not for a passing breath—
This is Forget-me-not and love.

Although not nearly so satisfactory as *Acme,* this poem indicates that Christina had some renewed source of nourishment, for apparent are a freshness of energy and an uncharacteristic optimism. But the next poem, written July 12, shows another abrupt change of attitude. In *Look on This Picture and on This,* love is portrayed as a turbulent maelstrom of emotions in which sexual hostility, jealousy, self-pity, and self-contempt each strives for dominance. If we turn to the factual record, we find a single clue leading to a possible explanation of these oscillations: a June 28 entry in Brown's diary informs us that Scott was again in London.

William hesitated about including *Look on This Picture* in the collected *Poems.* Suggesting (because of the name Eva) that it was inspired by Maturin's *The Women,* he admitted that, were this not the case, he would have been "embarrassed to guess what could have directed my sister's pen to so singular a subject and treatment." But the Maturin influence is evident in her poetry of the late 1840's, and it is doubtful whether a decade later Christina would have returned to her early interest in this author.

As the better part of discretion, William did omit twenty-three of the original forty-six triplets which appear in manuscript. The deleted stanzas

are much more personal, violent, and revealing than those he printed. Their frenzied melodramatic tone, passionate and unrestrained, confirms the impression of emotional autobiography which the printed version suggests. There is about them an urgency, a sense of the immediate present, as though they had been dashed off at white heat in the frantic attempt to capture the essence of an important personal experience and to put it down in writing before it evaporated. Although these unpublished stanzas do not add to Christina's stature as a poet, they cannot be disregarded in the record of her life. Moreover, their very spontaneity gives them an interest lacking in the more polished and revised production.

Not the Maturin novel but the title discloses the theme. *Look on This Picture and on This* is recognizable as a line slightly altered from *Hamlet:*

Look here, upon this picture, and on this
The counterfeit presentment of two brothers.

In Christina's poem the two women in a man's life are similarly compared and contrasted. The lover in addressing his former mistress, whom he has abandoned for a new love, attempts to justify his desertion by somewhat cruelly describing to her the superior charms of her rival, a woman who like Pauline Trevelyan is hazel-eyed and distinguished by a regal bearing and a commanding manner:

You have seen her hazel eyes, her warm dark skin,
Dark hair—but oh those hazel eyes a devil is dancing in:—
You, my saint, lead up to heaven, she lures down to sin.

But although the lover is fascinated by his new love, he still cannot make us his mind to quit the old:

*If we talk: I love you, do you love me again?—
Tho' your lips speak it's her voice I flush to hear so plain
Say! Love you? Yes, I love you, love can neither change nor wane.
What shall I choose, what can I choose for you and her and me;
With you the haven of rest, with her the tossing miry sea;
Time's love with her, or choose with you love's all eternity.*

To this restatement of the second of two choices, the injured mistress replies, "Why struggle, I have given you up," and adds resentfully, pressing into service the familiar symbols of the feast, the snapped cord, and the broken cup:

Take again your pledges, snap the cord, and break the cup.
Feast you with your temptation, for I in heaven will sup.

Momentarily remorseful, the lover gives us in his reply a picture of the deserted mistress, one which bears a strong resemblance to the poet herself:

Can I bear to think upon you strong to break not bend,
Pale with inner intense passion, silent to the end,
Bear to leave you, bear to grieve you, O my dove, my friend?

But shortly afterwards he relieves his feeling of guilt by a violent outburst of temper, by jeers and sadistic taunts:

*Did you think to sit in safety, to watch me torn and tost
Struggling like a mad dog, watch her tempting doubly lost?
Howl you, you wretched woman, for your flimsy hopes are crost.

Be still, tho' you may writhe you shall hear the branding truth
You who thought to sit in judgment on our souls forsooth
To sit in frigid judgment on our ripe luxuriant youth.*

Did I love? Never from the first cold day to this:
You are not sufficient, for my aim of life, my bliss;
You are not sufficient, but I found the one that is.

*The wine of love that warms me from this life's mortal chill:
Drunk with love, I drink again, athirst I drink my fill;
Lapped in love I care not doth it make alive or kill.*

Thereupon follows a quick shift of mood as the lover, flavoring brutality with tenderness, acknowledges his love:

Then did I never love you?—ah the sting struck home at last.
You are drooping, fainting, dying—the worst of death is past—
A light is on your face from the nearing heaven forecast.

Never?—yes I loved you then: I loved, the word still charms:
For the first time, last time, lie here in my heart, my arms,
For the first last time, as if I shielded you from harms.

*I trampled you, poor dove, to death; you clung to me, I spurned.
I taunted you, I tortured you, while you sat still and yearned:—
Oh lesson taught in anguish but in double anguish learned.*

For after all I loved you, loved you then, I love you yet:
Listen, love, I love you: see, the seal of truth is set
On my face, with tears—you cannot see? then feel them wet.

The remainder of the poem, in which the prevailing tone is one of self-pity, narrates the ascent and glorification of the dove trampled to death. The revenge of the abused mistress consists of her renewed power of choice, her ability to escape the torment of jealousy by dying. Once beatified, it is she who holds the lovers in her power, and in exercising Christian forgiveness, she takes a subtle vengeance.

How much of this tempestuous scene could actually have occurred and how much of it was invented must remain an enigma. It merely raises again the puzzling problem of the proportionate relation of fact to fiction in the work of an imaginative writer.

VIII

That autumn Scott went again to Paris, stopping over in London on his way back. On September 30 Christina turned out *The Lowest Room,* a long poem concerned partially although not wholly with personal problems. Originally entitled *A Fight over the Body of Homer,* this poem lacks the unity of structure we are accustomed to find in Christina's work. Two separate and seemingly unrelated issues are dealt with. First, she weighs and contrasts the domestic happiness of the married woman with the self-dedication of the artist. Second, she contrasts the virile attraction of the pagan Homeric age with the puritanical ethos of Victorian Christianity. Once again the royal lover flashes into the picture, in the image of the Homeric "crest-rearing kings with whistling spears" who

Hated with intenser hate
And loved with fuller love

than the men of the nineteenth century, who are "stunted from heroic growth." But like the prudent crocodile, such heroes as Achilles were violent and lawless, hence less than human. Although Christina rejects in this poem the romantic ideal of the "crest-rearing king," one senses the irresistible attraction the type had for her.

Like other of the poems, this also contains omissions which do not appear in the printed text. The unpublished opening stanzas are stronger and more vigorous than the published variant:

*Amen: the sting of fear is past,
Cast out and no more burdensome;
There can be no such pang as this
In all the years to come.

No more such wrestling in my soul
No more such heart-break out of sight,
From dawning of my longdrawn day
Until it draws to night.* [6]

Three other omitted stanzas occurring toward the end of the poem give us a still further clue to Christina's mood that autumn. Anger and self-pity and the desire for revenge have been succeeded by a quiet and weary acceptance:

*Still worn indeed I am and pale,
Yet lightened of a clog of care;
Contented with my goodly lot
For God has placed me there.

Rejoicing at my sister's joy,
In sympathy with young and old,
Feeding and trimming mine own fire
Tho' all the world was cold.

No longer bitter with my friend
Who cannot guess what I conceal,
Who cannot bind the secret sore
I never own to feel.*

In October Scott returned to London, dining at Lady Trevelyan's request with Ruskin and afterwards accompanying Gabriel and him to the Working Men's College in Red Lion Square, where both men taught art. There is no indication on the record of a meeting between Scott and Christina, but like *Look on This Picture,* her *Light Love* of October 28 dramatizes another love crisis between hostile lovers. Once again an abandoned mistress, described in the poem as "a mateless dove," reproaches her lover for having left her for a more alluring rival.

After Sunset, written a month later (November 26), has an entirely different tone. In the manuscript notebook pages 65–69 are torn out, leaving only the following two stanzas as an interesting fragment of a lost poem:

*To make it glad with a goodly crop:
Even so One wiser deals with me:—
Amen, say I: if He chose to lop
Branch after branch of my leaféd tree
In its own ripe season more fruit shall be.

Tenfold fruit in the time of fruit,
In the time of corn and wine and oil,
Sound at the core, firm at the root;
Repaying the years and years of toil,
Repaying the blood that fed the soil.*

Other devotional poems of the period, such as *After This Judgment, Not Yours But You,* and the first of the linked series of *New Year Ditties,* all confirm the impression that Christina was regaining self-confidence as she turned her painful experience into spiritual profit.

IX

But major emotional problems are not quickly resolved, and that she was still fighting cobwebs is revealed by two poems of December, *A Triad* and *Love from the North.* The former, dated December 18, is again haunted by the specter of the other woman, but in this poem the wife appears for the first time as well. In the summer of 1856 Mrs. Scott had been invited to dine *"en famille"* with Christina and William.[7] References to Mrs. Scott appear in the record more frequently as the years go by, and one gathers that the dinner *"en famille"* was the beginning of the cordial and close relationship that developed later between Christina and Scott's wife.

Three women in pursuit of love are contrasted in *A Triad.* The

first, like a honey-sweetened bee, drones rich and fat on love. Like the successful rival in *Look on This Picture* and *Light Love,* she is crimson and glowing and flushed with love. The second, a "sluggish wife," smooth and soft as a tinted hyacinth, grows "gross in soulless love." The third, a virgin, "blue with famine after love," finally perishes for the lack of it.

That *A Triad* was shocking to Victorian sensibilities is not surprising. "For voluptuous passion," said *The Spectator* later, it "could have been written by Dante Gabriel Rossetti." And yet the sonnet is harmless enough. It was the honesty with which Christina exposed what she once described in a different connection as "the feminine boldness and directness of aim," which distressed her contemporaries.[8]

The day after finishing this sonnet, she wrote *Love from the North,* originally called *In the Days of the Sea-Kings.* In this ballad another of her crest-rearing kings with whistling spears, this time a Viking, seizes another man's bride at the altar and carries her off without asking her consent, but nonetheless winning her love. By now such a suitor, combination of the demon lover and the royal wooer, is a stock figure in Christina's poetry. Although this ballad must be regarded primarily as wish-fantasy, the skeletal structure of the real world of fact may as usual be perceived through the tissue of medieval legendry. As we have seen, not only did Swinburne and Lady Trevelyan call Scott "a sea-king" at various times, but he himself painted a picture he entitled *The Sea-King's Funeral* (exhibited in 1865).

Moreover, Christina's description of the Viking as "a strong man from the North" with "eyes of dangerous grey" is confirmed by a self-portrait of Scott which shows his face in middle life as rugged and dignified, with boldly carved features, a high forehead, and eyes which were both sinister and commanding. "Grave" and "earnest" were the epithets Carlyle and George Henry Lewes used to describe him, but the impression of strength, of gravity and austere beauty, in Scott's face is contradicted by the outlaw's eyes. William relates an anecdote which places peculiar emphasis upon the disturbing quality of Scott's eyes. One summer when the two men were traveling together in Italy, a Pisan woman who shared their compartment on the train kept staring at Scott with furtive uneasiness. At length, frightened by the sinister expression of his clear, blue-gray eyes, she whispered to William that his companion surely "had the evil eye." An echo of this remark, which became a legendary joke in the Rossetti circle, reverberates in a line from Christina's ballad of 1866, *Cannot Sweeten:* "I slew my love with an evil eye."

Love from the North was the last of the 1856 poems. During the first half of the year, in pieces such as *Shut Out, It Is Over, Acme,* and others, the poet persistently dwelt upon the theme of solitary grief over the loss of love. But upon Scott's reappearance in June, a new element entered her poetry. *Look on This Picture, Light Love,* and *Love from*

the North may not be examples of Christina's best work, but they are charged with life and emotional action. The static, solitary gray landscape of *Cobwebs* has altered to one dynamic with human figures engaged in struggle. Emotionally speaking, Christina has reëntered the world of living people.

What is equally apparent is that, despite her disillusionment, she had by no means freed herself from her obsessive passion. The last stanza of *Love from the North* hints at the possibility of a lovers' reconciliation. Perhaps, as the lines suggest, the "Visitor from the North" (Holman Hunt's phrase for Scott) overrode Christina's misgivings once again; and, helplessly in love, she submitted to what was after all her heart's desire:

He took me in his strong white arms,
He bore me on his horse away
O'er crag, morass, and hairbreadth pass,
But never asked me yea or nay.

He made me fast with book and bell,
With links of love he makes me stay;
Till now I've neither heart nor power
Nor will nor wish to say him nay.

❁ 6 ❁

"A PENT-UP CONFLAGRATION"

1857–1858

During the first six months of 1857 Scott continued to maintain a brisk correspondence with Christina's brothers, calling William's attention to a recent work by an unknown American poet, *Leaves of Grass*—"the queerest, the most startling and in some ways the most catholic of new oracles"—and telling Gabriel about the commission he had succeeded in getting for Woolner to do the sculptured marble group in the central hall at Wallington. He himself had been commissioned by Lady Trevelyan to decorate Wallington Hall with murals from British history, a project which took him from 1856 to 1861 to complete, and which, needless to say, obliged him to spend the major portion of his free time at Wallington.

By June he had finished his *St. Cuthbert on Farne Island,* the first picture in the historical series, and had gone to Oxford to see the Arthurian murals with which Gabriel and his new Oxford friends, William Morris and Ned Jones (Sir Edward Burne-Jones), were decorating the walls of Oxford's Union Debating Room, in Scott's opinion "simply the most unmitigated fiasco that ever was made by a parcel of men of genius."

He undoubtedly went to London as well, for he was exhibiting several of his pictures with the former PRB painters at what was called "the Pre-Raphaelite Exhibition" at Russell Square; and he would have wanted to oversee their hanging, and in general make arrangements for his own participation in the show.

As ever, Christina's poetry shows what might be described as a seismic sensitivity to his presence in her vicinity. In *One Day* of June 6 she is still quietly brooding over the past, recalling nostalgically when "we" met and when "we" parted ("they" in the published version):

When shall we meet?—I cannot tell
Indeed when we shall meet again,
But meet we shall in Paradise:
For this we wait I wait in pain.

But by June 30 the past has been overturned and swept away in one of those sudden upheavals that periodically disrupted her inner landscape. Although no impression of the devastating event, whatever it may have been, is to be found in the external record of her life, it deposited its traces in her poetry. *Introspective* and *A Better Resurrection,* both written on June 30, remain as the evidence of a once vital eruption.

But if the two poems are characterized by the same emotional intensity, they differ strikingly in execution. Whereas *Introspective* reads as though it had been passionately spilled out from the spontaneous overflow of a full heart, *A Better Resurrection* displays the steady control of the artist whose critical capacity is at work shaping the molten materials of experience into aesthetic design.

Like others of Christina's poems, *Introspective* is recapitulative; but instead of dramatizing the crisis-event, in this poem she dramatizes the effect it had upon her:

I wish it were over the terrible pain
Pang after pang again and again:
First the shattering ruining blow,
Then the probing steady and slow.

Did I wince? I did not faint:
My soul broke but was not bent:
Up I stand like a blasted tree
By the shore of the shivering sea.

On my boughs neither leaf nor fruit,
Nor sap in my uttermost root,
Brooding in an anguish dumb
On the short past and the long to-come.

Dumb I was when the ruin fell,
Dumb I remain and will never tell:
O my soul, I talk with thee,
But not another the sight must see.

I did not start when the torture stung,
I did not faint when the torture wrung:
Let it come tenfold if come it must,
But I will not groan when I bite the dust.

In observing the verbal resemblance between what in 1850 William called "the staggering blow," and what in 1857 Christina described as "the shattering ruining blow," we are struck by a marked similarity in phrasing. What, if any, is the connection between the two events?

Separated in time by seven years, the only link appears to be the emotional force of the two shocks. The intensity with which Christina felt them suggests that they were delivered by the same person, the man who of all others had the power to hurt her. The first blow, the revelation of

Scott's marriage, was unintentional; and for the second, his attraction toward another woman, he might also have disclaimed responsibility. He probably felt that by making it clear to Christina that their affair was finished he was acting honorably and unequivocally, for she herself had refused love when it was offered to her. He understood, if she did not, that inevitably old love affairs end and new ones begin. He was enjoying himself at Wallington Hall and he intended to continue to do so, without any reproaches or accusations or unpleasant scenes to mar his pleasure. Wasn't it kinder to end the relationship decisively than to allow it to linger on in a moribund state?

The mood of grief and despair pervading *Introspective* is also evident in the opening stanza of *A Better Resurrection*. But the spiritual movement which in turn shapes the artistic design develops quite differently in the second of the two poems. In *Introspective* two opposing currents check one another. The scream of agonized pain is countered by the bravado of defiant pride. It was all very well for Christina to boast that she would not groan when she bit the dust; but to save herself, more was required. A positive spiritual impulse, not of reckless defiance, but of faith, of courageous affirmation, was needed.

As we read *A Better Resurrection,* we sense the labor involved in such a process—the strain, the effort, the summoning of vast reserves of spiritual energy in order to build of suffering a bridge over which to make the perilous crossing to an unknown bank. This crucial and creative work at the level of personality is given aesthetic expression in the poem, as material shapes and is in turn shaped by structure:

I have no wit, no words, no tears;
My heart within me like a stone
Is numbed too much for hopes or fears.
Look right, look left, I dwell alone;
I lift mine eyes, but dimmed with grief
No everlasting hills I see;
My life is in the falling leaf:
O Jesus quicken me.

My life is like a faded leaf,
My harvest dwindled to a husk:
Truly my life is void and brief
And tedious in the barren dusk:
My life is like a frozen thing,
No bud nor greenness can I see;
Yet rise it shall the sap of Spring;
O Jesus rise in me.

My life is like a broken bowl,
A broken bowl that cannot hold
One drop of water for my soul
Or cordial for the searching cold;

Cast in the fire the perished thing;
Melt and remould it, till it be
A royal cup for Him my King:
O Jesus drink of me.

Here also are two movements, the centric and the counter movement, but instead of checking one another, as they do in *Introspective,* they blend into a dissonant harmony. The negative or countercurrent which initiates each stanza is expressed in a series of rapidly shifting images, sharp, dynamic, bold—clear as black shadows on a sunlit wall. But the positive or centric current seizes and transforms the imagery at the conclusion of each stanza, so that by means of the varied refrain, a crescendo effect rising to a climax in the third stanza is achieved.

Besides the imagery, Christina's skillful control of verse texture and her choice of diction reveal a mature artistry lacking in *Introspective,* a rather remarkable distinction when we recall that both poems were written on the same day. Some time that June day, in the hours that separated *Introspective* from *A Better Resurrection,* Christina accomplished an inner work of no little magnitude, of which *A Better Resurrection* is the fruit and the record.

II

In July Scott went back not to Newcastle but to Wallington Hall, leaving ruin and desolation behind him in London. For Christina the long summer days must have passed in monotonous succession as, waging her battle in solitude, she tried to face with courage her loneliness and loss. *A Peal of Bells* of July 7 is in effect a threnody for love.

Again in this piece, as so often in Christina's poetry, the sensuous joys of love are represented as a feast, at which "Golden fruit, fresh-plucked and ripe" is the *plat du jour.* The speaker calls for wine, flowers, silver bells, scented lamps hung on golden orange trees, golden plates heaped with fruit. But with the tolling of the bell, she realizes with bewilderment that "My feast's a show, my lights are dim," and the bowl which once "sparkled to the brim" is now drained and broken.

In the meanwhile Scott was enjoying himself at Wallington Hall. The contrast between his life and Christina's that summer could not have been more striking. Basking in the luxury of gracious country living in a great house, Scott was petted and made much of by pretty women. Under his direction Lady Trevelyan and her young house guest, Miss Capel Lofft (the second Lady Trevelyan after Pauline's death), were painting the saloon of the great hall. The three of them formed an intimate and congenial circle. They worked together, they relaxed together, amusing themselves agreeably in the fragrant garden and the spacious drawing room. Sharing the same tastes, they took drives around the countryside, read the same books, and admired the same prints.

Later in the summer they were joined by Swinburne, then a youth, who was spending his holiday on his grandfather's estate nearby. He enlivened their company and entertained them by his brilliant and eccentric wit. With his "aureole of fiery hair and his pale and arrogant face," he reminded Scott of an Uccello portrait; but his behavior Scott considered that of a spoiled child. This probably meant that Swinburne was getting more than what Scott thought his fair share of attention from the women.

With these interesting distractions, Scott obviously had no time for Christina. We may assume that, having dealt her the shattering, ruinous blow, he promptly forgot her. But the wound was still throbbing, as her poem of August 27 reveals. Concerning *The Heart Knows Its Own Bitterness* (the second poem of that title), William wrote: "Few things written by Christina contain more of her innermost self than this."

As a result of laboring and striving for "pleasure with a restless will," the speaker finds herself left "beggared sense and soul." Therefore:

Of all my past this is the sum—
I will not lean on child of man,
To give, to give, not to receive!
I long to pour myself, my soul,
Not to keep back or count or leave,
But king with king to give the whole.
I long for one to stir my deep—
I have had enough of help and gift—
I long for one to search and sift
Myself, to take myself and keep.

This passionate utterance is followed by a sudden outbreak of the hostility observable in some of the 1856 poems. Using the symbolic language of religious eroticism, the speaker castigates with all-too-human resentment the earthly lover who has failed her.

You scratch my surface with your pin,
You stroke me smooth with hushing breath:
Nay pierce, nay probe, nay dig within,
Probe my quick core and sound my depth.
You call me with a puny call,
You talk, you smile, you nothing do:
How should I spend my heart on you,
My heart that so outweighs you all?

III

After another enigmatic reference to her secret in *Day Dreams* of September 8, four days later Christina wrote a strange and lurid little fragment she called *Nightmare,* which William discovered after her death. The page containing the middle portion of the poem is torn out of the notebook, and only the first and last part are left:

I have a *love* in ghostland—
Early found, ah me how early lost!—

Blood-red seaweeds drip along that coastland
By the strong sea wrenched and tost. . . .

If I wake he *rides* me like a nightmare:
I feel my hair stand up, my body creep:
Without light I see a blasting sight there,
See a secret I must keep.

William's substitution in the printed text of two mild and conventional words for the two more psychologically revealing words in manuscript becomes in context a highly significant alteration. The published variant reads "friend" for "love" in the first line, and the inoffensive verb "hunts" replaces the forceful verb "rides" in the fifth line.

After *Nightmare* Christina wrote two short lyrics, and then on November 8 *Memory I,* another of the important linked poems which are guideposts to her inner life. This poem, as William observes, is "a remarkable utterance." Again, as in *Introspective,* she appears concerned not so much with the external event that inspired the poem, important as it must have been to her, as with its effect upon her. In general, for her purpose—the purpose of poetry—the externals of fact were not significant. The emotional or spiritual essence of fact was all that she cared to extract for a poem. In *Memory I,* not the happening but her response to it gives the poem its moving quality:

I nursed it in my bosom while it lived,
I hid it in my heart when it was dead.
In joy I sat alone; even so I grieved
Alone, and nothing said.

I shut the door to face the naked truth,
I stood alone—I faced the truth alone,
Stripped bare of self-regard or forms of ruth
Till first and last were shown.

I took the perfect balances and weighed;
No shaking of my hand disturbed the poise;
Weighed, found it wanting: not a word I said,
But silent made my choice.

None know the choice I made; I make it still.
None know the choice I made and broke my heart,
Breaking my idol: I have braced my will
Once, chosen for once my part.

I broke it at a blow, I laid it cold,
Crushed in my deep heart where it used to live.
My heart dies inch by inch; the time grows old,
Grows old in which I grieve.

What is "the naked truth" that had to be faced so ruthlessly? Could it be that momentarily Christina was sufficiently clear-sighted to understand

her lover's weakness and to regard her situation realistically? Either Scott did not love her at all—and he might have said this in June—or he loved her in his own way, a way which had caused her suffering in the past and would probably continue to do so in the future.

That the choice consisted of breaking her idol is obvious from the text of the poem. But its underlying significance becomes clearer when considered in the light of a passage from *Letter and Spirit,* her devotional prose commentary upon the Ten Commandments. In this work she puts forward the view that the breaking of the Sixth, Seventh, and Eighth Commandments are breaches of the Second Commandment, which forbids the worship of graven images:

> The idolater substitutes in his heart and worship something material in lieu of God; and as being material, akin to himself and unlike God: the murderer, the sensualist, the thief, substitutes for his neighbour or for the well-being of that neighbour some personal indulgence or acquisition of his own: each postpones God or man to self.

To violate the Seventh Commandment (adultery), even by committing the sin already in the heart, was "to act in direct defiance of God." For, "the phraseology of the Old Testament systematically connects idolatry with breaches of the Seventh Commandment." But does it? Christina supports her assertion by quoting Deuteronomy 7:25, 26, but the example is hardly adequate evidence.

She herself suspected that hers was a personal rather than a traditional interpretation of Scripture, for she was careful to qualify her statement by adding, "And if that be not mere fancifulness which seeks to trace a parallel between the Second and Seventh Commandments . . . ," thereby confirming the impression that she made the connection by way of an emotional rather than a logical association of ideas.

If this were all, if *Memory I* had not been followed only ten days later by the rich, exuberant, joyous *Birthday*—if decisions were always implemented and life struggles won in a single resolute engagement—the business of living might be simpler than it is. And had Christina held firmly to the choice stated in *Memory I,* she might have avoided the anguish and the exhausting conflict of a decade; but she might also have failed to write some of her best poetry.

In a poet less subjective the surprising transition in mood from *Memory I* to *Birthday* could be regarded as purely fortuitous, but in view of the close organic connection between Christina's life and her poetry, such an explanation, which explains nothing, is unsatisfactory. As love poems, both should be regarded equally as emotional autobiography. William, for one, does not think that *Birthday* was written in an emotional vacuum. "I have been asked more than once," he admits, "whether I could account for the outburst of exuberant joy evidenced in this celebrated lyric; I am unable to do so. . . . It is of course possible to infer

that *Birthday* is a mere piece of poetical composition, not testifying to any corresponding emotion of its author at the time; but I am hardly prepared to think that."

What, then, had occurred to inspire this ecstatic poem in praise of the kind of love Christina had seemingly rejected only ten days earlier? There is no record of Scott's movements in the autumn of 1857. But if he had come to London again, if they had met, this time with happier results, the mood of *Birthday* could be accounted for.

After Christina's ordeal of the past three years, an assurance from Scott that he still loved her would have been sufficient to send her spirits soaring. Experiencing once again the restorative nourishment of that "secret manna" which had sustained her at Frome-Selwood, she might indeed have regarded her unexpected happiness as a new birth. The poem itself is a lyric of purely triumphant exultation at the fulfillment of earthly love. Love's ecstatic gratification is expressed in a swift succession of vivid images, all decorative and richly sensuous:

My heart is like a singing bird
Whose nest is in a watered shoot:
My heart is like an apple-tree
Whose boughs are bent with thickset fruit;
My heart is like a rainbow shell
That paddles in a halcyon sea;
My heart is gladder than all these
Because my love is come to me.

Raise me a dais of silk and down;
Hang it with vair and purple dyes;
Carve it with doves and pomegranates
And peacocks with a hundred eyes;
Work it in gold and silver grapes,
In leaves and silver fleurs-de-lys;
Because the birthday of my life
Is come, my love is come to me.

IV

Within the week Christina turned out two other poems, one at least almost as well known as *Birthday*. Both written on November 23, they are *Winter: My Secret* and *An Apple-Gathering*, the latter another of her enigmatic allegories. Despite the aroma of spring-like fragrance this delicate poem exudes, a haunting uneasiness shadows its clear, vivid colors. The symbolism of the fruit-bearing apple tree of *Birthday* is again apparent, but in different perspective.

The speaker complains that she has despoiled herself of the fruit of her full harvest by plucking her pretty pink blossoms in the springtime and wearing them in her hair:

Then in due season when I went to see
I found no apples there.

Furthermore, the maidens who have let their blossoms ripen into fruit are a reproach to the speaker, particularly plump Gertrude, who has already found the stronger hand than hers to carry her heavy basket of apples.

At this point the speaker suddenly breaks into the allegory with the reproachful question,

Ah Willie, Willie, *is* my love less worth [1]
Than apples with their green leaves piled above?
I counted rosiest apples on the earth
Of far less worth than love.

So once it was with me you stooped to talk
Laughing and listening in this very lane;
To think that by this way we used to walk
We shall not walk again!

Different in mood and tone is the cheerful, roguish, bantering *Winter: My Secret,* originally called *Nonsense,* in which the poet gives the impression that she is well satisfied with herself and the world. Evidently the bracing tonic responsible for *Birthday* was still having an invigorating effect, for in *Winter* she gaily boasts about the very secret which terrified her in *Nightmare:*

I tell my secret: No indeed, not I:
Perhaps some day, who knows?
But not today; it froze, and blows and snows
And you're too curious; fie!
You want to hear it? well:
Only my secret's mine, and I won't tell.
Or, after all, perhaps there's none:
Suppose there is no secret after all,
But just my fun.

That there is no secret is of course a possibility we cannot altogether disregard, but the following lines make it improbable:

Today's a nipping day, a biting day;
In which one wants a shawl,
A veil, a cloak, and other wraps:
I cannot ope to every one who taps,
And let the draughts come whistling through my hall;
Come bounding, and surrounding me,
Come buffeting, astounding me,
Nipping and clipping through my wraps and all.
I wear my mask for warmth.

The last line is the important one. Her playful allusion to a shawl, a veil, a cloak, and finally to a mask confirms the growing suspicion that

she had a large collection of such disguises which she donned one after the other—no doubt for warmth, as she says.

V

Her mood of jubilance did not last long. *An Apple-Gathering* had already foreshadowed approaching clouds, and now in the spring of 1858 they began to gather. If Scott had given her reassurance, it was only temporarily. He had by no means banished the specter of the other woman haunting Christina's 1856 poems, for she appears again in the ballad *Maude Clare,* which for publication Christina cut down from the original forty-three to twelve stanzas.[2]

In this piece, "My Lord, pale with inner strife," weds a great lady of small stature while still loving the village girl who is "taller by the head" than his bride. In the deleted opening stanzas human love is linked to matings in nature, those of the pigeon or dove and the lark, the latter traditionally the symbol of the poet:

*The fields were white with lily buds
White gleamed the lily beck,
Each mated pigeon plumed the pomp
Of his metallic neck;

A lark sat brooding in the corn,
Her mate sang in the height,
From heaven he sent clear notes to her
Of love and full delight.*

The ballad continues in traditional question and answer style:

*'Is it a wedding you're going to,
Maude Clare, that you're so fine?'
'Oh its [*sic*] the wedding I'm going to
Of a prosperous friend of mine.'—

'I'll break no bread, I'll eat no salt,
I'll pledge no toast in wine,
For it's the wedding I'm going to
Of a false false love of mine.'—*

Maude Clare's derisive wedding gift to the fortunate bride is

my share of a fickle heart
Mine of a paltry love.

One of the bride's attractions is her wealth, a point made several times. Observing Maude Clare in his wedding train,

*Lord Thomas shook when he met her face,
He flushed when he met her eye,
He stepped towards her a single step
And smothered a single sigh—

He cared not to meet her eyes again
And he dared not touch her hand,
For Maude Clare for all she was so fair
Had never an inch of land.*

And again,

*'For you have purchased him with gold,'—
Her words cut sharp and slow:
'For its [*sic*] your gold he took you for,'—
She said and turned to go.*

In witnessing the ceremony Maude Clare shows the same proud, silent discipline as the discarded heroine of *Look on This Picture:*

*Never a word said pale Maude Clare.
But she stood up rigid then,
She sang no praise, she prayed no prayer,
And she uttered no amen.*

The two concluding stanzas differ in manuscript and in print. In the published variant, which does not appear in the notebook, the bride defies and challenges her rival:

'And what you leave,' said Nell, 'I'll take,
And what you spurn I'll wear;
For he's my lord for better and worse,
And him I love, Maude Clare.

'Yea, though you're taller by the head,
More wise, and much more fair,
I'll love him till he loves me best—
Me best of all, Maude Clare.'

But as originally conceived, the bride is unaware of Maude Clare's attachment:

*'I never guessed you loved my lord,
I never heard your wrong;
You should have spoken before the priest
Had made our tie so strong.

You should have stood up in the Church
To claim your rights before;
You should have parted us in the Church
Or kept silence evermore.'*

This ballad is followed by a poem missing in manuscript, of which only the title is extant. But the title, "Jealousy Is as Cruel as the Grave," hints at the reason Christina might have torn out the pages. By April loneliness is again the dominant note in her poetry:

I dwell alone I dwell alone alone,
Whilst full my river flows down to the sea,

Gilded with flashing boats
That bring no friend to me:
O love-songs, gurgling from a hundred throats,
O love-pangs, let me be.

Her complaint in this poem, *Autumn,* is that she suffers from famine in the midst of plenty. While all are being lavishly satisfied, she alone endures privation. She could not help observing, as she wrote in *Convent Threshold* (1858), that

Milk-white, wine-flushed, among the vines,
Up and down, leaping, to and fro,
Most glad, most full, made strong with wines,
Blooming as peaches pearled with dew,
Their golden windy hair afloat,
Love music warbling in their throat,
Young men and women come and go.

It was true that in her circle almost all the young men and women were mating, or trying to. As we have seen, Maria's "warm heart" had been engaged by an unresponsive Ruskin. Next, she showed a preference for the Pre-Raphaelite painter Charles Collins, brother of the novelist Wilkie Collins. Again it came to nothing. During these years William was betrothed to "a lady not my junior," for whom, to use his own discreet language, he had "conceived a genuine affection." Gabriel's various love affairs were too numerous to be kept track of. Besides his lovely but neurotic Lizzie, there were Fanny Cornforth, his model—lush, vulgar, beautiful, and possibly also at this time the dark and queenly beauty, Jane Burden, later the wife of William Morris. Georgina Macdonald, afterwards Lady Burne-Jones, then sixteen and, as Lizzie said of her, "like a sweetmeat," had become engaged to her Edward. Wherever Christina looked, she saw what in *Autumn* she described as the "love-promising," the "slim gleaming maidens" whose love songs awoke "singing echoes in my land." No wonder she complained,

My trees are not in flower,
I have no bower,
And gusty creaks my tower,
And lonesome, very lonesome is my strand.

In such a predicament she had only one recourse. Remembering her glimpses of the more stable love she had celebrated in *A Better Resurrection* and *The Heart Knows Its Own Bitterness,* she turned her back upon the gleaming maidens and their love music, and in the strenuous effort to silence the siren call of the senses, attempted to identify herself with the wise virgins who patiently trim their lamps and await a different love call. Such an effort to spiritualize her need for love may be perceived in the following lines from *Advent Moon* (May 2), one of her best-loved religious poems:

We weep because the night is long,
We laugh for day shall rise,
We sing a slow contented song
And knock at Paradise.
Weeping, we hold Him fast Who wept
For us, we hold Him fast:
And will not let Him go except
He bless us first and last.

Weeping we hold Him fast to-night;
We will not let Him go
Till daybreak smite our wearied sight
And summer smite the snow:
Then figs shall bud, and dove with dove
Shall coo the lifelong day;
Then He shall say, 'Arise, my love,
My fair one, come away.'

VI

But a month after she closed her ears to the seductive "love-songs, gurgling from a hundred throats," she received an invitation to visit the Scotts at Newcastle.

She must have regarded the invitation with mixed feelings. If the spring poems are an indication, she had lost faith in Scott again, lapsing into dejection and loneliness. But although he may have neglected her, his summons showed that he had not forgotten her.

Apparently she felt no hesitation about accepting the invitation and did not realize what she fully understood years later: "Whatever leads to sensual temptation a rule of avoidance, rather than of self-conquest, or even of self-restraint, is a sound and scriptural rule."

The temptation theme, originally sounded in *Three Enemies* (1851) and *The World* (1854), from now on appears with increasing frequency in both the poetry and the prose. Christina wrote about it not as one academically concerned about a theological question, but as one who had herself crossed Dante's flaming path of arrowy fire, the last barrier to Paradise. In Canto 25 of the *Purgatorio,* Dante and Virgil, struggling through Purgatory, are drawn close to the Seventh Circle, that of lust. Spirits, glowing and flaming, plunge and leap into the great fire which hurdles the path. Virgil advises Dante to keep guard and place "the curb tight over the eyes." But, says Dante,

> *Summae Deus clementiae* at the core
> Of the great burning I heard chanted, so
> That to turn thither it made me hunger more.[3]

Goblin Market (1859), *Amor Mundi* (1865), and *Sœur Louise de la Misericorde* (B. 1882) are only a few of the many poems in which the temptation theme is treated. The problem turns up in the prose works

as well. In *Annus Domini* (1874) Christina acknowledges as major temptations the seductions of the flesh and (as in *Three Enemies*) the allurements of the world, but for the devil she substitutes angry rebellion, a form of temptation to which, as she admitted upon more than one occasion, she herself was peculiarly susceptible. In *Time Flies* (1885) she portrays temptation figuratively as Satan's sieve. In theological terms which nevertheless suggest an accepted insight of modern psychology, she writes:

> For he can never . . . destroy us, unless we first make a covenant with death . . . Meanwhile he is doing us an actual service by bringing to the surface what already lurks within. However tormenting and humiliating declared leprosy may be, it is less desperate than suppressed leprosy.

Possibly her Newcastle visit brought to the surface much which for years had been lurking within. But at the time this psychological insight must have been still hidden from her. Doubtless she walked toward her temptation with open arms, inviting it to allure her from the path she had chosen. Untempered as yet, she veered dangerously near the rim of the Seventh Circle, perhaps was even singed by the hot blast; and irresistibly attracted, she may have longed with Dante to plunge into the great fire populous with other spirits, not recognizing it as paradoxically "the very fire . . . which must one day try every man's work, of what sort it is." [4]

The place chosen for Christina's ordeal was in those years a quaint and staid old Northumbrian town, described by Scott as a place in which "half-timbered mullioned-windowed old houses" were jostled by elaborate new edifices in "the 'Italian' style," where in the aristocratic quarters "dull, cozy whist evenings were always going on in dingy drawing rooms full of old furniture and china, lit as much by the great blazing fires as by the still prevailing wax candles."

Scott had managed to ferret out whatever interesting people were to be found at Newcastle, and among the friends Christina met at his house were Dora Greenwell, the poet, with whom she afterwards corresponded; Carmichael, the painter; Robert Bewick, son of the famous wood engraver; and Thomas Dixon, the artistic cork cutter who "discovered" Walt Whitman for Scott, and subsequently for William Rossetti.[5]

The Newcastle visit was one of the rare spots of happiness in Christina's life. Even Mackenzie Bell, that most circumspect of biographers, comments upon the "especial pleasure" a Newcastle visit gave her. Although Bell, informed by William, speaks of three such visits, the record reveals only the one of June, 1858.

We hear a good deal about picnics and feasts in the poetry of the period. Two poems, one the unpublished *Verses on a Picnic near Sunderland,* and the other the well-known anthology piece *At Home,* originally

entitled *After the Picnic,* treat the subject. It is impossible to say whether the two poems refer to the same picnic, but, whereas *At Home* is an expression of deeply felt experience, the Sunderland piece is no more than jog-trot doggerel. It has, however, a certain interest for its deftly detailed sketch of the outing:

*Mr. and Mrs. Scott and I,
With Mr. Manson, Editor,
And of the social Proctors four,
Agreed the season to defy.

We mustered forces at the Rail,
Struck hands, and made our interests one. . . .

From Newcastle to Sunderland
Upon a misty morn in June
We took the train: on either hand
Grimed streets were changed for meadows soon.

Umbrellas, tarts, and sandwiches,
Sustained our spirits' temperate flow,
With potted jam, and cold as snow,
Rough-coated sunburst oranges.* [6]

A marginal jotting in the manuscript notebook informs us that *At Home* was also written "after a Newcastle picnic," which, William explains, "must no doubt have been held in company with the Bell Scotts." In this lyric Christina describes the "feasting" she enjoyed at Newcastle, the abundance that more than made up for the earlier dearth:

Feasting beneath green orange-boughs;
From hand to hand they pushed the wine,
They sucked the pulp of plum and peach;
They sang, they jested, and they laughed,
For each was loved of each.

But this visit, like all others, had to end. It must have been a painful wrench for her to part from Scott after having lived in his house so joyously. In the few short weeks of her visit they could have grown together so intimately that to separate was like tearing skin from skin in a newly healed wound. The difficulty of facing again the separate life after knowing the warmth and fullness of repletion is poignantly expressed in Christina's linked poem *Parting After Parting* of June 15. Originally called *Good-bye,* it was marked in the manuscript notebook, "Written in the train from Newcastle." In commenting upon the circumstance, William once again attempts to guide the reader's mind along the road of an acceptable interpretation of the lyric. "This," he is referring to her marginal note to the poem, "implies that Christina was then

'parting' from her friends, the Bell Scotts of Newcastle, and her visit then being terminated, was returning home to London. It may thus be seen," William continues smoothly, "that the intensity of feeling here expressed really originated in a very slight occurrence—the occurrence itself merely served the poet's turn as a suggestion of highly serious matters."

Undoubtedly to an unmarried woman of twenty-eight her emotional life is a highly serious matter. From what we know of Christina's experience, the "intensity of feeling" needs no elaborate theological explanation. That she was leaving Scott, after having known the rare happiness of sharing a life with him, even temporarily, is excuse enough for the passion communicated with such noble restraint.

Furthermore, that the poem has personal rather than theological implications comes out more clearly in the original text than in the printed variant, which, toned down considerably, is more formal in structure and generalized in tone: [7]

> *Parting after parting
> All one's life long:
> It's a bitter pang, parting
> While love and life are strong.
>
> Parting after parting
> Sore fear and sore sore pain
> Till one dreads the pang of meeting
> More than of parting again.*
>
> When shall the day break
> When this thing shall not be?
> When shall the earth be born
> That hath no more sea:
> The time that is not time
> But all eternity:—

A common complaint of lovers is "Had we but world enough and time." Love, as Marvell knew, requires eternity for its full expression. Only the slow and leisurely pace of centuries can satisfy the need of lovers to explore and savor one another completely. With the quick flashing by of day and night, they feel that sense of harassed interruption, the heavy hand on the shoulder that hurries them toward the grave where none embrace.

VII

At home Christina had the leisure to absorb her experience. It took some two weeks before she was ready to write about it. And then what she had once, in a different connection, described as "the restlessness of a pent-up conflagration" was suddenly released and given poetic form. William calls June 29 a "red-letter day in Christina's poetic calendar," for on that day she either produced or completed three outstanding poems.

They are *Up-hill, To-day and To-morrow,* and *At Home.*[8] Not only are these three lyrics different in tone and content from *Parting,* but they are also sharply distinguished from one another. Taken as a whole, what they suggest is that something happened after Christina's Newcastle visit which radically altered her view of it.

According to Scott's diary notebook, he was in Oxford again that June. Christina's visit to Newcastle ended on June 15, and, since he would not have left while she was his guest, he probably went to Oxford later in the month, and then on to London. If he were in love and like Christina, also suffered from the sore loss and the "sore sore pain" of parting, he might well have followed her to London. No less than Christina, he must have been aware of Time's wingéd chariot; and, although granting that eternity was preferable for the enjoyment of love, as a practical man Scott would not have scorned the more accessible expedient of overtaking and pinning down the racing hours.

Assuming that he did follow Christina to London, what kind of reception did he meet with there? Was she overjoyed to see him, prepared to carry on the same happy and harmonious relationship they had evidently enjoyed at Newcastle? From the June 29 poems and those written subsequently, we have to conclude that the contrary was the case.

Scott declared in his autobiography that all his life he had "tried for confiding affection from both men and women," and "had made many attempts to realise it without success." This may have been one of his attempts that failed. But if he was rebuffed, it was not because Christina did not love him, but because in the fortnight or so that had elapsed since she left Newcastle, she had come to look upon her visit there in a new light.

She had evidently come to the realization that the downhill path leads but to the "scaled and hooded worm." The seductive ease of the descent is the theme of *Amor Mundi,* which, although written some years later than *Up-hill,* is placed immediately before *Up-hill* in her first published collection of poems—"a significant juxtaposition," in William's opinion, and "done no doubt with intention." If we take the two poems together as a study in contrast, *Up-hill* complements *Amor Mundi,* for it points out the difficulty of the returning ascent compared to the dizzy and voluptuous dreaminess of the descent:

> Does the road wind up-hill all the way?
> Yes, to the very end.
> Will the day's journey take the whole long day?
> From morn to night, my friend.

Such are the opening lines of this impressive poem, which Dorothy Stuart has called "technically . . . almost perfect." It was another reminder of

the choice defined in the earlier poems. Christina was beginning to learn that the idol had to be smashed not once, but again and again, if one was to lead the dedicated life.

But she also realized that to do so brought on each time a fresh and ruinous death. In *At Home,* written the same day, the desolation and loss following the renunciation of love are described as a death of the spirit. And yet the renunciation is not complete because the spirit still yearns earthward, still hovers near the warmth of the much-frequented house where it has once known shelter and love. It sees the participants at the picnic still at table, still vigorously enjoying today and planning for tomorrow: "Their lives stood full at blessed noon." Only the forgotten ghost is of yesterday.[9]

The core of the conflict is found in the phrase, "Sad / To stay and yet to part how loth." A note of ambiguity has complicated the simple sorrow of *Parting.* The speaker's comparison of herself to a guest whose visit is limited to the short period of a day describes Christina's own brief stay in Scott's house.

The third poem which William assigns to Christina's red-letter day is *To-day and To-morrow.* Much worked over and revised, with parts of it borrowed for another poem entitled *Spring Fancies* (published in *Macmillan's Magazine,* April, 1865), this poem, like others we have looked at, is more personal as originally conceived than it appears in its final and revised form. Notable is the change from the first to the third person. The opening lines celebrate the happy and spontaneous mating life of nature in the spring:

All the world is out in leaf,
Half the world in flower.
I have waited weeks and weeks
For this special hour:
*Wake O rosy face and bloom
From thy rosy bower.*

All the world is making love:
Bird to bird in bushes,
Beast to beast in glades, and frog
To frog among the rushes:
*Wake, and whilst I tell my love
Blush consenting blushes.* [10]

But in the second part there is a steep drop to a mood of leaden desolation:

I wish I were dead, my foe,
My friend, I wish I were dead,
With a stone at my tired feet
And a stone at my tired head.

In the pleasant April days
Half the world will stir and sing,
But half the world will slug and rot
For all the sap of Spring.

Although these lines may recall Christina's childhood horror at discovering the dead mouse devoured by worms in the Holmer Green garden, the deeper reason for this abruptly arbitrary shift in mood lies in the contrast between life, expressed through the mating impulse, and death. It is the old grief of *Autumn,* the anguished protest against celibacy in a mating world. Deprived of love at its full tide, the speaker can see only the alternative of death.

What are we to make of these three poems written shortly after the Newcastle visit? Later poems of the summer and autumn belong to the same group, in that they all recapitulate symbolically the events of June. The relationship has evidently suffered another severe strain and is again in jeopardy. Another choice is called for: the man seems to have presented the woman with an ultimatum and, when she rejects it, he leaves. At times it appears that the decision to end the relationship is made by the woman, and at other times by the man.

The facts themselves are too elusive to be captured. What emerges is more like the confused report coming from a battlefield. It is perfectly clear that an engagement is being fought, that there are wounds and bloodshed, but just what is taking place within the line of battle—a shifting, swaying line—just which side is repulsing which in the locked struggle, just where victory is to be located in the embattled area, is far from clear.

We do not get much help in reconstructing events from the June 29 poems. These three lyrics relate the emotional effect of the crisis, but tell us little or nothing about it. For the narrative pattern we must turn to the later poems. Even hidden behind allegory and symbolism, the structure of the story is there. It is a story Christina was to tell again and again, in different versions and under different aspects. She changed one mask for another, but the face behind was always the one face whose features were her own.

❁ 7 ❁

CONFLAGRATION: "A GOLDEN FIRE"

1858–1859

Just as Christina at times sought refuge in her old adolescent expedient of illness when the pressures of life became too severe, so when the problems of love became too tangled and complicated for a solution, she often turned back to an earlier emotional evasion, withdrawal from the conflict. *Convent Threshold* (July 9), which she wrote a month after leaving Newcastle and ten days after the June 29 poems, returns to the theme of *A Novice* and *Three Nuns.* Again in this poem a nun is forced to choose between love and the cloister, and once again her choice is the renunciation of love and the vow of celibacy.

Although William maintained that in *Convent Threshold* the situation dealt with was an imaginary one, even Dorothy Stuart found it hard to believe that this sumptuous poem with its rich imagery, its emotional force, its bold rhythms and fierce freedom of expression was written between love affairs and had no anchor in experience. Gabriel praised it as "a splendid piece of feminine ascetic passion"; Alice Meynell, who had herself known the agony of renouncing an unpromising love, called it "an immortal song of love and . . . cry of more than earthly fear"; and it inspired Gerard Manley Hopkins to write a reply which he called *A Voice from the World,* "Fragments of an Answer to Miss Rossetti's *Convent Threshold.*"

The form is that of the dramatic monologue, and for the purpose of convenience we may divide this long poem into three parts. The first part sets forth the theme of guilt and repentance. The second develops the theme symbolically by means of two successive dream visions. The third, by dealing with the problem of renunciation, draws a conclusion. This is followed by a coda, a brief closing movement of resolution.

The sensational opening has almost the sound of clashing cymbals:

> There's blood between us, love, my love,
> There's father's blood, there's brother's blood:
> And blood's a bar I cannot pass.

I choose the stairs that mount above,
Stair after golden-skyward stair,
To city and to sea of glass.

Like the feast symbol, the scriptural image of the "sea of glass" is one Scott also used, and it appears in his intimate journal of 1854 as a symbol of chastity. In *Convent Threshold* it symbolizes the purifying and regenerating agent:

My lily feet are soiled with mud,
With scarlet mud which tells a tale
Of hope that was, of guilt that was,
Of love that shall not yet avail;
Alas, my heart, if I could bare
My heart, this selfsame stain is there:
I seek the sea of glass and fire
To wash the spot, to burn the snare;
Lo, stairs are meant to lift us higher:
Mount with me, mount the kindled stair.

The invitation to repentance recurs later in the poem. The speaker, still enmeshed in cobwebs, cannot face salvation alone. Like Gabriel's Blessed Damozel, she yearns to have the beloved lover with her in Paradise. To this end, she implores him to repent, as she has done, to "kneel, wrestle, knock, do violence, pray." She exhorts him, "By all the gifts we took and gave," to "Repent, repent, and be forgiven."

The difficulty the speaker experiences in starting the strenuous uphill climb after letting herself go on the downhill path of *Amor Mundi* suggests the kind of emotional agitation Christina herself might have experienced after leaving Newcastle:

You sinned with me a pleasant sin:
Repent with me, for I repent.
Woe's me that lore I must unlearn!
Woe's me that easy way we went,
So rugged when I would return.

And in what follows we get a glimpse of what could have happened when Scott came to London for Christina, and in the place of the joyful reception he expected, met with a rebuff:

I turn from you my cheeks and eyes,
My hair which you shall see no more—
Alas for *joys* that went before,[1]
For joy that dies, for love that dies!

With the line, "I tell you what I dreamed last night," the speaker relates her two dream visions. The first depicts a Faustian spirit who lusting after knowledge learns in the end that knowledge is but love:

A spirit with transfigured face
Fire-footed clomb an infinite space.

In the notebook the first line appears as "A spirit with a dulcimer," an obvious borrowing from *Kubla Khan.* The "transfigured face," then, was a second thought, a revision intended to remove the Coleridgean tincture.

Thirsting for knowledge, the fire-footed spirit mounts shrieking, "Give me light!" and, although light and more light is poured upon him, he is insatiable:

> Still 'Give me light,' he shrieked; and dipped
> His thirsty face, and drank a sea.

William interprets the poem as no more than a dramatic monologue dealing with an imaginary Eloise and Abelard situation, arguing that "a spirit with transfigured face" would not have been introduced "unless the writer had had in her mind some personage, such as Abelard, of exceptionally subtle and searching intellect." But we have seen that "transfigured" was an afterthought; and in any case, the lordly and fiery spirit of the dream vision could have had for a prototype instead of Abelard another medieval scholar, equally noted for his insatiable interest in knowledge: the Duns Scotus who provided Scott with the nickname by which he was familiarly and affectionately known in the Rossetti circle.

This fire-footed spirit is another of Christina's kingly heroes, another of her royal lovers. He leaves the throne and takes from "aching brows the aureole crown." He "exults in exceeding might." If we hesitate to accept Scott with all his human frailties as the original—and it is William who proposes an original—we should remember that his ermine cloak was woven from a synthetic fabric of Christina's invention, and that it was she who bestowed it on him.

We may not even be willing to grant that Scott was a man of "exceptionally subtle and searching intellect," and yet we ought not to forget that he impressed the Rossettis as such, Gabriel and William as well as Christina. And apart from the idealizing process through which a woman's love would glorify him, he occasionally did reveal in his writing sufficient originality and penetration to permit such a conception of him. William described him as "essentially a 'thinking man.'" To Gabriel he was "the best of philosophic and poetic natures, a man of the truest genius . . ." A writer for *The Athenæum* not only spoke appreciatively of his "keen Scottish wit," but further characterized him as "able, energetic, and acute," and "serious in his purposes."

After the Faustian spirit in the poem finally comprehends that "knowledge is strong, but love is sweet," the second dream vision is narrated. For vivid and concrete mortuary imagery, its like is not to be found anywhere in nineteenth-century poetry:

> I tell you what I dreamed last night.
> It was not dark, it was not light.
> Cold dews had drenched my plenteous hair

Through clay; you came to seek me there,
And, 'Do you dream of me?' you said.
My heart was dust that used to leap
To you; I answered half asleep,
'My pillow is damp, my sheets are red,
There's a leaden tester to my bed:
Find you a warmer playfellow,
A warmer pillow for your head,
A kinder love to love than mine.'
You wrung your hands; while I, like lead,
Crushed downwards through the sodden earth:
*Outside the world reeled drunk with mirth
But you reeled drunk with tears like wine.*

The third part of the poem, returning to reality, depicts the cost of renouncing love, the suffering and the sleepless nights Christina herself might have experienced after sending Scott away:

For all night long I dreamed of you:
I woke and prayed against my will,
Then slept, to dream of you again.
At length I rose and knelt and prayed.
I cannot write the words I said,
My words were slow, my tears were few:
But through the dark my silence spoke
Like thunder. When this morning broke,
My face was pinched, my hair was grey,
And frozen blood was on the sill
Where stifling in my struggle I lay.

The poem closes on a note of hope which ushers in a new theme in Christina's poetry, one that was to grow more conspicuous with the years. The full chord is struck for the first time in *Convent Threshold,* although a suggestion of it has already sounded in *One Day* and other short lyrics. Love on earth can be renounced, but preferably for the recompense of reunion in heaven. Lovers who in this life have given up the love that fails to satisfy will win each other through Christian love in a newer, completer, more rapturous and intense life, to which this one is but a prelude.

There we shall meet as once we met
And love with old familiar love,

is the unexpected ending to this strange and powerful poem.

II

During the remainder of the summer and well into autumn, poems such as *A Burden, Yet a Little While,* and *The Love of Christ Which Passeth Knowledge* indicate that the painful struggle dramatized so strikingly in *Convent Threshold* was continuing without abatement. In *A*

Shadow of Dorothea (November 11) another golden-haired, lily-footed Blessed Damozel yearns toward the earthly lover who likewise strains up to reach her, but is held back by earthly ties. On the same day Christina wrote a poem which, appearing in the collected edition under the title *By the Sea,* has a note by William explaining that the stanzas reproduced were originally part of a longer poem decidedly more personal, called *A Yawn.* The printed verses suggest a Northern seascape, of the kind Christina might have observed during her Newcastle visit. Of the omitted stanzas, the first two are of particular interest as a prelude to *From House to Home,* the long allegorical poem written five days later. The mood is one of lethargy, of the dull, dejected boredom that often follows upon a moral resolution which demands sacrifice of an erotic goal:

> *I grow so weary: is it death
> This awful woeful weariness?
> It is a weight to heave my breath,
> A weight to wake, a weight to sleep;
> I have no heart to work or weep.
>
> The sunshine teazes and the dark;
> Only the twilight dulls my grief:
> Is this the Ark, the strong safe Ark,
> On the tempestuous drowning sea
> Whose crested courses foam for me?*

On November 19 she produced in *From House to Home* (originally called "Sorrow not as those who have no hope") one of the most important poems of her career. Somewhat neglected by critics who find it even more of a riddle than *Prince's Progress,* this arresting poem has always been a particular favorite of the Rossetti family. "I have always regarded this poem as one of my sister's most manifest masterpieces," said William. Gabriel found it too good to be omitted from her first volume of collected poems, though he wondered if something "could not . . . be done to make it less like *The Palace of Art.*" William's daughter, Helen Rossetti Angeli, considers it one of her aunt's "very greatest" achievements, and one which additionally reveals "so much of Christina's feeling." William admits, "That it is in part a personal utterance is a fact too plain to need exposition." And he adds that in all his sister's poems of that summer and autumn there is evidence "of a spirit sorely wrung and clinging for dear life to a hope not of this world."

But having thus aroused the reader's curiosity and being either unable or unwilling to gratify it, he merely directs the reader's attention to page liii of his "Memoir" to the *Works.* If we follow this hint and turn to the reference, what do we find? A passage describing Charles Bagot Cayley's role in Christina's "hushed life-drama." We learn that she "may have known him as far back as 1847 or so, and again in 1854 [the date the

elder Rossetti died]: but the two did not meet much until some such date as 1860." If that is so, how can the 1858 *From House to Home* and the cluster of associated poems be related to Cayley? Are we to assume that Christina had been in love with him for years prior to 1858, that they had known together the kind of tempestuous and passionate love described in *Look on This Picture, Convent Threshold,* and *From House to Home* as well as in the shorter love poems, and that in a crisis she had renounced him—all before he started his placid and decorous courtship in the early 1860's? [2]

But if the admittedly autobiographical *From House to Home,* like *Convent Threshold* and the other 1858 poems which give evidence of "a spirit sorely wrung," can be interpreted as the poet's symbolic recapitulation of the June crisis in the light of all that led up to it, the pieces of the puzzle fall into place, and no inexplicable contradictions remain to mystify us.

III

One reason *From House to Home* has been slighted by critics, who following Gabriel's lead are in general content to draw attention to its resemblances to Tennyson's *Palace of Art,* is that on the surface it appears confused and incoherent. But that is because its structure has not been properly understood.[3] It has a logical design of its own and may even be analyzed in terms of dialectical reasoning, like *The Ancient Mariner.* Both the thesis and the antithesis are clearly if figuratively stated in the opening stanzas:

> The first was like a dream through summer heat,
> The second like a tedious, numbing swoon.

And,

> The first part was a tissue of hugged lies:
> The second was its ruin fraught with pain.

"The first" can be read as a reference to the Newcastle visit, and "the second" to its sequel so vividly described in the third part of *Convent Threshold.* For the first part, portrayed as an earthly paradise which lures the speaker from her goal, Christina borrows the Tennysonian imagery:

> My castle [4] stood of white transparent glass
> Glittering and frail with many a fretted spire,
> But when the summer sunset came to pass
> It kindled into fire.

But she also uses nature imagery to convey an even more vivid impression of the earthly paradise. It is "an undulating green," with meadows and avenues of stately trees. Filled with living things, it is a place where all the little creatures she loved could flourish and thrive unmolested—birds,

insects, animals of all kinds. It is in fact exactly the opposite of the lifeless, stagnant landscape of *Cobwebs*. In this innocent and animated Eden,

> Often-times one like an angel walked with me,
> With spirit-discerning eyes like *subtle fire* [5]
> But deep as the unfathomed endless sea,
> Fulfilling my desire.

The love of this couple, like that of the Brownings, is a communion of poets:

> We sang our songs together by the way,
> Calls and recalls and echoes of delight;
> So communed we together all the day
> And so in dreams by night.

Again love is portrayed as the picnic, the banquet, the feast:

> This only can I tell: that hour by hour
> I waxed more feastful, lifted up and glad.
> I felt no thorn prick when I plucked a flower,
> Felt not my friend was sad.

It is the man, not the woman, who finds something lacking in this Eden. What she regards as a feast he considers as fare too ethereal for earthly enjoyment. In the succeeding stanzas the woman, who relies gaily and confidently upon "To-morrow," is reminded by her lover that "To-night" is decisive. But she is not willing to grant that the future of their love depends upon its present fulfillment:

> 'To-morrow,' once I said to him with smiles.
> 'To-night,' he answered gravely; and was dumb,
> But pointed out the stones that numbered miles
> And miles and miles to come.
>
> 'Not so,' I said, 'to-morrow shall be sweet:
> To-night is not so sweet as coming days.'
> Then first I saw that he had turned his feet,
> Had turned from me his face.

The withdrawal and ensuing separation are described in terms of dynamic distance, which is in effect a spatial conception of time:

> Running and flying miles and miles he went.

Christina frequently uses this odd but very modern means to depict an emotional state. Time symbolically represented in terms of expanding space also is her method of portraying an emotional condition in poems such as *Autumn, At Home, Maiden Song, Sleep at Sea, I Followed Thee, My God,* and others.

But, although the lover is speeding rapidly away from the woman who

has refused his ultimatum of "To-night," he pauses once to look back, to beckon,

> And cry: 'Come home, O love, from *punishment*,' [6]

clearly an invitation to reconsider her refusal. Irony is concealed in the use of the word *home* in this context, for the whole purpose of the poem is to suggest that earthly love is but the "house," and that heavenly love is the real "home."

In *Convent Threshold* it is the woman who has turned away; in this poem it is the man. But now it becomes clear why he has turned away. In reality no contradiction exists. In both poems the woman rejects her lover, consciously in *Convent Threshold,* less consciously in *From House to Home*. But in both cases she is forced to face the consequence:

> That night destroyed me like an avalanche,
> One night turned all my summer back to snow:
> Next morning not a bird upon my branch,
> Not a lamb woke below.

The earthly paradise, the "first part," has been destroyed, leveled at a stroke, and the speaker is back again in the land of *Cobwebs:*

> No bird, no lamb, no living breathing thing;
> No squirrel scampered on my breezy lawn,
> No mouse lodged by his hoard: all joys took wing
> And fled before that dawn.

But the imagery of *Cobwebs,* which merely conveys a sense of blank desolation, is inadequate to communicate the complex of emotions resulting from this wrench: the frenzied resistance, the rebellion, the fierce despair, and blind, dumb agony, which when it becomes unendurable, results in "the tedious, numbing swoon," which is the "second part."

> O love, I knew that I should meet my love,
> Should find my love no more.
>
> 'My love no more,' I muttered, stunned with pain:
> I shed no tear, I wrung no passionate hand,
> Till something whispered: 'You shall meet again,
> Meet in a distant land.'
>
> Then with a cry like famine I arose;
> I lit my candle, searched from room to room,
> Searched up and down; a war of winds that froze
> Swept through the blank of gloom.
>
> I searched day after day, night after night;
> Scant change there came to me of night or day:
> 'No more,' I wailed, 'no more:' and trimmed my light,
> And gnashed but did not pray,

Until my heart broke and my spirit broke:
Upon the frost-bound floor I stumbled, fell,
And moaned: 'It is enough: Withhold the stroke.
Farewell, O love, farewell.'

With the next line, "Then life swooned from me," the antithesis begins. As the woman lies unconscious, spirits and angels cluster around her, and this supernatural intervention ushers in the antithetic movement. As in *The Ancient Mariner,* spirits debate about the destiny of the prostrate soul. Shall she be released from pain by "blessed death"? Or must she continue to live?

One answered: 'Not so: she must live again;
Strengthen thou her to live.'

This is accomplished by showing the unconscious speaker a vision, that of a woman

Most singularly pale, and passing fair, [7]
And sad beyond expression.

It is in fact a vision of the speaker herself, not as she was but as she might become, in her potential. The contrast appears in the lines,

I stood upon the outer ground,
She stood on inner ground that budded flowers.

But the flowers bloom on thorns and the thorns tear the woman's feet. Although she hears derisive laughter and shouts of ridicule,

She bled and wept, yet did not shrink; her strength
Was strung up until daybreak of delight:
She measured measureless sorrow towards its length
And breadth, and depth, and height.

Apparent again is Christina's skill in communicating a spiritual condition by giving it the concrete dimensions of the visible world.

Despite a "chain of living links," which connects the woman in the vision with heaven, the speaker begins to despair. Portrayed as lying still unconscious in the swoon, she hears the supernatural debate about her destiny resumed, and the verdict:

'Faith quakes in the tempest shock—
Strengthen her soul again!'

After this short break in continuity which serves to keep the two levels of the speaker's personality distinct, the dream vision is taken up again:

I saw a cup sent down and come to her
Brimful of loathing and of bitterness:
She drank with livid lips that seemed to stir
The depth, not make it less.

But as she drank I spied a hand distil
New wine and virgin honey: making it
First bitter-sweet, then sweet indeed, until
She tasted only sweet.

Her lips and cheeks waxed rosy-fresh and young;
Drinking she sang, 'My soul shall nothing want.'

While this transformation is going on, the dreamer hears mystical chants and songs. At the supernatural word of command, "earth and heaven were rolled up like a scroll," and a second vision is revealed to the speaker, the vision of a Dantean Paradise. At this point the synthesis begins:

Multitudes—multitudes—stood up in bliss,
Made equal to the angels, glorious, fair;
With harps, palms, wedding-garments, kiss of peace,
And crowned and haloed hair.

From now on, the *Paradiso* of the *Commedia* is closely followed. It will be recalled that in his great poem Dante uses fire imagery to convey his conception of divine love. Impulses of affection cause the heavenly spirits, which are portrayed as pure flames, to glow even brighter as love kindles them. These spirits, inhabitants of Paradise, express the intensity of their love by a luminescent flaming or "a melody of flame." As Dante mounts higher, he observes that in each sphere the spirits burn with ever-increasing brightness, until finally through the circle of Intelligences, portrayed as rings of revolving fire, he glimpses the Divine Essence, which to human eyes is apparent only as a burning point of blinding light. It is this symbolism we find in Christina's conception of Paradise:

Tier beyond tier they rose and rose and rose
So high that it was dreadful, flames with flames.

In her system of symbolism sun and moon generally represent sexual reciprocity, the feminine radiance of the moon reflecting and complementing the masculine power and beauty of the sun. But this symbol, like that of the feast, can take on a religious hue:

Each face looked one way like a moon new-lit,
Each face looked one way towards its Sun of Love;
Drank love and bathed in love and mirrored it
And knew no end thereof.

Among the heavenly throng, "all loving, loved of all; but loving best and best beloved of Christ," the dreamer recognizes

that one who lost her love in pain,
Who trod on thorns, who drank the loathesome cup;
The lost in night, in day was found again;
The fallen was lifted up.

In this way the poem is held together by the portrait of the woman who whether she be speaker, dreamer, or object of a vision is always the same, always the one person we cannot fail to recognize—always Christina herself.

IV

Formally, this poem follows a pattern similar to that of *Convent Threshold.* In both pieces the condition, which is the "first part," is initially described; the consequent, the "second part," is developed in each case by means of two succeeding dream visions; and finally, the resolution appears as the conclusion drawn from experience.

In *From House to Home* the resolution is reached logically, as the paradoxical end of the dialectical process. Reconciliation can be achieved only as a result of conflicting and contradictory experience.

> Therefore, O friend, I would not if I might
> Rebuild my house of lies. . . .
>
> Therefore in patience I possess my soul:
> Yea, therefore as a flint I set my face. . . .
>
> These thorns are sharp, yet I can tread on them;
> This cup is loathesome, yet He makes it sweet.

Once before, in *Introspective,* we met with this boast of fortitude. In that equally revealing poem the speaker likewise prides herself upon not fainting when the torture starts and not groaning when she bites the dust. But she braces herself to meet the "shattering ruining blow" with her own strength, with no help other than human courage to sustain her. In *From House to Home* the speaker calls to her aid supernatural strength. In some ways, the poet's spiritual progress along the uphill road can be measured by the change in attitude reflected in the two poems written within a year and a half of one another, *Introspective* in June, 1857, and *From House to Home* in November, 1858.

The latter closes on a note of triumphant faith. Closely paraphrasing Scriptures (Isaiah 61:1–3), the poem states as a perennial renewal the old promise that unto them that mourn in Zion will be given

> Beauty for ashes, oil of joy for grief,
> Garment of praise for spirit of heaviness.[8]

Fortified, then, by the firmness of her faith, the speaker can disregard the present. Sorrow and suffering can be accepted. Today can be endured for the sake of tomorrow. The poem ends with a lyrical and exalted expression of Christian optimism:

Although to-day I fade as doth a leaf,
I languish and grow less,

Although to-day He prunes my twigs with pain,
Yet doth His blood nourish and warm my root:
To-morrow I shall put forth buds again
And clothe myself with fruit.

Although to-day I walk in tedious ways,
To-day His staff is turned into a rod,
Yet will I wait for Him the appointed days
And stay upon my God.

V

William tells us that the two poems his sister wrote immediately before *Goblin Market* showed "more than a normal amount of melancholy and self-reproach." They were *L.E.L.* and *Ash Wednesday,* both written in March, 1859. In the first of the two pieces Christina dons a double mask: the title refers not only to the popular contemporary poetess who signed her verses with her initials, but also to Mrs. Browning's poem about her, *L.E.L.'s Last Question*. William, however, points out what is obvious, that his sister's poem "related to herself and not at all to the poetess, L.E.L.," whose volume of poems, incidentally, Scott edited.

The piece was originally called *Spring,* but when the publishing stage came on, says William, "Christina preferred to retire behind a cloud and so renamed the poem L.E.L., as if it were intended to express the emotions proper to that now perhaps unduly forgotten poetess." It was "the merest *fancy* title for a dejected outpouring of Christina's own," he confided to Bell. Some years later she herself admitted to Gabriel that she was too fond of her "pet name" for the poem to consider changing it.

The question naturally arises, why should the poem require such an elaborate protective device?

According to my reconstruction of events, Christina sent Scott away the preceding June, a renunciation which culminated in the religious exaltation with which *From House to Home* concludes. It often happens that a momentous decision of this sort will raise a heroic nature to a pitch of rapturous enthusiasm in which every sacrifice seems possible. But human beings cannot live on perpetual heights: the enthusiasm wanes, the rapture dwindles in the light of common day, and there is a gradual leveling off of emotion. The years in which a resolve is to be implemented loom ahead in slow, gray tedium. The goal of glory, once clear and bright, becomes dimmed in a gathering fog and finally obscured. This is the psychological state of which Christina gives us a glimpse in *L.E.L.:*

Downstairs I laugh, I sport and jest with all;
But in my solitary room above

I turn my face in silence to the wall;
My heart is breaking for a little love. . . .

All love, are loved, save only I; their hearts
Beat warm with love and joy, beat full thereof:
They cannot guess, who play the pleasant parts,
My heart is breaking for a little love.
While bee hives wake and whirr
And rabbit thins his fur
In living spring that sets the world astir.

I deck myself with silks and jewelry,
I plume myself like any mated dove:
They praise my rustling show, and never see
My heart is breaking for a little love.[9]

The plumes and rustling show probably signify the poetry. During these years the artist fattened and flourished at the expense of the woman. Once again, as in *A Triad,* the hungry cry for love is expressed with an honest directness seldom heard in feminine accents in mid-Victorian poetry. But for all her courage, even she had recourse to the camouflage of the title.

Ash Wednesday, the other poem of March, picks up the fruit tree symbolism which concludes *From House to Home.* Despite the painful pruning, as yet no bud had appeared:

I show as a blot
Blood hath cleanséd not,
As a barren spot
In thy fruitful lot.

Yet,

who
Save Thou shall give me dew
Shall feed my root with blood
And stir my sap for good?—

She could not have foreseen how soon her wish was to be granted. The knife was whetted and waiting. Compared to what was in store for her, the first "shattering ruining blow" had merely grazed the surface. This time the blow was to strike at the very root of her life, and it would be her own blood, her own tears, that would feed and water that root, forcing upward the dearly purchased sap which was to flow with such powerful vitality through *Goblin Market.*

VI

For a vain man who has been rejected, the injury to his self-esteem can often only be rectified by the hasty substitution of another woman to

supply the nourishment without which his vanity droops and dies. It did not take Scott long to find consolation elsewhere. Ten months after Christina's Newcastle visit, on March 18 to be exact, he "had a visit from a lady some few years over thirty," whose name he had not heard before. "She wanted to find a new interest in life, and thought to find it in art," he tells us. Attracted by her face and voice, he devoted himself "to answering this desire of hers," and "from day to day the interest on either side increased."

Alice Boyd, the lady in question, proved to be a more formidable rival than Lady Trevelyan had ever been. Descendant of an ancient and aristocratic Scottish family, she was, according to Gabriel, "a rarely precious woman," and according to Christina herself, "the prettiest handsome woman I ever met!" Himself an egoist, Scott particularly prized in Alice Boyd her unselfishness and nobility of character. Eager to please, she "enjoyed others' happiness and others' ideas exactly as if they were her own," said Scott. Moreover, she did not have a jealous disposition.

Freedom from jealousy in a woman was an undoubted advantage to a man like Scott. "Common prudence," he protested, "is always howling against turning from one study to another, from one love to another, from one form of art to another"; and he snorted indignantly at what Ford Madox Ford said was the Pre-Raphaelite maxim, "Let the shoemaker stick to his last." What is more, Scott put his theory into practice: he turned from study to study, from one art form, painting, to another, poetry, and he turned with equal ease from one love to another, sometimes maintaining relations with two or more women simultaneously. "It may be," he said complacently, "that few can do this without losing their way, coming to grief; it requires tact to hold half a dozen lines without allowing them to tangle, or to ride six horses as they do in the circus."

His own skill at this kind of management was masterly. Each of the women in his life knew about the others. He introduced them to each other, and sometimes they became warm friends. He conducted his emotional affairs with a bold and truly regal disregard of conventional attitudes and mores.

How soon Christina found out about what he discreetly called his "friendship at first sight," is uncertain. She must have known by the time she finished *Goblin Market* on April 27, for this famous poem is in essence another recapitulation of emotional experience.

VII

In common with other such enduring works of art as *The Faerie Queene*, *Gulliver's Travels*, and *Alice in Wonderland*, *Goblin Market* has many levels of meaning.[10] At the narrative level it offers a charming and delicate fairy tale to delight a child, if a somewhat precocious one. At the symbolic and allegorical level, it conveys certain Christian ethical

assumptions. At the psychological level, it suggests emotional experience universally valid.

Unlike the other long autobiographical poems we have been examining, this one, Christina's masterpiece, has no hero. No fiery intellectual such as is found in *Convent Threshold,* no poet-lover similar to the one who first shares and then shatters the speaker's earthly paradise in *From House to Home,* no tardy and loitering prince failing to make hymeneal progress grace this work. It can hardly be said to have a heroine, for the sisters, Laura and Lizzie, between them share the narrative interest. Golden-haired, ivory-skinned, "like two blossoms on one stem," they seem but different aspects of the same maiden. They may in fact be regarded as Christina's version of sacred and profane love. For once in her poetry, she presents love in large, abstract, general terms. But although the individual contours are lacking, no poem of hers is more clearly based upon personal experience.

Despite the fact that William remembered that he had often heard her say she did not mean anything profound by this fairy tale and it was not to be taken as a moral apologue,[11] he himself freely admitted finding "the incidents . . . suggestive," and in his comments about the poem encouraged an interpretation at a deeper level than that of a fairy tale fantasy. Although modern critics have been inclined to drop the whole matter of meaning and to regard the poem as a Pre-Raphaelite masterpiece which combines a realistic use of detail with the vague symbolism and religiosity of *A Blessed Damozel,* in interpreting the poem it would seem more fruitful to pay attention to William's various hints and admissions, particularly since Christina herself, for reasons of her own, wished to discourage explication. Indeed, these very reasons are what give the poem its organizing principle.

Once *Goblin Market* is read as the complex, rich, and meaningful work it actually is, the prevalent critical view that the poem has the bright, clear, obvious pigmentation and the lightly woven surface texture of a Pre-Raphaelite painting will no longer be tenable. An analysis of the poem in the light of the emotional facts in Christina's life will reveal that the symbolism, vague and suggestive as it may appear, actually has the same underlying contact with reality that her other poems display. Ford Madox Ford once remarked that, although love among the Pre-Raphaelites was a romantic and glamorous affair of generalizations, Christina alone regarded it concretely and individually.

VIII

The story is simple. Two lovely sisters are tempted by the little goblin merchants who haunt the glens and woods and toward evening allure unwary maidens with fruit, rich, glowing, delicious to the taste. Lizzie resists; Laura succumbs to temptation. Once the victim has tasted the

fruit, she is tormented by a wild craving for a second taste, but this the goblin merchants never grant. Fearing for Laura's life, Lizzie braves the seductions of the goblins, exposing herself to their tempting wares, so that she may secure the "fiery antidote" to save her sister's life. The antidote is the fruit itself. The goblins taunt, tease, maul, and torment Lizzie, but she stands firm amidst the turmoil. At length she triumphs, and with the rich juices smeared over her face, she runs home to let Laura kiss and suck them off her cheeks and chin. A second taste gratifies Laura's longing. She is saved, and the poem concludes with the well-known tribute to a sister.

Temptation, in both its human and its theological sense, is the thematic core of *Goblin Market*. Even more than in *Convent Threshold,* described by Alice Meynell as "a song of penitence for love that yet praises love more fervently than would a chorus hymeneal," *Goblin Market* celebrates by condemning sensuous passion. Seldom in nineteenth-century poetry, even in the verse of Dante Gabriel or of Swinburne, has the lure of the senses been so convincingly portrayed. Indirection is Christina's method, and its subtlety and delicacy can be appreciated only when *Goblin Market* is compared to poems as frankly and openly sensuous as Rossetti's *Eden Bower* and *Troy Town,* or Swinburne's *Dolores.* The symbolism in which Christina veils her own tribute to Eros is all the more persuasive in that it is rooted in both the legendry of pagan German romanticism and the morality of the Christian tradition.

To Mackenzie Bell, William admitted that the main subject of the poem was the problem of temptation. We have observed that this was a moral problem which interested Christina to the extent of treating it in both her poetry and prose over a span of some thirty-five years. Despite her denial of a "profound or ulterior meaning" in *Goblin Market,* said William, "one can discern that it implies at any rate this much—that to succumb to temptation makes one a victim to that same temptation. . . ."

In *Goblin Market* temptation is symbolized by the fruit, the great traditional symbol of sin and temptation in the Bible. Clearly the fruit sold by the goblin merchants, those "bloom-down-cheeked peaches," the "rare pears," and "bright fire-like barberries," the iced melons, and the sun-ripened citrons from the South, of which the taste brings decay and death, are the forbidden fruit of Scriptures. They belong to the order of fruit which tempted Eve, and which in Revelation (18:14) appears as "the fruit that thy soul lusteth after." In Christina's poem Laura even asks Lizzie if she has tasted "for my sake the fruit forbidden?"

Fruit also appears as the symbolic inducement to sin in St. Augustine's *Confessions.* In this work, one of Christina's early favorites, the plucking of the forbidden fruit is dramatized and symbolized in the famous pear

tree incident. As a young lad, Augustine with his comrades steals the ripe pears from the farmer's tree. For Augustine, this irresponsible act of a mischievous boy represents the first free choice of the evil will.

Although in *Goblin Market* the powerful lure of love is primarily represented by the traditional symbol of fruit, it is also symbolized by the goblin men of Teutonic fairy lore, the elves, dwarfs, and little men that B. Ifor Evans thought Christina found ready-made in Keightley's collection of fairy tales and in William Allingham's poem *The Fairies*.[12] But one hardly needs to go back either to Keightley or to Allingham for the little merchant men. In 1840 when Christina was ten years old, Dr. Adolf Heimann, a family friend, offered to teach the four Rossetti children German in exchange for Italian lessons from the elder Rossetti, then professor of Italian at King's College, London. With her brothers and sister, Christina studied German with Dr. Heimann for three years. Her first simple reading assignment in that language was the *Sagen und Mährchen,* the popular collection of folk and fairy lore in which the customary Teutonic dwarf makes a frequent appearance.

What distinguishes Christina's little men from the conventional figure of the dwarf is their partial resemblance to animals:

> One had a cat's face
> One whisked a tail,
> One tramped at a rat's pace
> One crawled like a snail,
> One like a wombat prowled obtuse and furry,
> One like a ratel tumbled hurry skurry.

We have seen that in *From House to Home,* written only six months before *Goblin Market,* such small animals form part of the speaker's earthly paradise, which is thus described: [13]

> My trees were full of songs and flowers and fruit;
> Their branches spread a city to the air
> And mice lodged in their root.
>
> My heath lay farther off, where lizards lived
> In strange metallic mail, just spied and gone;
> Like darted lightnings here and there perceived
> But nowhere dwelt upon.
>
> Frogs and fat toads were there to hop or plod
> And propagate in peace, an uncouth crew,
> Where velvet-headed rushes rustling nod
> And spill the morning dew.
>
> All caterpillars throve beneath my rule,
> With snails and slugs in corners out of sight;
> I never marred the curious sudden stool
> That perfects in a night.

Safe in his excavated gallery
The burrowing mole groped on from year to year;
No harmless hedgehog curled because of me
His prickly back for fear.

This innocent Eden strikes one as a child's rather than an adult's conception of the earthly paradise, and in fact probably originated in Christina's childhood memories of Holmer Green in Buckinghamshire.

As a child, then, she could have found the originals both of the fruit and the animal-faced goblins in the cottage grounds which were her "familiar haunt" and "inexhaustible delight," in the days when she roamed the orchards and waited for the strawberries to ripen with Maria and frequented the ponds and watched the frogs with her brothers. From William's reminiscences of the common childhood shared by the four Rossettis as well as from her own random recollections in *Time Flies,* we can be sure that she had ample opportunity to observe directly the frogs, toads, snails, mice, cats, rabbits, squirrels, and pigeons that invariably make up her earthly paradise. Such animal images grafted upon the imaginary German dwarfs and elves of the *Sagen und Mährchen* could have resulted in the poetic conception of the goblin merchants.

The question then arises, if she was so partial to these small animals dear to her childhood, why in *Goblin Market* did she portray them in such sinister guise, as the agents of evil and the vendors of temptation?

For the purpose of the poem itself, no contradiction exists. The joys of the earthly paradise must be renounced if one is to achieve spiritual redemption. The lusciousness of the forbidden fruit and the charm of the little animal-faced goblins are but different aspects of nature, the core of which is sexual passion. "Nature worshipped under divers aspects," Christina wrote in *Letter and Spirit,* "exacts under each aspect her victims; or rather, man's consciousness of guilt invests her with a punitive energy backed by a will to punish greater than he can bear."

But if she recognized and acknowledged the dangerous potentialities inherent in sexual love, she did not puritanically condemn it as such. At the conclusion of *Goblin Market* both sisters, Laura as well as Lizzie, are portrayed as happily married women with children of their own, to whom they relate the old tale. By such a traditionally "happy" ending, Christina seems to be implying that neither the fruit nor the animals are in themselves harmful, although in the poem one is the object and the other the agent of temptation; it is only "man's consciousness of guilt"—that is, the Christian concept of guilt incurred through sin embedded in the evil will—which charges them with a dangerous and punitive malignity. In short, man is his own destroyer.

Christina was explicit on this point—man's capacity for self-destruction—in *The Face of the Deep:*

> There is a mystery of evil which I suppose no man during his tenure of mortal life will ever fathom. But there is a second mystery of evil . . . I pursuing my own evil from point to point find that it leads me not outward amid a host of foes laid against me, but inward within myself: it is not mine enemy that doeth me this dishonour, neither is it mine adversary that magnifieth himself against me: it is I, it is not another, not primarily any other; it is I who undo, defile, deface myself. True, I am summoned to wrestle on my own scale against principalities, powers, rulers of the darkness of this world, spiritual wickedness in high places; but none of these can crush me unless I simultaneously undermine my own citadel. . . . Nothing outside myself can destroy me by main force and in my own despite.

How well this philosophy is illustrated in *Goblin Market* appears in Christina's conception of the two sisters. Both are equally tempted. One resists. The other succumbs. Laura is destroyed by her own weakness, not by goblin fruit. Even the taste of goblin fruit which the little men force upon Lizzie's lips does not corrupt her whose strength is formidable enough to put the goblins themselves to rout.

IX

The poem opens with the sisters exposed at dusk to the cries of the goblins. Hearing them, Lizzie "veiled her blushes." The two sisters crouch close together "with tingling cheeks and finger tips." Obviously these girls understand the call; their antennae feel love in the air. So certain is it what the goblins mean that

> Lizzie covered up her eyes,
> Covered close lest they should look,

thereby following Virgil's advice to Dante in the *Purgatorio,* to keep guard "with the curb tight over the eyes" when coming to the great fire. Laura, however, takes a covetous peep at the goblin men and their "evil gifts."

Ready and eager for love, she stretches out her gleaming neck, looks, and listens. She attracts her own temptation. And then as the goblin merchants, sniffing a victim, turn and troop "backwards up the mossy glen," Laura assists in her own undoing. She does this primarily by means of her imagination. In *Letter and Spirit* Christina said that "the seduction of imaginative emotion" was frequently an inducement to sin. And again in *The Face of the Deep:* "How shall a heart preserve its purity if once the rein be given to imagination; if vivid pictures be conjured up, and stormy or melting emotions indulged?"

Perceiving that Laura, through the instrumentality of her imagination, is ready for love, one of the little men "began to weave a crown." Another offered "the golden weight / Of dish and fruit . . ."—an obvious invita-

tion to the feast. Although the crown symbol appears only once, the familiar feast symbol, as might be expected, runs throughout the poem. The sensuous joys of love, for which Laura pays with the products of her own body, a curl and a tear, are described as a lustful feasting on the fruit:

> Then sucked their fruit globes fair or red.
> Sweeter than honey from the rock,
> Stronger than man-rejoicing wine,
> Clearer than water flowed that juice;
> She never tasted such before,
> How should it cloy with length of use?
> She sucked and sucked and sucked the more
> Fruits which the unknown orchard bore;
> She sucked until her lips were sore;
> Then flung the emptied rinds away.

But satiety does not come with repletion. After the feasting, Laura complains to Lizzie that

> I ate and ate my fill,
> Yet my mouth waters still,

a common lover's complaint.

Retribution follows swiftly as Laura begins to suffer and starve from the lack of the exhilarating fruit upon which she has fed so sweetly. "Like a leaping flame," she goes again with Lizzie to the goblin-haunted glen, alert for the sound of the "sugar-baited words." In lines which recall *Listening* (*Two Choices*), Laura is shown

> Listening ever, but not catching the customary cry.

After Laura's fall, Lizzie is invited by the goblins to "sit down and feast with us," clearly an inducement to erotic pleasure. Later she is told by them that "our feast is but beginning." After Lizzie has risked her own peace of mind to bring Laura the antidote, its first effect is to make Laura "loathe the feast."

That there may be no doubt about what the symbolic fruit is intended to represent, Christina describes its effect upon another girl victim:

> She thought of Jeannie in her grave,
> Who should have been a bride:
> But who for joys brides hope to have
> Fell sick and died.

In this stanza, again the distinction we have already observed is drawn between the two sorts of love, that which is domestic and legitimate, and the other, the outlawed love.

Elsewhere in the poem love itself is stigmatized as the "poison-cup" and the "poisoned fount" of the earlier poems:

Their fruits like honey to the throat
But poison in the blood.

Now we begin to understand why, for Laura, the fulfillment of love is followed by the passionate and rebellious anguish of love frustrated. Denied sight and sound of the goblins, perishing for another taste of their deadly fruit, Laura pines and sickens. Like the heroines of *From House to Home* and *Convent Threshold,* who likewise suffer from the deprivation of love, Laura

Then sat up in a passionate yearning,
And gnashed her teeth for baulked desire, and wept
As if her heart would break.

In *From House to Home* "baulked desire" is also the cause of weeping and the gnashing of teeth; and in *Convent Threshold* the novice who has sent away her lover spends the kind of wakeful, feverish nights familiar to Laura.

X

"No woman," observed C. M. Bowra in discussing another poem of Christina's, "could write with this terrible directness if she did not to some degree know the experience which she describes." [14] Indeed, it is difficult to believe that these poems could be derived from the imaginative fantasy of an untried woman who has put together her ideas about love from observation and books.

And yet a Christina Rossetti experienced in the passion of love and understanding the bereaved torment of one who has been deprived of love is totally unlike the conventional portrait that has come down to us. The legendary figure of the saintly recluse is typified in Ellen A. Proctor's biographical sketch of Christina written soon after her death. Miss Proctor's Christina "never realised evil." Living a sheltered and retired life like that of a nun, she was guarded carefully from all contact with evil.[15]

Christina herself granted that "some innocent souls there are who from cradle to grave remain as it were veiled and cloistered from knowledge of evil," but clearly she did not consider herself one of their number. Like Milton in the *Areopagitica,* she could not praise such a fugitive and cloistered virtue: "For most persons contact with evil and consequently knowledge of evil being unavoidable . . . they must achieve a more difficult sanctity, touching pitch yet continuing clean, enduring evil communications yet without corruption . . . ," she wrote in *The Face of the Deep.* But how difficult she knew this to be is evident from another statement in the same work: "Evil knowledge acquired in one wilful moment of curiosity may harass and haunt us to the end of our time."

It is Lizzie who must achieve the "more difficult sanctity," who must gain a knowledge of evil and still remain pure. And so she must sally

out to seek her adversary on that field "which is not without dust and heat." Fearing for Laura's life, she goes back to the glen at dusk in order to obtain "the fiery antidote." She dares the elfin men; she seduces the seducers. But she finds out what her creator undoubtedly knew from actual experience, that nature balked and frustrated takes a terrible revenge. The goblins scratch and grunt and snarl at Lizzie. They lash her with their tails, they claw and hustle her, they

> Twitched out her hair by the roots,
> Stamped upon her tender feet,
> Held her hands and squeezed their fruits
> Against her mouth to make her eat.

But Lizzie, no longer a youngling in the contemplation of evil, wears out the little evil people by her resistance. Disregarding her aches and bruises, the love-juices smeared triumphantly over her face, lodging in her dimples and streaking her neck, Lizzie runs home rejoicing to give the antidote to Laura.

> Hug me, kiss me, suck my juices
> Squeezed from goblin fruits for you,
> Goblin pulp and goblin dew.
> Eat me, drink me, love me,

she cries exultantly.

When Laura tastes again love's juices, this time vicariously from the face of Lizzie, her human redeemer, she reacts violently to the antidote:

> Her lips began to scorch,
> That juice was wormwood to her tongue.

Like the woman in the dream vision of *From House to Home* who deprived of love was likewise forced to drain the bitter and loathesome cup, Laura "gorges on bitterness without a name."

A passage from *The Face of the Deep* throws additional light upon Laura's condition:

> . . . the knowledge of foulness welcomed, entertained, gloated over, breeds in us foulness like itself; it acts like blood poison which, infused from without, turns the man himself, or the woman herself, to a death-struck mass of corruption.

The reference to blood poison provides the clue. If we recall that Christina had already compared the effect of the honey-tasting goblin fruit to "poison in the blood," and that much earlier she had used the figures of the poisoned fount and the poison-cup to describe love, we will have no difficulty in identifying the corrupting and death-bringing "foulness." The source of Laura's malady now becomes increasingly comprehensible.

Laura's extreme torment of repentance, brought on by the antidote which, paradoxically, is no more than love itself, at last reaches the pitch

of the unendurable and results in her loss of consciousness, the swoon of the speaker in *From House to Home*. Lizzie, a human angel, watches by Laura's bedside during her perilous crisis of soul, just as superhuman agents watch by the swooner of *From House to Home*.

At this point one of Christina's leading concepts begins to emerge: the paradox of love as both destroyer and redeemer. Nowhere is this concept dramatized with more striking originality and imaginative power than in *Goblin Market;* but what distinguishes this long narrative poem from the many short lyrics expressing the same idea is that here human rather than divine love is the agent of redemption. Christina's bold application of the Eucharistic principle to a human relationship may be detected in Lizzie's invitation to Laura to "Eat me, drink me, love me." [16] For despite its bizarre features, Lizzie's act is nonetheless a sacrifice. Her love brings Laura back from spiritual death; and in her traffic with the goblins she hazards the kind of human suffering that results from an insatiable craving of the unsatisfied appetite, Laura's own affliction.

The conception of love as both destructive and redemptive was not original with Christina. But like Dante, from whom she probably derived it, she uses fire symbolism to reinforce it. We have observed that in the *Commedia* fire imagery expresses both carnal and divine love. When Dante and Virgil arrive at the Seventh Circle of Purgatory, they see those spirits who, having indulged their lusts on earth, must thereafter plunge into and burn in the great fire. But the higher Dante mounts in Paradise, the more clearly he perceives that divine love is also fire. Christina, we recall, borrowed this symbolic representation of divine love as pure flame for the synthesis of *From House to Home*. And now in *Goblin Market* she uses the Dantean fire symbolism to emphasize through imagery the Dantean concept of the paradoxical nature of love. Laura is "most like a leaping flame" in her wild longing for love. And when it is denied her,

> She dwindled, as the fair full moon doth turn
> To swift decay and burn
> Her fire away.

And Lizzie, white and golden, standing firmly in the midst of the goblins' cruel attack, is figuratively

> Like a beacon left alone
> In a hoary roaring sea
> Sending up a golden fire.

XI

It would be a mistake to identify Christina herself with either Laura or Lizzie. And yet one senses that she uses both her heroines to express her own attitude toward the moral question she raises in the poem. If at times we are inclined to read into Lizzie Christina's own integrity and

firmness of character, we should remember that Lizzie has been identified with Maria Rossetti. Christina even dedicated the poem to her sister M. F. R., and she concluded it with the significant tribute,

> For there is no friend like a sister
> In calm or stormy weather;
> To cheer one on the tedious way,
> To fetch one if one goes astray,
> To lift one if one totters down,
> To strengthen whilst one stands.

William did not doubt that Christina had some good reason for her dedication, "but what it was I know not." Yet when Bell questioned him closely on this point, William was more explicit. "I don't remember that there was at that time any personal circumstances of a marked kind," he said, "but I certainly think (with you) that the lines at the close, 'There is nothing like a sister,' etc. indicate *something:* apparently C. considered herself to be chargeable with some sort of spiritual backsliding, against which Maria's influence had been exerted beneficially."

We have seen, however, that "personal circumstances of a marked kind" actually did occur a little over a month before Christina wrote *Goblin Market.* On March 18 Scott met a woman with whom he fell in love almost at first sight. On April 27 Christina finished *Goblin Market.* Allowing some time for Scott's new attachment to have become known to her and additional time for her to have reacted to it, to have assimilated it artistically, we may conclude that forty days would not be too long a lapse of time between the two events.[17] Gabriel and William must have found out about Scott's new friendship almost immediately, for he lived on terms of fraternal intimacy with the Rossetti brothers, and he was a man more inclined to boast about his love affairs than to keep them secret. If he told Gabriel and William about Alice within the fortnight, the Rossetti sisters could have learned about her shortly thereafter. Possibly Maria was the first to be informed, and it might have been through her agency that Christina was told. At any rate, not much longer than a month intervened between what may be called "a personal circumstance of a marked kind" and the writing of *Goblin Market.*

That Scott could have "turned from one love to another" with such apparent ease must have been a serious shock to Christina. His behavior would have shown her the unstable nature of his earlier attachment to her, would have revealed the depth of the abyss into which she had almost plunged, the peril of the temptation from which, like Laura, she had been saved.

Was it Maria who saved her? If so, when? And in what manner? Although these questions cannot be conclusively answered, we ought to take William's word for it that Christina's tribute to her sister at the end of *Goblin Market* "indicated something." Perhaps, as has been sug-

gested, it was Maria who informed Christina about Scott's new love. If so, the strait-laced Maria would not have been the one to have omitted pointing out the moral lesson. She may even have been responsible for breaking up Christina's friendship with Scott after the Newcastle visit. Possibly after Christina's return to London in June, 1858, Maria wrestled with her to prevent that "spiritual backsliding" she both desired and feared.

Although the theme of the spiritual rescue of one sister by another has not been conspicuously emphasized in critical discussions of *Goblin Market,* it has not gone unnoticed. Violet Hunt, who professed to know a great deal about the personal affairs of the Rossettis, alludes to it in her *Wife of Rossetti.* Asserting she has discovered Christina's "well-kept secret," Miss Hunt reveals her assumption as though it were fact, writing,

> Maria did not, like Lizzie to save Laura, hold converse with goblin men on the hillside, and eat their delicious deadly fruits. But for a week of nights, the kind, sonsy creature crouched on the mat by the house door and saved her sister from the horrors of an elopement with a man who belonged to another.

This man Miss Hunt identifies as James Collinson. "For Collinson, when she threw him over . . . consoled himself"; but apparently inadequately, for, according to this writer, some nine years later he returned, a married man, to ask Christina to elope with him. Despite the fact that this absurd story has gained credence with some writers, one need not consider it seriously, so wildly does it veer away from probability.[18]

XII

That Maria's intervention was of an active and positive nature is suggested not only by *Goblin Market* but by two poems written the following year which have as their theme the interference of one sister in the love affair of another. But instead of regarding the interfering sister as a human redeemer, the saved sister in the two ballads of 1860, *Sister Maude* and *The Noble Sisters,* resents the other's meddling. In fact, the tone of *Sister Maude* is noticeably vindictive:

> Who told my mother of my shame
> Who told my father of my dear?
> O who but Maude, my sister Maude,
> Who lurked to spy and peer.

The Noble Sisters is almost a travesty upon the *Goblin Market* situation. One sister sends away all the messengers of her sister's lover, the falcon, the ruddy hound, the pretty page. Finally she turns the lover himself from the door, thereby bringing down upon herself the angry denunciation of the saved one:

'Fie, sister fie, a wicked lie,
A lie, a wicked lie!
I have none other love but him,
Nor will have till I die.
And you have turned him from our door,
And stabbed him with a lie:
I will go seek him thro' the world
In sorrow till I die.'

These two poems together with several others were originally included in Christina's *Goblin Market* volume, but were omitted from subsequent editions. William thought she considered "the moral tone" of all four pieces open to reproach, and hence omitted them. But even by Victorian standards this judgment is hardly applicable to *Sister Maude*. In preparing the first collected edition of her poetry in 1875, Christina wrote to her publisher, "The sheets came safely to hand, and I am getting on with fusion, etc.; but I notice a few poems (e.g. 'Sister Maude') I do not want to reprint at all. . . ." [19]

What was her reason for not wishing *Sister Maude* in particular to appear in the collection? Could she have feared that the ballad might be construed as showing an attitude of resentment, even temporary resentment, against a sister she loved dearly and had long ago forgiven for any well-meant meddling?

But in 1860 she might have wished that Maria had restrained herself from exerting her influence, no matter how beneficially, against the "spiritual backsliding." At thirty a woman may find it inconvenient and provoking to be rescued so vigorously and enthusiastically that she is left to stand a lonely beacon in a hoary roaring sea and to send up her golden fire undefiled.

8

"A SLACKENING FIRE"

1860–1863

One of the four poems excluded from later editions of *Goblin Market* was *Cousin Kate,* and we can understand how it might have offended Victorian sensibilities. Kate, another of what Dorothy Stuart has called Christina Rossetti's "mateless doves," is a simple cottage maiden whose lordly lover has deserted her for a great lady. Like the deserted mistress in *Light Love,* the abandoned one in *Cousin Kate* has also borne her lord a son out of wedlock, but in this ballad her child is her triumph over her unfruitful rival.

This is the first of the 1860 poems to treat the subject of the unwed mother and the illegitimate child. That Christina's interest in the subject was expressed not only in her poetry but also in her life appears in the fact that from 1860 to 1870 she did social work at the St. Mary Magdalen Home for Fallen Women on Highgate Hill. Whether the personal contact with the women at this institution stimulated her interest in the social problem,[1] or whether a previous interest led her to work with the women is an open question. It is of course a fact that the religious consciousness in the nineteenth century was zealously concerned about the related problems of prostitution and the restoration of "fallen women," and that they were regarded as particularly the work of the nineteenth-century sisterhoods, in which both Christina and Maria took such a vital interest. But what is curious is that Christina's ten-year connection with Highgate was her only serious attempt at social work at a time when literary people in general and Christina's own circle in particular were greatly exercised about the problems of the working classes.

Two pieces which reflect her interest in Highgate are the long narrative poem *Iniquity* (originally entitled *Under the Rose*) and the sonnet *From Sunset to Rise Star. Iniquity,* a dramatic monologue, traces the effect upon a young girl of her mother's youthful transgression. Although the work is not outstanding, Christina's treatment of the subject, which is frank, real-

istic, unsentimental, and psychologically convincing, seems decades ahead of the mid-century Victorian novelists on the same subject.[2]

Ironically, Gabriel objected to both subject and treatment, advising Christina not to include the poem in her 1866 volume. "As regards the unpleasant-sided subject," she replied, "I freely admit it: and if you think the performance coarse or what-not, pray eject it . . . though I thought U. the R. [*Iniquity*] might read its own lesson, but likely I misjudge."

But whereas she was willing to defer to Gabriel's judgment about the subject matter, she was inclined to fight for the principle at issue: the artist's freedom to select his own material, with no conventional restrictions:

> But do you know, even if we throw U. the R. overboard, and whilst I endorse your opinion of the unavoidable and indeed much-to-be-desired unreality of women's work on many social matters, I yet incline to include within the female range such an attempt as this. . . . Moreover, the sketch only gives the girl's own deductions, feelings and semi-resolutions; granted such premises as hers, and right or wrong it seems to me she might easily arrive at such conclusions: and whilst it may truly be urged that unless white could be black and Heaven Hell my experience (thank God) precludes me from hers, I yet don't see why 'the Poet mind' should be less able to construct her from its own inner consciousness than a hundred other unknown quantities.

The poetic mind again projected itself into the feelings of a "fallen woman" in the sonnet *From Sunset to Rise Star*. In her manuscript notebook Christina marked in the margin of this poem, "House of Charity." Assuming the reference was to Highgate, William commented, "It may perhaps be inferred that Christina wrote this sonnet as if it were an utterance of one of these women, not of herself. Yet one hesitates to think so, for the sonnet has a tone which seems deeply personal."

What are we to make of such a statement? Does William intend to imply that Christina felt a kinship with the women of Highgate? If so, why? And yet if we keep *Goblin Market* in view as we look at these poems of the 1860's, it seems evident that she did not consider the gap between herself and the Highgate penitents so wide as to appear incomprehensible. That such an attitude ran counter to the spirit of the times is evident from the liberal-minded Canon T. T. Carter's instructions to the sisters of the Clewer community, which he founded, a sisterhood which had as "its primary work . . . the restoration of fallen women." Although the nuns were advised to show pity and tenderness toward the penitents, "yet nevertheless they will preserve such distance and propriety of demeanour as become ladies dealing with persons of inferior rank, and fallen even from that rank by their sins." [3]

Such an appeal to class distinctions, even on a moral basis, could have had little interest for Christina. Possibly her poetic imagination, which

was singularly free from the conventional Victorian prejudices, did not draw too fine a distinction between the desire and the deed!

II

It was not altogether by chance that Christina's charitable work at Highgate began the first summer Scott spent with Alice Boyd at Penkill Castle in Ayrshire. Although Alice's brother was present as a chaperon, Scott and Alice spent the summer exploring the gift of intimacy that had come to them so unexpectedly. They painted together by the rushing Penquapple Stream in the deep glen. Scott read aloud his poetry to Alice in the fragrant, old-fashioned garden. Evenings they played three-handed whist with Alice's brother before the great fireplace. Picturesque and isolated, the medieval castle overlooking the sea was an ideal setting for the development of a love affair. Scott thought that at last he had found "the perfect friendship" he had been seeking all his life.

Mrs. Scott naturally remained behind in London. From there she wrote her husband chatty, gossipy little letters containing news of their friends, and particularly of Christina Rossetti. Scott's wife assumed that, despite his new interest, he would still want to hear news of Christina.

Whether he wished it or not, he was kept well informed about her activities that summer. He learned that his wife and Christina had attended All Saints' Church together and afterwards had gone to look at Woolner's sculptured marble group designed for Wallington Hall. The same evening Mrs. Scott, possibly accompanied by Christina, went to an evening party and heard young Mrs. Burne-Jones sing *Greensleeves,* while the beautiful Mrs. William Morris dwarfed "all we little women" by her stature. A few days later Mrs. Scott found Christina at Highgate. Now an "Associate," she was wearing the dress, "which is very simple, elegant even; black, with hanging sleeves, a muslin cap with lace edging, quite becoming to her with the veil."

During the early Highgate period Christina's poetic production was far below her usual standard, both in quantity and quality. After *Goblin Market* she wrote nothing for five months. Then a trickle of verse appeared with *Spring, A Christmas Carol,* and *What Good Shall My Life Do Me?* Some time that autumn she wrote a poem called *The Massacre of Perugia,* of which only a fragment is extant. In its original form it must have been a lengthy poem, for according to Christina's neat table of contents in the 1859–1860 Dennis notebook, it ran from pages 48 to 61. What led in the first place to her interest in this Italian subject, off the main track of her usual concerns, and then what caused her to destroy the poem (if she did—it may have been William) cannot be explained.

> *A trumpet pealed thro' France. Then Italy
> Stirred, shook, from sea to sea.
> Then many cities broke

Their lawful yoke.
Then in an evil hour
Perugia on her fort-crowned hill . . .*

During 1860 only four poems appear in the notebook. It was not until the end of the year, with the distinguished poem *Passing Away* (the third and last of the linked series of *Old and New Year Ditties*), that Christina began to write with anything resembling her former power. Many years later William called this work her "chef d'oeuvre, and the finest sacred poem (me judice) in the language." In thanking him for the compliment, she said it was a poem she also rated "high among the works of that author!"

What is noteworthy about the poem is that the rhythm, diction, and word-order express the thought and emotion so naturally and with such inevitable rightness that one scarcely observes the technical triumph of monorhyme sustained throughout:

Passing away (saith the World) passing away:
Chances, beauty and youth, sapped day by day:
Thy life never continueth in one stay.
Is the eye waxen dim, is the dark hair changing to grey
That hath won neither laurel nor bay?
I shall clothe myself in Spring and bud in May:
Thou, root-stricken, shalt not rebuild thy decay
On my bosom for aye.
Then I answered: Yea—

Passing away (saith my Soul) passing away:
With its burden of fear and hope of labour and play.
Hearken what the past doth witness and say:
Rust in thy gold, a moth is in thy array,
A canker is in thy bud, thy leaf must decay.
At midnight, at cockcrow, at morning, one certain day
Lo the Bridegroom shall come and shall not delay;
Watch thou and pray.
Then I answered: Yea—

Passing away (saith my God) passing away:
Winter passeth after the long delay:
New grapes on the vine, new figs on the tender spray,
Turtle calleth turtle in Heaven's May.
Though I tarry, wait for Me, trust Me, watch and pray.
Arise, come away, night is past and lo it is day,
My love, My sister, My spouse, thou shalt hear Me say—
Then I answered: Yea—

Although by now Christina had already written some of her best poetry, her work had not yet been published except for the 1847 Polidori volume and in magazines. But as 1861 got under way, this was to be remedied.

In January Gabriel sent Ruskin her poem "about the Two Girls and the Goblins," and asked him to recommend it to Thackeray's *Cornhill Magazine*. Outraged by the metrical irregularities of Christina's verse, Ruskin flatly declined. "Your sister should exercise herself in the severest commonplace of meter until she can write as the public likes," Ruskin preached unctuously to Gabriel; "then if she puts in her observation and passion all will become precious. But she must have Form first." Gabriel sent the letter to William with the brief remark, "Most senseless, I think," an opinion posterity has endorsed.

While Ruskin was deliberating, Alexander Macmillan, co-founder with his brother of the publishing house, read *Up-hill,* which Gabriel described as Christina's "lively little song of the Tomb," and at once heralded Christina as an exciting new poet. He published *Up-hill* in the February issue of his magazine, and asked to see more of her work. Gabriel, by now convinced that her poems were "so unusually excellent that there could be little doubt ever of their finding a publisher, not to speak of a public," advised her to get them together in printable form immediately. Both he and William were disappointed to learn that she had destroyed *Folio Q* ("perhaps the best tale she ever wrote in prose," said William) because it seemed to raise a "dangerous moral question." But Gabriel was relieved to know that at least she had a considerable amount of poetry available in manuscript.

In June William took his mother and Christina to France for a short holiday, her first trip to the Continent. Although she enjoyed such tourist diversions as the hill and church of Notre Dame de Bonsecours near Rouen and "the splendid effect of sunshine after storm from near Avranches," her greatest pleasure was derived from the huge Persian cat attached to their hotel in Normandy, which she always referred to as "the Cat of St. Lô," and which, Maria told Swinburne some eleven years later, obtained admiration and milk from their eyes and hands, and "has lived on as a family tradition ever since."

III

By October Macmillan had made up his mind to publish Christina, and shortly thereafter Gabriel received from him the following letter:

> I was hoping to have seen you one of these Thursdays to talk about your sister's poems. I quite think a selection of them would have a chance—or to put it more truly that with some omissions they might do. At least I would run the risk of a small edition, with the two designs which you kindly offer.
>
> My idea is to make an exceedingly pretty little volume, and to bring it out as a small Christmas Book. This would give it every chance of coming right to the public. If the public prove a wise and discerning public and take a great fancy to it, we could soon give them an adequate supply.

> The attraction of the volume would be the *Goblin Market,* and this I think should furnish any designs. But we must, of course, leave that to you. If you would be so good as to look in next Thursday, I would go over the poems and indicate what seems to me to be needful to be left out.
>
> I enclose a rough specimen of the sort of style I thought of printing it in.
>
> I took the liberty of reading the *Goblin Market* aloud to a number of people belonging to a small working-man's society here. They seemed at first to wonder whether I was making fun of them; by degrees they got as still as death, and when I finished there was a tremendous burst of applause. I wish Miss Rossetti could have heard it.
>
> A quaint wood-cut-initial—not elaborate and *not* sprawling down the page, but with a queer goblin, say, grinning at a sweet, patient woman-face—or something else of the kind would make a nice addition.[4]

The remainder of the autumn Christina was correcting proof for the volume, which Macmillan scheduled for spring instead of Christmas publication. Writing to William, Scott said he was very pleased to hear that Christina was having a collection of her poems published: "Everyone's familiar may say with Charles V, 'Time and I against the world.' "

He did not write his congratulations directly to Christina but relayed them through her brother. And she in turn was equally reticent in speaking of him. In a letter of 1861, written to William while he was visiting the Scotts at Newcastle, she sent her love to "dear Mrs. Scott," but omitted mention of Mr. Scott, who had more claim upon her friendship.

In this letter of October 26 occurs the first reference to Charles Cayley since Christina had made a note of his call in the family diary at the time of her father's death in 1854. Cayley's two sisters have paid her a visit, she tells William, and goes on to describe them with her usual wit and felicity of phrasing. It is clear that this formal call was the opening salvo in Cayley's campaign of the 1860's to win the younger Miss Rossetti as his wife.

And beginning about this time a new *persona dramatis* enters her poetry, a man whose attentions she was bent upon discouraging.

> I'd rather answer 'No,' to fifty Johns
> Than answer 'Yes' to you,

she snaps brusquely in *No, Thank You, John* of 1860.[5] The tone has been altered to one of sweet reasonableness in *Promises Like Piecrusts* (1861), but obviously the same woman is trying to get rid of the same man:

> For I cannot know your past,
> And of mine what can you know?
>
> You, so warm, may once have been
> Warm towards another one:
> I, so cold, may once have seen
> Sunlight, once have felt the sun.

At the same time she was writing poetry which repeats the old complaint of *Autumn* and *L.E.L.*, "My heart is starving for a little love." It appears in the 1861 piece, *The Fairy Prince Who Arrived Too Late,* which, published in *Macmillan's Magazine* (1863), later became the thematic nucleus for the 1865 *Prince's Progress:*

Too late for love, too late for joy,
Too late, too late!
You loitered on the road too long,
You trifled at the gate.
The enchanted dove upon her branch
Died without a mate.

The enchanted princess in her tower
Slept, died, behind the grate;
Her heart was starving all this while
You made it wait.

The symbol of the enchanted princess or dove also appears in *The Royal Princess,* a poem of October, 1861, written only eleven days after the *Fairy Prince* stanzas. Although this long narrative poem has as its subject the class conflict originating in the glaring contrast between riches and poverty in Disraeli's Two Englands, the poet's real interest, as usual, lies outside the arena of social controversy. The matter comes out more clearly in the deleted than in the published stanzas. It is the emotional problem, the princess's feeling of isolation in the midst of her splendor, which gives the poem its structural focus.

Complaining that she is "alone by day, alone by night, alone days without end," the princess asserts that despite her silk and jewels, she

Would rather be a peasant with her baby at her breast
For all I shine so like the sun, and am purple like the west.

As things are, she looks upon herself as "a poor dove that must not coo," and an "eagle which must not soar." We have already observed that the dove was one of Christina's special symbols for herself. The eagle was another. Indeed, the two winged creatures epitomize the two widely opposite aspects of her nature, her gentleness and her power.

Belatedly the princess recognizes that the laborers in the fields and mines who work to satisfy her luxurious needs "are men, are men," though hitherto she has looked upon them as "lower than dog or horse." Sweeping into her father's banquet hall that evening, wearing "hereditary jewels" clustered in her hair and a golden chain, and carrying "a fan of rainbow feathers," she is stricken with guilt:

*Some bore gusty lights before me, some bore up my train:
'These are men, are men, are men;' throbbed my heart and brain.*

But curiously at this moment of crisis, her social concern slips into a celibate's self-pity:

*Not then nor ever any man, scaling the height above,
Struck fire, as flint from flint, and kindling nobly spake thereof:
'I love you, do you love me; high princess and love?'

Not then nor ever did I hear that softened special tone
Which whispers flattering in one ear unto one heart alone,
And wins the answer: 'Yes, I love: O Love what is a throne?'*

By now of course Christina herself was becoming something of a literary princess, surrounded by a royal circle of painters and poets; and one suspects that the blazing jewels, the silks, the purple that decorate the princess are the same kind of adornment as the plumes and "rustling show" of *L.E.L.,* in short, the poetry.

And the adulation bestowed upon genius was to become more evident with the publication of *Goblin Market* that March. Unfortunately Christina was not to taste her triumph to the full, for the preceding month, a family disaster occurred. Lizzie Siddal, whom Gabriel after prolonged delay had finally married in 1860, died from an overdose of laudanum, leaving him to the bitter self-reproaches which were the beginning of his long, tragic ordeal. He buried his poems in her coffin, fled from the Chatham Place studio that had been their home, and sought refuge from grief with Christina and their mother. Swinburne, Lizzie's warmest friend and admirer, both comforted him and shared his mourning.

The fates had decreed that Lizzie's bright day was done just as Christina's was dawning. The woman upon whom life had seemed to shower the choicest gifts, who had been lavishly loved by her husband and praised as a genius by the outstanding men of her age, vanished without leaving a trace upon her times. For her, even beauty and love had turned to dust and ashes. But while Lizzie's slight and sentimental poems, cherished only by Gabriel, were fading fast into oblivion, Christina's genius was gaining the recognition it deserved. With the publication of *Goblin Market,* she assumed the leading position in English letters that she never lost.

Looking back in retrospect, Gosse thought the *Goblin Market* volume revolutionary in its impact upon English verse. Together with Meredith, Swinburne, Rossetti, and William Morris, Christina was writing the "new poetry" of her day as distinguished from the conservative Tennysonian verse. Since the widespread success of *Idylls of the King,* the public had learned to favor the smooth bland rhythms and the well-bred, innocuous diction of the Tennysonian tradition. In mid-century, said Gosse, English poetry had become "a beautifully guarded park, in which, over smoothly shaven lawns, where gentle herds of fallow-deer were grazing, thrushes sang very discreetly from the boughs of ancestral trees. . . ."

The avant-garde poetry could not gain the public ear until ". . . at last came Christina Rossetti with her brilliant, fantastic, and profoundly original volume of *Goblin Market* in 1862, and achieved the earliest popular success for Pre-Raphaelite poetry." [6] Success eventually turned

to permanent fame as *Goblin Market* became acknowledged as a masterpiece—in Edith Sitwell's opinion still "perhaps the most perfect poem written by a woman in the English language." [7]

But at the time of publication, Christina seemed little concerned with this sudden upturn in her fortunes. Several unpublished letters written to her old friends, the Heimanns, shortly after her volume appeared disclose her state of mind. The first, to Mrs. Heimann, postmarked April 4, 1862, obviously accompanied a presentation copy. The poem discussed is the devotional piece *Christian and Jew* of July 9, 1858:

*My dear Mrs. Heimann

At length I have the satisfaction of begging your acceptance of my little book: pray receive it as a small expression of my very true love for you and yours, and let it serve as a remembrance between us of unfailing kindness on your part and affection on mine.

In the volume is one piece (p. 148) of which perhaps you might expect me to make no mention to you: yet this is the very one of which I will ask your permission to speak. I cannot bear to be for ever silent on the all-important topic of Christianity: indeed, how could I love you and yours as I do, having received so many favours at your hands, and felt so often your good example, without longing and praying for faith to be added to your works? Dear old friend, do not be offended with me; but believe that the love of Christ and of you all constrains me. If aught I have said offends you, be sure the offence lies in the words, not in the heart from which they come warm.*

The second letter, written April 29 to her former professor of German, is of very great interest, first, for the light it sheds upon the poet's own view of the relation between her private life and her poetry, and second, for her very rare defense against the persisting charge of morbidity:

*My dear Dr. Heimann

On the subject of my little book I have not received kinder or dearer letters than the two which you and your wife have sent me. But some of my verses have grieved you: I recall titles and subjects, and suspect *At Home* and *Shut Out,* of being amongst these offenders. If *sad and melancholy,* I suggest that few people reach the age of 31 without sad and melancholy experiences: if *despondent,* I take shame and blame to myself, as they show I have been unmindful of the daily love and mercy lavished upon me. But remember, please, that these and the rest have been written during a period of some 14 years, and under many varying influences of circumstances, health and spirits; that they are moreover not mainly the fruit of effort, but the record of sensation, fancy, and what not, much as these came and went. My next volume—should a next volume ever come to pass—may, I hope, show an improved tone of mind and feeling: but for the present, you must even accept the actual volume with all its shortcomings. . . .* [8]

IV

In the autumn of 1862 Gabriel, who had been drifting about anchorless since Lizzie's death, leased the residence called Tudor House at 16

Cheyne Walk in Chelsea, and from then on, the Rossetti circle had a center. The great years of Tudor House were from 1862 to 1870. During that time the most distinguished men and women in the Victorian world of art and letters gathered there to enjoy Gabriel's generous hospitality. Prosperous by now, he entertained on a lavish scale: during the winter in the great drawing room with its immense fireplace and its seven windows overlooking the Thames, during the summer outside in his luxurious garden tent surrounded by fruit trees and flowering bushes. His fabulous collection of rare blue china and Japanese prints, for which he and Whistler competed at Parisian auctions, his even more fabulous menagerie of beautiful and exotic beasts, who roamed the huge grounds at will and killed each other at their leisure, are all part of the Tudor House legend, which has survived as one of the more picturesque and romantic aspects of the drab Victorian scene.

At her brother's house Christina met everyone of importance in the artistic and literary world of London. For a time Meredith and Swinburne lived there as Gabriel's subtenants. Among the celebrated visitors were Whistler, Browning, Legros, Turgenev, Ruskin, Lewis Carroll, and Longfellow, who said once after admiring Gabriel's paintings that he should also like to meet the painter's brother, the famous poet.

At this time of her life Christina, now in her early thirties, was a charming and still youthful woman. Dark, slender, Italian in appearance, with an olive complexion and hazel eyes, she appeared to Grace Gilchrist, then a child, like "some fairy princess from the sunny south." At a later period, even after the years had taken their toll, William Sharp admired the rich coloring of her bronze-brown hair, the delicate olive pallor of her skin, the heavy, shapely, Madonna-like eyelids shading the "bright and alert look in her expressive azure-gray eyes, a color which often deepened to a dark, shadowy, velvety gray."

Much of her charm was undoubtedly due to what Sharp called "the bell-like sound of her voice, like that of resonant crystal," a voice described by Theodore Watts-Dunton as "precise, formal, yet as sweet as a silver bell." Grace Gilchrist likewise never forgot Christina's "beautiful Italian voice," with its "strange sweet inflection and silvery modulations." However, Sharp thought he discerned a touch of a Scottish rather than an Italian accent in her speech, "a peculiar lift of intonation . . . more suggestive of Edinburgh than of London." [9]

Certainly it is evident from contemporary accounts that in the 1860's Christina was an attractive woman indeed, with her extraordinary voice, her reserve, her shyness, her grace, her passion, and her dignity.

Among the more intimate friends who frequented Tudor House, says William, were "Scott and his wife, with at times Miss Boyd," and "of course the women of our own family. . . ."

Although Scott was still living in the North, the lure of London with

its friendships and literary activities was becoming increasingly hard for him to resist, and, with Tudor House as a magnet, he seems to have visited London even oftener than formerly. Seeing Christina at Tudor House, perhaps for the first time in several years, he probably became interested in her again. Doubtless a charming and famous woman poet, whose first published volume had proved a literary event, appeared more interesting in his eyes than the amateur scribbler of melancholy verse he had known since she was a girl. Unlike Maria, Christina did not occupy the position of merely a female relative of the great Rossetti; as a distinguished poet in her own right, she graced her brother's social functions as a personage among personages. Scott had always been fond of her; and now, in her gracious prime both as woman and poet, she would have appeared doubly desirable to him. According to his own flexible code, he would not have been offending Alice by letting Christina know she still attracted him.

"Parted friends coming in contact at long intervals are like the characters of a play," he wrote; "the living drama maintains its interest at every reappearance." Though he considered it likely that those friendships based on intellectual interests alone were likely to fade, those rooted "in habits of feeling rather than thinking . . . may be perennial."

V

Shortly after Gabriel leased Tudor House in the winter of 1862, Christina began writing *Il Rosseggiar Dell' Oriente* (*The Reddening Dawn*), her series of Italian love poems. Never intended for publication, they were locked away in what William called "the jealous seclusion of her writing-desk" during her lifetime; and it was only after her death that William found them among the personal papers in her desk. He first published them untranslated in her posthumously printed 1896 *New Poems.*

The opening two lyrics of the series were written within a few weeks of one another in December and January of 1862–1863, the third some time in 1864, and the remainder not until 1867–1868. As poems written for herself and not for public consumption, these lyrics composed in Italian may be taken as an altogether subjective expression of personal feeling.

In fact, so obviously do they stand as emotional autobiography that they presented an embarrassing problem to William in his dual capacity of brother and editor. What was he to do with them? How make them available to the public without giving away his sister's secret?

Cayley was the expedient he hit upon. "I forget what may have been the occurrence which brought Cayley and Christina together towards the end of 1862," he remarked, "but soon Cayley was paying her some marked attentions." He goes on to say, "Clearly Christina loved him before the year 1863 had begun, for she wrote at various dates a series of composi-

tions in Italian verse, which she kept together under the title of Il Rosseggiar Dell' Oriente; and the first of these, dated December, 1862, evinces the state of her feelings unmistakably."

It is true that the poem evinces most unmistakably the state of Christina's feelings, but it would be strange if they had been evoked by Cayley, than whom "a more complete specimen . . . of the abstracted scholar in appearance and manner . . . could hardly be conceived." An unproductive philologist, who made no contribution to the study of linguistics at a time when it was making such rapid advances, this "singularly unworldly person," as William describes him,

> smiled much in a furtive sort of way, as if there were some joke which he alone appreciated in full, but into some inkling of which he was willing to induct the less perceptive bystander. To laugh was not his style. Cayley's costume was always shabby and out of date, yet with a kind of prim decorum in it too. His manner was absent-minded in the extreme. If anything was said to him, he would often pause so long before replying that one was inclined to 'give it up,' but at last the answer came in a tone between hurry and confusion, with an articulation far from easy to follow. In truth one viewed his advent with some apprehension, only too conscious that some degree of embarrassment was sure to ensue.

It can be seen that he was hardly the kind of man to inspire a hopeless and enduring passion in a woman of Christina's temperament.

But let us look at the poem which reveals her feelings so unmistakably:

Goodbye—, sweet friend;
Love does not become me,
Since my heart was killed
By the beloved lover.
Yet for the other life
I consecrate to you my hopes;
For this one, remembrances
Oh, so very many.[10]

There are several reasons why this lyric could not have been addressed to Cayley. First, he was living in London at the time, and had but recently begun to court Christina. Why, then, would she be bidding him farewell? Second, if he had only started to pay her "some marked attentions" toward the end of 1862, as William states, how could she by December have reasonably complained that he had already killed her heart? Why would she speak of memories at all? How could there be a question of "remembrances . . . so very many" with a lover whose attentions had been of such recent date? But her allusions to the many memories shared and a hurt to the death inflicted by a "beloved lover" is readily understood in the light of a decade-long relationship of love and suffering. It is not likely that a Cayley could have had the power to cause her that kind of suffering, and neither William nor Christina her-

self ever suggested that he did. Besides, in this lyric we find again a reference to reunion in heaven, a theme which, initially introduced in *Convent Threshold* of 1858, was to become increasingly evident in her poetry as the years rolled on.

The second Italian lyric may be taken as a companion piece to the first:

> In a new spring
> Is born the ancient genius;
> Love insinuates 'Hope'—
> Yet I do not say it.
>
> If Love tells you, 'Love,'
> If he encourages you, friend,
> Swearing, 'That heart is yours'—
> Yet I do not say it.
>
> Nay indeed, that heart,
> Who knows whether it is worth a fig?
> I believe it, at least I hope it;
> Yet I do not say it.

The central question here is the identity of "that heart" which may be worthless, after all. If it is Cayley's, why would Christina doubt the worth of his affections? As a lover, the man was yet unproved. But Scott had hurt her repeatedly; he could well have been the "beloved lover" who had killed her heart, and she would have had good reason to wonder whether he was worth the suffering he had caused her.

But an oblique light is further shed upon this piece by the two devotional poems she wrote at approximately the same time. The devotional poems express two distinct and succeeding moods, one a state of perturbation and distress, the other a mood of devout thankfulness at having escaped a threatened danger. In the first, *Out of the Deep* (December 17, 1862), which begins,

> Have mercy, Thou my God—mercy, my God!
> For I can hardly bear life day by day,

she complains that, although she prays for grace, her sins unpray her prayer. "A traitor slung back from the goal," she implores divine aid in her anguish of mind: "Lord, I repent—help Thou my helpless loss." The second poem, written on January 13, is like a sigh of gratitude for deliverance:

> Thank God, who spared me what I feared!
> Once more I gird myself to run.
> Thy promise stands, Thou Faithful One.
> Horror of darkness disappeared
> At length: once more I see the sun.

And dare to wait in hope for Spring
To face and bear the Winter's cold:
The dead cocoon shall yet unfold
And give to light the living wing:
There's hidden sap beneath that mould.

What was it that Christina feared so greatly and was spared? What was the horror of darkness? Nothing in her external life provides the clue. Surely she could not have regarded the decorous courtship of Cayley, a respectable man of her circle, as a calamity deserving such strong language.

But fear of another "spiritual backsliding," of another temptation, another invitation to partake of goblin fruit, perhaps this time much harder to refuse, another crisis of passion requiring another costly choice—all this turbulent complex of emotions might well have appeared to her as a horror of darkness she would have been thankful to escape.

In the context of the two Italian love poems written at the same time, these devotional verses do suggest that Christina was facing an emotional crisis of some sort in the winter of 1862–1863. Could it have been brought about by one of Scott's periodic visits to London? During December Gabriel, who was in Newcastle to paint a portrait of Mrs. T. H. Leathart, was Scott's house guest, but he returned to London shortly after Christmas. There is a likelihood either that Scott accompanied him to London for the holiday season, or, what is more probable, that he intended to do so, and then changed his mind.[11]

Possibly Christina's feeling for him, repressed since his affair with Alice, had thrilled to life again as the result of his renewed attentions; and, both anticipating and dreading another meeting, she feared that she might prove as susceptible as she had ever been to the potency of the old fascination. As the two Italian lyrics indicate, she could not forget her experience with him in the past, the mingled pain and ecstasy his love had always brought her. Who would deliberately choose to fall back into a familiar trap, or consciously wander again into the maze of a blind alley already explored? Very likely in the years since 1859 she had achieved a certain tranquillity of mind and a steadfastness of direction in her religious life, and these she would have wanted to preserve. No wonder she felt threatened as she sensed again the approach of that powerful countercurrent of love and desire. No wonder that, recognizing the irresistible lure of "the ancient genius," she fought to escape the danger, and thanked her God when, as she believed, it had passed her by.

VI

Card-playing had been one of the favorite diversions of the four Rossettis when they were children, "the juvenile card party" which Hone recommended in his *Every-Day Book* as a source of "innocent amusement"

and "harmless mirth." Each child would identify himself with a different suit, and Christina's was always diamonds.

We are reminded of this childhood game in reading her 1863 poem *A Queen of Hearts,* which uses card symbolism to portray the triumph of a rival. In this piece Christina assigns hearts to the other woman, and to herself, as a suit appropriate to her portion in life, she assigns not diamonds but clubs. She admitted to Gabriel some years later that this poem (originally called *Flora*) was personal, but protested it was not "as open to comment as *My Secret*":

> How comes it, Flora, that whenever we
> Play cards together, you invariably,
> However the pack parts,
> Still hold the Queen of Hearts? . . .
>
> I cut and shuffle; shuffle, cut, again;
> But all my cutting, shuffling, proves in vain:
> Vain hope, vain forethought too;
> That Queen still falls to you. . . .
>
> I cheated once; I made a private notch
> In Heart-Queen's back, and kept a lynx-eyed watch;
> Yet such another back
> Deceived me in the pack;
> The Queen of Clubs assumed by arts unknown
> An imitative dint that seemed my own.

We know that Scott and Alice frequently whiled away their evenings with a game of whist, usually with Gabriel and whomever they could get for a fourth. Since such evening whist games often took place at Tudor House, Christina, who was particularly fond of whist, might occasionally have taken a hand at card parties no longer juvenile.

Two other poems of the period confirm the impression that she was troubled by the thought of a rival. In *Helen Grey* (February 23, 1863) a woman portrayed as handsome, witty, and beloved is told rather waspishly to come down from her height and take a lowlier place,

> For years cannot be kept at bay,
> And fading years will make you old;
> Then in their turn will men seem cold,
> When you yourself are nipped and grey.

In *Beauty Is Vain* (1864) the speaker asks the rhetorical question,

> Shall a woman exalt her face
> Because it gives delight?

And draws the significant conclusion that even if such a woman were as lovely as the rose or the lily, "she'd be but one of three."

One can perceive the tinge of jealousy in these poems, and it would have been remarkable had Christina been altogether free from it. Even if Scott had shown renewed interest in her that winter, she could not have ignored the fact that Alice had a prior claim upon him. And whereas in the poems of the 1850's Lady Trevelyan's nebulous and waving outlines are generally concealed behind various symbolic disguises, in those of the 1860's the rival's personality emerges with the clear contours of a living woman.

VII

We have seen that in *Beauty Is Vain* even the loveliest of women is reminded she is "but one of three." And now in *Maiden Song* of July the trio of women evident in *A Triad* reappears. But in this poem the three women who sing of love are poets. It is interesting to note that during these years Christina herself was linked in the public mind to a feminine "poetic trio," of whom the other two were Jean Ingelow and Dora Greenwell. The anonymous writer of an *Athenæum* article, printed August 8, 1897, recalls a somewhat silly fancy needlework contest which was suggested in the mid-'sixties, with Miss Greenwell challenging the other two members of the trio to show that they were as competent with the needle as with the pen. Although Christina tactfully but firmly declined to be drawn into the undignified and typically Victorian competition, the conception of a poetic trio of women appears in her *Maiden Song*.

Written shortly after her initial visit of June to Anne Gilchrist at Brookbank, Surrey, this poem, which Gladstone repeated by heart at a social function, owes much of its springlike quality, its suggestion of the fresh English countryside in June, to the rustic environment of Brookbank, where in addition to enjoying country life Christina also "battened"—her expression—upon her hostess's volume of Plato.

Like Dora Greenwell, Mrs. Gilchrist was another of the women Scott introduced to the Rossettis. It was through him that the Rossetti brothers first met her husband Alexander Gilchrist, and when he died in 1861 and his widow undertook to complete his unfinished *Life of Blake,* the Rossetti men offered their aid. It was Scott too who reviewed the biography upon its publication. William and Anne Gilchrist became warm friends during their collaboration on the *Life,* and in 1863 she told him to bring his sister to Brookbank for a visit. This he did, and Mrs. Gilchrist confessed herself "altogether charmed with Miss Rossetti—there is a sweetness, an unaffected simplicity and gentleness, with all her gifts that is very winning—and I hope to see more of her."

Perhaps it was the pleasant, relaxed atmosphere of Brookbank, the very house in which George Eliot wrote a good part of her *Middlemarch,* that lent *Maiden Song* its note of genial tranquillity. Although it follows in structure the design of *A Triad,* the tone is very different. Light, grace-

ful, assured, radiantly serene, it is altogether without a trace of the bitter realism and subdued fury that give *A Triad* its distinctive quality. All three maidens, who weave their songs of love, secure husbands through the magic of their poetry, but it is Margaret, the supreme poet of the trio, who wins a king for her mate. In this fairy-tale romance the royal lover is attracted by Margaret's gift for lyric poetry as Scott earlier was attracted to his "Mignon" as much for her lyric power as for her beauty. Margaret

> Sang a golden-bearded king
> Straightway to her feet,
> Sang him silent where he knelt
> In eager anguish sweet.

Moreover, we learn that Scott himself took an interest in the composition of this poem. Christina told Gabriel that the name of Meggan for one of her three girls "was suggested by Scotus to me, and comes out of a Welsh song book."

Shortly after Christina's return to London, the Reverend Shipley requested permission to reprint some of her religious poems in the anthology he was preparing, the *Lyra Eucharistica.* Undecided whether this mark of recognition would add to her professional stature, she consulted her publisher, "the staunch Mac," writing on July 2,

> Will you favour me by letting me know whether my compliance with his request is likely in any degree to injure the sale of your [*Goblin Market*] edition . . . because on this entirely depends my answering *yes* or *no.*
>
> Pray pardon my troubling you for advice on a point which very likely does not affect you at all, and can seem of importance only to a person small in the literary world as I am.[12]

Apparently Macmillan offered no objection, for two of Christina's poems (*The Offering of the New Law* and *I Will Lift Up Mine Eyes to the Hills*) appeared in the first edition of the Shipley anthology and two more in the second edition the following year.

That she was going through one of her recurrent periods of self-abasement is evident not only from the estimate of her position in the literary world expressed in the July 2 letter, but also from the poem she wrote on July 25, which expresses what may be regarded as an excess of Christian humility:

> Give me the lowest place: or if for me
> That lowest place be too high, make one more low
> Where I may sit and see
> My God and love Thee so.

William had this stanza inscribed upon his sister's tombstone as a summing up of the meaning of her life—an unfortunate choice. In considering its appropriateness as an epitaph, he should have made sure that the

poem struck more than a temporary attitude. In one sense Christina's striving for humbleness was a negative admission of pride. Writing in *Seek and Find* (1879), she herself alluded to her never-ending struggle to subdue a proud, masterful, rebellious spirit:

> To be humble is delightful for it is to be at peace and full of contentment: to *become* humble is far from delightful . . . When we ask God to humble us we must not wince if His instrument of discipline be some individual no better than ourselves.

Was Alice Boyd such an individual? If Christina was still teaching herself "that life-long lesson of the past"—how not to be first—she would have been obliged to consider Alice not as a rival but as an instrument chosen for her disciplining.

On the day she wrote *The Lowest Place* she also turned out *The Poor Ghost,* in which once again she presses into service the traditional form of the ballad as a vehicle for expressing personal emotion. The sad ghost of the piece is a first cousin to the forlorn spirit who haunts the picnic in *At Home*. The perpetual dialogue between lovers, so constant a feature of Christina's verse, is resumed, as the man begs the ghost of his deceased love not to haunt him, but to remain decently in her grave:

> 'Indeed I loved you; I love you yet,
> If you will stay where your bed is set,
> Where I have planted a violet,
> Which the wind waves, which the dew makes wet.'

Although the disillusioned ghost promises to return to her leaden bed,

> 'Never doubt I will leave you alone
> And not wake you rattling bone for bone,'

she points out to her lover that it was he, not she, who revived their buried love:

> 'But why did your tears soak through the clay? [13]
> And why did your sobs wake me where I lay?
> I was away, far enough away:
> Let me sleep now till the Judgment Day.'

VIII

One evening that autumn while attending a party at the home of Mrs. Virtue Tebbs, a friend of the family, Christina noticed in her hostess's fine collection of old Venetian glass a pair of exquisite antique Grecian vases, "mended, I believe, though to all intents flawless, portly, and oxidized." Observing them more closely, she realized that it was the centuries-old process of oxidation that was responsible for the beauty of their coloring. "Placed as they were aloft in my friend's drawing-room," she commented in *Time Flies,* "one might stand for sunrise, the other for moonrise. *Sunrise* was brilliant as the most gorgeous pheasant; *moonrise* as

exquisite as the most harmonious pigeon. I cannot exaggerate, I can only misrepresent their appearance."

Some weeks later she paid a visit to her Uncle Henry Polydore (he had Anglicized the family name) at Cheltenham. Although during this visit she dutifully admired the "old priory church and the view-commanding hill" of Malvern, what attracted her and caught her attention was a broken bottle she saw lying in a ditch. "With these unrivalled vases in my memory, I one day rescued from an English roadside ditch a broken bottle: and it was also oxidized! So, at least I concluded: for in a minor key it too displayed a variety of iridescent tints, a sort of dull rainbow." As she pondered over this experience, she came to the conclusion that "there are many more English ditches than Greek islands, many more modern broken bottles than antique lustrous vases. If it is well for the few to rejoice in sunrise and moonrise, it is no less well for the many to be thankful for dim rainbows."

With the sun-moon symbolism as a clue, we can infer that she associated the paired vases in their burning radiance with Scott and Alice, triumphantly self-contained in their reciprocal splendor, and herself with the broken bottle, which although not prized like the rare vases had in the process of slow burning nonetheless acquired a delicate and iridescent if dimmer beauty of its own.

Such a conception of herself, as the dim rainbow and the broken bottle, further colors the poetry of the autumn, some of the devotional pieces suggesting a mood of self-disparagement which even prayer is powerless to allay:

> Have I not striven, my God, and watched and prayed?
> Have I not wrestled in mine agony?
> Wherefore still turn Thy Face of Grace from me?

The two poems which follow hint at the cause for dejection, although *Margery,* written in October, conceals the personal reference by a mask of objectivity. A fictitious speaker, in discussing impersonally the plight of a lovesick girl, asks, what shall we do with Margery, Margery "who lies and cries upon her bed," who moans in her sleep and will not eat, and all because of a man?

> A foolish girl, to love a man
> And let him know she loved him so!
> She should have tried a different plan:
> Have loved, but not have let him know;
> Then he perhaps had loved her so.

A note of indignation creeps in, as the speaker protests,

> Were I that man for whom she cares,
> I would not cost her tears and prayers.

And again, more strongly:

Yet this I say and I maintain:
Were I the man she's fretting for,
I should my very self abhor
If I could leave her to her pain,
Uncomforted, to tears and pain.

The problem of the rival is the theme of *Last Night,* written in November:

Where were you last night? I watched at the gate;
I went down early, I stayed down late.
Were you snug at home, I should like to know,
Or were you in the coppice wheedling Kate?

The broken bottle symbolism casts an oblique shadow in the following (deleted) stanzas, thereby linking them to Christina's Cheltenham visit earlier in the autumn:

*We met first as strangers, we part friend from friend,
Each to travel his own road to his own end:
But let broken be broken; indeed I put no faith
In the quack who sets up to patch and mend.

Broken is broken while the world stands,
Gone is gone, tho' one compass seas and lands,
We shall meet often, but not as we met;
And shake hands, but as to-day we loose hands.*

With the speaker's challenge to her lover to "speak up like a man" and tell her the truth, which of the two he loves the better, her rival or herself, the poem concludes with the poignantly revealing lines,

Just my love and one word to Kate—
Not to let time slip if she means to mate;
For even such a thing has been known
As to miss the chance while we weigh and wait.

Palazzo Polidori, Orvieto

Gabriele and Frances Rossetti
by Dante Gabriel Rossetti

Christina as a child by
Filippo Pistrucci, 1837

Pencil portraits of Christina
by Dante Gabriel Rossetti,
ca. 1846 and 1847

Holmer Green before 1839

"The Girlhood of Mary Virgin"
by Dante Gabriel Rossetti, 1848–1849

Cartoon for Christ Church
memorial window

"William B. Scott aetat 21"
by his brother, David Scott

Portrait of Christina
by Dante Gabriel Rossetti, 1848

Crayon portrait of William Bell Scott
by Dante Gabriel Rossetti, 1852

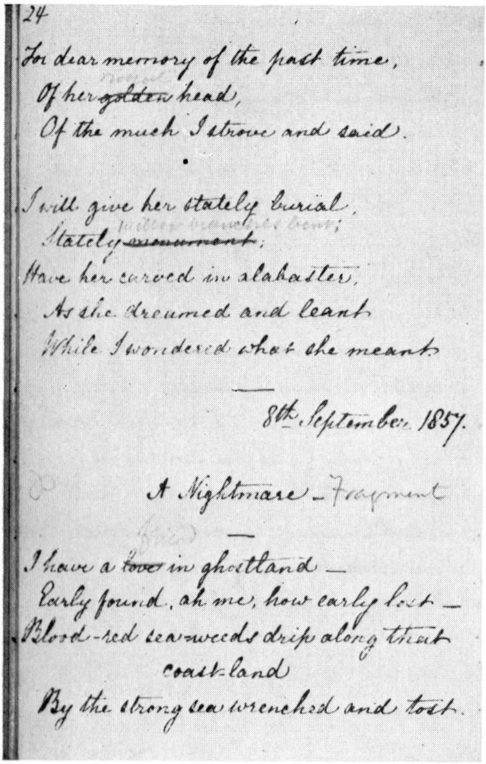

24

For dear memory of the past time,
 Of her ~~golden~~ [bright] head,
 Of the much I strove and said.

I will give her stately burial,
 Stately ~~monument~~; [willow branches bent;]
Have her carved in alabaster,
 As she dreamed and leant
 While I wondered what she meant.

—

8th September 1857.

A Nightmare – [Fragment]

—

I have a ~~love~~ [friend] in ghostland –
 Early found, ah me, how early lost –
Blood-red seaweeds drip along that
 coast-land
 By the strong sea wrenched and tost.

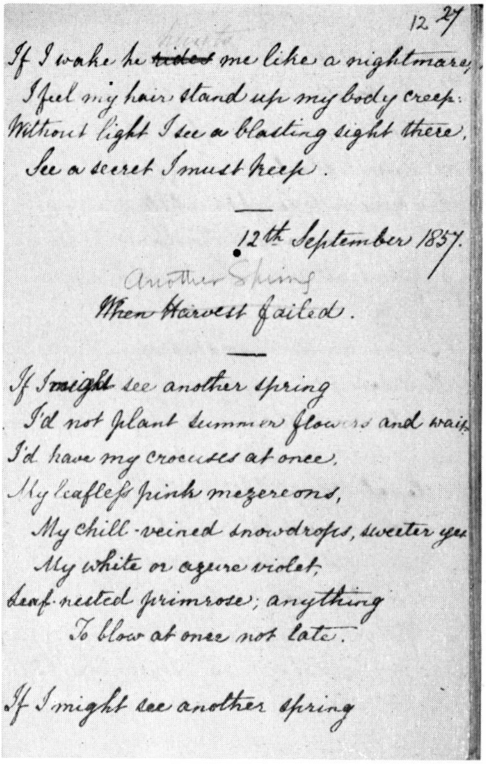

12 27

If I wake he ~~rides~~ [hunts] me like a nightmare;
 I feel my hair stand up my body creep:
Without light I see a blasting sight there,
 See a secret I must keep.

—

12th September 1857.

[Another Spring]
~~When Harvest failed.~~

—

If I ~~might~~ see another spring
 I'd not plant summer flowers and wait:
I'd have my crocuses at once,
My leafless pink mezereons,
 My chill-veined snowdrops, sweeter yet;
 My white or azure violet,
Leaf-nested primrose; anything
 To blow at once not late.

If I might see another spring

A Nightmare (September 12, 1857) and *Goodbye* (June 15, 1858)

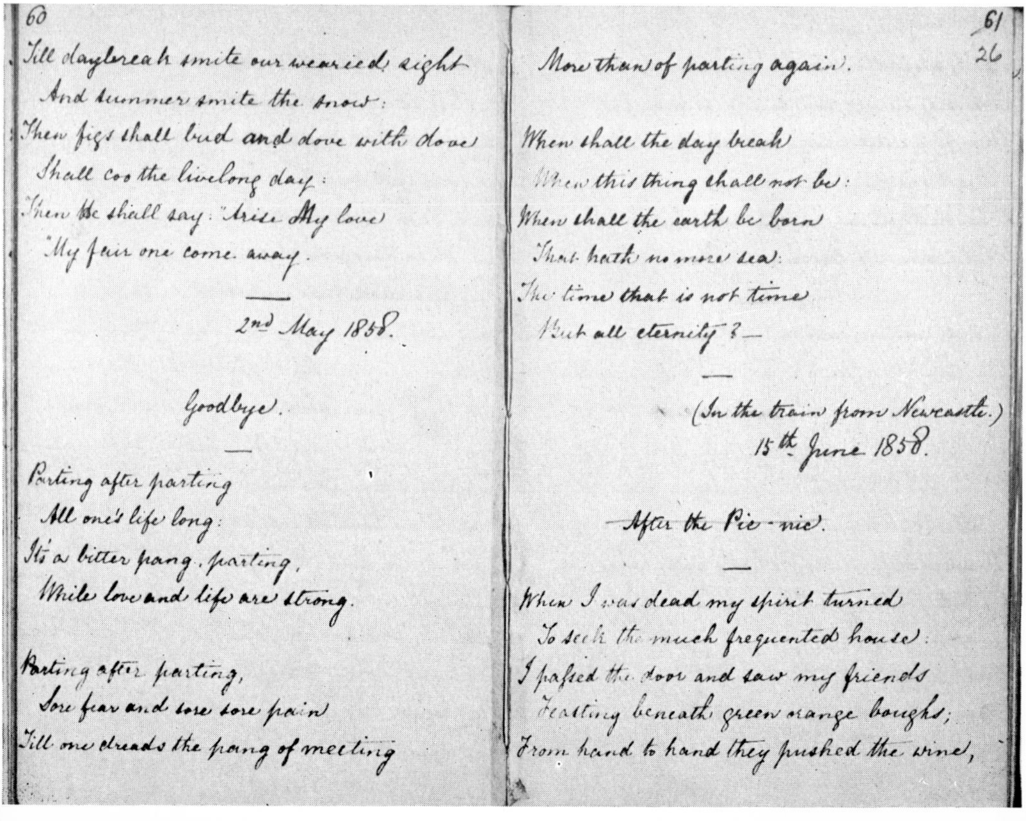

60

Till daybreak smite our wearied sight
 And summer smite the snow:
Then figs shall bud and dove with dove
 Shall coo the livelong day:
Then He shall say: "Arise My love
 "My fair one come away.

—

2nd May 1858.

Goodbye.

—

Parting after parting
 All one's life long:
It's a bitter pang, parting,
 While love and life are strong.

Parting after parting,
 Sore fear and sore sore pain
Till one dreads the pang of meeting

61
26

More than of parting again.

When shall the day break
 When this thing shall not be:
When shall the earth be born
 That hath no more sea:
The time that is not time
 But all eternity? –

—

(In the train from Newcastle.)
15th June 1858.

~~After the Pic-nic.~~

—

When I was dead my spirit turned
 To seek the much frequented house:
I passed the door and saw my friends
 Feasting beneath green orange boughs;
From hand to hand they pushed the wine,

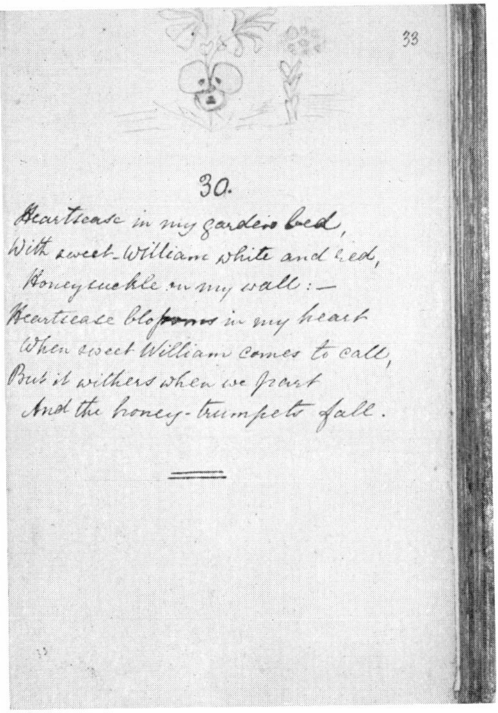

33

30.

Heartsease in my garden bed,
With sweet-William white and red,
Honeysuckle on my wall:—
Heartsease blossoms in my heart
When sweet William comes to call,
But it withers when we part
And the honey-trumpets fall.

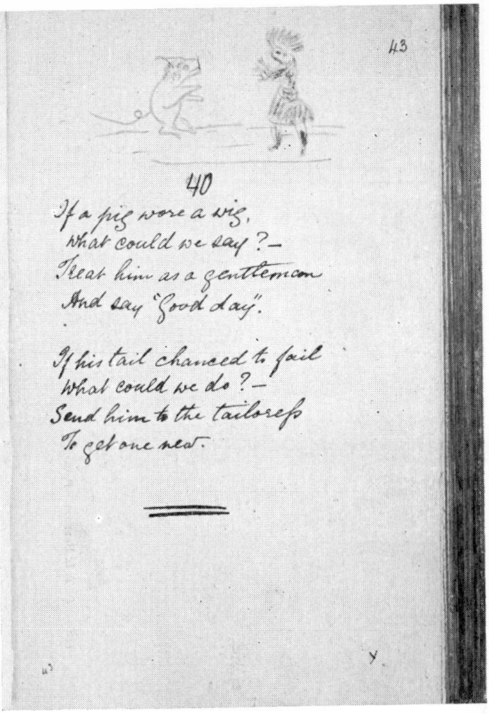

43

40

If a pig wore a wig,
What could we say?—
Treat him as a gentleman
And say "Good day".

If his tail chanced to fail
What could we do?—
Send him to the tailoress
To get one new.

Sing-Song poems (1870) and excerpts from *Look on This Picture* (July 12, 1856)

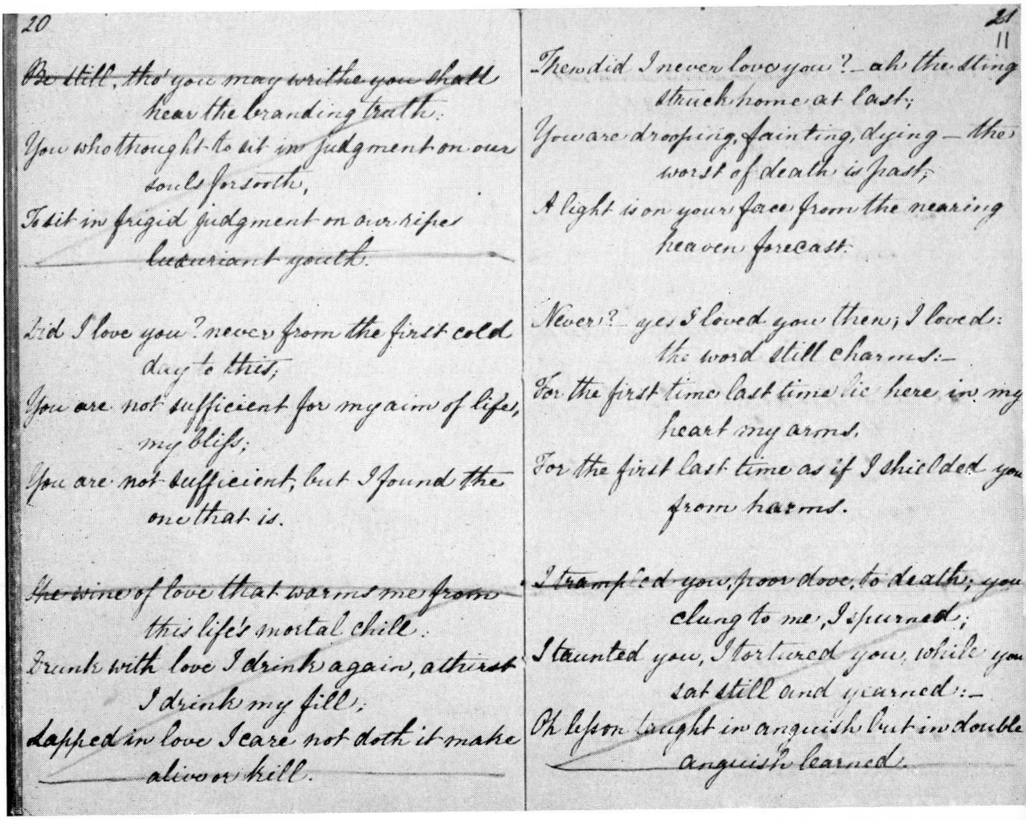

20

Be still, tho' you may writhe you shall hear the branding truth.
You who thought to sit in judgment on our souls forsooth,
To sit in frigid judgment on our ripe luxuriant youth.

Did I love you? never from the first cold day to this;
You are not sufficient for my aim of life, my bliss;
You are not sufficient, but I found the one that is.

The wine of love that warms me from this life's mortal chill:
Drunk with love I drink again, athirst I drink my fill;
Lapped in love I care not doth it make alive or kill.

21
11

Then did I never love you?—ah the sting struck home at last;
You are drooping, fainting, dying—the worst of death is past;
A light is on your face from the nearing heaven forecast.

Never?—yes I loved you then; I loved: the word still charms:—
For the first time last time lie here in my heart my arms,
For the first last time as if I shielded you from harms.

I trampled you, poor dove, to death; you clung to me, I spurned;
I taunted you, I tortured you, while you sat still and yearned:—
Oh lesson taught in anguish but in double anguish learned.

Self-portrait of William Bell Scott, 1868

William Michael Rossetti
by Julia Margaret Cameron

Penkill Castle near Girvan, Ayrshire

Christina Rossetti, 1863

Garden of 16 Cheyne Walk:
Christina, Maria, Frances,
and Dante Gabriel Rossetti

Chalk portrait of Christina
by Dante Gabriel Rossetti, 1877

9

"REFINE WITH FIRE"

1864

As 1863 drew to a close, Scott was considering a move which was to have a far-reaching effect upon Christina's life and hence upon her work. That year the Government Schools of Art were in the process of reorganization, and in the reshuffling the men originally appointed to their posts by the Board of Trade, of whom Scott was one, were replaced. Although he was retained as a government employee, his work at Newcastle was finished, and he saw no further reason to remain there. During the past few years he had been feeling the need for a more stimulating society than that offered by the provincial northern city, and the time now seemed opportune for him to return to London and settle there permanently. He reminded himself that "the acres of flatness in Wordsworth belong to the country life he led: his innovations and inspired work to his association with Coleridge and others."

The beginning of November he sold at auction his household furnishings, paintings, and other valuables, and on November 12, amidst a blaze of newspaper publicity, he was given a farewell banquet by his students and the townspeople. At Lady Trevelyan's suggestion the subscription raised in his behalf by his friends took the form of a commission to paint a picture for the city, "the work being at once a testimonial to Mr. Scott," as a newspaper report had it," and a memento of his long residence and the esteem in which he is held." Scott chose as his subject "The Building of the New Castle: the Origin of the Town"; and the picture was eventually hung in the rooms of the Literary and Philosophical Society.

This lucrative commission, engineered by his old friend of Wallington Hall, changed Scott's plans to the extent that he remained in Newcastle until his picture was finished. From the Newcastle *Daily Journal* we learn that by April 5 the work was well under way and by the early part of July was virtually completed. Christina must have known of Scott's plans by December of 1863, for at the end of that month she wrote Dora Greenwell that if "our dear Scotts" move away from the North, her pros-

pect of meeting Miss Greenwell again would "dwindle to the altogether vague."

From this casual reference to Newcastle visits one would assume that there was more than one. This brings us back to Bell's assertion that Christina visited the Scotts at Newcastle no less than three times, with, Bell adds, "especial pleasure." However, no evidence other than this statement exists of any but the June, 1858, visit. By 1864, as we shall see, Scott and his wife were already settled in London, and there was no further possibility of Newcastle visits.

Although by the end of December Christina was aware of Scott's intended move, she did not know how long the commissioned picture would detain him in the North, and she must have been disappointed to learn that he would not be coming to London after all until later in the year.

II

The poetry she wrote in the winter and spring of 1864 reveals that, whatever the cause may have been, she was laboring under the stress of some deeply felt disturbance. The earliest of the group of poems which William thought showed unusual "dejection and self-reproach" was *What Would I Give?* of January 20. But in William's opinion the entire group, which included as well *Come Unto Me, Who Shall Deliver Me?* and *In Patience,* "give evidence of a period of spiritual depression and self-reproof" in his sister's life. He offers no explanation of why she would have been feeling exceptionally dejected at this time; and perhaps he did not know.

In diction and structure *What Would I Give?* bears a striking resemblance to *A Better Resurrection* of June, 1857. The condensed generalization of the latter,

> I have no wit, no words, no tears;
> My heart within me like a stone
> Is numbed too much for hopes or fears,

is developed into a more elaborate logical design in the former:

> What would I give for a heart of flesh to warm me through,
> Instead of this heart of stone ice-cold whatever I do:
> Hard and cold and small, of all hearts the worst of all.
>
> What would I give for words, if only words would come;
> But now in its misery my spirit has fallen dumb.
> O merry friends, go your way, I have never a word to say.
>
> What would I give for tears, not smiles but scalding tears,
> To wash the black mark clean, and to thaw the frost of years,
> To wash the stain ingrain, and to make me clean again.

If we cannot be satisfied with interpreting these lines as an expression solely of conventional Christian doctrine, the question then arises, what in Christina's personal life could have urged her to give utterance to such a strongly felt sense of guilt. What black mark, what stain, what secret involution of years could have oppressed the conscience of a woman so blameless in all her acts and human relationships?

Such questions are at the core of the enigma that is Christina Rossetti.

Of the four poems mentioned by William, by far the bitterest and the most chilling is *Who Shall Deliver Me?* (March 1):

God strengthen me to bear myself:
That heaviest weight of all to bear,
Inalienable weight of care.

All others are outside myself;
I lock the door and bar them out,
The turmoil, tedium, gad-about.

I lock my door upon myself,
And bar them out; but who shall wall
Self from myself, most loathed of all? . . .

God harden me against myself
This coward with pathetic voice,
Who craves for ease, and rest and joys:

Myself, arch-traitor to myself;
My hollowest friend, my deadliest foe,
My clog whatever road I go.

Read in the context of a prose passage from *Time Flies,* this bleakly bitter poem shows up in clearer focus. One summer night, Christina relates, she was staying at Meads, the Convalescent Hospital at Eastbourne run by the Anglican All Saints' Sisterhood, which Maria later joined. The little room she occupied was far from cheerful; the wall, bare and undecorated, was dingy in the flickering gaslight. As she lay on her hard cot that warm summer night, arms folded behind her head, eyes staring straight ahead of her, she observed that suddenly on the blankness of the wall "appeared a spider, himself dark and defined, his shadow no less dark and scarcely if at all less defined." As she watched,

> They jerked, zigzagged, advanced, retreated, he and his shadow, posturing in ungainly indissoluble harmony. He seemed exasperated, fascinated, desperately endeavouring and utterly hopeless.
>
> What could it mean? One meaning and one only suggested itself. That spider saw without recognising his black double and was mad to disengage himself from the horrible pursuing inalienable presence.

> To me this self-haunted spider . . . remains isolated irretrievably with his own horrible loathesome self.

It is psychologically very interesting that but "one meaning and one only suggested itself" to Christina from this commonplace incident. To how many people would a spider and his shadow on the wall suggest self-hatred? Certainly not to anyone who was not already given to it. But it is obvious that here Christina identifies herself with the "self-haunted" spider.

Throughout the spring she continued to grapple with her "black double," her mood one of vacillation and doubt. *In Patience* of March 19 conveys the impression that she was trying to tap familiar spiritual resources, but without much success. Despite the confident opening lines,

> I will not faint, but trust in God
> Who this my lot hath given,

the weary tone of the verse belies the brave words and suggests that she was trying to force religious feeling, that she was groping half-heartedly for aid she did not actually want.

III

That she was under a severe strain of some sort is obvious. Was it related in any way to Scott's projected move? We learn from an entry in G. P. Boyce's diary that Scott was in London for a short time that spring and on March 23 dined at Tudor House with Gabriel. The record further reveals Scott's presence at a family dinner at the Rossettis' on April 6.[1]

However, this must have been a preliminary trip, for if he was to finish his picture by July, he would have had to remain in Newcastle to work on it the remainder of the spring. And in April we find Christina writing two poems which dramatize the mood of a woman who is watching and waiting for the arrival of the man she loves.

The Ghost's Petition (originally entitled *A Return*), written the day after Scott dined at her house, opens on a note of strained and expectant hope: "There's a footstep coming; look out and see." Although the footstep turns out to be an imaginary one, the speaker in this ballad—a waiting woman—insists,

> 'But he promised that he would come:
> To-night, to-morrow, in joy or sorrow,
> He must keep his word, and must come home.

Despite disappointment, she refuses to give up her vigil:

> 'I shall sit here awhile, and watch;
> Listening, hoping, for one hand groping
> In deep shadow to find the latch.'

In *A Pause,* written at Frome-Selwood in 1853, the arrival of the lover is likewise portrayed in terms of the familiar hand groping for the well-known latch.

Hoping Against Hope (called *If* in manuscript) is "a genuine lyric cry," as Christina once described another of her poems. Written April 12, presumably after Scott went back to Newcastle, it expresses the same poignant longing and emotional intensity as *Parting After Parting:*

If he would come to-day to-day to-day,
Oh what a day to-day would be;
But now he's away, miles and miles away
From me across the sea. . . .

I have a sister, I have a brother,
A faithful hound, a tame white dove;
But I had another, once I had another,
And I miss him my love my love.[2]

Her mood that spring alternated between despair and elation. Such vacillating uncertainty is reflected in *Sunshine,* written May 31. Despite a light tone, the poem indicates that once again she was balancing and weighing her chance for happiness:

'There's little sunshine in my heart
Slack to spring, lead to sink:
There's little sunshine in the world,
I think.

'There's glow of sunshine in my heart
(Cool wind, cool the glow):
There's flood of sunshine in the world,
I know.'

In the third and last stanza these contradictory statements are checked one against the other, and the poem concludes in the playfully enigmatic tone of *My Secret:*

Now if of these one spoke the truth,
One spoke more or less;
But which was which I will not tell:
You guess.

Just what could she have expected from Scott's return to London? She knew that he spent almost all his time with Alice now: winters Alice lived in Newcastle as the Scotts' guest; summers she and Scott spent together at Penkill Castle. Surely Christina should have realized that she had nothing to hope for from his presence in London, and perhaps when she regarded her situation realistically she did realize it. But so perverse

is starved love and so optimistic its speculations, that even knowing the circumstances, she might have looked forward to his arrival, possibly at times even allowing herself to feast upon the fantasies and the forbidden possibilities that in more reasonable moments she recognized for the empty daydreams they were.

IV

The vacillation perceptible in the poetry of the period also appears in Christina's management of her professional affairs that spring. Despite critical acclaim and popular interest, *Goblin Market,* like many seminal works in literature, did not immediately warrant a second edition. And although Alexander Macmillan was still firmly of the opinion that in Christina he had a poet of the very first rank, and he consequently encouraged her to produce another volume of verse, she herself was more inclined to feel the public pulse before following up her initial success with a subsequent offering. Her first impulse was to resist any well-intentioned effort to push her off course, for she realized that her poetic production could not be artificially stimulated but must come about naturally, as a fruit of her inner life. In acknowledging payment of three pounds, three shillings for the publication of her poem *One Day* in *Macmillan's Magazine,* she wrote the publisher on December 1, 1863: [3]

My dear Mr. Macmillan

I enclose my receipt and many thanks for the checque—and many more thanks for the kind words of encouragement you give me. Miss Proctor [Adelaide] I am not afraid of: but Miss Ingelow (judging by extracts; I have not yet seen the actual volume)—would be a formidable rival to most men, and to any woman. Indeed I have been bewailing that she did not publish with you.

Few things within the range of probability would give me greater pleasure than to see in print my second volume: but I am sadly convinced that I have not by me materials, equal both in quantity and quality, to what are already before the public. And, if one conviction can go beyond another, I am yet more firmly convinced that my system of not writing against the grain is the right one, at any rate as concerns myself. Had a second edition of *Goblin Market* been called for, one considerably augmented would have been at once feasible: but a second volume must I fear stand over to the indefinite future.

But Gabriel as well as Macmillan was urging her to get together another volume of verse, and since, as she told her brother, his opinion had "scale-dipping weight" with her, she reconsidered, and on April 4 requested the publisher to return one of her manuscript notebooks, "as I really want it for use." Four days later she wrote optimistically:

My dear Mr. Macmillan

I received my little book quite safely, thank you.

I am in great hopes of being able to put a volume together, and will see about it;—indeed some calculations of length, etc., already

made point in the right direction. Mr. Masson [editor of *Macmillan's Magazine*] has 2 little things of mine in hand; and you may think whether I am not happy to attain fame (!) and guineas by means of the Magazine.

But after looking over the contents of the little black book, she changed her mind again. "Don't think me a perfect weathercock," she apologized to Gabriel on May 7. "But why rush before the public with an immature volume? I really think of not communicating at all with Mac at present; but waiting the requisite number of months (or years as the case may be) until I have a sufficiency of quality as well as quantity. Is this not the best plan? If meanwhile my things become *remains* that need be no bugbear to scare me into premature publicity."

Aside from the pressure exerted by both Gabriel and Macmillan, another influence was apparently operating to produce Christina's indecisiveness. It is apparent from her letter of December 1 to Macmillan that she looked upon Jean Ingelow as a rival poet worthy of challenge. Like herself, this rising young poet had caused something of a stir in the literary world with her first published volume of verse. Even Gabriel was moved to inquire of William Allingham, "Have you seen a new volume of poems by one Jean Ingelow?" adding, "Really there seems a good deal in it." To Dora Greenwell Christina confided that she had not yet read the volume, "but reviews with copious extracts have made me aware of a new eminent name having arisen among us. I want to know who she is, what she is like, where she lives. . . ."

Although as a girl Christina had given up chess because the game aroused her competitive eagerness to win, discipline in one direction sometimes has the unfortunate result of producing an outbreak in another. It was not always easy for Christina to repress the innate spirit of robust aggressiveness she had inherited from her grandmother. Possibly such unexpected competition from the newest and not least brilliant member of "the poetic trio" acted as a stimulus to put on the second performance which her publisher and brother were already urging upon her.

Macmillan made the next move. The first edition of *Goblin Market*, which had sold steadily if slowly, being now exhausted, the publisher professed himself ready to run off a second edition, thus strategically meeting Christina's chief objection to the proposal for a new volume. That he raised the question again is evident from Christina's answer, which although undated, was probably written in June when she received her semiannual check. Her acknowledgment of it in this letter reveals the financial arrangements she had with her publisher as well as her continuing hesitation about the new volume:

My dear Mr. Macmillan

I enclose my receipt for half profits: with my grateful thanks, as I

am sure I could have no sort of claim upon them when you alone ran the risk.

Of course I shall delight in 2nd edition of *Goblin Market.* About possible vol. 2 I will write again, please, in a few days; meanwhile am sincerely gratified at what you say so kindly.

We cannot tell just when the succeeding letter, also undated, was written; but so far as Christina was concerned, it definitely if temporarily closed the question of the new volume:

My dear Mr. Macmillan

I have weighed and measured, but alas! vol. 2 is not ready. Pray pardon my delay in letting you know this, but I only to-day arrived at this final conclusion.

Hoping for a different result some day

Sincerely yours
Christina G. Rossetti

V

Although we know that Scott moved to London some time in 1864, the exact date of his arrival is not ascertainable. Christina's poems suggest that up to May 31, when she wrote *Sunshine,* she was waiting for him and by the 11th of June, the dateline of *Meeting,* he had arrived. *Meeting* is the second part of the linked poem *Parting After Parting,* written on the train after her Newcastle visit of 1858. But of the original four stanzas of *Meeting,* she extracted only the last for the published version of her linked poem:

To meet, worth living for;
Worth dying for, to meet;
To meet, worth parting for,
Bitter forgot in sweet:
To meet, worth parting before,
Never to part more.

Yet these lines tell only half the story. For the other half we must turn to the first three stanzas not joined to the linked poem and not published in Christina's lifetime:

If we shall live, we live;
If we shall die, we die;
If we live we shall meet again;
But to-night, good-bye.
One word, let one be heard—
What, not one word?

If we sleep, we shall wake again
And see to-morrow's light;
If we wake, we shall meet again;
But to-night, good night.

Good night, my lost and found—
Still not a sound?

If we live, we must part;
If we die, we part in pain;
If we die, we shall part
Only to meet again.
By those tears on either cheek,
To-morrow you will speak.

What are we to make of this? The lines do not easily yield to interpretation. But what is perfectly clear is that the lover in *Meeting,* the man the poet addresses as her "lost and found," and the man from whom she parted in 1858 with "sore fear and sore sore pain" are one and the same man. That man could be only William Bell Scott. He was "lost" after June, 1858, and "found" again in 1864, the year Scott established his permanent residence in London. If he had not been the man addressed in *Meeting,* what reason could Christina have had for joining the last stanza of this poem to the 1858 *Parting,* which she wrote upon leaving him? Unless, of course, one wishes to believe that she had nothing in mind and that she fitted the two verses together on a random impulse.[4]

But if she had been building up hopes of a genuine reunion, she was to be disappointed. The much-anticipated "meeting" apparently turned out to be a painful and anticlimactic one. Both *Meeting* and *Twice* suggest that Scott refused to acknowledge it as the emotional sequent of that parting six years earlier, that he failed to fulfill those half-promises of renewing the relationship at which he had probably hinted in the winter of 1862–1863, when he and Christina were meeting socially at Tudor House.

A careful reading of *Meeting* discloses a situation in which, although the man is silent, refusing to speak, the woman believes that "the tears on either cheek" betray him. If we interpret this poem as a personal statement—and indeed, how else can it be interpreted?—we may assume that Christina took the tears for evidence that the man addressed shared her own emotional agitation, and that for her they symbolized a still existing bond. With such a premise, she could draw the conclusion that despite all, he still loved her. Therefore the veiled threat, "To-morrow you will speak," can be taken as her resolve to wait no longer but to plunge into the crisis and force the issue.

Twice has been interpreted by C. M. Bowra and others as a reference to Christina's two love affairs, with Collinson and with Cayley.[5] But the poem itself does not support such a reading. There is nothing ambiguous about it except perhaps the order in which it appears in the MS notebook, coming as it does between *Sunshine* and *Meeting,* and carrying no more definite dateline than June, 1864. But in content it is one of the least obscure of Christina's productions. What she meant she wrote down

in this poem lucidly and directly, without the aid of symbolism or allegory. And if we read it with *Meeting* in mind, we are gradually enlightened about the feeling-event motivating both poems: we find out what took place on that "to-morrow" she had resolved would once and for all determine the future. Like all tomorrows, it soon became a today, and then a yesterday—but one which remained fresh in Christina's memory all the years of her life.

I took my heart in my hand,
(O my love, O my love,)
I said: Let me fall or stand,
Let me live or die,
But this once hear me speak—
(O my love, O my love,)—
Yet a woman's words are weak;—
You should speak, not I.

You took my heart in your hand
With a friendly smile,
With a critical eye you scanned;
Then you set it down,
And said: It is still unripe,
Better wait awhile;
Wait while the skylarks pipe,
Till the corn grows brown.

As you set it down it broke;
Broke, but I did not wince;
I smiled at the speech you spoke,
At your judgment that I heard:
But I have not often smiled
Since then, nor questioned since,
Nor cared for corn-flowers wild,
Nor sung with the singing bird.

It is clear enough that these three stanzas refer to one love, a woman's love for a man, a love which he rejects. In the stanzas which follow, no reference at all is made to a second love for a different man. The first time the speaker offers her heart to a man; the second time to her God. The "Twice" of the title alludes as plainly as poetic language can to two loves, one human and the other divine:

I take my heart in my hand,
O my God, O my God,
My broken heart in my hand:
Thou hast seen, judge Thou.
My hope was written in sand,
O my God, O my God:
Now let Thy judgment stand,
Yea judge me now.

This contemned of a man,
This, marred one heedless day,
This heart take Thou to scan
Both within and without:
Refine with fire its gold,
Purge Thou its dross away,
Yea hold it in Thy hold,
Whence none can pluck it out.

I take my heart in my hand
(I shall not die, but live),
Before Thy Face I stand,
I, for Thou callest such:
All that I have I bring,
All that I am I give,
Smile Thou and I shall sing,
But shall not question much.

We see now what may have occurred. Still in love, Christina was asking of Scott something he could not give. At one time his flame might have leaped in answer to her own. He might have taken her, might have given her back rich gifts in return for hers. But now because of Alice, it was impossible. And yet presumably he felt the old tender affection, which was why he had wept when they met. He might have grieved over her grief and for her sake have regretted that time and a new love had swept them apart.

Nevertheless he must have felt uncomfortable and wished she had not forced the issue in a scene which could have been only painful and embarrassing. She wanted the truth, but out of pity he could not give it to her, direct and uncompromising, as she demanded it. Or perhaps—for one does not really understand Scott or his motives—perhaps it was not pity that kept him from being honest with Christina, but something else. He may have been reluctant to lose her irrevocably. The fragrant essence of a rare love he knew he could not fully reciprocate might still have been a scent too sweet and delicate to relinquish entirely. And so he evaded, postponed, delayed, thrusting her away with one hand and holding her fast with the other.

But at this crisis in her "womanly life" Christina was not to be confused. She saw through the man's weak words and his friendly intentions, and spurned them for the crumbs they were. Once more she resolved to repudiate this earthly love which had brought only sorrow and suffering, to fling it off like a worn garment, to pour the passion of her nature into the new bottle which would not break like the old.

She had achieved her wish; they had met again; and now as she walked through the fire of her own feeding, flames crackling around her, she tasted on her lips the bitterness of ashes. What kind of relationship they

would have in the future was unpredictable. Scott, the pleasant addition to a brilliant circle of which she was a part, the intimate friend of both her brothers, Scott, her "lost and found," now accessible as he had never been—Scott must have seemed farther away, more inaccessible and remote than ever before.

VI

Throughout the summer the climax of the June meeting haunted Christina's imagination. In various poems of the period we see her holding it up to the light, turning it around for a new view, looking at it from a distance, and then bringing it into closer focus. In each of the two following pieces the significant event is described in slightly different perspective:

He looked at her with a smile,
She looked at him with a sigh,
Both paused to look awhile;
Then he passed by,
Passed by and whistled a tune;
She stood silent and still:
It was the sunniest day in June,
Yet one felt a chill.

We met hand to hand,
We clasped hands close and fast,
As close as oak and ivy stand:
But it is past;
Come day, come night, day comes at last.

We loosed hand from hand,
We parted face from face;
Each went his way to his own land
At his own pace,
Each went to fill his separate place.

If we should meet one day
If both should not forget,
We shall clasp hands the accustomed way,
As when we met
So long ago, as I remember yet.[6]

The restraint of these two lyrics, as well as of the devotional poem *None with Him* (June 14), is not evident in the turbulent and powerful dramatic monologue *By the Waters of Babylon,* which Christina originally called *In Captivity* and wrote only two and a half weeks after *Meeting.* In this poem the fictitious mask of the exiled Jew bewailing his banishment provides the protective covering for an outburst of despair and

violent grief that in its subjectivity recalls *From House to Home.* Exiled, forsaken, desolate, and accursed, the speaker, protesting that "strangers press the olives that are mine," gropes in darkness, searching for a lost God:

> How doth my heart that is so wrung not burst
> When I remember that my way was plain,
> And that God's candle lit me at the first.
> Whilst now I grope in darkness, grope in vain,
> Desiring but to find Him Who is lost,
> To find Him once again, but once again!

But as the summer progressed, the poems took on a steadier, calmer, and more objective tone. Perhaps the increasing recognition as a poet that came during the summer, though not a satisfying substitute for love, was at least a continuing source of comfort. It was undoubtedly pleasant to read in the *Fraser's* article Gabriel sent her that she was looked upon as one of the best women poets of the nineteenth century, a category that included Mrs. Browning. It was also agreeable to feel that she was for once appreciated for the right reasons, her "racy originality," her "bold, vigorous, peculiar daring," her reserve of strong emotion felt but expressed with disciplined artistry. Keeping the poet instead of himself in view, this critic thought that "certain of her poems are marked by an air of composure, of quiet scorn, of tender trifling . . . possibly assumed as the mask of a mood of deeper feeling which she cannot afford to disclose. . . ." [7]

During this summer she met Gerard Manley Hopkins at the house of the Reverend Gurney, vicar of St. Barnabas, Pimlico, whose acquaintance she had made at "a haymaking party at Mitcham." Hopkins was an avowed admirer of her work. Not only did he write an "Answer" to her *Convent Threshold,* but he studied her poetry as a model for his own work and quoted passages from her poems in his personal letters. He was particularly impressed by certain of her technical devices, such as her use of assonance and what he described as "licenses in rhyme," by which he meant rhyme to the eye but not the ear.[8]

Her two most interesting poems of the summer, *A Sketch* and *Songs in a Cornfield,* suggest a mood very different from the tragic intensity of the June poems. *A Sketch* (August 15) has the same playful, bantering tone as *My Secret* and is as transparently autobiographical:

> The blindest buzzard that I know
> Does not wear wings to spread and stir,
> Nor does my special mole wear fur
> And grub among the roots below;
> He sports a tail indeed, but then
> It's to a coat; he's man with men;
> His quill becomes a pen.

In other points our friend's a mole,
A buzzard, beyond scope of speech:
He sees not what's within his reach,
Misreads the part, so reads in vain,
Ignores the whole though patent plain,
Misreads both parts again.

My blindest buzzard that I know,
My special mole, when will you see?
Oh no, you must not look at me,
There's nothing hid for me to show.
I might show facts as plain as day;
But since your eyes are blind you'd say,
'Where? What?' and turn away.

William thought this poem needed some explaining; thereupon he once again produced the convenient Cayley. "It is clear that the person here bantered was Charles Bagot Cayley," he states, and goes on to suggest that "This *Sketch* might apparently be interpolated, by a reader of *Il Rosseggiar dell' Oriente,* between Nos. 2 and 3 of that series." Nothing could be more misleading. All that *A Sketch* has in common with the Italian poems is that both are addressed to a man Christina loved.

That this man is the same one addressed in *Meeting* and *Twice* can be taken for granted. Having written a poem like *Twice* in June, it is not likely that a woman as serious as Christina would in August have fallen in love with a different man and addressed him in the jaunty, intimate, bantering tone of *A Sketch.* No, if Cayley is to be taken as the suitor in this poem, he must also be the lover in *Meeting,* linked to *Parting After Parting,* and *Twice,* and we have seen that this is chronologically impossible and highly improbable. When Christina tells us as definitely as she does in *Twice* that she has had only two loves, one human and the other divine, we must believe her.

The tone and the animal symbolism in *A Sketch* deserve some notice. If it appears surprising that Christina had recovered sufficiently from her shattering experience of June to regard her emotional situation humorously, we should remember that not only did she have a strongly developed sense of humor, but she also possessed the rarer capacity to laugh at herself. If she had been seeing Scott all through the summer at Tudor House and elsewhere, no doubt the habitual social contact had filed away some of the tragedy and tension. But although the prevailing tone of *A Sketch* is one of quizzical blandness, an undertone of both tenderness and affectionate intimacy is not lacking.

We know from earlier poems, such as *My Dream* and *Goblin Market,* that Christina was given to using animal symbolism. The prudent crocodile and the demonic goat of the 1850's are now in the 1860's replaced as erotic symbols by a buzzard and a mole. But before inquiring what the

two animal symbols have in common, we may pause for a moment to consider what Christina actually tells us about the mole. He is "man with men," and his quill "becomes" a pen ("is cut to a pen" in the published version).

Although from this we might assume that he is a writer, the quill was also used by the nineteenth-century engraver. In Christina's prose tale for children, *Speaking Likenesses* (1874), one of the more objectionable of the young guests at the small heroine's birthday party is "Quills, the Engraver." He is a boy who "bristled with prickly quills like a porcupine." And indeed, "The Porcupine" was Lady Trevelyan's nickname for Scott.

Later in the narrative the children play a somewhat nightmarish game of Self-Help (Scott was at one time an enthusiastic advocate of the Self-Culture movement) in which the boys are "the players, the girls the played." In this game the boys are allowed to use "natural advantages such as quill or fishhook." And in the even "more dreadful sport of Hunt the Pincushion," in which the bewildered little heroine finds herself the pincushion, the use of "pricking quills" is permitted.

One cannot say whether Christina was aware of the erotic significance of these symbols, but it is not unlikely that Scott, who was early trained in his father's workshop as an engraver and practiced the art throughout his career, is the hidden original of both Quills, the engraver in *Speaking Likenesses* who can "prick and scratch with some permanence of result," and her "special mole," her "man with men" in *A Sketch*.

But what distinguishes both buzzard and mole in *A Sketch* is their blindness. William has pointed out Cayley's unobservant blindness, his absent-minded woolgathering that resulted from his solitary habits. But that is not the kind of blindness Christina is referring to in the poem. The buzzard-mole "sees not what's within his reach." He fails to relate part to part or to the whole, and so misreads a woman's message of love.

Now in a man's relationship with a woman this kind of failure may be either an unconscious or a willful blindness. He may choose to misread the parts and to ignore the whole. He may deliberately refuse to speak, as did the man addressed in *Meeting*. Scott in fact may have appeared blind to Christina's message not because he was incapable of seeing but because it was his conscious policy to shut his eyes to her meaning.

Buzzards are generally noted not so much for their blindness as for their voraciousness. A buzzard might well have in common with a monarch crocodile "an inexorable appetite." But like the fabulous crocodile, this particular buzzard, more mythological than zoological, belongs strictly within the context of the poem itself, and should not be considered apart from it. In any case, the symbol is hardly appropriate to the mild and inoffensive Cayley.

If Cayley does not qualify for the original in this poem, it does not

follow that he fails to appear in Christina's poetry of the period. The rejected suitor, it so happens, is the subject of *Jessie Cameron,* written in October, which relates the story of a rebuffed lover's supernatural revenge upon the woman who spurned him. Like Christina, whom Lady Burne-Jones described as "gently caustic of tongue," her heroine in this ballad is kind-hearted,

> But somewhat heedless with her tongue
> And apt at causing pain.

Again, as in some of the earlier poems, a courted woman tries to make a man understand that she does not love him, telling him with unconcealed bluntness,

> For me you're not the man of men
> I've other plans are planned.

If we compare these lines to those in the first of the undated *Monna Innominata* sonnets,

> For one man is my world of all the men
> This wide world holds; O love, my world is you,

we are confirmed in the impression that two men, one a major and the other a minor figure, filled Christina's emotional horizon. She never ceased to love and to long for the one; and from time to time she impatiently took cognizance of the other's devotion.

VII

Resilient though she had shown herself, Christina's mood of relative cheerfulness scarcely outlasted the summer. Despite a coppery-gold autumnal serenity of tone, *Songs in a Cornfield* (August 26) is befogged by a melancholy that is to grow more pronounced as the autumn months pass. It appears in the refrain which is the theme of the poem,

> Take the wheat to your bosom,
> But not a false false love;

and with gossamer delicacy in the following stanza which in rhythm and diction is not unlike a medieval lyric,

> Out in the fields
> Summer heat gloweth,
> Out in the fields
> Summer wind bloweth,
> Out in the fields
> Summer friend showeth,
> Out in the fields
> Summer wheat groweth,

and particularly in the deleted stanza which in manuscript concludes the poem:

*But death will keep her secret,
Turf will veil her face,
She will lie at rest at rest
In her resting place.
No more reaping
Wheat thro' the harvest day,
No more weeping
False lover gone away:
It may be sleeping
As dove sleeps in her nest;
It may be keeping
Watch yet at rest.* [9]

As autumn proceeded, the trace of melancholy deepened into a darker dejection, and with *Despised and Rejected* of October 10 we are back again in the somber and tragic shadow of *Who Shall Deliver Me?* and *By the Waters of Babylon*. This powerful poem, among the most moving of Christina's devotional poems, opens with the stark lament,

My sun has set, I dwell
In darkness as a dead man out of sight;
And none remains, not one, that I should tell
To him mine evil plight
This bitter night.
I will make fast my door
That hollow friends may trouble me no more.

The speaker is unable to see a difference between the hollow friends and Jesus, the unrecognized Friend who begs for admittance. Deaf and stony-hearted, as one who seeks to isolate herself from both human and divine intercourse, she drives the Stranger from her door:

But all night long that voice spake urgently:
'Open to Me.'—
Still harping in mine ears:
'Rise, let Me in.'
Pleading with tears:
'Open to Me, that I may come to thee.'
While the dew dropped, while the dark hours were cold;
'My Feet bleed, see My Face,
See My Hands bleed that bring thee grace,
My Heart doth bleed for thee,—
Open to Me.'

So till the break of day:
Then died away
That voice, in silence as of sorrow;
Then footsteps echoing like a sigh
Passed me by,

Lingering footsteps slow to pass.
On the morrow
I saw upon the grass
Each footprint marked in blood, and on my door
The mark of blood for evermore.

Other poems of the autumn, such as *If I Had Words* and *Weary in Well-Doing,* though less perfectly realized, show the same grief and heaviness of spirit. Although in November Christina appears to have been "unwell"—as we learn from Gabriel's letter of the 12th—on the 14th she turned out one of her most brilliant poems, the glittering and incandescent *Birds of Paradise:*

Golden-winged, silver-winged,
Winged with flashing flame,
Such a flight of birds I saw,
Birds without a name:
Singing songs in their own tongue—
Windy-winged they came. . . .

The wings of flame emitted sparks
With a cadenced clang:
Their silver wings tinkled,
Their golden wings rang,
The wind it whistled through their wings
Where in heaven they sang. . . .

As usual, Scott had spent his autumn holiday at Penkill with Alice, but her brother's illness had prevented her from returning to London with him, and so in November he appeared alone. Could Christina's outburst of lyrical ecstasy, so joyful in its expression, have been related to his return, alone, unhampered by the restriction of Alice's presence?

If so, she was to be disappointed once again. For it was with Alice, and no one else, that Scott looked forward to enjoying his first winter resident in the metropolis, and he was daily awaiting her arrival. This Christina must have soon found out. Any hope she might have cherished for a renewal of the old relationship was therefore crushed.

How deeply she felt this disappointment may be inferred from the fact that again she drifted into one of her mysterious illnesses. Throughout her life emotional disturbances were paralleled by poor health. But unlike the usual run of psychosomatic ailments, which though they often meet a deep-seated psychic need show but little practical purpose, her disorders seem to have served a practical end. In one instance, they had prevented her from "governessing *en permanence,*" and in another from becoming the unwilling wife of Collinson. Could the present collapse as well have been the result of another attempt to solve a hard problem her own way? For she knew that sooner or later, the social ties within the circle being

as close as they were, she would be required to meet Alice by Scott's side. Possibly she thought it preferable to remove herself from a situation fraught with potential pain.

And so we are not surprised to hear of her spending the winter in the seaside town of Hastings, "nursing a peccant chest," which after showing some improvement refused to mend, and, as she put it, "entered a protest against being considered well."

❁ 10 ❁

FIERY EMBERS

1865–1866

In many ways Hastings was a good idea. The three months of her stay there were remarkably productive ones for Christina. In addition to writing *Prince's Progress* and turning out a number of noteworthy poems, she swiftly and decisively, with no more hesitation or nonsense, put together the second volume of poems Gabriel and Macmillan had been urging upon her. With her brother's aid she had it ready for publication by April.

Besides their patient prodding, several other incentives induced her to action. For one thing, there was the increasing stimulus of a rival poet's success. Jean Ingelow's eighth edition, she told Gabriel, was imparting "a becoming green tinge" to her own complexion. Secondly, she was anxious for early publication for her mother's sake. Mrs. Rossetti was aging, and, knowing her "intense enjoyment of our performances," Christina feared that "by indefinite delay I should miss the pleasure of thus giving pleasure to our Mother, to whom of course I shall dedicate."

She knew that Mrs. Rossetti would be likely also to derive pleasure from the appearance of the second edition of *Goblin Market* with Gabriel's distinctive illustrations, which Macmillan was rushing through the press. "Your speed is mine as regards the date of issuing edition 2," she told him early in January, "but February sounds near and pleasant." She directed him to continue sending the proofs to 166 Albany Street, where they would have "the advantage of my sister's revision as well as of my own." That Gabriel also took a hand in the proofreading is evident from his letter of January 11 to Macmillan requesting that the reprinting of Sheet M (containing *Sleep at Sea* and *From House to Home*) be held up until Christina could make the change he had suggested.

In fact, wherever one looks during the Hastings period, one can detect Gabriel's giant footstrides imprinted upon Christina's sandy shore. His correspondence both with his sister and with her publisher reveals the extent to which he assumed responsibility for her literary career. Completely supervising the publication of her forthcoming two volumes, the

second edition of *Goblin Market* and the new *Prince's Progress* collection, he illustrated them himself, designed their bindings for which he selected the color, supervised the printing (he found it "very bad" in the first *Goblin* edition), and, in short, saw both books through the press.

His assistance in helping Christina organize the new volume was so thorough that it amounted almost to collaboration. As we shall see, they carried on what was practically a daily correspondence about the contents and arrangement of the new volume. Indeed, Gabriel must be held accountable for many of the revisions and alterations which, appearing in the 1866 volume, were incorporated into the final printed text of the *Works*. A number of the deletions we have noted resulted from his advice. He told Christina which poems to include and which to omit, suggested drastic changes in existing poems, rescued early poems from oblivion and eliminated later ones, criticized the style and tone of others, tried to induce her to alter the structure of her *Prince's Progress,* and, of all things, to write an epic poem. Finally one day she had to remind him that despite her gratitude for his invaluable aid, she had to follow her own system of work. "I do seriously question whether I possess the working-power with which you credit me," she told him, "and whether all the painstaking at my command would result in work better than—in fact half so good as —what I have actually done on the other system. It is vain comparing my powers (!) with yours (a remark I have never been called upon to make to any one but yourself)."

Whether Gabriel's tampering with her poetry improved or marred it is open to question—and would need to be decided upon the basis of each individual poem rather than the work as a whole—but assuredly without his obsessive but selfless devotion to her cause she would not have been able to accomplish what she did in such a short time.

He failed her in only one respect, and that was his delay in supplying the woodcuts to illustrate the new volume, causing publication to be held over until the following year. But in the spring of 1865 he had begun work on his *Blue Bower* and was reluctant to put it aside for Christina's illustrations. She took the delay good-naturedly, assuring him that she would wait a year for his woodcuts, if need be, "though (in a whisper) six months would better please me." But she admitted that her Prince, "having dawdled so long on his own account," could not "grumble at awaiting your pleasure; and mine too, for your protecting woodcuts help me to face my small public. . . ."

Her modesty should not be taken at face value, for the size of her public was increasing steadily. The Reverends Baynes and Shipley asked to use her poems in their respective anthologies. Her verses, now in demand by magazines other than *Macmillan's,* were praised by critical journals, set to music ("the more of my things get set to music the better pleased I am," she declared), and used as subjects for painting by prominent

artists. Sandys chose her *Amor Mundi* to illustrate for *Shilling Magazine.* As the former editor of *Once a Week,* Samuel Lucas, now editor of *Shilling,* had rejected her poems, and she therefore considered it "rather a triumph . . . Mr. Lucas wanting me, the Pariah of *Once a Week.*"[1] As for "the opportune *Times* notice" of January 11, "Of course I am crowing!" she exulted to Gabriel.

He was less enthusiastic about "the welcome *Times,*" as Christina called it. "Considering the high estimate," he complained to Macmillan, "there might have been a line or two more." A sentence in the review which read, "Miss Rossetti can point to finished work—to which it would be difficult to mend," aroused his sense of the ludicrous, and he sent Christina a cartoon representing her on the warpath, flourishing a hammer with grim excitement, destroying furniture and hurling bank notes with irresponsible abandon into the fireplace. She responded with a demure cartoon of her own: two hands raised in astonishment and admiration, underlined by the comment, "Such is my attitude vis-a-vis of the historic record of my finished work."

At one point, as a gesture of gratitude to Gabriel for his aid, she proposed including Lizzie Siddal's verses in her new volume. But after reading her sister-in-law's poems, she changed her mind and returned them to her brother with the diplomatic remark that "between your volume and mine, their due post of honour is in yours." Although she found them "beautiful," were they not, she inquired, "almost too hopelessly sad for publication *en masse?*"

Well aware that this kind of criticism ill became one whose own poetry was open to the charge of morbidity (indeed, Lizzie's verses were almost a travesty upon Christina's), she added that by comparison her own "bogieism" was jovial. And after dipping into Jean Ingelow's enviable eighth edition, which she had taken with her to Hastings, she observed that her own "groans" were certainly not as dismal as some of Miss Ingelow's "of oppressive memory." Apparently the writing of depressing poetry was a prevailing preference among mid-Victorian young women with literary inclinations.

II

"Perhaps there is no pleasanter watering-place in England . . . than Hastings, on the Sussex coast," is the way Christina begins her prose fiction tale, "The Waves of This Troublesome World." The story is set in Hastings, and her description of it gives us a good idea of her impression of the place:

> The old town, nestling in a long, narrow valley, flanked by the East and West Hills, looks down upon the sea. At the valley mouth, on the shingly beach, stands the fish-market, where boatmen disembark the fruit of daily toil; where traffic is briskly plied, and maybe haggling

> rages; where bare-legged children dodge in and out between the stalls; where now and then a traveling show—dwarf, giant, or whatnot—arrests for brief days its wanderings.

Besides Jean Ingelow's poems, she "lugged down" with her to Hastings six volumes of Plato, reading material which she looked forward to as "a prolonged mental feast." Time certainly could not have hung heavy on her hands, for in addition to reading Plato, correcting proof for *Goblin Market,* writing the long *Prince's Progress* and many short poems (she wrote seven the week of February 17, three in one day), and planning and arranging the contents of the new volume, she also set herself the task of doing "some of the subordinate work down here in my hermitage" for the Italian exercise book Maria was preparing for publication. For company in her hermitage she had the society of her Uncle Henry Polydore and her cousin Henrietta, both of whom were spending the early part of the winter in Hastings. Her mother also paid a short visit.

But in between intervals of hard work, she found the leisure for that kind of aimless relaxation which, as Keats knew, is frequently the optimum condition for poetic production. She has given us in her prose fiction story an impression of the sense-stirring "sights, sounds, and smells" to be enjoyed in a walk along the East Cliff toward Ecclesbourne:

> There was the scent of a hayfield, the sweetness of dog-roses and honeysuckle, the fragrance of thyme beneath their feet; there were chirpings in the hedges, scattered skylarks in the air, a murmur of waves; there was blue sky above their heads, bright living green and golden sunshine around them, glittering sea far down below the cliff, flowers in the grass and about the hedges, butterflies here, there, and everywhere.

Gabriel once described the cliffs of Hastings as "lazy . . . all grown with grass and herbage." Sea and sky, he told Allingham, appear one through the mists, "and if you half shut your eyes, as of course you do, there is no swearing as to the distant sail as boat or bird, while just under one's feet the near boats stand together immovable as if the shadows clogged them. . . ."

Strolling along such lazy sea cliffs on a sun-misted day, perhaps Christina descended the steep cliff steps to the rocky beach below, and then pausing to rest, sat down on the huge stone she described in her prose tale as hollowed out like an armchair, and, drawing out her little black notebook, wrote down the following poems, the second composed shortly after her thirty-fifth birthday:

1

I loved my love from green of Spring
Until sere Autumn's fall:
But now that leaves are withering
How should one love at all?

My heart's too small[2]
For hunger, cold, love, everything. . . .

I loved my love—alas to see
That this should be, alas!
I thought that this could scarcely be,
Yet it has come to pass:
Sweet sweet love was,
Now bitter bitter grown to me.

2

Lord, it was well with me in time gone by
That cometh not again,
When I was fresh and cheerful, who but I?
I fresh, I cheerful: worn with pain
Now, out of sight and out of heart;
O Lord, how long?—

She spent a lonely and unfestive Christmas, dining "on a potion or two." Comparing herself to the wistful ghost of *At Home,* she told her family that "if unbeknown I could look in upon you sucking pulp of (metaphorical) plums and peaches, I should not fear the fate of my own Bogie."

It was in Hastings, while working on *Prince's Progress,* that she wrote the second part of *Memory,* the linked poem begun in 1857. In *Memory I* she had asserted that she had smashed her human idol, broken it at a single blow, and buried it "crushed in my deep heart where it used to live." But in the eight years which had elapsed since then, she had discovered that decisions which affect the deep heart are not made with a single violent blow. Her idol had arisen in all its virility again and again. Each successive blow felled but failed to slay it.

Now with Scott's actual and Alice's potential presence no longer a threat to her emotional equilibrium, at Hastings she was able to consider her problem more dispassionately, to hold it up for review, so to speak.

By the winter of 1865 she seems to have accepted the fact that the love she had sought so often to vanquish had become a condition of her life. But the condition was not easy to live with, for Scott's love had not brought her fulfillment or satisfaction in the past, and was not likely to do so in the future. In *Memory II* we see her groping for a modus vivendi. If union on this earth is impossible—so her reasoning went—there is still the chance for reunion in heaven. Although this Rossettian answer was hardly a new one for Christina (it appeared in *Convent Threshold*), she takes a fresh grasp of it in *Memory II* as both solution and consolation:

I have a room whereinto no one enters
Save I myself alone:
There sits a blessed memory on a throne,
There my life centres;

While winter comes and goes—oh tedious comer!—
And while its nip-wind blows;
While bloom the bloodless lily and warm rose
Of lavish summer.

If any should force entrance he might see there
One buried yet not dead,
Before whose face I no more bow my head
Or bend my knee there;

But often in my worn life's autumn weather
I watch there with clear eyes
And think how it will be in Paradise
When we're together.

III

This secret room, center of Christina's emotional life, may be recognized, draped though it is in obscure allegory and symbolism, in *Prince's Progress.* Like other of Christina's major poems, this one also follows in its theme and structure the emotional pattern of her life. The bride, the "enchanted dove," and the "enchanted princess" of the other poems, like the speaker in *L.E.L.,* starves to death for the lack of love while awaiting the royal lover who delays claiming her until it is too late.

The prince's hazardous pilgrimage to win his bride provides the narrative pattern. This pilgrimage is a "wonderful voyage," of the kind found in medieval romance. The obstacles to the prince's progress arise from his own character. This royal lover is "strong of limb if of purpose weak." Like Scott, he cannot resist women; and also like Scott in his later years, he is subject to the same kind of genial inertia, being fond of "taking his ease on cushion and mat." [3]

Summoned at length by the love song of the princess, which reaches him not through his senses but through an intuitive faculty, the prince arouses himself and goes forth to win her. On his way he is detained by two women and an old alchemist. The first of the women is an "alluring milkmaid." The second rescues him from the rising tides of passion in which he almost perishes. The old alchemist in dying supplies the prince with the precious elixir of life brewed in his cave. Although the prince realizes that this is the elixir he should share with his bride, his true love, he squanders it on the second woman. By the time he has completed his voyage and reached his bride's palace, she is dead. For his bride he has arrived "too late for life, too late for joy," though he himself seems to have had his full share of it during his travels.

This, then, is the essential framework of the poem, another recapitulation of experience. Present once again are the stock characters of the royal lover and the trio of women. But unlike the Margarets and the Marians, the heroine in this poem is sharply distinguished and isolated from her sisters-in-love. She is the real mate, the intended, the recognized

bride of the royal prince; the other two women are merely incidental diversions in his life.

To get at the emotional content of this poem, it is necessary to pierce through the thick veil of symbolism which heavily overlies the narrative pattern. Although toward the end of her life Christina told Gosse that she intended neither *Goblin Market* nor *Prince's Progress* as allegory,[4] at the time of writing the latter work she nevertheless admitted quite freely and frankly to the use of symbolism. For instance, in answering Gabriel's objection to the word "aftermath" in stanza 49, she justified its use by explaining that it gave "a subtle hint by symbol" of its meaning. Not, she added, that she "expected the general public to catch these refined clues; but there they are for minds such as mine."

One of the more obvious of these refined clues is the poppy symbolism which, appearing throughout the poem, gives it unity. The red and white poppies symbolize the race between love (life) and death, the theme of the poem:

> Red and white poppies grow at her feet.
> The blood-red wait for sweet summer heat,
> Wrapped in bud-coats, hairy and neat; [5]
> But the white buds swell, one day they will burst,
> Will open their death cups drowsy and sweet:—
> Which will open the first?

Death here is the penalty for the failure of love. The final fate of the princess deprived of love is symbolized by the "white poppies she must bear." Her bier is strewn with white poppies, the sleep-inducing flower, for "your roses are too red," her waiting women tell the stricken prince whose loitering was responsible for his bride's death.

Another refined clue may be perceived in the figure of the milkmaid, the first woman to detain the prince. Obviously a denizen of the dusky glen of *Goblin Market,* she resembles Coleridge's sinister enchantress in *Christabel:*

> Was it milk now, or was it cream?
> Was she maid, or an evil dream?
> Her eyes began to glitter and gleam:
> He would have gone, but he stayed instead;
> Green they gleamed as he looked in them:
> 'Give me my fee,' she said.—

Just as Laura in *Goblin Market* was tempted by fruit, so in this poem the prince is tempted by milk, of which the symbolic significance is at once apparent. In both poems evil is disguised as life-giving nourishment. Love is still the poison-cup.

In return for her jug of milk, the enchantress (hazel-eyed) demands as her fee either the full moon,

Or else sit under this apple-tree
Here for one idle day by my side.

We have noted the sexual significance attached to both the fruit-bearing tree and the sun and moon in Christina's system of symbolism. And of fruit-bearing trees, the apple tree appears the most frequently in her poetry as a fertility symbol, in *Birthday,* for instance, and *An Apple-Gathering.* Hence, the alternatives the milkmaid offers the prince are not so unrelated as they appear at first glance. What she is demanding as her fee is either pregnancy (the full moon) or sexual dalliance under the symbolic apple tree. Naturally the prince, a traveler, chooses the apple tree.

At length he awakens from the enchantment and resumes his journey toward his waiting bride. Now he must pass through a bleak and arid country, a land which in its blank desolation recalls that of *Cobwebs:*

A land of chasm and rent, a land
Of rugged blackness on either hand: . . .

A lifeless land, a loveless land.

But it is "a tedious land for a social Prince," and the errant knight is dissatisfied with its endless labyrinths and its frightening solitudes. Attracted by a light, he wanders into the cave of an ancient alchemist who is brewing in his fiery caldron the elixir of life. In return for his keep, the Prince plies the bellows and feeds the glowing fire for the alchemist, who informs him that only one thing is lacking to complete the broth. Not even the "pinch of virgin soil" which he stirs into the pot can supply the lack. The missing ingredient is death, and this the alchemist himself finally contributes when he dies, and

The dead hand slipped, the dead fingers dipped
In the broth as the dead man slipped:—
That same instant, a rosy red
Flushed the steam, and quivered and clipped
Round the dead old head.

The prince, seeing his host lifeless, fills a phial with the dearly purchased broth, and departs. The death of the old man has freed the young one for life, as the death of Scott's mother in 1852 liberated him for a freer existence.

Instead of hastening on his way to share the elixir with his waiting bride, the prince takes a nap: "He can sleep who holdeth her cheap." But once again the bride's insistent summons, ringing and sobbing through his sleep, awakens the prince, and he resumes his journey.

Finding himself in a flowering country, he begins to feel the need for another woman:

It's oh for a second maiden, at least
To bear the flagon, and taste it too,
And flavour the feast.

While the prince is seeking a second maiden to share with him his "feast," he is almost drowned by the sudden rise of turbulent waters. "Bursting, bubbling, swelling the flow," the great waters thunder down upon him from the heights, and sweep him away in a "dizzying whirl."

Clutching his phial desperately, the prince almost goes down, but in the nick of time he is saved and rescued from the floodwaters by women:

Kind hands do and undo,
Kind voices whisper and coo.

Like another Don Juan, he comes back to life under female ministrations, and out of the haze of pleasant femininity he distinguishes his Haidee:

But one propped his head that drooped awry:
Till his eyes oped, and at unaware
They met eye to eye.

Oh a moon face in a shadowy place,
And a light touch and a winsome grace,
And a thrilling tender voice which says:
'Safe from waters that seek the sea—
Cold waters by rugged ways—
Safe with me.'

Again the prince dallies, postpones, lingers, loses the hour of bridal consummation. But Christina quite understands.

Had he stayed to weigh and scan
He had been more or less than a man.

He does "what a young man can," speaks of toil and duty and obligations, and yet he dawdles the golden hours away, breaking the promise to his bride,

The promise promised so long ago
The long promise, has not been kept.

Eventually the prince is again recalled to his aim, and starts afresh on his "tedious road." This time he must scale huge, inaccessible, snow-crowned mountains of rock. Black and forbidding though those unvisited and frozen peaks may be, he is not the man to be intimidated by them:

Up he went where the goat scarce clings,
Up where the eagle folds her wings,
Past the green line of living things,
Where the sun cannot warm the cold,—
Up he went as a flame enrings
Where there seems no hold.

The goat, the eagle, the sun are all familiar symbols. The frozen peak probably represents Christina's view of her own situation, one of austere

isolation from the warming rays which, wherever they penetrate, produce the fertile green.

At last the prince approaches the palace gate, but instead of a lovely bride fresh to greet him, he encounters his betrothed's bier as it is carried out by "veiled figures." The chorus of waiting women in reproaching the bridegroom for his tardiness point up the moral of the tale. It is to be sure a very special moral, not at all universal but applicable only to Christina's particular situation:

> Ten years ago, five years ago,
> One year ago,
> Even then you had arrived in time,
> Though somewhat slow:
> Then you had known her living face
> Which now you cannot know.
> The frozen fountain would have leaped,
> The buds gone on to blow,
> *And life have been a cordial 'Yes,'
> Instead of a dreary 'no.'* [6]

Shortly before the conclusion, the narrative flow of the poem is interrupted by a digression which is intended as a description of the lonely princess, but which in the light of contemporary descriptions of Christina should be read as another self-portrait like that in *The Royal Princess.* It is Christina's voice with which the princess speaks, the voice admired by Grace Gilchrist and William Sharp, and described by William as "uncommonly fine in tone and modulation." Christina's bearing, which Watts-Dunton thought displayed the quality of "poetic courtesy," and which William said reflected "her character in its dignity and modesty," is also apparent in the princess's quiet reserve:

> We never heard her speak in haste;
> Her tones were sweet,
> And modulated just so much
> As it was meet:
> Her heart sat silent through the noise
> And concourse of the street.
> There was no hurry in her hands,
> No hurry in her feet;
> There was no bliss drew nigh to her,
> That she might run to greet.

But despite a pervasive tone of subdued melancholy, the underlying attitude in this long poem is one of optimism, for Christina makes it clear that neither of the two women who detain the prince is his true love. It is neither the milkmaid nor the lady who rescues the prince from the rising waters, but the waiting princess, starved for love, who is his real beloved. Not even the second woman is a serious rival; she is merely someone with whom the prince is pleasantly wasting his time.

If we assume the correspondence of the women in the poem with those

in Scott's life, we may conclude that, despite the disillusionment to which Christina had given utterance in *Twice,* she still believed that she and not Alice was Scott's real love. That she could have persisted in such a belief in the face of all evidence to the contrary can be explained only by the fact that, when the emotions are involved, it is too fatally easy to believe what one wishes were true.

But disillusionment is not necessarily absent from *Prince's Progress.* The poem is in effect a bitter comment upon the failure of earthly love and the deficiency of the earthly bridegroom whose dalliance is responsible for his bride's death. Both hope and disappointment are present in this poem as separate elements that do not blend.

Symbolically the death of the princess represents the renunciation (or deprivation) of love, a theme to which Christina was committed. *Long Barren* (February 21), another of the poems she turned out while composing *Prince's Progress,* treats the same theme more directly. Once again in this poem we see the transmutation process in operation. Using the symbolic fruit tree as an organizing principle, she writes:

> Thou who didst hang upon a barren tree,
> My God, for me,
> Though I till now be barren, now at length
> Lord, give me strength
> To bring forth fruit to Thee.
>
> Thou who didst bear for me the crown of thorn
> Spitting and scorn,
> Tho' I till now have put forth thorns, yet now
> Strengthen me Thou
> That better fruit be borne.

At thirty-five Christina was a woman still young enough for childbearing and one, moreover, who had on hand in Cayley a respectable suitor willing to marry her. It was at this age, in the prime of her womanhood, that she renounced biological for spiritual fruitfulness.

IV

Her voluminous correspondence with Gabriel, relating both to the composition of *Prince's Progress* and to the organization of the collection of which it was to be the showpiece, gives us a behind-the-scenes glimpse into the working methods of the two poets, illuminates their divergent approaches to their art, and reveals the extent to which Christina consulted her illustrious brother about literary matters.

"True, O Brother," she wrote in a letter of December 23, shortly after her arrival in Hastings, "my Alchemist still shivers in the blank of mere possibility; but I have so far overcome my feelings and disregarded my nerves as to unloose the Prince, so that wrapping-paper may no longer

bar his 'progress.'" Not until January 16 was she able to report, "This morning out came the Prince, but the Alchemist makes himself scarce, and I must bide his time." Two weeks later she produced "an Alchemist reeking from the crucible . . . Please read him if you have the energy; then, when you return him to me, I must give a thorough look-over to the annotated *Prince*. . . . He's not precisely the Alchemist I prefigured, but thus he came and thus he must stay: you know my system of work."

Apparently Gabriel did not altogether share her own confidence in her system of work, for—remembering perhaps Ruskin's stricture on the irregular rhythm of *Goblin Market*—he objected to what he called "the metric jolt" in the new poem. She replied that she could not see her way clear to discard it, however unfortunate the original selection of such rhythm may have been. But, she added encouragingly, "we will file and polish."

Gabriel and Ruskin were not alone in criticizing Christina's unorthodoxy with metrics, for an *Athenæum* reviewer regretted that "Miss Rossetti who is, when she chooses, a mistress of verbal harmony, should at times employ discords . . . which . . . result in harshness." Tastes change, and to the twentieth-century ear such unexpected discords and sudden "metric jolts" are more appealing than the smooth melodic line preferred by most Victorian poets and their readers.

The structure of *Prince's Progress* as well as its rhythm came in for rigorous criticism at Gabriel's hands. One of his proposals to improve the plot was the introduction of a tournament as a narrative device. His sister shuddered at the very idea: "How shall I express my sentiments about the terrible tournament? Not a phrase to be relied on, not a correct knowledge on the subject, not the faintest impulse of inspiration, incites me to the tilt: and looming before me in horrible bugbeardom stand TWO tournaments in Tennyson's *Idylls*." Defending the existing structure, which she briefly outlined,[7] she pointed out that her "actual *Prince* seems to me invested with a certain artistic congruity of construction not lightly to be despised," and she concluded breezily, "See how the subtle elements balance each other, and fuse into a noble conglom!"

But in the end she was willing to concede that her *Prince* lacked "the special felicity (!) of my *Goblins*," a verdict with which criticism has agreed. The falling off can be attributed to the fact that the earlier poem was in the nature of a volcanic eruption from explosive inner pressure, whereas the later work was a response to external pressure and was written as much for the sake of producing another volume of poetry as for satisfying the creative drive.

Her Hastings letters disclose the extent to which she was worried about the length of "vol. 2," as she called the new collection. Counting pages in December, she told Gabriel that she had about 120 available, a fact which "cheers though not inebriates." At one time she had "a puerile

fancy" to make the new volume equal in length to *Goblin Market,* but this she soon abandoned.

Brother and sister were soon battling in friendly fashion about which of Christina's poems should go into the volume. Many that Gabriel disliked were favorites of Christina's, some of which she threatened to reinsert "WHEN publishing day comes around." Such was her "Captive Jew," as they called *By the Waters of Babylon,* which she wanted to retain chiefly because it was written in *terza rima,* and "I am inclined to show fight for at least one *Terza-rima* in honour of our Italian element." When Gabriel proved stubborn, they compromised on *After This the Judgment,* also written in terza rima.

Another poem Gabriel rejected was *The Lowest Room,* which he compared derisively to the work of Isa Craig and Adelaide Proctor. *"Lowest Room* pray eject if you really think such a course advantageous," Christina replied, "though I can't agree with you: still it won't dismay me that you should do so; I am not stung into obstinacy even by the Isa and Adelaide taunt in which I acknowledge an element of truth." She herself thought the poem not without "a certain Patmorean flavour." But rather than that of Coventry Patmore, Gabriel detected in it echoes of "the Barrett-Browning" style, which was all very well for those poets, but was "utterly foreign" to Christina's primary impulses. This "taint . . . of modern vicious style" he described as a kind of "falsetto muscularity." He found a good deal of it likewise in *No, Thank You, John* and *The Royal Princess,* but thought the latter too good to omit.

Again Christina disagreed, characterizing *The Royal Princess* as "rather a spite of mine." Nevertheless, after deleting a number of stanzas (some of which we have examined), she followed Gabriel's advice and kept it in the volume. She retained the following stanza over his objection that it resembled too closely some lines in Keats' *Isabella.*[8]

Some to work on roads, canals; some to man his ships;
Some to smart in mines beneath sharp overseers' whips;
Some to trap fur-beasts in lands where utmost winter nips.

"Is it so very like Keats?" she inquired, and then confessed that she had never read *Isabella* and was therefore altogether unacquainted with the lines in question.

Other of Gabriel's rejects were *The Bourne, Come and See,* and *Easter Even.* The first Christina wanted to retain because "Mac" liked it and it had been set to music by Alice Macdonald, Lady Burne-Jones' sister, later the mother of Rudyard Kipling. She promised to alter "the queer rhythm" of the second. And as for *Easter Even,* she had, she said, no particular liking for it, but she wanted it to appear in the volume because "Mrs. Scott told me that Scotus was struck by it quite remarkably in Mr. Shipley's volume where it is. . . ."

Among the poems included in the new volume were *Songs in a Cornfield* ("one of my own favourites, so I am especially gratified by your and Mr. Swinburne's praise"); *Jessie Cameron* ("Stanza 2 I cannot consent to sacrifice; to my conception of the plot and characters it really is essential: concede me that stanza 2 with good grace"); *The Ghost's Petition* ("Please cut it short, as you suggest"); *L.E.L.* ("adopted, your enormous improvement"); *Last Night* ("metre slightly doctored"); *By the Sea* ("has superseded *A Yawn;* for which however I retain a sneaking kindness").

By now it should be evident that, although Christina may have been the "spontaneous" poet William claims she was, she revised and rewrote her poems much as any other working poet does. A good example of the kind of carpentry work (fitting and joining, knocking out and nailing together) her poems frequently underwent is the piece called *Spring Fancies,* published in the April, 1865, issue of *Macmillan's Magazine:*

> How is it possible [she wrote Gabriel] that not only you recognize No. 1 of *Spring Fancies,*[9] but resuscitate defunct lines from memory? The great original stands as *The Spring Quiet* in a little book dated 1847; a little book so primitive that for aught I know you did not drag its depths for G[oblin] M[arket] vol.: whence pray do not deduce that it contains other treasures, for I am not aware that it does. I will send you an exact copy of its primeval form: then will you most kindly set it right from printed copy? but suppressing fifth lines and keeping extra stanzas as you judge best. Or, on second thought, I will retain certain alterations which I know are in the printed copy and which were the result of mature reflection, and will make the sea-stanza come last, as you put it; but I must still trust to your kindness to compare and alter it by the printed copy, in case I get a word here or there wrong.

Taking his sister's negative hint, Gabriel did dredge the depths of the Polidori volume, from which he extricated *Vanity of Vanities, Gone for Ever,* and a sonnet; whereupon Christina remarked with irony that she thought it not necessary this time to resort to the 1847 *Dead City* in the interests of bulk, though to be sure, "I have but to launch forth into the rag-and-bone store; thence, by main force, something must emerge."

Although she reminded Gabriel "that to make up Vol. 2 we must have recourse to some not skimmed by you as cream," she told him that she did have on hand "one or two new little things" which would fill up space. They were *Grown and Flown, Eve* (which ultimately became one of her best-liked pieces), and *Dost Thou Not Care?* all written at Hastings. And in addition to the title poem, she also had another work of considerable length in *Under the Rose* (*Iniquity*), which if it "passed muster" would, she hoped, "stop the gap single-handed." But despite what she described as its "not un-Crabbed aspect," Gabriel was dissatisfied with it, for on March 13 she "meekly" returned the poem "pruned and re-written to order." Still it did not meet with his approval, and on March 31,

"after six well-defined and several paroxysms of stamping, foaming, hair-uprooting," she agreed to "suppress that 'screech,'" whatever it may have been.

V

The work, both creative and editorial, which had been executed at such high speed, exhausted her, and she told Gabriel, "I hope after this vol. (if this vol. becomes a vol.) people will respect my nerves, and not hint for a long long while at any possibility of vol. 3. I am sure my poor brain must lie fallow and take its ease, if I am to keep up to my own mark."

Her achievement is all the more remarkable in that she was still fighting ill health. Worried by her "violent and persistent cough," William began to talk of taking her to Italy in the spring. An Italian cousin, Teodorico Pietrocola-Rossetti, upon hearing that she had brought up blood, was convinced that she was already in the second stage of tuberculosis and that nothing would save her but ass's milk, phosphorus, and wood fires. Christina herself reported her health "a little hobbly . . . but in an uninteresting way not alarming."

She was, she said, acquiring "the tone along with the habits of a hermit." Becoming somewhat restive under her isolation, she looked forward to a promised visit from Jean Ingelow, although she had to admit that "prospective Jean Ingelow inspires me with some trepidation." Such timidity in forming new friendships was not unusual, for as she once told a correspondent, "I, you know of old, am a social shortcomer." A few days later, however, she took a more sensible view of the visit: *"To be tooked and well shooked* is what I eminently need socially, so Jean Ingelow will be quite appropriate treatment, should she transpire: she has not yet done so." Another week passed, but "still no Jean Ingelow." Finally at the end of March "Miss Ingelow *wrote* . . . not called because her Brother has been having scarlatina. So precautionarily we don't visit; but talk and shake hands if we meet, which has happened once."

On March 23 both *The Athenæum* and *The Morning Star* carried announcements of the forthcoming *Prince's Progress* volume which Macmillan had not even seen, let alone approved. Embarrassed, Christina wrote him, "How either got in I know not. But though they take your acceptance for granted . . . I don't."

She was hoping to get through with the proofs by May, "in case that Fata Morgana of delight, my sight of Italy with William, should by any manner of means come to pass," and she therefore wrote Macmillan,

> I shall be most especially pleased if you will begin on Vol. 2 when it gets to you; if, that is, you are not disappointed in it. It seems not impossible (though so pleasant as to suggest improbability) that by the end of May I may go with William to get my first glimpse of Italy:

> could it anyhow be managed that my proof labours should be over by then? in case of need.[10]

A similar appeal to Gabriel resulted in his promptly dispatching the manuscript and the following note to the publisher on April 4:

> With this I post to you (by book post) the M.S. of *The Prince's Progress and Other Poems.* Christina is anxious to get on with the printing immediately as it is not unlikely that she may be going to Italy in May and would like to see all the proofs before then. I wish you'd always send a proof to me at the same time as to her, and not print off till *both* are returned to you. . . .

VI

Viewed in retrospect, Christina's productivity during her three months' stay at Hastings was due as much to the recovery of her emotional health as it was to her enforced solitude. By March she had traveled so far from the black mood of self-loathing in which she had written *Who Shall Deliver Me?* of the preceding spring that she could half-playfully warn Gabriel not to tamper with her personality. "Please make your emendations," she wrote about *Prince's Progress,* "and I can correct them over the coals in the proofs: only don't make vast changes as 'I am I.' "

Toward the end of March she began to look forward to leaving Hastings, and by April she was home, commenting ruefully on her "woeful phizz" and declining with thanks Gabriel's offer of half a dozen bottles of strengthening Madeira. Such a delicacy, fit for the discriminating palate of connoisseurs, she said, was "altogether lost on a Goth who knows not wine from wine, and who lumps all subtle distinctions in the simple definition 'Nice.' " On the whole, she was glad to be home, for "was there ever yet a snail who preferred the bravest nautilus floating to his own convenient shell?" Although her health showed definite improvement, she told Anne Gilchrist, her looks "didn't earn her many compliments."

Both Rossetti and Ford Madox Brown were entertaining a good deal that spring, and Scott, always observant of a woman's appearance, was frequently to be met with at their parties. Christina would naturally have wished to look her best for him, especially as he was still going about alone this season or accompanied only by Mrs. Scott. Alice was in mourning for her brother, who had died at Scott's house that February, and she was not attending social functions. Lady Burne-Jones mentions Scott as one of the distinguished guests who were present at Rossetti's dinner party of April 12. If it had not been Passion Week, Christina would have been there too, but, as she explained to Gabriel, "An old rule shuts me up from feasts and such-like during Lent. . . ." However, she did attend the supper party Brown gave for the French painter Legros and later the spring exhibition of Brown's paintings.

But although she was undoubtedly glad to get back into the reassuring

bustle of London activities, she seems to have derived little satisfaction and less profit from her excursions into social life, and William hoped that the forthcoming trip to Italy, to which she was looking forward with so much pleasure, might improve her condition, which he suspected had an emotional as well as a physical basis. Christina herself was of the opinion that

> Perhaps a change may after all
> Prove best for her: to leave behind
> These home-sights seen time out of mind;
> To get beyond the narrow wall
> Of home, and learn home is not all.
>
> Perhaps in this way she may forget,
> Not all at once, but in a while:
> May come to wonder how she set
> Her heart on this slight thing, and smile
> At her own folly, in a while.

Busy with last-minute preparations for her trip, she asked Gabriel to handle the business details connected with the publication of her new volume, "my wish being for the same terms as Goblin Market," and so on April 28 he wrote Macmillan,

> I find on inquiry that my sister is very anxious not to dispense with the 2 drawings I promised her—So I think we must then wait till I can do them which shall be as soon as possible.
>
> I asked her the other day what business arrangements she had made with you as to this new volume, and found that nothing had been said to the point. I therefore got her leave to say a word. Now couldn't you be a good fairy and give her something down for this edition, say £100? You know she *is* a good poet, and some day people will know it. That's so true that it comes in rhyme of itself! She's going to Italy and would find a little moneybag useful.

Macmillan must have refused emphatically, for a puzzled Christina wrote Gabriel,

> Mr. Macmillan writes under a complete misapprehension as to my Italian tour-fund, precarious indeed if it depended on P.P. instead of on unfailing family bounty. However, now I will write direct to him and set matters as straight as words can set them. I am perfectly willing to let vol. 2. appear on the same terms as vol. 1., and very likely these terms are both what will suit him best and what in the long run will do at least as well for me as any others. So please wash your hands of the vexatious business; I will settle it now myself with him. What made him combine my Italian holiday with the proceeds of vol. 2. I know not: it may have been a guess founded on (apparent) probability, or he may have supposed that my motive in wishing to get through the proofs before setting off was to bag the money,—of course it *was* merely not to delay publication.[11]

VII

The Italian trip took a little over a month, from May 22 to June 26. The three of them, William, "Mamma," and Christina, went to Paris by Calais on "a very heavy dark morning with a little lightning and thunder, following a remarkably sultry day." She was "charmed with Paris," where they stayed at the Hôtel de Normandie ("8 fr. each per day"), visited the Louvre, the Théâtre Français, Notre Dame, and the usual tourist attractions, leaving for Switzerland on the 26th of May. Although Christina admitted later to Anne Gilchrist that on the whole she preferred "nature treasures" to art treasures, on this trip she managed to see "glorious specimens of both classes." She and William returned again and again to the Cathedral at Langres, although even here Christina seems to have enjoyed the view from the lower parapet more than the architectural features.

Traveling to Lucerne on "a grey, sunless, at times showery afternoon succeeding considerable heat," Christina felt increasingly depressed as she approached the mountains. Was it because "their mass and loftiness dwarf all physical magnitudes familiar to most eyes," or because "their sublimity impresses us like want of sympathy"? Whatever the reason, "Saddened and weary," she tells us, "I ended one delightful day's journey in Switzerland and passed indoors, losing sight for a moment of the mountains." But a glance out her window overlooking the lake brought them back again into view: "And lo! the evening flush had turned snow to rose, and sorrow and sadness fled away."

An even more impressive experience was to follow. "A small party of us," she wrote in *Time Flies,* "crossed the Alps into Italy by the Pass of Mt. Gothard. We did not tunnel our way like worms through its dense substance. We surmounted its crest, like eagles." Expressed prosaically, it was in the private carriage William had hired at Flülen from where they had commenced the ascent up to Andermatt. On the way up they observed with pleasure the red pigs and the Alpine roses, more like rhododendrons; and then suddenly, to Christina's extreme delight, "at a certain point of the ascent Mount St. Gothard bloomed into an actual garden of forget-me-nots." She gazed in rapture: "Unforgotten and never to be forgotten that lovely lavish efflorescence which made earth cerulean as the sky":

The mountains in their overwhelming might
Moved me to sadness when I saw them first,
And afterwards they moved me to delight;
Struck harmonies from silent chords which burst
Out into song, a song by memory nursed;
For ever unrenewed by touch or sight
Sleeps the keen magic of each day or night,
In pleasure and in wonder then immersed.

All Switzerland behind us on the ascent,
All Italy before us, we plunged down
St. Gothard, garden of forget-me-not:
Yet why should such a flower choose such a spot?
Could we forget that way which once we went
Though not one flower had bloomed to weave its crown?

They stayed overnight at Andermatt and left the next morning for Bellinzona. The sight of a very pretty Italian girl at the hotel drew from William the judicious remark that "the *personnel* of the inhabitants changes markedly for the better as soon as one passes from the German to the Italian side of the mountains." Christina too showed "intense relief and pleasure," said William, when she saw "lovable Italian faces and heard musical Italian speech at Bellinzona after the somewhat hard and nipped quality of the German Swiss." Rejoicing in her Italian blood, she described Italy's people as "a noble people" and its very cattle "of high-born aspect." The pigs, however, she found "exceptionally mean and repulsive" and the Italian poppies not nearly so vivid and rich in color as the English wild scarlet poppies.

A brief sojourn at Lake Como on a rare night in June provided another of the unforgettable experiences destined to bloom into a sonnet. Out on the lake, with William and the young Italian boatman talking politics —Garibaldi and the Austrians—Christina listened dreamily to the song of a nightingale trilling from a distant starlit hill:

A host of things I take on trust: I take
The nightingale on trust, for few and far
Between those actual summer moments are
When I have heard what melody they make.
So chanced it once at Como on the Lake:
But all things, then, waxed musical; each star
Sang on its course, each breeze sang on its car,
All harmonies sang to senses wide awake.
All things in tune, myself not out of tune,
Those nightingales were nightingales indeed:
Yet truly an owl had satisfied my need,
And wrought a rapture underneath that moon,
Or simple sparrow chirping from a reed;
For June that night glowed like a doubled June.

After a few days at Brescia and Verona, the travelers started for home, going by way of the Sflügen. As they descended a mountain side by side with a mountain torrent, William caught sight of "a slight spraybow" in the midst of the plunging waters which Christina regretfully missed. "That single natural foambow which I might have beheld and espied not, is the one to which may attach a tingle of regret . . . ," she wrote in *Time Flies.* Although had she not missed the experience, a sonnet might have resulted, even so she was able to evoke it in the poetic prose of *Seek and Find:* "Such streams descend with murmur, tumult and thunder, in crystal

expanses, in ripples, leaps and eddies, in darkness and light, in clearness and whiteness, and foam and foam-bow."

The Italian trip awakened the warmer, deeper Italian chords in Christina's temperament, that sensuous side of her nature she sternly suppressed. One of the group of poems she called *En Route* expresses both her "passionate delight" in Italy and her regret at leaving it:

Farewell, land of love, Italy
Sister-land of Paradise:
With mine own feet I have trodden thee,
Have seen thee with mine own eyes.

Her awareness of the contending elements in her nature, which she rightly attributed to the differing national strains she had inherited, appears in *Italia io ti saluto,* written in London some time in July. Italy, which she must leave, is the "sweet South" of emotional richness, and England, to which she returns, is the "bleak North" of moral responsibility:

To see no more the country half my own,
Nor hear the half familiar speech,
Amen, I say; I turn to that bleak North
Whence I came forth—
The South lies out of reach.

But when our swallows fly back to the South,
To the sweet South, to the sweet South,
The tears may come again into my eyes
On the old wise,
And the sweet name to my mouth.

VIII

Once back in London, Christina found that nothing had changed during her absence, not even she. William reported to Macmillan that, although the trip had been "a great delight" to them all, "its effect upon Christina's health . . . did not produce the sensible improvement I had hoped for." And he told F. G. Stephens in September that, although she was reasonably well, he could not observe any "fundamental change such as might save her from getting very unwell again at any time especially in the chill and damps now approaching. . . ." In fact, it did not take long before she relapsed into her usual autumnal depression, writing lines such as,

Faded and all-forsaken
I weep as I have never wept.
Oh it was summer when I slept,
It's winter now I waken.

Scott was spending the autumn at Penkill with Alice, who upon her brother's death had inherited the family seat. With no male heir to an

illustrious line (which included Boyds who had fought under Wallace and Bruce and in the fifteenth century a Regent Boyd whose son had secured the Orkney Islands for Scotland), it looked as though an old Girvan prophecy would be fulfilled:

> When the last leaf draps frae the auld aish tree
> The Penkill Boyds maun cease to be.

That summer Alice's coachman had pointed out the withered stump of the "auld aish tree" on the road to Girvan. Hoping to defeat the prophecy in symbol if not in fact, Scott and Alice stopped the carriage, got out, and plucked a fresh green shoot from the withered stump. This they took back with them to Penkill and planted in the heated greenhouse of the garden, but it drooped and died at the end of the second season.

Although Alice, like Christina, was still young enough to marry, she too had made her choice, and so long as Scott could not marry her, she preferred to remain unwedded and childless. Barrenness was his gift to both the women who loved him.

Returning to London in November, Scott found William enthusiastic about the spiritualistic seances he had been attending. The medium was a Mrs. Marshall, a former washwoman and follower of Joanna Southcott. William prevailed upon Scott to accompany him to Mrs. Marshall's, and at his first table-rapping session Scott attempted to communicate with Alice's brother. The following year, when Lady Trevelyan died, he again resorted to Mrs. Marshall in the effort to reach his friend's departed spirit.

The interest in "spirit-rapping" had started in England in the 1850's and had reached a fashionable climax in the mid-'sixties. Despite their professed skepticism, both Scott and the Rossetti brothers half-believed in the possible communication with the dead. Once William thought he had got hold of his Uncle John Polidori, whom he questioned about Byron: another time he asked the "bogey" of Lizzie Siddal what would be the outcome of Christina's illness. Lizzie did not know.

Both William and Gabriel attended the fashionable seances of the American Davenport brothers, who in 1864 were "electrifying London" by their amazing psychic feats. Of them all, Christina alone was not taken in. Upon hearing her brothers' reports of the seances, she suspected what later turned out to be the case, that "simple imposture" was the "missing key" to the inexplicable. "Please God," she vowed, "I will have nothing to do with spiritualism, whether it be imposture or a black art; or with mesmerism, lest I clog my free will; or with hypnotism, lest wilful self-surrender become my road to evil choice. . . ."

IX

Whether Christina saw much of Scott that autumn is uncertain, but not very likely. Shortly after returning to London, he had started work on the windows of the South Kensington Museum's Ceramic Gallery,

which the government had commissioned him to decorate, a task which occupied him for the next three years. If anyone wanted Scott, Gabriel said, he could always be found "in the deserts of stucco which he . . . inhabits."

As autumn deepened into winter, Gabriel bestirred himself to work on the illustrations for *Prince's Progress,* scheduled for Christmas publication. Although early in December Christina observed with satisfaction that "now my vol. seems really on the eve of coming out," by the sixteenth she was writing regretfully to Macmillan that "as for the old sore: you know the woodcuts cannot be ready for Xmas?—I hardly know how to ask you now to keep back *P.P.* after your 'few days' advertisement;—yet if you agree with me in thinking Gabriel's designs too desirable to forego, I will try to follow your example of patience under disappointment."

Not long after this, she received from Roberts Brothers of Boston a "liberal proposal" to publish her work in America, an offer she "gladly" accepted in January.[12] It was Jean Ingelow who had put her in touch with the American publishers, and, although she was not in the habit of forming close friendships with women, relying mainly upon her family for intimate companionship, at this period she seems to have made some effort to associate with the women poets who sought her company. In addition to Miss Ingelow and Dora Greenwell, for whom the Rossettis gave a dinner party ("a most estimable and superior woman," said William, but with a "middle-aged and by no means fascinating exterior"), Christina also made a slight endeavor to cultivate Isa Craig, introducing her to Macmillan and requesting Gabriel to illustrate one of her poems. "Alarms Excursions. Recater Vague! . . . I couldn't do it," he replied.

Instead, he sent her to C. Fairfax Murray, who, though "a very young artist," was "an extremely promising one," and, if given the job of illustrating Miss Craig's poems for *Argosy,* would be sure to do it creditably.

Christina was not writing much poetry this year, probably allowing her "poor brain" to "lie fallow," and, with the exception of *A Dirge,* a threnody for love, she produced little of high quality. Throughout the winter and spring we find her repeating melodiously melancholy variations on the theme of *A Dirge,* the death of love. Like her enchanted bride in *Prince's Progress,* she felt that she had no bliss to run and greet, and that the loveless life was not worth living. Even spring did little to relieve the mauve-gray monotony of her verse. She complained in May that

> I am weary of my life
> Through the long sultry day, . . .
>
> I am weary of my life
> Through the slow tedious night.

One would think that the publication of her "vol.," now at last imminent, might have brightened her outlook, but seemingly literary

prestige belonged to the order of external events, which, unless they were associated with the feeling events of her inner world, did not touch her deeply. By the end of March Gabriel had finally finished the block for the illustrations, and he sent it to Scott's friend W. J. Linton to be engraved, cautioning Macmillan in April to be sure that "thorough care" was taken with the printing, as "Goblin Market was so ill done in this respect as to be a fresh annoyance every time I see a copy."

By the first week of June he was able to announce to his aunt, Charlotte Polidori, that Christina's book was out at last and that she herself was in Scotland.

X

A life, when wound up, accelerates, just as conversely it slows down and stagnates when Fortune's finger fails to touch the mechanism. Gifts were suddenly showered into Christina's lap that summer. Not only was she to enjoy the fruits of her Hastings labor in the critical acclaim which greeted *Prince's Progress,* but in the invitation to visit Penkill, which arrived that June, she could discern, if she chose, Scott's acknowledgment of the long promise and his intention to keep it indirectly.

The invitation was one of three, for with her growing fame, hostesses were vying with one another to get her to their country houses. The mother of the painter Val Prinsep held out as bait a meeting with Tennyson if Christina would visit her at the Isle of Wight, and Anne Gilchrist was urging her to return again to Brookbank. But it was the Penkill invitation which brought the greatest surprise as well as unexpected joy.

What prompted it? Although it came from Alice, she was undoubtedly acceding to Scott's wish. Had his interest in Christina revived, then, as the result of some incident or occasion of which we have no record? Or should his summons be regarded as merely another tribute to her increasing importance in the literary world? But since theirs was one of those "perennial friendships" rooted in what Scot called "habits of feeling rather than thinking," he as well as she might have felt the need to renew it from time to time by fresh contact.

She did not hesitate about which invitation to accept. Declining Mrs. Gilchrist's hospitality, she wrote, "If the end of my Penkill sojourn deprives me of seeing you, its beginning mulcts me of a visit to the Isle of Wight, in which I was promised to meet Tennyson—poor me! . . . However, I am not certain that in any case I should have screwed myself up to accept it, as I am shy amongst strangers and think things formidable. . . ." [13] Despite the amenities, she had no intention of going to the Isle of Wight. Not the chance to meet all the poet laureates in English literature could have kept her away from Penkill that June.

What, then, did she expect from the visit?

When she had been Scott's guest at Newcastle, there had been no Alice

Boyd in his life. Evidently that time as this, Mrs. Scott did not count as an obstacle to her husband's friendships. But at Penkill Alice Boyd would be very much present; in fact, it was not Scott's but Alice's home Christina would be visiting. The woman she must have guessed was Scott's mistress was to be her hostess. Under the circumstances, why would she have gone at all?

She might have foreseen that some risk would be involved in a prolonged stay of weeks under the same roof with a man she had loved for so long and who knew so well, when he chose, how to revive *amor dormente*. She could of course have believed that by now she had her emotions well under control. She might even have regarded the prospective visit as a challenge to her powers of resistance, still not comprehending at thirty-six what she knew with certainty at the age of sixty-three, that "it were rash to reckon any temptation assuredly past, while the liability to all temptation remains."

What is more likely is that she was convinced she had permanently renounced any hope for or possibility of physical union, that Scott knew it as well as she, and that was why he had Alice; and therefore whatever feeling she retained for him had become spiritualized beyond the desire of the senses. Even if she had reason to fear that her affection could take on again a sensuous hue, was not Alice's very presence at Penkill an additional safeguard?

But such reasoning would have been the conscious process through which she would have justified a course of action she obviously desired and intended to follow. The truth is, she wanted to go to Penkill. Whatever her conscious motives may have been, her less conscious drives undoubtedly dominated her decision. She firmly intended to go to Penkill and spend six weeks near Scott. Although she might have been far from clear what benefit she hoped to derive from such proximity, the proximity itself could have been the chief inducement.

Even if another woman had a prior claim upon him, even if the conditions of her visit entailed the sharing of him with that woman, perhaps to the extent of feeding upon the crumbs from the feast, it is unlikely that she would have surrendered without a struggle the unexpected gift with which life had presented her. Everything in her character indicates that she had the courage as well as "the feminine boldness and directness of aim" which would cause her willingly to risk the pain along with the pleasure.

XI

What were her thoughts, as in company with Scott's wife, she journeyed northward into Ayrshire and Alice's territory? Though the Scottish hill line had once been pointed out to her (possibly during one of the Newcastle visits), she had never before crossed the border.

Was she excited as the carriage from Ayr, to which she had changed at the Kilmarnock junction, turned at length into the gates of Penkill, drove briskly down the beech-lined avenue, and rolled to a stop in front of the round turrets and stone walls of the medieval castle? There, in front of her, was the place she had tried so often to visualize, described by Scott as "the old Scotch house with its gray walls chequered by the shade of great trees, and jackdaws sitting forever on its vane or towers."

What prospect awaited her within those walls?

❋ 11 ❋

"A SELF-KINDLING, SELF-DEVOURING LOVE"

1866

"As spring advances into summer," said Scott, "and my work at South Kensington draws to a close, we prepare to emigrate to Scotland." Alice generally went on ahead to prepare the castle for occupancy, and then Scott, either alone or accompanied by his wife, followed shortly thereafter. In 1866 he wrote to Swinburne on May 22, "I go to Scotland today on the 5 o'clock train." A week later Christina and Mrs. Scott arrived.

Situated a few miles inland from the coastal town of Girvan on the Firth of Clyde, past the winding road which skirts the Old Dailly churchyard, Penkill Castle is built on a hill overlooking the sea, high above Penquapple Glen. In this glen where during the summer Scott and Alice set up their easels and painted together, runs the stream celebrated by Gabriel in his poem, *The Stream's Secret,* of which the title, said Scott, was "grabbolozzied by D.G.R." from a poem of his own.

The rushing of these hidden waters and the soughing of the wind in the ancient trees are the only sounds to disturb or rather to blend into the rural stillness, what Scott once called "the absolute silence of the country after Chelsea." But the silence is relative, not absolute, for once the visitor accustoms himself to it, "sounds inaudible in London to the human sense begin to grow on the ear. The silence becomes animated with charming, soothing characteristic sounds, the air is filled with the hum of insects, the fine winnowing of small birds' wings, the rustle of a dress on the grass." The sun-warmed air, fresh with the moist woodland fragrance of running water, is in June additionally sweetened by the delicate, powdery scent of the first-blooming roses, mingled with alyssum and the more overpowering perfume of the aggressive honeysuckle.

"You are not badly off," Christina wrote William, who was then visiting Naples, "if you are only in country as fine as this." Wherever she looked, her eye met green grassland, gently sloping hillside meadows where cattle and sheep grazed, or the stretches of rich farmland which supplied the Penkill table. In the distance she could see the rooftops and

church spires of Girvan, and beyond them the open sea, with the conical rock of Ailsa Crag jutting out on the horizon like a huge mountain.

The castle itself, seen from afar as a brown, indigenous mound, looked as though it had always been there, and indeed, it had lasted through storms and blasts for over four centuries. The original medieval structure, a peel or square tower of four stories, with thick walls and corner turrets equipped for defense, had been added to according to their tastes by successive Boyds. Abandoned in the eighteenth century, the castle fell into decay—becoming one of the picturesque ruins dear to the Augustan heart—until its restoration in the nineteenth century by Spencer Boyd, Alice's brother. It was he who built the new round stone tower adjacent to the square one, glazed the windows, added a wing, and constructed the famous winding stone staircase to replace the old spiral stairway of feudal days.

In former times when Scotch noblemen had been desperadoes and outlaws, the Boyds, who rustled cattle from their neighbors, smuggled rum, or fled Cromwell's men in the Civil War, entered their stronghold by climbing up a ladder to the second story and crawling in through a tiny, squat door built deep inside the tower wall, and then pulling the ladder up after them. Their neighbors' cattle they hid in the small, dark, dungeon-like chamber leading off the central hall, used by Alice's housekeeper as a storehouse for her jams, jellies, and preserves.

Christina's first glimpse of the interior of the castle was through the heavy oak door studded with iron nails which swung slowly open to admit her. As she exchanged greetings with her hostess and Scott, she could have observed over the entrance the carved coat of arms of the Earl of Kilmarnock, who was beheaded in the Tower for supporting the Stuart Pretender in 1745. Opposite the door hung a medieval suit of armor, another reminder of the family's ancient heritage.

"Miss Boyd makes me very welcome and comfortable," she wrote William, once she was unpacked and settled, "and the Scotts don't need comment from me." As to quarters, "I suspect I exceed you, inhabiting as I do an apartment like the best bedroom in Tudor House on a large scale." This could have been the luxurious Laird's bedroom off the first landing, or more probably, the spacious guest apartment over it, which with its carved black oak fireplace and massive chests, its recessed windows hung with crimson velvet curtains, and its hand-embroidered canopy over the carved four-poster would have impressed her as no less splendid. In fact, she found it disturbingly so, for she had not been at Penkill long before she moved up to the top-story bedroom in the square tower, formerly the Ladies' Bower. "Ailsa Crag," she continued, "is a wonderfully poetic object continually in sight. Of small fry, jackdraws perch near the windows, and rabbits parade in full view of the house. The glen is lovely. And to crown all, we are having pleasant mild summer."

This statement is nothing if not noncommittal. And yet she was never again in her life to experience an emotional climate which so nearly approached that of "pleasant mild summer" as those June weeks at Penkill. Evidently Scott and Alice agreed beforehand to do all within their power to make her visit memorable. This meant some self-effacement on Alice's part and considerable attentiveness on Scott's. With Alice's permission, then, he exerted himself to be as cordial, as tender and charming, to Christina as propriety would allow.

That summer he was just beginning to paint the murals for the great circular stone staircase recently completed. He took as his subject the medieval poem, *The King's Quair,* and shortly after Christina's arrival, he asked her to pose for Lady Jane, the heroine of the courtly romance, whom King James I loves and sighs for during his captivity at Windsor. Nothing could have been designed to give Christina greater pleasure than this congenial occupation as Scott's model, one which required her to spend a good portion of each day in his company and enabled her to enjoy that comradely intimacy which is so frequently the outgrowth of working hours shared.

She appears in several of the murals as Lady Jane. In one she is the slim and graceful central figure in the foreground of the Court of Venus, standing hand outstretched, head drooping, before the seated figures near the fountain. In another she is the winsome figure half in profile, dreaming in the garden, attended by her ladies and unaware of the winged angel who kneels to one side of her. Her likeness may still be detected through the flaking of the oil pigments which Scott tried to make enduring through the use of encaustic. However, the chill damp of the stone walls which never dry has caused the first of these frescoes to deteriorate more rapidly than some of the others more fortunately placed. The portraits higher up the staircase of Alice as Minerva and of Scott himself as a blue-eyed courtier in the foreground are better preserved.

Although, as William once put it, "No Rossetti ever indulged in verbal fireworks in letter-writing," Christina's happiness shines through the reserve of her cautiously worded letters. Comparing Penkill to Naples, where William was, she wrote Anne Gilchrist that not even "the glories and beauties of most beautiful Naples" could match the "quiet fertile comeliness of Penkill" at the close of day. "And when beyond the immediate greenness, a gorgeous sunset glorifies the sea distance, one scarcely need desire aught more exquisite in the world."

We also learn from her letters that she was being congratulated on her "looks and *fat.*" This probably means that she was once again receiving from Scott the compliments she had missed upon her return from Hastings in 1865. Undoubtedly Penkill, and not Hastings or even Italy, offered the kind of restorative treatment her health needed.

To complete her abundance even literary success was not lacking. The

long-delayed publication of *Prince's Progress* finally took place the first week in June. "This morning," she wrote William on June 4, *"Pr Pr* actually came to breakfast—blemished to my sorrow, by perhaps the worst misprint of all left uncorrected." This was the punctuation error mentioned by Gabriel in his letter to Macmillan of December 3, 1865, an error which occurring "in a very beautiful poem [*Songs in a Cornfield*] is well worth a cancel in my opinion." [1]

Nerving herself to face the inevitable reviews, she told Mrs. Gilchrist with a touch of irony that she was glad her health had become "so very tolerable that I may be all the braver to undergo the lash." She need not have been anxious, for on the whole the reviews were favorable. Those appearing in *The Saturday Review* and *The Athenæum* are typical, however, of the brand of unprofitable criticism in which Victorian reviewers occasionally indulged. Whereas *The Saturday Review* pronounced "Miss Rossetti's poems . . . of the kind which recall Shelley's definition of poetry as 'a record of the best and happiest moments of the best and happiest minds,'" *The Athenæum* regretted "that the tone of Miss Rossetti's poetry—always, be it remembered, religiously submissive—should be that of the dirge rather than that of the anthem." [2]

Although the sole poem we can be sure she wrote at Penkill is not a dirge, neither is it an anthem nor a record of her best and happiest moments. Dated June 11, 1866, it is chiefly notable as the last of her precisely dated poems, the final entry in her series of seventeen black notebooks. *Song* (*What Comes?* in MS.) is a somber little piece quite different in spirit from the animated gaiety of her letters. Even this mild pleasant summer of Penkill was not without dark, rain-filled clouds. Obviously not all Scott's beaming compliments and attentions could conceal from her the unhappy reality of her position at Penkill, a reality obliquely acknowledged in *Song:*

Oh what comes over the sea
Shoals and quicksands past;
And what comes home to me,
Sailing slow, sailing fast?

A wind comes over the sea
With a moan in its blast;
But nothing comes home to me,
Sailing slow, sailing fast.

II

Very likely another poem bearing only the general 1866 dateline was written at Penkill that summer. Entitled *Verses to W. B. Scott dos-à-dos,* it is one of the two poems Christina addressed openly to Scott. No longer extant, it is the only poem she wrote after 1859 that William omitted from both the *New Poems* and the *Works.*[3] He may have decided not to

publish it either because it was not a good poem or—and this is more probable—he thought it too personal to appear in print.

The phrase *dos-à-dos* could be taken as Christina's acknowledgment that it was with Alice, and not with her, that Scott was to be paired (though it could also be interpreted in the contrary sense). Despite the fact that she was living under the same roof with him and seeing him daily, they obviously did not share a life together, as they had at Newcastle. If Scott shared a life with anyone, it was with Alice. And at Penkill, as in London, Christina continued to lead her usual life of withdrawn solitude, a life she once stigmatized as "the one besetting trial of man," a trial "how keen and how unsuited to our constitution" could not be imagined by any who had not experienced it.

In *Time Flies*[4] we are given an insight into the details and solitary satisfactions of such a life:

> Once in Scotland, while staying at a hospitable friend's castle, I observed, crossing the floor of my bedroom, a rural insect. I will call it, though I daresay it was not one in strictness, a pill millepede.
>
> Towards my co-tenant I felt a sort of good will not inconsistent with an impulse to eject it through the window.
>
> I stooped and took it up, when in a moment a swarm of baby millepedes occupied my hand in their parent's company.
>
> Surprised, but resolute, I hurried on, and carried out my scheme successfully; observing the juniors retire into cracks outside the window as adroitly as if they had been centenarians.

Further on, she speaks of "that self-same bedchamber" where she would "answer matutinal taps," supposing herself called, "and lo! it was only a tapping of jackdaws or of starlings lodged in the turrets."

It is the lot of the lonely to answer imaginary matutinal taps. But Christina knew that Scott was in the habit of waking up very early of a summer morning and prowling restlessly around the house to find a readable book he could take back to bed with him. He has described such mornings in both prose and verse:

Vaguely at dawn within the temperate clime
Of glimmering half-sleep, in this chamber high,
I heard the jackdaws in their loopholes nigh,
Fitfully stir: as yet it scarce was time
Of dawning, but the nestlings' hungry chime
Awoke me, and the old birds soon had flown;
Then was a perfect lull, and I went down
Into deep slumber beneath dreams or rhyme.

But suddenly renewed, the clamouring grows,
The callow beaklings clamouring every one,
The grey-heads had returned with worm and fly;
I looked up and the room was like a rose,
Above the hill-top was the brave young sun,
The world was still as in an ecstasy.

On one such morning, said Scott with a painter's appreciation of nature,

> the landscape was as still as the house within. The sky was white, the sun unspeakably white, making the shadows of the trees faintly chequer the smooth green terrace. On the point of one of the leaves of a great aloe below, perched a thrush, silent and motionless; two wild rabbits were sitting on the green terrace still as if they were carved in stone. In the clear air every leaf on every tree had an individuality, and every pebble on the walk, as if shade and even colour were defects of nature, yet there was a luminosity at that hour that gave a peculiar unity to the whole scene.

It is unlikely, however, that he summoned Christina to enjoy such fresh beauties of early morning with him. He might have done so once, at Newcastle. But the time for that had passed. Engrossed now in his own sensibilities and freed by his satisfying relationship with Alice from that tormenting dependence upon another's moves to which Christina was still subject, he had little need of her. If she had been expecting "matutinal taps," probably they never came.

The turret apartment at the top of the square tower is still referred to at Penkill as "Christina's room." It is also known as "the Windy Room," for in winter the coastal gales whistle and howl around the former bower room, the walls of which Alice had appropriately decorated with a pattern of wind-swept leaves. In the seventeenth century it had been a bridal chamber, but in the summer of 1866 it was a lonely celibate's refuge.

From the old-fashioned garden below, Christina was often seen standing in front of the little four-cornered window which, Arthur Hughes tells us, "exactly framed her." Her habitual position was to lean forward, "elbows on the sill, hands supporting her face," and she could be seen for hours "meditating and composing."

But she could see as well as be seen. Her room commanded a view of the garden with its sundial, moss-covered stone benches, and lattice arbors overarched by roses, of the dark leafy depths of the glen, of Girvan stretching out into the distance, and further, beyond the town, the sea and Ailsa Crag. "Doves at windows," she observed, "command a much wider horizon than moles on hillocks, whilst a mole who takes his ease or grubs inside a hillock, what chance has he for seeing?"

One recalls the mole of *A Sketch* and the tardy Prince who enjoyed "taking his ease on cushion and mat." In a letter to Miss Losh, Alice's aunt, Gabriel described Scott at Penkill as "a double-distilled drone," who nevertheless managed to complete his biography of Dürer. "He seems in composing it to have been seized every now and then with his constitutional somnolence but to have gone on writing all the same." Al-

though Scott remained productive in both art and literature almost to the end of his life, his indolence increased with advancing years.

III

But without such a relaxed attitude, Scott might have found his position that summer too strenuous for enjoyment. It would have required all his tact and all his skill at "holding half a dozen lines without allowing them to tangle" in order to control a situation so delicate and precariously balanced as the one in which he found himself. It is true that the four who made up the Penkill house party were all highly civilized people, but even at that, Scott was a man living in a house with three women who loved him. Mrs. Scott, a shadowy figure in the background (neighborhood gossip had it that she hated Penkill), claimed no possessive rights, and Alice, Scott insists, was without jealousy. But what of Christina?

At one time, in the winter of 1862–1863, ripples of jealousy had occasionally ruffled the surface of her poetry. But at Penkill she was Alice's guest, and she had gone there knowing what she had to expect. The warmth of her eulogy of Alice to Mrs. Gilchrist does not show any tinge of jealousy toward this erstwhile "Queen of Hearts." Miss Boyd, she wrote, her "dear hostess at Penkill Castle . . . might charm you if you knew her. Perhaps she is the prettiest handsome woman I ever met, both styles being combined in her fine face." And to F. S. Ellis, the publisher, she described Alice in 1870 as "a very special friend of mine."

Was she, then, altogether free from jealousy?

In writing *Prince's Progress* the year before, she had managed to minimize the importance of the second woman who detains the royal lover, regarding her as a hazard only slightly more serious than the alluring milkmaid. But such an attitude would no longer have corresponded to Christina's grasp of reality in 1866. At Penkill she could not blind herself to Alice's importance in Scott's life. He once said that in his "perfect friendship" with Alice not a misunderstood word or wish ever divided them. In many ways, theirs was an ideal relationship.

As several years earlier the beauty of a pair of matched antique vases in Mrs. Virtue Tebbs' drawing room had suggested to Christina the reciprocal radiance of sexual love, so a seashell, possibly picked up at Girvan, symbolized for her the potentialities inherent in the kind of ideal union she saw before her daily. Such a union was like "a most exquisite shell, composed of two halves, which joined together make up one flawless heart":

> Each separate half is beautiful, shaded with darker and lighter rose tints, worked in grooves and curves, and finished with a notched edge. Yet each by itself remains obviously imperfect and purposeless.

> Join them together and notch fits into notch; each brings out, proves, achieves, the perfection of the other.
>
> Does such an illustration seem to excel and shame the possibilities of even the highest and purest human love?

Another time she expressed the same idea more starkly and simply: "Where two bodies touch, the dividing line is imaginary."

Are we, then, to suppose that she ceased to struggle, and that bowing to the inevitable she surrendered Scott to Alice without further protest?

We have seen that for a number of years she had been consoling herself with the prospect of reunion in eternity. In another, a more perfect, life, unflawed by the flux and change and grief of this one, she counted upon the eternal meeting unmarred by partings. The thematic chord of reunion in paradise had been struck again and again, in poem after poem, and it was to swell to a full crescendo in the *Monna Innominata* sonnet sequence and the Italian love poems. But even this consolation was ultimately to be denied her. And it was at Penkill that summer that her faith in the possibility of such reunions was initially undermined.

For the inescapable fact that Scott loved Alice, not lightly but deeply and fully, must have brought Christina to the consideration that, if there were to be reunions of loved ones after death, Scott would have to be joined to Alice Boyd, the woman he loved and who was in all but name his wife, and not to Christina.

But such a stern concession to reality did not come about all at once. As the poems of the next ten years testify, Christina resisted the truth stubbornly, refused to acknowledge it, struggled with all the energy at her command to preserve the illusory hope. An army in retreat, she nevertheless fought valiantly to defend each position she was forced to fall back upon. The record of this strange battle is found in the *Monna Innominata* sonnet sequence and the *Il Rosseggiar dell' Oriente.*

IV

Although in a sonnet sequence external facts do not always correspond to emotional attitudes, we may assume that the *Monna Innominata* sequence is in the main a subjective expression of emotion rather than an exercise of the literary imagination in the form of a recognized poetic convention. In this assumption we would be supported by William, who repeatedly stated that his sister's love sonnets were inspired by a real and not an imaginary person.

Christina, conversely, wished to conceal the personal reference, and therefore provided a prose foreword for the sequence which would place the sonnets in a medieval rather than a contemporary frame. One would expect William to protect his sister's attempt at anonymity; instead, he exposes her stratagem with what seems like undue emphasis:

> To anyone to whom it was granted to be behind the scenes of Christina Rossetti's life, and to how few this was granted—it is not merely probable but certain that this 'sonnet of sonnets' was a personal utterance—an intensely personal one. The introductory prose-note about 'many a lady sharing her lover's poetic aptitude,' etc. is a blind—not an untruthful blind, for it alleges nothing that is not reasonable and on the surface, correct, but still a blind interposed to draw attention from the writer in her proper person.

It is, he continues, "indisputable that the real veritable speaker in these sonnets is Christina herself, giving expression to her love for Charles Cayley."

What could have been the motive behind William's uncharacteristic eagerness to instruct Christina's reading public about her love affairs? The answer is obvious. Far from exposing his sister, as appears at first glance, William as usual was actually shielding her. Upon their publication in 1881 the sonnets gave rise to a speculative curiosity which increased over the years, and in order to spike the accumulating gossip, William finally attached the sonnets to the name of a respectable suitor.

It may be seen that Christina was not the only Rossetti adept at producing masks. For this one William would have had a traditional precedent in Dante's *La Vita Nuova,* which Gabriel translated. In that work Dante tells us that he screened his love for Beatrice from the gossiping world by pretending to be in love with a different lady.

But in addition to serving as a mask or a "screen for the truth" (Gabriel's translation of Dante's phrase), Christina's prose foreword, the mask behind the mask, as it were, has another function, one which attaches the sonnet sequence firmly to the contemporary world of existing reality by inviting comparison of the sonnets to Mrs. Browning's *Sonnets from the Portuguese.* If Elizabeth Barrett Browning had had an unhappy instead of a happy love, Christina suggests, she might have written genuine poetry springing from deep feeling rather than literary poetry resulting from cultivated art. The supposition is that Christina regarded her own work, rooted in strong feeling rather than in conventional literary attitudes, as the product of an unhappy love:

> Beatrice, immortalized by 'altissimo poeta . . . cotanto amante'; Laura, celebrated by a great though an inferior bard—have alike paid the exceptional penalty of exceptional honour, and have come down to us resplendent with charms, but (at least to my apprehension) scant of attractiveness.
>
> These heroines of world-wide fame were preceded by a bevy of unnamed ladies 'donne innominate' sung by a school of less conspicuous poets; and in that land and that period which gave simultaneous birth to Catholics, to Albigenses, and to Troubadours, one can imagine many a lady as sharing her lover's poetic aptitude, while the barrier between them might be one held sacred by both, yet not such as to render mutual love incompatible with mutual honour.

> Had such a lady spoken for herself, the portrait left us might have appeared more tender, if less dignified, than any drawn even by a devoted friend. Or had the Great Poetess of our own day and nation only been unhappy instead of happy, her circumstances would have invited her to bequeath to us, in lieu of the 'Portuguese Sonnets,' an inimitable 'donna innominata' drawn not from fancy but from feeling, and worthy to occupy a niche beside Beatrice and Laura.[5]

The reference to the barrier is frequently interpreted as an allusion to the religious difference that kept Christina from marrying Cayley. But if that is so, why did she go to the trouble of constructing the elaborate and ingeniously contrived frame of courtly love? In the troubadour poetry of courtly love the barrier which generally separated lovers was the marriage of one of the lovers to someone else. Such was the practical though not the emotional barrier which separated Dante from Beatrice and Petrarch from Laura. It was the kind of barrier which, though "held sacred by both," was "yet not such as to render mutual love incompatible with mutual honour."

V

Until June, 1866, Christina's manuscripts are all extant and dated. After that, "few precise dates are traceable." To all the undated or approximately dated poems written after the publication of *Prince's Progress* (1866) and before the publication of Christina's *Pageant* volume (1881), William affixes the dateline "Before 1882," explaining, however, that a poem so dated was not necessarily written shortly before 1882, but that it may have been written at any time between June, 1866, and April, 1881.

Although for this reason the *Monna Innominata* sonnets, which first appeared in the *Pageant* volume, cannot be dated with accuracy, and some were probably written in 1869–1870, as I intend to show, I believe the greater number of them were composed in the autumn and winter of 1866, and represent Christina's initial response to the Penkill experience.

We have noted that, although she was happy during her stay at the castle, she spent much of her time alone, "meditating and composing," and the one poem we know she wrote at Penkill has a tone of resigned sadness. Perceiving, as she was bound to do, the genuineness of Scott's and Alice's relationship, she would have been obliged to shift and readjust her own attitude, with the result that her conflict was brought into new focus. But the change seemingly took place slowly, in the deeper strata of her mind, and only gradually arose to surface recognition. Her first spontaneous response to the Penkill visit seems to have been a fresh resurgence of love.

If, before accepting Alice's invitation, she had thought it possible to

live under the same roof with a man she had loved for so many years without again responding to him, she must have soon recognized her error. Indeed, the sonnets themselves convey the impression that she wrote them in the first flush of renewed love. "Emotion melts so naturally into words," Dorothy Stuart observes, "that to read these poems is like listening to the secret rhythms of the heart."

Like the linked poems, these sonnets by reason of the poet's strongly expressed wish require consideration as a group rather than as single units. In requesting that a poem which formed part of a series or group be reprinted in its "entirety" and not extracted and reproduced out of its own context, Christina explicitly mentioned the *Monna Innominata* sonnets.[6]

In the first sonnet she takes up again the recurrent theme of parting and meeting, a perennial lament in her love poetry. But here the separation is one of days rather than months or years, as in some of the earlier poems. There are regular meetings, widely spaced though they may appear to the unsatisfied craving of greedy love:

> Come back to me, who wait and watch for you:—
> Or come not yet, for it is over then,
> And long it is before you come again,
> So far between my pleasures are and few.
> While, when you come not, what I do I do
> Thinking 'Now when he comes,' my sweetest 'when:'
> For one man is my world of all the men
> This wide world holds; O love, my world is you.
> Howbeit, to meet you grows almost a pang
> Because the pang of parting comes so soon;
> My hope hangs waning, waxing, like a moon
> Between the heavenly days on which we meet:
> Ah me, but where are now the songs I sang
> When life was sweet because you called them sweet?

The last two lines suggest that the speaker was by no means indifferent to her lover's admiration of her work and that his praise in fact stimulated poetic productivity.

The second sonnet, reaching back into the unrecorded past, seeks to fix in time the genesis of love:

> I wish I could remember that first day,
> First hour, first moment of your meeting me,
> If bright or dim the season, it might be
> Summer or Winter for aught I can say;
> So unrecorded did it slip away,
> So blind was I to see and to foresee,
> So dull to mark the budding of my tree
> That would not blossom yet for many a May.
> If only I could recollect it, such
> A day of days! I let it come and go

As traceless as a thaw of bygone snow;
It seemed to mean so little, meant so much;
If only now I could recall that touch,
First touch of hand in hand—Did one but know!

The fourth sonnet also deals with the remembrance of things past. If, taking some liberty with the printed arrangement of the sequence, we wish to follow the principle of emotional logic which unifies the individual sonnets into relevant autobiographical coherence, we may read the fourth before the third sonnet. Here, as in others of the poems, the concrete measurements of the sensible world are applied to something so intangible as a human relationship:

I loved you first: but afterwards your love
Outsoaring mine, sang such a loftier song
As drowned the friendly cooings of my dove.
Which owes the other most? my love was long,
And yours one moment seemed to wax more strong;
I loved and guessed at you, you construed me
And loved me for what might or might not be—
Nay, weights and measures do us both a wrong.

This concept of equity provides the framework for the development of the thought in the sestet: because unity is the whole force behind love, and its aim as well, love has its own special kind of equity:

For verily love knows not 'mine' or 'thine;'
With separate 'I' and 'thou' free love has done,
For one is both and both are one in love:
Rich love knows nought of 'thine that is not mine;'
Both have the strength and both the length thereof,
Both of us, of the love which makes us one.

But this noble conception of love, akin to that in Shakespeare's sonnets, remains but an ideal difficult to achieve on this earth. Not in real life, but only in dreams, are lovers so united. The third sonnet reveals that love such as Christina celebrates is still only the stuff of dreams:

I dream of you to wake: would that I might
Dream of you and not wake but slumber on;
Nor find with dreams the dear companion gone,
As Summer ended Summer birds take flight.
In happy dreams I hold you full in sight,
I blush again who waking look so wan;
Brighter than sunniest day that ever shone,
In happy dreams your smile makes day of night.
Thus only in a dream we give and take
The faith that maketh rich who take or give;
If thus to sleep is sweeter than to wake,
To die were surely sweeter than to live,
Though there be nothing new beneath the sun.

The dream image of the lover as companion probably had its roots in the Penkill experience. During that brief summer's happiness (to which the love dream is compared) Scott was a daily companion whom she saw not only at meals and in periods of relaxation but during his working hours as well; and of what other man in her life can this be said?

The ideality of love compared to its paltry realization in the actual world is again her theme in the seventh sonnet. Although the splendor and equity of human love are reaffirmed in the octave,

> 'Love me, for I love you'—and answer me,
> 'Love me, for I love you'—so shall we stand
> As happy equals in the flowering land
> Of love, that knows not a dividing sea.
> Love builds the house on rock and not on sand,
> Love laughs what while the winds rave desperately;
> And who hath found love's citadel unmanned?
> And who hath held in bonds love's liberty?

in the sestet we learn again that in the real world all is quite different. There fear, jealousy, the ache of separation cloud the glory:

> My heart's a coward though my words are brave—
> We meet so seldom, yet we surely part
> So often; there's a problem for your art!
> Still I find comfort in His book, who saith,
> Though Jealousy be cruel as the grave,
> And death be strong, yet love is strong as death.

The concluding lines give us an insight into the peculiar pathos and tension of Christina's situation at Penkill: love, never free to express itself fully except in dreams, must always contend with its death-dealing enemy, the jealousy which threatens its very existence.

The sixth sonnet is important for several reasons. First, it states Christina's attitude toward the relation of human to divine love. Second, it continues or resumes a discussion belonging to the past, but on a more profound and serious level than in the earlier poems. In replying to a lover who has reproached her for not placing him first, the speaker raises the old question of the choice treated in *Memory* and *Twice:*

> Trust me, I have not earned your dear rebuke,
> I love, as you would have me, God the most;
> Would lose not Him, but you, must one be lost,
> Nor with Lot's wife cast back a faithless look
> Unready to forego what I forsook;
> This say I, having counted up the cost,
> This, though I be the feeblest of God's host,
> The sorriest sheep Christ shepherds with His crook.
> Yet while I love my God the most, I deem
> That I can never love you overmuch;
> I love Him more, so let me love you too;
> Yea, as I apprehend it, love is such

I cannot love you if I love not Him,
I cannot love Him if I love not you.

If during the Penkill sittings Christina and Scott had discussed their relationship of years, perhaps even analyzing it, he might well have pointed out to her that it was she who in 1858 had rejected him, not he who had given her up. To this she could have replied that if so, it was not from lack of love. In the pages of *The Face of the Deep* she posed the question, "What is in truth my own ideal of love?" and gave the answer, "Such love, at once an affection and a mystery, would sacrifice not myself alone but the beloved object also to his . . . highest good." It is easy to understand that a conviction of this sort expressed to Scott could hardly have aroused his enthusiasm. A man who preferred the warmth and earthly comfort of companionship in this comfortable world was not likely to appreciate such a lofty conception of love, particularly if he found himself designated as the sacrificial object of it.

But that she found the struggle to choose God before the beloved a costly one is revealed in sonnets nine and twelve. With the nostalgic opening lines of the ninth,

Thinking of you, and all that was, and all
That might have been and now can never be,

the very core of her conflict is exposed, as weakness follows upon strength, discouragement upon firmness, sick regret upon resolution:

For woe is me who walk so apt to fall,
So apt to shrink afraid, so apt to flee,
Apt to lie down and die (ah, woe is me!)
Faithless and hopeless turning to the wall.

But as so often before, she is able to summon the spiritual toughness to turn defeat into triumph at the point of disaster:

And yet not hopeless quite nor faithless quite,
Because not loveless; love may toil all night,
But take at morning; wrestle till the break
Of day, but then wield power with God and man:—
So take I heart of grace as best I can,
Ready to spend and be spent for your sake.

The general statement in the last line takes on a crucial specificity in the twelfth sonnet:

If there be any one can take my place
And make you happy whom I grieve to grieve,
Think not that I can grudge it, but believe
I do commend you to that nobler grace,
That readier wit than mine, that sweeter face;
Yea, since your riches make me rich, conceive
I too am crowned, while bridal crowns I weave,

And thread the bridal dance with jocund pace.
For if I did not love you, it might be
That I should grudge you some one dear delight;
But since the heart is yours that was mine own,
Your pleasure is my pleasure, right my right,
Your honourable freedom makes me free,
And you companioned I am not alone.

Such, then, was the larger vision produced dialectically by the night's toil and struggle described so vividly in the ninth sonnet. In *Convent Threshold* and *From House to Home* there had also been wrestling in the night and the achievement of a solution, but on a less mature level. In the former a Blessed Damozel ascends to a golden Heaven alone, and yearns earthward toward an earthbound lover. In the latter a Christian sufferer, bereft of her lover, bleeds and drinks the bitter cup in solitary anguish, and then achieves sanctity in a Dantean Paradise enringed by the flames of impersonal love. In both these earlier poems the solution ignores the human lover. In soaring, Christina turns her back upon the earthly responsibilities of relationship which require action and decision here on this earth.

"Once loaded with the responsibility of life, we can never shift it off," she wrote in *Seek and Find*. And in sonnet twelve she faces such responsibility without shirking. "Rich love," the abstraction of the other sonnets, here becomes concrete, here is illustrated not in words but in the act, in the offering up of that most precious of all possessions, the gratification of the self.

But consistency is not to be expected in human behavior, and Christina could not always reach up to her highest grasp. Though in the twelfth sonnet she is able to identify herself with the beloved so completely that she can even rejoice in the happiness he finds with another woman, in the preceding sonnet, the eleventh, falling back to her old position, she makes it clear that she "foregoes" her love for this mortal life only, but that her claim extends beyond the grave into that infinitely more real existence of which (she learned from Plato) this one is but a pale shadow. She will give up the man she loves for the present but not for the future life:

Many in aftertimes will say of you
'He loved her'—while of me what will they say?
Not that I loved you more than just in play,
For fashion's sake as idle women do.
Even let them prate; who know not what we knew
Of love and parting in exceeding pain,
Of parting hopeless here to meet again,
Hopeless on earth, and heaven is out of view.
But by my heart of love laid bare to you,
My love that you can make not void nor vain,
Love that foregoes you but to claim anew

Beyond this passage of the gate of death,
I charge you at the Judgment make it plain
My love of you was life and not a breath.

This tendency toward *contemptu mundi* was a prevailing one in Christina's thought. Interpreting in a wider sense her father's feeling of exile from his native country, she looked upon herself as an impatient exile upon this earth. Spiritually she was coiled and tensed, ready at any moment the lever was released to spring and hurtle into eternity. Now if this existence is but a temporary as it is a temporal one, if it be but a brief segment of another stabler, more permanent state, then to relinquish dear joys temporarily is not to renounce them. In short, if the immortal and not the mortal life is the real one, it is not to give them up at all.

Therefore what in the twelfth sonnet appears as a selfless act of sacrifice is more in the nature of a practical bargain, like denying oneself a present luxury in the interests of future security. In staking her claim to her lover's immortal spirit, Christina agrees to give up all rights to and interest in his corporeal being. He may entertain himself in any way he chooses on this unsubstantial earth. In sonnet twelve the poet pictures his relationship with the other woman not as a serious attachment, but as one of "dear delight," of "pleasure." He has found a playmate, that is all, much as Christina's unprogressive prince found a new playmate in the maiden who rescued him from the floodwaters. Bridal crowns and bridal dances are but features of the amorous festival; they do not signify a solemn and serious joining of lives. For this reason, Christina is able to participate in the celebration, assured that for her is reserved the better part.

After the publication of the sonnets in her *Pageant* volume in 1881, she was gratified by Scott's praise of them. She told Gabriel that "Scotus sent me up a warm admiring word on 'Monna'" through his wife. This word of recognition meant much to her, acknowledging as it did the gift and offering of herself concealed in the sonnets. "We often hide what is deepest and dearest in us," she said in *The Face of the Deep,* "yet one friend has cognizance of it."

VI

William has persuaded generations of readers that this one friend was Cayley, who proposed shortly after Christina's return from Penkill, in September, 1866, and was promptly refused.

Admirers of Christina have always found it puzzling why, if she loved Cayley, she did not marry him. William offers two explanations. First, Cayley was incapable of supporting a wife. Second, his religious beliefs were unacceptable to Christina. The latter, according to William, weighed more heavily in the scale: "The ultimate decision rested upon religious

grounds alone. As in the previous case [the reference is to Collinson] she made the whole affair a matter of conscience, to be determined by considerations of religious faith."

But whereas Collinson was Roman Catholic, Cayley was Anglican. Even if he tended in his thinking toward the Broad Church liberalism of the day, he remained within the Establishment. Furthermore, Christina herself was anything but a rigid dogmatist. She was quite accustomed to religious heterodoxy in her own family. Her revered mother, though a stricter Anglican than she, had married a Roman Catholic, as had her grandmother, Anna Louise Pierce. The two brothers she loved were agnostics. In three of her poems (*Home by Different Ways, Jerusalem Is Built of Gold,* and *Slain in Their High Places*) she expressed views of broad-minded toleration of religious differences. In *The Face of the Deep* she was even more explicit:

> Cannot we—I at least can learn much from the devotion of Catholic Rome, the immutability of Catholic Greece, the philanthropic piety of Quakerism, the zeal of many a 'protestant.' And when the Anglican Church has acquired and reduced to practice each virtue from every such source, holding fast meanwhile to her own goodly heritage of gifts and graces, then may those others likewise learn much from her: until to every Church, congregation, soul, God be All in all.

Is it likely that a woman who held these views would have refused to marry a man she loved because his belief in all its details was not the same as her own?

In discussing her earlier rejection of Collinson, William conceded that her religious convictions were not arbitrary enough "to make marriage with a Roman Catholic, in itself, distasteful to her, or contrary to her sense of duty." How much less, then, would she have regarded religious differences within the Established church as a reason sufficient to prevent marriage with a man she loved. If Cayley's religious liberalism had been the only obstacle, conceivably she might have hoped to open his mind to her own light.

Upon Cayley's declaring himself, says William, "she must no doubt have probed his faith, and found it either strictly wrong or woefully defective. So she declined his suit, but without ceasing to see and cherish him as a friend."

For an explanation of human conduct in terms of rigorous cause and effect, nothing could be simpler. No slow, ambiguous, vacillating movements here. No losing and gaining of ground. No puzzling incompleteness such as we find in real life. This cut-and-dried version of human behavior not only eliminates dynamic process but also fails to explain much of the poetry we have been examining, poetry covering a spread of at least sixteen years.

The last part of William's statement, that Christina continued to see

Cayley and to cherish him as a friend, is true. The older she became, the more she cherished him. If in 1860–1861 he had inspired verses such as *No, Thank You, John* and *Promises Like Piecrusts,* or even in 1864 *Jessie Cameron,* he was undoubtedly held in higher esteem by 1866. His steady and undemanding devotion evoked gratitude, if not love. Christina was thirty-six now, almost past the age for conventional courtship, and she found it comforting to have on hand a suitor whose affection and admiration for her never faltered.

Although her letter of September 11 to William does not tell us why she refused Cayley, it supplies a few clues. She wrote it in reply to William's generous offer to support her husband and her in the event of a marriage. It is an unusually emotional letter for Christina (who generally expressed emotion in poetry, not letter writing), but a good deal of the emotion is due to her realization of the brotherly sacrifice William was prepared to make for her. She knew that he was not earning enough to support two families. What his offer meant was that he was willing to give up marriage and children for himself in order to make them possible for her.

DEAR WILLIAM

I am writing as I walk along the road with a party.

I can't tell you what I feel at your most more than brotherly letter. Of course I am not *merely* the happier for what has occurred, but I gain much in knowing how much I am loved beyond my deserts. As to money, I might be selfish enough to wish that were the only bar, but you see from my point of view it is not. Now I am at least unselfish enough altogether to deprecate seeing C. B. C. continually (with nothing but mere feeling to offer) to his hamper and discomfort: but, if he likes to see me, God knows I like to see him, and any kindness you will show him will only be additional kindness loaded on me.

I prefer writing before we meet, though you're not very formidable.

Apparently she did not consider Cayley's economic inadequacy a good reason for not marrying him. On the contrary, she wished she could have looked upon his lack of money as the only bar. If this remark appears ambiguous, that is because we are not looking at Christina's situation through her eyes. An offer had been made to her. It was an invitation to the normal domestic happiness which as a woman she by no means undervalued. It meant the possibility of children. She may have felt, and with good reason, that Cayley's proposal would be her last chance at matrimony. No wonder she wished that no bar at all existed, or that it could have been such a mildly practical one as the lack of money.

But we have seen that the religious bar, if there was one, also could not have provided a strong enough motive for her refusal, had she loved Cayley. The most plausible explanation of the existing bar is that it was a preceding commitment. She did not feel free to bestow her love for the simple reason that it was already given to another man. Her heart was

engaged, not temporarily, as she herself assures us, but beyond this life, for eternity.

And in order to follow her reasoning further and understand why she thought it selfish to continue seeing Cayley "with nothing but mere feeling to offer," we should remember that she was convinced, as she wrote in the fifth *Monna Innominata* sonnet and elsewhere, that "woman is the helpmeet made for man." If this is true, then in return for a man's full love, much more is required of a woman than "mere feeling." What is required of her, if she is to meet love with love, is responsibility for the shared life. But this was the kind of responsibility she felt she could not assume in her relationship with Cayley. Not loving him wholly and fully, without reservations, she did not feel capable of being his helpmeet; hence, she could not be his wife.

VII

For these reasons the "bar" to her marriage with Cayley was not unrelated to the "barrier" which could separate a *donna innominata* with poetic aptitude, whether of the thirteenth or the nineteenth century, from the man she loved. An existing wife was indeed a formidable "barrier" that not all the feeling in the world could wish away. And a woman who was convinced that in the sexual relationship the feminine role was that of helpmeet and not that of mistress would not be likely to indulge in a passionate affair for its own sake. Even before Alice's appearance, the barrier of a wife had prohibited Christina from assuming the role that Alice later gladly filled.

And yet, as she knew, feeling could not be turned on and off like a faucet. It did not even have the opportunity to dribble away and evaporate through prolonged separation. The expedient of absence, which she had tried, had provided only a temporary remedy, not a permanent cure. The difficulty of her position is that she was forced into constant contact with Scott because of his close friendship with her brothers and his own wish to be regarded as an intimate of the Rossetti family circle. There was no escaping him. Wherever she went between 1866 and 1870, she was sure to meet him.

A glance at William's diary discloses how intimately Scott lived with the Rossetti brothers during these years. William records dining with Scott, visiting Scott and being visited by him, chatting with Scott about Shelley, whose works William was then editing, and gossiping with him at Tudor House about Ruskin's infatuation with Rose la Touche or Whistler's expulsion from the Burlington Club. Constant references to him are to be found in Gabriel's letters of the period. In one, an undated letter to his mother, Gabriel invites her and Christina to dine with him at seven on Saturday:

*. . . Come at 6 (when I send my model away) or as much sooner as you like, since you can spend the interval very agreeably in the garden which is jollier and jollier.

The Scotts are coming, so do not miss doing so also if you possibly can.* [7]

Was the last bit of information intended for Christina? One wonders how much Gabriel knew about his sister's inner life and suspects that he knew a great deal, more perhaps than William. A perceptive man, with the poet's chameleon-like sensitivity to the hidden life of others, possibly he understood Christina's need and offered her this opportunity to meet the "one man" who "of all the men this wide world holds" possessed the power to give her the maximum of pleasure and of pain.

These were the years she resumed writing her Italian love lyrics, the *Il Rosseggiar dell' Oriente* series, which she had begun in 1862 and dropped in 1864. The series, recommencing in January, 1867, and concluding August, 1868, was not intended for publication. In order to ensure privacy, she wrote the poems in a foreign language and locked them away secretly in her desk, where William stumbled upon them after her death and published them.

❋ 12 ❋

"THOU WHOLE BURNT-OFFERING"

1867–1870

Although Christina was seeing a good deal of Scott during the late 'sixties, the Italian poems suggest that their real meetings still took place only in the imaginary world of her fantasy. The social encounters in the world of actuality undoubtedly fed the flames and probably provided the incentive for the writing of the Italian poems, but in no sense did these conventional meetings offer the opportunity for a shared emotional relationship. And so Christina's passion flourished and dug its deep roots in that subsoil which also nourished her poetry.

The first two poems of the Italian series, *Amor Dormente?* and *Amor Si Sveglia?* were written in the winter of 1862–1863. The third, undated in manuscript, is a slight and rather unimportant piece. The fourth, with which the series recommences, is called *Blumine Risponde.* Blumen, it will be remembered, is the name of the woman beloved by Carlyle's Teufelsdröckh in *Sartor Resartus.*[1] In this lyric Christina returns to the theme of reunion in Paradise, the problem which engrossed her in the English sonnets. One day, she hopes, she will again meet her lover in the *eterna Pace,* which then would offer no longer peace but delight. Yet if she should meet him in the cursed circle, she would grieve more for him than for herself. By the cursed circle she probably means the second circle in the Inferno, where lovers are tempest-blown. Although her goal is not sexual union on this earth but spiritual reunion in eternity, nevertheless it is on this earth that she suffers:

> For you my life lies half-dead,
> For you I stay awake nights,
> And I dampen the bed with tears.

The theme appears again in the very title of the fifth lyric, *"Lassù fia caro il riverderci"* ("Up There It Will Be Sweet to See Each Other"), also written in January. In the opening lines the paradox of the be-

loved friend, both "lost and not lost," suggests the phrasing "my lost and found" in *Meeting,* written the year Scott returned to London:

> Sweet heart of mine lost and not lost
> Sweet life of mine who leaves me in death,
> Friend and more than friend, I salute you.
> Remember me; for blind and short
> Were my hopes, but they were yours.
> Do not scorn this harsh fate of mine.
> Let me say it, 'His hopes
> Like mine languished this winter'—
> Yet I will resign myself, that which was was.
> Let me say it again, 'With him I discern
> The day that is born of frozen eve,
> A long heaven beyond a short hell,
> Beyond winter, spring.

The man who scorns her "harsh fate" in this poem is presumably the one who administers the "dear rebuke" in the sixth *Monna Innominata* sonnet. Possibly at Penkill Scott criticized Christina's ascetic way of life, which to him would have appeared a very harsh fate indeed.

As emotional autobiography, one of the most interesting of the series is the *Iddio C'Illumini* ("God Enlighten Us") of March. Longer than the others, it contains one of Christina's few direct references to a guilty love and also another admission of jealousy. Furthermore, it sounds a new note, one to be frequently repeated as the years pass: the religious concern for the lover's salvation:

> When the time comes for us to depart
> Each taking his separate road,
> A moment will come, the final moment
> Whenever that may be:
>
> The one treading an unknown track,
> The other following his wonted path,
> Let no shame be born on our faces then
> Nor within our breast remorse.
>
> Be it that you go first quite alone,
> Or be it that I precede you on that path,
> Let us remember that we have spoken
> The truth always.

The difficulty of associating such lines with Cayley is manifest. Why would Christina exhort him to feel no guilt at the final moment? Nothing in their decorous relationship even remotely suggests a cause for shame or remorse. But such an exhortation to Scott, with the full memory of years behind it, has a poignant appropriateness. Behind the verse are the weight and pressure of a complex relationship of decades:

How much I loved you, how much! And I should not
Have expressed the love that I felt for you:
More, much more than I told you
I loved you in my heart.

More of happiness, more of hope:
I do not speak of life that is of little worth:
Bitter-sweet you were in remembrance
To me jealous.

But to me you preferred virtue,
Truth, friend: and will you not know
Whom you loved in the end? Only the flower unfolds
At the sun's rays.

If more than me you loved the truth
Jesus was that unknown love of yours:—
Jesus, Who unknown spoke to him,
Conquer his heart.

Was it at Penkill that Christina told Scott she loved him? And upon that occasion, in contrast to an earlier one, did he give her the honest truth in exchange for her courage? If, as *Twice* implies, he had been taken by surprise in 1864 and in the place of the truth had offered evasions and lame excuses, at Penkill, where Christina came by his own wish, he would have been ready for her. And if she again "expressed the love" she felt for him, he might have thought it kinder in the long run to give her the truth she wanted—the truth that because of his existing attachment and her former rejection of him a love relationship between them was no longer possible.

For Christina the truth in any of its forms was always God. The Christian abstraction, God is Truth, was never abstract for her. It meant that even one weak in faith who adhered to truth was accessible to the religious influence. And for her, Love is Truth was the second premise leading to the inevitable conclusion.

"Yet now and then two who have differed—and two who differ cannot both hold the entire truth—have loved on faithfully, believing and hoping the best of each other . . . ," she wrote. "In such a case where both have loved the Truth and have accounted it 'great . . . and mighty above all things,' there surely remains a strong consolation of hope to flee unto. For can an utter alien from God love Truth and make sacrifices for Truth's sake?"

II

The movement of her mind can be followed in the two lyrics of April, as she seeks to make palatable the truth Scott had not spared her. Both treat the problem of the other woman. The sonnet *Non son io la rosa*

ma vi stetti appresso ("I Am Not the Rose But I Was Near It") is sixth in the series:

Happy house where many times by now
Sits my love speaking and also laughing.
Happy woman sitting by him,
Cheer him with what you do and say.
Happy garden where I strolled
Thinking of him, thinking and not speaking,—
Happy day when I betake myself
Where strolling I thought of him.
But if he be there when I return,
If he welcomes me with his sweet smile,
Every little bird will sing,
The rose will blush in her charming face:—
God give us that day in eternity,
May he give us for that garden paradise.

The happy house and the happy garden point to Penkill, and the happy woman to Alice Boyd. She is the rose with the charming face who adorns that garden. Whatever pain Christina may have experienced in Penkill has faded into oblivion, as pain will, and only the nostalgic memory of pleasure remains. Happiness is centered in that one house and that one garden where her beloved friend has found his own happiness.

The seventh poem, *Lassuso il caro Fiore* ("The Dear Flower Above"), continues in the same vein. The charming rose of the preceding sonnet is the dear flower of this piece, also written in April:

If God taught you
His own Love thus,
I would yield you, my heart,
To the dear Flower.
The dear Flower calls to you,
'Make me happy one day';—
The dear Flower who loves you
Asks you for love.

Although in the English sonnets the lover is likewise relinquished to the rival, limitations are set to the sacrifice. But in the remainder of the *Lassuso* Christina takes the next and much more difficult step, and gives up her lover to the other woman in the real and beautiful world to come as well as in this less satisfactory one:

That flower in paradise
Blooms for you still;
Yes, you will see again that face,
You will be happy.
Of the grief that has been
You will ask, 'Where is it?'
For the past will pass
In one moment.

And Christina? What may she expect in this Heaven of her own creating?

I, as a John the Baptist
Will praise God:
Your much beloved Love
Will be your reward,
And your saved soul
Mine.

The scriptural simile is a striking one, but it has a traditional precedent in *La Vita Nuova*. It will be recalled that in the twenty-fourth chapter Dante explains that another lady walks before his Beatrice by virtue only of her name, Joan, "taken from that John who went before his True Light. . . ."

In assigning the subsidiary role to herself in Heaven as well as on earth, Christina well knew what she was giving up. If we are inclined to feel that she was sacrificing a chimera, an impossible dream, we must realize that to her it was spiritual reality. For years she had been clinging to the hope of reunion in Paradise, and now she was required to relinquish that hope as well. And, she may have inquired, to what purpose?

The answer appears sporadically in both prose and poetry as the deepest and most serious statement of her life. In *The Face of the Deep:* "The gold which I offer Thee must be purified in the fire; fire of self-denial, of self-sacrifice, of love. . . ." In *Letter and Spirit:* ". . . Take heed to purify our hearts by love, as well as to cleanse our hands through fear; and not by a tepid love, but by a self-kindling, self-devouring love." In *An 'Immurata' Sister:*

Sparks fly upward, toward their fount of fire,
Kindling, flashing, hovering:—
Kindle, flash, my soul; mount higher and higher
Thou whole burnt-offering.

To such stern spirits their religion offers not soft consolation, but the heroic opportunity for total self-immolation.

III

After the spring of 1867 Christina wrote no more Italian poems until August. Earlier that year she had accepted an assignment from John Murray to translate from the Italian a work on brick architecture in Italy, and in April she received her remuneration of £21 from the publisher. She also received from Roberts Brothers, her American publishers, the sum of £38.10, which represented her 10 per cent share of the profit from the approximately 3000 copies of *Prince's Progress* sold in the United States the year following the end of the Civil War.

Fortunately, her financial ledger was not an accurate reflection of her literary reputation, which always outstripped her income. The journals

continued to praise her work, "a highly laudatory notice" appearing in *The Examiner* on October 6, 1866. The Reverend Dodgson's [2] friend, a Mr. Rivington, competed with Gabriel's aristocratic friends, Lady Waterford and Mrs. Boyle, for the privilege of illustrating her books. Several paintings inspired by her verses were on exhibition at the Dudley Gallery during February. She refused Elliot and Fry's request to photograph her for their famous women series; and so noted had she become that Elihu Burritt, known as the American "literary blacksmith," made her the object of a literary pilgrimage in August.

With the death in February, 1867, of Aunt Margaret Polidori, who for years had occupied an apartment in the Rossetti household, the family began to consider a change of residence. A good old soul with a tart temper, Aunt Margaret was remembered for her piety—she attended services at Christ Church twice a day—and for her fits of hysterical laughter. After her death, the house in Albany Street must have seemed strangely silent, so accustomed had its occupants become to hearing the spectral peals of her hyena-like laughter, which would suddenly ring out over the house and stop just as suddenly. Not until May would Mrs. Rossetti consent to move; finally, toward the end of June the family left Albany Street for their new home at 56 Euston Square, where Christina was to spend the next nine years of her life. "Miss C. Rossetti . . . calls attention to her change of address," she wrote Macmillan on July 1.

William was in Penkill during July. If Christina had been looking for another invitation that summer, none came. By August she was complaining in an Italian lyric that the bird of love, whose thorny nest was on a cold shore, was "faithful to the unfaithful." But the *Amicizia,* also written in August, reveals that she was viewing her problem from a slightly different perspective. Friendship, not as a substitute for love, but as a hidden expression of it, was possibly the solution:

Let friendship come and be welcome,
Let her come, but let not Love depart for this:
Both dwell in the gentle heart
Which refuses not shelter to pilgrims.
She a docile and accomplished handmaid,
And he no tyrant but a pious lord:
Let him reign hidden and not show himself outwardly,
Let her reveal herself in due humility.
To-day and also to-morrow for friendship,
And after to-morrow too if you wish,
For it brings sweet, not bitter things:
And then let there come, but not with moon or sun,
The day of love, day of great delight,
Day that dawns never again to set.

The last three lines nevertheless disclose her stubborn reluctance to accept the idea of total renunciation she had proposed to herself. They

show her still struggling, still groping for a less arbitrary way out of her predicament. Perhaps reunion in Paradise does not necessarily need to take place on a sexual basis. Possibly the matings in this life (the sun and moon) need not be perpetuated into eternity, but, on the contrary, friends may be allowed to look forward to being reunited with friends on that "day of love." In this way Christina's mind, no mean instrument, subtly attempted to work its way out of the logical dilemma in which she had trapped herself.

The concern for her lover's salvation expressed in the *Iddio* tends to become increasingly conspicuous in the later lyrics of the series. It may be partially accounted for by the appearance of a new spiritual influence in her life. It was through Scott that she met the Reverend Dr. Littledale, a noted High Church controversialist. William met him for the first time at Scott's dinner table September 5 and was surprised to find him a jovial Irishman with a broad brogue, fond of jokes and wit and much addicted to writing humorous verses to his friends. It was only after Christina was on terms of intimate friendship with him that she learned what the clergyman's good-humored sociability never revealed: he was a seriously sick and ailing man.

As Scott's close friend, Dr. Littledale was interested in his spiritual welfare, and this might have provided the favorable framework for the development of the friendship with Christina. As two fervent Christians who loved Scott, both were undoubtedly distressed by his agnosticism, which grew stronger as the years passed.

Perhaps at the September 5 dinner party Scott and the High Church clergyman might have debated the question of religious faith, for such debates were frequent and fashionable in the 1860's. If Scott had wanted to arouse his friend to battle ("my dear Reverend but humourous Dr. Littledale") and to display his polemical prowess for the intellectual entertainment of his dinner guests, he himself would have overstated and exaggerated his own position as a means of drawing out Littledale.

If Christina was present, she would have been grieved and dismayed at this plain evidence of Scott's spiritual darkness. Although she would have sat quietly by and said nothing—it was not her way to participate in such discussions—later at home she would have had recourse to prayer. Perhaps she unlocked the writing desk in which she secreted her Italian poems, and in the dark, quiet hours of the night wrote these lines which bear the September date line:

What shall I give Thee, my good Lord Jesus?
I will give Thee that which I love best:
Accept it, Jesus my Lord,
My only sweet love, nay my heart;
Accept it for Thine Own, may it be precious to Thee;
Accept it for my sake, save my spouse.
It is all I have, Lord, do not deprecate it.

IV

The thirteenth lyric, the *Finestra Mia Orientale,* opens with the lines,

> I turn my face toward the dawn,
> Toward the south, where he lives:—

The poem is marked "In Illness" ("In Mallattia"), and in it Christina expresses her hidden longing for the one healing presence denied her. Lonely and uncomforted, she cannot ask for that solace. Only in poetry, in lines she is confident no one will ever see, does she feel free to reveal a desire destined to expend itself in words—unsatisfactory substitute for the warming human contact of flesh with flesh:

> Weak and tired, I turn toward you:
> What can this be that I feel, friend?
> I gather every sweet memory of you,—
> How much I would tell you! and yet I say nothing.
> Through the long days I grieve for you:
> If we were only together in a fertile land!

"Fertile" or "fruitful" (*aprico*) approximates in translation the adjective Christina selected to describe Penkill in 1866: the "quiet fertile comeliness of Penkill." But to wish that she and her lover were together in a fruitful land holds an implication much deeper than a fleeting allusion to Penkill. Or rather, it contains both allusions, the lesser within the greater.

The *Finestra* was written in October. By February of the following year her illness had taken a turn for the worse. Dr. Jenner, her physician, told her she had congestion of one lung. She had been subject to pulmonary ailments more or less throughout her life, but, as we have seen, it was chiefly during periods of emotional stress that latent susceptibilities burgeoned into symptoms. Accumulating strain and tightening tension are evident in the Italian lyric she wrote in February while under Dr. Jenner's care:

> O slow bitter time!—
> When will you come, my heart,
> When, but when?
> Dear as you are to me
> If I were as dear to you,
> Would I go seeking you?

Nevertheless the title of this short piece, *Eppure Allora Venivi* ("And Yet Then You Came"), suggests that despite her sad impatience, she obtained her moments of gratification.

Per Preferenza of March consists of three stanzas which in manuscript Christina marked "Supposto" ("Supposed"), "Accertato" ("Ascertained"), and "Dedotto" ("Deducted"). "There must have been in her head some whimsical notion of logical sequence or what not," William observed, and

then, adding to the enigma, "I can understand it to some extent without discussing it."

As a pattern of emotional association if not logical sequence, the arrangement is not without a continuity of its own. In the first stanza Christina expresses envy of her lover's feminine relatives, the women who have the right to love him.

> Yet their advantage
> I should not want for myself

is her half-humorous conclusion. In the second she exults that at last the beloved man knows with certainty that she loves him. But she wishes she could see from time to time "that grave aspect" of his, a phrase peculiarly applicable to Scott, whom Carlyle called "a grave, earnest man" and George Henry Lewes "the grave and high-minded Scott."

In the third stanza she returns again to the theme of the *Amicizia*. Once more the two alternative and perhaps complementary solutions to her problem are proposed: friendship as an expression of love, and reunion in Paradise:

> This is still sweeter
> Than the other, it seems to me:
> Indeed I wish to be
> Either all or nothing to you; [1]
> Nor do I want to complain too much
> That we are separated now,
> If one day in Paradise
> You will rejoice with me.

By *this* is meant friendship, as distinct from love, the *other*. The statement of the first two lines, however, is contradicted by that in the next two. That Christina herself was aware of the ambiguity is evident from the footnote she attached to the fourth line, which further confuses rather than clarifies the issue:

> [1] But no, if not a lover, be my friend:
> What I will be to you I am not predicting.

Even more puzzling is the fact that the lyric concludes on the familiar note of hope abandoned in the *Lassuso*. But of course Christina was writing for herself, not for the critics, and she was interested not so much in imposing upon herself the requirement for logic and clarity as in adequately and for her own purpose expressing an attitude that in itself was far from clear. She was searching for a satisfactory solution to a crucial emotional problem, and one can detect the flash of her mind as it darts in pursuit, first in one direction and then in another.

V

In February the Rossettis gave an evening party which Browning attended, "looking," said William, "exceedingly well, and behaving most cordially and affably." A few weeks later the great man called again at Euston Square, this time talking with enthusiasm about his intelligent owl who kissed him "gently all over the face with its beak" and tweaked his hair. He reported with satisfaction that because of Swinburne's growing popularity, Tennyson's books were not selling so well.

If Christina was present, she might not have appreciated the jab at Tennyson, for whom she had great respect. In acknowledging payment for her poem *Mother Country,* which Macmillan published in his magazine that March, she told him she considered it "honorably formidable to appear in one no. with Tennyson." Her two poems sharing the May number with the Laureate's *Lucretius* were *A Smile and a Sigh* and *Dead Hope.*

That spring she and her mother paid a short visit to her uncle, Henry Polydore, in Cheltenham. Before leaving she wrote the following Italian lyric, which bears the March, 1868, dateline, and has the puzzling marginal note in Italian, *"Se fossi andata a Hastings":*

I say good-bye to you,
My friend,
For weeks
That seem long:
I recommend to you
From time to time
Square circles
Oblong ideas.

At first glance this odd little piece may appear obscure, but a relevant passage from her book *Time Flies* (published in 1885) gives a clue to the private symbolism:

> 'A square man in a round hole,'—we behold him incompatible, irreconcileable, a standing incongruity.
>
> This world is full of square men in round holes; of persons unsuited to their post, calling, circumstances.
>
> What is our square man to do? Clearly one of two things: he must either get out of his round hole, or else he must stay in it.
>
> If he can get out by any lawful exit, let him up and begone, and betake himself to a square habitat.
>
> But for one cubic man who can shift quarters, there may be a million who cannot.

What, then, she inquires, is the solution for the man who can neither escape from nor change his environment? "He can turn that very misfit into account by sitting loose among his surroundings," is her answer.

On the other hand, there is the plight of the round man in the square

hole. Such a one necessarily "abides cramped, dwarfed; he cannot expand evenly and harmoniously in all directions with perfect balance of parts. Wherever he expands he is liable to graze and get jammed against prison confines." Ought he, in that case, to feel comfortable? Or in modern terms, should he make the effort to adjust to his environment? It is the poet, society's perennial rebel, who gives the uncompromising reply:

> We do not expect a caged eagle to look comfortable. We rather expect him to exhibit noble indignant aspiration and the perpetual protest of baulked latent power.

The image of the caged eagle is a transparent one. But in a larger sense both the problems she raises in the passage are her own, and the several expedients she proposes are the alternative solutions to the practical problem of how to live in an unlivable world. Applied more specifically to her own emotional predicament, to sit loose among one's surroundings might be to accept friendship as love's expression or substitute. To exhibit "the perpetual protest of baulked latent power" might be to express through poetry a disdain of this life's frugal gifts, while keeping one's powerful wings in readiness for a flight into freer horizons.

At times, however, both solutions are apt to manifest a recalcitrance to reality. As some of the Italian poems, notably the *Lassuso,* display Christina's strength, others, like the short *Ripetizione* of June, reveal her weakness. This touching little piece shows a shrinking of horizons. The wings are stilled; the head is bowed; and one gigantic figure looms striding across the skyline:

> I thought I would see you again, and I am still waiting for you;
> From day to day I always long for you:
> When shall I see you again, my beloved heart,
> When but when?

VI

Although Alice had already left for Penkill, Scott remained in London during July, a month of what Gabriel called "murderous weather." Despite the wilting heat, probably both Scott and Christina were present at Ford Madox Brown's party the first week in July, which Christina had promised to attend "if well enough." Afterwards Gabriel described the affair in a letter to Alice: "Last Tuesday Brown gave a monster party to 120 friends and foes. It went off very well, however, people managing to amuse each other exactly according as they happened to be packed, making the most of the person next to them, like pickpockets at a hanging, till they got shoved on to someone else."

Brown's parties were noted for their lavishness and the occasional hilarious malapropisms of their host. There was no doubt, he once told his delighted guests, that Mary Queen of Scots "had a real feeling for Boswell." It is Lady Burne-Jones who has preserved this and other anecdotal gems

in Brown's collection. Her impressionistic recollection of these parties conjures up "a slender vision of Swinburne in evening dress"; Whistler "looking ten times more like a Frenchman than Legros"; Gabriel "in a magnificent mood . . . bringing pleasure to great and small by his beautiful urbanity, a prince among men"; and "Christina Rossetti, gently caustic of tongue."

The oppressive weather continued until the last week in July. Suddenly on the 24th the weather changed, and the coolness which brought Londoners relief from the sweltering heat was, said Gabriel, "a return to life." The day must have brought Christina a double return to life, for on that evening Scott and his wife dined at Euston Square.

Shortly thereafter, in August, she took up the Italian poems again, and the three she wrote that month close the series. In the sonnet *Amico e più che Amico* ("Friend and More than Friend"), she reaches a tentative but significant conclusion, the first fruit of her long conflict:

My Heart to whom turns my other heart
As a magnet to the pole, and fails to find you,
The birth of my new life
Took place with tears, with shouts and grief.[3]
But the bitter pain was for me the prelude
To gentle hope that sings and broods;
Yes, he who knows not sorrow does not experience love,
And he who fails to experience love does not live.
O you who are in God for me, but after God,
All my earth and enough of heaven,
Think if it is not a grief for me behind a veil
To speak and never tell you that I long for you:—
Say it to yourself, my sweet heart,
If you still love me tell yourself that I love you.

The reference to the veil hints again at the hidden reason that prevents her from speaking freely of her love. But behind all the disguises, the various masks and veils—that of a medieval *donna innominata* in the sonnets, a contemporary poetess in *L.E.L.,* and a Maturin heroine in *Look on This Picture*—is the unchanging identity of the face in the mirror, reflecting its own image through every disguise.

The twentieth Italian poem, likewise a sonnet, not only subordinates earthly to divine love, as in the *Amico,* but condemns earthly love as unsubstantial vanity:

Gentle wind that towards the south
Keeps blowing, carry please a sigh of mine,
Saying to One what I dare not say,
With a sigh tell him this:
She who said a 'No,' wishing a 'Yes'
(Wishing and not wishing—why say it again?)
She sends you word: It is vanity the flourishing
Of the life we lead here.

Hear what she says weeping: It is vanity
Which brings to birth and puts to death this earthly love;
Come raise your eyes, I want to raise them,
Toward the realm where not in vain
One loves God as much as one is able
And all creation in loving charity [*carità*].

Merely as a matter of geographical interest, Notting Hill, where Scott lived, and the South Kensington Museum, where he worked, are south of Euston Square. But the message sent southward to the lover is of less significance than Christina's comment in parentheses. *"Volendo e non volendo—a che ridir?"* epitomizes the very essence of her conflict, the tragic vacillation that pulled her in both directions at once and was responsible for creating the tension in both her life and her poetry, a tension which is reflected in the lean, stripped tautness of her verse at its best.

The last of the Italian poems reflects again this vacillation, and is in effect a retraction of the *Lassuso.* In the first of the two short stanzas she courageously acknowledges the truth, that truth she could have heard from Scott at Penkill. But looking at it directly, she cannot bear the sight of its hard, naked, ugly face, and so in the second stanza she retreats to her former position, the old familiar, comforting assurance of reunion in Paradise:

I loved you more than you loved me:—
Amen, if so wished God our Lord;
Amen, although my heart is breaking,
Lord Jesus.

But Thou Who recordeth and knoweth all,
Thou Who hast died through love,
In the other world give me that heart
I loved so much.

And so as the *Il Rosseggiar dell' Oriente* closes, we see Christina still fighting fiercely to claim in Heaven her lost happiness on earth.

VII

Scott in his essay on *The King's Quair* gives us a few relevant facts about the life of King James I, those bearing upon his composition of the poem, and concludes that "*The King's Quair* is autobiographic . . . as all our best poetry is, or ought to be." In the light of this remark one does not hesitate to attribute autobiographic significance to Scott's own series of sonnets he called *Parted Love* and eventually published in his *Poet's Harvest Home* volume of 1882. The Penkill manuscript notebooks (A8 and A9) show that he rewrote and changed the five sonnets in the series over and over again before publishing three of them. Unless an earlier version exists, they were originally written during 1868–1869, not

long after Christina wrote her Italian lyrics. The first is *Parted Love,* the title later given to the series,[4] and is dated Christmas eve, 1868:

*No cypress-wreath nor outward signs of grief:
But I may cry as in a dream, and flee
After the god whose back is turned to me,
And touch his wings and plead for some relief;
And draw perhaps an arrow
Of shining shafts for days and years to come
When morn and vesper shall be no more [illegible]
And all my life reclothed with flower and leaf.*

Opening "Memory's casket," the poet turns "the withered petals o'er and o'er," recalling "the perfume of that hair" he may no longer touch and the beauty of the "white neck" which now appears to him as no more than a faintly bright picture glowing in the darkness.

The tone of poignant pain and quiet sorrow which distinguishes this sonnet conveys a sense of irreparable loss and suggests that he as well as Christina still felt reverberations of the anguish originally experienced at the loss of the one irreplaceable person.

Another sonnet in the group recalls Christina's *Echo* (see above, pp. 90–91):

Come back! the hot sun makes our lips athirst;
Come back! thy dreams may recreate the past;
Come back! and smooth again this heart's long strife.[5]

The sonnet called *Evening* has as its theme reunion in Paradise. Again the poet regrets the loss of a loved woman whose memory seems to haunt him. Other friends may come and go, he writes, and the toys of life succeed one another, but they can never supplant that one lasting image which remains with him:

In vain I wish again within these arms
To fold thee, once more feel there those shoulders soft
And solid, but that is no more to be:
Unless perchance—(*speak low*) beyond all harms
I may walk with thee in God's other croft,
When this world shall the darkling mirror be.

Although Scott also wrote love poems to Alice, these, written after he had been living with her almost a decade, reflect the shadow of another woman to whose loss he seems to have been unreconciled. What makes *Evening* so curious is that in expressing his hope of becoming reunited with this woman after death, he was contradicting his own materialistic convictions.

VIII

The three Rossettis seem never to have been guests at Penkill at the same time. Each was invited in turn, Christina in 1866, William in 1867,

Gabriel in 1868, Christina the summer of 1869, and Gabriel the autumn of the same year.

It was in 1868 that Gabriel first began to be seriously affected by insomnia and incipient blindness, the initial symptoms of his later collapse. Unable to paint and hence to fulfill his commitments, he felt an understandable anxiety which only aggravated his nervous condition; and Scott and Alice hoped that a prolonged rest at Penkill would restore his health. Scott claimed it was he who that summer reawakened Gabriel's latent interest in poetry and who convinced him that he was a poet by birthright, not a painter.

Scott's attitude toward his "dear friend" Gabriel is more than puzzling. On the one hand, he seemed to be genuinely fond of his guest and concerned about his condition. On the other hand, he himself contributed, whether consciously or not, to Gabriel's steady deterioration, and regarded him with secret contempt while doing so. But Scott's character was far from simple, and much of his complexity arose from his inability to understand his own motives.

Night after night the two men emptied "endless tumblers . . . of whiskey-toddy," and Gabriel brought out and "danced" before them, for his own relief and Scott's callous amusement, what the latter called Gabriel's "fearful skeletons in the closet." But in the brotherly haze of affection brought on by companionable drinking, Scott may have made a few indiscreet confidences of his own. In describing to Mrs. Rossetti some months later the group of his sonnets to be published in *Fortnightly,* Gabriel told her they were "such a lively band of bogies that they may join with the skeletons of Christina's various closets and entertain you by a ballet," the only time any one other than Christina herself ever suggested there were skeletons in her closet.

Another visitor at Penkill that summer was old Miss Losh, Alice's aunt, "a nice, cheerful, intelligent old thing," said Gabriel. Her daily delight was to watch him smash his breakfast eggs on the plate and all over the damask tablecloth. "You see, Alice dear," she explained, "he is not like one of us, he is a great man, can't attend to trifles, is always occupied with great ideas." To enable him to occupy himself even more fully with great ideas, the old lady generously offered to subsidize him. Gabriel just as generously refused, although he accepted a loan from her.[6]

Absent in person from the Penkill house party that summer, Christina nonetheless contributed to its entertainment, her poetry sharing the evening honors with Shakespeare and whist. "I read a vast amount of Christina aloud the other evening," Gabriel wrote his mother, "which was much enjoyed, though everyone knew it already. . . ." Among the poems known and enjoyed by the company was *L.E.L.* with its refrain of "My heart is breaking for a little love."

During the reading Miss Losh was much struck by the line, "And rabbit

thins his fur," for in her own observation she knew that female rabbits, when expecting a brood, pull off some of their own fur to make a soft bed for the young. Gabriel had remarked the same habit in his Chelsea rabbits, and in a letter to his mother inquired if this was what Christina had intended. If so, he thought she should change the gender of the pronoun from *his* to *its*, "for *her* would not come in well."

In a postscript, possibly meant for Christina, he added that "Scotus's pictures are now quite finished and look fine. There is a hedgehog together with other beasts, in the last one, which would delight Christina." In the Penkill circle not only was Scott called "The Porcupine," but he was also known as "The Hedgehog," the leading animal image in Christina's *Speaking Likenesses* (1874). In this guileless child's story one of the small heroine's birthday gifts was "a gilt pincushion like a hedgehog"; and in the dream-nightmare which follows, the Engraver, the most disturbing male element, "bristled with prickly quills like a porcupine, and raised or depressed them at pleasure. . . ." [7]

IX

That autumn Scott returned to London with Gabriel, leaving Alice behind at Penkill. Gabriel expressed his gratitude for Penkill hospitality by writing her chatty little letters, mainly about Scott, but in one of them he mentioned that Christina was "a good deal better—indeed very well for her." She herself, however, told Macmillan that she still clung to her "invalid habits," and refrained from visiting more than was necessary.

But in February she made a point of attending a concert at St. James's Hall where the featured work was her own *Songs in a Cornfield* made into a cantata by C. A. Macfarren. Although the new work was respectfully received—the audience demanding an encore of the "Swallow Song"—William thought the performance a pretty dreary affair, both words and music, and rightly doubted that it would become a popular success.

We hear from Mrs. Gilchrist (whose "incredible enthusiasm" about Walt Whitman mildly astonished William) that in April the Rossettis gave a dinner party. Among the guests were Ford Madox Brown's daughter Lucy, destined to be the future Mrs. William Rossetti, and "a gifted man of the name of Cayley." Although Scott may or may not have been one of the dinner guests (Mrs. Gilchrist does not mention his name), he was a frequent visitor at Euston Square that spring. The record is silent about his and Christina's friendship during the first six months of 1869, but on July 8 an entry in William's diary informs us that "Christina went off with the Scotts, to spend a month or more at Penkill." Once there, she seems to have forgot her "invalid habits" and, in William's words, was "uncommonly well, capable of taking goodish walks, etc."

The home circle rejoiced at receiving "good news" of her. Gabriel wrote

Alice that he was glad to hear "Christina is enjoying herself with you, and I inferred a suppressed groan from the creaking joints of Scotus made to walk. I suppose some 'small deer' must have turned up to make Christina so happy. Perhaps even a hedgehog may have taught her that all tears are not born of sorrow."

We do not know what poetry Christina wrote at Penkill that summer, if indeed she wrote any. Oral tradition has it that she composed many of her *Sing-Song* nursery rhymes there. But of the poems she wrote after the visit—those dated 1869 and 1870—a number are love lyrics. Such are *Confluents, Autumn Violets, An Echo from Willowwood,* and *By Way of Remembrance.*

Confluents, approved by Gabriel as "lovely and penetrating in its cadence," has the same tone of exalted passion and quiet ecstasy as some of the *Monna Innominata* sonnets. Putting aside for once the veil behind which, she had complained in the *Amico,* she was obliged to conceal her love, and "unveiled utterly," she gives full expression to the intensity of her love. But, although the emotion flows freely, the control of structured imagery and logical design is imposed upon it, so that the total effect is one of dignified simplicity almost classical in its restraint:

As rivers seek the sea,
Much more deep than they,
So my soul seeks thee
Far away.
As running rivers moan
On their course alone,
So I moan
Left alone.

As the delicate rose
To the sun's sweet strength
Doth herself unclose
Breadth and length;
So spreads my heart to thee
Unveiled utterly,
I to thee,
Utterly.

As the morning dew exhales
Sunwards pure and free
So my spirit fails
After thee.
As dew leaves not a trace
On the green earth's face;
I, no trace
On thy face.

Its goal the river knows,
Dewdrops find a way,

Sunlight cheers the rose
In her day:
Shall I, lone sorrow past,
Find thee at the last?
Sorrow past
Thee at last?

The sonnet *Autumn Violets* has the same poignant quality and suggests that Christina's happiness at Penkill held its own alloy. Three years had passed since her first visit. Living again with Scott and Alice in the domestic intimacy of one household, she would have been forced to the fresh recognition that theirs was no temporary love affair but a permanent alliance, a marriage, like that of George Eliot and Lewes. And although they loved her and wanted to include her in their own warm, happy, enclosing circle, she felt that she was still the outsider at the circumference, not at the glowing center of their lives. This comprehension of her position is revealed most movingly in the concluding sestet of the sonnet, particularly in the final striking image of Ruth, which, besides carrying the weight of the scriptural allusion, has rich associations with Keats's *Ode to a Nightingale:*

Keep violets for the spring, and love for youth,
Love that should dwell with beauty, mirth and hope:
Or if a later sadder love be born,
Let this not look for grace beyond its scope,
But give itself, nor plead for answering truth—
A grateful Ruth tho' gleaning scanty corn.

Her gratitude for being allowed to glean the stray sheaves from the Penkill abundance also appears in these Italian lines she wrote on the flap of an envelope dated 1869 and sent to Penkill with some verses:

*Quanto a Le grata io sono
L'Umil dirà simplicità del dono.* [8]

An Echo from Willowwood (c. 1870) has for its motto a line from Gabriel's *Willowwood* sonnets, "O ye, all ye that walk in willowwood." The theme is again the separation of lovers:

Two gazed into a pool, he gazed and she,
Not hand in hand, yet heart in heart, I think,
Pale and reluctant on the water's brink,
As on the brink of parting which must be.
Each eyed the other's aspect, she and he,
Each felt one hungering heart leap up and sink,
Each tasted the bitterness which both must drink,
There on the brink of life's dividing sea.
Lilies upon the surface, deep below
Two wistful faces craving each for each,
Resolute and reluctant without speech:—
A sudden ripple made the faces flow,

One moment joined, to vanish out of reach:
So those hearts joined, and ah were parted so.

William has told us that this sonnet "may possibly be intended to refer to the love and marriage of my brother and Miss Siddal, and to her early death in 1862, or"—and it is a significant *or*—"it may (which I think far more probable) be intended for a wholly different train of events." What those events were he does not explain.

Professor Doughty in his *A Victorian Romantic: Dante Gabriel Rossetti* has interpreted the poem as Christina's comment upon her brother's love for Mrs. William Morris, assuming that "the wholly different train of events" probably referred to "the relations between Janey Morris and Rossetti." However, there is no reason to believe that Christina was treating her brother's love relationship rather than her own. As the title of her sonnet hints, she found in her own experience an echo of his. Like Gabriel, Christina was no stranger to willowwood: its "bitter banks" and "fathom-depth of soulstruck widowhood" were well known to her. The sonnet is in effect an acknowledgment of the bond between the emotionally shipwrecked. In a letter to Gabriel written many years later, she was to emphasize even more pointedly the parallelism of their experience.

But despite the similarity of temperament, a resemblance of genetic structure which in itself might have brought about a similarity of experience, there was a striking difference between brother and sister, due primarily to the way in which they handled experience. His motto on his stationary was "Bend, do not break." But confronted with the stress and conflict of an insupportable situation, whatever it may have been, he broke because he was unable to bend. The reverse was true of Christina, whose religious discipline enabled her to endure with more fortitude the successive blows of a lifetime.

X

An important work belonging to the 1869–1870 period is Christina's *By Way of Remembrance,* a group of four sonnets. Written in October, 1870, this series would seem to be a result of the second Penkill visit just as the *Monna Innominata* sonnet sequence and the Italian love poems were in all probability the result of the first. The emotional focus of all three groups is similar; theme and treatment are related; and, to make the resemblance even more pronounced, one of the *Remembrance* sonnets has the same sestet as one of the *Monna* sonnets.

The first *Remembrance* sonnet picks up again and develops the concept of love's equity, subject of the fourth and the seventh *Monna* sonnets:

Remember, if I claim too much of you,
I claim it of my brother and my friend:
Have patience with me till the hidden end—
Bitter or sweet, in mercy shut from view.

Pay me my due; though I to pay your due
Am all too poor, and past what will can mend.

Though love refuses to admit inequality in the exchange of gifts, somehow in the weighing the balance has shifted more heavily to the man's side, and so

Thus of your bounty you must give and lend,
Still unrepaid by aught I look to do.

In the next sonnet of the series Christina tries to imagine what reunion in Paradise might really be like. What will be the nature of the delicate balance of relationships in the hereafter? Will she be on hand

To sit down in your glory and to share
Your gladness, glowing as a virgin bride?

Will there be one Dantean blaze of dazzling love, without sun and moon,

Or will another, dearer, fairer-eyed,
Sit nigher to you in your jubilee,
And mindful one of other will you be
Borne higher and higher on joy's ebbless tide?

And if this is the way it is to be, what place should she assign to herself in the Heaven of her own invention?

It is fascinating to watch her mind in action as it grapples once again with a problem never settled. Unable to convince herself that reunion in Paradise will take place on a nonsexual basis, she is, then, of necessity obliged to assume that man and wife will be reunited. In that case, what will become of her? Her very faith in the power of love and in immortality has forced her into a logical position which withers her hopes, root of her emotional vitality. There is only one egress from the logical trap, the same one which always presents itself: she must give up personal gratification in Heaven as she has on earth. In the twelfth *Monna* sonnet she had declared,

If there be anyone can take my place
And make you happy whom I grieve to grieve,
Think not I can grudge it, . . .

and now in the second *Remembrance* sonnet, picking up the key word *grudge,* she writes,

Yea, if I love, I will not grudge you this:
I too shall float upon that heavenly sea
And sing my joyful praises without ache;
Your overflow of joy shall gladden me,
My whole heart shall sing praises for your sake,
And find its fulfillment in your bliss.

The third *Remembrance* sonnet need not detain us. It deals in a somewhat theological manner with the nature of resurrection, which for Chris-

tina always preserved personality, the identity of the individual: not for her was the mystic's concept of merging into an unknowable Absolute. In her view God, the original Giver of personality, did not take it away; on the contrary, once the individual had surrendered personality, He enlarged and enriched it.

The fourth sonnet shows continuity with the second: the problem seemingly resolved with such a triumphant flourish is brought into the closer focus which reveals its factual texture. Here the microscope rather than the telescope is the lens of vision. It was all very well to sing joyful praises for another's bliss in a golden and glittering *Paradiso,* but life still remained to be lived out soberly on this earth.

The opening lines of this sonnet, a blunt and undisguised declaration of love as plain and forthright in expression as the second sonnet is ornate, propose an answer similar to that suggested in *Autumn Violets:* if a woman must, she can live and be nourished on gleanings:

> I love you and you know it—this at least,
> This comfort is mine own in all my pain:
> You know it, and can never doubt again,
> And love's mere self is a continual feast:
> Not oath of mine nor blessing-word of priest
> Could make my love more certain or more plain.

After two transitional lines completing the octave comes the queer sestet, so different in tone and attitude from what has preceded that it sounds like another poem. And that, in fact, is what it is. It is, surprisingly, the sestet of the tenth *Monna Innominata* sonnet:

> Life wanes; and when Love folds his wings above
> Tired joy, and less we feel his conscious pulse,
> Let us go fall asleep, dear Friend, in peace;—
> A little while, and age and sorrow cease;
> A little while, and love reborn annuls
> Loss and decay and death—and all is love.[9]

With the fading of feeling, that diminution of the "conscious pulse" that beats to love, vitality begins to ebb, the stream dries, and life slows down.

This is likewise the substance of the last *Monna Innominata* sonnet, the fourteenth, which like the *Remembrance* group may have been written as an aftermath of the second Penkill visit. In fact, the tenth, thirteenth, and fourteenth *Monna* sonnets have more in common with the poetry written in 1869–1870 than with that of the earlier period. The sonnet which closes the *Monna Innominata* sequence would seem, then, to be a product of the later period:

> Youth gone, and beauty gone if ever there
> Dwelt beauty in so poor a face as this;
> Youth gone and beauty, what remains of bliss?
> I will not bind fresh roses in my hair,

To shame a cheek at best but little fair,—
Leave youth his roses, who can bear a thorn,—
I will not seek for blossoms anywhere,
Except such common flowers as blow with corn.
Youth gone and beauty gone, what doth remain?
The longing of a heart pent up forlorn,
A silent heart whose silence loves and longs;
The silence of a heart which sang its songs
While youth and beauty made a summer morn,
Silence of love that cannot sing again.

In 1870 Christina was forty. She was still single, still childless, still lonely, and still in love. Obviously her fame as a poet had not compensated for her deprivations as a woman. The question she felt obliged to ask herself at this stage was, did she regret her life—its indecisions, its sacrifices made and recalled and made again, its anguishes, and its austere rewards? Was it worthwhile to have lived? to have loved? Would she have been willing to go through it all again, if she had had her life to live over?

In the *Amico* she had stated that he who does not know sorrow does not experience love, and he who does not experience love has not lived. This insight she reaffirms in *They Desire a Better Country,* another poem of the 1869–1870 period:

I would not if I could undo my past,
Tho' for its sake my future is a blank;
My past for which I have myself to thank,
For all its faults and follies first and last.
I would not cast anew the lot once cast,
Or launch a second ship for one that sank,
Or drug with sweets the bitterness I drank,
Or break by feasting my perpetual fast.

Once again, as in *Memory* and *Twice,* she tells us that she had only one love in her life. If the first ship sank, she could not and would not launch a second. There was no Collinson–Cayley succession of attachments. She cast one lot, launched one ship; she gambled, and lost. But she had no regrets. She was willing to drink unsweetened the bitter cup of *From House to Home*. If feasting was not in the cards, then she fasted. She did not go, hungry, from one table to another looking for new banquets:

I would not if I could: for much more dear
Is one remembrance than a hundred joys.

Despite the pain and the disillusionment, then, she was still willing to endorse her life, to declare it worth living. This is a robust acceptance quite different from that pale negation of life and love that many critics have considered her most characteristic attitude.

❅ 13 ❅

"IF EVER THE FIRE REKINDLES"

1869–1870

In the summer of 1869, shortly after Christina's return from Penkill, she found herself the subject of an article in *Tinsley's Magazine,* the first of three articles about the Rossettis in the "Criticism on Contemporaries" series.[1] Within the family circle the series occasioned a good deal of excitement and curious speculation about the anonymous author's identity. "Some one who knows *something* about us," William conceded, "but who I have not the least idea." By September, when the second article appeared, the author was known to be "a man named Forman." He was of course H. Buxton-Forman.

He praised the Rossetti tone in general for its chastity and elegance, though he thought William occasionally showed inelegancies and "uncouthness" in his diction, but he took Christina to task for her use of slang and colloquialism. Forgetting what his generation should have learned from the *Preface to the Lyrical Ballads,* Forman cited the lines,

One hauls a basket
One lugs a dish

as an example of faulty diction likely to steer the poet of *Goblin Market* into "the shallows of commonplace." Today, critics like F. R. Leavis have found its closeness to colloquial speech one of the chief charms of Christina's diction. A goblin may "lug" a dish just as she herself "lugs" to Hastings her six volumes of Plato. And when she dons her singing robes, she can be as formal and ceremonious in the use of language as the next poet.

Despite "a genuine poetic gift," Forman continued, she could not be ranked with Mrs. Browning. In one respect only did she exceed the latter, and that was in her "sense of execution," which Forman attributed to her literary training by her father and brothers. He cites *Birthday* as an example of her careful workmanship, but then, confusing execution and subject matter, he praises that lyric for its "healthy happiness and the

ringing melody of a joyful young heart." No wonder the painter Frederick Shields complained that the author of the *Tinsley* article was "deaf to what is best" in Christina and "forces the sweetest notes from her."

Forman reserved his highest praise for Gabriel, whom he treated in the September issue. Deploring the fact that the poet's work was known only from the sonnets he had published in *Fortnightly,* Forman urged Gabriel to bring out a collection of verse, "the sooner the better." We cannot say that Forman's exhortation to publish decisively influenced Gabriel's resolve to recover the volume of poems he had buried in Lizzie's coffin, for in August he had already discussed the possibility of the exhumation with Charles Augustus Howell,[2] his friend and confidential agent in the art world, but Forman's rapturous enthusiasm was undoubtedly a factor.

What is more likely is that the article about Christina awoke his ambition to achieve immediate recognition as a poet. She was given precedence in the series because so far she had produced more poetry than either of her brothers, but in Forman's opinion even she had not yet written enough "to prove her worth as a poet." And all that Gabriel had before the public as evidence of his own worth was the 1861 *Early Italian Poets* and the *Fortnightly* group of sonnets. As a producing poet, his sister was well ahead of him.

II

Shortly after Christina returned from Penkill, Gabriel went there. Finding him "more hypochondriacal than ever," Scott once more helped him to "drown his anxieties in Scotch"; and their nightly "sederunts," as Scott called them, became even more prolonged than they had been the preceding autumn.[3] Despite the drinking bouts and the warm weather, "almost too hot for walking," both men accomplished a good deal that autumn, Gabriel rewriting some of his early poems from memory and composing new ones for the volume he was then getting ready for private printing, Scott "working in his steady though leisurely way" at his sketches for the South Kensington Museum windows, his illustrations of Burns's poems ("really most beautiful in invention and high feeling," said Gabriel), and his life of Dürer. Evenings, before the drinking started, they devoted to reading aloud and criticizing one another's work. Frequently Gabriel revised his poetry in accordance with Scott's critical suggestions.

Once Scott had finished with the poems, Gabriel sent them to Euston Square for further critical comment; and it then became Christina's turn to reciprocate for the aid Gabriel had given her with *Prince's Progress.* "If Christina would read my things, and give any hints that occur to her, I would be thankful," Gabriel wrote William, who was also pressed into service. Did she have any suggestions for "the *next* revise"? And would she kindly read proof for him? Whatever one Rossetti produced in the

creative field had the benefit of three other penetrating minds at work on it, a fact which does much to explain the Rossettis' remarkable accomplishment as a family.

With a record of such productive labor within a six-week period, it is hard to credit Scott's assertion that Gabriel at this time was mentally unbalanced. A clear and unmuddled head is required to perform "the fundamental brainwork of poetry." Yet it was during the 1869 Penkill visit that the two celebrated incidents occurred which caused Scott to doubt Gabriel's sanity. The first was what Scott described as his suicidal urge to hurl himself into the black depths of the whirlpool called the Devil's Punchbowl in Lady Glen. The second was his strange insistence that a tame chaffinch he found on the hilly road to Barr was the spirit of his dead wife.

That same year, 1869, Christina wrote an elegy to Alice's pet chaffinch (deceased), but whether this was the chaffinch of Gabriel's delusion is an open question. Scott thought that Gabriel's bird was a tame creature which had escaped from some cage. Possibly later in the autumn, after Gabriel's departure, Alice found the tame bird on the road one day, picked it up, took it home with her, and kept it for a pet, naming it Bouby and cherishing it until its death. However that may have been, Christina clearly did not connect the bird with her brother. The gay though tender tone, the almost frivolous treatment in her elegy, does not show the awareness that would have been inevitable had she known of the associations the chaffinch had for Gabriel: [4]

Gone to his rest
Bright little Bouby!
Build green his nest
Where sun and dew be,
Nor snails molest

*A cheerful sage,
Simple, light-hearted:
In ripe old age
He has departed
And ta'en his wage.

Dear for himself;
Dear for another
Past price of pelf;
—(Ah, dearest Mother!)—
Song-singing elf.*

O daisies, grow
Lightly above him,
Strike root and blow:
For some who love him
Would have it so.

Returning to the castle after the chaffinch incident, Scott and Gabriel were told by Alice that the house bell had mysteriously rung, without any visible human presence to account for it, a circumstance which seemed to confirm Gabriel's belief in the supernatural sequence of events. Later that autumn his own "bogey" contributed to the haunted-house legendry that began to accumulate about the old Scotch castle. They still tell the story at Penkill that once Gabriel had definitely decided to "dig out" his poems, he came down one morning with his valise fully packed and went into the dining room where Scott and Alice were finishing breakfast. "Wot? Ye off, Gabby?" said Scott. Gabriel nodded and said briefly, "London." He then left, but days and weeks after his departure, the occupants of the castle could plainly hear his footsteps pacing the drawing room above the library (where he worked) and his voice reciting his poetry. A visiting clergyman, hearing the footsteps and the voice, asked Alice if she had a guest upstairs.

Although Scott and Gabriel appeared to be better friends than ever that autumn, the currents were already forming that led to the rift of later years. Scott thought of himself at this time as Gabriel's "keeper" and later as his "banker." And, although Gabriel described Scott to Frederick Shields as "the best of philosophic and poetic natures, a man of the truest genius, and one of my oldest companions," he complained to William that Scott was always "against" him. Significantly, he refused to return to Penkill after this visit. And when William urged him to do so some years later, Gabriel protested that he had been "molested" there.[5]

Jealousy was the motive behind Scott's growing animosity. Early in life he had looked upon himself as a "poet *nascitur non fit*," but as the years passed, and no recognition of the sort he craved was forthcoming, he became "increasingly haunted by the consciousness of having missed my mark."

Not only Gabriel, but Christina as well, was achieving eminence in an art in which Scott had long aspired to excel. Seeing his friends sprint ahead of him in the race for immortality, himself forced to fall back, no wonder he turned for comforting assurance to a woman like Alice Boyd who offered no serious competition in the arts.

III

During the time he was at Penkill Gabriel was arranging with Howell and the solicitor Virtue Tebbs (owner of the Greek vases) for the exhumation of his poetry, which took place in October.[6] In her 1850 prose fiction tale *Maude,* Christina had prefigured the entombment of poetry: the story ends with the burial of the deceased young heroine's poems in her coffin. William drew attention to this striking coincidence in the preface to his edition of *Maude* (1897), but, although he suggests, he does not definitely say that the fictitious episode influenced Gabriel's own action

at the time of Lizzie's death in 1862. If so, by 1869 Gabriel clearly recognized the gesture for the romanticism that it was. The concept of the entombment of poetry, like that of a Blessed Damozel longing for reunion in Paradise, is pervasively Rossettian. Possibly both these concepts originated in speculative childhood discussions among the four Rossettis, fed, no doubt, by their reading in romantic literature.

It was also while he was at Penkill that Gabriel purchased, sight unseen, a wombat, "the greatest lark you can imagine," William wrote, once he had seen it. Christina went into equal ecstasies, immediately writing a poem in Italian to *"L'Uumibatto,"* which she sent to Gabriel with the explanatory couplet in English,

When wombats do inspire
I strike my disused lyre.

Thanking her for the "shrine in the Italian taste" with which she had honored his wombat, he proclaimed the new pet "a joy, a triumph, a delight, a madness!" Or, more prosaically, "a round furry ball with a head something between a bear and a guinea-pig, no legs, human feet with heels like anybody else . . . no tail . . . and most endearing habits." A babe as yet, his coat was still rough, "although," Gabriel assured Miss Losh in a letter, "the Consummate Wombat is quite smooth, and such he will be when adult."

But the little creature was not destined to reach adulthood. Its decline proceeded apace with Gabriel's, even to the initial symptoms of blindness. Ill during October while the exhumation and afterwards the disinfection of the moldy pages of poetry were taking place, the animal finally died in November at a time when Gabriel, deeply shaken by the strain he had undergone, was himself showing signs of collapse.

All through October, however, his poetic activity continued unabated. And as soon as he wrote a new poem for his forthcoming volume, he hurried over to Euston Square to read it to the family. Christina listened to the erotic poems with her customary bland courtesy, but the serpent-sex symbolism in *Eden Bower* proved too much for her, and with Maria she fled from the room, much to Gabriel's delight. The incident went the rounds, Gabriel relating it with glee to Scott, who, relishing it in turn, relayed it back to William.

By October 20 Scott was back in London. Alice stayed on at Penkill. The letters he wrote to her there during October and November give us a close view of events as they occurred throughout the remainder of the autumn.[7] On October 25 he wrote:

*DEAREST,

Please send the whiskey immediately, as I have not a drop, and don't want to buy any. Gabriel the other night had the Cape brandy and I suppose did not like it very much. Gabriel is writing no more. 'The

> Orchard Pit' has made no way. But he has got *the book*. It was so decayed through the *middle* part of the pages that he has had to *copy it himself*. A queer sensation it must give him. However, he is quite well, and has got all the poems now. I am going one day soon to meet Hake at his dinner table.*

Like Scott himself, Dr. T. G. Hake, who was to prove his friendship during a crisis, was one of the men whose acquaintance Gabriel initially sought through being attracted to his literary work.

In Scott's letter of November 5 we learn that "the whiskey came all right, with catsup and pickles." He apologizes for the delay in sending off the letter, explaining that he dined at Gabriel's and stayed overnight:

> *At Gabriel's it was very jolly, a large party of men including Algernon, who gradually became noisy, then rampant, then unmanageable, and lastly inarticulate and helpless. Next morning he turned up at breakfast, however, his breakfast being sherry.
>
> I have sent in the design for the next window at South Kensington. Tomorrow—, Saturday, we go to dine at Euston Square, and on Tuesday I am to have a number of the set in the evening.*

On November 10 he demands, "Whatever is keeping you until the 22nd?" Again he "had a lot of men in," including the Rossetti brothers and Brown. Gabriel was already "making chaff" about the recent death of his beloved wombat, parodying his own *Parted Love* sonnet in the following lines:

> Oh, how the family affections combat
> Within this heart, and each hour flings a bomb at
> My burning soul; neither from owl nor from bat
> Can peace be to me now I've lost my Wombat.

In this letter we learn for the first time of a plan on foot for a party to visit the Continent in the spring:

> *Letitia [Scott's wife] of course keeps talking about it, and Christina seems to continue in the same mind. The other day at Fitzroy Square [Brown's house] she ventilated the scheme, and as I was to go to Nurnberg when she and Christina went to Italy, William volunteered . . . to go there with me. The other day she said we could not go and enjoy ourselves if you staid at home, whereon I took the chance and suggested that you might be induced to go to Nurnberg. Now this proposal of William's seems as if everyone will infallibly hail it as the right thing.*

The plans for the Continental trip came to nothing, and not until 1873 was a similar traveling party arranged, but by then it was too late for Christina to join it, for she was ill and unable to travel. Although her health had improved greatly during 1869, in October she became worried about a slight discoloration around her eyes. When she consulted Sir William Jenner about it, he appeared much more interested in the condition of her chest, "conspicuously better" than it had been, but still de-

serving of precautions. Thus despite her own vigilance, the first sign of that thyroidic disorder which was to cause her so much trouble in the 1870's went unheeded and unchecked.

On the 19th Scott wrote Alice that if she arrived in London on Thursday, the 22nd, as planned, she would find "William, Christina, Maria, Littledale and his wife, and probably the Woolners . . . at dinner." Alice did arrive on the 22nd, in time to attend Scott's dinner party, at which Dr. Littledale, William noted in his diary, discussed recent developments in Anglo-Catholicism.

Conversions from the English Church, he said, were rarer than they had been a few years previously, "the aspirations of the more Roman-tending Anglicans being now fairly met in their own Church." This helps to explain why Christina was never tempted to become a Roman Catholic, but throughout her life was content to remain in what she once called "the beloved Anglican Church of my Baptism."

IV

Although in the couplet about the wombat she had referred to a "disused lyre," a number of the poems we have looked at, including *By Way of Remembrance,* were written in the 1869–1870 period, and it was in 1870 that she wrote *Sing-Song*. The little book of nursery rhymes and children's songs, which Gabriel thought "divinely lovely," and she herself said contained some of her "best songs," proved to be one of her most popular productions; and it has remained in our literature as a classic of its kind. Unlike *Speaking Likenesses,* which admittedly she turned out "with an eye to the market," *Sing-Song* was not written for commercial purposes. That it appeared in print at the height of the vogue for nonsense stories and verses—it was reviewed in *The Academy* with *Through the Looking Glass* and Lear's *More Nonsense*—is a matter of luck rather than of intention. She wrote this group of gay, charming, and delicate little verses as a means of personal expression, as she did her more serious poetry.

She dedicated the verses "without permission to the baby who suggested them." This baby has been variously identified—as Arthur Hughes' son and Cayley's nephew—but more probably it belongs to the immortal order of Charles Lamb's dream-children. Although Christina was supposed to be not particularly fond of children and had herself confessed that she was "deficient in the nice motherly ways which win and ought to win a child's heart," these little songs and jingles could have been written only by an adult who had a genuine appreciation of the child's point of view. Theodore Watts-Dunton once observed the sympathetic bond which existed between Christina and small creatures such as puppies, kittens, and birds; and there was very much the same kind of bond between her and very young children. In the verses household pets share the domestic

scene with the baby, each little creature receiving its due in affection according to its need and nature:

The dog lies in his kennel
And puss purrs on the rug,
And baby perches on my knee
For me to love and hug.

Pat the dog and stroke the cat,
Each in its degree;
And cuddle and kiss my baby,
And baby kiss me.

A composite picture of the Lovable Baby emerges from these pages: the bald head, pink cheeks, and coral pink mouth, the sleepily winking round blue eyes, the elbow "furrowed with dimples," and the fat creased wrist:

My baby has a mottled fist,
My baby has a neck in creases;
My baby kisses and is kissed,
For he's the very thing for kisses.

The blissful nursery intimacy of contented mother and child appears in lullabies meant to be softly murmured and crooned at bedtime:

Lullaby, oh Lullaby!
Flowers are closed and lambs are sleeping;
Lullaby, oh Lullaby!
Stars are up, the moon is peeping;
Lullaby, oh Lullaby!
While the birds are silence keeping,
(Lullaby, oh lullaby!)
Sleep, my baby, fall a-sleeping,
Lullaby, oh lullaby!

Love me,—I love you,
Love me, my baby;
Sing it high, sing it low,
Sing it as may be.

Mother's arms under you,
Her eyes above you;
Sing it high, sing it low,
Love me,—I love you.

You are my one, and I have not another;
Sleep soft, my darling, my trouble and treasure;
Sleep warm and soft in the arms of your mother,
Dreaming of pretty things, dreaming of pleasure.

The small disagreements attendant upon nursery discipline give a touch of daily realism to the idealized domestic intimacy:

> Baby cry—
> Oh fie!—
> At the physic in the cup;
> Gulp it twice
> And gulp it thrice,
> Baby gulp it up.

Not only babies but also chubby toddlers and older children are found in this miscellaneous assortment of one hundred and twenty-one songs, riddles, puzzles, nursery jingles, of the kind Christina herself had enjoyed as a child in Hone's *Every-Day Book*. We come upon them, children of all ages, sometimes listening for the postman's knock, sometimes digging in the sand, or watching wrens and robins who are

> Building, perching, pecking, fluttering,
> Everywhere.

We see them playing at King and Queen, observing snails and hopping frogs, pigs, rabbits, the "brown and furry Caterpillar," or the toadstool "that comes up in the night"; we watch them fidgeting at a task, counting in rhyme, catching ladybugs, wandering aimlessly in the daisied meadows of spring, or dreaming by the "windy sea" in an autumnal apple orchard. We see them romping wildly and weeping without cause—in short, expressing in all their moods and activities the life of children, a life at once simple and very complex. These little poems catch the very essence of childhood and recreate the wonder and the freshness of its world.

For Christina the verses served a twofold function. They enabled her to recover and relive the happy past, the lost and loved security of her own bright childhood on Charlotte Street and in the country, and in that sense they provided an escape from the problems of adult life. But they also supplied another of her ideal worlds of the imagination which made up for the deficiency of the actual world. Just as the *Monna Innominata* sonnets, the by-product of an unhappy love, pose an ideal order in which "rich love" can give and take in perfect equilibrium, without the disturbing elements which upset the balance in the real world, so *Sing-Song*, in its own way also a by-product of frustrated love, similarly constructs an ideal order which both parallels and purifies from its defects the real world.

And as the features of that world of reality are nonetheless limned in the sonnet sequence, so in *Sing-Song* the structure of the adult world of existent emotion is occasionally glimpsed through the gay and ingenuous rhythms. In a light-hearted child's verse we find the juxtaposition of heartsease, a flower which appears in Scott's early verse as an erotic symbol, and sweet william, with its punning allusion to both flower and lover:

Heartsease in my garden bed,
With sweetwilliam white and red,
Honeysuckle on my wall:—
When sweet William comes to call;
But it withers when we part,
And the honey-trumpets fall.

In other of Christina's poems heartsease is associated with love-lies-bleeding, as in the following lines:

Heartsease I found, where Love-lies-bleeding
Empurpled on the ground.[8]

The adult point of view is equally apparent in this poem:

If hope grew on a bush,
And *love* grew on a tree [9]
What a nosegay for the plucking
There would be!

But oh! in windy autumn,
When frail flowers wither
What should we do for *love* and joy,
Fading together?

And finally in the delicately chiseled miniature work of the nursery rhymes the familiar intertwined themes of parted love and reunion occasionally cast their adult shadow on the sunny brightness of the surrounding verses, as in the following:

'Goodbye in fear, goodbye in sorrow,
Goodbye, and all in vain,
Never to meet again, my dear—'
'Never to part again.'
'Goodbye to-day, goodbye to-morrow,
Goodbye till earth shall wane,
Never to meet again, my dear—'
'Never to part again.'

V

In 1870 Christina was also working on "Commonplace," the long prose fiction story which she completed on March 5 and which gave the title to her collection of short stories published in June. From the publishing history of this volume, it is evident that, just as the title poem in *Prince's Progress* was written for the sake of a second volume of poetry, so "Commonplace" was produced to supply sufficient bulk for the collection of prose fiction tales.

Many of these stories had been written years earlier, and some of them had been printed in magazines. "The Lost Titian" appeared in *Crayon* (1856), "Hero" in *Argosy* (January, 1866), "A Safe Investment," "Pros and Cons," and "The Waves of This Troublesome World" all in *Churchman's*

Shilling in 1867.[10] "Nick" had been written as early as 1853 at Frome. Of the remainder of the volume, only Swinburne's favorite, "Vanna's Twins," and "Commonplace" were new.

Like Gabriel's "Hand and Soul," "The Lost Titian" is a story of the art world, and it is perhaps the most finished piece in the volume. In the sensuous richness of the prose style, peculiarly appropriate to the Venetian Renaissance setting, the poet of *Goblin Market* and *Birthday* is recognizable, particularly in this passage describing Titian's studio:

> The studio was elegant with clusters of flowers, sumptuous with crimson, gold-bordered hangings, and luxurious with cushions and perfumes. From the walls peeped pictured fruit and fruit-like faces, between the curtains and in the corners gleamed moonlight-tinted statues; whilst on the easel reposed the beauty of the evening, overhung by budding boughs, and illuminated by an alabaster lamp burning scented oil. Strewn about the apartment lay musical instruments and packs of cards. On the table were silver dishes, filled with leaves and choice fruits; wonderful vessels of Venetian glass, containing rare wines and iced waters; and footless goblets, which allowed the guest no choice but to drain his bumper.

Titian's model for his recently completed masterpiece, the "beauty of the evening," was a hazel-eyed woman; for, comments the author, "blue eyes are not always in season; hazel eyes, like hazel nuts, have their season also."

The theme of the story is the difficulty of accepting the second place in life and art, a problem which in 1856 was disturbing Christina and which she also treated in *The Lowest Room,* a poem written that year. Gianni, the second-best painter in Venice, is corroded by envy and he hopes to destroy the great Titian's reputation by hiding the latter's most recent masterpiece from the acclaiming world.

A stanza from *The Lowest Room* could well be the motto for the prose fiction tale:

> *I may be second, but not first;
> I cannot be the first of all.
> This weighs on me, this wearies me,
> I stumble like to fall.*

The envy that arises from vanity is likewise the theme of two other stories in the volume, "Nick" and "Hero." Both these fairy tale fantasies possess the same bold brilliance and imaginative originality that distinguish Christina's best poetry ("Your 'Hero' is splendid," Gabriel told her, "you ought to write more such things"). No mention of Ovid occurs in any record of Christina's reading, but in both tales the leading dramatic device is metamorphosis, which to be sure she could also have found in *The Arabian Nights,* a reading staple of her childhood. But what is peculiarly individual about her use of the device is the moral purpose

underlying it. Through the mechanism of wishes granted by fairy magic, both Nick and Hero undergo sanative experience through a series of metamorphoses which change the very structure of their personalities. The ill-tempered and envious Nick is altered in turn to a sparrow, a dog, a stick, fire, and finally a rich old miser, only to wish himself back again to his own shape, but regenerated. Hero's wish, "to become the supreme object of admiration," is likewise granted, and, as a magnificently blazing diamond (Christina's own identifying suit in the juvenile card games), she is the object of universal desire. After a rapid sequence of changes, all of which modify her, she renounces the vanity of self-gratification, and chooses love rather than admiration.

Least interesting in the volume are the factual stories, which for the most part are as sentimental and didactic as the general run of mediocre Victorian prose fiction. An exception is the slight sketch "Pros and Cons," published in 1867 and probably written while Christina was still living at 166 Albany Street and attending Christ Church. In 1866 the Reverend Burrows, then incumbent, was striving to overcome the opposition of his parishioners to the abolition of pew rents at Christ Church. Christina's sketch, which dramatizes an incident in Burrows' struggle, is not without a certain tart satire upon the existent class structure of the English church in the mid-'sixties. Solidly united, the parishioners protest over tea in the Rectory drawing room at their vicar's High Church innovations, of which the abolition of pew rents is the least supportable:

> We have borne with chants, with a surpliced choir, with daily services, but we will not bear to see all our rights trampled under foot, and all our time-hallowed usages set at nought. The tendency of the day is to level social distinctions and to elevate unduly the lower orders. In this parish at least let us combine to keep up wise barriers between class and class, and to maintain that fundamental principle practically bowed to all over our happy England, that what you can pay for you can purchase.

As early as 1867 Roberts Brothers of Boston had proposed to bring out these tales in a collection, but nothing further was done, and in April, 1869, Christina wrote to them, asking that her pieces, those both in manuscript and in print, be returned to her, "as we have not duplicates of all of them by us." But not until February, 1870, did she return to the idea of bringing out a collection of prose fiction stories.

The first mention of the project occurs in a letter Gabriel wrote to Swinburne on February 21. He had, he said, not yet seen the principal story ("Commonplace"), but had heard at home that it was remarkable. Once he read "Commonplace," however, he was less enthusiastic. "Not dangerously exciting to the nervous system," he pronounced it, but "very good and far from uninteresting" for all that. He thought it "rather in the Miss Austen vein."

But in the field of the novel Christina could offer Jane Austen no competition. As a piece of realistic fiction, the work does not show much development from the 1850 *Maude*. The narrative comes to life chiefly when the heroine's emotional conflict is treated.

Christina drew heavily upon the materials of her own life for this tale of her middle age. A lonely woman's sadness is contrasted with the happy contentment of a mated pair. Lovers' poignant partings are followed by disappointing reunions. The chief action of the plot concerns the heroine's struggle to conquer her love for a married man while concealing it from the others who make up their social circle of friends and relatives.

The characters are also derived from Christina's intimate circle. Alan Hartley, the man Lucy Charlmont loves, "handsome and clever on the surface, if not deep within," has Scott's fascination of manner with women, his "ready good-nature which seemed to make every one a principal person in his regard," his "want of deep or definite purpose," and his careless disregard of consequences. A Cayley also haunts this tale. He is Tresham, the good, solid, faithful suitor whom Lucy knows she ought to marry (and finally does), could she forget the fascinating Alan. Subsidiary characters likewise show the particular traits and the individualizing idiosyncrasies of Christina's relatives and friends: there is a lively, facetious Dr. Littledale, who puns in verse; a garrulous, long-winded, but harmless chatterer of commonplaces like Mrs. Scott; a poised and intelligent elder sister whose air of authority and steadfastness to moral ideals are Maria's; and finally, in Alan's new wife, "this winning little woman who had won the only man Lucy ever cared for," but whom even Lucy herself "liked rather than disliked," an Alice Boyd.

The setting too partakes of the scenery of Christina's familiar environment, shifting back and forth from a seaside town like Newcastle to a Notting Hill residence in London. Notting Hill parties ("all was peace and plenty, smiles and wax candles, at Kensington") and Newcastle picnics held in Penkill glens are all part of the fictitious landscape.

Despite the unimportance of this work as literature, its autobiographical value is high. The portrayal of Alan Hartley gives us a picture of Scott, not as he was, but as he would have appeared to Christina—cordial, handsome, tender, attentive, a Scott whose warmth of manner toward her, even in Alice's presence, implied so much more than friendliness. And Lucy Charlmont, whose point of view the author presents, provides an unequaled insight into Christina's own attitudes. It is all there: the meetings during rare visits, the painful partings, the man's eventual return to become a permanent part of the woman's social circle, but with another woman by his side; the woman's responsiveness to the charm of close intimacy during those "delightful Junes" of the visits; her succeeding misinterpretation of the man's motives, followed by her painful disillusionment and the deep disappointment of love unfulfilled; the result-

ing tension, the unendurable strain of concealing her love from the world and from her lover; the morbid fear of continuing to love a man who belonged to another woman; the struggle to free herself from a "dangerous charm"; and lastly, the dawning suspicion, quickly dismissed, that the man may be a shallow egoist, not worth the loving.

VI

Gabriel was not happy at seeing his gifted sister devote herself to writing fiction. Her "proper business," he reminded her, was "to write poetry, and not *Commonplaces*." To this she replied somewhat testily that it was "impossible to go on singing to one's one-stringed lyre." And if he thought that a wider range of interests and new themes might stimulate greater poetic productivity, he might as well know that "It is not in me, and therefore it will never come out of me, to turn to politics or philanthropy with Mrs. Browning: such many-sidedness I leave to a greater than I, and having said my say, may well sit silent. 'Give me the withered leaves I chose' "—a quotation from her early lyric, *Roses for the Flush of Youth*—"may include the dog-eared leaves of one's first, last, and only book. If ever the fire rekindles availably, *tanto meglio per me:* at the worst, I suppose a few posthumous groans may be found amongst my remains."

Another time she said that "the whole subject of youthful poems grows anxious in middle age . . . one is so different, and yet so vividly the same." In a moment of discouragement she confided to Macmillan that the fire had died out and she knew of no bellows potent enough to revive it. She told Gosse that she was a "great believer in the genuine poetic impulse belonging (very often) to spring and not to the autumn of life, and some established reputations fail to shake me in this opinion"; and added, "If so one feels the possibility to stand in one's own case, then I vote that the grace of silence succeed the grace of song. By all of which," she concluded with a touch of playfulness, "I do not bind myself to unbroken silence."

From these and similar remarks, it is evident that, once she was past forty, she felt that the major part of her work was already finished and that the poetic incandescence was dimming. But whatever power controls human destinies had other plans in store for her. Another of the devastating shocks which periodically dislocated her emotional life and disturbed her creative equilibrium was in preparation. Although this was to be the most destructive of all the tremors and the one requiring the greatest recuperative power, it, like the others, was to quicken her poetry and give it a regenerative force.

❄ 14 ❄

"A DISENKINDLED FIRE"

1870–1872

It was chiefly due to Gabriel's maneuvers that in the spring of 1870 Christina changed publishers. Of her own accord she would not have left the man she called the "staunch Mac" and her "friendly publisher." Gabriel's idea was to gather together under one publishing banner—that of F. S. Ellis—"a little knot of congenial writers," that is, a literary coterie of producing poets. This was the same agglutinative tendency responsible for the formation of the PRB and other of Gabriel's cliques. For a time he succeeded in his latest endeavor, and Ellis could boast of having in his literary stable Gabriel, Christina, Swinburne, Morris, and Scott.

In fact, it was Scott who started the move toward Ellis, then a leading bookseller in Covent Garden just beginning to gain a reputation as an enterprising publisher. In February, 1869, Scott sold Ellis his unfinished translation of Dürer's diary, and in September Gabriel began to consider Ellis as the man to be entrusted with the publication of his recovered poems. He immortalized Ellis in the well-known limerick,

> There's a publishing party named Ellis
> Who's addicted to poets with bellies:
> He has at least two—
> One in fact, one in view—
> And God knows what will happen to Ellis.

Morris was the poet already captured by Ellis, and either Gabriel himself or Swinburne the one in view. In December Gabriel asked Swinburne if he was really going to publish his *Songs Before Sunrise* with Ellis. He himself, he said, was almost resolved to go along with Ellis, "but should feel a great deal relieved if Topsy [Morris] was not E's only other author, as he is so fearfully prolific that one would feel like the mouse looking upon the mountain. . . ." If Swinburne, and possibly Ruskin as well, would publish with Ellis, "the position would become tenable."

By February Gabriel was persuading Christina to leave Macmillan and join the newly forming Ellis group. Knowing Swinburne's almost obsessive

admiration for his sister and her work, Gabriel dangled her before the younger poet as bait, writing on the 21st,

> I hope you are going to give your new book to Ellis, who I think is really a straightforward fellow and deserves to publish for us all. It would be most pleasant to concentrate our forces. My sister is now going to him with a joint edition of her old things (including additions) and also with a book of 101 Nursery Rhymes (illustrated by herself!) which she has lately produced—admirable things, alternating between the merest babyism and a sort of Blakish wisdom and tenderness. I believe no one could have written anything so absolutely right for babies but herself. She will also have a volume of prose tales ready soon. . . . She has resolved to leave Macmillan after a degree of meanness in his proposal which was really laughable. Ellis will pay much better—indeed I believe as well as can be managed.

William's account of Christina's transactions with her publishers is less highly colored and more factual. On the same day Gabriel was writing to Swinburne William noted in his diary:

> Christina has lately been discussing with Macmillan about the publication of a volume of Nursery-rhymes which she has written, and the republication of her two old volumes. M[acmillan]'s terms are obviously meagre; Gabriel has consulted Ellis about it, and writes this morning that E[llis] offers £100 for the old poems, and some proportional sum for the new—a great advance on M[acmillan]. This has determined C[hristina] to transfer the publication of her books from M. and no doubt to E.

Two days later, on February 23, Christina herself approached Ellis:

> SIR
>
> I understand from my brother Mr. Rossetti that you are desirous of seeing some Nursery Rhymes I have just completed, and which I send you by book post. I shall be very glad if we can come to terms for their publication. I fear you may have misconceived what the illustrations amount to, as they are merely my own scratches and I cannot draw: but I send you the M.S. just as it stands.
>
> As regards the complete edition of my former vols., this cannot be gone into until the matter has been discussed with Mr. Macmillan, in whose hands is a large remainder of the 2nd ed. of Goblin Market. But my brother promises me to call on Mr. Macmillan and see what can be done some day.
>
> The terms you named to Mr. Rossetti (¼ price of edition) I shall be very glad to accept, if you continue in the same mind.
>
> Begging the favour of an early reply, I remain
>
> Faithfully yours
>
> Christina G. Rossetti [1]

It did not take Ellis long to decide. Even before reading the manuscript of *Sing-Song,* he made Christina an offer, which she promptly accepted. On February 25, only two days after her letter opening negotiations, she wrote that she accepted his terms "very gladly," adding as a precau-

tionary measure, "By which however I beg not to bind myself never at any future time to publish them otherwise, though of course I have not the slightest present idea of so doing." In view of what happened subsequently, this reservation proved a canny bit of foresight.

Either William was not informed of this letter or he thought it not binding upon his sister, for on the 28th, while Gabriel was writing to William Allingham that Christina was leaving "Mac" and was going to publish with Ellis, William was still dickering with Macmillan, using Ellis' offer as a bargaining wedge. He thought it very likely that Macmillan would shortly "raise his offer" to Christina.

The next letter written on the 28th was Christina's to Ellis. In the light of William's negotiations, it is a masterpiece of subtle diplomacy. But of course by now her position with regard to both publishers had become complicated by the fact that her brothers were working at cross-purposes, William's idea being for Christina to remain with Macmillan but get more money out of him, and Gabriel's for her to pick a quarrel in order to quit him and swell the ranks of Ellis poets. That she herself felt decidedly uncomfortable in the Machiavellian role forced upon her is evident from her letter:

Dear Sir

My brother is now engaged in attempting to arrange matters as to the large remainder of 'Goblin Market' with Mr. Macmillan, and as I cannot foresee the result I let you know this, lest, pending such an arrangement, you should see fit to take no further steps as to 'Sing Song.' I for my part should be very glad at once to carry out our terms as stated in my letter of the 25th. Pray favour me with a reply and believe me

Truly yours

Although on March 2 William was still bargaining with Macmillan, presenting him "with a comparative statement of the offers made to Christina by himself and Ellis . . . ," she determined to wait no longer, but to get one bird in hand before both flew away. She therefore wrote to Ellis on March 3,

I most gladly close with the terms settled between us, and prefer waiting till publication to having any sum in advance. As for fixing a time for the book to come out, I only meant to fix such a time as shall ensure the business not dragging on indefinitely: suppose we say that the agreement between us lapses if 'Sing Song' is not published by 1st July 1871? I will conclude that you assent to this unless I hear from you to the contrary. Your plan for illustrating 'Sing Song' pleases me, and I do indeed see the call for added bulk. You will I trust oblige me in due course by letting me correct the proofs.

I am now waiting for Macmillan's answer, my brother having twice called on him about my former volumes; and when I myself know I will also let you know. . . .

As it turned out, she displayed a shrewd business sense in setting a terminal date for the publication of the volume, although her immediate motive was undoubtedly to leave the door open for a return to Macmillan, if need be.

Her next letter (March 7) reveals that Ellis had been making certain discreet inquiries of his own, for she indignantly denies that her nursery rhymes were " 'declined' " by Macmillan. "But perhaps as the business was not transacted immediately with Mr. Craik he though a partner [since 1865], was not aware of every detail."

Adding that she was still waiting to hear from Macmillan on the subject of *Goblin Market,* she also mentions for the first time in this letter the volume of prose tales which she hopes to send Ellis as soon as she has completed the leading story, and she brings up again the question of an illustrator for *Sing-Song*. Although she had tentatively agreed to Ellis' proposal that C. Fairfax Murray design the woodcuts, a new suggestion, put forward by Scott, that Alice be the illustrator, was enthusiastically endorsed by her. Receptive to his wishes as always, she wrote to Ellis:

> About the illustrations to the Nursery Rhymes, my brother Mr. Rossetti wrote to me two days ago: 'S. was mentioning to me an idea that Miss Boyd would have been very glad to put those things on the blocks for your Nursery Rhymes. I fancy she would really probably do them with more fun and zest than Murray though perhaps not so artistically—Her ideas for beast drawings are good as you know.' I just tell you this, though I fear it may be too late. Miss Boyd, who has exhibited more than once is a most particular friend of mine: ⟨and it would have been very nice⟩ but of course the point is for you conclusively to decide. . . .

For his part, Ellis still wanted Murray, but he was willing to defer to a new writer's preference by compromising, a solution Christina eagerly accepted, since it still gave her the opportunity to gratify Scott by sharing her own preëminence with Alice:

> I am extremely pleased both that Mr. Murray should do some of my illustrations, and that Miss Boyd should (if as I trust she will) undertake the rest. Her address is
>
> 33 Elgin Road
> Notting Hill—W
>
> After what my brother has said it is needless for *me* to express admiration of her talents. I am sending her your note, so that if you open direct communication with her you will find the way paved: or perhaps she will write first to you. No, on second thoughts, I suppose she might prefer not writing first.
>
> I hope very soon to send you my little prose volume, but have not quite finished copying the principal story. Mr. Macmillan has not written yet about the volume of verse. It struck me, after receiving the hint you kindly gave me as to utilizing the remaining copies of Goblin Market, that after all I fear it will be impossible to incorporate them in an 'entire' edition: for it seems that *at most* not more than 450 copies remain on hand, and I suppose it might not answer to publish so

> small an edition as 450,—besides the doubt whether there really are so many. In short I know not what to do about it all. . . .

To this letter she added the postscript, "I believe Miss Boyd is so sure to undertake the Sing Song illustrations, that the sooner she has them in hand the better."

II

And so Christina, influenced by her desire to please both Scott and her brother, allowed her career to be bent to the private purposes of the two men. At the time she could not suspect the harm she was doing herself, and was undoubtedly only too glad to be able to do them a service. But the disastrous effect of permitting her affections to govern her professional life was soon to be apparent.

At the moment, however, her affairs had never looked so promising. Ellis was bringing out *Sing-Song,* was sure to publish *Commonplace,* and possibly a collected edition as well. She had already derived considerable financial advantage from the change in publishers, and would doubtless soon realize further profits from the new arrangement.

Not only were her own prospects bright, but those of her intimate circle were equally so. Alice, already at work on the woodcuts, through Christina's agency was being given the chance to make a name for herself as an illustrator. Maria was writing *The Shadow of Dante* (published in 1872), her contribution to Dante studies, the work upon which her slight claim to fame rests. As the result of his Shelley publications, William was gaining increased prestige as a critic, editor, and man of letters. And Gabriel was getting ready his volume of poems, which Ellis had scheduled for late April publication. He had secluded himself at Scalands, the country house of his friend Mrs. Bodichon (the former Barbara Leigh Smith), and his only companion there was the American, W. J. Stillman, who at this time introduced him to chloral as a remedy for insomnia. His literary friends, including Swinburne, Morris, Joseph Knight (then editor of the Sunday *Times,* later to be Rossetti's first biographer), Dr. Hake, Scott, Sidney Colvin, and others, were preparing the laudatory reviews which were to launch the volume to the immediate and brilliant success for which it was destined.

By the third week in March Christina had finished "Commonplace" and sent it to Gabriel. Although he approved it as "very good at first glance," as "likely to take," and "far from uninteresting," his praise has a tepid ring. He was of course absorbed in his own affairs which were rapidly approaching a climax, but, as we have seen, he also thought that writing such prose tales diverted his sister's energies from her "proper business" of writing poetry.

Nonetheless he looked after her interests with his usual energy of

purpose, writing Ellis on the 23rd that he had finished her story and predicted "a good success" for it. "Have you my sister's stories," he asked three days later, "and how do you like them?"

Ellis liked them well enough to undertake publication, and on the 29th Christina wrote that she would be very glad to close with his terms, which were the same he had offered for *Sing-Song,* one-fourth the published price for 500 copies. She was sorry he didn't like the title of "Commonplace," for "what else to name the every-day story I know not. I have been turning titles over in my head at intervals all day, and can't think of a one." She advanced Maria's suggestion, "Births, Deaths and Marriages," but Ellis found that title even drearier than the objectionable "Commonplace."

When he proposed that she fill out the volume with more tales, she replied, "As regards my writing an additional story to increase bulk, perhaps you with me will shrink from the expedient when I tell you that the 6 you have in hand are nearly all the prose I have written between '52 and '70!" In closing, however, she said she would try to scrape up "2 more trifles in print." Though they were very short, they were "better than nothing." Presumably these were two of the three tales published in *Churchman's Shilling* in 1867.

On the same day she wrote Macmillan the letter which with one exception closed their correspondence for the next four years. The friendly tone of it, however, shows that she had no wish to burn her bridges behind her:

> DEAR MR. MACMILLAN
>
> I have been fancying you were going to write to me as the result of my brother's calling upon you, and I have not had a letter. So if I do not shortly hear from you I will conclude that the complete edition question has been dropped for the present. My Nursery Rhymes are in hand and I hope promise to look pretty.
>
> What a winter! This March is very like January. When will the world grow green again?

Although by April she was reading final proof, Ellis was still asking for changes in "Commonplace." Among others he suggested that Christina specify how Lucy Charlmont's father had made his fortune. Faced with this problem and knowing little about financial matters, Christina took a hint from Scott's speculations on the stock market, the way he cannily transferred his £1400 "from Egyptian and American stock and back again so as to get both dividends," and wrote to Ellis:

> We will, if you please, make Mr. Charlmont 'come' unexpectedly into *some hundreds* a 'year' p.q. As to his *speculations,* I imagine him doing such things as buying in and selling out at lucky moments, though not otherwise than as a perfectly upright man may do. Do you think this too much, or that my word does not convey my meaning? If the latter,

I bow to your superior business knowledge, and will let ⟨him⟩ it be that he 'invested his savings profitably'. . . .

III

On April 25 Gabriel's 1870 *Poems* appeared. Within the week the first edition of almost a thousand copies had been sold, and Ellis was going to press with a second thousand. No wonder Frances Rossetti exulted to her son, "These are palmy days when poetry can produce £300 a month. What would Milton and a host of other worthies say to it?" [2]

With Ellis unable to meet the demand for Gabriel's *Poems* and about to publish both Christina's new volumes, relations between the Rossettis and the publisher could not have been more cordial. All was love, harmony, congratulations. At Euston Square it was decided to put the business relationship upon a social basis, and Christina therefore wrote the following note on April 29:

DEAR MR. ELLIS

I do not know whether it is monstrous to imagine you wasting 4 o'clock next Tuesday afternoon on a kettledrum; but I should like our acquaintance to get beyond knowing each other's handwriting by sight, and I hope a few kind friends will favour us at the time indicated. The week following I expect to leave town.

If I blunder in asking you pray pardon

Yours truly
Christina G. Rossetti

Not only did Ellis gladly present himself at the Euston Square tea party, where he met Alice Boyd, whom Christina had told him he would find "amongst our small circle of friends," but he also sent Christina "a handsome check" in advance of publication. After the tea, Frances Rossetti reported to Gabriel that she had met Mr. Ellis, and that he was "a fine-looking Englishman."

Commonplace was published on May 7. A few days later Christina left for Folkestone, where she stayed until mid-July. Her object apparently was to leave London before the reviewing began, an affair she always dreaded as a nerve-shattering ordeal. In this case her precaution was wisely taken, for the contrast between the dazzling success of Gabriel's *Poems,* going through edition after edition, and the dismal failure of her own volume could not have been more striking.

Ellis was discouraged by the public's indifference to *Commonplace* and even more by the woeful inadequacy of Alice's illustrations for *Sing-Song,* now manifest; and he therefore hesitated to bring out the nursery rhymes. He could not have objected to Alice's "beasts," which, as Gabriel had foreseen, were drawn with charm and skill—her ducks, birds, caterpillars, snails, rabbits, and frogs live on the pages with an innocent vitality of their own—but she could not draw the human figure, and her babies and young children were disastrous. A series of four letters written that

spring by the publisher to Alice reveal his increasing loss of confidence in the market value of *Sing-Song*.[3]

On April 16 and 20 he was still going ahead with publication plans, sending Alice supplies of plates and having those she had completed called for and delivered to him. By May 14 he had cooled off, and by May 25 he was writing to Alice, then at Penkill, "that he was really ashamed to think how long I have left your letter unanswered." Although he still spoke glibly of proofs and plates, his excuses—"I have been so very much engaged with a variety of things that I have not been able to give this book so much attention as I ought to have done"—and his polite chattiness about the countryside and art barely covered his disinclination to proceed with publication as planned. His concluding sentence indicates where his real interest lay. "You will be glad to hear that Rossetti's book continues to sell—to say that it has far exceeded my expectations would be a moderate phrase to use. . . ."

By the beginning of June it was clear to Christina that Ellis was reluctant to follow up one publishing failure with another uncertain venture by the same author. They had already discussed Alice's illustrations; and the problem of what to do about them without offending Alice, and therefore Scott, was a troublesome one. But Christina correctly surmised that she herself presented an even more difficult problem to Ellis, for at this juncture he would have been anxious to avoid anything that would have marred his cordial relations with Rossetti. In receiving her long letter of June 1, the publisher must have been grateful for her gift of tact, which in this instance took the form of plain speaking, because it extricated him from an embarrassing position. The capacity to face the hard truth without flinching, not always shown in her emotional affairs, is here evident, as she draws the obvious conclusion from the failure of her most recent publication:

Dear Mr. Ellis

I enclose a P.O.O. for the money portion of my debt to you, cordially acknowledging the liberality with which you have all along treated me. Pray believe that my wish for some commercial success with both my volumes, regards your interest as well as my own. I still hope that favourable reviews may rescue 'Commonplace' from oblivion; but am sorry to say I know not of any such definite prospect, beyond a rumour that the 'Pall Mall' means to treat me well. However, I trust it is not yet too late for hope.

I ventured to mention my brother Gabriel's remarks to you; but certainly I do not venture to urge them, sharing as I do, neither risk nor responsibility. It strikes me that if anything could be done to lessen the evil we both perceive, it might be to suggest to Miss Boyd to make no more *large* figure designs; thus the bulk of the illustrations might be rescued from the misfortune which has already befallen some: but I merely mention this as what has occurred to me. Now pray allow me to mention something of more importance. I can readily imagine that if

> 'Commonplace' proves a total failure, 'Sing-Song' may dwindle to a very serious risk: and therefore I beg you at once, if you deem the step prudent, to put a stop to all further outlay on the rhymes, until you can judge whether my name is marketable. It would probably not be long before you could give me a final answer as to 'Sing-Song,' after which of course I should be at liberty to try its fortunes elsewhere, if I thought it worth while.
>
> Congratulations on the marked success of my brother's volume. . . .

But not even favorable reviews could rescue *Commonplace* from a deserved oblivion. In general the reviewers, although well-intentioned (some of them were Gabriel's friends), did Christina a disservice by praising her book for the wrong reasons. For instance, the review in the *Athenæum* of June 4—"slipshod" but "quotable," said Gabriel—pointed out that the title piece, wholesome and simple, lacked the sensational and startling qualities which gratified the public taste in Mr. Disraeli's "tawdry romance" *Lothair*. Understandably a story which consisted "of the most ordinary incidents of commonplace life," as the review put it, with "commonplace characters," lacked attraction for the buying public which went right on giving its money for *Lothair* instead. But how right Ellis had been to object to the title!

Colvin, writing in the *Pall Mall Gazette* June 7 (Ellis had advertised in both these journals), called attention to the resemblance between Miss Rossetti and Mrs. Gaskell, particularly in their "art of painting with moral grays." This and the further observation that in Christina's story there was "little room for the exciting elements of fiction" were enough to dampen the interest of any prospective reader.

The Sunday *Times* of June 12 did better by her, the reviewer discerning in her prose the qualities which distinguished her poetry. Describing the title story as "a gilded commonplace," he assumed that Christina wished "to prove that in life there is no commonplace," the tragic element in human existence giving the superficially commonplace richness and beauty. Possibly this perceptive review was written by Joseph Knight, for Gabriel used the same strategy in arranging for a favorable reception of his sister's published work as for his own. In her case, however, "the skillful scheming"—William's phrase for it—failed to produce similar results. The one time she had allowed herself to be completely led by Gabriel, her professional affairs had taken a ruinous turn. Not only was *Commonplace* a failure and *Sing-Song* shelved as a result, but, having sacrificed her satisfactory relationship of eight years with Macmillan, she was, though a recognized poet, left in the humiliating position of being without a publisher.

The last of her 1870 letters to Ellis, written from Folkestone (undated), sets the seal upon this unfortunate episode which only five months earlier had been so full of bright promise:

Dear Mr. Ellis

I am so sorry for all the money you have spent on Sing Song, which may well hide its diminished head for one while. If ever its publication comes in question again, do you think it would be worth while doing what Gabriel thinks feasible? omitting the ugly human beings, but making use of the pretty beasts and flowers. Thank you gratefully for not mentioning my name, though if the slightest difficulty as to truth arises I beg you to bring me in unsparingly even to Miss Boyd.

I have not seen the Churchman's Shilling Magazine, and should have supposed it might have had a warm word for me. Pazienza!

No, I went by the Sunday Times . . . and a few others which you probably know. Still I am glad that even so many, though so few, copies have sold. We are not all D.G.R.s

Sincerely yours
Christina G. Rossetti

IV

Despite this professional setback, Christina's life flowed along smoothly and on the whole pleasantly for the remainder of 1870. She had accepted Scott's relationship with Alice as a *de facto* situation, and she anticipated settling down to enjoy a comfortable friendship, which, as she had foreseen in the *Amico,* would serve as love's expedient expression.

By 1870 Scott had finished painting the windows of the South Kensington Museum's Ceramic Gallery, a work which had occupied him for three years, and, as a reward for his labors, he proposed to buy himself a house. The one he had in mind was situated on the other side of Tudor House, at the Chelsea end of the old wooden bridge to Battersea. Bellevue House was a picturesque eighteenth-century mansion originally designed by the Adam brothers. It had a garden on the other side of the road leading down to the river, a vinery behind the house, and a music room that had once contained Handel's organ. Scott hoped to get the house cheap because Chelsea was such an undesirable residential section. "I am sure the locality is so against it," he wrote Alice, "that their chances of a sale are few. If I bought it to let it would be a bad investment. . . ."

He asked Virtue Tebbs, the solicitor who had been so useful to Gabriel in the matter of the exhumation, to transact the business for him while he was at Penkill. Early in June he instructed Tebbs to offer £1400 for the house, to be paid in November. This was the sum he had been using for speculation, and it was then invested in Berlin Water Works shares and Egyptian government bonds. Scott's intention was to increase his capital investment by November, then sell, and put his money in the Chelsea property.

But he had not counted upon the outbreak of the Franco-Prussian War that summer. One day in July as he was driving through Girvan with Alice, he heard of the sudden declaration of war, and trembled for his

investments. At the advance of the French army, his Berlin Water Works shares crashed, only to rally as the French cavalry was turned back. With the threat of Russia in the East, his Egyptian bonds were in danger, but this crisis passed too, and he had the satisfaction of watching the value of his Egyptians soar higher than ever. That autumn was the most exciting in his life. The war was for him an exhilarating spectacle he could read about in the daily newspaper while enjoying the peaceful summer seclusion of the Penkill garden. For obvious reasons his sympathies were on the side of Germany, whereas, he observed with contempt, "the vast mediocrity, literary or other, went in for France."

Christina was one of those who favored the cause of France, though in writing her two poems entitled *The German-French Campaign,* she declared that her aim was to express "human sympathy, not political bias." Nevertheless her human sympathy was definitely on the side of what in *To-day for Me* she called "Sister France," "Vine-clad France," and "Broken France." This poem with its skillful variations in monorhyme—"the best thing said in verse on the subject," Gabriel pronounced it—concludes on a note of prognosis so characteristic of Christina that it can be regarded as almost her signature:

A time there is for change and chance:
Who next shall drink the trembling cup,
Wring out its dregs and suck them up
After France?

Profiting by the fortunes of war, Scott was enabled through the defeat of France to meet his obligation on Bellevue House in November. He moved in the beginning of January, 1871, and Alice, but presumably not his wife, joined him shortly thereafter. He installed his books and his early Italian and German prints, began redecorating, and felt, as he put it, that the "hermit crab" had at last grown a permanent shell. Gabriel told Miss Losh that "Scotus exists all day long in that Paradise of pottering, which . . . is so sweet to him." As next-door neighbors, Gabriel and Scott were on daily visiting terms, and the three-handed whist games (sometimes with the painter Boyce as a fourth) before the marble fireplace in the drafty old eighteenth-century mansion became an evening institution.

This neighborliness extended northward to Euston Square. Often after an exhausting day's labor before the easel, Gabriel would look in at Bellevue House, hoping for a rubber, only to be told that Scott and Alice were visiting the family at Euston Square. Such opportunities for unlimited social intercourse must have been gratifying to Christina, providing her (though in the way of sublimation) with the emotional stability heretofore lacking in her life. She could increasingly regard Scott as her

"brother" and her "friend." He knew she loved him. His acceptance of her love and his tenderness because of it (whether he returned it or not was his own affair) gave her a certain amount of satisfaction, for wasn't "love's mere self a continual feast"?

V

But her quiet contentment was not to last. Sometimes a life falls into a circle of disaster, which then whirls downward with an inevitability and an acceleration the individual is powerless to stop. At such times, unable to control the direction his life has quite suddenly and inexplicably taken, the individual appears to be a helpless and passive spectator of his own ruin.

In Christina's case, the disappointment of her literary hopes consequent upon her change of publishers served as the first warning of trouble ahead. But, as usual, such signposts are not recognizable as such until events have swept by them; and then they are visible only in retrospect. Beginning in 1870 Christina was subject to a series of misfortunes she did nothing to incur but which simply happened to her. Unless we wish to regard her decision to leave Macmillan as a fault of judgment starting the movement of calamity which governed her life for the next few years, we cannot hold her responsible for her afflictions. Like Job, she did not create her own disasters, though also like the Biblical hero, she had to endure them.

The first mention of the strange thyroidic disease which afflicted her occurs in her letter of February, 1871, to Gabriel. Some weeks earlier he had asked her to read and criticize Dr. Hake's new volume of poetry, the author being anxious to know the impression it would make "on a lady of acute mind." She kept the volume around the house for a long time, and finally returned it with the explanation that she had lost herself "in its mazes, and perished in its quag." Still, she tried to do what was expected of her in the way of criticizing the various poems: in one she recognized beauty, "but how about meaning?" In concluding she apologized, "Perhaps if I had not been pulled down by my abscess I might be more pointed; as it is, please pardon generalities."

In April she began to be troubled by severe shooting pains, which Dr. Jenner diagnosed as neuralgia. By April 28 she was writing to Gabriel in a hand as shaky as that of an old woman, "Sir W. Jenner saw me last Saturday and pronounced me seriously ill: to avoid stairs I am confined to the drawing room floor. . . . Please attribute intolerable hideousness in part to weakness."

But, although her symptoms began to grow daily more alarming, she refused to stay in bed. She insisted upon arising at her usual hour, dressing herself, and attending to her daily domestic chores. Before long, however,

this became impossible, and she was forced to resign herself to lying about on the sofa.

On May 5, despite her physician's assurance that there was no immediate danger, William felt increasingly uneasy about her condition, which appeared "extremely serious" to him. She rallied, however, in the weeks that followed, and by May 12 Gabriel was expressing delight at her improvement.

A letter she wrote to Ellis on March 1 reveals that, despite illness, she was still engaged in literary work, though not of a productive nature:

> DEAR MR. ELLIS
>
> I am unfortunately obliged once more to trouble you about Sing-Song. This morning I looked through the Rhymes with an eye to business, and was very sorry to find 22 of them missing. I am sure of this because the whole set is numbered in sequence. The strayed *nos* are: [follows a list of the missing poems].
>
> Would it be possible for you to recover them anywhere and restore them to me? I fear my poor little book is troublesome to you ⟨nearly⟩ even as it were in its grave; but pray believe me that it is so quite against my will. I should like as soon as well may be to hear from you on the subject.

Some time during that spring, struggling with pain and sickness, she managed to get her nursery rhymes in order and accepted for publication by George Routledge, for by April 26 the brothers Dalziel had been engaged to engrave the woodcuts, and shortly thereafter Arthur Hughes was selected as the illustrator. It may have been Scott who introduced Christina to Routledge, who was bringing out his own *Gems of Modern Belgian Art.* At any rate Christina now had the satisfaction of knowing that her book would be published. The fortunes of *Sing-Song,* in some queer way inextricably linked with Christina's illness, advanced in the same ratio as she herself declined in health and strength.

It was not until many months had elapsed that Dr. Jenner recognized in her symptoms the incipient stages of the rare Graves' disease. He persisted in believing she would benefit from a change of air, and so on June 6 she moved with her mother to lodgings at 17 Christ Church Road in Hampstead Heath. Upon her return six weeks later, better but far from well, Dr. Jenner ordered her off again, this time to Folkestone for the sea air. In London she caught a cold, and this indisposition allowed her a brief respite from the tedious journeying about from place to place, the inevitable prescription for nineteenth-century invalids.

During the week she remained at home she received the second proofs of *Sing-Song* with Hughes' illustrations ("Mr. Hughes continues charming"), helped Maria choose a frontispiece for her *Shadow of Dante,* to be published in August, and entertained Cayley at dinner, lending him her presentation copy of Joaquin Miller's *Song of the Sierras.*

At Folkestone, where she remained through September, she corrected

proof, writing to her publisher that she hoped "the delightfully early period at which you think S.S. may be ready will not entail too great a pressure of haste on Mr. Hughes," a polite way of pointing out what William had already noticed, evidence of "speedy execution" in some of the illustrations. Asserting that Christina's book took up his whole time, Hughes explained that at the beginning he had worked in a fairly leisurely fashion, but before long the Dalziels were demanding ten designs a week; and the first week, at their request, he had even furnished twenty.

Christina was not unappreciative of his efforts. In fact, so grateful did she feel to her illustrator, whose "cuts deserve to sell the volume," that she requested the Dalziel brothers to print his name "in larger print on the title page." She was particularly partial to Hughes' designs on pages 93 and 94; these were *Who Has Seen the Wind?* and *The Horses of the Sea.*

From Folkestone she wrote William that it looked as though she were gaining ground: the abscess had disappeared; her appetite had improved; she walked more steadily. "Still I am weak," she admitted, "and less ornamental than society may justly demand. . . ."

VI

This was understatement. By October 8 she was back in London, "feeling pretty so-so," William told Stephens, "but looking very bad." A few weeks later he reported in a letter to Stephens that she "continues pretty fair: not well, but not worse than she often is at times she is not, *for her,* very bad. As to looks, she continues amiss." And, when Gabriel returned from Kelmscott Manor, which he shared with the William Morrises, he was shocked to find his sister "completely altered and looking suddenly 10 years older." It was no wonder that he was startled at the change in her appearance, for—as she explained apologetically—during her entire illness she had seen her brother only twice, "his nocturnal habits" not being "adapted to a sickroom." [4]

But, as the autumn weeks passed, Christina held her own, and Gabriel, observing that she was on the whole "much in her usual state as to health and spirits," considered the worst over. The much desired and long postponed publication of her nursery rhymes, scheduled for November, undoubtedly helped to cheer her.

On October 24 she was well enough to attend with Gabriel a small but select dinner party at Scott's house, where she met Edmund Gosse, then an ambitious young man starting a literary career, who hoped that social intercourse with such literary figures as "Miss and Mr. Rossetti" might be "useful" to him.[5]

But her release from physical suffering did not outlast the month. By the last week in October she noticed an odd swelling in her throat. Sir

William Jenner was away, and in his absence she consulted a Dr. Fox, who prescribed digitalis. "In this house of late," William wrote Macmillan, "there has been much sickness—Christina entirely prostrated for months, and still in a state causing great distress and anxiety. . . ." By the first week in November the swelling in her throat had increased to alarming proportions, and she was unable to swallow without difficulty.

Throughout November she continued in what William called "a very deplorable state." Besides the swelling in her throat, which did not subside, she had "a fluttering at the heart" that caused stifling sensations and sometimes loss of consciousness. She was also tormented by violent headaches, and her hands shook like those of a very old, palsied woman, so that she could not even hold a pencil between her fingers.

William was forced to admit that "as regard appearance, she is a total wreck for the present, and I greatly fear this change may prove permanent." Her hair was falling out, so that she had to wear a cap. Her skin had turned a dry, rusty brown. Her eyes protruded wildly. Her features had become sharply thin in sunken cheeks. Her voice was entirely altered. "But with all these disasters—and she is fully alive to every one of them," said William, "her spirits are not so bad as might have been expected; she shows a really admirable constancy, and the worst shafts of Fate find her their equal."

On November 18 she received her author's copy of *Sing-Song*. In the midst of her suffering it was a triumphant moment when she first held the finished volume in her shaking hands. Seldom had a literary birth proved more difficult. But despite all obstacles and hindrances, she had brought her book through to life, and at this dark hour it was a visible symbol of her achievement.

VII

Yet such consolation was only momentary. In her condition poetry and publication seemed like the remote occupations of the red-cheeked healthy, with a firm hold on life. Feeling herself sinking daily, she needed stronger and more solid support than the mere assurance of literary success. In her extremity, beyond human aid, she turned for help where she had always found it; and much of the poetry dated "Before 1882" reflects the experience of this gloomy period when her only recourse was prayer:

I have not sought Thee, I have not found Thee,
I have not thirsted for Thee:
And now cold billows of death surround me,
Buffeting billows of death astound me,—
Wilt Thou look upon, wilt Thou see
Thy perishing me?

The suffering endured in long, sleepless, pain-haunted nights left its mark on these lines:

Blackness of darkness this, but not for aye;
Darkness that even in gathering fleeteth fast,
Blackness of blackest darkness close to day.
Lord Jesus, through Thy darkened pillar cast
Thy gracious eyes all-seeing cast on me
Until this tyranny be overpast.

Sir William, now back from his holiday, held consultations with Dr. Fox, and finally they identified Christina's sickness as the very rare exophthalmic bronchocele, called Graves' disease, a malady so rare that both physicians had seen only two other cases of it. As the disease developed in all its horror, Christina had to fight not only the malady, but worse, the fear and despair it engendered. Often she felt that medical assistance was of little use to her; only divine aid could save her.

Thy Will I will, I Thy desire desire;
Let not the waters close above my head,
Uphold me that I sink not in this mire:
For flesh and blood are frail and sore afraid:
And young I am, unsatisfied and young,
With memories, hopes, with cravings all unfed,
My song half sung, its sweetest notes unsung. . . .

In the last line may be discerned the unmistakable cry of the poet with work still to do.

During the endlessly tedious, slow-moving hours in the sickroom she pondered over the cause of her suffering. What had she done to deserve such a grotesque affliction?

Was I a careless woman set at ease
That this so bitter cup is brimmed for me?

But it was futile to rebel, to resist one's apportioned lot. The immediate problem was to learn how to bear

Pain and weariness, aching eyes and head,
Pain and weariness all the day and night.

One could of course look for minimal compensations:

. . . the pillow's soft on my smooth soft bed,
And fresh air blows in, and mother shades the light.

But they were only superficially satisfying. At a deeper level it was necessary to seek out the source of suffering, and from the Exemplar learn how to endure it:

Thou, O Lord, in pain hadst no pillow soft,
In Thy weary pain, in Thine agony:
But a cross of shame held Thee up aloft
Where thy very mother could do nought for Thee.

Therefore she must school herself, in devout emulation, patiently to submit to her own suffering "till all days and nights and patient suffering cease."

Another utterance which gives voice to the terrible despair of this period reflects even more powerfully the agony of spirit she was undergoing:

Lord, I am waiting, weeping, watching for Thee:
My youth and hope lie by me buried and dead,
My wandering love hath not where to lay its head
Except Thou say 'Come to Me.'

My noon is ended, abolished from life and light,
My noon is ended, ended and done away,
My sun went down in the hours that still were day,
And my lingering day is night.

Her humiliation at still craving human love at a time when her ruined appearance left her little hope of obtaining it is apparent in this cry of abject distress:

O God Who before the beginning hast seen the end,
Who hast made me flesh and blood, not frost and not fire,
Who hast filled me full of needs and love and desire
And a heart that craves a friend,— . . .

Turn Thy gracious eyes on me and think no scorn
Of me, not even of me.
Beside Thy Cross I hang on my cross in shame,
My wounds, weakness, extremity cry to Thee.

VIII

By December she was, said William, "looking decidedly not quite so miserable in the face." He even observed "some little diminution of the thinness and starting eyes." When Dr. Fox examined his patient, he confirmed William's optimism: she was definitely better. In fact, so marked was her improvement that she could once again turn her mind to business, writing on December 1 in a fairly firm and steady hand,

DEAR MR. MACMILLAN,
I received with surprise this evening a little sum on my *Goblin Market* about which I no longer thought at all as a source of profit. Thank you and please accept my receipt ⟨appended⟩ enclosed. I am sorry to see so many Goblins still in the market, as otherwise the small remainder of *Prince's Progress* we could have dealt with.
If you have seen *SingSong* I hope you have admired the beautiful illustrations which charm my brother Dante.

Fortunately for Christina in her precarious state of health, the reviews could not have been more enthusiastic. This time her brother's friends

did not let her down. The Sunday *Times* of December 16 (probably Knight again) pronounced her the leading woman poet of her day, *Sing-Song* displaying that "imaginative power" united with "supreme delicacy and tenderness" which marked all her work. Colvin, writing in *The Academy* on January 15, called the volume "one of the most exquisite in its class ever seen . . ."

One of the Dalziels predicted to Dr. Hake that the verses would become and remain "household words." The doctor himself confided to Gabriel that he had read *Sing-Song* "with a rapture that makes me wish myself a loving, listening child." Arthur Hughes, whose illustrations received as much attention from reviewers as Christina's text, merely commented that the book had "a horrid blue cover." [6]

But despite the paean of praise, it is doubtful whether Christina made much money out of *Sing-Song*. According to agreement, she received 10 per cent on each copy sold. Although Roberts Brothers published it in the United States, Routledge did not bring out a second edition until 1878. The third edition was by Macmillan in 1893. After Christina's death, it continued to be reprinted at intervals, and maintained a modest but steady volume of sales well into the twentieth century.

All during this time, throughout the excitement of publication and reviewing, Christina kept fairly well. As previously, she was afforded a few months of relief before the screws were tightened again. A peculiarity of her disease was the way it relaxed its grip upon its victims at intervals. To the Rossettis it must have seemed like a hideous monster out of some Teutonic folk tale, a malignant monster which toys dangerously with its captives before devouring them.

By March Christina was again in its clutches. Dr. Jenner assured the family that the disease was seldom fatal, but that the chief danger arose from exhaustion. "Of this," said William, "there have been of late very distressing symptoms in Christina—almost total want of appetite, prostration of strength, and very frequent vomiting."

In the middle of April Maria saw Christina's throat uncovered for the first time in months; and she expressed herself as "agreeably surprised" to find how very much the swelling had diminished, and how much less marked was the discoloration. She said one might almost take the throat for its natural shape. But Christina's condition failed to justify this outburst of optimism. On the contrary, she grew steadily worse. Her doctors ordered her to keep to her bed. Unable to take nourishment, she had to be fed small amounts of food every two hours to keep up her strength.

Factual reading, chiefly history and biography, subjects she had avoided almost all her life, appealed to her at this time. Her mother read aloud Southey's *Life of Nelson,* and she herself, when able, read Goldsmith's *History of Greece.*

As the weeks passed, she showed "no real rally of physical energy." It

looked to William as though the process of exhaustion was advancing "with fatal and frightful steadiness." On May 15 the family "felt very uneasy about Christina all the earlier part of the day, as . . . she was in a terribly low condition, accompanied with frequent vomitings."

But shortly afterwards, her voice, so strained and enfeebled all through the spring, began to recover its former tone and quality. Gradually she also regained command of her ability to concentrate. What astonished William the most and aroused his enthusiastic admiration was his sister's heroic fortitude. Throughout the harrowing experience her strength of mind, he said with pride, continued "to maintain an admirable triumph over all physical suffering and prostration."

IX

Misfortune seemed to strike simultaneously at various members of the Rossetti circle. Each man and woman of the formerly gay and brilliant group was struggling with his own particular trial. As every generation, so this one was reluctantly descending the slopes of middle age toward that last lonely outpost where those few left in ranks decimated daily face the last grim prospect.

Scott, who had suffered all his life from periodic attacks of "nervous despair," which he did not hesitate to call "a mental disease . . . one of my most perplexing and dangerous enemies," now fell into a state of dejection which caused Holman Hunt to write from the Holy Land, "I am sorry to believe your assurance that you are amongst the unhappy ones of the earth." Hunt in turn reported himself cheerless, friendless, and feverish with anxiety about work that was leading him "coffinward." Brown was fighting fiercely to carry on his own labors in the midst of "distressing illnesses and harassing cares." Alice, suddenly faced with financial ruin, was threatened with the loss of her beloved Penkill.[7]

And Gabriel, having made the discovery that the anonymous attack upon his poetry in the *Contemporary Review* was by Robert Buchanan, lashed himself into a fury and brooded savagely upon revenge.[8] Although he fought back, giving as good as he got, Buchanan's intemperate criticism acted upon him like slow poison, and Scott thought that Gabriel, like Keats, was letting himself "be snuffed out by an article."

In May of 1872 came Buchanan's second attack, this time in the form of a virulent pamphlet expanding and developing his "Fleshly School of Poetry" thesis in the *Contemporary*. Although Gabriel was at the prime of his powers both as painter and as poet, and in the full enjoyment of his success in both fields, he was nevertheless in a highly nervous condition bordering upon psychosis. According to his biographer, "A victim of drug, drink, and passion, he was increasingly succumbing to paranoid tendencies. . . ." [9] Although this exaggerated description seems to be but part of the truth, Gabriel was undoubtedly in a state of abnormal excitement

which intensified his receptivity to any evil the outside world might inflict upon him; and Buchanan's second attack was a deadly blow from which he never fully recovered.

The crisis and collapse came during the weekend of June 2. Alarmed by Gabriel's wild talk, William hurried next door to fetch Scott, who, said William, "as usual, acted in the spirit of the truest and kindest friendship." To both men Gabriel appeared to be "partially insane." Later William concluded that the hypochondria resulting from overdoses of chloral and alcohol was the real secret of his brother's "frenzied collapse." In this emergency Dr. Hake appeared and took charge of Gabriel, carrying him off to his own house in Roehampton.

The culmination of a weekend of gruesome horrors was reached on Saturday night, when, unbeknown to the others, Gabriel swallowed the contents of a bottle of laudanum (the drug that had killed his wife), and at once fell into a deep and deadly sleep that lasted almost twenty-four hours and from which he could not be aroused.

In the crisis that followed, it was William's harrowing duty to go to town as fast as a fly would carry him and fetch his mother and Maria from Euston Square. There was no question of fetching Christina. A bed-ridden invalid herself, she had to remain at Euston Square while her mother and Maria hurriedly packed a few necessaries and went out with William to the waiting fly. Aunt Eliza, who lived nearby in Bloomsbury, was hastily summoned to look after Christina.

At the time William came for his mother and sister, it had not yet been discovered that Gabriel had taken laudanum, and Dr. Hake diagnosed his collapse as a stroke of serous apoplexy. Such an affliction could result in either death or the loss of reason, and it was feared that Gabriel could not live through the night.

X

This was the prospect Christina had to face in an hour when her own life, said William, "was hanging by a thread." Once the family had departed, she was left alone but for the elderly aunt. Lying in her sick chamber in the desolate, darkening house, what could her thoughts have been?

Above all, she regretted her own helplessness in the face of the family disaster. In the time of crisis, when now if ever she was needed, her own discouraging illness, so prolonged, so wasting in its effects, bound her to the bed as with thongs of iron. What kind of night could she have spent, with the black hours crawling slowly by, bringing in their wake—what?

Did she look for a cause-and-effect relationship in this new calamity? Once before in a poem of 1854, written immediately after her father's death, she had invited divine retribution for her "sin." And now in the light of this new suffering, did she turn once again to that "special self-

sifting" which she thought "scrupulous Christians" should never neglect?

Although she and Gabriel were the chief sufferers, the others had not been spared—the innocent had to suffer alike with the guilty. *Mea culpa?* is the relentless question the stern conscience never spares itself. Who, then, was guilty—Gabriel, herself, or both of them? Or neither? But no. Surely there was guilt somewhere, for there was punishment. And in a religious frame of reference there is no room for the random element or for the miscarriage of divine justice.

Pursuing, then, this kind of logic, did her mind, always so adept at relating the unrelated (a poet's business) seek for the obscure, underlying spiritual connection between the two seemingly unrelated misfortunes, her own and her brother's illness? According to the moral law operative in the spiritual life, transgression—or what she called Christian sin—was always a cause producing an effect. The effect she could plainly see. The cause?

Although no evidence exists that she ever reproached Gabriel for what Ruskin called his "disorderly" way of life, this does not mean that she was unaware of his inability to deny himself any kind of sensual gratification. She could not have been blind to the fact that her brother's susceptibility to women, freely indulged, was to a large extent responsible for his drift toward self-destruction. Why, then, did she never interfere? Why did she not in some way try to prevent the steady deterioration that she as well as Gabriel's friends could not but perceive? She herself admitted in *Time Flies* that under certain circumstances a person was obliged to interfere:

> Impossible as in reality it is to avoid exercising personal influence, there is yet a restricted sense in which it may be withheld to the grievous hurt of those whose due it is; just as a lantern may be placed so as to hide its light; such withholding amounts not to neutrality but to evil influence: the lantern which does not cast light casts shadow.

How, then, could she have justified her own withholding?

If, in the process of her scrupulous "self-sifting," she had detected in her own nature a moral flaw similar to Gabriel's, perhaps in her case sternly and valiantly dealt with, but a corrosion nonetheless, would she not have felt that the stamp of this one defect restrained her from exerting personal influence? If she had recognized that her own susceptibility to what in *Convent Threshold* she had called "the pleasant sin" had proved to be the central problem of her own life, could she, without being hypocritical, have reproached Gabriel for sharing that particular fault? She had, as we have seen, already acknowledged the bond in *An Echo from Willowwood,* and was to do so again.

Although her mind was too subtle to have directly inferred that she was to blame for Gabriel's collapse, she might have felt that in some way, perhaps by being herself imperfect, she had failed him; and that whereas, because of her superior spiritual enlightenment, she had the greater moral

responsibility, he was undergoing the harsher punishment. A sonnet dated "Before 1882" suggests such a line of reasoning. It reflects the kind of anguish she experienced that crisis weekend of June 2, when, close to death herself and not knowing at what hour she would receive news of Gabriel's death, she kept the night's vigil alone:

I have done I know not what,—what have I done?
My brother's blood, my brother's soul, doth cry:
And I find no defence, find no reply,
No courage more to run this race I run,
Not knowing what I have done, have left undone;
Ah me, these awful unknown hours that fly,
Fruitless it may be, fleeting fruitless by,
Rank with death-savour underneath the sun!
For what avails it that I did not know
The deed I did? what profits me the plea
That had I known I had not wronged him so?
Lord Jesus Christ, my God, him pity Thou;
Lord, if it may be, pity also me:
In judgment pity, and in death, and now.

XI

Monday afternoon Gabriel awoke from his almost lethal trance. As soon as possible, William sent a reassuring word to Christina, which she at once acknowledged with gratitude:

My own dear William

Thank you warmly for your note received before 4 last night: it helped me—with its comparatively hopeful news—to get soundly to sleep at last. . . . I know not (having heard of one fearful alternative) what to hope: but with my whole heart I commit our extremity to Almighty God.

With the crisis safely passed and Gabriel's life no longer in danger, Mamma and Maria came home, leaving Gabriel in charge of William, Dr. Hake, and Scott. But with the subsiding of the emotional excitement that had sustained her during the weekend ordeal, Christina was left with that sickening feeling of let-down emptiness which often follows upon a crisis that digs deep into reserves of energy.

And with the relieving knowledge that Gabriel was out of danger came the restricting return to her own dismal existence. She knew that she was by no means out of the long black tunnel of her own disease. Weeks and months of patient endurance of pain still stretched ahead of her. Exhausted, depressed, unhappy about her ruined looks—that calamity carelessly added to calamities—she felt at this time that the noon of her life had indeed darkened to shade; that the sun of desire which at its meridian had warmed her and fired her creative powers, had lost its life-giving heat; and all that remained was the anticipation of the slow, loveless decline of a long afternoon.

This exhaustion of spent passion pervades *Sœur Louise de la Misericorde*.[10] And yet beneath its tone of tragic disillusionment can be felt the faint but still persisting throb of the vital pulse, the creative rhythm that would stop beating only with the cessation of life itself.

In this arresting dramatic monologue, in which once again Christina hides her own features behind the nun's veil, she turns for her theme and refrain to the words of the Preacher, which had inspired so much of her youthful poetry: vanity of vanities—all is vanity! But what had once been the immature cry of a girl whose unjaded eyes saw only the world's lack of perfection became for the mature woman the deep, heartfelt groan of a soul bruised and torn by experience:

I have desired, and I have been desired:
But now the days are over of desire,
Now dust and dying embers mock my fire:
Where is the hire for which my life was hired?
Oh vanity of vanities, desire!

Longing and love, pangs of a perished pleasure,
Longing and love, a disenkindled fire,
And memory a bottomless gulf of mire,
And love a fount of tears outrunning measure:
Oh vanity of vanities, desire!

Now from my heart, love's deathbed, trickles, trickles
Drop by drop slowly, drop by drop of fire,
The dross of life, of love, of spent desire:
Alas my rose of life gone all to prickles!
Oh vanity of vanities, desire!

Oh vanity of vanities, desire!
Stunting my hope which might have strained up higher,
Turning my garden-plot to barren mire;
Oh death-struck love, oh disenkindled fire,
Oh vanity of vanities, desire!

15

"DUST AND DYING EMBERS"?

1872–1876

During the summer both Christina and Gabriel slowly recovered, Gabriel in Scotland, cared for by the Hakes, father and son, and Christina at Glottenham in Sussex. Early in July her doctor had sent her to Hampstead Heath for the fresh air, but, unable to find ground-floor lodgings with a garden, she had to be satisfied with an apartment on the first floor. Since she was not yet permitted to climb stairs, this meant she was restricted to sitting out on the balcony. Such inactivity was depressing, and after a time she left for Sussex, accompanied by her mother.

But an invalid's life is bound to be colorless, and Glottenham proved almost as monotonous as Hampstead. Her chief pleasure there was an occasional game of croquet, a pleasure she was soon deprived of because the walking about made her feet swell. "One day here is so very like another," she wrote William in August, "that there is not much news for a letter even to my brother of brothers." Such news as there was she related: two robins were haunting the garden; emmets had appeared in swarms. No wonder she wrote the early part of September, "Please do not think me obstinate for returning home with Mamma on the 11th. . . . I feel languid and sometimes low here."

Yet despite her discouragement, she had gradually mended throughout the summer, leaving her illness behind her like some hideous shroud. And as daily life, which had been wrenched and distorted into nightmare patterns for the past eighteen months, imperceptibly smoothed itself back into normal contours, she began to take stock of her losses. The most visible was the loss of her good looks. She told William that "*Pro* you will find me fatter; *contra* of a fearful brownness." All her adult life her mirror had shown her the reflection of a sweetly delicate face. Now it revealed to her an image almost unrecognizable, with protruding eyes, sunken cheeks, and skin the color of parched adobe.

> All things that pass
> Are woman's looking-glass;

Thy show her how her bloom must fade,
And she herself be laid
With withered roses in the shade;
With withered roses and the fallen peach,
Unlovely, out of reach
Of summer joy that was.

With her realistic appraisal of human relationships, tinged as it was by pessimism, she understood that her ability to retain masculine interest had with this disadvantage shrunk to an alarming margin. How could Scott's affection, never very loyal, although enduring, withstand such a cruel attack upon her beauty?

Alas, alas, mine earthly love, alas.
For whom I thought to don the garments white
And white wreath of a bride, this rugged pass
Hath utterly divorced me from thy care.
Yea, I am to thee as a shattered glass
Worthless, with no more beauty lodging there,
Abhorred, lest I involve thee in my doom: . . .

Dear, what hast thou in common with a tomb?
I bow my head in silence, I make haste
Alone, I make haste out into the dark,
My life and youth and hope all run to waste.
Is this my body cold and stiff and stark,
Ashes made ashes, earth becoming earth,
Is this a prize for a man to make his mark?

Still, by the third week in September she was back in London and well enough to go with the rest of the family to greet Gabriel at Euston Station between trains, on his way from Perth to Kelmscott. Later in the autumn the faithful Cayley, whose loyal devotion never faltered, sent her several sonnets about the birth of Venus, which in October she acknowledged by her own sonnet, *Venus's Looking-Glass.*

This piece, with its lyrical lightness and Renaissance charm, would seem unrelated to the somber mood of these years but for the mirror image which appears so prominently in her poetry of the 'seventies. The sonnet itself recalls happier times, delicately evoking the memory of Christina's first Penkill visit, when she posed to Scott for Lady Jane in "The Court of Venus":

I marked where lovely Venus and her court
With song and dance and merry laugh went by;
Weightless, their wingless feet seemed made to fly,
Bound from the ground, and in mid air to sport.
Left far behind I heard the dolphins snort,
Tracking their goddess with a wistful eye,
Around whose head white doves rose, wheeling high
Or low, and cooed after their tender sort.

All this I saw in Spring. Through summer heat
I saw the lovely Queen of Love no more.
But when flushed Autumn through the woodlands went
I spied sweet Venus walk amid the wheat:
Whom seeing, every harvester gave o'er
His toil, and laught and hoped and was content.

She called the next sonnet to be written *Love-Lies-Bleeding,* and intended at one time to link it to the Venus sonnet by changing the title of the latter to "Love-in-Idleness," remarking that it should be read "with an eye to the next one." But the two sonnets have little in common except that love is the subject of both. Did she wish to associate them for the sake of contrast? It is undeniable that with the second sonnet we leave the world of serene, classic ideality and are back once more in the real world of pain, of separation, and suffering:

Love, that is dead and buried, yesterday
Out of his grave rose up before my face;
No recognition in his look, no trace
Of memory in his eyes dust-dimmed and grey;
While I, remembering, found no word to say,
But felt my quickened heart leap in its place;
Caught afterglow thrown back from long-set days,
Caught echoes of all music past away.
Was this indeed to meet?—I mind me yet
In youth we met when hope and love were quick,
We parted with hope dead but love alive:
I mind me how we parted then heart-sick,
Remembering, loving, hopeless, weak to strive:—
Was this to meet? Not so, we have not met.

But, if she had seen "the lovely Queen of Love" for the first time in the fresh springtime of her youth, lost sight of her in the summer (from 1858 to 1866), only to catch another enchanting glimpse of her during the ripe autumn of maturity, by 1872, the date of these sonnets, she despaired of ever spying "sweet Venus" again.

Had a meeting with Scott taken place in between the writing of the two sonnets? Had he, as she feared, failed to recognize in her careworn face, ravaged by sickness and suffering, traces of the beauty he admired? Had his response been not even pity for her misfortune, but the usual masculine indifference to a plain face?

As in 1864, so now the theme of meeting and separation haunts her poetry. The title *Meeting,* used for the 1864 linked poem, graces another piece dated "Circa 1875," setting the tone for the others in which the same theme is treated: *One Foot on Sea . . . , Parted, He and She, Brandons Both,* and *Mariana. Meeting* begins with the lines,

I said good-bye in hope;
But, now we meet again,

I have no hope at all
Of anything but pain,—
Our parting and our meeting
Alike in vain.

The ballad *One Foot on Sea* . . . narrates in the form of dialogue the same mournful tale of love and parting. To the woman's plaintive query,

'Oh tell me once and tell me twice
And tell me thrice to make it plain,
When we who part this weary day,
When we who part shall meet again,'

the man returns the inflexible answer,

'When windflowers blossom on the sea
And fishes skim along the plain.'

II

But Christina was too resilient to accept such an answer as final. In the middle life of a woman the two forces of renewal and decay are simultaneously active. No sooner does she reconcile herself to the inevitability of aging than a new surge of life flooding through her organism creates juvenescence, though temporarily.

So it was with her. As her health improved, she began to recover her looks. William observed with relief that her eyes, which had protruded so painfully, were returning to their normal size and shape. Mrs. Scott too told Alice that there was a great improvement in Christina's appearance. By April she herself thought she was "very well . . . all things considered." By June she could report with complacency that her looks had "met with some amount of approval." A few weeks spent with Gabriel at Kelmscott in July enlivened her still more. He was delighted to see that she "plucked up in an extraordinary way," looked well, and was "quite active and natural again," for the first time in two and a half years.

With her appearance restored to something of its former comeliness and her energy returning, she rallied to the extent of hoping that "sweet Venus" might favor her with another late visitation. *Touching 'Never'* argues that

Because you never yet have loved me, dear
Think you you never can nor ever will?
Surely while life remains hope lingers still,
Hope the last blossom of life's dying year.

And to support the argument an earlier concept, that of equity in love, is introduced:

If you had loved me, I not loving you,
If you had urged me with the tender plea

Of what our unknown years to come might do
(Eternal years, if Time should count too few),
I would have owned the point you pressed on me
Was possible, or probable, or true.

But love cannot be summoned by a closely reasoned argument. As for the blossoms of hope, they wither and die long before life itself comes to an end. The unornamented truth, as Christina saw more clearly in *The Willow Shade,* was that those

Who set their heart upon a hope
That never comes to pass
Droop in the end like fading heliotrope,
The sun's wan looking-glass.

Who set their will upon a whim
Clung to through good and ill
Are wrecked alike whether they sink or swim,
Or hit or miss their will.

And yet such sad self-knowledge brings scant comfort to the craving heart. Fortunately, the increasing pressure of years eventually blunts the sharp fierceness of the willing and the wanting, dampens raging optimism, and induces those who have lived a sufficient time upon this earth to relinquish—though with regret—the passionate life of youth. Now that she was in her forties, moving toward a fifth decade, Christina began to weary of a struggle she had never fully relished, even as a young woman.

Long have I longed, till I am tired
Of longing and desire;
Farewell my points in vain desired,
My dying fire;
Farewell all things that die and fail and tire,

she wrote in *Till To-morrow.*

A number of the *Later Life* sonnets have the same note of diminished vitality. This sequence, published in the 1881 *Pageant* volume, lacks the unity and continuity of the *Monna Innominata* sequence, which appeared in the same volume. Though the *Later Life* group is not biographically important as a whole, some single sonnets are of particular interest, and a few can be assigned to certain periods. One of these is *Later Life 18,* a revised version of *Cor Mio,* written in 1875. Both sonnets have the same sestet. But, whereas *Cor Mio* is a love poem, beginning,

Still sometimes in my secret heart of hearts
I say 'Cor Mio' when I remember you,
And thus I yield us both one tender due,
Welding one whole of two divided parts,

Later Life 18 is more impersonal, its octave more in harmony with the autumnal weariness of the common sestet, which is as follows:

So late in Autumn one forgets the Spring,
Forgets the Summer with its opulence,
The callow birds that long have found a wing,
The swallows that more lately gat them hence:
Will anything like Spring, will anything
Like Summer, rouse one day the slumbering sense?

Later Life 17 begins in the same prevailing gray tone, but with an added touch of nostalgia for the past:

Something this foggy day, a something which
Is neither of this fog nor of to-day,
Has set me dreaming of the winds that play
Past certain cliffs, along one certain beach,
And turn the topmost edge of waves to spray:
Ah pleasant pebbly strand so far away,
So out of reach while quite within my reach,
As out of reach as India or Cathay!

One of the interesting features of this sonnet is the sudden shift in mood which explodes it in the middle and makes the sestet appear to be a separate fragment. Assuming that Christina was not up to her old trick of pulling a sestet out of one sonnet to use for another, we may explain the sharp difference between the two parts by the supposition that a consideration of the past, rich and exotic like India or Cathay, brings about a violent reaction to the present. As we have seen in *Birthday* and other poems, for Christina joy and happiness took on the quality of the sumptuous, the luxurious, something rich and strange, and out of reach. By comparison to the past, the present is meager and unendurably bleak:

I am sick of where I am and where I am not,
I am sick of foresight and of memory,
I am sick of all I have and all I see,
I am sick of self, and there is nothing new;
Oh weary impatient patience of my lot!—
Thus with myself: how fares it, Friends, with you?

And yet the new currents were forming, although Christina did not as yet feel them; new tides were pushing and surging up from the deep; great forces were preparing to sweep onto her shore and in their ebbing to carry away with them all the dear familiar landmarks of the here and now.

III

At first only placid ripples appeared on the surface. In a letter of April, 1873, Christina mentioned that Ford Madox Brown's daughter Lucy had called. "What a delightful person she is!" was her enthusiastic comment. In May William spent his holiday in Italy with the Scotts and Alice, and at the last moment Lucy Brown was invited to join their party.

"Old Scotus seems quite sulky about it," Gabriel observed, adding quickly that he shouldn't like the remark to get back to Scott, who was "able to hate one now on the slightest provocation." But William, who was attracted to Lucy, determined to have her along; and by the time they all returned to England, he had resolved not to part with her again. "My dear Lucy," Christina wrote in July from Kelmscott, "I should like to be a dozen years younger, and worthier in every way of becoming your sister; but such as I am, be sure of my loving welcome to you as my dear sister and friend."

William's and Lucy's engagement, which united the two families, friends for so many years, appeared a stroke of good fortune to all. During the summer there was much dining together and visiting back and forth and sharing of prenuptial festivities. Christina found Lucy as "sweet and engaging as ever," and she foresaw only "the promise of happiness to come."

In preparation for the arrival of the bride, the house at Euston Square underwent a flurry of renovations and repairs. The household, William reported, was "pretty nearly topsy-turvy, as there are painters and plasterers about the house, and various interchanges of rooms going on—books turned out into passages in a desolate condition—etc."

But even before the wedding, which took place the following spring, clouds darkened the sugary blue of the domestic sky. Christina's surprising letter of November 5 blows up the amenities without previous warning:

> My dear William,
>
> I am truly sorry for my ebullition of temper this morning (and for a hundred other faults), and not the less so if it makes what follows seem merely a second and more serious instance.
>
> My sleeping in the library cannot but have made evident to you how improper a person I am to occupy any room next a dining-room. My cough (which surprised Lucy, as I found afterwards, the other day at dinner) . . . makes it unseemly for me to be continually and unavoidably within earshot of Lucy and her guests. *You* I do not mention, so completely have you accommodated yourself to the trying circumstances of my health: but, when a 'love paramount' reigns amongst us, even you may find such toleration an impossibility. I must tell you that not merely am I labouring under a serious relapse into heart-complaint and consequent throat-enlargement (for which I am again under Sir William Jenner's care), but even that what appeared the source of my first illness has formed again, and may for aught I can warrant once more have serious issues.
>
> The drift of all this is that (through no preference for me over you as you may well believe, but because of my frail state which lays me open to emergencies requiring help from which may you long be exempt) our Mother, if I am reduced to forego all your brotherly bounty provides for me, will of her own unhesitating choice remove with me. We believe that from all sources we shall have enough be-

tween us, and you know that our standard of comfort does not include all the show demanded by modern luxury. I have very little doubt that an arrangement may be entered into which shall lodge us under one roof with my Aunts; thus securing to us no despicable amount of cheerful companionship, and of ready aid in sickness.

Dear William, I should not wonder if you had been feeling this obvious difficulty very uncomfortably, yet out of filial and brotherly goodness had not chosen to start it: if so, I cannot rejoice enough that my perceptions have woke up to some purpose.

I do not know whether any possible modification (compatible with all our interests, and not least with Lucy's) may occur to you as to arrangements; to me, I confess, there scarcely seems any way out of the difficulty short of a separation. Perhaps in a day or so you will let Mamma or me know what you judge best.

Of course Mamma is in grief and anxiety; her tender heart receives all stabs from every side.—If you wonder at my writing instead of speaking, please remember my nerves and other weak points.

Although this letter proposes an immediate separation of the family, as a matter of fact Christina did not carry out her intention of moving for another two years. After the wedding in March, 1874, she and her mother continued to live at Euston Square with the newly married couple, though in William's decorous words, "the harmony in the household was not unflawed, and was sometimes rather jarringly interrupted." The fault, he infers, was his bride's, for "no two persons could be less encroaching or less interfering, or more observant of the rightful rule that the wife is the mistress of the house, than my mother and sister." On the other hand, Brown had brought up his daughter to be a freethinker like himself, and William believed that Lucy's agnosticism may have been a source of friction, though, to be sure, both he and Gabriel were likewise agnostics.

The chief trouble was between Christina and Lucy. Two different attitudes toward life clashed. Lucy, not quite thirty, was gay, worldly, ambitious, and Christina's seriousness and religious intensity offended her. "To do anything whatsoever," Christina remarked once, "even to serve God 'with all strength', brings us into collision with that modern civilized standard of good breeding and good taste which bids us avoid extremes." Too her invalid habits were distasteful to her sister-in-law. But the deeper source of the antagonism lay in the fact that the two women whose attitudes toward life were incompatible were fond of the same man. From the beginning Lucy, who wanted William all to herself, resented his reverent adoration of his sister and the admiring affection she felt for her "brother of brothers." The strong bond uniting the two since birth had to be broken if the forty-five-year-old William was to be married in the true sense of the word. Lucy understood that she must wean him away from his family, and particularly from his gifted younger sister, before she could have a husband in him.

IV

It was in the autumn of 1873 that Maria determined to join the Anglican Sisterhood of All Saints, Margaret Street. Possibly what she called "Lucy's enthronement as bride" at Euston Square influenced her decision to some extent, but the thought of taking such a step had long been in her mind. From her youth she as well as Christina had been susceptible to the radiation of the Park Village Sisterhood on Albany Street. As we have seen, she had worked actively in one of its social service organizations, the Young Women's Friendly Society, which under the leadership of the Honorable Mrs. Chambers of Christ Church devoted itself to the welfare of servant girls in the parish.[1] But, whereas Christina imaginatively dramatized the conventual personality in her poetry, Maria, more inclined to direct action, herself became a nun.

It was as obvious to her as to Christina that with the advent of Lucy the unity of the family, heart and center of their lives, was fragmented. But, unlike Christina, Maria did not have the resource of poetry, as a life apart from life, with which to fill the vacuum. An extremely able woman, her talents lay in the direction of both scholarship and social work, and the life of a Sister offered her an outlet for latent energies unabsorbed by the restricting domestic life of an unmarried woman. A. M. Allchin and others have pointed out that the Oxford movement, in which the Anglican sisterhoods had their spiritual roots, played an important initial role in the emancipation of women in England. The sisterhoods presented a wide variety of opportunities to women in the fields of teaching, nursing, social work, and community organization. Far from retiring from the world during her novitiate, Maria actually entered it for the first time; and in her brief years as a sister distinguished herself in a number of ways. It was she who first translated for the order the Day Hours of the Roman Breviary, which with some revisions became the standard work of its kind, being reissued in 1923 as *A Book of Day Hours for the Use of Religious Societies.*

Christina's long illness may likewise have proved a factor in Maria's decision. Sir William Jenner, pioneer in vaccination for smallpox, was closely associated with the Margaret Street Sisterhood, and during his visits to Christina Maria would have had ample opportunity to learn from him about the work of the Sisterhood and Miss Brownlow, its Mother Superior and Foundress.

But deeper motives undoubtedly precipitated her into a course of action she might otherwise have postponed indefinitely. Her profession as a novice coincided with the onset of the serious illness which was to end her life. Just as the fate of *Sing-Song* was entwined with the progress of Christina's disease, so the most important step in Maria's life was intimately connected with her own mortal illness. Perhaps Christina's

severe trial had pointed out to her the precariousness of human life. Possibly she felt within her own organism a secret, hidden ill, grim warning not to delay, but to use her life to the full before it was cut short.

It was in May, 1873, while Lucy and William were courting under Italian skies, that Maria had experienced the first symptoms of an internal tumor. In September she announced her intention of joining the All Saints Sisterhood. Seeing Maria for the first time in her nun's habit, with the black scapular and veil, and the stiff white collar and wimple, Christina pronounced her "a decided lark."

"Though I am glad that Maria should carry out her long desire of becoming a Sister," Frances Rossetti confided to Gabriel, "I miss her company and conversation very much; besides I am not easy about her health." Of course nobody, she added loyally, could be "more loving and helpful than Christina is to me and I rejoice in the possession of her." [2]

Maria's new profession brought her unexpected happiness. "I cannot tell you, my dear Gabriel," she said, "what a blessed life this is; peace and love really do reign throughout the house." Another time she explained to him that "human love is a figure of that which, being at once Divine and human, satisfies the soul as nothing else can. What that is in this most blessed life, when all is given up for it, cannot be expressed . . ."

V

After four years, the rift in Christina's relations with Macmillan was healed in 1874. That year he published *Speaking Likenesses* (orginally called *Nowhere*) and the following year a collected edition of her poetry. She first broached the subject of the prose work she described as "merely a Christmas trifle, would-be in the *Alice* style with an eye to the market," in a letter of February 3: [3]

> DEAR MR. MACMILLAN
> I have tried to write a little prose story, such as might I think do for a child's Xmas volume, and if you would allow me to send it to you to be looked at you would truly oblige me. Properly speaking, it consists of 3 short stories in a common framework,—but the whole is not long.
> A statement received a short time ago from your office shows me that Goblin Market is not so very far apparently from selling off,—and glad I am, and also, of the 5–9–0 in prospect, especially as I have just now a wedding present to make [to William and Lucy]. . . .

Macmillan did not wait twenty-four hours before replying in a way that Christina must have found highly flattering, for she wrote on February 4:

> Thank you very much. Here is my little story on trial.
> Will you think me too eccentric for returning—but with a cordial sense of your liberal kindness—your cheque (herein) for 15£, & begging you to favour me by substituting for it one for that precise £5–9–0 which is all that I have earned? I have more than enough for my

> wedding present, & like to feel that in the future an odd sovereign or two may now & then drop in.
>
> The possibility of your thinking proper some day to reprint my 2 vols. in one, is really gratifying to me as you may suppose: but as to additional matter, I fear there will be little indeed to offer you. . . .

On April 20 she wrote that she would gladly accept his offer for *Nowhere,* "not having expected such success with you just now." But her experience with *Commonplace* had taught her caution in dealing with a publisher. Not only was she wary of placing herself under financial obligation by accepting a check for future royalties, but she was also careful to set a terminal date for publication and to reserve copyright. "The only supplementary point I should like to suggest would be that we fix a time by which it is to be published, and after which in want of non-publication the copyright simply and without any further process reverts to me. Suppose we say it shall be out on or before the 31st December of this year:—otherwise, etc."

She received no immediate answer to this letter, and it was only through an announcement in *The Athenæum* that she learned her book was to be published. "Funnily enough," she told Gabriel, "I did not know matters were concluded between Mac and me, but now I hope they are." A week later she expressed her relief to William: "I have heard again from Mr. Macmillan, and find he is treating with Mr. Arthur Hughes about illustrating my Christmas story; so of course *this* is accepted, to my great contentment."

Now that the book was scheduled for publication, Gabriel objected to the title, "unlucky because of that free-thinking book called *Erewhon,* which is 'Nowhere' inverted. The title would seem a little stale; I should change it." Whereupon Christina wrote Macmillan,

> And then I really must adopt 'Speaking Likenesses' as my title, this having met with some approval in my circle. Very likely you did not so deeply ponder my text as to remark that my small heroines perpetually encounter 'speaking (literally *speaking*) likenesses' or embodiments or caricatures of themselves or their faults. I think the title boasts of some point and neatness.

In addition to this work, Christina's first book of devotional prose was published in 1874. *Annus Domini,* for which her friend the Reverend Burrows wrote an introductory note, was brought out by the firm of James Parker and Company in April. Brown's gifted nineteen-year-old son Nolly (Oliver Madox Brown), who was visiting Gabriel when Christina's presentation copy arrived, was "struck by the beauty of the prayers." What impressed Gabriel was not the prose but the high quality of the single poem included in the volume (*Wrestling*), which he pronounced "most excellent, like all Christina's religious poetry."

Approbation also came from another quarter. "I hear Mrs. Scott with

Miss Boyd have called in Euston Square since we left," Christina wrote from Eastbourne, where she and her mother were staying with Maria, "and that the former likes my little book, I having sent it to her." She might have been hoping for an expression of approval from Mr. Scott as well, but clearly the volume was not quite the thing to appeal to him.

Speaking Likenesses appeared in November, in time to catch the Christmas trade. Christina observed in annoyance that Macmillan had used his own judgment about a matter in which she felt she should have been consulted. Evidently he had made the mistake of underestimating her meticulous precision about language, an area in which she could consider no compromise. But as he read the following letter (undated), he must have recognized with surprise that the silken folds of gentleness and courtesy in Christina's nature covered a hard core of firmness:

> Thank you cordially for my book which pleased me much, & of which your gift of 6 copies was most welcome. I only hope the public appetite will not be satisfied with 6 or 60, but crave on for 600 or 6000 at least!
>
> But Gabriel writes me that I ought to beg a *cancel* of the *titlepage:* & though I don't know how to ask this of you, I will own that 'with pictures thereof' is so different from the 'with (so many) illustrations' which I had thought of, that I feel uneasiness at the different form being read as my own. I don't think 'thereof' happy in this particular context. Then the *List of Illustrations* treats my subjects as I should not have treated them: the word 'fairy' I should altogether have excluded as not appropriate to my story—I should have aimed at greater neatness & brevity,—& not least I should (as who would not?) have described the *last* on the list in other terms. ["Maggie drinks tea and eats buttered toast with Grannie."] In short, I am now deploring that the *Titlepage* & *List of Illustrations* were not shown me in proof, even if in the first instance I was not called upon to supply the latter.
>
> What shall we do? Cannot something be done to remedy these oversights & soothe my anxiety?
>
> Do please reassure
> Yours in trouble

But the publisher, who had his own hard core, did nothing to reassure his anxious author, and the first edition still retains the flaws to which Christina had objected.

VI

However, the disagreement between author and publisher did not mar their otherwise cordial relations, and by the beginning of 1875 Christina felt sure enough of Macmillan to request of him a favorable reception for a friend's book of children's verses, which in her opinion had a certain "takingness." In her subsequent letter of January 26 she thanks him for letting the friend "know her doom without delay," and then gets on to her own affairs:

> To lapse to the private and personal. I am glad if there is any prospect of another edition of my verses being wanted some day, & one nice fattish volume takes my fancy. Have any more of the last copies of 'Goblin Market' sold? I have not received our usual statement this Xmas, as you may recollect.
>
> I am pleased to hear of more than 1000 'Speaking Likenesses' having been disposed of: truth to tell, I had feared the reviews might this time have done me a very real injury with the buying public; but, for me, such a sale is certainly not bad. I have been thinking over the terms you originally offered me & which were settled between us, that I should have 35£ & no further property or interest in the book: so I understood the arrangement to stand. Well, at this point of partial success, perhaps I may fairly suggest that if after all you should prefer our returning to our old system of half profits—the profits at this moment being for aught I know 0—I shall be most happy to fall back on those familiar terms, & run the risk of something or nothing as the case may be. I may get *more,* I know, by some incalculable contingency; but I count on no such results: I may equally get *less* or get *nothing.* In short, if you leave present terms to stand, I shall like my 35£: or if you change to halves, I shall like them perhaps on the whole better. Very likely such a suggestion is simply monstrous from a business point of view: but if so, I am sure you are enough my friend to excuse my business ignorance.
>
> Now let us get away from the fog of business into the sunshine of pleasure. I hope that much health & enjoyment await you & Mrs. Macmillan in *our* lovely Italy. Pray assure her that I do not forget having . . . once met her at my kind friends' the Leifchilds': but I have since then gone through so much illness as may suffice to colour soberly the rest of my days; & what with one thing & another, I am now disposed to ask rather that some who kindly recollect me should continue their remembrance than that they should readmit me of [*sic*] their acquaintance. Will she then, & will you, accept my very cordial compliments in lieu of my visit?

This long letter brought an immediate response. Macmillan gave Christina everything she wanted, including the old terms of half profits and the retention of copyright for herself. "By all means," she then wrote on January 30, "let us take in hand, if you please, a general reprint of my verses, fusing all into 1 volume. . . . So soon as I hear from you quite conclusively, I will look up what waifs and strays I can from Magazines, & forward them to you: of *never-printed* pieces, I fear I shall scarcely find one or two for use." [4] It was no good looking back to *The Germ,* for "the 'Germ' has contributed what it had to contribute, curious old book that it is."

Her reluctance, evident in the January 26 letter, to establish social relations with her publisher (perhaps she was unpleasantly reminded of the Ellis tea) led her not only to sidestep all his invitations but even to avoid business appointments with him. "Your visit will always be a favour,—" she wrote in August, "mine to your Office (where I have never

yet been) looks a little formidable. Pending either event, I feel inclined to write my notions on our joint subject of interest." To this she added the postscript, "I fear the 'formidableness' of your office may rather seem to you laziness in myself: but pray wink at so subtle a distinction." Another time, in sending a title page, she said she had thought of bringing it to his office herself, but suddenly she had remembered another engagement.

"What you say of Miss Rossetti is most true," Macmillan told a correspondent. "She is very subjective. But so *fine,* I think. Every word *tells* enough and no more. I once told her that all her poems were so *sad* and she said she did not wonder I felt it so. I have only seen her two or three times and she was very bright and interesting, but she is very delicate in health. She is a true artist and will live." [5]

VII

Upon the publication of the collected poems in 1875, Christina was gratified to "see more stir is excited by my new ed. than I anticipated." Again Gabriel's friends proved their devotion. When Watts-Dunton wanted to "do" her for the *Examiner,* Gabriel assured him that she was "safe in the hands of Gosse," to whom she subsequently wrote,

> Save me from my friends! You are certainly up in your subject, and as I *might* have fared worse in other hands I will not regret that rival reviewer who was hindered from saying his say. As to the lamented early lyrics, I do not suppose myself to be the person least tenderly reminiscent of them; but it at any rate appears to be the commoner fault amongst verse-writers to write what is not worth writing, than to suppress what would merit hearers. . . .

"Rummaging" in his copy for poems not heretofore included in a volume, Gabriel singled out for praise the Venus sonnet ("most exquisite") and *Amor Mundi* ("one of your choicest masterpieces"), but regretted the inclusion of *My Secret, The Queen of Hearts,* and *No, Thank You, John* on the grounds that they were too personal to appear in print. We may recall that he also objected to the latter because he thought it shared with *The Royal Princess* and *The Lowest Room* the taint of the Browning–Barrett "modern vicious style." In respect to this, he wondered if Jean Ingelow too had not been an influence. Christina reminded him that *The Lowest Room* had been written long before she knew Jean Ingelow; therefore "Miss J.I. could not have misled me anywhither."

That year Scott as well as Christina published a volume of new poems, which he shrewdly dedicated to Gabriel Rossetti, Swinburne, and Morris. One result of this literary dragnet was an article in *Macmillan's* entitled, "William Bell Scott and Modern British Poetry," written by William Rossetti "to promote the repute of my old friend."

The summer of 1875 Christina visited Maria at the All Saints' Mission Home at Clifton, near Bristol, where she had the opportunity of renewing her old friendshp with Dora Greenwell, then living in the vicinity of Bristol, who was, said Christina, "far more dilapidated than myself, poor thing." But despite shattered health, Miss Greenwell's "large-mindedness" still impressed Christina and afforded her the intellectual stimulation otherwise lacking in the decorous, provincial town she described as "Cheltenhamy."

For amusement she had the Bristol Zoo. Her lifelong love of animals, whose innocent antics she could observe firsthand at the zoo, led her at this time to push actively a petition against that "horror of horrors, Vivisection." Hearing that chloroform was not used in experiments with animals, she felt obliged to lend her support in opposition to what she called "a cruelty of revolting magnitude." An early poem (1853) reveals the basis for her strongly felt prejudice:

> Innocent eyes not ours
> Are made to look on flowers,
> Eyes of small birds and insects small:
> Morn after summer morn
> The sweet rose on her thorn
> Opens her bosom to them all.
> The least and last of things
> That soar on quivering wings,
> Or crawl among the grass blades out of sight,
> Have just as clear a right
> To their appointed portion of delight
> As Queens or Kings.

It was in the interests of justice and the sanctity of life that she objected to a practice which, despite its unpleasant aspect, has done much to advance the study of medical science.

She came home from Bristol that September in time to rejoice at the appearance of the first shoot of new life within her own family. "We have a niece!" she reported jubilantly to Gabriel on the 21st. But as invariably in family chronicles, life marched in on the heels of death. The birth of Olive, the eldest of William's and Lucy's five children, occurred only ten months after the death of "Nolly" Brown, before he had reached his twentieth year. He had shown extraordinary precocity as both artist and writer, his novel *Gabriel Denver* having been published shortly before his death. The whole family, including Christina, felt the shock of his loss and Brown's grief.

Christmas of 1875 Christina spent with Gabriel at Aldwick Lodge near Bognor. Of the immediate family, only Maria was absent. Her novitiate had ended the preceding month. "Poor Maggie is parting with her grayish hair next Sunday," Gabriel told Scott, "and annexing the kingdom of heaven for good." Despite his levity, he was genuinely con-

cerned about her, and couldn't understand why she would refuse his invitation for Christmas. "I grieve to think how lonely she will be on Christmas-day without her family," he protested to Frances.

Maria wrote him a long letter Christmas eve trying to explain. She hoped to reconcile him to her choice by giving him an insight into the nun's life, a life in which self-denial is transmuted into austere joy.

VIII

The year 1876 opened placidly enough, with Christina making scrapbooks for sick children in her spare time and evenings playing whist with her mother and two aging aunts at Bloomsbury Square. But in July Maria's condition caused Miss Brownlow increasing anxiety, and the Mother Superior sent her to Eastbourne for treatment.

At the same time the domestic problem at Euston Square reached a long-pending crisis. "Our Euston Square home-party is broken up!" Christina announced to Gabriel, adding that she and her mother would probably move some time that autumn. "I suppose it may be best to regroup ourselves, and of course we part friends. William is cut up, I think, at losing our dearest Mother; but I am evidently unpleasing to Lucy, and could we exchange personalities, I have no doubt I should then feel with her feelings."

By September it was settled that Christina and her mother would share a residence with the two aunts at 30 Torrington Square. In telling Lucy of her plans, Christina made the first of her many friendly overtures to her brother's wife. "I hope," she wrote, "that when two roofs shelter us and when faults which I regret are no longer your daily trial, that we may regain some of that liking which we had as friends, and which I should wish to be only the more tender and warm now that we are sisters. Don't, please, despair of my doing better." Despite his tight-lipped reserve about the family quarrel, William could not help commenting, "Christina here takes the blame to herself, and imputes none to her correspondent. There might be something to remark about this, but the less said the better." Frances, however, confided to Gabriel, "By this change Christina and I hope to avoid mutual annoyances between ourselves and Lucy, and I think it will promote the comfort of most generous and affectionate William. . . ."

In October Christina settled down with the three elderly ladies in Torrington Square. "Our move has proved less horrible than I prefigured," she told William. "Now we are far on towards shaking down in our fresh groove, and it promises to prove a suitable and comfortable one." But from the first, Torrington Square, Christina's residence for the next eighteen years, was a house of death. Beginning with Maria (who, though not living at home, was dying when the family moved into

the house), one by one the elderly Torrington Square inmates died, until only Christina was left.

Maria sank rapidly, but astonished all by the serenity with which she faced death. "She is heavenly-minded, brave and calm," said Christina; "indeed the grief is ours, and the dread ours, rather than hers." An operation was deemed necessary in October, and Christina warned William that he must be prepared for anything. Maria rallied a little, and survived a second operation. But on November 24 Christina wrote Gabriel, "You see my black edge. This afternoon (at between half past 1 and a quarter to 2 about) our dear Maria died peacefully. . . ."

Two days later she followed with a dryly competent letter to William, informing him in great detail about the funeral arrangements and concluding with a word of caution as to Gabriel:

> *Last night I answered a letter from Gabriel; & told him from our Mother that she advised him to attend the preliminary service in the Chapel only, & *not* to go to the Cemetery: the latter is of course distressingly public, & the Sisters' habits render a funeral exceptionally noticeable. I do not know what he is likely to decide, but I dread the Cemetery for him with all his peculiar feelings: I count on your, not my, writing him ⟨the⟩ all necessary particulars.* [6]

Much has been said about Maria's harmful influence upon Christina. Gosse thought it was like "that of Newton upon Cowper, a species of police surveillance exercised by a hard, convinced mind over a softer and more fanciful one." Such a statement merely reveals his lack of insight into the character of either sister, for Maria's mind was no more inflexible than Christina's was soft and fanciful. What they had in common was a stern devoutness combined with a playful brightness of spirit, qualities which seem logically irreconcileable but which can and do exist side by side in life.

Unfortunately, Christina herself inadvertently contributed to the Gosse legend. Posterity's conception of Maria as a narrow-minded, gloomy fanatic partially originated in Christina's frequently quoted verbal portrait of her sister in *Time Flies.* Maria, she wrote, "shrank from entering the Mummy Room at the British Museum under a vivid realisation of how the general resurrection might occur even as one stood among those solemn corpses turned into a sight for sightseers."

But despite this vignette which has indelibly fixed Maria's character for future generations, Gabriel pronounced her "the healthiest in mind and cheeriest of us all, with William coming next, and Christina and I nowhere." In the depths of her fatal illness, she could still write a bright little letter playfully calling Christina the "crowned Queen of Dears." And on her deathbed she unsentimentally scoffed at what she called "the hood and hatband" style of mourning. "Why make everything as hope-

less looking as possible?" was her common-sense query. The loss of such a hardy spirit was bound to diminish Christina's resources, though with her usual discipline she kept her grief to herself. Gabriel told Swinburne admiringly that his mother and Christina "bear their loss *well*—in the truest sense of the word."

In this time of sorrow Scott unexpectedly showed his worth as a friend. His note to William, written the day after Maria's death, must have been a source of comfort to Christina, though she might have smiled as she read that "there was something between Maria's practice in life and my own, in the way of duty, that made, I used to fancy, a kind of bond between us. . . ." But no trace of self-regard appeared in the healing formality of his closing sentence, only affection, expressed with simple dignity: "Letitia has already conveyed my sympathy . . . in a note to Christina. I now offer it by my own hand." A few days later she was gratified to read in the *Examiner* what Gabriel described as "a most loving little notice of Maria, written by dear old Scotus. . . ." [7]

Despite Christina's forebodings, Maria's funeral turned out to be a relatively cheerful affair. In later years Christina liked to recall that "loving mourners followed her, hymns were sung at her grave, the November day brightened, and the sun (I vividly remember) made a miniature rainbow in my eyelashes."

IX

But the Christmas of 1876 could not have been a happy one for Christina, as the family all gathered at William's house to participate in holiday festivities for which they had little enthusiasm. Parted from her sister by the white barrier of "the separating sea," temporarily estranged from William by his marriage, unable to reach Gabriel, who was gradually drifting away from them all on strange currents, with only chloral to keep him afloat, Christina viewed her old home at Euston Square, now Lucy's domain, with a heavy heart.

Events over which she had no control were drying out the juices of her life, crushing and aging her. Even her home, the comfort of her sanctuary, that "nest love-hidden from ills," had been taken from her. Cast down, the resilience of youth gone, ordeals braved and passed to no purpose, ahead the gray years of aging—she had little left but the faith that itself often deserted her:

> Lord, I believe, help Thou mine unbelief:
> Lord, I repent, help mine impenitence:
> Hide not Thy Face from me, nor spurn me hence,
> Nor utterly despise me in my grief;
> Nor say me nay, who worship with the thief
> Bemoaning my so long lost innocence.[8]

Always in extremity she turned to prayer as her only active means of facing reality. For her, prayer was no ritual, no formula, but a living, ever freshly flowing current which could galvanize her exhausted and burned-out spirit. It was a means of reorganizing her personality after successive defeats. And the defeats which kept appearing now so rapidly one after the other (for fame, worldly success lose their reality in the face of sickness and death) at times seemed to her as effects arising from one cause, consequences of one guilt, retributions symptomatic of that underlying disorder in the world which she found reflected in herself:

I peered within, and saw a world of sin;
Upward, and saw a world of righteousness;
Downward, and saw darkness and flame begin
Which no man can express.

I girt me up, I gat me up to flee
From face of darkness and devouring flame:
And fled I had, but guilt is loading me
With dust of death and shame.

In this and others of her devotional poems echoes are rung from George Herbert, from Crashaw, from the later Donne. Like the great seventeenth-century religious poets, she too lived a submerged life, fathoms below the surface, a life intense and violent, but one which seldom penetrates into the annals of day-to-day living. In seeking to plumb these depths, we cannot expect any aid from the factual record, which is silent about this as about so many important aspects of Christina's life. Once again we must turn to the poetry, which as the years pass increasingly reveals the anguish of a turbulent and hidden spiritual struggle incomprehensible to the secular mind:

Alas my Lord
How should I wrestle all the livelong night
With Thee my God, my strength and my delight?

How can it need
So agonized an effort and a strain
To make Thy Face of mercy shine again?

How can it need
Such wringing out of breathless prayer to move
Thee to Thy wonted love, when Thou art Love?

❋ 16 ❋

"STRIKE A FLINT"

1877–1880

On New Year's day of 1877 Christina received from Cayley the gift of a brightly scaled Sussex sea mouse preserved in spirits of wine, which she acknowledged with a light little poem she called *My Mouse*. From time to time he had been sending her other little oddities as gifts, an article from *The Times* about wombats or a translation of an obscure fourteenth-century Italian sonnet. Occasionally he would call at Torrington Square, stay to tea, and join in the evening game of whist. The closer Christina approached fifty, the more she valued this quiet, steady, loyal, and undemanding relationship. Cayley's devotion may not have been what she had early expected from life, but it was what she got, and in these later years she was not given to underestimating any of life's free gifts, no matter how unexciting they might be.

She celebrated the beginning of a new year by sending Gabriel a long poem she had recently completed, with the jaunty remark, "I doubt if you will unearth one to eclipse it. Moreover," she added, "if I remember the mood in which I wrote it, it is something of a genuine 'lyric cry,' and such I will back against all skilled labor." The poem was probably *Mirrors of Life and Death,* published in *The Athenæum* on March 17, where it was read and admired by Gerard Manley Hopkins. Encouraged that she could still utter "a genuine 'lyric cry,'" she was discovering, to her satisfaction, that the poetic fires had been banked, not extinguished; and this self-confidence is reflected in the *Mirrors,* in which the perennial glass image of the 'seventies is the symbolic device which unifies the poem. Hopkins, who described it as "lovely" and quoted passages from it in his letters, mistook the title for "Symbols of Life and Death," an understandable error, for in the work all Christina's special symbols are arrayed and passed in review.[1]

For her, symbolism—which she used with conscious purpose—had a philosophical and religious as well as an aesthetic function. It offered an escape from the self. It was one means through which man could force

his way out of a self-enclosed universe into the greater freedom afforded him by identification with the cosmos. "Man burdened by the unbearable burden of self grows wearied," she wrote in *Letter and Spirit,* "has recourse to vivid symbols." Interpreted symbolically, Nature reflects the spiritual unity permeating the universe: sky, sun, clouds are "terrene mirrors," or "earthly pictures with heavenly meanings" through which man experiences a renewing unity with nature.

Thus the external world of nature symbolizes the inner world of the spirit. Christina visualizes "the two worlds, visible and invisible" as "doubling" against each other: "Wind, water, fire, the sun, a star, a vine, a door, a lamb . . . will shadow forth mysteries." This Platonic conception of nature providing an endless series of "terrene mirrors" as images of a nonsensuous reality is the theme of *Mirrors of Life and Death.* Stated in the opening stanza,

> The mystery of Life, the mystery
> Of Death, I see
> Darkly as in a glass;
> Their shadows pass,
> And talk with me,

the theme is developed through a succession of images in the remaining nineteen stanzas. In this omnium-gatherum may be recognized such familiar symbols as the rose with thorns, the eagle, the dove, the sun and moon, the separating sea, the blooming fruit tree fed by hidden sap, and the barren desert.

Of animal symbols, the mouse and the mole appear the most conspicuously. Gabriel objected to them as an intrusion of the commonplace into a formal poem, but Christina asked him to "wink at her m. and m.," from which she was unable to "wean" herself:

> *I have thickened my skin and toughened the glass of my house sufficiently to bear some fraternal stone-throwing. Let us resume our subject—& if possible finish it off.
>
> Stanzas 1, 2, shall very willingly & with my hearty concurrence change places. My mouse and my mole I incline to cling to, on grounds that seem to me of some weight. Still, if you will let me have 'Mirrors' back, I will consider my point before deciding. For really I think I might just as well have it & the rest back, & transact what little business remains to be done straight with the *Athenæum,* instead of troubling you. . . .* [2]

She does not explain the reason she wished to retain her mouse and mole, but clearly the two symbols had for her some personal significance. We suspect that her symbol for Scott was a mole; and perhaps Cayley's New Year's gift of a sea mouse, which arrived as she was finishing the poem, suggested to her such a creature as an appropriate and amusing symbol for the man whose manner and demeanor were not unmouse-like.

As a concession to Gabriel's criticism, she said she would weave in "a few fresh mirrors," which she hoped would "tone down any abruptness of the m. and m." But at no time did she consider eliminating them.

II

If Cayley would have been disconcerted to find himself represented in Christina's system of symbolism by a mouse, Scott would have been even more astonished to find himself represented symbolically by a mole. There is always a discrepancy between our own image of ourself and the image we reflect upon others. Scott's self-portrait, as he draws it in the *Notes,* resembles that of an aging prince still "taking his ease on cushion and mat," and incidentally making no progress. Young-looking at sixty-four, Scott thought the reason he had been able to preserve his youthful appearance was that he "now took all things easy."

He has told us in the 1854 autobiography that once in the Tuileries he had had his fortune told by a "magician in a white beard and tall red hat," who, by means of "an oracular homunculus in a bottle," predicted that, although he would never be powerfully rich, he would want for nothing, would live long, and enjoy *"une felicité parfaite,"* by virtue of his desires. Furthermore, *"à soixante ans l'amour n'aura pas encore eteint le flambeaux que vous eclaire depuis longtemps."*

It was true that, still virile at sixty, Scott enjoyed sexual felicity with a woman twenty years younger than he, and that in addition he had the satisfaction to his vanity of retaining the lifelong affection of one of the most gifted women of her day. No wonder that in reading over the 1854 volume before destroying it in 1877, he added as a concluding note to the soothing prognosis, which had been unaccountably fulfilled, "So then I may be very well content. I close the book, turn round my chair, manufacture a cigarette, and gladly make a bonfire of all the dusty letters and notebooks. There they go roaring up the chimney. . . ."

Fortunately, a few unpublished poems by Christina escaped the flames and have been preserved among the Penkill papers. One was the 1868 poem to Alice's chaffinch. Another, dated May 4, was probably written in 1877. The black border showing that Christina was still in mourning for Maria, her allusion to the unseasonable cold (May that year was "chilly and stormy"), and the mention of Alice's relatives, the Courtneys, who often visited Scott's Bellevue House after 1876, all seem to point to 1877 as the year of composition:

*My carrier pigeon is a 'fancy' pigeon,
Less tangible than midgeon;
A sympathetic love,—yet not a Cupid
Not pert nor stupid,
Heart-warm and snug tho' May Day deals in zeroes,
A well-known Eros.
On windless wings by flight untried forever

Outspeed the speeding river,
From Torrington remote to utmost Chelsea
(Do what I tell ye!—)
Carry a heart of love and thanks and blisses,
A beak of kisses,
Past Piccadilly's hills and populous valleys,
Past every human head that more or less is
Begirt with tawny tresses,
Past every house, to sumptuous Bellevue Palace;
There greet the courteous Courtneys with politeness,
And the dear Scotts with affectionate brightness,
And give a kiss to dark-locked Alice.*

Although Gabriel and Scott were still neighbors in "utmost Chelsea," a certain coolness was developing between them. Increasingly critical of Gabriel, Scott complained that all the "new men" surrounding his old friend interfered with their former comradeship. By "new men" Scott meant Gosse, Watts, William Sharp, and later Hall Caine. Undoubtedly Scott's grievance was not so much that they took up Rossetti's time as that, despite illness, he proved still able to attract powerfully another generation of literary men.

Many of these men became in time Christina's devoted admirers as well as her brother's, and none more so than Theodore Watts (known as Watts-Dunton), who originally felt such awe of Gabriel's sister that he shrank from meeting her. In his eyes she was and remained to the end a saint, although, after knowing her better, he modified his idea of her to that of a "playful saint." At the same time he was fully alive to her charm as a woman, which he attributed chiefly to her "youthfulness of soul and temperament," a quality that "in the truly adorable woman is invulnerable to age."

It was in the summer of 1877 that Watts came to know Christina well. The previous summer she and her mother had spent in the sickroom at Eastbourne nursing a dying Maria. This year, with a renewal of Gabriel's illness, complicated by an operation and the usual menace of chloral, they were fated to spend another summer in another sickroom. At Cheyne Walk, Watts was in constant attendance upon Gabriel except for the times when Christina and her mother relieved him. "No words of mine," he said, "could convey the effect of having these two ladies moving about the house—a very dark house. They seemed to shed a new kind of light in every room and passage." [3]

Directly contradicting this picture of serenity and peace is Brown's report to his daughter that chaos and absurdity reigned at Cheyne Walk, "and it would require nothing short of my being placed in authority by the commissioner of Lunacy to stop it . . ." What was more, "Gabriel tells me his mother and Christina are converting him to Xtianty—and in *his* state as to the philosophy I see no harm in that, and perhaps they

would feel more free to impress him if I were not in the way, though from his general conduct he seems more fitted to turn Turk. . . ." Although nothing came of Christina's efforts at conversion, the initial impression had been grooved, and during Gabriel's last illness he was to ask for a priest and absolution.

A few weeks later he and Brown left for Herne Bay, where Christina and her mother were to join them. But, Brown confided to Lucy, "I am sorry to say he begins to begrudge the near approach of his mother and sister—I tell him that he ought to love them and be happy in being able to have them with him—to which he agrees but adds that their company will be exceedingly dull and that when they come he ought to have *someone* besides to modify their extreme quietude."

Of the opinion that Gabriel was not yet "fit to be left to himself," Brown stayed on even after the arrival of the women, remaining until he was satisfied that "for the present he is well cared for in the company of his mother and sister, which very likely is as good as any could be got for him—because with his mother 77 and Christina scarcely yet restored from her illness he is forced in some degree to restrain his lamentable ways and speeches."

After Brown's departure Christina was appointed housekeeper. She missed him and was "selfishly ready to wish him back here a dozen times a day to hand him over the housekeeping and be encouraged by his influence over Gabriel." Subsequently Frederick Shields was pressed into service to provide the stimulating society Gabriel thought he needed. "A nearer view of Mr. Shields has added to our esteem for him," a grateful Frances declared. Christina too appreciated the extent of the artist's sacrifice in giving up his own work and responsibilities to help care for Gabriel, and this was the beginning of the admiration and affection she felt for him throughout the remainder of her life.

Once she was settled in Hunter's Forestall, the house Gabriel had rented, she joined the Herne Bay Lending Library, taking out a copy of Cunningham's *Lives* and "a nice old edition with plates of 'Plutarch's Lives' " to read aloud to Gabriel. On pleasant afternoons they drove out in a carriage; "and a little whist," she reported to William, "helps on the evenings fairly." But how to get Gabriel through the nights was the real problem. As a last desperate measure, they tried buttermilk, recommended as a remedy for insomnia. For a while it helped. Christina was convinced that it would have proved efficacious in what she described as Gabriel's "longdrawn agony of sleeplessness," had he not "unhappily" used it to excess and so "rapidly exhausted its sedative virtue." Still, by the end of August she was encouraged to see that he no longer sat "in that attitude of dreadful dejection with drooping head," and that sometimes even "a shadow of the old fun breaks out and lights up all for the moment."

Nevertheless it was a trying time, for the sick man was difficult to please.

Despite what Frances called "a very anxious position," they tried to "bear up" and do their best. The chief burden fell upon Christina, who felt obliged to keep up her mother's and Gabriel's spirits as well as her own. No less than Gabriel, her mother needed "every cheerful influence within reach," she confided to William.

One of the most cheerful of influences was news of William's baby son Arthur, born the preceding February. "Mamma quite warms towards her little grandson," Christina reported to William, "and I should not wonder if in the long run he supersedes his small elder in some hearts." Then came surprisingly a significant admission: "It is the lot of us 'lone lorn females' to sing second in life, tho' not in music. . . ."

III

Was she, then, willing to be elbowed aside in life so long as she excelled in poetry? Since the beginning of the year her confidence in her powers as a poet had been slowly returning. And at Hunter's Forestall poetry provided that cheering influence of which she too was so much in need. There she wrote *An October Garden* and probably the two long poems *An Old World Thicket* and *The Thread of Life,* both dated "Before 1881." All three poems reflect the beauty of nature, which like poetry afforded Christina some relief from the monotony of the sickroom.

Watts has told us how he persuaded her to come out with him one chilly gray dawn to see her first sunrise in the country. The pageant was heralded by the twittering of awakening birds in the green hedgerows. Gradually, as they watched, the cold night grays turned to a delicate apple-green, lighted by lilac bars. Then the sky deepened to a dark, gold-sprayed salmon red, as the sun slowly rose from behind the elms. Falling upon a sheet of silver mist in the meadow in which cows were lying, the risen sun fired it to a sheet of dazzling gold, which, says Watts, "made each brown patch on each cow's coat gleam like burnished copper." Christina watched the splendid scene in silent awe, her lips moving but the words unintelligible to Watts. Afterwards she admitted that a sunrise surpassed even a sunset.

But she also had ample opportunity to observe many a fine sunset that summer in Kent. One of these, or a blended impression of them all, probably provided the raw material for the memorable sunset which concludes *An Old World Thicket.* In this poem as well as in *The Thread of Life* the scenery, the scents, the live creatures all suggest September in the country. Both poems show an unusual sensitivity to nature, and they also reveal evidence of a new influence, that of the Romantic poets.

Was Christina turning to them at this time for answers she could not find elsewhere? The solution to the still unsolved problem of how to live an unlivable life is in *An Old World Thicket* provided by a combination of the Wordsworthian concept of the healing power of nature and Chris-

tian optimism; and in *The Thread of Life* by Coleridgean existentialism. These Romantic poets are so insistently and hauntingly present in both works that the two poems can in a sense be regarded as Christina's equivalent of an *Intimations* and a *Dejection* ode.

This suggests that she was reading Wordsworth and Coleridge that summer. Either she had rediscovered them for herself, or through Gabriel's influence her interest in them was reawakened. William has told us that in the long run his brother "perhaps enjoyed and revered Coleridge beyond any other modern poet whatsoever." Gabriel himself admitted worshiping Coleridge "on the right side idolatry." Although he did not rate Wordsworth highly, in general grudging him "every vote he got," he made an exception of the *Intimations Ode,* which no one, he declared to Hall Caine, could regard with "more special and unique homage" than he did.[4] It seems likely, then, that the influence of the Romantics reached Christina that autumn through her brother. Living so closely with him, she could well have absorbed his enthusiasm.

An Old World Thicket begins with an idyllic, typically romantic picture of nature. The first six of its thirty-seven stanzas describe the speaker's perception of natural beauty through the senses: like Wordsworth of the *Ode,* she protests that she *hears* and *sees,* but cannot *feel* the beauty of nature surrounding her, "the silver aspen trembling delicately," the birds "like downy emeralds," the murmuring waters which "spread a sense of freshness through the air."

The reason appears in the next six stanzas. In her mood of darkness and desolation, she is affronted by the beauty of a nature oblivious to suffering. Unable to shut out the general sounds of rejoicing, she then succeeds in imposing her own mood upon nature. Beneath the serene beauty she discerns "a universal sound of lamentation." All that live groan in anguish and travail. Suffering and injustice rule the universe. Responding to what appears external in the world but is in reality within herself, she feels a surge of rage and rebellion:

> My heart then rose a rebel against light,
> Scouring all earth and heaven and depth and height,
> Ingathering wrath to wrath and night to night.

Further on, her oscillations in mood are passed in review and briefly summarized:

> Rage to despair; and now despair had turned
> Back to self-pity and mere weariness,
> With yearnings like a smouldering fire that burned
> And might grow more or less,
> And might die out or wax to white excess.

Precisely at the moment when all hangs in the balance, an event from the natural world dips the scale. A flock of sheep approaches through the

trees. The speaker hears the pattering fall of feet, a bell, and bleatings. And then a second natural event, coinciding with the first, enhances its significance through the symbolic "doubling" that gave nature its meaning for Christina:

Then I looked up. The wood lay in a glow
From golden sunset and from ruddy sky;
The sun had stooped to earth though once so high;
Had stooped to earth, in slow
Warm dying loveliness brought near and low.

Although the calm and dazzling luminosity of the sunset is thereupon described literally, the symbolic "doubling" is always apparent. The miracle of individuality, a Christian concept, is symbolized in this beautiful description:

Each twig was tipped with gold, each leaf was edged
And veined with gold from the gold-flooded west;
Each mother-bird and mate-bird, and unfledged
Nestling, and curious nest,
Displayed a gilded moss or beak or breast.

In the midst of this splendor, the "home-ward flock" is glimpsed between the trees, led by the patriarchal ram with the tinkling bell. In this poem, then, through the reconciling loveliness of nature, which always mirrors a parallel spiritual state, Christina reached a religiously oriented resolution. It was the kind of solution toward which she was groping in these years. A vision by no means lasting or steady, more like a mirage, it appeared and vanished, only to reappear as an ever-receding goal.

IV

If the Wordsworthian concept of the healing power of nature provides the instrument for reconciliation in *An Old World Thicket,* Coleridge's Anglican existentialism is the agency in *The Thread of Life.* Although the English poet has not been linked to the nineteenth-century Danish existential tradition, a number of his leading ideas, scattered throughout his philosophical and religious writings, fall within the existential frame of reference, for example, his recognition of the need for total commitment and his perception of the relationship between faith and personal identity. Although we do not know if Christina was familiar with Coleridge's prose works (probably she was not), both these ideas, closely interwoven, are to be found throughout her poetry and her prose. Nowhere are they more clearly expressed than in the three sonnets she called *The Thread of Life.*

In 1879 she was to write in *Seek and Find,* "Once loaded with the responsibility of life we can never shift it off, never repudiate our identity,

never force our way back into the nothingness whence we emerged." But it is in *The Face of the Deep* that we find the fully matured statement of her Protestant existentialism, which is expressed poetically in *The Thread of Life:*

> Concerning Himself, God Almighty proclaimed of old: 'I AM THAT I AM,' and man's inherent feeling of personality seems in some sort to attest and correspond to this revelation: I who am myself cannot but be myself. I am what God has constituted me: so that however I may have modified myself, yet do I remain that same I; it is I who live, it is I who must die, it is I who must rise again at the last day. I rising out of my grave must carry on that very life which was mine before I died, and of which death itself could not altogether snap the thread. Who I was I am, who I am I am, who I am I must be for ever and ever.
>
> I the sinner of to-day am the sinner of all the yesterdays of my life. I may loathe myself or be amazed at myself, but I cannot unself myself for ever and ever.

The "thread of life" is of course the binding unity of personal identity. Christina develops this idea in the three sonnets joined under that title. In the first she notes with Matthew Arnold the aloofness and self-dependence of the natural world, which seems to impose the lesson of stoicism upon man. But this answer is unsatisfactory chiefly because it closes off the escape from self-imprisonment through human love:

> But who from thy self-chain shall set thee free?
> What heart shall touch thy heart, what hand thy hand?

In the second sonnet, nature, no longer remote, is the nature of *An Old World Thicket,* the flowering, leafy, bird-serenaded summer world of stream-moistened woods. Absorbing it through her senses, Christina asks with Wordsworth and Coleridge the question crucial for the poet:

> Then gaze I at the merrymaking crew,
> And smile a moment and a moment sigh,
> Thinking, why can I not rejoice with you?

But, although she recognizes with Coleridge that the loveliness of nature resides in the beholder's perception of it—that famous shaping power of the imagination—her answer is not his. For her, the only possible answer is an existential acceptance of selfhood:

> But soon I put the foolish fancy by:
> I am not what I have nor what I do;
> But what I was I am, I am even I.

And in the last of the three sonnets she draws the existential conclusion from such a premise: the self is the only possession of value which man has, and this rare gift he may present in religious reciprocity to his Maker. If the conception seems imbued with the Coleridgean philosophy,

the imagery is Christina's own, the same she used to describe the relationship of human donor to divine recipient in *A Better Resurrection.* Here she writes,

> Therefore myself is that one only thing
> I hold to use or waste, to keep or give;
> My sole possession every day I live,
> And still mine own, while moons and seasons bring
> From crudeness ripeness mellow and sanative;
> Ever mine own, till Death shall ply his sieve;
> And still mine own, when saints break grave and sing.
> And this myself as king unto my King
> I give, to Him Who gave Himself for me;
> Who gives Himself to me, and bids me sing
> A sweet new song of His redeemed set free;
> He bids me sing, O Death where is thy sting?
> And sing, O grave, where is thy victory?

In this sonnet we find not only the concept of personal identity, which is based upon an awareness of "the responsibility of life," linked to religious commitment but also related to poetic productivity. Christina seems to be saying that, once the poet can establish the relationship of the individual I am to the greater I AM (to use Coleridgean terms), not through self-sacrifice but through the royal presentation of himself to a greater than self, he receives in turn as a divine gift the freshening through faith of the poetic impulse.

Thus, for the sentimental self-abnegation of the late 'sixties she substituted in the 'seventies a self-exaltation which, arising not from pride of ego but from the full acknowledgment of the dignity of personality, was more in harmony with the requirements of her development in her mature years.

V

By September there was a marked improvement in Gabriel's condition. Frances reported to William that he "looks better, is stronger, more cheerful, more talkative, indulges indeed in his old jokes, nasal American stories, and even sings sotto voce in his drives."

One reason for his improvement, or perhaps a result of it, was that he felt able to work again. He made the well-known chalk drawing of his mother's head in part profile, sketching in Christina's profile behind her mother's as an afterthought. In addition, he made two other chalk drawings of Christina, both excellent likenesses of her at the age of forty-seven. Somber in mood and in color (browns and purple-grays), the portraits clearly reveal "traces of her Italian beauty," as Arthur Symons called it. The face is a delicate oval, firm in contour, still unlined, showing little effects of the thyroidic disease which had once created such havoc with her looks. The eyes are large, full-lidded, and only slightly protuberant.

An expression of austere strength overlies the beauty of the chiseled features, a reminder that what Lionel Johnson described as "her fair stern philosophy" could not be achieved without leaving its mark upon her face.

The constant presence of human society also helped Gabriel's recovery. He enjoyed the company of Christina and his mother more than he had anticipated, and, with the additional visits of friends, he was relieved from that devastating solitude which at Tudor House was destroying him even more than chloral, and of which he never ceased complaining. "We have told him that should our living with him prove any alleviation we would consent to do so," Frances worried, "but neither he nor we have arrived at any conclusion." The problem of money was harassing him at this time, and he knew he could decrease his expenses by living with Christina and his mother; he knew also that "utter solitude, if I return to such in London, may be well nigh fatal." On the other hand, he feared that his feminine relatives would curtail his freedom. "My ways are not theirs, and they would get anxious and uneasy," he confided to Fanny Cornforth. Indeed, she was the chief obstacle to such an arrangement. The habit of sleeping with her (even after she became Mrs. Schott) had for years been as much a part of Gabriel's normal life as chloral, and, though she could not cure the evil of solitude, she could mitigate its worst effects. One of his difficulties was the fact that what for him was a normal way of living—insomnia, chloral, whisky, nightly prowls, fierce and unremitting bouts of labor, and Fanny—was regarded by others as highly abnormal.

At one time he considered giving Christina and her mother the entire first floor of Tudor House to themselves. In this way he would manage to have both privacy and company. But in the long run, he could not bring himself to tolerate the disadvantages of family life, and in November he was to return once more to the depressing solitude he both dreaded and embraced.

Despite his decision, he parted reluctantly from Christina and their mother, and, although they planned on returning to London on November 3, he begged them to stay on for another few days. Of course they did, and Christina thereby gained the opportunity of observing "a large beautiful butterfly" in the garden, which obligingly remained "fixed for some time on a scabiosa" so that she could see at close range its black velvet body and red-striped wings tipped with bright blue and gray. She went into the house declaring herself "its ardent admirer."

While she was at Hunter's Forestall, Watts sent her poem, *An October Garden,* to *The Athenæum,* which accepted it at once. "Capital!" she exclaimed upon receiving her check of £5. "I hear too that the Athenæum inclines toward a second piece," she wrote William; "all cheery in the way of business." Through his good offices *The Dublin University Magazine* (its title later shortened to *The University Magazine*) also asked her

for a contribution. Before sending a poem, she wondered whether she ought "to forewarn the D.U.M. that I invariably reserve copyright." Like many writers at this time, she was becoming increasingly copyright conscious.

VI

For the next few years Christina's life was uneventful. The custom of spending Christmas with Gabriel, initiated in 1876, continued. "If we were apart this Christmas," he warned his mother and sister in 1877, "I should view it as a bad omen." Another year she told him that if he would provide a bottle of dye, she would tone down his slippers on Boxing-Day.

Summers she spent at some country or seaside town such as Walton-on-the-Naze or Seafort. Cayley called and wrote at intervals. She continued to see Scott from time to time, though her visits to Bellevue House were more frequent than his to Torrington Square, but that was probably because she could combine a call upon Scott with a visit to Gabriel when she went to Chelsea. Upon one occasion she told her brother, "Mamma is so impressed with the beauty of to-day for you as a long working day, & all is so doubtful as to the hour at which we may leave the Scotts, that with her very best love she announces that we will *not* have the pleasure of visiting you & your studio this afternoon. . . ." [5]

Misunderstandings with Lucy continued, with Christina tactfully trying to smooth them over in order to keep relations on as friendly a basis as possible. Both she and her mother derived so much pleasure from "the family babies" that she was particularly anxious to avoid friction on their account. She was especially partial to curly-headed Arthur, who was said to "take after" her, and whom she described proudly as her "one nephew, a precious little man."

But sometimes the children were themselves a cause of fresh dissension. Once when three-year-old Olive was visiting at Torrington Square, she got her fat, mischievous little fingers on Christina's working copy of *Sing-Song,* which she was then translating into Italian "in a really exquisite way," said Gabriel admiringly. Naturally the book had to be snatched away from the child, and Christina tried to make amends by buying another copy of *Sing-Song,* which she presented to Olive's parents with the unfortunate remark, "So now Olive may do her worst!"

It is impossible to please those to whom we are unpleasing, and, as a result of this incident, Christina fell into a fresh trap. Lucy took offense and threatened to put a stop to the little girl's visits to Torrington Square. Christina had to use all her persuasive diplomacy to prevent her sister-in-law from carrying out her intention. "I quite admire our clever little Olive," she assured Lucy, "and am really glad she should be imbued with *Sing-Songs;* and the more at ease she is among us, some of her nearest

relatives, the better; and if some day she comes to love me as well as to be familiar with me, that will be better still. . . ." Then came the real point: "You do not know how much pleasure moreover you will retrench from Mamma's quiet days if you check Olive's coming here or her perfect freedom when she is here. . . ."

Although she was "charmed at the good success" of her translation with Gabriel, after a time she admitted that it needed "a better Italian than I to translate the whole series: think of me writhing helpless before 'Heartsease in my garden-bed.' . . ." The better Italian was soon forthcoming in the Florentine cousin, Teodoro Pietrocola–Rossetti, who undertook to translate *Sing-Song,* calling it *Ninna-Nanna.* Privately Christina told Gabriel that she liked some of her own translations better than her cousin's, though "his No. 5 beats me hollow."

While working on her translation, she added stanzas to existing poems and wrote the new ones dated "Before 1894." On the flyleaf of the first edition [6] she wrote *Playing at Bob Cherry* and *Brownie, Brownie,* and on the back flyleaf, *I Am a King* and the couplet which introduces still another fresh image for her ever-recurrent fire symbolism:

> Stroke a flint, and there is nothing to admire;
> Strike a flint, and forthwith flash out sparks of fire.

VII

One day, having received from an Egyptian acquaintance a mummied head and hand in a glass case, William offered to lend it to Christina, "who used to have a penchant for such lively objects." She declined with thanks, explaining that she "could not feel easy at keeping bits of my fellow-human-creatures as curiosities," and reminding him of Maria's distaste for the Museum Mummy Room.

Three years had passed since her sister's death, but Maria's memory was still green in her heart, still as fresh as the flowers she faithfully placed on her grave. She studied carefully Maria's *Shadow of Dante,* quoting passages from it in her own works and making copious marginal notes, which in their entirety give the impression of a continuous dialogue with her sister, uninterrupted by death.

That she herself was forty-nine now, the age at which Maria had died, seemed in her eyes to strengthen and renew the bond; and the recollection of Maria's scrupulosity in the small details of daily living inspired her to emulation. She herself suggests this motive as the reason for writing the following curious letter to Alice Boyd in 1879. In itself the incident seems unimportant. What is significant is that Christina remembered it for ten years:

My dear Alice

I have long been worried by one reminiscence connected with ever-

charming Penkill,—why should I not lighten my heart by a frank avowal?

I quite forget—at least, I do not clearly recollect the name of the then Incumbent of Girvan, but I remember you disliked him and thought ill of him. Do you remember his calling one day on me? I then said (I mean, such was what I said mixed with what I left unsaid) it was through my fault, for that doubtless a letter I had written asking him about a service had been misunderstood—at least quite probably so—as meaning that I was a grandee residing awhile in your Castle. This letter was really so worded as to invite such a misconception. I said this or something feeble of the kind: but I do not think you ever believed me so as to clear him from a charge of impertinence towards yourself in presenting himself more than uninvited under your roof. Please now do believe that so it was: perhaps I did not say so clearly before *to you,* indeed I am convinced I did not say it convincingly: but now I do say it: I beg you to transfer all odium from one you dislike to one (oh conceit!) who do⟨es⟩ not even now expect to become an object of your dislike. You may well wonder what has set me writing at last: partly it may be that I am now of almost the exact age at which dear Maria died, and I would fain (God helping me) become more like her.

This is no secret from the dear Scotts—pray give them my love if they are with you.

And love on if you can
Your Affectionate
Christina G. Rossetti [7]

During these years she was writing her devotional prose works and reading Richard Hooker and Thomas Fuller, both of whom she quotes in *Called to Be Saints* (1880). Although this volume was published a year later than *Seek and Find,* it was written some years earlier and offered to Macmillan on November 4, 1876: "I have by me a completed work, a sort of devotional reading-book for the red-letter Saints' Days, which of course is longing to see the light & which I shall be glad if you will consent to look at." Macmillan was not interested in publishing it, and the book had to wait another four years to find a publisher.

"No graver slur could attach to my book than would be a reputation for prevalent originality," she declared in her preface, "The Key to My Book." Admitting she was not writing for the learned, "lacking as I do learning and critical practice," she warned scholars that she had used no text "more recondite" than the Authorized Version.

But if her source material was confined to the Bible, her prose style shows, in addition to Revelations, the influence of Fuller and Hooker. Indeed, the fifth book of Hooker's *The Ecclesiastical Polity* provides its motto. The sonority and stately rhythms of the rhetorical prose of the great Anglican divines resound in her sentence-paragraphs, of which the following is an example:

Alas for Herod, against whom blood more innocent than the blood of Abel cried out for Vengeance; who killed those very saints and

martyrs that could not pray for their murderer; who, greedy as Balaam, yet not for any reward, forestalled the possibilities of God's eternal councils, and with impious hands snatched at a share in the slaying of Christ.

Traces of this prose style with its involved sentence structure, its balance and antithesis, its parallelism, and sweeping climax also appear in *Seek and Find* (1879). Christina was not unaware of the Latinate element in her devotional prose, for, when Gabriel expressed his hope that *Seek and Find* would contain some new poems, she replied, "Sad to say, my little book . . . is exclusive prose: yet I flatter myself some of it is that prose which I fancy our Italian half inclines us to indite."

To William, who wondered what she had been working on that summer, she wrote that she could at last shed "a gleam of light on some of those mysterious literary avocations at which you have occasionally caught me." *Seek and Find,* she said, was "a small work on the 'Benedicite,'" and she had sold it, copyright and all, to the Society for the Propagation of Christian Knowledge for £40.[8] It had "one solitary footnote," for which the authoritative source was "our dear good Maria."

In addition to bringing out this work and *Called to Be Saints,* the S.P.C.K. also published Christina's later devotional prose volumes, *Letter and Spirit* (1883), *Time Flies* (1885), and *The Face of the Deep* (1892). When Gabriel protested at such particularly committed publication, she made the oft-quoted remark, "I don't think harm will acrue to me from my SPCK books, even to my standing: if it did, I should still be glad to throw my grain of dust into the religious scale."

That she meant what she said is further evident by her withdrawal in 1878 of her contribution to *The University Magazine* because its editorial policy was distasteful to her. "I could never be at my ease or happy in literary company with persons who look down upon what I look up to," she wrote Keningale Cook, the editor. "I have not *played* at Xtianity, and therefore cannot play at unbelief."

As for the S.P.C.K., actually it was doing her a favor to publish books which, having slight literary appeal, could count upon but a limited number of readers. Macmillan wanted no part of these books, nor did any other commercial publisher. But when the poetic impulse deserted Christina ("Just because poetry *is* a gift . . . I am not surprised to find myself unable to summon it at will and use it according to my choice"), she still had a means of expression in these devotional works and a small public which liked them. In this way, she could write down the thoughts which she brooded over during the last fifteen years of her life.

But even the faithful S.P.C.K. refused to publish her undated "Notes" on Genesis and Exodus (extant but still unpublished),[9] probably because they were too fragmentary and unorganized. Among them, however, may be found occasional striking or original observations suggested to her by

the matter of the Old Testament, which, in accordance with current practice, she read for its symbolic relationship to the New Testament.

One of the biographically most interesting sections is her comment on Exodus 1:22, "And Pharaoh charged all his people saying, Every son that is born ye shall cast into the river, and every daughter ye shall save alive":

> *There seems to be a sense in which from the Fall downwards the penalty of death has been laid on man and of life on woman. To Eve: 'I will greatly multiply thy sorrow and thy conception; in sorrow thou shalt bring forth children:'—to Adam: Unto dust shalt thou return.' The mere name *Eve* was 'the mother of all living,' or it may be (?) of the Living One. May it so be that in this distinction is hidden the true key which supersedes any need of an 'Immaculate Conception,' that from the father alone is derived the stock and essence of the child; the mother, transmitting her own humanity, contributing no more than the nourishment, development, style so to say. The father active, the mother receptive. Thus dead Adam must be the father of a dead child: the Living God the Father of the Living Son. Thus 'Who can bring a clean thing out of the unclean? Not one,' —would darkly set forth the same immutable fact: (All this I write down craving pity and pardon of God for Xt's sake if I err).
>
> And if so not Pharaoh's impious decrees alone, but the course of nature and the necessities of civilization typify the same fact. In their native wildness the male animals are the combatants and champions, the female the passive charge and prize. Under human dominion the male half of domestic breeds is maimed and consumed; the female, far more largely at least, preserved and made much of. In wars, whether sacred or secular the men are *many times* exterminated, the women spared.*

The concept of the maimed male as the carrier of death in the genic process, with his partner, the living mother, spared for the sorrow of childbearing, reveals a psychologically curious attitude toward the respective functions of the sexes. Are we to assume that Christina considered the female the stable and enduring spiritual element, source of spiritual as well as of physical life, whereas the expendable male represents the mortal and perishable element?

VIII

Probably she was jotting down these "Notes" while working on *Seek and Find,* for the same ideas appear in both works. In the latter, which reads more like a lyrical prose poem than a sober exegesis, she gives evidence of having familiarized herself with the prevalent scientific theories of her day. Using the Benedicite as a framework, she seeks in some respects to find a synthesis of science and religion. For her, the great schism which was disturbing Victorian intellectuals existed only by virtue of the limitation of men's minds. "Let us not exercise ourselves in matters beyond our present powers of estimate," she warns, "lest amid the shallows (not the depths) of science we make shipwreck of our faith." It was important to

keep from "confusing probabilities with certainties and opinions with beliefs." Over and over again she makes the distinction between "false science"—the "apparent facts of science"—and true science, between "miscalled reason," which deduces nothingness from a living universe, and that intellectual power which can "gauge height and depth, deduce cause from effect, and track out the invisible by clue of the visible"; and which in so doing leads not to disbelief but to reverence and faith.

Unlike many of her contemporaries, she finds the discoveries of science in the fields of geology, evolutionary biology, and astronomy not incompatible with religious truth as revealed in the Bible. For example, she points out that the assumption of "pre-Adamic convulsions," of " 'a great earthquake, such as was not since men were upon th earth' " is supported by geological evidence. And in both *Seek and Find* and the Exodus notes she applies the "vast periods theory" to the Biblical account of Creation. If the six days of Creation are regarded as geological periods, "not as days of 24 hours each, but as lapses of time by us unmeasured and immeasureable," our whole conception both of Creation and of Biblical time must become altered. Thinking in this way, we may conceive of the seventh day, God's sabbath, as a vast geological period not yet completed, in fact the very "current period . . . in which we are all living and dying." And, to possible objections, she replies in the Exodus notes:

> *Is it necessary . . . (suppose there be any truth in the vast periods theory), to estimate the Seventh Day according to the same standard as the preceding Six? That Seventh alone fell within the cognizance of man and might therefore be subjected to his scale . . . I would even venture to consider (humbly and submissively to the truth whatever that may be) whether this actual cycle is not itself God's Sabbath: this cycle in which the natural laws He originally enacted are as it were fulfilling themselves; in which His creatures run their course and attain their prefixed end while He (so to say) stands aside and lets them by the energies with which once for all He endowed them to do their work, make or mar their future, reach the sum of their weight, number, measure. . . .*

Again in *Seek and Find,* when dealing with the symbolic significance of fish in the Gospels, she shows some knowledge both of the terms and the facts of evolutionary science, as it was then understood. In tracing man's descent from fish, she writes, "Though a comparison of both skeletons reveals to us modifications of an identical structure, yet on the surface the two living organisms have scarcely or have not a limb in common." Nevertheless in the Gospels, "fishes are constituted representatives of men." Quoting from Matthew and Luke, she implies that in this one respect at least the Gospels would complement rather than contradict the findings of evolutionary biology.

But it is the new astronomy, still in its infancy, which has the greatest fascination for her. "I have read how matter can be exploded, or at the

least can be conceived of as exploded from the sun, with such tremendous force as to carry it beyond the radius of solar attraction," she writes in *Time Flies.* Elsewhere in the same work she asks, "Who has not rejoiced at the ever familiar, ever marvellous aspect of the stars? Those resplendent orbs remote, abiding . . . ," and adds:

> But now science, endeavouring to account for certain recurrent obscurations of one or more of such luminaries, suggests that among them and with them may be revolving other non-luminous bodies; which interposing periodically between individuals of the bright host and our planet, diminish from time to time the light proceeding from one or another; and again, by advancing along an assigned orbit, reveal their original brightness.

The subject attracts her equally in *Seek and Find,* where she writes,

> Our globe which once seemed large is now but a small planet among planets, while not one of our group of planets is large compared with its central sun; and the sun itself may be no more than a sub-centre, it and all its systems coursing but as satellites and sub-satellites around a general centre; and this again,—what of this? Is even this remote centre truly central, or is it no more than yet another sub-centre revolving around some point of overruling attraction?

Thus anticipating hypotheses not yet advanced, she concludes, "While knowledge runs apace, ignorance keeps ahead of knowledge."

Yet even "we who occupy comparative shallows of intelligence" cannot only reap the benefits but can also enjoy the aesthetic delights of science:

> We can marvel over the many tints of the heavenly bodies, ruddy, empurpled, golden, or by contrast pale; we can understand the conclusion, though we cannot follow the process by which analysis of a ray certifies various component elements as existing in the orb which emits it; we can realise mentally how galaxies, which by reason of remoteness present to our eyes a mere modification of sky-colour, are truly a host of distinct luminaries; we can long to know more of belts and atmospheres; we can ponder reverently over interstellar spaces so vast as to exhaust the attractive force of suns and more than suns.

But in so doing, "we can make of what we know and of what we know not stepping-stones toward heaven, adoring our Creator for all that He is and that His creatures are not; adoring Him also for what many of our fellows already are, and for what we ourselves are and may become."

Clearly this is a doctrine of optimism which endeavors to reconcile the facts of the material universe, as discoverable by science, with a belief in human potentialities and a serene confidence in the existence of a Divine Power. Not for Christina the pessimism and premature despair of *Locksley Hall* and *Dover Beach.* In her view modern science could not only enlarge the extent of knowledge but could also deepen the depth of faith; and in seeking the one, she believed, we may well find the other.

IX

These, then, were the reflections which occupied Christina as she stepped over the edge of fifty. The legend that she occupied a narrow, self-regarding sphere in her maturer years is simply not true. She loved universal nature, of which human nature is a part, and sought help in understanding it, both from science and from religion. In fact, unlike Gabriel, who increasingly withdrew into himself and seldom bothered his head about matters not concerned with art and literature, intellectually she ranged more widely as her social participations contracted.

She also differed from her brother in retaining her capacity to regard the human spectacle as diverting. Despite the vulgarities of Eastbourne, where she spent the summer of 1880 with her mother, the clamorous over-spilling of life at the seaside resort awakened a responsive chord within her. "The horrors of this place," she wrote Gabriel, "would certainly overwhelm you,—its idlers, brass bands, nigger minstrels of British breed, and other attractions; but I, more frivolous, am in a degree amused."

By now English and American critics had become aware that there were two geniuses in the Rossetti family, and comparisons between them began to appear increasingly in the literary journals. In America Christina was preferred to Gabriel. *The Atlantic Monthly* considered her "a more original bard" than her brother; and Emerson told Scott that Americans did not care for Rossetti's poetry—it was too exotic—"but we like Christina's religious pieces."

In England, however, Gabriel took the lead, and Alice Meynell's unsigned article in *The Pen* (July, 1880) exalted him far above his sister. But if he feared that she might feel slighted, she soon put his mind at rest. "Don't think me such a goose as to feel keenly mortified at being put below you, the head of our house in so many ways," she wrote upon reading the article. When shortly thereafter the journal ceased to exist, Gabriel facetiously suggested that excessive praise of himself had led to its being "snuffed out by an article."

But whatever literary rivalry existed between brother and sister was all on paper. In life, their relations were closer and fonder than they had ever been. With the decline in Gabriel's health, he tended to become more emotionally dependent upon Christina than formerly, and she in turn, sensing his need, became more deeply attached to him. One time when a visit of hers failed to materialize, he was seized by a sudden unreasonable panic until a note explaining her absence arrived. In thanking her for her "sisterly missives," he said that it made "life less bleak as it advances to find the old care and love still prompt to hand."

Scott, too, despite a cooling off in their intimacy, helped to keep at bay the solitude Gabriel feared and dreaded. Scott often spent the evening with him, he told his mother, and was always "intellectual and interest-

ing." Although Christina did not see Scott very often, news of him, which reached her through her brothers, continued to shed the bright glow of the past over the less vibrant present. Hearing of his enthusiasm about Gabriel's new ballad, *The White Ship,* she commented that it was "no wonder the poem had won Penkill laurels," adding, "Scottish laurels those. . . ."

And that the old bond still had the power to move her to an inspired performance is evident from a sonnet (*Later Life 9*), which suggests the nature of her relationship with Scott during these years. It is one of the few poems which directly reflects her interest in astronomy, and for this reason I assign it to 1879 or thereabouts, the year she was writing *Seek and Find.* The star imagery here is treated with astronomical precision rather than with the dreamy vagueness of conventional verse, the point of view being that of the telescope which probes the skies rather than the romantic imagination which probes the psyche. Developing in terms of contrast a single sustained metaphor, Christina describes the kind of invisible communication that may continue to exist between those whose lives touch at no tangible point:

Star Sirius and the Pole Star dwell afar
Beyond the drawings each of other's strength.
One blazes through the brief bright summer's length
Lavishing life-heat from a flaming car;
While one unchangeable upon a throne
Broods o'er the frozen heart of earth alone,
Content to reign the bright particular star
Of some who wander or of some who groan.
They own no drawings each of other's strength,
Nor vibrate in a visible sympathy,
Nor veer along their courses each toward each:
Yet are their orbits pitched in harmony
Of one dear heaven, across whose depth and length
Mayhap they talk together without speech.[10]

17

"FORTHWITH FLASH OUT SPARKS OF FIRE"

1881–1882

The winter of 1880–1881 was marked by severe blizzards. Although the weather hindered Christina and her mother, now eighty, from joining Gabriel for their customary Christmas celebration in Chelsea, it did not prevent Christina a few weeks later from venturing out to brave the unprecedented cold, which kept everyone within doors, in order to visit Scott, who was ill that winter. Gabriel's own perennial poor health provided an additional incentive for the excursion, but it was her anxiety for Scott as much as for her brother that brought her out in the depth of winter. "At the worst,—and that will be by no means bad—" she wrote Gabriel, "I can combine a visit to Mrs. Scotus with my own visitation of you; and as Scotus has been ill, my doing so would be obviously neat and appropriate." According to an entry in the diary she was then keeping for her mother,[1] it was on January 13 that she made the trip to Chelsea, "lunched at the Scotts and called on Gabriel."

But Alice, not Christina, was at the core of Scott's life, and on March 18, while another snowstorm froze the opening daffodils and crocuses, the convalescent Scott wrote a sentimental poem to Alice, marking that "day of days," the anniversary of their first meeting in 1859. Despite graying hair, he wrote,

> Your smile is still as bright as long ago,
> We still are gathering shells on life's seashore,
> We still can walk like children hand in hand,
> Friendship and love beside us evermore.

Although Christina had no opportunity to read these lines, she had observed the kind of pleasant, relaxed existence they celebrated, and she took a different view of the shell-gathering on the seashore: the leisurely, idle summers at Penkill, the snug and cozy winters at Bellevue House, with Scott and Alice placidly playing bezique by the library fire, while outside the storms and blasts of winter raged. In *Pastime* she contrasts

such a pointless life with one which, though "wrecked," was at least strenuous and meaningful:

A boat amid the ripples, drifting, rocking;
Two idle people, without pause or aim;
While in the ominous West there gathers darkness
Flushed with flame.

A hay-cock in a hay-field, backing, lapping;
Two drowsy people pillowed round-about;
While in the ominous West across the darkness
Flame leaps out.

Better a wrecked life than a life so aimless,
Better a wrecked life than a life so soft:
The ominous West glooms thundering, with its fire
Lit aloft.

But, although she might have disapproved of Scott's way of life, which she clearly saw led to intellectual and moral torpor, she was committed to the principle that she herself stated in *Time Flies,* "Once loving, we cannot love too long." Despite Scott's flaws and weaknesses, her abiding affection for him never faltered, revealing itself not only in that tender solicitude which could bring her out in the icy depths of winter to inquire about his health (or perhaps merely to see him), but in an equally tender regard for his fame. When she noticed that his poems had not been proposed along with hers and Gabriel's in Samuel Waddington's anthology of sonnets by living authors, she had Gabriel write to the editor and call his attention to the omission: "In the list sent to my sister I do not see W. B. Scott or Philip Marston. Both will no doubt be applied to." [2]

She might have particularly wished for some recognition of Scott's position in English letters in view of the fact that she was to have a new collection of poems published that summer, thus widening the already wide distance between their respective achievements in poetry. It was becoming increasingly evident, not only to Christina but to Scott himself, that, while the three Rossettis were sprinting ahead in the race for immortality, he was lagging behind. Some years later, bitter and disappointed, he complained to William, "As for Watts, he wrote me a year ago that he was going to give me a critical lift, and place me *once for all* in the place among poets of this age that belongs of right to me! He has never mentioned me in print since. Why is this?" [3]

II

It was in 1879 that Christina had first started to prepare for publication her *Pageant* volume. That year her relations with Macmillan reached another crisis, and once again her brothers thought it necessary to take a

hand in her business affairs, even going to the length of requesting Watts, a solicitor by profession, to represent her.

Some time earlier she had written to Macmillan inquiring what had happened to her 1875 volume of collected poems. Had it sold at all or had it "suffered under the general trade depression and failed"? More than once she had been asked how her last edition had fared, "and I never know." Macmillan thereupon sent her "an acceptable little check" and the information that the 1875 volume had not paid off. But without consulting her, he had been applying the proceeds from the 1875 volume to make up the deficit on the 1866 *Prince's Progress.*

It was this to which Gabriel and William objected. Watts wanted the facts, and in her letter to Gabriel of December 26, 1879, Christina provided them:

> *It seems less formidable to write to *you* than straight to Mr. Watts, whose good will has my warm thanks. So far as I recollect, the 'Goblin Market' business stands thus (N.B. Whenever I talk of *'I said'* you must understand *'I wrote':* for I have not met Mac for years.)—When the last unstereotyped edition of Goblin Market was within about half a dozen copies of exhaustion, Mr. Macmillan wrote to me proposing a new edition. I said yes. 'Prince's Progress, Etc.', long out of print were [*sic*] to be included. I carefully wrote out in my letter a statement of our old original terms (*his* the whole expense and risk; at least I meant *expense,* and I am sure I defined risk: and any profits to be halved *between us*), and begged him to let me have a written answer accepting definitely these terms. No answer whatever did I receive: but proofs came, and I dropped the subject of terms. When statement of sale began coming in, I perceived that the fresh ed. was paying off the old debt on 'Prince's Progress': well and good. In time this debt was paid off, and at last a little money came in. In the course of the summer a friend wanting a copy of my vol. was informed that there were no copies at the moment but that there soon would be some. After a period of ignorance on my part what this meant, I found out (by a sort of chance in our correspondence) from Mr. Macmillan that more copies could and would shortly be issued, because the last ed. had been stereotyped: without my being consulted; yet doubtless on the supposition that I should ⟨be pleased⟩ consent, as ⟨I am⟩ of course I should.
>
> This is the whole story; and evidently the reissue is now on sale, because I know of a copy recently bought. . . .* [4]

It can be seen that the publisher had done nothing illegal or even unethical, though he had acted somewhat arbitrarily. Nonetheless Gabriel and William thought that Watts ought to see Macmillan with the purpose of putting "business-matters . . . on a business-footing." But, although Christina expressed her "affectionate gratitude" to her two "very brotherly brothers," she remembered the muddle they had made of her affairs in 1870, and she did not want to run the risk of another unpleasant break with her publisher just as she was "hugging hopes of getting to-

gether before long enough verse for a *small* fresh volume." She agreed to let Watts speak to Macmillan, but "only and absolutely in the most amicable manner. Nothing would make me have recourse to law: this is a statement at once preliminary and final."

The matter was cleared up without undermining Christina's "position of cordial personal friendship with my friendly publisher" (whom she so seldom saw), and when she sounded him out about publishing the new *Pageant* volume in 1881, he responded promptly and favorably. "I am very glad your business transaction with Macmillan has proved so easy," Gabriel wrote on January 5 of that year, adding, "and could not have doubted its proving so. My book [*Ballads and Sonnets,* published by Ellis and White] lags and drags in the printer's hands. I hope yours may not do so."

The remainder of the winter and during the spring she was working steadily on the manuscript, though, from her entries in her mother's diary, one would not suspect it. The record reveals her leading a leisurely social and domestic life, receiving and returning calls, attending services either at All Saints' Church at Gordon Square or Christ's Church, Woburn Square, shopping on Regent Street, walking or driving in Regent's Park or Hyde Park with her mother and aunts, visiting Brompton cemetery to "place a pink everlasting on dear Maria's Grave," visiting William and Lucy, whose twins Michael and Mary had been born in April, entertaining old friends such as Shields, Scott, Cayley, Mrs. Heimann, Dr. Littledale, and others at dinner or "tea and a rubber of whist."

We learn from the diary that on the 28th of January the drawing-room ceiling fell down and had to be replastered and freshly papered, and that on February 24 she attended vespers at the newly opened Chapel of St. Katherine in Queen's Square, with Dr. Littledale officiating. On April 8 appears the notation that "Miss Boyd and Mr. Scott spent the evening with us; Mrs. Scott, tho' invited, being too unwell [!] to accompany them."

Later in the month Christina and her mother visited Highgate Penitentiary, where, she wrote, "the Warden, cordial as ever, took us into one of the [caprooms] where girls (some enter as early as 9 or 10 years old) are kept apart from the elder penitents. He showed us a pretty patchwork of their making, and attributes much of such premature depravity to the bringing together hundreds of boys and girls in close proximity in the schools."

On May 2 and 23, the diary informs us, "Mr. Cayley called"; and on May 19 "Christina lunched at the Scotts, with also Miss Boyd, and the two Miss Courtneys." There is no further mention of Scott, who left shortly thereafter for Penkill, until his return in October.

On June 1, after litany, "Christina went into the vestry and signed the petition to both Houses of Parliament in favour of not altering the oath

required of Members, a concession which would work on behalf of atheists." On the 22nd she and her mother visited Shields' studio and saw "with delight and admiration" his cartoons for the stained glass windows in the Duke of Westminster's Chapel at Eaton. And on the 23rd she was revaccinated by Dr. Stewart, "Sir W. Jenner having so advised."

III

All these diary entries in Christina's handwriting provide no key to her personal life or important concerns. We hear nothing about the publication of her *Pageant* volume, the outstanding event in her year, and one which, she admitted to William, put her "somewhat in a quake, a fresh volume being a formidable upset of nerves."

She had finished the volume, and on April 18 offered it to Macmillan on the old terms. For answer, he sent her a contract form to be filled out. "Thank you for welcoming my offered M.S.," she wrote on the 20th, "and I hope and dare to say we shall come to one mind." But

> Copyright is my hobby: with it I cannot part. If it is of any value I think I have the first claim upon it, & if it is none it may gracefully be left to me!
>
> So, you see, I cannot proceed to sign the proposed Form, either for my old volume or for my new. Please write back something that may help matters forward. I am, thank you, so wonderfully stronger than I used to be that I could easily call at the Office & talk the business over with you: but I think one often gets on better & keeps more to one's point in a letter.[5]

Macmillan assured her she would not lose copyright, and she thereupon signified her willingness to sign, writing on the 23rd,

> Your assurance that I do not lose copyright reconciles me to *the* Form for both volumes. So please send me such a Form as you propose, either for each edition or for all editions as you like best. I see with satisfaction that you erase the clause about *corrections,* so trust I may improve my text as often as I please: will it not be so? There remains really nothing to discuss verbally: I hope I worried you less than I worried myself by misunderstanding business terms. My brother's wife has just presented us all with *twins!* So the minutest prospective gains become of double value, & I cling to my dear copyright more than ever—if possible and so to say.

As for stereotyping, the issue raised in 1879, "I am sure," she wrote on April 26, "you will do me the favour of judging what is best for our common interest." And then she added in a burst of irrepressible enthusiasm, "I think it looks grand to be stereotyped!"

The business was finally concluded on the 27th. Expressing herself as delighted with everything, she returned the form and its duplicate, both signed, with the playful remark, "Perhaps you suspected I was not quite so ready!"

She reported with satisfaction her successful handling of the transaction to her brothers, telling Gabriel that she was "quite pleased about Macmillan, because he said *yes* without asking to see the M.S. or making a single enquiry as to either bulk or subject"; and announcing to William, " 'Io anche—'! At last I took the plunge and sent in some poems to Macmillan, who before he saw accepted them. . . ." Although the inevitable ordeal of another public performance now loomed up ahead, she remarked that, unlike William's recent production, the book could not possibly "turn out TWINS!"

IV

As usual, she arranged to be away from London when her new volume was published and reviewed. With her mother and two aunts she spent July in Sevenoaks, renting for the month Fayremead, which she described as "quite a gentleman's house, commodiously and even elegantly furnished," an establishment "far superior to our customary scale of accommodation." But with the four of them "clubbing together," she felt they could afford the steep rent of four guineas a week. "Nor are we divorced from our dear whist!" she observed complacently, "there being four of us."

William and Lucy, with their "nice little flock" of five children, were spending their holiday at Littlehampton; and Christina wrote William that she hoped the air there would not "prove *gouty,* or *bilious,* or *coughified,* or *diarrheaed,*" these all being ailments which had afflicted the family. Of all the children, Christina's favorite at this time was "my pet Helen," born in 1879, "an endearing little dear."

On July 20 she wrote William, "Only think, my Poems are to come out next Monday. . . . I should have fancied this moment was between 2 publishing seasons, but it seems unlikely that a sane publisher should not understand his business better than I do." In another letter, this time to Lucy, she confessed that she was "glad to be away at this formidable literary crisis, and to let my storm blow over before my return: for tho' I like to bring out a fresh volume, it strains one's nerves to do so."

But delay at the binder's resulted in postponement of publication, thus straining her nerves even tauter. She heard from Macmillan that her volume was sure to appear before the middle of August. "Of course I feel this fresh plunge into publicity formidable," she wrote Gabriel on the 4th, "but I must (at the worst) 'grin and bear it.' " She added that she had considered sending her new volume to Watts, "for friendship's sake and in acknowledgment of kindness—but forebore, lest he should suppose I aimed at disarming him. I daresay he is acute at reading and even at divining motives, so I hope he will not misconceive mine if ever he thinks about them one way or the other!"

Watts was to review the volume for *The Athenæum,* and Hall Caine,

who had recently come to live with Gabriel, for *The Academy*. "I rather wince in prospect of Mr. Watts and Mr. Caine," she worried. But she need not have feared. Both Gabriel's friends launched the new volume with paeans of praise, singling out for particular notice the *Monna Innominata* sonnet sequence, which was easily the outstanding success in the volume. In fact, so exclusively was it mentioned in the reviews that Christina ironically pointed out that there was a second set of sonnets (*Later Life*) in the book she thought also worthy of some attention. Gabriel was "deeply impressed by the beauty of the *Monna Innominata* series," and so was Watts; as for Swinburne, his delight "amounted to screaming and dancing ecstasy," said Gabriel with cynical amusement.[6]

V

But the "warm admiring word on 'Mona' " Scott sent through his wife particularly pleased her. Her book arrived at Penkill by post at a time when he was bored. In recalling to him memories of the past, the sonnets set dormant currents vibrating, which started him dreaming again. Like Christina, he had his own secret room to which no one but himself had access.

His letter of August 26 to Gabriel, though discreetly worded, hints that he felt himself better qualified than most to appreciate Christina's sonnets:

> *My dear Gabriel
> Here we, that is AB, Letitia, and myself, are shut up yesterday and today by rain, and in need of something more interesting than a lot of tragedies, old and new, we are reading. Fortunately yesterday's post brought Christina's Pageant . . . which [is] highly appreciated . . . [and] has set me thinking about you and yours.
> Christina's book is rich in beautiful thoughts, but sometimes a little puzzling in execution. The Donna Innominata is truly a great thing to have done, these 14 sonnets are to me in a high degree noble and delightful. Perhaps knowing Christina so well makes me feel and understand them, and so enter into and delight in them more than I might were they by an unknown to me. The series appears to be equal or superior to anything she has done, or anyone has done.*

Moreover, her performance evidently inspired him to try once more for fame as a poet. As he brooded over the volume of poems and their author, a flying spark from her genius enkindled a brief blaze of his own talent, all but smothered under the busy activities with which he concealed his deficiencies from himself. Whatever the cause, that autumn he wrote the hundred or so poems he published in the spring under the title *A Poet's Harvest Home*. "In all these pieces," he told Gabriel, "I have endeavored to express myself, my way of thinking and feeling." They came, he said, "really spontaneously." To Swinburne he said the same thing: "Every one was produced with a spontaneity and energy, quite a new experience,

to me." Furthermore, "They (for the major part) record, or relate to actial [*sic*] incidents."

One of these poems based upon "actial" experience he called *Rose-Leaves;* it was written in answer to Christina's poem *Summer Is Ended,* which she probably composed during or after her illness of 1872. The opening lines of her poem are a bitter and anguished protest against the inevitable process of aging, which ruthlessly sweeps away a woman's beauty as the first autumn wind scatters the last petals of the overripe rose which has till then arrested time and held firmly its form:

> To think that this meaningless thing was ever a rose,
> Scentless, colourless, *this!*

As Scott read these lines, he was profoundly moved by Christina's fury of self-hatred, and he understood at last what the loss of youth and beauty had meant to her, and why. Belatedly he sought to console her for the theft of the years and to assure her that he himself sometimes, retiring to his secret room, opened "memory's casket" and nostalgically sifted through the "withered petals" which for him as for her still held the fragrant scent of past passion:

> Once a rose ever a rose, we say,
> A loved one who loved us
> Remains beloved though gone from our day—
> It must be thus:
> The Past is sweetly laid away.
>
> Sere and sealed for a day and a year,
> Smell it, Christina, I pray:
> So nature deals with its children dear,
> So memory deals alway
> God's memory also never fear.

Before this poem appeared in print, Scott sent it to Christina with dried rose leaves. She preserved and cherished it. Four years later she copied it out on a blank end leaf of her *Pageant* volume, writing under the poem,

W. B. Scott—Penkill
Sent with dried rose leaves.
(*see* p. 104)

If we turn to page 104 of the first edition of *The Pageant,* we find her poem *Summer Is Ended.*[7]

VI

But by now Christina had already passed her fifty-first birthday and was growing stouter. She herself observed with dry humor that "a fat poetess is incongruous, especially when seated by the grave of a buried hope."

In the same spirit of self-mockery she drew a verbal caricature of herself as November in *The Months,* the pageant for children which gave her 1881 volume its title:

> Here comes my youngest sister, looking dim
> And grim,
> With dismal ways.

"Pray appreciate the portrait," she wrote Gabriel, who responded with the sardonic limerick,

> There's a female bard grim as a fakeer,
> Who daily grows shakier and shakier—

That her self-portrait was not wholly exaggerated is evident from contemporary accounts. "Christina Rossetti affected the least picturesque of black garments for daily use," said Ford Madox Ford (Hueffer), "whilst on occasions of a festive nature she would go as far as a pearl-grey watered silk." Gosse found her a truly formidable figure: not only her dowdiness in dress, which was "really distressing and hard to bear from the high priestess of Pre-Raphaelitism," but even more, her lack of small talk and her manner, shy and portentously solemn, which made social intercourse with her painful. Once, when Macmillan accused her in jest of having "cut" him, she replied soberly, "Pray do not even joke about my having 'cut' you. I hope I am incapable of cutting any friend, and certainly I shall not pick out one who treats me so kindly."

That September Gabriel went to the English Lake Country with Caine and Fanny Cornforth, though, according to Christina's decorous entry in her mother's diary, only two of the party of three were "staying in the Vale of St. John, near Keswick, in a lovely old place which enchants Gabriel."

But he was too ill to remain enchanted for long, and was glad to get back to Cheyne Walk. He arrived in October during a week of storms and cold winds. On her way to litany, Christina had been "buffeted . . . by the stormy wind," which subsequently blew the roof off the house where Cayley lodged. Gabriel and Caine reached London in the cold, dreary dawn. At Cheyne Walk the blinds were still down when they entered. As Gabriel, assisted by Caine, crossed the gloomy threshold, he murmured with a sigh of relief, "Thank God! Home at last, and never shall I leave it again!"

By the end of October, when Scott returned from Penkill, Gabriel was a very sick man. Stopping by Tudor House shortly after his arrival, Scott was "shocked to find the dear old Gabriel prostrate on the old sofa we had so often in the earlier times seen filled with genial friends," with no one to look after or to attempt to cheer "the man whose spirits were down to zero."

Scott's own method of cheering Gabriel was curious. He had brought

along his recently completed poems to read aloud and had anticipated a cozy, companionable evening by the fire, whisky toddies on hand, reading and afterwards discussing his work with a sympathetic friend. Instead, "When he and I were alone, he wept and complained and made unkind speeches, or showed me things he thought would wound me," such as a recent sketch of the Sphinx which satirized Scott's own youthful illustration of the same subject for his *Year of the World.*

It was not a satisfactory substitute for the kind of evening Scott had expected, and he probably showed his annoyance, for Gabriel suddenly turned hostile. "Lying on the sofa dying, as he was," Scott tells us, "I saw that singular expression of ferocity that used to take possession of his face if he surmised a quarrel was coming." Scott says that he refused to take up the gauntlet, though perhaps he did not conceal his opinion that Gabriel's drawing had deteriorated as a result of his illness. Such criticism, expressed or implied, would have been sure to infuriate Gabriel.

We can hardly give Scott the credit he takes to himself for avoiding an unpleasant scene with a sick man. As old age crept upon him, Scott began to settle down into the mold of a stubborn, crusty, selfish, and quarrelsome old man. "For myself," he said irritably, "I never was among the well known men in London, and never tried to be."

This lack of recognition and his failure to live up to his own expectations may have been the cause of his resentment, not only of his contemporaries but also of the younger men pushing their way into the ranks of literature, men like Gosse and Caine. Annoyed by what he called Gosse's "cheeky impertinence," he warned William that the young man was "becoming the most dangerous of busybodies and turns up everywhere," including Scott's own dinner table. Even angrier at Caine, whose "penny-a-liner leader" about him gave the impression he was an unknown person struggling with difficulties, he told Watts that, although Caine meant "the horror" to be of service to him, it was obvious that Caine had "no ideas on poetry and nothing to say," and was "the most unfit person" he knew "to be trusted with literary work."

Neither Caine nor Gosse suspected the depths of his hostility, but Gabriel, more sensitive to the subtle nuances of relationship, intuitively recognized that beneath Scott's show of friendliness lurked that "devil lying *perdu* in each of us"; and the presence at his sickbed of this old companion who so persistently misunderstood him was one of his minor trials during his last days on earth. But, because by then he had become morosely suspicious of all his friends, no attention was paid to his resentment of "that damned old beast Scott."

VII

Toward the end of November Gabriel's condition reached a crisis which at first seemed to be more psychological than physical. He seemed to be ever sinking deeper and deeper into the bottomless quicksands of

melancholy. On the 26th Christina, "going to early dinner at the Scotts," afterwards "called on Gabriel whom she found glad to see her, but weak and much depressed," she wrote in the diary. A nurse, Mrs. Abrey, had been engaged, and both Watts—that "hero of friendship," as Gabriel called him—and Caine were on hand. Returning to Tudor House a few days later, Christina persuaded her brother to take a little walk around the garden, and together they circled "the reduced but still pleasant little garden" twelve times, Gabriel leaning on her arm.

His distress of mind showed itself in a strange remorse about his youthful treatment of his father. "No wonder that in weakness and suffering," Christina remarked sympathetically, "such a reminiscence haunts weary days and sleepless hours of double darkness." More than the others she was able to sympathize with Gabriel and to feel with his feelings, for she had not forgot her own weary days and sleepless hours in 1872. Only religious faith had enabled her to bear her burden, and now she longed to make that same comfort available to her brother. "How exceedingly I wish," she said to William, that "Mr. Burrows or one like him had access to the nearly-closed precincts: you must laugh at me if you will, but I really think a noble spiritual influence might do what no common sense, foresight of ruin, affection of friends, could secure."

A week later she wrote her frequently quoted letter of December 2. Probing the core of the old wound in order to expose the scar to Gabriel, she assured him in this most frankly self-revealing of all her letters that she, as well as he, had her haunted memories and harassing anxieties:

> My dearest Gabriel
>
> I write because I cannot but write, for you are continually in my thoughts and always in my heart, much more in our Mother's who sends you her love and dear blessing.
>
> I want to assure you that, however harassed by memory or anxiety you may be, I have (more or less) heretofore gone through the same ordeal. I have borne myself till I became unbearable to myself, and then I have found help in confession and absolution and spiritual counsel, and relief inexpressible. Twice in my life I tried to suffice myself with measures short of this, but nothing would do; the first time was of course in my youth before my general confession, the second time was when circumstances had led me (rightly or wrongly) to break off the practice. But now for years past I have resumed the habit, and I hope not to continue it profitlessly.
>
> ' 'Tis like frail man to love to walk on high,
> But to be lowly is to be like God,'
>
> is a couplet (Isaac Williams) I thoroughly assent to.
>
> I ease my own heart by telling you all this, and I hope I do not weary yours. Don't think of me merely as the younger sister whose glaring faults are known to you, but as a devoted friend also.

Shortly thereafter she spoke to Canon Burrows, who called, probably at her request, and it was at this time that Gabriel astonished his friends

by asking for a priest to whom he might confess.[8] Scott, who considered this request another of Gabriel's "hallucinations," like the chaffinch incident, reminded him of his lifelong agnosticism, but Gabriel insisted that he didn't care about that: "I can make nothing of Christianity, but I . . . want a confessor to give me absolution for my sins." Scott could only smile at such "medievalism," as he called it, but her brother's desire must have gratified Christina.

Although William assumed it was a Roman Catholic priest Gabriel wanted—merely because he had always thought Gabriel more receptive to Catholicism than to Protestantism—no evidence exists that he asked for a Roman rather than an Anglo-Catholic priest. We have seen that in 1877 Christina and her mother had tried to convert him to Christianity, and, in his very great trouble of mind during this last, fatal illness, their lifelong Anglican faith, in which he too had been brought up, would have been the particular form of religion to which he would have turned rather than one which could not claim the emotional strength of early ties reinforced by later persuasion. Hall Caine, in describing his lonely dinner with Gabriel on Christmas Day, relates that, when the bells rang out from the neighboring churches, Gabriel "spoke with emotion of his mother and sister . . . and how they were supported through their sore trials by religious resignation."

It was, then, through emotion and not conviction that he was feeling his way toward Christian belief, but his shifting and capricious moods were not a sufficiently solid foundation for a genuine conversion. After his one outcry, he did not mention the matter again. "Each soul is saved by itself, not able to carry its nearest and dearest with it," Christina had observed in the Exodus notes, and the truth of the observation must have struck her anew at this time.

A bad cold confined her to the house during the holiday season. Unable to make the usual visit to Chelsea, Christina wrote Gabriel on Christmas Day,

> * If I had seen you yesterday I need not have troubled you with a Christmas love letter! As it is, accept the expression of my affectionate good will and wishes in choice autograph form. I hope soon to come again and see you and find you better, but for the moment my cough keeps me within doors. I have not even been to Church. . . .*

Had she known it, this was to be her brother's last Christmas on earth.

VIII

Urged by his physician and William, toward the end of January Gabriel went to Birchington-on-Sea in Kent. Some instinct must have told him that this was his journey to the grave, for at every stage of the trip he protested that he wanted to go home, and, once he was installed at West-

cliff Bungalow (loaned him by John P. Seddon), he took an immediate dislike to the house and insisted upon returning to Cheyne Walk. Against his better judgment, he was prevailed upon to stay.

Although he was accompanied by his nurse, Mrs. Abrey, Caine, and Caine's thirteen-year-old sister Lily, and was visited from time to time by Watts and Shields, he waited impatiently for his mother and Christina to join him. Delayed because of Mrs. Rossetti's illness, they did not arrive until the beginning of March. Shortly before leaving London, Christina wrote to William, appealing for a more sympathetic understanding of Gabriel's condition. In common with Scott, William Morris, and others of their circle, William suspected that his brother's critical illness was in large part imaginary. Never once did Christina fall into such an error. The closest to him in a kinship of temperament as well as of blood, and with her own experience of illness to support her poet's sensitivity to the feelings of others, she was able to judge Gabriel's condition from first to last. "Pray do not ascribe all his doings and non-doings to foundationless fidgetiness, poor dear fellow," she pleaded. "Don't you think neither you nor I can quite appreciate all he is undergoing at present, what between wrecked health at least in some measure, nerves which appear to falsify facts, and most anxious money-matters? It is trying to have to do with him at times, but what must it be TO BE himself?"

That she felt pain at watching his suffering may be taken for granted, but not a hint of this appears in her letters to William from Birchington, which in general were an unflinching and dryly factual account of Gabriel's progressive deterioration. "This is all grievous for you to read," she wrote. "But I on the spot must write as I hear."

On March 14, after "a delightful walk on the cliff: seagulls and very large daisies in abundance," she came back to the bungalow and had a talk with Mrs. Abrey, who thought that, instead of improving, Gabriel was steadily retrogressing. Christina too suspected that "some terrible mischief" lurked in his constitution. Again she urged William not to doubt the *"reality* of poor dear Gabriel's illness: do not let any theory or any opinion influence you to entertain such a doubt." [9]

Although on March 17 she thought Gabriel "rather better than worse since Sunday," by the 24th she saw that he was "going back apparently rather than going forward," and was "comfortless . . . sinking . . . and wasted away." The weather, which till then had been "mild and beautiful," suddenly changed to wintry cold, with stormy days of wind, rain, sunshine, and hail. "On Sunday morning," she reported in a letter to William, "I struggled home from church in what *felt* like danger to my life from a storm of wind which began to rage after I got there: three times I was driven to take refuge in cottages, and at last was most happy in being able to procure a shut-up fly. . . ." William sent this letter on to Lucy (who was visiting her father in Manchester) with the comment. "The

tussle against the wind on Sunday last . . . must have been no trifle in her condition and tendency of health. I hope I may not on Saturday find her still suffering from its effects."

But by the following weekend she had recovered and was none the worse for her adventure. "Well enough," William told Lucy, "though saddened and anxious, of course." During his two-day visit Christina heard from him about the performance at Hanover Square of the new *Goblin Market* cantata composed by E. Aguilar. She learned also that John H. Ingram wanted her to write the life of Mrs. Browning in his *Eminent Women* series, but both she and William agreed that she was "temporarily out of the running" as far as doing any writing went. Then, according to a letter of April 2 from William to his wife, Christina told him "that Scotus is confined to the house these few days, and attended by a medical man—having somehow hurt his leg." Although Christina may have been made uneasy by the accident, William gathered that it was "not a grave affair."

Although Dr. Harris, the local physician attending Gabriel, spoke of the possibility of softening of the brain, neither Christina nor William could detect any sign of it. "In spirits I find G. of course low," William confided to Lucy, "but not so painfully gloomy as he has been at times: he talks with perfect good sense, and listened to Christina reading a novel until he fell asleep. . . ." The novel was probably Wilkie Collins' *Moonstone,* which was the last novel Christina read to Gabriel.

He lingered on for two more days. April 9 was Easter Sunday, but Christina, who had not left her dying brother's bedside all through the night, was too exhausted to attend church services. The vicar, Mr. Alcock, who had been visiting Gabriel regularly for the past few days, came again on Easter. Toward evening the family agreed to take turns watching by the sick man, who appeared to be sinking rapidly. Christina's shift was to have been from ten on; she was therefore not in the room when the crisis came. It was she, however, who wrote down in her mother's diary the account of Gabriel's last hours.

Shortly before half past nine the nurse and Watts finished putting a poultice on Gabriel's back. Watts left the room, and the nurse went over to stir the fire. Gabriel was sitting up in bed; his mother was rubbing his back. Suddenly he collapsed, "threw his arms out, screamed out loud two or three times close together, and then lay breathing but insensible."

No account of a death could be simpler and less sentimental than Christina's brief report of it: "All assembled around the bed. Mr. Shields flew for Dr. Harris and in the shortest time returned with him. Gabriel still breathed, but that was all. Dr. Harris once or twice said he still lived—then said he was dead."

IX

On Good Friday Gabriel had made his will. At first assuming that his property would be divided equally between William and Christina, he did not intend to make a will, but Watts reminded him that a will he had made many years ago, leaving everything to Lizzie, still existed, and that her family could have some legal claim upon it. Gabriel therefore made a new will, naming William and Christina as his legatees. But she wouldn't hear of it: she was "immoveable in her resolve" that her mother, not she, should be Gabriel's heir. And so another will had to be prepared, substituting Mrs. Rossetti's for Christina's name.[10] Christina's share of her brother's property was "any such small drawing or other article" as she might select as a memento.

Scott too was left the choice of a drawing. Confined to his house by his injured leg, he was unable to attend the funeral at Birchington, but he heard about it from Judge Vernon Lushington. The medieval gray church of country flint was situated on a hill overlooking the sea. The churchyard was bright with irises and wallflowers in bloom, and "close to Gabriel's grave there was a laurestinus and a lilac." Standing beside the grave, said Lushington, was "the old mother, supported by William on one side and Christina on the other—a most pathetic sight. She was very calm, extraordinarily calm, but whether from self-command or the passivity of age, I do not know—probably from both; but she followed all the proceedings with close interest."

It was a clear spring day, and, as the vicar read the funeral service, Lushington observed that the old gray shingle spire on the church tower pierced a pure blue April sky. About fifteen or twenty friends present listened to the simple service.

> Then we all looked into the resting-place of our friend, and thought and felt our last farewells—many flowers, azaleas and primroses, were thrown in. I saw William throw in his lily-of-the-valley. That is all I have to tell you. Sad it was, very sad, but simple and full of feeling, and the fresh beauty of the day made itself felt with all the rest. . . .

Later that evening the family with Shields returned to the churchyard to place on the new grave the magnificent wreath sent by Lady Mount-Temple. Then Christina gave her mother a bunch of woodspurge she had picked in the garden; and, while they all looked on, Mrs. Rossetti knelt down and laid on the grave the flower celebrated by Gabriel in his poem, *The Woodspurge:*

> The wind flapped loose, the wind was still,
> Shaken out dead from tree and hill:
> I had walked on at the wind's will,—
> I sat now, for the wind was still.

Between my knees my forehead was,—
My lips, drawn in, said not Alas!
My hair was over in the grass,
My naked ears heard the day pass.

My eyes, wide open, had the run
Of some ten weeds to fix upon;
Among those few, out of the sun,
The woodspurge flowered, three cups in one.

From perfect grief there need not be
Wisdom or even memory:
One thing then learnt remains to me,—
The woodspurge has a cup of three.

X

The day before Gabriel died saw the publication of Scott's new volume, *A Poet's Harvest Home*. Scott found the striking contrast between the revival of his own creative power at seventy and Rossetti's decline and final defeat at fifty-four immensely cheering. In the unequal race for fame, life was on his side. But he was to learn that Gabriel dead proved an even more formidable rival than Gabriel alive.

During April, however, while the Rossetti family was in mourning, he enjoyed to the full a brief spurt of prominence. A host of well-wishing friends, among them William Morris, Holman Hunt, Swinburne, and Dr. Littledale, wrote flattering letters of praise and congratulation. Arriving much later than the others, Christina's own tribute in verse added the last crowning touch of glory to Scott's winter triumph.

She had returned to London on April 15 after paying Gabriel her final respects in the poem *Birchington Churchyard,* and had been at home no more than three days before she made a special trip to Chelsea to see Scott. It was to him she turned in the freshness of her grief. On April 18, she noted in her mother's diary, she called at Bellevue House to inquire about Scott's health. He was not at home. She was told that he had gone to South Kensington for the day. As always, he was not available when she needed him the most.

That Cayley called upon her at Torrington Square to offer his condolences upon the same day she went to Chelsea to see Scott was one of those dramatic ironies more frequently arranged by the novelist than by life. She was absent to Cayley, as Scott had been to her.

Some days later Scott sent her a presentation copy of his new book. She acknowledged it in these lines:

My old admiration before I was twenty
Is predilect still, now promoted to se'enty.
My own demi-century plus an odd one
Some weight to my judgment may fairly impart.

Accept this faint flash of a smouldering fun,
The fun of a heavy old heart.

This piece, moving despite its self-conscious awkwardness, was published for the first time by Scott in his *Notes*. He introduced it by a passage calling attention to the duration of his decades-long friendship with Christina:

> Here is a trifle by Christina Rossetti, which has an exceedingly interesting reference to the first visit I paid to her household about thirty-five years ago, when I first saw her standing writing at a small high desk . . . 'before I was twenty' indicating her age pretty nearly at the epoch I mean.

18

"LOVE IS THE FIRE"

1882–1886

Before the dismantling of Gabriel's house and the sale of his effects at Christie's, Christina and her mother made a last painful pilgrimage to Chelsea. Each selected a favorite drawing and a volume from Gabriel's library for remembrance. As they left what Christina described as "the saddened house" with "the familiar old objects all about the rooms ready for the sale next week," they must have been haunted by the memory of the lurid splendor and the baffling futility of that life so dear to them and now removed. They must have asked one another, as mourners sometimes do, whether, if they could, they would will the dead back again into life. Christina for one had no doubts:

For who that feel this burden and this strain,
This wide vacuity of hope and heart,
Would bring their cherished well-beloved again:
To bleed with them and wince beneath the smart,
To have with stinted bliss such lavish bane,
To hold in lieu of all so poor a part?

That summer William Sharp (Fiona MacLeod to many of his readers) paid his first visit to Torrington Square in order to get material for his memoir of Gabriel. As he entered the drawing room Christina was reading aloud to her mother Southwell's *Burning Babe.* She looked up, and Sharp observed her "quick alighting glance," then its swift withdrawal as she indicated by a nod that he was to take a seat until she finished. Studying her as she read the poem in "her beautiful, mellifluous voice which articulated each word with such exquisite precision," Sharp observed the long heavy eyelids over the slightly protrusive azure-grey eyes, the rich brown hair now threaded with solitary white strands, the face not unlined yet still smooth and young in contour. As she came to the words, "Love is the fire, and sighs the smoke, the ashes shame and scorn," she paused and exchanged "an intimate and significant glance" with her mother. Impressed by this incident, Sharp sensed something momentous and hidden

in the unspoken communication between the two women, but, lacking the key, he was unable to unlock the door. That exchange of glances remained with him—vivid, enigmatic, apparently irrelevant, and yet he remembered and recorded it.[1]

The family, including Christina, warmly welcomed his intention to write a book about Gabriel. "I need not tell you," she wrote Macmillan, who was to publish it, "what an interest we are taking in Mr. Sharp's Memoir. Little did we think that our dear Gabriel would already become the subject of memorials." However, when Sharp also proposed to memorialize Christina's birthday by a sonnet in *The Athenæum,* her enthusiasm cooled. And when the poem failed of publication, she confided to William that, although Sharp had said he could explain the reason it had not appeared, "in my secret soul I suspect that reason of being the cogent one that it is not a good sonnet."

Swinburne offered his own tribute to Christina in a copy of his recently published volume *Tristram of Lyonesse,* "a valued gift," said Christina, but embarrassing since it was the fourth of his books he had given her, and "I not one hitherto to him." She had pasted strips of paper over the lines in the atheistic chorus in her copy of *Atalanta in Calydon;* and now, with the mischievous motive of edifying him (but not without misgivings that he might take offense), she presented him with a copy of *Called to Be Saints.* Neither edified nor offended, the atheistic poet acknowledged her gift "with consummate graciousness," and parried her thrust by suavely praising the verses to the Holy Innocents and to Sts. Barnabas, Phillip, and James.

He continued his professional homage by dedicating to her in 1883 his *Century of Roundels.* In a letter accompanying the presentation copy, he suggested that, if she found "the references to Dante and Farinata a propos of caverns in Guernsey . . . strange or far-fetched," she should visit them herself and see "that wonderful sight" so generally neglected by English tourists. Assuring him that she was "dipping about" in her "newly-acquired book of beauties," she wrote on June 9,

> *Thank you indeed for it, and for its dedication, where my name might well blush into red ink at the honour done it. The *last* result of my wondering over 'Dante' and 'Farinata' will (let us hope) be a will-o-the-wisp rivalry! I think I have quite done with travelling, or else I might hope some day to see Sark and Guernsey—but even then I should not gaze upon them with your eyes or your wealth of association: so home will do well enough for me.
>
> Very much your obliged
> Christina G. Rossetti *

The following year in his *Ballad of Appeal to Christina G. Rossetti* he entreated her to pour out once more "sweet water from the well of song." He sent it to her with a copy of *A Midsummer Holiday,* the volume

in which it appeared, and a polite note apologizing for addressing her publicly without permission and repeating in prose his hope that she would soon present the world with "a fresh gift of such verse as only you can give." To this she replied:

> *Thank you truly for so kind an estimate of me however little I may justify it. Pray believe that dumbness is not my *choice:* nor will I attempt to justify it with the parrot who screamed 'But I think the more.' And perhaps I may add that no one is more pleased than I am when by fits and starts I become vocal.*

One time in comparing some lines of Herrick's, which he admired, to the work of Herbert and Crashawe, Swinburne declared that they were "worthy of Miss Rossetti herself; and praise of such work can go no higher." [2]

II

The year following Gabriel's death was not a "vocal" one for her, but we have seen that an emotional crisis which drained her energy generally resulted in a poetically dry period. Besides, her time was taken up by several projects not of her own seeking. The first, helping William to collect and edit Gabriel's correspondence, she regarded less as a task than as a labor of love. Toward the end of September she and her mother began reading through Gabriel's letters, Christina destroying those she considered unfit for publication and marking with a blue pencil objectionable passages in others; but after a few days Mrs. Rossetti protested that she could not continue, for the pain was "too great." Nevertheless, a month later, with Christina's aid, the old lady resolutely took up the task again. As for Christina, she enjoyed "working away at copying Mamma's contingent of Gabriel's letters—such good old letters some of them, so loving—and so funny." A way of reliving Gabriel's life, it in a sense restored him to her. She admitted in *Time Flies* that occasionally she wished "a certain occupation at once sad and pleasant and dear to me, and at that moment inevitably drawing towards a close, could have lasted out through the remainder of my lifetime." [3]

In the summer of 1882 she also agreed to write one of the biographies for John H. Ingram's *Eminent Women* series. She at once rejected Adelaide Proctor, the first subject offered to her, explaining she had "for so long dropped out of literary society" that she felt incapable of dealing with it. She next objected to Mrs. Browning because she said she could not count upon Browning's coöperation, and furthermore she thoroughly sympathized with his reticence to disclose details of his married life. Mrs. Radcliffe, whose Gothic tales she had read avidly in adolescence, was more to her taste, but here the difficulty proved to be lack of material. After "Radcliffizing" at the British Museum during the summer of 1883, she gave up the project along with her promised £50 for the completed work.

"Someone else, I daresay, will gladly attempt the memoir," she told Ingram, "But I despair and withdraw."

Ingram himself suspected there was another reason for her retreat. "Miss Rossetti, I fear," he wrote William, "will never look with favour again upon the idea of writing a vol. for the *Series* after what you told her about my squabbling with my lady friends! After all, only two have been cantankerous, and, I assure you, my work has been no sinecure. . . ."[4]

But Christina's abortive attempt to write biography caused her to think about some of the problems inherent in the literary form; and a few scattered comments in her letters, though they in no way formulate a theory of biography, at least indicate her attitude toward such an undertaking.[5] When she was considering the life of Adelaide Proctor, she wrote Ingram that she assumed "a great part of the volume . . . must in the case of a quiet life, such as I suppose Miss Proctor's to have been, be made up of quotations from her unpublished verse or of available correspondence, should such come to light." And while she was collecting "Radcliffeana" she read with interest the *Memoir of Emily Brontë,* which had already been published in Ingram's series. "But does it strike you," she asked William, "as being in the main a memoir of Emily?" To an unknown correspondent who in 1883 had requested some biographical data about herself, she replied, "Pardon me as to the biographical details. If there are any, I am in favour of keeping them back at any rate till the *whole* (in my case quiet) life can be summed up with the final date."

She herself has not made it particularly easy to sum up her life, for in the same spirit in which she did away with those of Gabriel's letters she considered unfit for delivery to posterity, she deliberately and methodically destroyed her own letters as soon as they were answered. "She is one of those persons," William told Herbert Gilchrist, who "wd. bury letters and personal documents or details generally, into oblivion."

To Gosse, who wanted information about her life for his chapter "Christina Rossetti" in *Critical Kit-Kats,* she answered evasively, "Any definite question I am ready to respond to. But where is the definite point for a definite question?" She proposed that "instead of that exquisite drawing of Gabriel's which was taken—and please bear in mind by the pencil of a partial brother—as long ago as 1866," a plain photograph be substituted, one "done . . . in quite middle life, and so, presumably, a good deal like me still."

Her attitude toward the approach to a life of Dante Gabriel, which presented and still presents such difficult problems, sums up at a deeper level her view of the biographer's function. After Hall Caine's book appeared in 1882, she told Lucy that "considering the circumstances under which his experiences occurred, I think it may fairly be pronounced neither unkind nor unfriendly; but I hope some day to see the same and

a wider field traversed by some friend of older standing and consequently of far warmer affection towards his hero; who, whatever he was or was not, was lovable." And to Watts, when he entertained the project of writing Gabriel's life (see my Preface), she expressed the wish that if the necessity arose to "touch on painful subjects," he would treat them with truth and with tenderness.

III

We have seen that beginning in 1881 Christina showed an increasing concern about her "dear Copyright," which she called her "hobby." This growing awareness of her rights as an author was stimulated by and reflects the general interest the question was arousing in literary circles during the 'seventies and 'eighties. Although in England a writer was protected for forty-one years of his lifetime and seven years after his death, the inadequacy of such limited duration was becoming apparent. Furthermore, when hard-pressed, an author could and frequently did sell his copyright to a publisher and thus lose control of his literary property. Since no international agreement existed (the first Berne Convention was not signed until 1886), an author's works were commonly pirated in other countries, the worst abuses of English writers occurring in the United States.

The prevalent chaos brought out protests from powerful voices in the writing world, among them Herbert Spencer, T. H. Huxley, and Alexander Macmillan, all of whom were called as witnesses in the parliamentary debate following the report of the Copyright Commission of 1876. Spencer testified that his own works had begun to pay off only after twenty-four years. Macmillan, in addition to speaking before the House in favor of the copyright bill, published in the December, 1880, issue of his magazine an article by Grant Allen called "The Ethics of Copyright," which presented forcibly and lucidly the arguments for universal international copyright, an ideal partially but not altogether realized in our own day.

This, then, was the background to Christina's awareness of her own position as an author and her determination to protect her "dear Copyright" whenever possible. She was fortunate in having secured an American publisher in Roberts Brothers of Boston, but other problems connected with international copyright arose from time to time. One of these was the sale of a poem in 1882 to an American magazine. Unless the poem could get published in England as well, she would lose the English rights. She therefore wrote Macmillan on July 27:

> Is there a chance of your liking to have a Xmas Carol I have written (9 5-line stanzas) for your January Magazine? I seem indeed asking the question betimes, but somewhere I must endeavour to bring out this Carol which is coming out for Xmas in 'Wideawake' (Boston) and of which I want to secure to myself the English copyright. Thro' this

circumstance I am on the other hand bound not to get it published here before December 15.

Please favour me with a *yes* or *no,* as in default of you I must look elsewhere.

George Grove, then editor of the magazine, was willing to accept the carol (*A Holy Heavenly Chime*) without seeing it, and two days later, in writing to thank Macmillan for having used his "friendly influence" in her behalf, Christina observed, "I must hope that 'Wideawake' will not cross the Atlantic before my countermine is in working order."

Not until September did she send Grove the carol, and then she told him quite frankly that if he didn't like it, "Pray do not out of kindness hesitate to tell me so, as between this and January (*that* no. being the earliest in which I am at liberty to bring it out) I dare say I can find some humbler Magazine by aid of which to save my English copyright."

Grove liked the poem well enough to schedule it for publication in his January issue, but the Boston editor, being sufficiently wide awake to recognize Christina's "countermine," erected obstacles to English publication. In her letter of October 11 she attempted to explain the tangle to Grove:

Dear Sir

I feel very grateful for your kind answer when I have involved everything so vexatiously, and I shall be genuinely disappointed if the only course left open is to withdraw the Carol from Macmillan's Magazine, where I would far rather have had it appear than in Wide Awake. From the latter however it is obviously impossible that I should now secede, as I have been paid for the lines and have posted my receipt. Yet you will see how innocently I have involved matters (if so it be) when I tell you that the date before which I am engaged not to let the Carol appear in England was distinctly stated to me *"December 15"* and all along I have understood that it is equally to appear in the (so-called) *Xmas* no. of Wide Awake. The only thing I can think of now to do, is to write to the Editress Mrs. Ella Farman Pratt and ask her distinctly how the matter stands: at the worst I must put up with my own loss, and very reluctantly with what you obligingly treat as yours. So I will write to Boston, and in due course let you know the result.

On the same day she sat down and wrote to Mrs. Pratt.[6] Explaining that she had observed from the *Wide Awake* wrapper that the magazine appeared to have London offices, she inquired whether that indicated that the magazine was published in London as well as in Boston; and "if so, I must in common fairness explain my mistake to Mr. Macmillan's Editor." The two points she wanted cleared up were first, "whether or not any question of copyright forbids simultaneous publication by Mr. Lothrop [publisher of *Wide Awake*] in Boston and by Mr. Macmillan here in London?" And second, "whether Macmillan's Magazine issued on the 22nd or 23rd of December will in fact be *preceded* in the London market

by Wide Awake? for if so, it materially alters matters as I imagined them to exist."

We do not know what Mrs. Pratt answered, but on November 3 Christina acknowledged Grove's "forebearing note" and the "fatal enclosure" (probably her carol). Hoping to make amends for her share in "this vexatious business," she offered Macmillan another sonnet as a substitute for the carol. It was probably *A Wintry Sonnet,* published in the magazine's April, 1883, number, for that is the only poem of hers which appeared in *Macmillan's* that year.

IV

On September 21 she attended an informal dinner party at William's house, at which Cayley was one of the invited guests. On December 14 she dined with the Scotts and Alice, both events being duly recorded in the diary she kept for her mother. Seemingly of slight significance, these minor social activities are of interest for the later importance they assumed in Christina's consciousness during her critical last days on earth.

Cordial relations with Alice continued and grew even warmer as the years passed. Some months after Gabriel's death Christina sent her as a token of remembrance what may have been the brass plate of the sundial from his Cheyne Walk garden, asking her to "think of it as marking time somewhere in the beautiful place where you and Miss Losh cared for himself and his health so kindly." Alice responded with a gift of her own and an invitation to pay another visit to Penkill, which she had retained despite her earlier financial difficulties. Christina declined this invitation. "Though I cannot wish to visit the pretty old place now that it is no longer its real self to me," she wrote in reply, "I value in proportion the record of what it was. How beautiful all used to be!"

Early in 1883, less than a year after Gabriel died, another death occurred in the family. William lost his infant son Michael, one of the twins. Receiving a message from Lucy, "Christina went round between 10 and 11," she wrote in the journal, "found all in grief, and sat with poor William and Lucy till the baby died before 1 o'clock." Prior to its death, she baptized the infant with her own hands, explaining to Lucy subsequently that "baptism (where attainable) is the sole door I know of whereby entrance is promised into the happiness which eye has not seen nor ear heard neither heart of man conceived." It is to William's credit that he permitted his sister to perform this sacrament, for both he and Lucy were nonbelievers. Later Christina wrote a poem to the infant which expressed in verse the same faith she had evinced by her act.

Starting in 1883 she began to suffer from the plague of the famous, importunate solicitations for aid, some professional but most financial. At first she responded with generosity and enthusiasm, but as the years went

by and the number of beggars increased, she understood that she had to draw the line somewhere. That spring she befriended the first of the suppliants, a Dr. Olivieri, an Italian writer whom she had never met but whose cause had originally been taken up by Maria, then seconded by Gabriel—enough to recommend him to her care.

Next, a man named Gringer enlisted her sympathy because she understood from him that he had undergone "hard usage at hands so dear to me." But perhaps the worst offender of all was "poor Mr. William Bryant, of whose distressed circumstances," she confided to Macmillan in 1886, "impaired health, and ability to work in some department of literature, I entertain no doubt," but to whom she was provoked into writing several years later the following letter, undated:

> Dear Mr. Bryant
>
> Perhaps you deprecate my letters as—only in a limited sense—I do yours.
>
> *Pray do not* go on asking for the petty sums which fritter away my resources for helping you at a future moment. If you will not be firm I must endeavour to become so. When I promised you 3£ it was exclusively with the object of promoting your and your wife's fresh start at Manchester, and was limited to that contingency, which removal I hoped might relieve both you and myself. The 3£ are now reduced to £2.10.0; and I am neither willing to sink the sum yet further, nor to replace the deficit. So once more I warn you not to keep us both in the cold holding uncomfortable conversations. I cannot afford to assist you indefinitely, and it is my duty to live within my means. I heartily wish well to your wife and you, but my own ill doing by spending too much cannot be the right way of aiding you. Do not answer, as there is nothing to be answered.

The reason we have this letter is that Bryant sold all Christina's letters to an autograph dealer, and so profited doubly by her.[7]

It was Gosse who in 1883 opened to Christina what she called the "Dantesque door," by placing for her with *Century Magazine* her article, "Dante the Poet Illustrated out of the Poem." She began work on it in January, but it was not published until the following year (February, 1884). On January 30, 1883, she wrote Gosse,

> *I have got so far as to put pen to paper—not much further as yet. At the outset there besets me the temptation to weave in a word here and there from the *original* not the translated Dante: will my Editor tolerate this? So very much beauty evaporates with the loss of the musical Italian! but of course I must conform if needs be.
>
> Then again. I *hope* I may use one of the *terza rima* translations, say Cayley, instead of the National Longfellow. The only alternative translation which would in the least suit my views would be a Dayman; but I far prefer the other with which I am more familiar,—I prefer it, I mean, for my own use, and moreover I have it handy. Longfellow I do not possess, nor Dayman either.
>
> When I say I want to quote the original Italian, I only wish to do

> so when a few words or a line or two at most are in question: long passages, should any occur, I am ready to quote from Cayley.
>
> Will you oblige me by finding out these points for me, and by letting me know the result? I hope I shall not make you repent for having opened this Dantesque door to me!* [8]

She and her editor reached a compromise on her first question: she was permitted to quote lines from the original, but was obliged to supply the translation in parenthesis. She was also allowed to use Charles Cayley's *terza rima* translation of the *Commedia,* and she explained in her text that it was "not out of disrespect to Mr. Longfellow's blank verse translation," but because she preferred the cadence of *terza rima,* which "by adhering to the . . . ternary rhyme of the original poem, has gone far towards satisfying an ear rendered fastidious by Dante's own harmony of words. . . ."

Her documentation was on the whole a cozy, inner-circle affair. Not only did she use (and praise) her old friend's translation, but she also relied upon Maria's *Shadow of Dante* for her prose extracts. In her introduction she reviewed at length her family's achievements in Dantean scholarship: her father's analytical commentary upon the *Inferno,* Maria's contribution, Gabriel's translation "with a rare felicity" of the *Vita Nuova,* and William's blank verse translation of the *Inferno,* concluding with the graceful tribute, "I, who cannot lay claim to their learning, must approach my subject under cover of *'Mi valga . . . il grande amore'* ('May my great love avail me') leaving to them the more confident plea, *'Mi valva il lungo studio'* ('May my long study avail me')."

It took her many months to write her article. She herself admitted it was proceeding "at the pace of a lag-last snail"; and when it was finally finished, she apologized to Gosse for failing to be "over-prompt in grappling with 'Dante.' " Thanking him "for the friendly hand recognisable thro' the whole transaction," she said she was pleased with her check for 20 guineas, particularly since she was not sure that the article, consisting mainly of quotations, was worth that much. And should "the *Century* magnates" belatedly realize it, she was willing to refund part of the money. This scrupulosity does much to explain why, as she once observed, "We poets, judging by myself, are not an opulent race."

V

But most of her time and energy during the year following Gabriel's death were devoted to the aftermath of his affairs. His death, like the crashing fall of a giant redwood in the California forests, had repercussions within a wide area. Although his drawings brought in £2,800 at Christie's, the greater part of this sum had to be used to clear his debts. After the sale in May, plans had to be made for his gravestone and Mrs. Rossetti's memorial window to him at Birchington Church; and Christina

therefore spent July and August with her mother at Birchington attending to these matters. The gravestone was designed by F. M. Brown, and the stained glass window by Shields from Gabriel's cartoon for *Passover in the Holy Family.* Upon its completion a year later Christina pronounced it "a beautiful worth-waiting-for window." She was particularly pleased with "the homely little dog and puppies" in it.

Though she spent both the summers of 1883 and 1884 in Birchington, the past did not engage her interest exclusively. The future, personified in the new generation of Rossettis, was beginning to make its claim upon her as well. From Birchington she wrote the first of her many letters to her nephew Arthur, then spending his holiday at Herne Bay. At six years Arthur, as he appears in Christina's letter, was lively and frisky enough to have jumped right out of the pages of *Sing-Song,* from which he recited several songs "prettily," to the great delight of his grandmother, who rewarded him with an orange:

> MY DEAR ARTHUR
> This morning your Papa writes us word that you have been tumbling down and cutting that poor little thumb of yours and that your arm has had to be put safe in a sling. What a terrible little man you are for hurting yourself: now a head, and now a hand, and now I don't know what! I do hope the whole of my not large nephew will get safe back to London; without leaving a finger, or a thumb, or a nose, or any other outlying morsel behind.
> Give my love to your Mamma, please, and tell her that I hope she is better than when she left town. Grandmamma sends her love to her, and joins me in love to you and your three sisters. Why, as their one and only brother it becomes you to take care of them: and how will you manage that if you cannot take care of your own small self? I send you a book about a Cat's Teaparty in which 'Master Tabbie' has a fall worthy of someone I know! [9]

Like Arthur, little Helen also seems to be a child out of the imaginary world of *Sing-Song* or *Speaking Likenesses.* "She will have more spirit than any of the others," Christina predicted of her in the Italian words Grandfather Polidori had spoken about her so many years ago: *"Avrà più spirito di tutti."*

Olive, the eldest, was also showing the Rossetti precocity. An avid reader, she wrote a play about Theseus at ten and a drama in French at twelve. Among the memories of her childhood an incident involving Cayley remained vivid to the end of her life.

One day, she tells us, she went with her mother and the other children to the British Museum to look at the new ichthyosaurus which had been received but was not yet reassembled and ready for public display. On the way to the room where the big whale was kept, Lucy and her children met Cayley and invited him to join them. They entered the room, and the attendant in charge locked the door behind them from the inside.

They walked through the room, admired the whale's anatomy, which was scattered about in pieces, and then left through the opposite door, the attendant locking it after them. As they were walking down the corridor, Olive stopped suddenly and said, "But Mamma, where is Mr. Cayley?" Hurrying back to the locked room, they found him, like Jonah, deep in the interior of the whale, hands folded behind his back, gazing meditatively at the exhibit, totally unaware that the others had gone and he had been left behind.

Early in 1883 he wrote to Christina and asked her to be his heir and literary executrix. Touched by this final proof of her old friend's loyal affection, she expressed her willingness to be his literary executrix, providing his family did not mind, but refused to be his legatee. She remembered, not without remorse, that "Very likely there was a moment when —and no wonder—those who loved you best thought very severely of me," adding, "and indeed I deserved severity at my own hands,—I never seemed to get much at yours."

As for being named his heir, she would not hear of it. Although she did not want to accept what would so clearly place her in an equivocal position, she was careful not to wound Cayley's feelings. And so in delicately chosen phrases she reminded him that she could not reciprocate by making him her heir. Even should she inherit money (not a remote possibility, since both her mother and two aunts intended leaving her their property), she would, she said, feel obliged to recompense William for having supported her these twenty years, "and here at once is £2000 . . . I daresay you will trace, though I certainly have not stated what sort of train of thought set me upon saying all this." There was no doubt in her mind: her first loyalty belonged to William and his family.

As it turned out, however, she survived her old admirer. In December, 1883, Cayley died in the night of a heart attack. The following morning when Christina came home from church, Cayley's brother, who was Sadlerian Professor of Mathematics at Cambridge, was waiting in the drawing room to tell her of Charles' death. She went over to his house to see him for the last time and to lay a white wreath on his bed. A few days later she learned that he had bequeathed her the rights to all his (unremunerative) literary property and left her his "best writing-desk," together with the large packet of her letters which he had saved over the years. She accepted the writing-desk, and, according to her wont, requested the family to destroy the letters.

Although she was not unaffected by this death—quite the contrary, for on January 15 she made a special trip to Hastings to visit Cayley's grave —it was far from being the all-important event in her life William has claimed for it. Miss G. M. Hatton has pointed out that *One Sea-Side Grave,* supposedly addressed to Cayley's memory in 1884, was originally written in February, 1853, and hence had no connection with Cayley.[10]

We cannot doubt that he was in love with Christina, but that he continued to be "a living personality in Christina's heart up to the day when she also expired," as William asserted, is extremely dubious. We have seen that his role in her life had not been conspicuously important while he lived, and it is not likely she would have enshrined him in her heart after his death. He was not and could not possibly have been the broken idol of *Memory,* of which the first part was written before his appearance as a suitor (see pp. 113–114).

William let the public know the details of the primly proper romance for the first time in 1906, when he published his *Some Reminiscences,* of which the twentieth chapter is devoted to "Charles Cayley and Christina Rossetti." The initial reaction of the *Athenæum* critic who reviewed the book is typical of those that followed: "Though supposing ourselves pretty well *au fait* with the principal members of the Rossetti circle, we learn matters of much interest. Of the relations between Christina and James Collinson . . . we were aware. We hear, however, for the first time of a subsequent and no more prosperous attachment. . . ." The reviewer then repeats William's story, concluding, "For Cayley Miss Rossetti had a warm regard, suffused with as near an approach to passion as her nature could know. To him she dedicated [?] sonnets and poems included in her published works and on her death-bed she spoke of her love for him."

This is the official legend which, uncritically handed from one writer to another, has come down to us with the rigid encrustation of an unexamined but venerated belief. Accepted by subsequent generations as the unvarnished truth, it depends for veracity upon the single statement of a brother, who either was not fully informed about or chose to ignore the emotional facts of his sister's life. The deathbed confession of love, as we shall see, is likewise open to question, for it rests solely upon William's interpretation or, more probably, his misinterpretation of his dying sister's inaudible and at times confused references to the past. As for Christina's passionless nature, this is the impression a brother would wish to create. But the embalmed image of the ideal Victorian woman, sexless, decorous, and devout, with no wayward emotions or unregenerate passions, bears but little resemblance to the actual Christina Rossetti, the breathing, feeling, thinking woman, whose volcanic life seethed periodically beneath a cool white mantle of self-discipline.

That she did have a "warm regard" for Cayley, however, may be taken for granted. As the years passed, she had grown increasingly fond of him, and very likely she missed his unwavering devotion and his never-ceasing attentions at a time when her personal ties were being cut, one by one. Except for Scott, she had not formed many close relationships throughout her life, for her family had taken the place of intimates. In the midst of the many who at various times were attracted by her art or fame and

the few who admired her Christian integrity, Cayley stands forth as the friend who, valuing her chiefly for herself, had remained within sight all the middle years of her life. He had never been obtrusive, had always been reliably there, and had not ever given her cause for pain. It could not have been easy for her to lose him.

VI

But Death, to whom Christina had addressed so many of her early poems, was not to give her a long respite. As a reminder of her many vain longings and sighs for him in youth, of her many sentimental searches for his invisible reaches and her intimate surrender to him in pieces such as *Remember, When I am Dead, My Dearest, Dreamland, Two Thoughts of Death, Sweet Death,* and numerous others, this archetype of the demon lover struck again and again in his various forms before his last great assault.

In 1885 it looked as though Scott would be the next prize. The first warning came in April. "He had been working at the South Kensington at the examination of students' drawings," said Alice, "and did not feel well, but had no idea of anything serious being the matter till the 23rd of the month at three o'clock in the morning, when he was seized with frightful heart-spasms."

For the next six weeks his physician refused to allow him to leave his bed. By June, however, he had recovered, so that on the 10th Christina could report, "Today we utilized our fly by calling at the Scotts's, where I had the pleasure of seeing W. B. looking very fair all considered; he now takes and enjoys drives, and speaks cheerfully of his own health." In fact, so encouraging was his improvement that his physician gave him permission to leave for Scotland within the next few days.

But he had overestimated his own strength, for during the train trip with Alice to Girvan, he almost perished of another heart attack. "As the night advanced," Alice relates, "he became very cold, and at about three o'clock in the morning, when the train was going at great speed, he was attacked by a frightful heart-spasm, and I thought he was dying. I could hardly get the necessary medicines given, for the swinging of the carriage; a dreadful night of suffering it was. At last the paroxysm passed away, and though much exhausted and very weak, he appeared to have recovered by the time we got to our journey's end." A few days later at Penkill, however, he had another relapse, this time accompanied by congestion of the lungs; and he remained ill the rest of the summer. "Dear old W. B.," Woolner wrote William, "has had a narrow chance of his life, though happily he has pulled through."

The preceding February Christina had confided to a correspondent that she hoped to bring out a new book before very long, and later in the year *Time Flies* was published. After it appeared, she enjoyed making

punning allusions to its title in her personal letters. "No one has a better right than myself to bear in mind that 'time flies,' " was the way she began a birthday letter to nine-year-old Arthur. In another letter she told him that she was "taking Time by the forelock," despite her own testimony that "he 'flies.' " And she said to Lucy, "I felt an impulse to write to you on Saturday, but 'Time Flew' and it remained undone."

She gave the book the subtitle of "A Reading Diary," and organized it in the form of a daily journal. As we have seen from the numerous passages hitherto quoted from it, the book consists of miscellaneous notes and jottings: snatches of early recollections, religious musings, random observations upon a wide variety of subjects. For this reason, it is valuable as Christina's only attempt at informal autobiography. Its literary value, however, resides in the many new poems she published in it for the first time.

These are for the most part the poems William has dated "Before 1886." A number written after Scott's illness reveals that in 1885 she was unaccountably reopening a closed issue, debating once again the choice of her life, that decision which in important poems such as *Memory, Twice,* and *They Desire a Better Country* she had firmly declared she did not regret. The verse beginning, "Lie still, my restive heart, lie still," with its conclusion,

Lord, I had chosen another lot,
But then I had not chosen well,

chimes an echo of the old crisis. Again in the tumultuous *All Heaven Is Blazing Yet* the familiar anguish of indecision flames into a belated autumnal conflagration:

All heaven is blazing yet
With the meridian sun:
Make haste, unshadowing sun, make haste to set;
O lifeless life, have done.
I choose what once I chose;
What once I willed, I will:
Only the heart its own bereavement knows;
O clamorous heart, lie still.

That which I chose, I choose;
That which I willed, I will;
That which I once refused, I still refuse;
Oh hope deferred, be still.
That which I chose and choose
And will is Jesus' Will:
He hath not lost his life who seems to lose:
O hope deferred, hope still.

Hope deferred is the theme of another lyric which in *Time Flies* has the May 5 dateline: [11]

Love said nay, while Hope kept saying
All his sweetest say,
Hope so keen to start a-maying!—
Love said nay.

Love was bent to watch and pray:
Long the watching, long the praying:—
Hope grew drowsy, pale and grey.

Hope in dreams set off a-straying,
All his dreamworld flushed by May;
While unslumbering, praying, weighing
Love said nay.

What could the author of such verses have been hoping for at fifty-five? Long ago she had surrendered her hope of happiness on earth, and later, though stubbornly resisting, she had also finally relinquished her subsequent hope of reunion in Paradise. That by 1885 she had come to regard such a hope as an illusion of her dream world, perhaps a delusion, is suggested by the skeptical tone of the following lines:

Eternity holds rest in store,
Holds hope of long reunions:
But holds it what they hungered for
Together once?

The old wound, then, still festered. Seemingly still not wholly reconciled to the self-inflicted deprivation, she could not, despite all, quite give up what she had never taken. Hers was the dilemma which William James has called that of the divided heart. In describing the struggle of the religious to take the last remaining step in that self-surrender through which the mystic union with God is achieved, he wrote,

> So long as any secular safeguard is retained, so long as the surrender is incomplete, the vital crisis is not passed, fear still stands sentinel, and mistrust of the divine obtains: we hold by two anchors, looking to God, it is true, after a fashion, but also holding by our own proper machinations.

Long before James described this spiritual dilemma in *Varieties of Religious Experience,* Christina recognized and analyzed it as her own:

O foolishest fond folly of a heart
Divided, neither here nor there at rest!
That hankers after Heaven, but clings to earth:
That neither here nor there knows thorough mirth,
Half choosing, wholly missing, the good part:—
O fool among the foolish, in thy quest.

VII

In September Scott suffered another frightening heart spasm, from which he rallied; but in December congestion of the lungs brought on

still another, more severe attack, and his doctor forbade him to take the long train trip back to London. Doomed to spend an isolated winter in the medieval castle around which the icy sea blasts from the Firth of Clyde moaned and howled and roared, Scott, sorely missing his old friends and his cheerful London life, endeavored to occupy himself as best he could. Between attacks he made an etching of Gabriel's profile drawing of Alice, and that Christmas he sent prints of it to all his friends.

Prompt to acknowledge her own gift, Christina wrote Alice a long chatty letter on December 19, enclosing with it a seven-line poem inscribed "Grateful CGR to AB and WBS." [12]

> Hail, noble face of noble friend!—
> Hail, honoured master hand and dear!—
> On you may Christmas good descend
> And blessings of the unknown year
> So soon to overtake us here.
> Unknown, yet well known: I portend
> Love starts the course, love seals the end.

The letter accompanying the poem was tactfully designed to amuse and cheer Scott by giving him news of that world from which he was now excluded and to assure him that despite absence he still lived in Christina's heart and thoughts:

> My dear Alice
>
> A thousand warm thanks to yourself and W. B. for the beautiful gift I received yesterday, some posts before your card of kindness reached me. I rejoice in the mild weather which adds an opportune charm to charming Penkill,—unforgotten Penkill. Often have my Mother and I enquired at 92 [Bellevue House] after the health of the beloved absentee: our last call was on Tuesday when I heard a favourable report which you now confirm. . . .
>
> Once or twice, but not always, I have been fortunate in finding Mrs. Scott at home, but not so last Tuesday. She has talked of coming to see us, but no wonder if her courage has failed her in such weather as we have had,—lately bitterly cold, and since that steeped in mud.
>
> How I wish I had literary and artistic news in store. Let me scrape together a few scraps without dates. I don't know whether you keep up with the Hakes; but we of course do, such friends as they were to Gabriel. Well, last summer I stood Godmother to George Hakes' little firstborn *Ursula,* and thus we have again met once or twice. I find Dr. Hake is as devoted to literary pursuits as (perhaps) he ever was: without them he avows that life would lack interest, although he resides with the George Hakes and must I should think have cozy quarters there and a bright circle presided over by so attractive a 'Rose'—.
>
> One afternoon Mr. Sharp called to get *copyright* leave before bringing out a volume [compiled] of Sonnets: he looked very portly and prosperous. But very likely W. B. heard from him long ago on the very same subject, and thus I bring coals to dear old Newcastle!
>
> You have heard of poor Mrs. Gilchrist's death after great suffering? She can only have been about 57 years old, I think. I do not know anything of Grace or Herbert's plans.—Lately a photograph was sent up

of the Brown-Seddon design for the DGR memorial fountain [at Cheyne Walk], and I thought the architecture severe and pleasing; but about the main point, the head, I can say nothing as I understand the version then shown us has now been set aside. Indeed, it was no more than a rough sketch.—Did you hear of Mrs. Val Prinsep's dangerous illness at Venice? Since, I suppose, recovered, so as to be able to reach London; but at one moment she hung between life and death. And it is surmised from visiting her at Venice Mr. Leyland brought back seeds of typhoid fever which soon after his return to England prostrated him and occasioned great alarm: but he also, according to my last news, has rallied.

We of my home circle are a very sober little party and likely to keep a very sober Christmas. But certainly I am not hankering after gaieties and dissipations! Fancy me got up as 'the glass of fashion and the mould of form'!!! Having conjured up which figure of fun I contentedly settle down as your dowdy but

Affectionate

Christina G. Rossetti

The heart attacks which had begun in the spring of 1885 closed off with finality Scott's active days. From then on, except for rare occasions, he was confined to the house and compelled to live the life of an invalid. To fill the long dull days he took up again the writing of his autobiography, dropped in 1882, and, when his health permitted, maintained an active correspondence with a wide circle of friends.

VIII

He was still to be spared for a few years. But in the meantime Death swooped down suddenly and robbed Christina of another precious life. The winter of 1886 was again a severe one. In January Christina told William that the cold confined their mother to the house, "but we trot a little about the drawing-room, which is better than nothing. . . ." Mrs. Rossetti was now eighty-five, and, although Christina could shelter her from the white peril of winter, she could not shield her from the invisible dangers lurking within the home nest. One day in February Mrs. Rossetti fell and hurt her back. Although no bones were broken, her doctor confined her to bed. Christina, who confessed to being "full of anxiety," feared "the exhaustion of her strength, so frail at 85."

As March passed and Mrs. Rossetti showed no improvement, Christina resigned herself to the inevitable. "I see my dearest Mother suffer much, though very patiently," she said. "I could not wish her to suffer on indefinitely for my own selfish sake. God's will be done."

Within a few days an entry appeared in the old family diary which had recorded with events of Gabriele's, Maria's, and Dante Gabriel's last days: "I, Christina Rossetti, happy and unhappy daughter of so dear a saint, write the last words. Not till nearly half an hour after noon on April

8 . . . did my dearest Mother cease from suffering. . . . At the moment of death William, Nurse, Mr. Stewart [the doctor] and I, were present."

To Lucy, then traveling in Italy, Christina admitted that it had become "a different world since last I wrote to you. Yet I rejoice that it is I who am left in grief of this separation, and not my dearest Mother." But writing again, two days later, she said, "Please do not fancy me bearing this bitter trial so much better than I really am bearing it."

Her tribute to the woman who had given her the dubious gift of life, from whom in fifty-six years she had seldom been separated, and who in her embattled stride through life had kept beside her, shoulder to shoulder, is best expressed in the dedicatory sonnet originally written for the *Pageant* volume but later appropriately inserted by William as the dedication to the *Poetical Works:*

Sonnets are full of love, and this my tome
Has many sonnets: so here now shall be
One sonnet more, a love sonnet, from me
To her whose heart is my heart's quiet home,
To my first Love, my Mother, on whose knee
I learnt love-lore that is not troublesome;
Whose service is my special dignity,
And she my lodestar while I go and come.
And so because you love me, and because
I love you, Mother, I have woven a wreath
Of rhymes wherewith to crown your honoured name:
In you not fourscore years can dim the flame
Of love, whose blessed glow transcends the laws
Of time and change and mortal life and death.

Now Christina was left alone with her aged aunts. Death, who was gradually crowding out the living inmates at Torrington Square, had already selected for his next victim Aunt Charlotte, frail and invalided, but, said Christina, still "looking like a rose" on her eighty-sixth birthday. Although Christina was glad to keep her elderly and infirm relatives under her protective wing, she never pretended that they provided her with companionship. After the loss of her mother, she had no one left to share her life with, and she had to learn to "build of loneliness thy secret nest."

Although at first she protested with the weariness of emotion spent again and again on the same kind of grief, "One sorrow more? I thought the tale complete," eventually she discovered that, besides loneliness, other materials were available for the building of her nest, among them paradox and patience. "One sorrow more" became modified to

Sorrow hath a double voice,
Sharp to-day but sweet to-morrow,

which developed into the paradoxical conception, "Joy is but Sorrow," and conversely, "Pain is but Pleasure," until she could utter the challenge,

Turn, transfigured Pain,
Sweetheart, turn again,
For fair thou art as moonrise after rain,

and even say with Donne, "Death, Be not Proud":

This Life we live is dead for all its breath;
Death's self it is, set off on pilgrimage,
Travelling with tottering steps the first short stage:
The second stage is one mere desert dust
Where Death sits veiled amid creation's rust:—
Unveil thy face, O Death who art not Death.

But how many graves there were now for her to place her wreathes of flowers upon—Maria's, Gabriel's, Cayley's, her mother's—as many as once there had been living doors to open at her approach and living hearts to warm her:

They lie at rest, our blessed dead;
The dews drop cool above their head,
They knew not when fleet summer fled.

Together all, yet each alone;
Each laid at rest beneath his own
Smooth turf or white allotted stone. . . .

God be with you, our great and small,
Our loves, our best beloved of all,
Our own beyond the salt sea-wall.

❋ 19 ❋

"SCALING HEAVEN BY FIRE"

1886–1892

With Mrs. Rossetti gone and Scott invalided at Penkill, William was Christina's last remaining emotional connection with the world. "So long as I have you I have one very dear person left," she told him. Another time she wrote, "To see you the other day so unexpectedly was an oasis in what it would be thankless to call my *desert,* tho' the phrase would be neat." She expressed the wish to Arthur that he might "grow up as kind and dear a brother" to his sisters "as your precious Father has been to me." And once, when William was starting out on a short trip, she confided to Lucy that "a great slice of my heart travels about with him now, he being the only one of his own standing left to me. . . ."

But Lucy's consent was necessary to keep the old bond intact. Between 1886 and 1890 Christina's patient efforts to conciliate and to win over Lucy, to make a close friend and dear sister of her brother's wife, are touching in their unconscious revelation of her deep need for human love. The secret nest was fragile after all, despite the strength of the material that went into its construction.

Upon her mother's death Christina had inherited the family fortune, which accumulating over the years amounted to a fair sum, and she knew that she was also to inherit more upon the decease of her two aged aunts. She thereupon promptly assured Lucy that not only did she intend to reimburse William in her will to the amount of at least the £2,000 he had spent for her support all these years, but did she survive him, "I should (so far as I foresee at present) feel that his claim lapses in full to yourself or to the children." With the reconciliation between the sisters-in-law effected upon so practical a basis, it was celebrated by Christina's dining at William's house in October, "an incident perhaps unprecedented these four years," William remarked.

After the peacemaking dinner, Christina continued to make friendly overtures to Lucy, writing her sister-in-law cheerful, chatty, affectionate letters which had as their topics Lucy's children and Lucy's interests. A

letter to William begins with the apology, "I am sure Lucy will accept my love and sanction my writing to you at this time, as I have written once to her and to you not at all." In another letter addressed to Lucy she said that William's note was "so charming that I felt tempted to swerve from my propriety and write to him twice running! But," she added diplomatically, "your prior and welcome claim I deliberately honour, and indeed I should be very short-sighted to forfeit by neglect a continuance of 'your esteemed favours.'" It was to these favors that she owed what she called the chief pleasure of her last years—to see William's "good face from time to time." In 1891 she closed a letter to Lucy with the admission that she had been secretly hoping she would see William yesterday, "and he came."

With Lucy's consent, then, she could have a share in William. The Shelley Society, of which he was then the president, met in the vicinity of Torrington Square on Wednesday evenings, and at her invitation he had formed the habit of taking a meal with her on his "Shelley nights," a weekly event which meant much to her. "You are welcome on the most *cupboard love* terms, always and every way welcome," she assured him. She would give him a cup of tea and show him books she thought might interest him; and, chatting quietly together, they would recover the flavor if not the fact of their cherished but lost intimacy.

All this delicate maneuvering and tactful conciliation for ends which were after all so ordinary—just the affectionate connection with an elderly brother and his family—required patience. But this was a technique for living which Christina had been teaching herself over the years. "Exhaust this world and its resources," she said in *Time Flies;* "this done, if spiritual life survives the soul will learn patience. Sit aloof and look down on the world; viewed from aloof and aloft the world's hollowness becomes apparent: this realised, the living soul strikes root in patience."

And yet without poetry, that creative expression which became increasingly vigorous and flourishing as her personal life narrowed and dwindled, patience—a negative virtue which sometimes parches and tames rich natures such as Christina's—might have left her sterile. Perhaps poetry even more than patience was the real reconciling agent for her.

> A hundred thousand birds salute the day:—
> One solitary bird salutes the night:
> Its mellow grieving wiles our grief away,
> And tunes our weary watches to delight;
> It seems to sing the thoughts we cannot say,
> To know and sing them, and to set them right,

she wrote in *Later Life.*

Once, in attempting to characterize his sister's personality briefly and

impressionistically, Gabriel wrote, "Christina—the isolation of a bird, remote, minute, and distinct, shy like a bird."

Not long after her mother's death she began to work on *The Face of the Deep,* which, however, was not published until 1892. Referring to it in a letter to Watts on November 22, 1886, she wrote:

> *Dear Mr. Watts
>
> Why was I so mysterious the other day about my literary occupation? From short wits perhaps, but certainly not from unfriendship!
>
> Having rallied my wits the matter is yet, you may say, not worth resuming.
>
> All I am doing is reading and thinking over part of the New Testament [Revelations], writing down what I can as I go along. I work at prose and help myself forward with little bits of verse. What I am doing is (I hope) for my own profit, nor do I in the least know that it will ever become an available 'book.' At present, as you may divine, I am not likely to draw much upon the simply imaginative.
>
> Pray do not take the trouble of answering—there is nothing truly to answer. This is but the end of an incomplete sentence in our pleasant conversation.* [1]

Hearing from Macmillan a few days later that a Miss M. A. Woods had asked permission to include *Goblin Market* in a school poetry book the firm was bringing out, she reiterated her strong objection to the current practice of reproducing poetry in snatches and snippets, writing on November 24,

> As to *Goblin Market* is it possible that Miss Woods wishes to reprint the *entire* text? If this is indeed her and your wish I consent,—but on no account if any portion whatever is to be omitted. *G.M.* seems to me bulky, and I observe abridgements (one or more) in the First Reading Book: wherefore it behoves me to forestall any risk of like treatment. I now make a point of refusing extracts, even in the case of my Sonnet of Sonnets some of which would fairly stand alone: so please do not think me disobliging in this particular case.[2]

II

Wild and tempestuous storms, raging throughout December, closed the year of 1886. "Such a winter as we Londoners are having!" Christina exclaimed, and described in a letter to Arthur "the storm of wind and snow" that occurred shortly after Christmas. "And tho' I have not been about to see half the damage which I read of in the Gazette, here in Torrington Sq. and close by in Woburn Sq. trees are damaged and broken, —one tree is split as if by an axe. This morning our gardener is at work tidying up."

The severe winter had a serious effect upon her health. By January she was in such low spirits that she actually believed her aged and infirm aunts would survive her. "What the precise illness is I don't gather,"

William puzzled, but he clearly perceived that the prospect of death was not alarming to his sister, but "on the contrary, consolatory."

Her physician ordered her to Torquay for the remainder of the winter (a French acquaintance circulated the report that Miss Rossetti had gone to *la Turquie*). Taking lodgings in Abbey Road for a guinea a week, she looked forward to reveling in "lizard-like laziness," but for that kind of relaxation the sun is needed, and Torquay, though on the southern coast, turned out to be both cold and hilly. The following letter to Aunt Eliza, written on February 21 shortly after her arrival, provides an interesting glimpse of her at Devon:

> *After all it is an excellent thing that circumstances opposed your visiting Torquay; for if you found Brighton hilly, what would you say to this! It would be out of the question your walking as far as any seaside seat from this lodging: *I* find it toilsome, and for you it would be downright dangerous unless we say simply impossible. But when you are seated as I was to-day, beautiful indeed is the view. Yet it is not my own predilect phase of sea beauty, for the bay is so much enclosed as strongly to resemble a lake while my delight is boundless expanse. Still one must be very prejudiced and very thankless not to enjoy what it *is* without cavilling at what it is not. Seagulls were in sight to-day, those noble birds. Houses are perched and trees grow at all sorts of altitudes, and slopes and steps allure one or dismay one up or down as the case may be. Vegetation is as prominent a feature as in an inland situation. I do not think I shall ever descend to the water's edge, especially as the handiest point I know of seems *sandy* rather than *shingly* which latter forms my favourite hunting ground. I know my way about fairly now for ordinary practical purposes . . .
>
> Of *letters* I have received a nice one from Mrs. Heimann . . . an assurance from the SPCK that my *double s* [probably for Rossetti] shall be seen to for the annual Report, a request from Miss Tynan [Katherine Tynan Hinkson], poetess for leave to dedicate her forthcoming volume to me as well as to William: *yes* say I. And a note from Alice for which I thank her being glad of the news it imparts. . . .
>
> My warm love to good Aunt Charlotte: I am prepared to cope with the illegible.*

While she was at Torquay a severe earthquake shook the Riviera, where William was staying with his family. Greatly alarmed by exaggerated press reports of damage, she telegraphed him, and he wired back a reassuring reply. "Your blessed telegram yesterday afternoon between 5 and 6 o'clock has eased me of a burden," she wrote upon receiving it. "My love to Lucy, who I hope is not suffering from shock and makeshift quarters, and to Olive, and to Arthur whose attack of pain and illness I hear of with regret,—I wonder whether he is half such a coward as I am at the dentist's. . . . What an awful awestriking experience an earthquake must be. . . ."

March was an even more disagreeable month in Torquay than February had been. Although the natives predicted that warm weather was sure to

follow shortly, Christina decided to leave. "3 weeks hence perhaps the residents may find their mouths 'full of the warm south—' " she wrote Lucy, "residents, but not I, for . . . I am going home next Tuesday week." One resident who probably encouraged her to await the spring in Devon was Herbert Coleridge's sister Edith, who, learning she was in Torquay, immediately called upon her. But not even the prospect of congenial company could induce her to remain.

She thought, however, that as a result of her holiday, she had "made a 10 years' stride both as to looks and feelings," and consequently again felt ready "to bear the wear and tear of daily life."

Indicative of her recovery was her energetic proposal to Lucy that she teach the children Italian by correspondence. "What specially urges me to write this afternoon," she began a letter of April 29, "is the wish to know whether you would care for O. and A. to write me a weekly Italian letter from Bournemouth, for me to correct as well as may be and return. My Italian is somewhat *rule of thumb,* but doubtless would enable me to do somewhat towards keeping up what they have acquired. If you think such *imperfect* help worth accepting, it awaits your and their commands. Of course William is as Italian as myself, but I dare say his many occupations disincline him to come forward as pedagogue. . . ."

The lessons got underway, with Christina advising O. and A. to learn by heart the auxiliary verbs *essere* and *avere,* if they had not already done so. This simple lesson in auxiliary verbs had far-reaching consequences for Olive, who was to marry an Italian and spend sixty years of her life in Italy. But as the correspondence course proceeded, Christina lost confidence in her pedagogic ability. "I fear I sent back Olive's and Arthur's very creditable letters in one mass of confusion," she confided remorsefully to Lucy. "Even whilst seeing what is amiss and what is wanting, I have no call whereby to evoke grammatical rules from my inner consciousness."

By the following year, however, both teacher and pupils had advanced to the stage of conducting their correspondence in what Christina called the ancestral *"bella lingua."* In one of her letters she teases Arthur about his error in miscalling a bunch of flowers (*mazzo*) a cane of flowers (*mazza*), and she concludes with the almost untranslatable Italian expression of loving affection, *"Tua zia amorevole."*

That she took seriously her role of pedagogue to William's children is further evident from her careful choice of literature for them. Each child received from her books appropriate to his age and development. At ten Arthur was given a copy of *Robinson Crusoe* with Stothard's illustrations and a nine-volume Plutarch, and at twelve a "Pictorial Geography." Olive, mature at fourteen, was presented with an illustrated Metastasio in Italian (one of Christina's own favorite poets in her youth) and Maria's *Shadow of Dante,* "a work," said her aunt, "written from a

fund of knowledge far wider and deeper than could be compressed into its pages, eloquent and elegant, the fruit of a fine mind and a noble soul." Ten-year-old Helen received the gift of a book called *Dodo,* about "a disagreeable little girl . . . whom I recommend you not to be like!" Mary, still too young to be edified by books, was entertained by what Christina called "feline literature."

This consisted mainly of tall tales about the doings of cats and kittens, and during the 1880's we hear much of Muff, Christina's huge semi-Persian tabby, described by Gabriel as "a carroty cat," and of Muff's innumerable and successive generations of kittens. In the autumn of 1888 Muff gave birth to "a spectacled and a tabby kitten," which was soon old enough to be given away. In February Christina reported that "the spectacled kitten was pronounced pretty (!) in its new home, and . . . it touches and I believe takes into its mouth some white mice (its fellow citizens) without injuring them."

Other examples of her "feline literature" likewise display the quality of fantasy and fable. "Tell Mary for me that I have heard of a brandy-drinking cat. Poor puss was taken ill and milk and brandy tried. It rallied. When afterwards plain milk was offered it, it declined till brandy was added!" Or: "I happened to mention our pretty long-haired puss the other day to a friend, and she tells me in answer of a cat who when its master lay dying laid at his door first a mouse and then a bird to tempt his appetite: a funny feline idea of tempting fare, certainly, if such was the cat's motive."

But after a time she began to suspect that this kind of literature was losing its charm for the children. "Perhaps Helen is outgrowing *kittens,*" she wrote Lucy, "but Mary is still young enough (!) to be told that we have 2 new ones: one grey tabby, the other black with dabs of tortoise shell: this latter promises well. Both are promised, so we are very fortunate in housing kittens. 'Kittens' suggests that I have reached the dregs of news. . . ."

William had now replaced Gabriel as head of the family; and he filled the role of paterfamilias far more capably than Gabriel ever had. "I bear in mind that you are head of the house and in many ways my better," Christina wrote to him after a slight dispute, "so don't brand me as impertinent." It was to the "head of the house" that she naturally turned when puzzled by financial matters which, now that she had inherited money, she had to cope with. "Income tax pursues not to say persecutes me," she complained in January, 1889. "See enclosure,—besides which there was one interim 'Demand' which I repudiated and of which I never told you. Vainly too have I declared myself a woman and not a man. Weakest minded of my sex I am only too glad to betake myself to you for rescue. Please, if you can, somehow convince some one of my having

paid what I owed and being a transparently blameless victim: 'Drive' is enough to drive one frantic. . . ."

By May she seems to have mastered the mystery of forms. "Once more, our friend the Income Tax!" was her gay beginning to a letter of May 27. "However this time I seem so [illegible] a goose that unless you think otherwise and interpose, I shall fill up my Form and send in my Return by the 10th—rather before, of course—all by myself like a rational being." But as she puzzled over the figures, pen in hand, she observed ruefully that "To my regret, the poetry of impulse has been succeeded by the prose of calculation."

Although to some extent William and his family lessened her burden of loneliness during these years, he was in the mid-career of an active and prolific man of letters, and Lucy and her children lived abroad most of the time, so she did not see much of them after all.

In the autumn of 1890, when the family moved from Endsleigh Gardens to St. Edmund's Terrace, they stayed with her at Torrington Square in the interim between residences. "I have just lately been having my brother and his family (6 in number) staying here," she wrote her friend Ellen Proctor on October 30; "this made a great change and *stir up* in my quiet habits." Nevertheless, she was delighted at the pleasant intrusion, and, said William, provided "a genuine sense of home" for them.

But the children were growing up. Gone were the days when Arthur would recite a verse from *Sing-Song* "prettily." One by one, each child left behind the kitten-and-nursery-rhyme stage, even little Mary. When in 1892 Christina was told that Arthur and Olive had successfully passed their chemistry examination for Oxford, she exclaimed, "The babies of yesterday are the sages of to-day!"

As for *Sing-Song,* it was in little demand by the new generation of babies. Christina told William that a bookseller whom Lucy asked for a copy had "failed to unearth that obscure tome." Lucy suggested that Christina send the bookseller her publisher's name, and shortly thereafter she replied,

> *I did your flattering behest forthwith, and can only hope that that faulty tradesman has acquired permanently so valuable an item of information. I do regret the chronic eclipse of 'Singsong' but must class that work with unfound pearls and unquarried gems: cash would be more cheerful, but meanwhile conceit is something! *

III

In 1887 the controversial question of the treatment of Gabriel's biography agitated the Rossetti circle. Christina was twice approached with the suggestion that she write a life of her brother, "but I hold inflexibly aloof," she said, and advised William to do the same. Although he did

not write Gabriel's biography until 1895 (by which time he was convinced that Watts would never do it), he had something to say about his brother in his preface to the 1886 *Collected Works.* This, together with Knight's biography in 1887 and other brief memoirs, started the controversy which still simmers.

Scott, immured at Penkill and working on his own *Autobiographical Notes,* was irritated by the whitewashing of Gabriel's reputation, and he resolved to reveal the other side of the picture in his own memoirs. Although viewing it differently, friend and foe alike remarked upon the posthumous glorification of Gabriel. "Have you . . . read Gilchrist's book or Knight's life of D.G.R.?" Madox Brown asked Lucy. "The latter is 'coleur de rose' indeed; in fact both in his book and in Gilchrist's poor Gabriel is painted a kind of angel: all the better for the family say I." [3] Scott's attitude, though equally subjective, assumed the guise of disinterested impartiality apparent in this letter of July 19:

> *My Dear W.M.R.
>
> I was truly delighted to have your letter with its genial air of the old-time pervading it. Except my own brother David, who was my tyrant and occasional bully, no friend was so much to me as Gabriel, and still I must say, these two men are in the history of my life the two great and able men I have known. I had to write my brother's life and I tried to convey a picture of the hero sufficiently just and yet sufficiently noble. I tried to make a biography that was a work of art, and had my subject been, as Gabriel would have admitted in a similar treatment, romantic and even mystical, I fancy the book would have made a greater impression. As it was, however, I have had in the course of years, many evidences to prove the memoir a work of lasting interest. I thought you had a chance of doing something of an extraordinary kind with poor dear G's biography but you misunderstood me, I think. Except that, I have given you no reason to suppose me deficient in affectionate regard for Gabriel.—But to drop this question. I shall be very grateful for your sending me the late edition, of what you call the whole works, which I have no doubt will be of lasting interest to me for the remainder of my life. My next birthday 2 months hence makes me 76 which is pretty well is it not? . . .*

He concludes by inquiring if he should send a copy of his etchings to Knight, and adds, "I propose to send [one] to Christina, but have not yet. . . ."

In a letter to Watts dated July 27, he takes up the subject again, at the same time revealing his egoistic sensitivity to rebuffs from the great:

> *Many thanks for your second note. Glad you like my etchings from the pictures, and what I say of Knight's book.
>
> I have had some interesting correspondence with W. M. R. caused by my sending him a copy. Perhaps you know I think his line of treatment of Gabriel's personality and social life quite a wrong line. He knew my view of what he was doing and getting others to do, long ago,

as I advised him soon after D.G.R.'s death to make a true history of him, a work of Art for History to preserve, an advice which he did not approve of. The letters that have lately passed between us refer to that advice. I think we are now better friends than we have been.

You mention your kind intention of taking with you my Etchings when visiting Tennyson. I would like to send him a copy, if you approve of my doing so. Long ago you gave me his address, when I intended to send him the little Harvest Home. I did not send it, because I had just sent it to Browning *who did not acknowledge it,* and I saw a paragraph in a paper that Lord T. on his accession to the peerage had given up replying to letters, or something of the kind, so I refrained from running any risk. The fact is, I suffer much more from insult [than] I receive pleasure from compliments, so I am shy of exposing myself to the chances of either . . .*

The next day he wrote to William thanking him for his gift of "your two excellent volumes, Complete Works of D.G.R., which I see every lover of poetry must possess himself of." Nevertheless he could not resist probing the sore spot again. "As for your own writing in the edition, I look upon it as an admirable and lovable piece of work, but not representing Gabriel. That touches the old subject between us, so I say no more."

William, however, proved not equally eager to drop the subject and apparently raised the issue sharply in his reply, for in Scott's letter of August 9 he hits back:

Regarding the difference between your views of how we should write D.G.R.'s history or internal nature I fancy no good would come of either talking or writing. But of the two talking would be best certainly. Did you read a review of Knight's book in the Academy? The impression evidently made on the mind of the dear creature who had written the little article was that the author of the Ballads, the sonnets, Jenny, and every other powerful poem, was the most amiable, innocent purist of the generation. I fancy your views have been adopted from F.M.B. who so delights in secrets and even in conspiracies, that a few more added to his collection are an addition to the pleasure of life to him!

The attack upon Brown was quite gratuitous, but Scott, like a wounded animal in his lair, was striking out in all directions: a few weeks later in a letter to Watts he attacked Matthew Arnold with equal virulence. The dispute with William did not, however, prevent him from asking permission to reprint Gabriel's letters in his *Notes,* a request generously granted. "Many thanks for your permission for my printing the series of letters from Kelmscott," Scott replied. "I shall take care that nothing offensive to any one is printed in them, and indeed there is nothing in them of that character scarcely, [and] the little there is I shall excise."

As the 1880's drew to a close, it was perceptible to Scott's friends that his life was also drawing to a close. "How frail poor old Scotus seems

now," Christina remarked to William in 1888, and a year later she wondered uneasily why she had "heard nothing of the dear old Scotts this long time."

He was alive but growing weaker, and he was no longer able to continue the active correspondence which had kept him in touch with his London life. Still the "social Prince" in sickness and old age, he felt his isolation as one of his more grievous afflictions, and he complained continuously of loneliness during the last years of his life. "Living here so much alone with Miss Boyd, the best of company indeed, but without the concussion of the robuster natures, after spending all my life in the society of sets or coteries . . . men closely associated and seeing each other daily, I sometimes get into a lowish key which prevents me from applying myself to anything whatever, and does not assist to get me out of the invalid groove," he confided to W. Minto.

To Minto he was "a very picturesque figure, propped up in the curiously carved bed in the tapestried chamber." In his scarlet biretta and cowl, he looked like an invalid Cardinal Inquisitor, "but far from inquisitorial was the laugh with which he capped our little jokes and anecdotes." The evening hours were the happiest of Scott's restricted day, the time "when the lamps were lit, a little square box ranged on the bed beside him, and placed thereon the glass of hot grog which was one of the milder features of the severe regimen." His "ever-vigilant nurse" Alice was in constant attendance.

His needs had changed, and Alice's role in his life had altered to meet them. He was an old man now, sick and worried about himself, and his youth lay far back in the past, much farther back than the youth of either Christina or Alice. So little interested in love was he now that, upon receiving from an old friend (possibly Linton) a newly published volume of verse, he exclaimed in surprise, "He is my age, yet all his later poems are on LOVE, a fack [*sic*] that baffles me to understand."

In 1890 his friends in London heard that he was dying. Unlike Gabriel at the point of death, he never renounced his agnosticism. And, since he was not able to meet death with the stern stoicism of more indomitable spirits, he was forced to confront the consequence of his own lifelong logical position with no comfort to fall back upon. From the report of those around him, it appears that his was no easy death.

Christina could not have failed to appreciate his dilemma. Although she was of the opinion that sometimes, as in the instance of St. Thomas, skepticism was a step toward faith ("Skepticism is a degree of unbelief: equally therefore it is a degree of belief"), she knew it was not likely to prove so in Scott's case. "Then if nothing remains which we may lawfully give," she wrote in *Seek and Find,* "at least our prayers can ascend on behalf of the friend who is as our own soul." And elsewhere: "If we are spirit-broken by doubts of our own, if we are half heart-broken by

a friend's doubts, let us beg faith for our friend and for ourself; only still more urgently let us beg love."[4]

IV

"In a life marked by so few external incidents, such matters as the deaths of relatives and friends count for much," William wrote in his "Memoir" of Christina. Although those he lists in his long "mortuary catalogue" are family deaths, the one exception is the death of Scott, "our friend ever since 1847," and "a man whom Christina viewed with great predilection."

Although she was not unprepared for his death, which took place on November 22, 1890, the final wrench was nonetheless a shock, for no amount of intellectual comprehension is sufficient to establish in the mind the fact of death until it is experienced emotionally. During the first few days she might have found comfort in that mysterious sense of the nearness of the dead which the living frequently feel immediately after a loss. At such times the presence of the dead, although invisible and intangible, seems nonetheless powerfully actual and existent. Paradoxically, the absent in life draw closer in death:

> In life our absent friend is far away:
> But death may bring our friend exceeding near,
> Show him familiar faces long so dear
> And lead him back in reach of words we say.
> He only cannot utter yea or nay
> In any voice accustomed to our ear;
> He only cannot make his face appear
> And turn the sun back on our shadowed day.

But as the presence of the dead receded and faded—as it does—Christina would have felt the need to review in retrospect this lifelong relationship. Now that all was finished, there could be no more sentimental glossing over of facts. The truth had to be faced: this relationship had brought her little happiness and much suffering. Most of the time it had lured her as a mirage into empty desert expanses. She had always fought it, never quite conquered her yearning for it. Yet now that Scott was gone, she was no doubt able to forgive the many hurts he had inflicted upon her. Inquiring in a *Later Life* sonnet whether Adam had loved his Eve from first to last, she answered firmly,

> I think so; as we love who works us ill,
> And wounds us to the quick, yet loves us still.
> Love pardons the unpardonable past.

"The more we do for any one the more we love them," Canon Burrows had said once in a sermon of 1859 at Christ Church, Albany Street; and it is this attitude we find expressed in the following passage from *Time*

Flies, in which may be recognized the enshrined idol of *Memory,* often broken, often crushed, repeatedly hurled down, but never dethroned:

> In the purest, loftiest, most spiritual heart of man or woman, oftentimes next to God Supreme, sits enshrined some one beloved sinful soul. . . .
>
> On behalf of such cherished souls no gift is grudged: not tears, or prayers, or agony of fear, or anguish of a lifetime. For their sakes hearts more precious than most precious alabaster are broken and pour forth fragrance, and drain out the last drops of life, and would and can keep back nothing, if so be their sacrifice may win acceptance.
>
> Of those who 'love much,' many love thus.

And then comes the crucial question: "Is not theirs a life worth living, leading up, and not down, to a death worth dying?"

V

After 1890 Christina gradually withdrew from the world and lived the existence of a recluse in what Ford Madox Ford described as her boxlike drawing room in the gloomy London square, "its windows brushed by the leaves, and darkened by the shade of those black-trunked London trees that are like a grim mockery of their green-boled sisters of the open country." Ford pictures her in that "cloistral seclusion" as "a black-robed figure, with clear-cut and olive features, dark hair, restrained and formal gestures, hands always folded in the lap, head always judicially a little on one side." To him she represented "the tranquil Religious . . . undergoing within herself always a fierce struggle between the pagan desire for life and an asceticism that, in its almost more than Calvinistic restraint, reached also a point of frenzy." [5]

To William, who worried about her solitary way of life, she said serenely, "Beautiful, delightful, noble, memorable as is the world you and yours frequent,—I yet am well content in my shady crevice: which crevice enjoys the unique advantage of being to my certain knowledge the place assigned me." Another time she told him she was glad he had "more happy and endeared ties" than she did; "otherwise I should be afraid of not wishing it for you any more than for myself, and for myself I do not wish it."

This was true. In her later years she regarded marriage as the lesser condition, and the spiritual state of even the happiest and most fortunate of wives as greatly inferior to that of the virgin. The wife, she wrote in *Letter and Spirit,* "sees not face to face, but . . . in a glass darkly." Husband and children, her earthly loves, are to her but the mirrors of her Maker. Faithful to "interests not her own," her sacrifices are second-hand, made to the "shadows cast by the reality" (a Platonic image). Whereas on the contrary,

> She whose heart is virginal abides aloft and aloof in spirit. . . . Her spiritual eyes behold the King in His beauty; wherefore she forgets, by comparison, her own people and her father's house. Her Maker is her Husband, endowing her with a name better than of sons and of daughters. . . . She loves Him with all her heart and soul and mind and strength; she is jealous that she cannot love Him more; her desire to love Him outruns her possibility, yet by outrunning enlarges it. She contemplates Him, and abhors herself in dust and ashes. . . . The air she breathes is too rare and keen for grosser persons. . . .

For those who achieve it, then, the dedicated life is not without compensation. The sacrifice, once made, loses the aspect of sacrifice, and—as Christina wrote in the Exodus notes—"the desert of the faithful sacrifice becomes the wilderness of our joyous feast."

Instead of the tension between asceticism and a pagan desire for life, or a starved and ugly frustration, at this stage of her development Christina had achieved an insight known to and experienced by many mystics; and she expressed it, according to the tradition of mystic literature, in the language of eroticism. We should therefore be careful of making superficial judgments and falling into the vulgar error of assuming she was a desiccated and sex-starved spinster.[6] Nothing could be further from the truth.

This is not to say that she did not occasionally suffer from her isolation. Not even a Christina Rossetti could exist perpetually in such a high, rarefied atmosphere so difficult for human respiration. Between flights of religious rapture, she too felt the common human need for companionship. At times it was painfully clear that

> Others have this or that, a love, a friend,
> A trusted teacher, a long-worked-for end,

all the homely consolations of this earthly life, whereas she had only the remote grandeur of her religious faith, only her invisible comfort which so unaccountably both descended and withdrew, only her assurance of Divine Love, an assurance yet baffling to the human intellect.

VI

As she approached sixty, she thought that on the whole she continued "to flourish in my own style, rather severe than florid." And on her sixtieth birthday she admitted to feeling very much as she had at fifty-nine, "though not quite so relieved and exhilarated by the circumstance as when at 30 I gazed into the looking-glass and discerned no marked change from 29."

She was reading Emily Dickinson, to whom she has often been compared. She thought Emily had "a wonderfully Blakean gift, but therewithal a startling recklessness of poetic ways and means." On the face of it this would appear to be a remarkable statement from a poet who

was herself noted for freedom of poetic expression, but she valued structure and logical design in a poem as much as what she called its "essence." In her opinion "form" and "essence" could not be separated. Though her critical terms are Victorian, her point of view is modern, for what she means is that in the total organization of a poem none of its elements can be isolated from the whole. She was also opposed to virtuosity, a brilliant technical display in poetry. "What is the use of *cleverness* in matters poetic?" she asked in commenting upon the work of a now forgotten poet.

When Aunt Charlotte died in 1890, Christina devoted herself to Aunt Eliza, the sole remaining relative of her mother's generation. Shortly after Charlotte's death, Watts wrote her a letter of condolence, to which she replied:

> •I truly value your praise. Yet it humbles me, knowing myself as I do. Thank you for recollecting us and expressing your kindness at a moment when friendship is particularly precious. I wish a day may come when instead of taxing your sympathy some of us may afford you pleasure. But advancing age and a narrowing circle are not very promising elements towards such an event. . . .
>
> And of course you will be welcome if ever you do come. Ten to one I should be at home ready to receive you tho' one good old Aunt still claims my care. Meanwhile I live, so to say, in a circle of the absent who inhabit either this world or the next: and if absence does not deprive me of their sympathy, never may it deprive them of mine!
>
> I hope you are in good health and rich in happiness.*

Despite her seclusion, the young writers of a new generation sought her out at Torrington Square and considered themselves honored by her friendship. Besides her circle of old and still loyal admirers, which included Watts, Sharp, Gosse, Swinburne, and Shields, all of whom continued to pay her homage, young people such as Lisa Wilson, Mackenzie Bell, and Katherine Tynan (later Mrs. Hinkson) were frequent callers at Torrington Square. Miss Tynan was "deferential enough," said Christina, "to puff me up like puff-paste." To Miss Tynan she confided that, although she had been "a very melancholy girl," she was now "a very cheerful old woman."

Miss Tynan, unimpressed, doubted it. Seen through her young eyes, Torrington Square was a house of silence and old age, a silence so heavy that it darkened as well as muffled sound. Despite Christina's pretensions to cheerfulness, which, she admitted to Sharp, one could "put over one's sadness like a veil—a bright shining veil," she deceived neither Miss Tynan nor the world.

She has been variously described during these latter years.[7] At first sight Miss Tynan had an impression of "short-petticoated sturdiness," but a second look convinced her that Christina "was not in the least bit sturdy." Miss Tynan found the "thick boots and short rough grey skirts" she affected oddly incongruous with "the spiritual face, with the heavily-

lidded eyes" which reminded her of an Italian nun's face. "Santa Christina shone like a light" in the dark room dimly lit by candles, Miss Tynan rhapsodized, and thought it a shame that this "flame-hearted saint" lived out her life in the gray streets of Bloomsbury.

Swinburne was equally enthusiastic if less rhetorical. He told his mother that "dear Miss Rossetti" was "one of the most naturally attractive and delightful people I ever met." There was "a mixture of frankness and gentleness in her manner—straightforward without brusquerie, and reserved without gaucherie—" which was altogether "natural and peculiar to her."

Gosse thought her a more intimidating figure. He recalled her "sitting alone, in the midst of a noisy drawing-room, like a pillar of cloud, a Sybil whom no one had the audacity to approach." To Ford Madox Ford she was, as we have seen, the mysterious, black-robed figure. Her nieces likewise found her an awe-inspiring personage. Helen was intimidated by her aunt's "impenetrable reserve" and "her gloomy religion not far removed from pessimism." Olive, older and more realistic, saw her aunt as "a short, stout, elderly woman with dark prominent eyes and heavy leaden complexion . . . dowdily dressed in black with an unbecoming bonnet set on her greying hair, making her way to and from the Church in Woburn Square where she was the regular occupant of a pew."

But, Olive added,

> if you had sat with her in her little back sitting-room as I have often done, you would be struck with the finely-cut features, rather reminiscent in profile of Dante's death mask, by the melancholy depths of her dark eyes gazing abstractedly into the world of ideas and emotions in which she lived, almost oblivious of her surroundings. And she would have an affectionate stroke for old Muff, the tabby who came to us after her death and whose kittens used to amuse her, and now and again some odd snatch of nursery rhyme or playful memory would bring a smile to her lips summoning up from the dead past a pale shadow of the sprightly Christina of far off days.

Virginia Woolf relates an anecdote which places Christina in an exceedingly queer light. At a tea given by her old friend Mrs. Virtue Tebbs, some remark, casual or flippant, was made about poetry; whereupon, reports Mrs. Woolf, "suddenly there uprose from a chair and paced forward into the centre of the room a little woman dressed in black, who announced solemnly, 'I am Christina Rossetti!' and having so said, returned to her chair." Mrs. Woolf interprets this curious act of self-assertion as Christina's awareness and statement of her poetic vocation, but, considering her shyness and reserve as well as her sense of propriety, it seems unlikely she would make a public show of it. Certainly the act itself is altogether uncharacteristic.

That she appeared eccentric at times is undeniable. Living alone in her

gloomy house, "and so much in the other world," as she put it, she was losing contact with this one. As happens so often in the case of the withdrawn personality, she was touchy and excruciatingly sensitive to slights, fancied or real. Coming home one afternoon from a reception at William's house, she immediately sat down and wrote to him, "Please give my love to Lucy and explain that I was on my way to say good-bye when the door at which I was presenting myself shut, and shut me out: I daresay she detects that I am still sufficiently shy to lose heart under such a rebuff." She closes with the revealing words, "Love to any who love me—but really that is quite un-Christian—to all who do and to any who don't." In the last phrase may be detected a faint glimmer of the latent hostility toward Lucy she had tried so hard and so successfully to repress.

VII

Six months after Scott's death the first signs of cancer appeared on Christina's chest and shoulder. Despite these ominous symptoms, she was assured by Mr. Stewart, her doctor, that there was no reason she could not live to be eighty. To William she observed dryly that she did not "run up like quicksilver at the announcement."

Although in reporting the state of her health to Mrs. Heimann in February, 1892, she said, "I go on, if not friskily, doggedly," by May her condition had become so serious that she had to undergo immediate surgery, an operation William described as "truly a formidable one." But as before—during her 1872 illness—again in this crisis she bore herself "like a heroine," said her admiring brother. The operation, pronounced successful, left her in a greatly weakened condition, and the remainder of the summer she alternated between her bed and the sofa, at times showing improvement, at other times relapse. Her convalescence at Brighton immediately after the operation was cheered by William's presence. "Thank you for the invaluable loan of William," she wrote Lucy; "he transforms our enforced expedition to quite a holiday."

The year 1892 marked the appearance of her "final performance" in print, the publication of *The Face of the Deep* by the Society for the Propagation of Christian Knowledge. This study of the Book of Revelation, which she had been working on for some six years, was published thirty years after *Goblin Market,* and the two works enclose her literary career as in a parenthesis.

Like others of her devotional prose volumes, this one also contains her meditations and observations about anything that took her interest while she was writing it. Like the others, it too includes a large selection of religious poems not previously published, some of them among the best products of her late years. Happening upon a review in an obscure journal called *The Rock,* she was amused to read that she had purposely refrained

from making her verse as good as she could. "Perhaps as devout self-denial?" was her ironic inquiry.

Scott also made his final literary bow in 1892 with his posthumously published *Autobiographical Notes,* edited by W. Minto. In a different sense, his was likewise a study in revelations. Christina's first intimation of the forthcoming work was a letter from Alice Boyd, requesting permission to use the 1882 poem Christina had addressed to Scott. She replied with cordial warmth:

> My dear Alice
>
> I ought indeed to be able to sympathize with anyone whose heart is in the other world, and surely not least with you who have been to me such a friend and who have shown me such lavish kindness. Accept my love, my sympathy, my best wishes for here and hereafter.
>
> It greatly pleases me to know that those lines gave W. B. a moment's pleasure, and their appearing in his Autobiography will dignify them and me. I did not know that his circle and the public had any such interesting memorial to look forward to.

This letter is a document of dramatic irony, for Scott's ill-natured attack upon Gabriel throughout the autobiography shocked and scandalized the Rossetti circle. Scott dead revealed as he had never done alive the treachery of which he was capable. No longer masked by the charm of his personality, his character shows through the printed pages with the impartiality of truth. In recording his jealous envy of Rossetti, in gloating over his friend's physical deterioration, and in pointing up his weaknesses and stigmatizing them as manias, Scott drew for posterity the self-portrait of a disgruntled and bitter egoist, one who could deceive himself as well as others, for he believed he was acting from the loftiest and most disinterested of motives.

The publication of the *Notes* had immediate repercussions. So violent was the storm of controversy which followed its appearance in November that William thought the attacks upon Scott "seriously embittered" Alice's remaining years. Swinburne, who considered himself maligned in the book, "dashed into tempestuous reprisals." William, no less resentful but more restrained, managed to avoid fierce recriminations, and expressed his indignation in relatively temperate terms.

But afterwards he heard from F. G. Stephens that Scott's autobiography was to have contained even more sensational disclosures than it did in the final published form. Writing on December 5, 1895, Stephens said:

> *I think you are invariably right about Scott's unhappy book, and I am not sure you know that this mixed concern was originally far more injurious than it is now. Scott himself, a good while before his death, told me that he intended to tell, without reserve or mercy, all he knew (or thought he knew) about G. He was resolved, he said, to let the world know the 'truth.' I remonstrated in the most stringent manner as to this, and finally left him with a remark that whatever he knew (or

> thought he knew) as to these matters he spoke of, had come to him in the confidence of friendship, and I denounced his purpose as strongly as I could. Later, he said to me that he had actually revised much of his materials, and he did so in such a manner as led me to think he had toned down his observations. Minto, too, moderated this but not a little before it was published, but of course, M. was not in a position to check any of S.'s 'facts' or opinions. He simply cut the text down, and by omitting parts which were obviously offensive, moderated the whole thing. M. promised me to insert a note explaining something about myself which Hunt had peevishly and unjustly told him of my conduct. The fact is Scott's knowledge was mostly at second hand, or derived from letters, and thus he could not conceive correctly much that was essential to a right opinion of what he heard indirectly. Besides, apart from many a fine point, Scott was pitiless and unfeeling now and then, [and could be] outrageously cruel. . . .* [8]

Christina did not know about this letter, for it was written after her death. What she did know was bad enough. Though it was still true for her that "Love pardons the unpardonable past," she could not have foreseen that from his grave Scott would arise in a vindictive resurrection to deal her another blow, the last of the many she had received at his hands. When William told her about Scott's attack upon Gabriel, "she refused to look at the book, swayed, I think," said William, "as much by respect for Scott's memory as for her brother's."

Although she declined to read her old friend's autobiography, she kept hoping she had been misinformed about its contents. "In last night's *St. James's Gazette,* there was a rather long article on Mr. Scott's book," she wrote William on November 29, "pleasant and laudatory and containing nothing obnoxious." But eventually she too had to accept the fact that the man they had all trusted for more than forty years had, in a sense, betrayed them to a curious public avid for sensational details.

This final hurt, the humiliation of realizing that all her life she had loved an unworthy man, could have been a crushing experience for a sensitive woman. For years she had put away from her with both hands the suspicion that the man was shallow, idle, and selfish, a suspicion to which she had given literary form in the fictitious character of Alan Hartley in "Commonplace."

But after the appearance of the *Notes,* she could have blinded herself no longer to Scott's true character. He was a man who overrating his own gifts was envious of those possessed by others. His was a warped and sour nature; and it had been only his charm and her habit of affection for him that had prevented her from recognizing it all along.

VIII

Severe as had been the wrench of final separation at the time of Scott's death, she had at least been left with the consolation of her memories

(which a reading of the *Notes* would have desecrated), and even more, with the assurance that her love, "the anguish of a lifetime," had been not without value in the total estimate of her life. But the disenchantment that followed robbed her of this comfort as well. She could easily have fancied that a Divine Lover was resolved to smash the last remaining vestige of an earthly rival's image—even if the jagged and broken pieces must lacerate an already grieving heart.

Once the last remaining prop for earthly love was removed, she found herself launched upon the deep, unable, even had she wished, to turn back. The dilemma of the "divided heart" had been painfully solved, and there was left

None other Lamb, none other Name,
None other Hope in heaven or earth or sea,
None other Hiding-place from guilt and shame,
None beside Thee.

My faith burns low, my hope burns low,
Only my heart's desire cries out in me
By the deep thunder of its want and woe,
Cries out to Thee.

Lord, Thou art Life tho' I be dead,
Love's Fire Thou art, however cold I be:
Nor heaven have I, nor place to lay my head,
Nor home, but Thee.

Her final disillusionment was a means of freeing herself at last from the bonds of that inauspicious love which throughout her adult life had shackled her spirit and weighted it earthward. But, "Crouch lowest, to spring highest," she had written in *The Face of the Deep;* and a late poem expresses even more urgently this inclination to take the dangerous leap into faith:

O Foolish Soul! to make thy count
For languid falls and much forgiven,
When like a flame thou mightest mount
To storm and carry heaven.

Such a soaring movement is much in evidence in her poetry of the 'nineties. It rises toward a crescendo of religious exaltation, much as the great rhythms in the Protestant music of Bach, Schütz, and Handel thunder upward in ever-accelerating waves of expanding ecstasy.

We find this rising rhythm expressed quietly and with restraint in *The Vigil of the Presentation:*

Long and dark the nights, dim and short the days,
Mounting weary heights on our weary ways,
Thee our God we praise all our nights and days,
Thee our God we praise.

Starting slowly, it gains momentum in *As the Sparks Fly Upward:*

Lord, grant us wills to trust Thee with such aim
Of hope and passionate craving of desire
That we may mount aspiring, and aspire
Still, while we mount; rejoicing in Thy name.
Yesterday, this day, day by day the same:
So sparks fly upward scaling heaven by fire,
Still mount and still attain not, yet draw nigher,
While they have being, to their fountain flame.

But it is in *Faint Yet Pursuing* that we feel the full force of the emotional power which provides the energy for the final liberating upthrust, the free soar into immortality:

Press onward, quickened souls, who mounting move,
Press onward, upward, fire with mounting fire;
Gathering volume of untold desire,
Press upward, homeward, dove with mounting dove.
Point me the excellent way that leads above;
Woo me with sequent will, me too to aspire;
With sequent heart, to follow higher and higher,
To follow all who follow on to Love.
Up the high steep, across the golden sill,
Up out of shadows into very light,
Up out of dwindling life to life aglow,
I watch you, my beloved, out of sight;—
Sight fails me, and my heart is watching still:
My heart fails, yet I follow on to know.

20

"SLEEPING AT LAST"

1894

With the publication by the S.P.C.K. of the 1893 *Verses* (collected from three devotional works), Christina was recognized as "one of the greatest living poets," and one of "the foremost poets of the age." [1] Within her lifetime she had won her niche in English poetry and had achieved the status of an immortal. But the 1893 volume had an overwhelming popular as well as critical success. By Christmas the first edition was sold out, and Christina heard that "there was no meeting the demand" for the *Verses*. In one shop alone thirty people were on the waiting list hoping to obtain their copies by Christmas; and the volume went through three editions before spring.

Of all her books, only this one remains undedicated. She had intended to dedicate it to William, but he objected that a person of his known antireligious views ought not to have a religious work dedicated to him. In that case, Christina said, she would leave it undedicated, but "you and I will know that in my heart thus it stands:—

To my dearest Brother
William Michael Rossetti
I commend these verses."

Unlike many poets who lose their capacities as they grow older, Christina continued to write good poetry until the year of her death. Despite the continual inroads of disease and weakness, her imaginative and intellectual powers showed no diminution. Indeed, some of her late lyrics are among her most notable productions. One reason for the sustained vitality of her genius is that the accumulating years brought not decay but continued growth. She experienced no hardening of the spiritual arteries.

The twig sprouteth,
The moth outeth,
The plant springeth,
The bird singeth:

Tho' little we sing to-day
Yet are we better than they;
Tho' growing with scarce a showing,
Yet, please God, we are growing,

she wrote in this 1893 piece which in the freshness of its feeling, its naïve rhythm, and archaic flavor is comparable to the best examples of the Middle English lyric. It reflects the luminous serenity which both Bell and Miss Tynan thought characteristic of Christina during her last years.

Much of this serenity can be attributed to her religious faith, which was also responsible for keeping alive within her the principle of growth. At this time of her life she seems to have achieved the tranquil assurance of divine love for which she had longed and struggled so many years but never before realized. Lines such as the following hint at a conviction of election lacking in her earlier work:

O Lord, when Thou didst call me, didst Thou know
My heart disheartened thro' and thro',
Still hankering after Egypt full in view
Where cucumbers and melons grow?
—'Yea, I knew.'—

But, Lord, when Thou didst choose me, didst Thou know
How marred I was and withered too,
Nor rose for sweetness nor for virtue rue,
Timid and rash, hasty and slow?
—'Yea, I knew.'—

My Lord, when Thou didst love me, didst Thou know?
How weak my efforts were, how few,
Tepid to love and impotent to do,
Envious to reap while slack to sow?
—'Yea, I knew.'—

Good Lord, Who knowest what I cannot know,
And dare not know, my false, my true,
My new, my old; Good Lord arise and do
If loving Thou hast known me so.
—'Yea, I knew.'—

This tendency toward the Protestant mystique should be sufficient to contradict the prevalent view that she was inherently Catholic in predisposition and that she would have been happier within the Catholic faith. Side by side with her Anglican deference to the authority of the Church was her extreme Protestant conception of the individual's relation to God as one that is personal, intimate, and unmediated.

Such an assurance that she had been singled out for the kind of loving discipline reserved for the elect did much to banish earlier doubts and fears, though, as we shall see, they were not permanently exorcised. Nevertheless, in the remaining few years of her life affirmation, not doubt

or even resignation, was the dominant note in her poetry. Poems such as *Lord, Grant Us Calm, While Christ Lay Dead the Widowed World, Safe Where I Cannot Lie Yet,* and many others suggest an attitude of quiet acceptance, of positive reconciliation:

> Death is not death, and therefore do I hope:
> Nor silence silence; and I therefore sing
> A very humble hopeful quiet psalm,
> Searching my heart-field for an offering;
> A handful of sun-courting heliotrope,
> Of myrrh a bundle, and a little balm.

II

After the death of Aunt Eliza in 1893 Christina was the sole occupant of 30 Torrington Square, except for her two servants and Muff. During the last year of her life she became particularly fond of one of Muff's newly born kittens, whose chief claim upon her was its weakness. Isolating it from the litter shortly after birth, she rubbed the tiny creature's hind legs with camphorated oil every day until finally it grew strong enough to live. "Such a pretty kitten," she told William, "with such rich fur. And it stood up yesterday at the fender and made the Y of our childhood."

Living as she did in "the circle of the absent," she would often let her mind dwell upon memories of those far-off days of her childhood, so full and active, so crowded with life compared to the soundless solitude of the present. The pretty, richly furred kitten recalled to her the cozy warmth and the security of 38 Charlotte Street. It brought back the picture of her father, weary after a day of lecturing at King's College and then giving private Italian lessons, dozing before dinner on the rug in front of the fireplace, the cat standing up on hind legs, front paws outstretched on the fender, warming its furry stomach, and the children, herself among them, playing quietly on the firelit floor and exclaiming in delight at the cat's resemblance to a living Y.

Although cancer had recurred in 1893, Christina's heart condition made a second operation inadvisable. She herself was "glad to escape the heavy expense of an operation and its context," and, although she knew that what she called "the mischief" was there, it was working slowly and not causing her undue discomfort. She went on from month to month without any grave complications setting in. During pleasant weather she let herself into the Square gardens, to which she had a key, and sat outside in the sunshine. Otherwise, she tended to her domestic affairs, read, meditated, wrote letters, held household services twice a day, attended Church regularly, and in William's opinion managed to get through the days "with placid contentment or resignation and not (I think) with any extreme tedium or lowness of spirit."

In September she spent a short time in Brighton in search of the health she knew she would never regain. From there she wrote the newly married

Katherine Tynan Hinkson, of her decided repugnance to the prevalent practice of interviewing celebrities:

17 Brunswick Road
Brighton
Sept. 14. [1893]

*Dear Mrs. Hinkson

I knew that you are married though not the date, and I have often thought of you, and be sure I wish you and yours fullness of happiness. My brother's address is 3 St. Edmund's Terrace
Regent's Park—N.W.
in case you should again want it.

Do come and see me,—only please do not 'interview' me. I own I feel this modern fashion highly distasteful, and am tenacious of my obscurity. Not, of course, that I have aught to say against my friends (or foes: only I trust I have none) writing whatever they please about me, only I cannot lay myself out for the purpose. So far do I carry this that I would very much rather *not* see the article before publication. I am very much of an invalid now and expect to remain so permanently, and this seaside holiday was taken for health's sake. In the course of next week I trust to be at home again, all the better for the change yet not improved beyond a certain point.

Always
Truly yours
Christina G. Rossetti* [2]

When Ford Madox Brown died in 1893, William urged her to take over Brown's house at No. 1 St. Edmund's Terrace so that she could be nearer to him and his family. But she saw little advantage in moving from one large house to another. "A number of empty rooms are not merely useless," she told him, "but depressing." As it was, she kept most of the rooms at Torrington Square locked, for there was no one but herself to use them. Often she dreamed of leaving the big gloomy house with its steep staircase now so hard for her to climb, with its closed rooms and dark silences, and leasing a small, pleasant cottage with a garden near Regent's Park, within walking distance of William's house. But this dream was never to be realized.

In April, 1894, Lucy, who had been ill for a number of years, died in Italy. She left all her property, including the house at St. Edmund's Terrace, to be divided among her four children. To William she bequeathed the crayon portrait of her that Gabriel had drawn in 1874. "I will not venture to say that I regret anything in Lucy's will," Christina remarked, but she understood very well what a humiliating position it had placed William in, and she longed to help him without wounding his pride. Now that he was a widower with four children to care for, she was available should he wish to join households, she told him, "available, that is, if life lasts so long."

Then lest she might have alarmed him, she added, "Do not suppose

by this I have fresh reason to anticipate a speedy end, but you and I know how precarious is all life and how doubly precarious mine has become. Mr. Stewart detects progress of the mischief, but I understand slow progress. . . ."

That June she told Mackenzie Bell that she had definitely decided to move away from Torrington Square by Michaelmas. But by then she had taken to her bed, never to rise again.

III

It is to Bell, who visited her regularly during the last six months of her life, that we are indebted for a final portrait of her. Although other of her contemporaries saw her as a short, stoutish woman, she seemed tall to Bell, perhaps because of "the commanding breadth of her brow" and the dignity of her bearing. To him both her appearance and her voice bespoke a woman of genius. Yet far from being formidable, she was "one of the most lovable women who ever lived."

She never wore ornaments. Usually she was "demurely attired in a black silk dress . . . relieved by some simple white frilling at the throat and wrists." Her hair, still abundant and dark except for a few inconspicuous gray strands, was generally covered by a cap.

But it was her voice which aroused Bell's most enthusiastic admiration. Although its inimitable charm eluded analysis, he attributed it in part to her precise pronunciation of syllables and in part to a hauntingly Italian inflection which reminded him of the speech of an educated foreigner.

After June she spent most of her time in the drawing room, which, with its tall western windows facing the square below, was the most cheerful and spacious room in the house. Although a few good pieces of Chippendale were scattered about, according to Victorian standards the room was comparatively bare. The small bookcase contained chiefly religious works and Mrs. Rossetti's favorite novels, those by Maria Edgeworth, Sir Walter Scott, and Dickens. The flowers sent by Christina's admirers always filled the room. Near the western windows was a miniature glass-house with ferns, which Christina tended herself so long as she was able.

The walls were hung with Gabriel's pictures, including the 1866 chalk drawing he had made of Christina. A prominent place was also given to the portrait of Frances Rossetti's favorite brother, Dr. John Polidori, Byron's traveling physician. But the picture that gave Christina the most pleasure during her last days was a copy of Shields' *The Good Shepherd,* which hung on the center wall facing the windows.

Bell observed with growing uneasiness that upon each of his successive visits she appeared to be a little weaker. Entering one sultry late afternoon in July, he was struck by the frailty of her appearance. He had just come from a fashionable literary tea, and after the noise and chatter he found

Christina's quiet drawing room restful and relaxing. Her couch had been wheeled under the windows. He presented his customary offering of flowers, and sat down beside her. Although she was cheerful and composed, he thought she showed signs of recent suffering. But it was not often that she would admit to pain. Once, however, she did ask Bell to pray for her, because "I have to suffer so *very* much."

As they chatted, the room was brightened by the last ripe glow of the setting sun. The rays, striking the pendant of the glass chandelier hanging from the ceiling, reflected brilliantly colored prisms on door and wall. The sun disappeared, and as the lavender shadows of the long summer twilight deepened, the noises in the square, a blend of children's cries, bird chirps, competing organ-grinders' music, and the crunch of carriage wheels gradually became hushed. The outline of the plane trees below darkened, the leaves silhouetted in lacy patterns against the dark violet sky. The mild, fragrant, summer evening air, coming in through the open windows, reminded Christina of her summers in the country, and she talked of Holmer Green and the effect it had had upon her youthful imagination.

She then asked Bell what he thought of Shields' *Good Shepherd;* and seemed pleased when he praised it. "That is the only representation of the subject I ever saw," she said, "which brings to mind at all adequately my conception of it." And then, after a pause, "You see, he does not treat sacred themes merely as an artist; they are part of his life. They are part of his life in a way that I have never known them to be of any other artist, and this is one cause of his marvellous power."

This penetrating observation provides a clue to the source of Christina's own power as a poet. The inseparable unity of experience and its expression in poetry is a particular attribute of her genius. By the 1890's such a quality had already become something of an anachronism, for the Aesthetes were starting the modern trend toward the disassociation of life and art which was to dominate the cultural life of the twentieth century. But what Christina lived she wrote, and her poetry is a record of that experience.

And now, with her life drawing to a close, she felt an increasing urgency to impart the insights she had acquired during her years of living. She had been in her time one of the bold explorers who penetrate to the penumbra of human experience. She had pushed into the untouched regions and seen the unfrequented places. In between explorations she had made a practice of reporting in the form of poetry to those at home. So far, her reports had been tentative. But was it not possible to reach some sort of conclusion before taking her leave?

Explorer though she might be, hers was the report of the poet, not the scientist. We have seen that in a *Later Life* sonnet she had already suggested that poetry could have a reconciling function. The poet, a

solitary bird, who amidst "the hundred thousand merry-making birds" alone saluted the night, was for his pains empowered "to sing the thoughts we cannot say." And by the very act of knowing and singing them, the poet somehow was enabled to "set them right."

This was the view she developed on a grander and more comprehensive scale in *Voices from Above,* a late poem, which depicting her final attitude before her mind became clogged by drugs and shadowed by dark fears, may be taken as her last report. In this lyric of praise for all creation, she affirms not only that the universe is harmonious, but that the poet's special function is both to participate in and to recreate through his art that essential harmony:

Voices from above and from beneath,
Voices of creation near and far,
Voices out of life and out of death,
Out of measureless space,
Sun, moon, star,
In oneness of contentment offering praise.

Heaven and earth and sea jubilant
Jubilant all things that dwell therein;
Filled to fullest overflow they chant,
Still roll onward, swell,
Still begin
Never flagging praise interminable.

Thou who must fall silent in a while,
Chant thy sweetest, gladdest, best, at once;
Sun thyself to-day, keep peace and smile;
By love upward send
Orisons,
Accounting love thy lot and love thine end.

IV

"It is a good thing really to do what I have to do *now,*" she told William in the spring of 1894 as she posted "certain little papers." What they were we do not know—William surmised "something for publication." Possibly she was sending off the last poem to be published in her lifetime, *The Way of the World,* which appeared in the *Magazine of Art* in July, 1894.

In August she took to her bed. Dr. Stewart tried to prepare William for what was coming, and he therefore heard "a very gloomy and alarming account" of his sister's condition. In addition to cancer she suffered from a functional irregularity of the heart, although there was no evidence of organic heart disease. Dropsy was an additional complication. Dr. Stewart further considered her extremely subject to hysteria. Mildly surprised at this diagnosis, William protested, "I can't say I should have discerned it for myself." He nevertheless instructed Bell in writing her

biography to mention the hysteria, of which the symptoms were apparent during her final illness, "particularly during semi-consciousness, chiefly manifesting themselves in cries. . . ."

This objective and subdued statement tells us little either about the cause or the nature of the cries which commencing about September 17 were a trial and annoyance to Christina's nearest neighbor.

Realizing that his sister's days on earth were numbered, William began to make regular entries in his diary after each visit to her.[3] Although his notations were chiefly of her physical deterioration, he also recorded "the shifting eddies of her mind," which included some very dark currents.

On September 3 he reported a gradual though not very marked "worsening" of her condition. Despite this, however, he and she had "a little earnest talk on matters of religion." Three days later he was shocked to find her "very low and exhausted . . . distinctly worse in the face than I had yet seen her." She said to him, "I should like to see you there," by which he gathered that she meant heaven.

Although subsequently she showed improvement, by September 8 he wrote that there was not "any real change of condition for the better." During his visit she discussed the provisions of her will: everything was to go to him, with the request that he set aside a certain stipulated sum for religious bequests.

In the middle of September a ghost arose to haunt her. A letter from Alice arrived, which William answered in the following fashion:

> MY DEAR MISS BOYD
>
> I saw my sister Christina the other day and opened and read to her your kind letter of the 11th. Christina, I regret to say, has been confined to bed for a month or so past, and is quite unable to write: she asked me to reply. It is too true that she is exceedingly ill—in fact she is undoubtedly dying, owing to a malady of the heart and other grave matters: I am sure she will never be out of bed again, and if her life lasts to the end of this year I shall be surprised.
>
> Christina wd. certainly like to avail herself of your most friendly offer to present to her that portrait of me wh. my beloved friend Scott painted many years ago. I will not conceal from you, dear Miss Boyd, that there are some things about Gabriel in that book of Scott's Reminiscences wh. I do not regard as either kind or friendly or even fair: yet this does not substantially affect the feeling wh. I always did and always [will] entertain for Scott. Christina has not read the book—knowing that it contains matters wh. she wd. not like and with wh. she prefers to remain unacquainted.
>
> Christina sends you her love and thanks—and I am sure you will accept my own expression of warm regard. I have had many sorrows lately, of wh. you no doubt know somewhat.[4]

Not long after this what William has called his sister's "troubles of soul" began. Dr. Stewart had advised moving her bed from the small stuffy back bedroom to the drawing room so that she could get fresh air.

As a sick chamber, the drawing room had the disadvantage, however, of being noisy—Bell reported hearing, during one of his visits, "the discordant noise from no fewer than three piano-organs"—and not only did the outside noises from the square come in, but sounds from within could be heard with equal distinctness by those outside. It was on October 31 that Mrs. Charlotte C. Sto[f]es, living at 31 Torrington Square, wrote the first of her two letters to William complaining about the disturbance which came from the house next door: [5]

*SIR

I sympathize deeply with Miss Rossetti and with you in the sad affliction which has befallen her. But I have come to town for three winters for my literary work, and have chosen this place because of its QUIETNESS. But since my return on the 17th September I have been perfectly unable to work, from the distressing screams that sound clear from her Drawing-room to mine, *especially* at the hours I have hitherto devoted to writing, between 8 and 11 p. m.

I gave notice to my landlady that I must go, and she naturally is unwilling to lose good permanent lodgers through no fault of her own, especially as she is well aware that no new lodger would stay a second night in the Drawing-room. She therefore urged me to write to see if nothing could be done.

As far as regards myself, if her bed were removed to the Back Drawing-room, the cries would not be heard clearly enough to disturb. I would remove my sitting-room but there is no gas at the back.

As far as regards Miss Rossetti, I have a strong suspicion that her screams occur when she is left alone. If, after paying a morning visit, you should unexpectedly return with a passkey between 8 and 10, you might determine this. It would be *very* inconvenient and expensive for me to remove, but the mental strain is killing me. . . . I am trying to support myself by literature, so you may understand and forgive the reason of my troubling you.*

Besides two servants, at this time Christina had in her employ Mrs. Harriet Read, the servant nurse who had tended Aunt Eliza at the last, and assuredly the devoted and responsible Mrs. Read would not have deserted her in the evenings. Possibly though in attendance, neither Mrs. Read nor the servants could do anything for their mistress when she was in such a state. Still, it was not until November 17 that a professional nurse was hired.

During the day, as Christina's neighbor pointed out, there was little or no sign of these hysterical symptoms. In general, throughout September and October William found his sister "perfectly conversible" on subjects that interested her and "fully capable of sustained talk." On October 3, for instance, she discussed with him the volume of Gabriel's letters he was editing, going over with him the list of old childhood acquaintances, rectifying errors, and reminding him of omissions. On the 9th she seemed "surprisingly cheerful," even reciting from memory one of her earliest poems, a little thing called *The Chinaman,* written when she was twelve.

But with the setting of the sun such efforts were no longer possible; and during the long, lonely evenings her rigid self-discipline broke down, allowing the floodwaters to rush in:

A dream there is wherein we are fain to scream,
While struggling with ourselves we cannot speak:
And much of all our waking life, as weak
And misconceived, eludes us like the dream.
For half life's seemings are not what they seem,
And vain the laughs we laugh, the shrieks we shriek.

On November 4 William heard again from Christina's neighbor:

*I must thank you for your kind letter. I would not have written you but that Miss [Walks] begged me to do so, and I knew that she was not herself good at the pen. It is because I feel so much for Miss Rossetti, that her screams overwhelm me so much. I am overworked, overanxious, sleepless, and far from well: and it distresses my little girls also. I would have been glad if I could have *helped;* but to sit alone and listen to cries one cannot soothe is distracting. That was the reason I had to give notice to leave. I did not think you could do anything but perhaps give instructions to her attendants not to leave her alone. I must say that there has been, during the last week, no long-continued fits of hysterical screaming in the evening. I did not know she was *so* ill. I trust you will pardon my letter, and receive my sympathy.

I am yours truly*

A discreet hint dropped to Christina about the complaints of the neighbors probably silenced her, thereby blocking off what might have been a channel of relief.

V

In October there was an unforeseen switch in physicians. Dr. Stewart, the family doctor who had taken care of Christina's mother and both her aged aunts and in whom she herself had the greatest confidence, was obliged for reasons of his own poor health to give up his practice and leave England. He was replaced by a Dr. Abbott Anderson. "She took the announcement placidly," William wrote in his journal, "though no doubt it must be unwelcome to her."

Despite this and her other misfortunes, from time to time flashes of her old sprightly playfulness appeared. One day quoting the line from *Macbeth,* "Thrice the brinded cat hath mewed," she remarked that, although a brinded cat was nothing more or less than a tabby cat, the effect would have been ruined had the poet written, "Thrice the tabby cat hath mewed." In the midst of sickness, her mind was still busy with its lifelong occupation, the employment of words. Another time she recited from memory *Charon,* the humorous verse which, written at Frome-Selwood in 1853, had amused and delighted Maria.

But by the first week in November she was no longer capable of such

playful excursions. On the 3rd William found her "more low and exhausted and less capable of sustained attention" than he had yet seen her; and by the 9th he feared she would not last out the week.

On that day she appeared to be sinking fast: her articulation was poor, she spoke with difficulty, and she seemed "very gloomy." William read aloud several letters from admirers, but she showed little interest in them. Apparently something troubled her. Speaking with an effort, she asked William's forgiveness for two old matters. One touched some incident that had occurred in their childhood. The other appeared to relate to Cayley, but William had great difficulty in understanding what she said because of her imperfect articulation, and he could not catch any of the details. What he thought she said was that she wanted his forgiveness for disregarding his wishes several years ago in regard either to taking lunch with the Cayleys or receiving Cayley at lunch, William was unable to make out which, but he distinctly heard her say, "I was so fond of him."

Other than William's supplementary statements, this seems to be the substance of Christina's deathbed confession of her love for Cayley, this poor flotsam of memory thrown up by her wandering wits. Since William himself admits he could not fully grasp what she was saying, all that emerges clearly is that she was suffering from a deeply felt sense of guilt which she somehow connected with disregarding William's wishes.

But even in her confused state of mind she could hardly have imagined that William disapproved of her seeing Cayley. She knew very well that it was William who had originally urged her to marry Cayley, and, instead of not wishing her to see him, William had, as we have seen, actually arranged for her to meet Cayley at his own house, at his own dinner table. Furthermore, Cayley had been in the habit of dropping by Torrington Square regularly for tea and whist (practically never for lunch) with the full approval of the family. Indeed, there was no reason for the family to disapprove.

While it is true that the emotions operate outside time—and therefore Christina could have thought of the early 1880's (Cayley died in 1883) as "several years ago"—they always spin on their own axis, and the center of their rotation is their fixed knowledge of the order of relevance. Even when dimming or fading consciousness blurs full self-recognition, the principles governing emotional relevance do not shift their position. Christina knew and had always known that Cayley was not the forbidden suitor, that William had never interfered or wanted to interfere with her seeing him, and, even when her mind was befogged, she was not likely to have shuffled these facts of her inner world like a pack of cards.

But if William knew about or even suspected her attachment to Scott, he assuredly would not have encouraged it, no matter how well he liked Scott. We have seen that she had often lunched with Scott, possibly ig-

noring William's disapproval to do so, and that at Scott's house she had sometimes met and lunched with the Courtneys, a name which sounds enough like the Cayleys for William to have mistaken it for such, especially since he was unable to understand the greater part of what his sister was saying. And although the Courtneys are occasionally mentioned in Christina's correspondence, there is no further reference to Cayley's sisters after Christina's first allusion to them in the early 1860's.

Possibly Alice's letter of September 11 had inadvertently opened the old wound and caused Christina to repeat the bitter self-reproaches with which she had doubtless tortured herself after the appearance of Scott's autobiography. On her deathbed all she could think of to excuse her culpable affection was the affection itself, the simple plea, "I was so fond of him." Although this may have been the last, it was not the first time she had expressed in words her fondness for Scott.

Either William misunderstood her garbled remarks or else he interpreted them to fit into his own preconceptions. After her death the *Saturday Review,* expressing the prevalent sentiment, wrote, "What a satisfaction it is to the lovers of her poetry to feel that there is nothing in her life to record unworthy of her high genius and her pure and noble work in verse." [6] Thus there was a further accretion to the romantic legend originated and circulated by William.

VI

Cheered by her brother's presence, Christina rallied a few days later to the extent of asking for "any entertaining bit of news." When William told her that he was making progress in writing the memoir of Gabriel to be published with the letters and that he was already up to the publication of *The Germ,* she looked pleased.

Once she interrupted to ask if there was really any sort of animal crawling on the sheet, and she appeared to accept William's explanation that it was a delusion. He then asked whether she would like to have him read from the Gospels, but she replied she was too far gone for that: sometimes when she tried to repeat the Lord's Prayer, her mind would wander. He next suggested that he bring her the kitten, but she shook her head, saying she was "past that" too. But before he left, she reminded him of his promise to take the kitten after her death.

"If I meet Mamma in the other world, shall I give her your love?" she asked. "Yes, to all," he replied, humoring her. Although we might draw the inference from this remark that she felt little doubt about personal immortality, such was not the case. Two opposing tendencies fought for domination of her mind during the last weeks. On the one hand, she still retained her traditional orthodox belief in the resurrection of the body, to which she gave expression in this verse of 1893:

Bone to his bone, grain to his grain of dust:
A numberless reunion shall make whole
Each blessed body for its blessed soul,
Refashioning the aspects of the just. . . .

Each with his own not with another's grace,
Each with his own not with another's heart,
Each with his own not with another's face,
Each dove-like soul mounts to his proper place:—
O faces unforgotten! if to part
Wrung sore, what will it be to reembrace?

On the other hand, she had an equally strong fear of death, not only the death of the body, but even more, the death of the spirit. If, as she firmly believed, life on earth was a trial, then the soul which had proved itself unworthy in this life lost its chance of salvation, of eternal survival in the life beyond this one. As for herself, she was not at all sure she had passed the test.

We find in a sonnet from *Later Life* both fears fused, that of physical disintegration and spiritual annihilation. In presaging the conditions of her own death, Christina reveals that, despite her Christian optimism, she regarded death naturalistically and was far from blind to its revolting features:

I have dreamed of Death:—what will it be to die
Not in a dream, but in the literal truth,
With all Death's adjuncts ghastly and uncouth,
The pang that is the last and the last sigh?
Too dulled, it may be, for a last good-bye,
Too comfortless for any one to soothe,
A helpless charmless spectacle of ruth
Through long last hours, so long while yet they fly.
So long to those who hopeless in their fear
Watch the slow breath and look for what they dread:
While I supine with ears that cease to hear,
With eyes that glaze, with heartpulse running down
(Alas! no saint rejoicing on her bed)
May miss the goal at last, may miss a crown.

As the dark, bleak, and foggy November days passed, each nightfall shortening by the length of one day more Christina's life span, her "spiritual outlook," as William calls it, became increasingly gloomy. This brother who despite all persisted in regarding her faith as "pure and absolute," unequivocal, and not subject to the stress of doubt, was naturally puzzled and distressed by the late streak of pessimism which showed itself so darkly in the end. He accounted for it by his conviction that her religion had "weighted her down at the last."

It was not her religion but her own conviction of unworthiness, of

failure, which oppressed her. On the contrary, her faith had been throughout her life and still was a source of nourishment greater than comfort. Possibly what weighed her down was the burden of guilt she had borne almost the whole of her mature life. From the time Scott had first entered the house on Charlotte Street, and like a malignant Mephistopheles had charmed and fascinated her, she had never known what it was to be free from feelings of guilt.

Repeatedly dwelt upon in her poetry, this sense of personal unworthiness has baffled and mystified her readers. If ever a life was blameless, praiseworthy, unstained by even the common run of blemishes, Christina Rossetti's was that life. What, then, could she have had to reproach herself with? Unless we wish to believe with William that her guilt had its origin in theological dogma or with Jung in some archetypal racial consciousness, we are obliged to account for it in some other way.

We may assume that, although her final disillusionment with Scott after the publication of his *Notes* had liberated her from the love which for over forty years had been her special cross, as death approached, she began to fear a just retribution. Alice's letter had probably brought to the surface long-buried memories, and as her vital forces became weakened by disease and opiates, this fear gained an increasing hold upon her. "How dreadful to be eternally wicked," she said to William, "for in hell you must be so eternally—not to speak of any question of torments." And she confided to Mrs. Read that her illness had humbled her: "I was so proud before."

William attributes the dark turn of her pessimism both to the opiates and to the regular visits of the Reverend Charles Gutch of St. Cyprians. Although this cleric was a fairly recent acquaintance,[7] he seems to have had a decided influence over her, and during her last days she came to rely increasingly upon his spiritual counsel. William, suspecting that he might be her father confessor, observed that after each of his visits she was left more cheerless and dejected than before his arrival. "He took it upon him to be austere, where all the conditions of the case called upon him to be soothing and solacing."

But if she had accused herself of "sin" in confessing her lifelong love, we could not expect a soothing leniency from a strait-laced Victorian clergyman of the type portrayed by Samuel Butler in *The Way of All Flesh*. Unable to appreciate a moral nature so self-responsible or to understand a personality so delicately organized, so complex and involuted as Christina's, he would have dealt with her as with the common run of sinners, applying the lash instead of the salve. And perhaps this was after all what she deeply wanted.

VII

On November 15 she was so weak and prostrate that William believed she could survive no more than a few days. But again he had underesti-

mated his sister's vitality, which was remarkable, for by the next day she had recovered sufficiently to be able to discuss with him and apply to herself the line from Young's *Night Thoughts*, "All men think all men mortal but themselves."

By the first of December it was apparent that she could not live out the year. William now wrote down with unsentimental precision the record of her day-to-day journey toward the grave, and it is to these pages that we must turn for a knowledge of the last weeks:

December 2. Christina this afternoon was a little drowsy. Said a few things in a very natural voice, better than often has been the case these three weeks or so. *Lord of the Isles* [she discussed Sir Walter Scott's poem of that title].

December 6. Christina very quiet and composed to-day, talking with presence of mind in a deliberate though very weak voice. She got me to look into the contents of her deed-box (will, spoons, etc.) and also gave me information as to the *provenance* of the principal articles of furniture in her (front-drawing) room. . . . She has some fancy about animals, 'like pussy-cats,' on a piece of black satin, 'looking about for sleep': but I think she understands that this is a mere fancy of an exhausted brain and frame.

December 7. To-day Christina was very placid, and capable of attending to whatever was said. It is remarkable how much her articulation has improved beyond what it was some fortnight or so ago.

December 17. Christina was not *so* bad to-day. After I had been standing a minute by her bedside she opened her eyes and addressed me in an affectionate and natural tone, and she was able to follow my reading of two longish letters. I fear her mind is always now possessed by gloomy ideas as to the world of spirits, but she has not for some weeks past said to me anything bearing in this direction. She has again taken some liquid nourishment.

December 25. Christina awake: taciturn, but not wholly silent. As usual now, she seems gloomy and distressed, but I find it difficult now to apprehend the precise cause. Religious ideas seem to me predominant herein.

December 27. Christina seemed to-day a little more self-possessed than yesterday. She did not speak. I come to the conclusion that she is constantly engaged in mental prayer, and though not unconscious of what is going on around her, will not take any express notice of it.

This was Thursday, December 27. The next morning she turned deadly cold, and Mrs. Read noticed a purple look on her face. Nonetheless, with great presence of mind Christina herself ordered restoratives and sent for Dr. Anderson. By the time he arrived she was better.

During the remainder of Friday those about her observed little change in her condition. She took nourishment and seemingly suffered little

pain. William visited her in the afternoon. He stood over her bed silently, but she did not recognize him. Mrs. Read was holding her hand. Her eyes were closed, but once or twice she opened them and gazed at her nurse with grateful affection. Before William left, he kissed her forehead. At the door he turned back for a last look. Christina's eyes were closed, and her lips were moving silently. Was she perhaps repeating to herself the following lines, among the last she had written?

Passing away the bliss,
The anguish passing away:
Thus it is
To-day.

She slept quietly through the night. At about 5 A.M. on Saturday, December 29, the housemaid came in as usual to relieve Mrs. Read. Whispering together, the two women agreed that their mistress appeared fully conscious and that her voice was stronger than it had been the preceding day. Still, Mrs. Read was uneasy. Although she had remained with Christina all through the night, she refused to be relieved. Instead, she remained sitting quietly by her bedside.

Between six and seven Mrs. Read observed that Christina's lips were moving perpetually and assumed that she was in prayer. The expression of her face was composed and tranquil. At that final moment could those dark fears haunting her last days have been banished? Was she hearing in all their majestic splendor the mighty opening chords of that divine music, of which hers had all her life been the devout echo?

Hark! the Alleluias of the great salvation,
Still beginning, never ending, still begin,
The thunder of an endless adoration:
Open ye the gates, that the righteous nation
Which have kept the truth may enter in.

Roll ye back, ye pearls, on your twelvefold station:
No more deaths to die, no more fights to win!
Lift your heads, ye gates, that the righteous nation,
Led by the Great Captain of their sole salvation,
Having kept the truth, may enter in.

Mrs. Read was the only person in the room with Christina when she died. At 7:25 by the nurse's watch on the table, she gave a faint sigh, and then ceased breathing.

A note among William's papers, unsigned but undoubtedly written by Christina's faithful nurse immediately after her death, reads: "Dear Miss Rossetti has passed peacefully away after Seven. Please Come." At eleven William, accompanied by Olive, arrived at Torrington Square. His sister's face was "peaceful, colour much sunken, but aspect not distressing." Later he wrote in his journal, "My noble, admirable Christina

passed away about 7.20 a.m. on Saturday (29). Far better so than that she should continue any longer in suffering of mind or of body."

Around noon Mackenzie Bell called, and at once observed that the blinds were drawn. Christina had left instructions that, should he call within a reasonable time after her death, he was to be taken up to see her. And now as he entered her drawing room, he remarked "how changed and yet unchanged" it was. The small narrow bed upon which she was lying—the same upon which her mother had died—had been moved directly under Shields' picture *The Good Shepherd,* and there were white flowers on the little table beside the bed. Mrs. Read "reverently uncovered the dear face, and as I looked once more upon it, I saw that though slightly emaciated, it was not greatly changed."

VIII

The funeral was held on January 2. Snow had fallen in the night, and the morning air had a wintry crispness. As Bell was about to enter Christ Church, Woburn Square, where the service was to be held, he saw the hearse containing the coffin draw up and stop before the western door of the church. It was met by the clergyman and surpliced choir. Covered with flowers and wreaths, the bier was borne solemnly to its place in front of the chancel while the sonorous chords of "O Rest in the Lord" rolled forth from the organ.

The service was concluded by the singing of stanzas from Christina's *Advent Moon,* which had been set to music for the occasion. To the solemn strains of *The Dead March* from *Saul* the coffin was raised from the foot of the chancel steps and slowly carried down the aisle. Outside the church door a crowd had gathered, members of the congregation and old friends such as Shields, Stephens, Hughes, Sharp, and many others who were waiting to pay their last respects to Christina as the funeral cortege departed for Highgate cemetery.

She was buried near her father and mother in the family plot. Besides William and his children, the only mourners present were Harriet Read, Watts, Lisa Wilson, and Bell. "A sprinkling of snow had remained on the ground," said Bell, "and as the closing words of the burial service were being read by Mr. Nash, the winter sunshine, gleaming through the leafless branches of some nearby trees, revealed all their delicate tracery, while a robin sang."

The little group of relatives and friends placed their wreaths on the coffin, and then it was lowered into the earth. The mourners departed, and left Christina Rossetti to her final rest: [8]

> Sleeping at last, the trouble and tumult over,
> Sleeping at last, the struggle and horror past,
> Cold and white, out of sight of friend and of lover,
> Sleeping at last.

No more a tired heart downcast or overcast,
No more pangs that wring or shifting fears that hover,
Sleeping at last in a dreamless sleep locked fast.

Fast asleep. Singing birds in their leafy cover
Cannot wake her, nor shake her the gusty blast,
Under the purple thyme and the purple clover
Sleeping at last.

APPENDIX

TWO LETTERS TO WILLIAM ROSSETTI

January 2. 1895

*My dear Mr. Rossetti,

It was with great sorrow that I saw recorded in the newspaper the death of dear Christina, which adds another heavy grief to those that you have of late had to bear.

We have comfort in knowing that her sufferings are now at an end, and with her firm belief in a future life we are sure she was more than willing to go. Although for years I have known we should never meet again there was always the feeling that one was honoured by her love and sympathy. I know of none other so good and noble.

With great regard
Yours very truly
Alice Boyd* [1]

The Pines
Putney Hill
London. S.W.
June 10th, 1895

My dear and always kind and true friend,

Watts had of course told me last evening about his interview with you in the morning, and your more than kind intention to give me the memorial of your sister which I shall always treasure as a really and naturally sacred relic. None other could be so precious as the table cover hallowed by her use at the very last. But even more precious than any relic is your assurance of her regard for me. I need not tell you, of all people, how deep was my admiration of her genius, or how sincere and cordial my feeling towards her, which I hope you will not think it presumptuous of me to say was nothing short of affection. Slight and short and intermittent as was our actual acquaintance or intercourse, no slighter word would at all express my sense of her beautiful nature and its inevitable spiritual attractiveness for anyone not utterly unworthy to breathe the same air with her. It is so difficult to express this

sort of impression (the very words imply that) that you will make allowance for my awkward attempt to do so.

Years ago I began an article on 'Sacred English Poetry' designed to lead up from the anonymous medieval writers of some of the sweetest hymns in the world, and on through Herbert and Vaughan (who was a *great* poet by fits and starts, and essentially more akin to her, I think, than anyone else) to the crowning close in Christina at her highest. The fragment long mislaid, I have now recovered: and as I might have ventured to hope that the tribute might possibly give her pleasure I should be more bitterly vexed and self-reproachful than I am if I did not remember that I never lost a chance of paying tribute to her 'in prose or rime.' I was amused and edified to read in a religious magazine that this was my one redeeming point—the man (wretch as he might otherwise be) who was so devoted to such a cause could not (in *this* world) be regarded as utterly lost. I think she might have liked my lines 'to a baby kinswoman . . .' Of course I am reminded of this by thinking of the author of the divine volume called 'Sing-Song.'

Ever affectionately yours
A. C. Swinburne

P.S. I was forgetting (what should be superfluous) to say that Watts *did* tell me how very kindly you had spoken of my verses written on New Year's Eve [Swinburne's tribute to Christina]. I wonder if you noticed, what I well remember, how exceptionally splendid the stars were; bigger and brighter and nearer-looking than usual. I am very glad you liked the verses.

A. C. S.[2]

NOTES

ABBREVIATIONS USED IN NOTES

Add. MSS	Additional Manuscripts, British Museum.
Angeli MSS	Owned by Mrs. Helen Rossetti Angeli.
Ash. MSS	The Ashley Library, British Museum Dept. of MSS., T. J. Wise Catalogue, 9 vols., London (1922–1927).
B.	Before.
Bissell MSS	Owned by E. E. Bissell.
Bod. MSS	Bodleian Library, Oxford.
Bod. Ross. MSS	On loan to the Bodleian; owned by Mrs. Helen R. Angeli. Consists of family documents, correspondence, holograph MSS. of poems, and the vast bulk of unpublished Rossetti papers, some of which William Rossetti had already prepared for publication.
Brit. Mus. MSS	British Museum.
Cockerell MSS	Owned by the late Sir Sidney Cockerell.
DGRFL	*Dante Gabriel Rossetti's Family Letters with a Memoir,* ed. W. M. Rossetti, 2 vols. (1895).
Dennis MSS	Owned by Mrs. Imogene Rossetti Dennis.
Fam. Lttrs.	*The Family Letters of Christina Georgina Rossetti,* ed. W. M. Rossetti (1908).
Half-Century	Henry W. Burrows, *A Half-Century of Christ Church, Albany Street* (1887), privately printed.
Heimann Corr.	Owned by the Wilmington Society of the Fine Arts, Delaware.
H.L. MSS	Huntington Library, San Marino, Calif.
Notes	William Bell Scott, *Autobiographical Notes,* ed. W. Minto, 2 vols. (1892).
N&Q	*Notes & Queries.*
Penn. Hist. Soc.	Pennsylvania Historical Society.
PMLA	Publications of the Modern Language Association of America.
Pnkll. MSS	Owned by Miss Evelyn Courtney-Boyd of Penkill Castle, Ayrshire.
Polidori Docs.	Polidori family documents; owned by Count Goffredo Polidori.
PRDL	*Pre-Raphaelite Diary and Letters,* ed. W. M. Rossetti (1900).

Remin.	W. M. Rossetti, *Some Reminiscences,* 2 vols. (1906).
Rossetti-Macmillan Letters	*The Rossetti-Macmillan Letters:* Some 133 Unpublished Letters Written to Alexander Macmillan, F. S. Ellis, and Others, by Dante Gabriel, William Michael, and Christina Rossetti, 1861–1889, ed. Lona Mosk Packer, Univ. of Calif. Press (1963).
Harold Ross. MSS	Owned by Harold Rossetti.
Ross. Pprs.	*The Rossetti Papers, 1862–1870,* ed. W. M. Rossetti (1903).
TLS	*Times Literary Supplement.*
WHR	*Western Humanities Review.*
Works	*The Poetical Works of Christina Georgina Rossetti, with Memoir and Notes,* ed. W. M. Rossetti (1904).

NOTES

PRELUDE (PAGES 1–8)

1. R. D. Waller, *The Rossetti Family, 1824–1854,* Univ. of Manchester, No. 217, Eng. Ser. No. 21 (1932), pp. 50–51. I am heavily indebted to Professor Waller's lively and scholarly work for much of the material in my early chapters. Additional works consulted in the introductory chapters and throughout are E. R. Vincent, *Gabriele Rossetti in England* (1936); Mackenzie Bell, *Christina Rossetti* (1898); and the following publications by William Michael Rossetti: *Dante Gabriel Rossetti, His Family Letters, with a Memoir,* 2 vols. (1895); *Some Reminiscences,* 2 vols. (1906); *Gabriele Rossetti, A Versified Autobiography* (1901); and *The Poetical Works of Christina Georgina Rossetti, with a Memoir and Notes* (1904).

2. Polidori Docs. The Palazzo Polidori, built in 1100, may still be seen in the city of Orvieto.

3. For further information about Dr. Polidori, see Henry R. Viets, "John William Polidori, M.D., and Lord Byron—A Brief Interlude in 1816," *New Eng. Journal of Medicine* (March 16, 1961), 264:553–557.

4. *Half-Century of Christ Church, Albany Steet,* privately printed by Henry W. Burrows (1887), and *St. Mary Magdalen, Munster Square, A Record,* pub. by the Soc. of SS Peter and Paul (n.d.).

CHAPTER 1 (PAGES 9–25)

1. "It is a mistake," writes Waller (*The Rossetti Family, 1824–1854* [1932]), "to think of Christina as a passionate nature strongly curbed. . . . It is impossible to understand Christina Rossetti at all unless one begins by realising that she was not in middle age [thirty?] 'too late for joy,' but was hardly born to it at all. She had not any firm hold on it, it lay always just beyond her grasp. Her nature was too tentative ever to impose terms on the world around; hence her fear of it, and her renunciation" (pp. 219–220).

Besides Professor Waller's study and the others already indicated (Chap. 1, n. 1) the works consulted in this chapter are Dorothy M. Stuart, *Christina Rossetti,* E.M.L. series (1930); Eleanor W. Thomas, *Christina Georgina Rossetti* (1931); Sir Edmund Gosse, *Critical Kit-Kats* (1896); William Sharp, "Some Reminiscences of Christina Rossetti," *Papers Critical and Reminiscent* (1912); C. M. Bowra, *The Romantic Imagination* (1949); Walter de la Mare, "Christina Rossetti," *Essays by Divers Hands,* ed. G. K. Chesterton (1923); William Hone, *Every-Day Book,* 3 vols. (1825); Helen Rossetti Angeli, "Aunt Christina," newspaper clipping (Dec. 5, 1930), source unknown; Geoffrey Rossetti, "Christina Rossetti," *Criterion,* ed. T. S. Eliot (October, 1930), No. 38, 10:95–117; Christina Rossetti, *Verses,* privately printed by Gaetano Polidori (1847); W. M. Rossetti, *The Rossetti Papers, 1862 to 1870* (1903), and *The Family Letters of Christina Geor-*

gina Rossetti (1908); Brit. Mus., Ash. MS 1386, and Bod. MS Don e 1/1; and *The Sacred Harp* (1836) with Christina's marginal notes and illustrations in pencil.

The incidents of Christina's childhood related in this chapter are drawn from *Time Flies* (1885). In a presentation copy, now at the University of Texas, Christina's marginal notes in pencil identify the persons and places not named in her text.

2. Such generalizing simplifications frequently prove ingenuous. It must be remembered that Dr. John Polidori was a maternal, not a paternal, relative. On the other hand, a Rossetti cousin, Teodorico Pietrocola, was a strait-laced, puritanical minister.

3. The book was originally presented in 1837 to "Master W. Rossetti" by his schoolmaster, the Reverend Paule, "for his improvement and good behavior." William gave it to Christina, Dec., 1844. Still extant, it is now in the library of Mr. and Mrs. Roderick O'Connor of Cheshire.

4. In Dr. Richard Garnett's *DNB* article about Christina, he called attention for the first time to "the taint of disease which clings to her most beautiful poetry, whether secular or religious, *Goblin Market* excepted." Later critics have been inclined to agree with Dr. Garnett, although Ford Madox Ford [Hueffer] engaged him in a prolonged argument about it, and Walter de la Mare called the charge of morbidity "a familiar parrot cry." (For an explanation of Ford's change of name, see *PMLA* [Dec., 1961], No. 5, 76:544–552.) Among modern critics opinion varies. Dorothy Stuart attributes the morbid note to Christina's anemia and the lack of fresh air on Charlotte Street. Eleanor W. Thomas believes that the young poet was merely exploiting the popular themes of her day, which were also treated by her contemporaries, such as Mrs. Caroline Norton, the Countess of Blessington, L.E.L., and Mrs. Hemans. Waller considers the morbidity a quality of Christina's temperament (see above, n. 1). But Fredegond Shove in *Christina Rossetti* (Cambridge, 1931) argues that, "although Christina Rossetti's poetry has quite often been criticised as morbid, I find a most unmorbid matter-of-fact acceptance of pain, sickness and the prospect of death or of old age to have been her strongest characteristic" (p. 29).

5. These lines are not listed in Appendix B of the *Works.*

6. *Rossetti-Macmillan Letters,* Lttr. 117 (Dec. 19, 1877); lttr. to Swinburne, Nov. 19, 1884, Brit. Mus., Ash. MS 1386, pp. 7–8.

CHAPTER 2 (PAGES 26–42)

1. Lttr. of Dec. 10, 1883, Penn. Hist. Soc., Gratz MS. See also *Rossetti-Macmillan Letters,* Lttrs. 133 and 150.

2. The three poems are joined in MS, and that is how they will be considered in the present work, with the sole reservation that each will be discussed in turn for its biographical relevance at the time it was written.

Both Dorothy Stuart and Eleanor W. Thomas place no importance upon the sequential aspect of the linked poems. Although Margaret Sawtell in her *Christina Rossetti* (1955) considers *Three Stages* as a group, her interpretation of the unifying principle as Christina's yearning after sanctity strains credulity (p. 27). Miss Thomas (p. 52) believes that the eighteen-year-old girl was longing for fame, for recognition as a poet, but it is doubtful whether the ambition for fame would have disturbed Christina's peace of mind seriously at the age of eighteen. Furthermore, although this kind of ambition characterized Gabriel at an early age, it was, if it existed at all, a recessive feature of Christina's personality.

3. Graham Hough, "Rossetti and the P.R.B.," *The Last Romantics* (1949), p.

43. Among the numerous works written about the Pre-Raphaelite movement (spelled in various ways), the most reliable first-hand accounts are those by Holman Hunt, *Pre-Raphaelitism and the Pre-Raphaelite Brotherhood,* 2 vols. (1905), and by William Rossetti, *DGRFL,* I, 110–178; *Ruskin: Rossetti: Pre-Raphaelitism: 1854–1862* (1899); and *The Pre-Raphaelite Diaries and Letters* (1900). In studying the MS of this last publication, now among the Rossetti papers on loan to the Bodleian Library (Bod. Ross. MS 95), I availed myself in some instances of passages left unpublished by William. Other studies which have contributed to this chapter are Ford Madox [Ford's] Hueffer's four works, *The Pre-Raphaelite Brotherhood* (1907), *Rossetti: A Critical Essay* (1896); *Ford Madox Brown* (1896); and *Ancient Lights* (1911); Harry Buxton Forman, "Pre-Raphælite Group," *Our Living Poets* (1871); and T. E. Welby, *The Victorian Romantics* (1929). Among modern estimates of the movement, the most valuable beside Hough's are Robin Ironsides, *Pre-Raphaelite Painters* (1948), and Howard Mumford Jones, "The Pre-Raphaelites," *The Victorian Poets,* ed. F. E. Faverty, Harvard Univ. Press (1956). D. S. R. Welland's *The Pre-Raphaelites in Literature and Art* (1953) is helpful in locating reproductions of original documents now out of print and hard to obtain.

4. Undated letter from Collinson to F. G. Stephens, Bod. MS Don e 57, fol. 1. The second letter partially quoted in my text (p. 41) may be found in the same collection, foll. 4–5. Christina's Pleaseley Hill correspondence is published in *Fam. Lttrs.,* under the Aug.–Sept., 1849, dateline. Unless otherwise stated, all quotations from Christina's published correspondence are taken from this source.

5. The sonnet was reproduced on the cover of each issue.

6. Dickens wrote, "In the foreground of the carpenter's shop is a hideous, wry-necked, blubbering, red-haired boy in a nightgown, who appears to have received a poke in the hand from the stick of another boy with whom he had been playing in an adjacent gutter, and to be holding it up for the contemplation of a kneeling woman so horrible in her ugliness that (supposing it were possible for a human creature to exist for a moment with that dislocated throat) she would stand out from the rest of the company as a monster in the vilest caberet in France or the lowest gin-shop in England." After reading this outburst, the Queen, unable to attend the Academy show, asked to have Millais' picture sent to her.

7. The privately printed pamphlets of Dodsworth's sermons are in the archives of Christ Church, Albany Street. They include sermons delivered at Christ Church, Jan. 27 and March 10, 1850; an address, "The Gorham Case Briefly Considered (n.d.); and "A Letter to the Rev. E. C. Pusey," dated May 7, 1850. For further information about the religious crisis in the 1850's, see R. W. Church, *The Oxford Movement* (1909); F. W. Cornish, *The English Church in the Nineteenth Century,* Vol. VIII, Part 1 (1910); and A. O. J. Cockshut, *Anglican Attitudes* (1959). Pusey's remark to Keble on the subject of Dodsworth's dereliction is quoted in T. J. Williams, *Priscilla Lydia Sellon* (1950), p. 102.

8. In a letter of August 8, 1850, she requested William to find out for her "whether Mr. Collinson is as delicate as he used to be." By "delicate," she probably meant his inability to stay awake.

CHAPTER 3 (PAGES 43–61)

1. I have seen what remains of the 1854 journal, now uncatalogued in the Penkill Castle library, Ayrshire, Scotland. The binding is intact, but most of the pages have been torn out and a few, burned around the edges, indicate they were rescued from the flames. This journal and Scott's *Autobiographical Notes,*

ed. W. Minto, 2 vols. (1892) have been my chief sources for information about Scott's early life. I was shown the journal through the kindness of Miss Evelyn Courtney-Boyd, the present "laird," who gave me permission to use the unpublished Penkill MSS for the purpose of this biography. Some of the Penkill Papers were published by John Purves in "Dante Gabriel Rossetti: Letters to Miss Alice Boyd," *Fortnightly Review* (May, 1928), and others I published in "Christina Rossetti and Alice Boyd of Penkill Castle," *TLS* (June 26, 1959), p. 389.

2. This frequently reproduced passage from the *Notes* (I, 247–248) has given rise to some confusion about the dating of Scott's acquaintance with the Rossettis. He gives the date of his initial visit as "about Christmas, 1847–48," but admits elsewhere that "the particular powers of memory I do not possess are those that command dates. Dates being out of my power, I may therefore go back or forward a little in my record" (I, 327). Although occasionally, lacking other sources, I have been forced to rely upon Scott for dates, I have regarded such evidence as inconclusive. However, his assertion that he first met Christina in the winter of 1847–1848 is confirmed by William (*Remin.*, I, 59, 131; *DGRFL*, I, 19) and by Hunt, and may therefore be accepted.

3. She expressed the same idea in a letter written over thirty years later (July 20, 1880): "May I deserve remembrance when my day comes, and then remembered or forgotten, it will be well with me."

4. Frequently reproduced in anthologies, this highly regarded lyric has been praised for its compression and economy of expression. Therefore it is of interest to note that originally it consisted of five stanzas, of which the first three were deleted for publication. They are as follows:

*They told me that she would not live
But how could I believe their word?
Her cheeks were redder than a rose;
And smoother than a curd.

Her eyes were full of a deep light,
Steady, unmoved by hope and fear:
And though indeed her voice was low,
It was so sweet and clear.

But now that she is gone before,
I trust I too shall follow fast:
And so I sit and sing her song,
And muse upon the past.*

Bod. MS Don e 1/5, pp. 37–38.

5. H. P. Liddon, *The Life of Edward Bouverie Pusey*, 4 vols. (1893–1897), III, 13–18. Other works consulted in this chapter are the following: Peter F. Anson, *The Call of the Cloister* (1955); A. M. Allchin, *The Silent Rebellion* (1958); Thomas Jay Williams, *Priscilla Lydia Sellon* (1950), and "A Lost Treasure," *Holy Cross Magazine* (April, 1956), No. 4, 67:100–104. I am particularly indebted to the Rev. Allchin of St. Mary Abbots Church, London, who supplied me with additional information about the Anglican sisterhoods.

6. This sonnet is listed as unpublished in Appendix B to the *Works* (No. 38), but Miss G. M. Hatton found it in the American edition of *Maude* (Chicago, 1897), p. 67.

7. Violet Hunt writes in her *Wife of Rossetti* (1932), "Conscious that her value was deeply impaired by the illness which deprived her of her looks and half her

wits, Miss Norquoy offered to release Scott from his engagement but he gallantly refused" (p. xlv n.).

8. If the engagement had been broken in May or June, why would there have been a delayed reaction to a "staggering blow" of four to five months earlier? Prolonged grieving over a lost love cannot be described as a staggering blow.

CHAPTER 4 (PAGES 62–85)

1. This scriptural image appears with striking effect in Christina's *Convent Threshold.* See my text, p. 128.

2. According to Ford Madox Hueffer's [Ford's] account of his grandfather, Brown taught at the North London Drawing School only between the years 1850 and 1852. *Ford Madox Brown* (1896), p. 79 n.

3. *Notes,* I, 233, 332–333.

4. Mackenzie Bell, *Christina Rossetti* (1898), p. 33.

5. Three days later in *Moonshine* Christina returned to the theme of the 1847 *Repining.* In this ballad again the demon lover, offering love and joy, carries off the maiden, only to present her with death and decay.

6. Bod. MS Don e 76. The letter, dated Thursday, mentions that Gabriel is moving to No. 14 Chatham Place, Blackfriars, which he did Nov. 23, 1852.

7. William explains that it was because the vicar, Dr. Bennett, was obligated for the living of Frome to the Marchioness of Bath, and hence might have been thought willing to sponsor Mrs. Rossetti's school. The implication is that Aunt Charlotte was instrumental in obtaining the living for the High Church clergyman, who as a result of his Puseyite sympathies had "been ousted" from St. Barnabas, Pimlico, during the disturbances there. But it was not like Frances Rossetti to pull up stakes upon such flimsy prospects, which as it turned out, did not materialize.

8. This poem is unlisted in Appendix B. It appears in Bod. MS Don e 1/8, pp. 9–17. It should not be confused with the printed poem also called *Annie.* In his note to *A Harvest,* William observes that "the poem as it originally stood is . . . by no means a bad one" (*Works,* p. 470).

9. The first stanza of this poem (No. 54 in Appendix B) appears as part of a late poem dated "Before 1886" (*Works,* p. 133).

10. The death motif, however, is not absent. Young Love drowses "away to poppied death." Keatsian in both verbal texture and ideology, the last two stanzas recall the *Ode to a Nightingale* and the *Ode to a Grecian Urn.* In 1849 Christina wrote a poem, *On Keats,* in which she praised the earlier poet as "the strong man grown weary of a race / Soon over."

11. Cf. CGR's *Maiden Song* (see my text, pp. 168–169). In describing her three lovely maidens, she wrote:

> Sun-glow flushed their comely cheeks
> Wind-play tossed their hair,
> Creeping things among the grass
> Stroked them here and there.

12. In *The Face of the Deep* (1892), p. 406, Christina wrote, "Dante in the Divina Commedia (*see* my sister's *A Shadow of Dante*) tells us how he 'dreamed of a woman stammering, squinting, lame of foot, maimed of hands, and ashy pale. He gazed on her, and lo! under his gaze her form straightened, her face flushed, her tongue loosened to the Siren's song.' " The passage occurs in Canto 19 of the *Purgatorio.* We have here an interesting instance of the long life of a

figure belonging to literary tradition. The concept of the Loathely Lady, probably of very ancient origin, was not only treated by Dante but appears as well in several of the English ballads (*The Marriage of Sir Gawain* and *The Wedding of Sir Gawain and Dame Ragnell*), in Chaucer's "Wyfe of Bath's Tale," and in Gower's "Tale of Florent" in his *Confessio Amantis*—only to reappear in the nineteenth century in Christina's sonnet.

CHAPTER 5 (PAGES 86–107)

1. The ballad is *Cannot Sweeten*. See my text, p. 106.

2. *Notes,* I, 231. Janet Camp Troxell, *Three Rossettis, Unpublished Letters to and from Dante Gabriel, Christina, William* (1937), pp. 44–45. The story is confirmed by Helen Rossetti Angeli in *Dante Gabriel Rossetti* (1949), p. 155.

3. W. M. Rossetti, *Ruskin: Rossetti: Preraphaelitism: 1854–1862* (1899), p. 49.

4. Marya Zaturenska in *Christina Rossetti* (1949) twists Brown's observation into an unfavorable and even malicious comment upon Christina, writing, "Christina would then take out her knitting—she seemed forever 'working at worsted'—and survey this changeling from the slums [Lizzie] with her brilliant hazel eyes; and under their heavy lids the fires of repressed cruelty would glow and linger . . ." (p. 96).

5. In the first edition of *Time Flies* (Aunt Eliza's presentation copy), Christina wrote in the margin (p. 77), "Maria with Ruskin." This copy is at the University of Texas, Humanities Research Center.

6. Cf. the published verses:

> Like flowers sequestered from the sun
> And wind of summer, day by day
> I dwindled paler, whilst my hair
> Showed the first tinge of grey.
>
> 'Oh what is life, that we should live?
> Or what is death, that we must die?
> A bursting bubble is our life:
> I also, what am I?'

7. Letter to F. G. Stephens, Bod. MS Don e 76, p. 54.

8. In Christina's devotional prose work of 1883, *Letter and Spirit,* Eve is described as "that first and typical woman . . . indulging quite innocently sundry refined tastes and aspirations, a castle-building spirit (if so it may be called), a feminine boldness and directness of aim combined with a no less feminine guessiness as to means" (p. 17).

The *Spectator* review (Feb. 29, 1896), 76:309–310, was occasioned by the posthumous publication of Christina's *New Poems* (1896), the first collection of Christina's poetry edited by William and one containing poems she left unpublished in her lifetime. After allowing *A Triad* to appear in her 1862 *Goblin Market* volume, she withdrew it from publication, but William included it in the *New Poems,* explaining to Mackenzie Bell, "I don't remember having heard her make any express statement about her motives for burking *A Triad;* but am clear that they proceeded more or less on a notion that the sonnet might be misconstrued or unfavourably construed, from a moral point of view" (Mackenzie Bell, *Christina Rossetti* [1898], p. 213).

When critics promptly raised the question of whether or not he was justified in printing poems his sister had withdrawn from publication, he defended him-

self as follows: "I myself apprehend that (both in the case of my sister and of other writers) there may have been a variety of reasons why poems did not get published in their lifetime, which reasons do not continue to operate posthumously to any valid extent; and that the person who comes into possession of the poems of the deceased has a full right—amounting in some instances almost to a duty—to publish what he considers to be good enough for the purpose, and to be unexceptional on other grounds" (*Works* [1904], p. viii).

CHAPTER 6 (PAGES 108–126)

1. "Was" in the published text. It will be recalled that Scott's first name was William.

2. It was first published in *Once a Week* (Nov. 5, 1859) 1:381–382, and sixteen of the forty-three stanzas were reproduced. Later, when Christina reprinted the poem in the 1862 *Goblin Market* volume, she reduced the number of stanzas to twelve.

3. Laurence Binyon translation.

4. "We must conclude that nowhere round this whole Terrace is there any break in the flame-wreathe," wrote Maria in her *Shadow of Dante* (1871), p. 176; "wherefore no penitent Shade but must needs pass through it, whether tainted or not with the special sin chastised by sojourning within it." In the margin of the presentation copy to Mrs. Rossetti, which came to Christina at her mother's death, she wrote, "May it also possibly have to do with 'flesh and blood cannot inherit the kingdom of God'—we shall all be changed?" This copy is now in the library of Mr. and Mrs. Harold Rossetti.

5. Thomas Dixon, a Sunderland man, ran across *Leaves of Grass* in the stock of an itinerant bookseller from America. He sent a copy to Scott, who drew William's attention to it, and this was the beginning of Walt Whitman's reputation in England. At mid-century, when interest in working-class problems was nearing its peak, with novelists producing such works as *Alton Locke, Hard Times,* and *Mary Barton,* with Ruskin, Rossetti, and Maurice teaching at a night school for working men, and Scott instructing artisans in drawing at his Government School of Design in Newcastle, a man such as Dixon, a cork cutter by trade but an artistic dilettante by preference, was held up in the Rossetti circle as the ideal working man. It was he to whom Ruskin addressed his "Letters to a Working Man" in *Time and Tide.* Dixon himself admitted that he owed all the great blessings which had enriched his life to Scott. Among these cultural blessings he counted the poetry of Christina Rossetti, which he thought had been written by Maria.

6. The Sunderland *Verses* do not appear in the MS notebook. William lists the poem as No. 59 in Appendix B and dates it 1859. My conjectural date of 1858, based upon the pattern of events, is more likely to be accurate. The text may be found in Miss G. M. Hatton's unpublished dissertation, Bod. MS B. Litt. d. 491, Feb. 16, 1955, p. 99.

7. Cf. *Works,* p. 200:

> Parting after parting,
> Sore loss and gnawing pain:
> Meeting grows half a sorrow
> Because of parting again.
> When shall the day break
> That these things shall not be?
> When shall new earth be ours

Without a sea,
And time that is not time
But eternity?

See also William's note, *ibid.*, p. 473.

8. *Up-hill* and part of *At Home* are in William's writing, Ash. MS 1364, notebook 2, pp. 61–62. The reason appears in William's note appended to the holograph MS of *Up-hill,* now in the Huntington Library: "Christina Rossetti, from the time when she first began writing verses, was in the habit of transcribing them into little notebooks, giving the date of composition. The leaf wh. contains 'Up-hill' (along with the conclusion of 'At Home') comes out of one of these note-books. It was purchased from me, soon after Christina's death, by Mr. F. H. Evans. . . ." Lttr. of May 11, 1895, H. L. MSS 6066 and 6067.

But, according to a letter William wrote to Thomas Wise on May 6, 1895 (Univ. of Texas Collection), he did not cut out the leaf containing *Up-hill* (though Evans had already purchased it) until, at Evans' request, he had first shown the manuscript notebook to Wise. Protesting that he by no means wished to sell the notebook ("it is interesting to myself, and may be of practical service hereafter"), William nevertheless mentioned the matter to Wise, in case the latter should wish to take "any definite steps." Apparently Wise did not care to do anything at the time, although later he acquired a number of the notebooks now in the Ashley Library. Unfortunately, notebook 2 remains mutilated and bereft of one of Christina's most important poems.

9. Cf. the lines in *Look on This Picture:*

*If you were dead I verily believe that you would haunt
The home you loved, the man you loved, you said you loved—avaunt.*

10. In the published version the third line reads, "Earth has waited weeks and weeks," and the concluding two lines of the first stanza are as follows:

Faint the rainbow comes and goes
On a sunny shower.

Since the revision in no way improves the poem, we may assume that once again Christina wished to tone down and modify a personal utterance.

CHAPTER 7 (PAGES 127–152)

1. "Joy" in revised version.

2. An example of the uncritical acceptance of prevailing assumptions is Thomas Burnett Swann's assertion that Christina's "most famous love poem to Cayley is 'A Birthday,'" written in 1857. (*Wonder and Whimsey, the Fantastic World of Christina Rossetti* [1960], p. 38.

3. Fredegond Shove devotes more space than other critics to a discussion of this poem, but shows not much more insight into its structure and meaning. She thinks that the martyred woman symbolizes the Christian Church, "the narrator, the poetess herself," and "the 'pleasure-place' . . . her ideal of the fair and happy life which for so many reasons had to be relinquished . . ." (*Christina Rossetti* [1931], p. 68).

4. In MS "palace" is crossed out and "mansion" written above it. "Castle" was substituted in the final revision.

5. The printed version reads "flames of fire."

6. "Banishment" in the printed text.

7. The text: "Incomparably pale, and almost fair."

8. Cf. the Authorized Version: "To appoint unto them that mourn in Zion, to give unto them beauty for ashes, the oil of joy for mourning, the garment of praise for the spirit of heaviness. . . ." Christina quotes this passage in *The Face of the Deep,* p. 361.

9. The first and third lines of each stanza are unrhymed in the original MS. It was Gabriel who "fitted the double rhymes as printed, with a brotherly request that I would use them," Christina wrote in her notebook. She thought it greatly improved the piece.

10. Much of the material on *Goblin Market* appeared in my article, "Symbol and Reality in Christina Rossetti's *Goblin Market*" in *PMLA* (Sept., 1958), No. 4, 73:375–386.

11. In 1893 she told Gosse that ". . . in my own intention Goblin Market was no allegory at all, so it does not surprise me that it is inexplicable in detail." Brit. Mus., Ash. MS B 1366. See my text, p. 198.

12. "The Sources of Christina Rossetti's 'Goblin Market,'" *Modern Language Review* (April, 1933), No. 2, 28:157–158.

13. Several months earlier Christina gave William a complete report of activities at the Regent's Park Zoological Garden: "Lizards are in strong force, tortoises active, alligators looking up. The weasel-headed armadillo as usual evaded us. A tree-frog came to light. . . . The blind wombat and neighbouring porcupine broke forth into short-lived hostilities, but apparently without permanent results. The young puma begins to bite" (*Fam. Lttrs.,* pp. 25–26).

14. *The Romantic Imagination,* p. 263. The poem referred to is *Twice.* See my text, pp. 181–183.

15. Ellen A. Proctor, *A Brief Memoir of Christina Georgina Rossetti* (London, 1895).

16. Cf. *A Better Resurrection;* see above, pp. 110–111.

17. We cannot suppose that the actual writing of *Goblin Market* was a lengthy process, for upon more than one occasion William has assured us that his sister's "habits of composition were eminently of the spontaneous kind," that she seldom meditated or deliberated before writing a poem, but on the contrary, after "something impelled her feeling or 'came into her head' she wrote rapidly, easily, and without hesitation almost as though her hand obeyed dictation" (*Works,* pp. lxviii–lxix; *New Poems,* ed. W. M. Rossetti [1896], pp. xii–xiii). And of all her long poems *Goblin Market* strikes the reader as the one most likely to have been produced in the mood of direct inspiration. I take it that she wrote the poem out as a whole first, and later made whatever revisions and alterations she deemed necessary. It would not have been impossible for a poet with her working habits to have turned out the approximately 550 lines within a week or so.

It is of course impossible to know whether the poem was written out first and then copied or whether Christina wrote it exactly as it appears in the Dennis notebook (March 21, 1859, to Dec. 31, 1860, pp. 3–38). The manuscript shows some revision, chiefly of diction, but not a great deal. In almost every instance the revisions improve the text. For example, in describing her merchant men Christina substitutes some other epithet for the original *quaint:* "Brother with <quaint> queer brother," and "Of <quaint> brisk fruit-merchant men." The most radical change occurs in the following lines, which read in MS:

*Lizzie hid her eyes with hands
That showed like curds of cream.
Laura reared her glossy head
And spoke like music of the stream,*

and in print,

Lizzie covered up her eyes,
Covered close lest they should look;
Laura reared her glossy head,
And whispered like the restless brook.

18. Zaturenska (pp. 59–60) and Sawtell (pp. 54–55) are the writers in question. For a refutation of Violet Hunt's allegation, see Helen Rossetti Angeli, *Dante Gabriel Rossetti* (1949), pp. 6 n. and 272.

19. *Rossetti-Macmillan Letters,* Lttr. 108 (dated Sat. morning [1875]). The other two poems Christina did not want reprinted were *A Triad* and *Cousin Kate.*

CHAPTER 8 (PAGES 153–172)

1. Gabriel's picture *Found* and Hunt's *Awakened Conscience* also deal with the subject. Scott's poem *Rosabel* (see my text, p. 45) is an earlier treatment. The subject, in fact, was one of those taken from "modern life," which Ruskin recommended to the painters.

2. One has only to compare the conception of the young girl in *Iniquity* to Dickens' "Little Em'ly" or Mrs. Gaskell's Ruth in order to appreciate the unconventionality of Christina's treatment.

3. A. M. Allchin, *The Silent Rebellion* (1958), p. 70. From Canon Burrows we learn that "one of the earliest institutions referred to in our old records has now vanished from the neighborhood. It was a house of refuge for fallen women maintained for several years in Camden Street and visited by one of the curates of Christ Church. I see it was started in 1852 by a contribution of £100 from the Church Penitentiary Association, but as I do not remember that it was ever helped through Christ Church funds, I think it must have been maintained at the expense, or through the exertions, of the Honorable Mrs. Chambers, the lady who superintended it. Probably it was removed when Mrs. Chambers left the neighborhood. What help we used afterwards to render to this cause was chiefly in connection with the Diocesan Penitentiary, St. Mary's, Highgate . . ." (*Half-Century of Christ Church, Albany Street* [1887], pp. 36–37).

At one time Maria belonged to Mrs. Chambers' Young Women's Friendly Society, which attempted to provide recreation and religious instruction for servant girls on their Sunday afternoons off. This was probably the indirect route through which Christina eventually found her way up to Highgate Hill.

4. *Letters of Alexander Macmillan,* ed. George A. Macmillan (1908), pp. 94–95.

5. The first two stanzas (published) of *John* are missing in MS. Pages 66–69 of the Dennis notebook are torn out, and the poem begins on the bottom half of p. 69. The preceding poem, of which part likewise is missing, is *The Noble Sisters,* which Christina lists in her table of contents as starting on p. 64. *John* is listed for pages 69–70.

John raises some perplexing problems. When some years later Gabriel objected to the inclusion of the poem in Christina's first collected edition because its tone appeared "utterly foreign" to her "primary impulses," she replied that, since "no such person existed or exists, I hope my indiscretion may be accounted the less." Yet William was certain that John "was not absolutely mythical," for after his sister's death, he discovered a pencil jotting to the effect that the "original John was obnoxious because he never gave scope for 'No thank you!' " He considered the original to be the marine painter John Brett, who in 1852 was "smitten" with Christina. But eight years is a long time for a woman to remember with immediate vividness the unwelcome advances of a suitor to whom she

is indifferent. Difficult as it is to reconcile Christina's conflicting statements, if we assume that in 1860 she had Cayley in mind instead of Brett, her reply to Gabriel that there was no such person as John would not swerve too far away from the truth.

6. Sir Edmund Gosse, *Algernon Charles Swinburne* (1917), pp. 134–137.

7. Edith Sitwell, *English Women* (1942), p. 41.

8. Bissell MS.

9. Grace Gilchrist, "Christina Rossetti," *Good Words* (1896), 37:822–826; William Sharp, "Some Reminiscences of Christina Rossetti," *Atlantic Monthly* (June, 1895), 75:736–749; Thomas G. Hake and Arthur Compton-Rickett, *Life and Letters of Theodore Watts-Dunton,* 2 vols. (1916), II, 42.

10. Trans. Charles Speroni. The Italian original may be found in the *Works,* pp. 447–453.

11. The evidence seems somewhat conflicting. A letter from Gabriel of December 28 (University of Texas Collection) establishes the fact that he was back in London by New Year's. Although Scott speaks of walking with Swinburne "by the much-resounding sea" at Tynemouth during the holiday season of 1862, Swinburne was at Wallington Hall with the Trevelyans between Christmas and New Year's. See Scott's *Notes,* II, 68–69, and Lang, *The Swinburne Letters,* 6 vols. (1959–1961), Vol. I, pp. 65–69.

12. *Rossetti-Macmillan Letters,* Lttr. 2 (July 2, 1863).

13. Cf. *Convent Threshold:*

> Cold dews had drenched my hair
> Through clay; you came to seek me there.

CHAPTER 9 (PAGES 173–191)

1. *Extracts from G. P. Boyce's Diaries, 1851–1875.* In the Old Water-colour Society's Club 19th Ann. Vol. (1941). Lttr. from William Rossetti to F. G. Stephens, Bod. MS Don e 76. The date is marked in pencil, 4/4/64.

2. The lines in MS have an altogether different rhythm from those in the printed version, owing to punctuation. In the first two lines the printed variant has a series of commas separating the repeated "to-days," and in the last line a comma similarly separates the repetition of "my love." The sense of breathless spontaneity is checked by carefully punctuating the series, and the emotion thereby conventionalized.

3. This and the following three letters appear as Letters 6, 10–12 in the *Rossetti-Macmillan Letters* (1963).

4. The revised version of *Parting After Parting* was first published in *Time Flies* under the May 30 dateline (p. 102), and *Meeting* in its shortened and altered form under the August 10 dateline (p. 153). They were not joined. They first appeared as a linked poem in Christina's 1890 *Verses.*

5. Bowra, *The Romantic Imagination,* p. 263. See my text, p. 181, and ch. 7, n. 14.

6. This poem forms the second part of the linked group, *Twilight Night,* started in 1863. It was originally written as a lyric in *Songs in a Cornfield.* But, in preparing her 1866 *Prince's Progress* for publication, Christina acted upon Gabriel's advice and took it out of *Cornfield,* substituting another lyric in its place. This one she joined to *Twilight Night,* first published posthumously in the *New Poems* (1896).

7. "Our Camp in the Woodland: A Day with the Gentle Poets," *Fraser's* (Aug., 1864), 70:204–214. The article is signed "A Campaigner at Home."

8. *Correspondence of Gerard Manley Hopkins and Richard Watson Dixon,* ed. Claude Colleer Abbott (1935), pp. 62, 77; *Notebooks and Papers,* ed. Humphrey House (1937), p. 246; *Further Letters of Gerard Manley Hopkins,* ed. C. C. Abbott (1938), p. 67. Austin Warren, discussing Hopkins in *The Kenyon Critics* (1945), says that Hopkins "felt the influence of Christina Rossetti and the male P.R.B.s at Oxford" (p. 9).

9. This poem, which has the familiar structural pattern of a group of women singing together about love, shows various changes. For a lyric with personal relevance (see above, n. 6) Christina substituted the relatively innocuous "swallow song" which appears in the printed text, a lyric similar to Tennyson's *O Swallow, Swallow* in *The Princess* and perhaps derived from it. She also changed the names of two of her feminine singers. The new names are Lettice and Rachel. The resemblance of the first to Letitia Scott's name should be noted. As for the second, Christina tells us in *Letter and Spirit* that Rachel "stands for our picture of the triumphant wife, whose sway over her husband's heart is legitimate and supreme . . . ," whereas "Leah, 'hated,' secondary, ever haunted . . . and ever humiliated by the fraud to which she owed her position, yet . . . loving her alienated husband . . . represents another and not rare class of wives," a class to which presumably Mrs. Scott belonged. Another time, in writing about Dante, Christina equated the loved Rachel with Beatrice and the unloved Gemma Donati, Dante's wife, with the equally unloved Leah. What all this suggests is that a third and still deeper level of comparison lurked beneath her several discussions of the loves of Jacob and Dante.

CHAPTER 10 (PAGES 192–216)

1. Samuel Lucas was editor of *Once a Week* until 1865, at which time he was succeeded by Edward Walford. For further information see William E. Buckler, " 'Once a Week' under Samuel Lucas, 1855–65," *PMLA* (Dec., 1952), No. 7, 67: 924–41.

The "opportune *Times* notice" was in the critical article, "Modern Poets," *Times* (Jan. 11, 1865), p. 12, col. 5. After discussing Browning, Tennyson, and Patmore, the writer turns to "the young rising brood of poets," of whom the two chief representatives are Jean Ingelow—"She is apt to be vague, and has not yet learned to be brief"—and Christina, whose work is "simpler, firmer, and deeper."

Among the unpublished sources used in this chapter are the Stephens Papers at the Bodleian, Don e 76. Published works are the *Rossetti-Macmillan Letters;* the *Ross. Pprs.;* Janet C. Troxell, *The Three Rossettis* (1937); Georgina Burne-Jones, *Memorials of Edward Burne-Jones,* 2 vols. (1912); Herbert H. Gilchrist, *Anne Gilchrist, Her Life and Writings* (1887) (see below, n. 13); and George Birbeck Hill, ed., *Letters of Dante Gabriel Rossetti to William Allingham, 1854–1870* (1897).

2. The text has "One's heart's too small . . ."

3. Gabriel frequently complained of Scott's inertia. *DGRFL,* II, 102, 103, 104, 197, *et passim.*

4. Lttr. of June 1, 1893, Brit. Mus., Ash. MS B 1366, p. 2. See above, ch. 7, n. 11.

5. When Gabriel objected to the modifier "hairy," Christina replied, *"Hairy* I cannot feel inclined to forego, as it portrays the bud in question." *Ross. Pprs.,* p. 88. She was an unusually close observer of detail in nature. R. D. Waller (*The Rossetti Family, 1824–54* [1932], pp. 165–166) and Dorothy M. Stuart (*Christina Rossetti* [1930], pp. 41–42) hold the contrary view: that she had little knowledge of nature and wrote about it in general terms.

6. The printed version reads,

The warm south wind would have awaked
To melt the snow,

a more conventional and less individually robust expression of the thought.

7. "1st, a prelude and outset; 2nd, an alluring milkmaid; 3rd, a trial of barren boredom; 4th, the social element again; 5th, barren boredom in a more uncompromising form; 6th, a wind-up and conclusion." *Ross. Pprs.*, p. 78. The reader may notice that my own analysis of the poem's structure differs somewhat. The design is more coherent and logically executed than CGR's brief summary would indicate.

8. DGR probably had in mind stanza 14:

And for them many a weary hand did swelt
In torched mines and noisy factories,
And many once-proud-quivered loins did melt
In blood from stinging whips. . . .

9. No. II of *Spring Fancies* (the second poem under that title) included parts of *Today and Tomorrow*. No. I was the 1847 *Spring Quiet* revised along the lines indicated in CGR's letter. It appeared as follows in *Macmillan's Magazine* (Apr., 1865), No. 66, 11:460:

Gone but were the winter,
Come were but the spring,
I would go to a covert
Where the birds sing
(Ding-ding, ding-a-ding).

Where in the whitethorn
Singeth the thrush,
And the robin sings
In a holly bush
(With his breast ablush).

Full of fresh scents
Are the budding boughs.
Arching high over
A cool green house
(Where doves coo the arouse).

There the sun shineth
Most shadily;
There sounds an echo
Of the far sea
Though far off it be.

10. This and the two following letters to Macmillan appear in the *Rossetti-Macmillan Letters* as Lttr. 41 (March 30, 1865) and Lttrs. 43 and 45.

11. Janet C. Troxell, *op. cit.*, p. 146.

12. For information about the firm, see the *Rossetti-Macmillan Letters,* Lttr. 53, n. 2.

13. Mrs. Troxell (p. 155) dates this letter to Mrs. Gilchrist (of which I have

given only the relevant excerpt) as 1869, thus reproducing the original error in Herbert Gilchrist's biography of his mother. The letter was written in 1866. I first questioned the accuracy of the dating because the letter is headed 166 Albany Street and the Rossettis moved from there to 56 Euston Square in the summer of 1867, and next, because Christina closes with a reference to William's expected arrival in Naples: "For all we know William may to-day have reached Naples, but we cannot calculate his movements with certainty" (Troxell, p. 157). According to William's diary, partially published in the *Ross. Pprs.* (pp. 187–191, 395–400), he traveled to Naples in June, 1866, but was in London all through June, 1869.

Some time after I had straightened out the date to my satisfaction, I happened upon Herbert Gilchrist's presentation copy of the *Life* of his mother to William in Mrs. Lucy Rossetti O'Connor's library. On p. 175 Gilchrist publishes an excerpt from another letter Christina wrote to his mother from Penkill during the summer of 1866, in which she again refers to William's visit to Naples. This letter Gilchrist dates 1869. William has underlined the sentence, "The home budget informs me that William is at home again, fresh from all the glories and beauties of most beautiful Naples," and has written in the margin, "I was in Naples / 66—The reference date of this letter must be wrong." In the same letter Gilchrist makes another error. Christina wrote, "I hope you know that my laggard book is out at last." Gilchrist identifies the work as *Commonplace,* which was not published until May, 1870. The "laggard book" of course is *Prince's Progress,* published in June, 1866, when Christina was at Penkill.

CHAPTER 11 (PAGES 217–236)

1. In the lines,

> The green snake hid her coil
> Where grass grew thickest, bird and beast
> Sought shadows as they could,

a period was inserted after *coil,* changing both the rhythm and the meaning. Gabriel proposed deleting the period after *coil* and placing it after *thickest* instead; but in a letter to Anne Gilchrist, requesting her to correct the mispunctuation in her printed copy, Christina wrote, "There should be no stop whatever after *coil* ('The green snake hid her coil') but a colon after *thickest* in the next line" (*Anne Gilchrist,* p. 160). However, a semicolon appears in the first collected edition of Christina's poetry (1875) and in the *Works* (p. 370). But see my article, "Christina Rossetti's *Songs in a Cornfield:* A Misprint Uncorrected," *N&Q* (March, 1962), n.s. 9:97–100.

2. *Sat. Review* (June 23, 1866), 22:761–62; *Athenæum* (June 23, 1866), p. 825.

3. He lists it as No. 60 in Appendix B.

4. In Aunt Eliza's annotated first edition, Christina underlined "friend's castle" and wrote in the margin, "Alice Boyd of Penkill" (p. 61). She also identified the succeeding incident as having taken place at Penkill (p. 62).

5. Christina protested that Hall Caine completely misunderstood the purport of her foreword. In reviewing the *Pageant* volume in *The Academy* (Aug. 27, 1881), No. 486, p. 152, he wrote:

> Surely it is a mistake to think that even 'occasional' poetry that is cheerful and hopeful must, by virtue of these subjective qualities be drawn merely from fancy; or that the poetry of which sadness is the governing constituent must of necessity be drawn from feeling. The brighter side of life has its appeal for the

imagination and its profound response in the affections, though it is true that unhappiness calls the utmost powers and passions into play. It may be doubtful whether Miss Rossetti is right in saying that, if the great poetess of our own day and nation had been unhappy instead of happy, she would have bequeathed to us, in lieu of the 'Portuguese Sonnets', a 'donna innominata' more worthy to occupy a niche beside Beatrice and Laura.

"Surely not only what I mean to say but what I do say," Christina insisted in a letter of Sept. 5, 1881, to Gabriel, "is, not that the Lady of those sonnets is surpassable, but that a 'donna innominata' by the same hand might well have been unsurpassable. The Lady in question, as she actually stands, I was not regarding as an 'innominata' at all,—because the latter type, according to the traditional figures I had in view, is surrounded by unlike circumstances" (*Fam. Lttrs.*, p. 98).

6. See above, pp. 28–29, and chap. 2, n. 1. Space forbids a detailed discussion of each sonnet in the series. Not all have biographical relevance. I have omitted a few because they are similar to those discussed, and one, the eighth, because as a dramatization of the Biblical Queen Esther story its relation to the sequence is slight. The tenth, thirteenth, and fourteenth are mentioned in connection with the 1870 poems, with which I believe they have more in common than with the earlier sonnets in the series. See below, pp. 257–258.

7. Cockerell MS.

CHAPTER 12 (PAGES 237–258)

1. In 1856 Brown noted in his diary, "CR called; she is reading Carlyle with her mother" (F. M. [Ford] Hueffer, *Ford Madox Brown* [1896], p. 131). The MS of *Il Rosseggiar dell' Oriente* is in the British Museum, Ash. MS 1367. See above, chap. 8, n. 10.

2. Lewis Carroll, who was responsible for the many photographs of the Rossettis and their friends taken in the Cheyne Walk garden.

3. The reference to the birth of a new life recalls *Birthday*. Although the 1857 lyric is an expression of purely ecstatic joy, Christina's elation was short-lived and was soon jostled off the scene by the "tears" and "shouts" of grief which followed her renunciation of love. But the birth into the new life may also be read as a dedication to the religious life, a sequel to the renunciation, and perhaps its cause.

4. It is also the title of a well-known sonnet in Gabriel Rossetti's *House of Life*.

5. Cf.:

> Come to me in the silence of the night;
> Come in the speaking silence of a dream;
> Come with soft rounded cheeks and eyes as bright . . .

6. For an account of this matter of the loan, which became highly controversial after Miss Losh's death, see Janet C. Troxell, *The Three Rossettis* (1937), pp. 80–108, and Mrs. Angeli's *Dante Gabriel Rossetti* (1949), pp. 153–155. In the Ashley Library there is a letter from Scott to Gabriel, dated Monday, Oct. 17, probably written in 1881 (for in it Scott acknowledges the presentation copy of Gabriel's *Ballads and Sonnets*, published that year). Scott writes, "Did I ever tell you the ending of the story of dear old Miss Losh and her friendship for you? Mrs. Pennell [Miss Losh's niece and executrix] found your sundry acknowledgments of money and asked Alice what she should do with them. Our dear friend said the thing took her by surprise but advised her to put them in the fire. This

between you and I, remember. She told me, but does not know I have told or am now telling you, so by no means [mention this] circumstance, and put this in the fire." Brit. Mus., Ash. MS 1482, pp. 33–34.

7. For a discussion of *Speaking Likenesses,* see "Not All Roses in the Victorian Nursery," *TLS* (May 29, 1959), p. xi, and my comment (June 5, 1959), p. 337. The writer of "Not All Roses . . ." describes *Speaking Likenesses* as "a surrealistic fantasy" with "a resolutely didactic purpose," and detects in it a ruthless exposition of "sex-war . . . with its bickering and jealousy." The chief rival who spoils the little heroine's birthday feast is the sinister Birthday Queen. When we recall that Christina's 1863 *Queen of Hearts* was originally called *Flora,* the name of the heroine in the 1874 *Speaking Likenesses,* and that it was she who trumped all the aces in the card game, it seems obvious that not only the Porcupine-Engraver but also the successful Birthday Queen had their originals in life. The birthday symbolism and the feast imagery need no explanation. See also p. 187, above.

8.

> The modest simplicity of the gift
> Will tell you how grateful I am to you.

9. I have no way of knowing whether this sestet was originally written for the *Remembrance* or the *Monna* sonnet. On the basis of internal evidence I would say the latter. The same use of personification, the same tone of subdued weariness and gray resignation occur in the octave of the *Monna* sonnet.

> Time flies, hope flags, life plies a wearied wing;
> Death following hard on life gains ground apace,

is the way the tenth *Monna* sonnet begins, quite different from the energetic elation with which the *Remembrance* sonnet commences. The phrase "Time flies" later became the title of Christina's devotional work published in 1885.

CHAPTER 13 (PAGES 259–272)

1. *Tinsley's Magazine* (Aug.–Oct., 1869), 5:59–69 (Christina); 142–151 (Gabriel); 276–281 (William).

2. For a lively and informed biography of this colorful and ingratiating adventure, see Helen Rossetti Angeli, *The Pre-Raphaelite Twilight* (1954). The large collection of Gabriel's letters to Howell at the University of Texas supplements this work.

3. During this visit Gabriel, restless and uneasy, longed for additional company. "But why don't you come?" he demanded of Miss Losh with a touch of hysterical impatience, and he insisted that Brown *"must* come instantly on receipt of this." Ignoring the succession of Gabriel's frantic pleas, Brown told his daughter Lucy that finally Rossetti had left off writing him "elaborately worked-out itineraries to Penkill Castle, followed by exhortations not to be a sneak but to start at once" (Janet C. Troxell, *The Three Rossettis* [1937], p. 89; *Ross. Pprs.,* pp. 453, 464).

4. This poem is listed as unpublished in the Penkill Library Catalogue (A9). However, with Miss Evelyn Courtney-Boyd's permission, I published the first and last stanzas in a special article in *TLS* (June 26, 1959), p. 389.

5. Letter from William to Lucy Rossetti, Aug. 8, 1877. Bod. Ross. MS 39.

6. For an account of Howell's part in the exhumation, see Troxell, *op. cit.,* pp. 108 ff.

7. Pnkll. MS, unlisted.

8. In Scott's poem *Sunday Morning Alone,* the flower symbolizes the relieving of sensual desire:

> Here where black earth bears heartsease, human eyes
> Converse, and passions cling with burning lips
> Dying together.

Poems by a Painter (1854), p. 70.

9. In the printed version "love" is changed to "joy" in the second line and to "hope' in the seventh.

10. "A Safe Investment" was written before 1865. The original in the Huntington Library (H.L. MS 6079) is inscribed in the author's hand, "Miss C. G. Rossetti. 45, Upper Albany Street, London, N.W." Although the residence remained the same, the address was changed toward the end of 1864 to 166 Albany Street. The last of Christina's letters with the Upper Albany Street heading appears in November, 1864. Beginning in the spring of 1865 both her letters and William's are headed 166 Albany Street.

CHAPTER 14 (PAGES 273–295)

1. Add. MS 41,130, p. 169. I have drawn upon this source for others of Christina's letters to Ellis quoted in this chapter and hereafter, supplementing it with Oswald Doughty's *Letters of Dante Gabriel Rossetti to His Publisher* (1928), derived from the same collection at the British Museum. See *Rossetti-Macmillan Letters,* Lttrs. 68–91, and *WHR* (Summer, 1962), No. 3, 16:243–253.

2. Bod. Ross. MS 22.

3. Pnkll. MS A 10. Alice Boyd's illustrations to *Sing-Song* are still extant and preserved in the Penkill library.

4. Bod. MS Don e 76, pp. 132–134. Letter from Christina Rossetti to Kate Howell; Humanities Research Center, University of Texas.

5. Evan Charteris, *The Life and Letters of Sir Edmund Gosse* (1931), p. 36.

6. Letters to D. G. Rossetti from T. S. Hake, December 9, 1871, and from Arthur Hughes, n.d., at the Humanities Research Center, University of Texas.

7. Alice discovered after her brother's death in 1864 that he had mortgaged Penkill. She was unable to meet the payments in 1871 because an ironwork in which she had a large investment went bankrupt and water came into the pit of the Tyne Main coal mine, of which she was a principal owner.

8. For an impartial account of the Rossetti-Buchanan feud, see John A. Cassidy, "Robert Buchanan and the Fleshly Controversy," *PMLA* (March, 1952), No. 2, 67:65–94.

9. Oswald Doughty, *A Victorian Romantic* (1960 ed.), p. 508.

10. Dated "B. 1882" but written in or before 1877. See *Fam. Lttrs.,* p. 66.

CHAPTER 15 (PAGES 296–314)

1. See above, chap. 8, n. 3.

2. Lttr. of Sept. 16, 1873, Bod. Ross. MS 22. Excerpts from Maria's letters to Gabriel are derived from Bod. Ross. MSS 33, 34.

3. Some of the letters to Macmillan reproduced in this section (305–306) were published in part by me in *TLS* (June 5, 1959). For the others see *The Rossetti-*

Macmillan Letters, Lttrs. 92–95, 97, 99 and n. 1. See also chap. 12, n. 7, of the present work.

4. But we have seen that she had a number of unpublished poems on hand, many of them too personal to be given to the world during her lifetime.

5. *Letters of Alexander Macmillan,* ed. George A. Macmillan (Edinburgh, 1908), p. 287.

6. Lttr. tentatively dated Nov. 26, 1876, Bod. Ross. MS 39.

7. *Examiner,* Dec. 2, 1876, no. 3592, p. 1354. Brit. Mus., Ash. MS 1436, IV, pp. 161–162. Bod. Ross. MS 39.

8. The poem is called *Cried Out with Tears.* The other two poems quoted in the remainder of the chapter are *Escape to the Mountain* and *Wrestling* (see above, p. 306).

CHAPTER 16 (PAGES 315–334)

1. "Miss Rossetti in her new volume (I have not seen it but I read this poem in the *Athenæum*) has a piece called 'Symbols of Life and Death,' I think, in which is quite a parallel line, 'Scarlet and golden and blue': you should see this lovely poem" (*Correspondence of . . . Hopkins and . . . Dixon,* ed. Claude C. Abbott [1935], p. 62). In another letter Hopkins quotes what he calls a "noble passage" from the same poem (*op. cit.,* p. 77). See above, chap. 9, n. 8.

2. Lttr. from Christina to Gabriel marked Tuesday, tentatively dated March 12, 1877. Brit. Mus., Ash. MS 1386, pp. 1–2; *Fam. Lttrs.,* p. 66.

3. Watts-Dunton's account of Christina may be found in his *Old Familiar Faces* (1916), pp. 177–207, and Thomas G. Hake's and Arthur Compton-Rickett's ed. of his *Life and Letters,* 2 vols. (1916), Vol. II, pp. 31–50. Material for the 1877 period is drawn from the Bod. Ross. MS 39, which includes Brown's letters of August to Lucy, and Christina's and Frances Rossetti's letters of Aug. and Sept., 1877, to William.

4. Hall Caine, *Recollections of Dante Gabriel Rossetti* (1882), pp. 146–166.

5. Bell, *Christina Georgina Rossetti* (1898), p. 68. A number of Christina's published letters quoted in the remaining chapters are derived from this source and the *Fam. Lttrs.*

6. "With an eye to its future I have concocted a *priceless Singsong* with marginal additions," Christina wrote William (*Fam. Lttrs.,* p. 167). "Indeed, I advise you not to disperse my library to the four winds without careful inspection of copies, lest you should squander unsuspected treasures here and there." After her death, William took possession of the "priceless" *Sing-Song* and refused to part with it "for any level of price." Upon his death it came to his daughter Signora Agresti, and when she died to her niece, Mrs. Lucy Rossetti O'Connor of Cheshire, to whom it now belongs.

7. Pnkll. MS, unlisted. Pub. by me in *TLS,* June 26, 1959, p. 389.

8. Before the volume was published, she sold Charles Fairfax Murray the printer's copy for £10. Her receipt, dated Aug. 23, 1879, is in the Murray Collection at the University of Texas.

9. Harold Ross. MS.

10. The sonnet was published in the *Pageant* volume in 1881. Although the original autograph volume is at the University of Texas, the holograph manuscript of *Later Life 9* and the other sonnets in the series is in the Huntington Library Collection (H.L. MS 6076). Originally called "One Star Differeth from Another Star," the sonnet shows few alterations and those chiefly in minor points of diction. I have reproduced the printed version in my text, in my opinion an improvement over the original.

CHAPTER 17 (PAGES 335–351)

1. Extracts from the diary have been published in the *Fam. Lttrs.*, App. 2, pp. 222 ff. However, Mrs. Helen Rossetti Angeli lent me the complete diary for the years 1881–1882; through her kindness I was therefore able to make use of the unpublished parts as well.

2. In a letter to Gabriel dated Thursday afternoon only, Christina wrote that she had said yes to Waddington's feeler for seven sonnets. She listed them as *After Death, A Dream, If Only, Autumn Violets, Rest, The World,* and *After Communion.* Humanities Research Center, University of Texas.

3. Bod. Ross. MS 47. Other sources contributing to this chapter are the *Rossetti-Macmillan Letters;* Bod. Ross. MSS 19 and 40; and Brit. Mus., Ash. MS 1482, containing Scott's correspondence.

4. Brit. Mus., Ash. MS 1363, pp. 2–3.

5. *Rossetti-Macmillan Letters,* Lttrs. 129 and n. and 130. For a further account of Macmillan's championship of copyright reform see my text, p. 356, and *Rossetti-Macmillan Letters,* Lttr. 101, n. 1.

6. The phrase "screaming and dancing," which appears in Bod. Ross. MS 19, was deleted from the letter published in *DGRFL,* Vol. II, p. 386. Gabriel was unstinting in his praise of Christina's work with the sonnet form. "Besides the unsurpassed quality . . . of her best sonnets," he told Hall Caine, "my sister has proved her poetic importance by solid and noble inventive work of many kinds, which I should be proud indeed to reckon among my life's claims" (Caine, *Recollections* [1882], p. 241). Another time he said, "I certainly think there must be 20 living writers (male and female—my sister a leader, I consider) who have written good sonnets . . ." (p. 243).

7. I am indebted to Mr. E. E. Bissell of Warwick for providing this information. He owns the dedication copy (from Christina to her mother; later, upon Mrs. Rossetti's death, a part of her own library), upon which she wrote out Scott's poem, with the reference to dried rose leaves and her own poem.

8. William, quoting Scott, gives the date as Nov. 21, but elsewhere he criticizes Scott's lack of accuracy about dates.

9. Doughty believes that Christina's appeal was a discreet reference to Lucy. *A Victorian Romantic,* p. 661.

10. Gabriel's last will, among the Rossetti papers on loan to the Bodleian, is dated April 8, 1882.

CHAPTER 18 (PAGES 352–370)

1. Sharp, "Some Reminiscences . . . ," *Atlantic Monthly* (June, 1885), 75:736–749. Additional sources for this chapter are Angeli MS; Pnkll. MSS; Bod. Ross. MSS 22, 40, 42, 44; Ash. MSS 1482, 1386, XA 4385, B II 1384; Add. MS 41,130; Penn. Hist. Soc., Gratz MS; Heimann Corr.; H.L. MS 11228; and *Rossetti-Macmillan Letters.*

2. For a detailed treatment of Christina's friendship with Swinburne, see my article, "Swinburne and Christina Rossetti: Atheist and Anglican," *Univ. of Toronto Quarterly* (Oct., 1963).

3. Bell (*Christina Georgina Rossetti* [1898], p. 171) identifies the "certain occupation" as Christina's contribution to William's edition of Gabriel's correspondence.

4. "Speaking to Ingram the other day," William wrote Anne Gilchrist, who

wrote the life of Mary Lamb for the series, "I found him likewise more than pleased with your book. He says too that you gave him no trouble—being herein exceptional among his lady-contributors" (Paull F. Baum and Clarence Gohdes, *Letters of William Michael Rossetti . . . to Anne Gilchrist* [1934]), p. 143. Ingram's letter to William in my text is dated Dec. 18, 1885, and may be found in Bod. Ross. MS 44, pp. 2–3.

5. For Christina's theory of biography I have drawn upon Mackenzie Bell, *op. cit.*, pp. 88–93; *Fam. Lttrs.*, p. 122; Lttr. of Dec. 10, 1883, Penn. Hist. Soc., Gratz MS; Baum and Gohdes, *op. cit.;* Ash. MS B II 1384, p. 137 (published in part in Gosse, *Critical Kit-Kats* [1896]); Lttr. of Apr. 3, 1883, Ash. MS 1386, pp. 17–18.

6. Troxell (*Three Rossettis . . .* [1937], p. 172). The carol appeared in *Wide-Awake* (Dec., 1882), pp. 102–103. For a complete account of the transaction, see *Rossetti-Macmillan Letters,* Lttrs. 138–143.

7. After her death, Bryant bothered William, whose letter of reply, refusing aid and reprimanding him for selling Christina's letters, was promptly offered to a dealer, who inserted the passage relating to Christina in his catalogue (*Remin.*, II, 510–511). Her letter to Bryant quoted in my text is derived from Ash. MS 1386, pp. 3–4. See also *Rossetti-Macmillan Letters,* Lttr. 149, n. 1, and S. Gorley Putt, "Christina Rossetti, Alms-giver," *English* (Autumn, 1961), pp. 222–223.

8. Lttr. of Jan. 30, 1883, Ash. MS B II, 1386, p. 135. For the article see *Century Magazine* (Feb., 1884), 27:566–573.

9. The complete series of Christina's hitherto unpublished letters to Arthur (Harold Ross. MS) appeared for the first time in my article, "Christina Rossetti's Correspondence with Her Nephew: Some Unpublished Letters," *N&Q* (Dec., 1959), n.s., no. 11, 6:425–432.

10. G. M. Hatton, Bod. MS B. Litt. d. 491, Feb. 16, 1955, App. B, p. 117. See my text, p. 72. But *One Seaside Grave* does include the last of the three stanzas comprising *From the Antique* of Feb. 8, 1853 (Bod. MS Don e 1/7, p. 59). The first stanza remained unpublished. The second provided the theme and structure for the later *One Seaside Grave,* but with alterations in the diction and imagery:

From the Antique (1853)	*One Seaside Grave* (1884)
Forgetful of the roses,	Unmindful of the roses,
Forgetful of the thorn;	Unmindful of the thorn,
So sleeping, as reposes	A reaper tired reposes
A child until the dawn.	Among his gathered corn:
So sleeping without morn.	So might I, till the morn!

11. Christina's marginal note in Aunt Eliza's copy: "My first roundel."

12. Pnkll. MS A 11. Both poem and letter were first published in *TLS* (June 26, 1959), p. 389.

CHAPTER 19 (PAGES 371–390)

1. Brit. Mus., Ash. MS 1386, p. 23. The unpublished material in the remainder of this chapter has been drawn from this source and from Bod. Ross. MS 47, supplemented by the other sources for unpublished material already referred to. Printed works include Mackenzie Bell, *Christina Rossetti* (1898); Janet C. Troxell, *The Three Rossettis* (1937); *Fam. Lttrs.;* Scott's *Notes;* and *Remin.*, II.

2. *Rossetti-Macmillan Letters,* Lttr. 150.

3. Lttr. of May 24, 1887, Bod. Ross. MS 47. Gilchrist's book is Herbert Gilchrist's biography of his mother, *Life of Anne Gilchrist,* published in 1887.

4. *Seek and Find,* p. 53; *Time Flies,* p. 245.

5. Ford Maddox [Ford] Hueffer, *Ancient Lights* (1911), p. 66. The American title is *Memories and Impressions.*

6. Among writers who have put forward this view are Violet Hunt and Marya Zaturenska. It is predominantly that of Virginia Moore in *Distinguished Women Writers* (1934).

7. Hueffer, *op. cit.;* Gosse, *Critical Kit-Kats* (1898), p. 158. Cecil Y. Lang, *The Swinburne Letters,* 6 vols. (1959–1961), Vol. VI, pp. 77–78. Katherine Tynan (Hinkson), two articles in *The Bookman:* "Christina Rossetti" (Feb., 1895), pp. 28–29, and "Santa Christina" (Jan., 1912), pp. 185–190. The latter, with a reproduction of Gabriel's 1866 portrait of his sister on the cover, is a special Christina Rossetti number. Virginia Woolf, "I Am Christina Rossetti," *Second Common Reader* (1932), pp. 260–261. Signora Olivia Rossetti Agresti, "The Anecdotage of an Interpreter," unpublished MS.

8. Lttr. 177, Dec. 10, 1895, Bod. MS Don e 76.

CHAPTER 20 (PAGES 391–408)

1. *Athenæum* (Dec. 16, 1893), pp. 842–843; *Sat. Review* (Feb. 22, 1896), 81:196.

2. University of Texas Collection. In Mrs. Hinkson's article in *The Bookman* (Feb., 1895) she mentions Christina's aversion to being interviewed. "I don't like the custom of interviewing," Mrs. Hinkson reports Christina as saying during the visit she paid her at Torrington Square, "because it leads to self-consciousness, and the interviewed person is always turning out the best side for the public" (p. 29). As Mrs. Hinkson was leaving, Christina thanked her again for giving up the idea of a formal interview.

3. The diary is partially reproduced in the Appendix to the *Fam. Lttrs.,* pp. 218–222. Additional accounts of Christina's closing days may be found in Bell, *Christina Rossetti* (1898), and in *Remin.,* Vol. II, pp. 530–542.

4. Lttr. of Sept. 17, 1894, Pnkll. MS, first published by me in *TLS,* June 26, 1959.

5. Letters of Oct. 31 and Nov. 4, 1894, Bod. Ross. MS 54.

6. *Op. cit.* This issue (Feb. 22, 1896) was the one in which William was castigated for publishing much of his sister's unpublished poetry in his edition of *New Poems.*

7. He shows up in the record only once previously, as the editor of an anthology of religious poetry to which Christina contributed in 1879. Bell, p. 344.

8. The holograph MS of this poem was exhibited under a glass case at the entrance to the Manuscript Room of the British Museum, 1958–1960. On back, under the dateline 13/2/95, William wrote, "I found these verses at Christina's house in a millboard case containing some recent memoranda, etc.—nothing of old date—the verses must I think be the last Christina ever wrote—perhaps late in 1893, or early in 1894."

APPENDIX (PAGES 409–410)

1. Bod. Ross. MS 55.

2. Brit. Mus., Ash. MS 5080, p. lxxiii. First published by Cecil Y. Lang, *The Swinburne Letters,* 6 vols. (1959–1961), Vol. VI, pp. 79–80.

SELECTIVE BIBLIOGRAPHY

MANUSCRIPT SOURCES

Mostly unpublished holographs, but includes some printed books with autograph notes.

I. Angeli Collection

A. The Rossetti Papers on loan to the Bodleian Library. The collection consists of family letters and documents, including thirty unpublished letters by Christina, seven by W. B. Scott, and a vast miscellaneous assortment written throughout the nineteenth and part of the twentieth century by members of the Rossetti family, their friends, acquaintances, and business associates. A number of these letters contain references to Christina and her work.

B. Unpublished portions of Christina's diary for her mother, 1881–1882.

C. Some unpublished pages of William M. Rossetti's diary.

D. Unpublished Memoirs, "Anecdotage of an Interpreter," by Olivia Madox Rossetti Agresti.

II. E. E. Bissell Collection

A. Two letters from Christina Rossetti to Mrs. Adolf Heimann. One letter to Dr. Heimann.

B. *A Pageant and Other Poems,* first edition belonging to Frances L. Rossetti, with autograph notes by Christina and William M. Rossetti.

III. Bodleian Library Collection

A. A series of nine notebooks containing Christina Rossetti's poems from 1845 to 1856.

B. Eight letters from Christina Rossetti to Miss May of 12 Chester Place, Regent's Park.

C. The F. G. Stephens Papers, including two letters from Christina Rossetti to F. G. Stephens, two letters from James Collinson, and five letters from W. M. Rossetti to Stephens.

D. Letter from Christina Rossetti to the Reverend Horder, published by Mackenzie Bell in *Christina Rossetti* (1898).

E. An edition of the unpublished poems of Christina Rossetti by G. M. Hatton (B. Litt. thesis, St. Hilda's College, 1955).

IV. British Museum Collection

A. Thomas J. Wise, *The Ashley Library:* A Catalogue of Printed Books, Manuscripts, and Autographed Letters Collected by Thomas James Wise, 9 vols. (1922–1927), printed for private circulation only. It lists the following Rossetti manuscripts:

1. Notebook containing Christina Rossetti's early poems from 1842 to 1845.
2. A series of six notebooks containing Christina Rossetti's poems from 1856 to 1866.
3. Bound holograph manuscript of *Sing-Song* with Christina Rossetti's illustrations in pencil.
4. Holograph poems: *An Apple Gathering, Mirrors of Life and Death, He and She.*
5. *Il Rosseggiar dell' Oriente,* a series of twenty-one holograph poems written in Italian (1862–1868) by Christina Rossetti (untranslated except for a few poems).
6. Four holograph sonnets, *By Way of Remembrance.*
7. A volume of thirteen unpublished letters from Christina Rossetti to A. C. Swinburne, D. G. Rossetti, T. Watts-Dunton, and Others.
8. Five letters from Christina Rossetti to Edmund Gosse, partially reproduced in *Critical Kit-Kats* (1896).
9. A letter from Christina Rossetti to D. G. Rossetti.
10. A letter from Christina Rossetti to A. C. Swinburne.
11. A volume of seventeen letters from W. B. Scott to A. C. Swinburne, T. Watts-Dunton, and others. Includes a letter from Alice Boyd to A. C. Swinburne.
12. A letter from Maria Rossetti to A. C. Swinburne.
13. A letter from W. M. Rossetti to A. C. Swinburne.
14. A volume of ten letters from D. G. Rossetti to A. C. Swinburne, 1869–1870.
15. Two letters from Frances L. Rossetti to D. G. Rossetti.
16. Letter from A. C. Swinburne to W. M. Rossetti referring to Christina, published by Cecil Y. Lang in *The Swinburne Letters,* 6 vols. (1959–1961).

B. An album containing fourteen letters from Christina Rossetti to F. S. Ellis and one to [William Bryant], published in part by L. M. Packer in *Western Humanities Review* (Summer, 1962).

C. Holograph poem by Christina Rossetti, *Sleeping at Last,* with W. M. Rossetti's autograph note relating to date of composition.

V. Sir Sidney Cockerell Collection

Among other items the collection includes an unpublished letter from Christina Rossetti to an unknown recipient, and two unpublished letters from D. G. Rossetti, one to Frances L. Rossetti, the other to an unknown recipient, as well as many other letters written by D. G. Rossetti, most of them published.

VI. Dennis Collection

A. Unpublished poem by Christina Rossetti with note by W. M. Rossetti (listed No. 59 in Appendix B to *Works*).

B. Notebook containing poems by Christina Rossetti from March 21, 1859, to Dec. 31, 1860. Includes holograph of *Goblin Market* with revisions and variations from the published text, and also includes an unpublished fragment (listed No. 58 in Appendix B to *Works*).

VII. Huntington Library Collection

A. Leaf from Christina Rossetti's manuscript notebook (Ashley Li-

brary 1364/3) containing holograph of *Up-hill* and W. M. Rossetti's explanatory note relating to purchase of the leaf.

B. Twenty-eight holograph sonnets by Christina Rossetti, *Later Life,* published in *A Pageant and Other Poems* (1881).

C. Holograph poem by Christina Rossetti, *Behold the Man.*

D. Prose tale by Christina Rossetti, "A Safe Investment," published in *Commonplace* (1870).

E. Prose tale by Christina Rossetti, *Maude* (written 1850, published 1897).

F. Six unpublished letters from Christina Rossetti to Frederick Locker, F. L. Furnivall, T. G. Hake, A. L. S., J. T. Fields, and Mrs. Fields.

G. Sir Walter Scott manuscript of *Harold the Hardy* with autographs, including a couplet by Christina Rossetti. Letter from W. M. Rossetti to Locker commenting on Christina's couplet.

H. Letter from D. G. to W. M. Rossetti.

I. A volume of letters from D. G. Rossetti to F. M. Brown, 1864.

J. Holograph essay by Edmund Gosse entitled, "Miss Christina Rossetti," first printed with alterations in *The Century Magazine* (June, 1893) and reproduced in *Critical Kit-Kats* (1896).

K. A volume consisting of a miscellaneous assortment of letters written by members of the Pre-Raphaelite Brotherhood.

VIII. MISCELLANEOUS

A. Letter from Maria Rossetti to Mrs. Bevir commenting on *The Divine Comedy,* owned by David Gould.

B. Letter from Christina Rossetti to Constance M. [Chohueler] in a first edition of *Pageant* (1881), owned by L. M. Packer.

IX. O'CONNOR LIBRARY COLLECTION

A. First edition of *Sing-Song* containing Italian translations by Christina Rossetti written in the margins, five additional poems (published in 1894), and some stanzas added in pencil to the printed verses.

B. *The Sacred Harp* (1836), an anthology of religious poetry, with Christina Rossetti's marginal comments in pencil.

C. Presentation copy of Herbert Gilchrist's *Life of Anne Gilchrist* to W. M. Rossetti; contains Rossetti's penciled correction of dates and other marginal notes.

X. PENKILL LIBRARY COLLECTION

A. Three unpublished poems by Christina Rossetti.

B. Three letters from Christina Rossetti to Alice Boyd. One letter from W. M. Rossetti to Alice Boyd discussing Christina. (This group partially reproduced by L. M. Packer in *TLS,* June 26, 1959.)

C. Fragment of W. B. Scott's unpublished 1854 autobiography.

D. A packet of unpublished letters from W. B. Scott to Alice Boyd, 1869–1870.

E. Four unpublished letters from F. S. Ellis to Alice Boyd.

F. Manuscript book containing Christina Rossetti's *Sing-Song* with Alice Boyd's illustrations.

G. Scrapbook inscribed "MS Poetry, 1869, 70, 71," containing W. B. Scott's poems and rough drafts of some poems by D. G. Rossetti.

H. Autograph album containing miscellaneous assortment of letters written to W. B. Scott.

I. Album containing newspaper clippings and criticism of W. B. Scott's pictures and literary works.

XI. Pennsylvania Historical Society

A. Three unpublished letters by Christina Rossetti, one to Miss Proctor, the others to unknown recipients.

B. Holograph MS of a poem, *Passing Away,* signed Christina G. Rossetti and sent with her compliments to Miss Graham.

XII. Polidori Documents

Contains photographed copies of papal bull and other documents pertaining to the history of the Polidori family, and written copies of baptismal and marriage records from the cathedral at Orvieto and various churches in Orvieto and Pisa. A letter of February 8, 1960, from Count Geoffredo Luigi Polidori gives information about the origin of the Polidori family in A.D. 800 and traces the family history to the present, citing relevant passages from various Italian publications.

XIII. Harold Rossetti Library Collection

A. An album containing William M. Rossetti's family correspondence. Contains many references to Christina Rossetti.

B. Twelve letters and a fragment from Christina Rossetti to Arthur Rossetti, 1886–1889, published in part by L. M. Packer, *N&Q* (Dec. 1959).

C. Christina Rossetti's Birthday Book.

D. Two letters from H. W. Longfellow to Maria Rossetti.

E. One letter from Charles B. Cayley to Maria Rossetti.

F. Copy of Main's *A Treasury of English Sonnets* containing Christina Rossetti's dedicatory sonnet to her mother, a letter from D. G. to Frances L. Rossetti, and two sonnets with illustrations by D. G. Rossetti.

G. Presentation copy of Maria Rossetti's *A Shadow of Dante* with copious marginal notes and illustrations in pencil by Christina Rossetti.

H. Manuscript notes by Christina Rossetti commenting on Genesis and Exodus.

I. A copy of Keble's *Christian Year* (1837) with illustrations in pencil and marginal notes by Christina Rossetti.

XIV. Oliver Rossetti Library Collection

A. Pencil drawing of an octopus by Christina Rossetti.

B. Another presentation copy of Maria Rossetti's *A Shadow of Dante* with marginal notes by Christina Rossetti commenting on the text.

XV. University of Texas Collection

A. Fifty-two letters from Christina to W. M. and D. G. Rossetti, C. A. and Kate Howell, the Dalziel brothers, C. F. Murray, Katherine (Tynan) Hinkson, Mrs. Garnett, Frederick Shields, and others.

B. An autograph volume, *Letter and Spirit* (1883), by Christina Rossetti.

C. An autograph volume, *A Pageant and Other Poems* (1881), by Christina Rossetti, with variations in the text from the published

version. The sonnet sequence *Later Life* not included (see Huntington Library Collection).

D. First edition of *Time Flies* (1885) by Christina Rossetti, containing author's marginal notes identifying persons and places mentioned in the text.

XVI. PRE-RAPHAELITE COLLECTION BELONGING TO THE WILMINGTON SOCIETY OF FINE ARTS.
Seven unpublished letters from Christina Rossetti to Mrs. Adolf Heimann.

XVII. YALE UNIVERSITY COLLECTION
Nine letters from Christina Rossetti to William Bryant; extracts published by S. G. Putt, *English* (Autumn, 1961).

PUBLISHED SOURCES

Unless otherwise stated, the place of publication of books is London.

I. BIBLIOGRAPHICAL AIDS

Anderson, J. P., Bibliography in *Christina Rossetti* by Mackenzie Bell (1898), pp. 339–353.

Bateson, F. W., ed., *The Cambridge Bibliography of English Literature,* 4 vols. (Cambridge, Eng., 1940), Vol. III and Supplement Vol. V.

Ehrsam, T. G., and R. H. Deily, *Bibliographies of Twelve Victorian Authors* (New York, 1936).

Fredeman, William E., *Pre-Raphaelitism: A Biblio-Critical Study* (Cambridge, Mass., in press).

Houghton, Walter, "British Periodicals of the Victorian Age: Bibliographies and Indexes," *Library Trends,* Vol. 7, No. 4 (April, 1959), pp. 554–565.

———, ed., *The Wellesley Index to Victorian Periodicals, 1824–1900* (in preparation).

Jones, Howard M., "The Pre-Raphaelites," in *The Victorian Poets,* ed. F. E. Faverty (Cambridge, Mass., 1956).

Templeman, William D., *Bibliographies of Studies in Victorian Literature for the Thirteen Years, 1932–1944* (Urbana, Ill., 1956).

"Victorian Bibliographies," in *Modern Philology* (1932–1956 [1933–1957]); in *Victorian Studies* (1957 [1958]).

Wise, T. J., *The Ashley Library,* a catalogue of printed books, manuscripts, and autograph letters, collected by Thomas James Wise, 11 vols. (1922–1936), printed for private circulation only. Vols. IV, VIII, IX (index vol.)

Wright, Austin, *Bibliographies of Studies in Victorian Literature for the Ten Years, 1945–1954* (Urbana, Ill., 1956).

II. CHRISTINA ROSSETTI

A. *Works*

1. POETRY

Verses by Christina G. Rossetti. Dedicated to her mother. Privately printed by Gaetano Polidori (1847).

Goblin Market, and Other Poems. With two designs by D. G. Rossetti (1862). 2nd. ed. (1865).

The Prince's Progress, and Other Poems. With two designs by D. G. Rossetti (1866).

Sing-Song, a Nursery Rhyme Book. With 120 illustrations by Arthur Hughes (1872).

Goblin Market, The Prince's Progress, and Other Poems. New ed. (1875).

A Pageant, and Other Poems (1881).

Poems. With four designs by D. G. Rossetti. New and enlarged ed. (1890).

Verses. Reprinted from *Called to be Saints, Time Flies,* and *The Face of the Deep* (1893).

New Poems, by Christina Rossetti hitherto unpublished or uncollected., ed. William Michael Rossetti (1896).

The Poetical Works of Christina Georgina Rossetti, with Memoir and Notes, ed. W. M. Rossetti (1904).

2. PROSE

Contributions to the *Imperial Dictionary of Universal Biography,* ed. John Francis Waller (1857–1863).

"Dante, an English Classic," *Churchman's Shilling Magazine,* Vol. II (1867), pp. 200–205.

Commonplace and Other Short Stories (1870).

Annus Domini, a prayer for each day of the year, founded on a text of Holy Scripture (1874).

Speaking Likenesses. With pictures . . . by Arthur Hughes (1874).

Seek and Find. A double series of short studies of the Benedicite (1879).

Called to be Saints: the Minor Festivals devotionally studied (1881).

Letter and Spirit. Notes on the Commandments (1883).

"Dante. The Poet illustrated out of the Poem," *The Century,* Vol. XXVII, N.S. Vol. V. (Feb., 1884), pp. 566–573.

Time Flies: a reading Diary (1885).

The Face of the Deep: a devotional commentary on the Apocalypse (1892).

The Rossetti Birthday Book, ed. Olivia Rossetti [Agresti] (1896).

Maude. With an introduction by W. M. Rossetti (1897). Written in 1850.

3. PUBLISHED CORRESPONDENCE. (Works cited contain one or more letters written by Christina Rossetti.)

Bell, Mackenzie, *Christina Rossetti* (1898).

Curti, M. E., "A Letter of Christina Rossetti," *Modern Language Notes,* Vol. LI, No. 7 (Nov., 1936), pp. 439–440.

Gilchrist, Herbert H., *Anne Gilchrist, Her Life and Writings,* with a Prefatory Note by W. M. Rossetti (1887).

Gosse, Sir Edmund, *Critical Kit-Kats* (1896).

Packer, Lona Mosk, "Christina Rossetti's Speaking Likenesses," *Times Literary Supplement* (June 5, 1959), p. 337.

———, "Christina Rossetti and Alice Boyd of Penkill Castle," *Times Literary Supplement* (June 26, 1959), p. 389.

———, "Christina Rossetti's Correspondence with Her Nephew: Some Unpublished Letters," *Notes & Queries,* N.S. Vol. 6, No. 11 [Vol. 204 of the continuous series] (Dec., 1959), pp. 425–432.

———, "F. S. Ellis and the Rossettis: A Publishing Venture and Misadventure," *Western Humanities Review,* Vol. XVI, No. 3 (Summer, 1962), pp. 243–253.

———, *The Rossetti-Macmillan Letters: Some 133 Unpublished Letters Written to Alexander Macmillan, F. S. Ellis, and Others, by Dante Gabriel, Christina, and William Michael Rossetti, 1861–1889* (Berkeley and Los Angeles: University of California Press, 1963).

"A Poetic Trio and Their Needlework," *Athenæum,* Part 2 (Nov. 8, 1897), pp. 193–194.

Putt, S. Gorley, "Christina Rossetti, Alms-giver," *English,* Vol. XIII (Autumn, 1961), pp. 222–223.

Rossetti, William Michael, ed., *Dante Gabriel Rossetti: His Family Letters, with a Memoir,* 2 vols. (1895).

———, *Ruskin: Rossetti: Preraphaelitism: 1854–1862* (1899).

———, *The Preraphaelite Diaries and Letters* (1900).

———, *The Rossetti Papers, 1862–70* (1903).

———, *The Family Letters of Christina Georgina Rossetti* (1908).

Troxell, Janet C., *Three Rossettis: Unpublished Letters to and from Dante Gabriel, Christina, William* (Cambridge, Mass., 1937).

B. *Biographical and Critical Studies*

Angeli, Helen Rossetti, "Aunt Christina: An Elusive Poet-Mystic" (Dec. 5, 1930). Newspaper clipping, source unknown.

Bell, Mackenzie, *Christina Rossetti* (1898).

Belloc, Elizabeth, "Christina Rossetti," *Catholic World,* Vol. 155 (Sept., 1942), pp. 674–678.

Birkhead, Edith, *Christina Rossetti and Her Poetry* (New York, 1930).

Bowra, C. M., "Christina Rossetti" in *The Romantic Imagination* (1949).

Campaigner at Home (anonymous). "Our Camp in the Woodland: A Day with the Gentle Poets," *Fraser's,* Vol. LXX (Aug., 1864), pp. 204–214.

Cary, Elizabeth L., *The Rossettis: Dante Gabriel and Christina* (New York, 1900).

Clutton-Brock, A., "Christina Rossetti," in *More Essays on Religion* (New York, 1928).

Dallas, Eneas Sweetland, "Modern Poets," *The Times* (Jan. 11, 1865), p. 12, col. 5.

De la Mare, Walter, "Christina Rossetti" in *Essays by Divers Hands, being the Transactions of the Society,* Royal Society of Literature, ed. G. K. Chesterton, N.S. Vol. VI (1926).

Dubslaff, Friedrich, *Die Sprächform der Lyrik Christina Rossettis,* (Halle, 1933).

Elton, Oliver, "The Rossettis," in *A Survey of English Literature, 1830–1880,* 2 vols. (1924).

Evans, B. Ifor, "The Sources of Christina Rossetti's 'Goblin Market,'" *Modern Language Review,* Vol. XXVIII (April, 1933), pp. 156–165.

Forman, Harry Buxton, "Criticism on Contemporaries," *Tinsley's,* Vol. V (Aug., Sept., Oct., 1869): Part 1 (Christina Rossetti), pp. 59–69; Part 2 (D. G. Rossetti), pp. 142–151; Part 3 (W. M. Rossetti), pp. 276–281. Reproduced in *Our Living Poets* (1871).

Garlitz, Barbara, "Christina Rossetti's Sing-Song and Nineteenth Century Children's Poetry," *PMLA,* Vol. LXX, No. 3 (June, 1955), pp. 539–543.

Garnett, Richard, "Christina Georgina Rossetti," in *Dictionary of National Biography,* Vol. XVII (1909).

Gilchrist, Grace, "Christina Rossetti," *Good Words,* Vol. XXXVII (Dec., 1896), pp. 822–826.

Gosse, Sir Edmund, "Christina Rossetti," *The Century,* Vol. XLVI, N.S. Vol. XXIV (June, 1893), pp. 211–217.

———, *Critical Kit-Kats* (1896).

Hinkson, Katherine (Tynan), "Some Reminiscences of Christina Rossetti," *The Bookman* [New York], Vol. I (Feb., 1895), pp. 28–29.

———, "Santa Christina," *The Bookman* [London], Vol. XLI Supp. (Jan., 1912), pp. 185–190.

Hueffer [Ford], Ford Madox, "Christina Rossetti and Pre-Raphaelite Love," in *Ancient Lights* (1911); published in the U.S. as *Memories and Impressions* (1911).

———, "The Character of Christina Rossetti," *Fortnightly Review,* Vol. XCV, N.S. Vol. LXXXIX (March, 1911), pp. 422–429.

Lewis, Naomi, "Introduction," in *Christina Rossetti,* Pocket Poets (1959), pp. 5–10.

Madeleva, Sister Mary M., "The Religious Poetry of the 19th Century," in *Chaucer's Nuns* (New York, 1925).

Mason, Eugene, "Two Christian Poets, Christina G. Rossetti and Paul Verlaine," in *A Book of Preferences in Literature* (1915).

Meynell, Alice, "Christina Rossetti," *New Review,* Vol. XII (Feb., 1895), pp. 201–206.

———, "Christina Rossetti," in *Prose and Poetry* (1947).

Moore, Virginia, "Christina Rossetti's Centennial," in *Distinguished Women Writers* (New York, 1934).

More, Paul Elmer, "Christina Rossetti," in *Shelburne Essays, Third Series* (New York, 1905).

Morse-Boycott, D. L., "Christina Rossetti," in *Lead, Kindly Light: Studies of the saints and heroes of the Oxford Movement* (New York, 1933).

Nash, Rev. J. J. Glendinning, *A Memorial Sermon Preached at Christ Church, Woburn Square, for the Late Christina Georgina Rossetti* (1895).

Noble, James Ashcroft, "The Burden of Christina Rossetti," in *Impressions and Memories* (1895).

Norton, Caroline, "Goblin Market and Other Poems," *Macmillan's,* Vol. VIII (Sept., 1863), pp. 65–69.

"Not All Roses in the Victorian Nursery," *Times Literary Supplement,* Children's Section (May 29, 1959), p. xi.

Packer, Lona Mosk, "Symbol and Reality in Christina Rossetti's *Goblin Market, PMLA,* Vol. LXXIII, No. 4, part 1 (Sept., 1958), pp. 375–385.

———, "The Protestant Existentialism of Christina Rossetti," *Notes & Queries,* N.S. Vol. 6, No. 6 [Vol. 204 of the continuous series] (June, 1959), pp. 213–215.

———, in *Collier's Encyclopedia,* Vol. XX, new ed. (1962), p. 225.

———, "Christina Rossetti's 'Songs in a Cornfield': A Misprint Uncorrected," *Notes & Queries,* N.S. Vol. 9, No. 3 [Vol. 207 of the continuous series] (March, 1962), pp. 97–100.

———, "Swinburne and Christina Rossetti: Atheist and Anglican," *University of Toronto Quarterly* (Oct., 1963).

(For additional studies see Packer under Christina Rossetti, Part II, A, 3, of the "Published Sources" of this Bibliography.)

Proctor, Ellen A., *A Brief Memoir of Christina Georgina Rossetti* (1895).

Ricks, Christopher, "'O Where Are You Going?': W. H. Auden and Christina Rossetti," *Notes & Queries,* N.S. Vol. 7, No. 12 [Vol. 205 of the continuous series] (Dec., 1960), p. 472.

Robb, Nesca A., "Christina Rossetti," in *Four in Exile* (1945).

Rossetti, Geoffrey," Christina Rossetti," *Criterion,* Vol. X, No. 38 (Oct., 1930), pp. 95–117.

Rossetti, William Michael, *Some Reminiscences,* 2 vols. (1906).

———, ed., "Memoir," *The Poetical Works of Christina Georgina Rossetti* (1904).

———, *Chambers Encyclopedia,* Vol. VIII (1895), p. 815.

(For additional studies see W. M. Rossetti under Christina Rossetti, Part II, A, 3, of the "Published Sources" in this Bibliography.)

Rota, Felicina, *Amore, Sogno e Morte nella Poesia di Christina Rossetti* (Toreno, 1953).

Sandars, Mary F., *The Life of Christina Rossetti* (1930).

Sawtell, Margaret, *Christina Rossetti* (1955).

Sharp, William, "The Rossettis," *Fortnightly Review,* Vol. XLV, N.S. Vol XXXIX (March 1, 1886), pp. 414–430.

———, "Some Reminiscences of Christina Rossetti," *Atlantic Monthly,* Vol. LXXV (June, 1895), pp. 736–749. Reproduced in his *Papers Critical and Reminiscent* (1912).

Shove, Fredegond, *Christina Rossetti* (Cambridge, Eng., 1931).

Shuster, George, *The Catholic Spirit in Modern English Literature* (1922).

Sitwell, Edith, *English Women* (1942).

Stedman, F. C., *Victorian Poets* (1887).

Stuart, Dorothy M., *Christina Rossetti,* English Men of Letters Series (1930).

Swann, Thomas Burnett, *Wonder and Whimsey, the Fantastic World of Christina Rossetti* (Francestown, N.H., 1960).

Swinburne, Algernon C., "Dedication to Christina Rossetti," in *A Century of Roundels* (1883).

———, "A Ballad of Appeal to Christina G. Rossetti," in *A Midsummer Holiday and Other Poems* (1884).

———, "A New Year's Eve," in *A Channel Passage and Other Poems* (1904).

Symons, Arthur, "Christina G. Rossetti," in *The Poets and the Poetry of the Nineteenth Century,* ed. A. H. Miles, Vol. VII (1891–1897).

———, "Christina Rossetti," in *Studies in Two Literatures* (1897).

———, "The Rossettis," in *Dramatis Personae* (1923).

Thomas, Eleanor W., *Christina Georgina Rossetti* (New York, 1931).

Waller, R. D., *The Rossetti Family, 1824–54,* No. XXXVII, English Series No. 21 (Manchester, Eng., 1932).

Watts-Dunton, Theodore, "Christina Rossetti," in *Old Familiar Faces* (1916).

Winwar, Frances, *The Rossettis and Their Circle* (1933).

Woolf, Virginia, "I Am Christina Rossetti," in *Second Common Reader* (1932).

———, *A Writer's Diary,* ed. Leonard Woolf (New York, 1953).

Zaturenska, Marya, *Christina Rossetti* (New York, 1949).

III. General

Allchin, A. M., *The Silent Rebellion* (1958).

Angeli, Helen Rossetti, *Rossetti, His Friends and His Enemies* (1949).

———, *The Pre-Raphaelite Twilight: The Story of Charles Augustus Howell* (1954).

Anson, Peter F., *The Call of the Cloister* (1955).

Bancroft, Samuel, and Mary R. *The English Pre-Raphaelite Collection* (Wilmington, Del., 1962).

Baum, Paull F., *Dante Gabriel Rossetti's Letters to Fanny Cornforth* (1940).

———, and Gohdes, Clarence, *Letters of William Michael Rossetti . . . to Anne Gilchrist* (Durham, N.C., 1934).

Beerbohm, Max, *Rossetti and His Circle* (1922).

Benson, Arthur C., *Rossetti* (1904).

Bickley, Francis, *The Pre-Raphaelite Comedy* (1932).

Boyce, G. B., *Extracts from G. B. Boyce's Diaries, 1851–1875,* in The Old Water-Colour Society's Club 19th Annual Vol. (1941).

Buckler, William E., "'Once a Week' Under Samuel Lucas, 1855–65," *PMLA,* Vol. LXVII, No. 7 (Dec., 1952), pp. 924–941.

B[urne]-J[ones], G[eorgina], *Memorials of Edward Burne-Jones,* 2 vols. (1904).

Burroughs (Burrows), Henry W., *Half-Century of Christ Church, Albany Street,* privately printed (1887). See also E. Worksworth.

Caine, Hall, *Recollections of Dante Gabriel Rossetti* (1882). Revised reprint, 1928.

Cassidy, John A., "Robert Buchanan and the Fleshly Controversy," *PMLA,* Vol. LXVII, No. 2 (March, 1952), pp. 65–94.

Charteris, Evan, *The Life and Letters of Sir Edmund Gosse* (1931).

Christ Church, Albany Street, *Parish Magazine* (Jan. and Feb., 1924).

Church, R. W., *The Oxford Movement* (1909).

The Church of St. Mary Magdalene, Munster Square, A Record, 1852–1927 (Society of Peter and Paul, n. d.).

Cockshut, A. O. J., *Anglican Attitudes* (1959).

Cornish, F. W., *The English Church in the Nineteenth Century,* Vol. VIII (1910).

Dante Alighieri, *The Divine Comedy,* trans. Laurence Binyon; ed. Paola Milano (1947).

———, *The Inferno,* trans. John Ciardi (New York, 1953).

———, "The New Life" (La Vita Nuova), trans. Dante Gabriel Rossetti in *The Early Italian Poets* (1861), rev. edition, *Dante and His Circle* (1874). Reprinted in *The Collected Works of Dante Gabriel Rossetti,* 2 vols. (1901), Vol. II, pp. 30–95.

Darton, Harvey, *Children's Books in England* (Cambridge, Eng., 1932).

Dodsworth, William, four pamphlets privately printed, now in the archives of Christ Church, Albany Street, London: Two Sermons (1850); An Address on the Gorham Case (n.d.); A Letter to the Rev. F. B. Pusey (May 7, 1850).

Doughty, Oswald, *Letters of Dante Gabriel Rossetti to His Publisher, F. S. Ellis* (1928).

———, *A Victorian Romantic: Dante Gabriel Rossetti* (1928); American ed. (New Haven, Conn., 1949); new ed. (1960).

Dunn, H. T., *Recollections of Dante Gabriel Rossetti and His Circle* (1904).

Eggleston, Edward, "The Blessings of Piracy," *Century,* Vol. XXIII, N.S. Vol. I (April, 1882), pp. 943–945.

Eliot, T. S., "Religion and Literature," in *Selected Essays* (1951).
Francis, John Collins, " 'Macmillan's Magazine,' " *Notes & Queries,* No. 8 [Eleventh Series] (Feb. 19, 1910), pp. 141–142.
Fredeman, William E., "Pre-Raphaelites in Caricature . . . ," *Burlington Magazine,* Vol. CII (Dec., 1960), pp. 523–529.
Gaunt, William, *The Pre-Raphaelite Tragedy* (1942).
The Germ (Jan., Feb., April, May, 1850).
———, "A Facsimile Reprint," with an introduction by W. M. Rossetti (1901).
Gilchrist, Alexander, *Life of William Blake,* 2 vols. (1863).
Glynn-Grylls, R., "The Correspondence of F. G. Stephens," *Times Literary Supplement* (April 5 and 12, 1957).
Goodman, Margaret, *Sisterhoods in the Church of England* (1863).
Gosse, Sir Edmund, *Algernon Charles Swinburne* (1917).
Hake, Thomas Gordon, *Memoirs of Eighty Years* (1892).
———, and Compton-Rickett, Arthur, eds., *Life and Letters of Theodore Watts-Dunton,* 2 vols. (1916).
———, *The Letters of A. C. Swinburne* (1918).
Hill, George Birbeck, ed., *Letters of Dante Gabriel Rossetti to William Allingham, 1854–70* (1897).
Hone, William, *The Every-Day Book,* 3 vols. (1825).
Hopkins, Gerard Manley, *Correspondence of Gerard Manley Hopkins and Richard Watson Dixon,* ed. Claude Colleer Abbott (Oxford, 1935).
———, *Notebooks and Papers,* ed. Humphrey House (Oxford, 1937).
———, *Further Letters of Gerard Manley Hopkins,* ed. Claude Colleer Abbott (Oxford, 1938). (See also below, Austin Warren.)
Horne, Herbert P., *William Bell Scott, Poet, Painter, and Critic.* Reprint from *The Hobby Horse* (1891).
Hough, Graham, *The Last Romantics* (1949).
Howitt, Mary, *An Autobiography,* ed. Margaret Howitt, 2 vols. (1889).
Hudson, Derek, "The Pre-Raphaelites," in *The Forgotten King* (1960).
Hueffer [Ford], Ford Madox. *Ford Madox Brown* (1896).
———, Rossetti, *A Critical Essay* (1896).
———, *The Pre-Raphaelite Brotherhood* (1907).
Hunt, Holman, *Pre-Raphaelitism and the Pre-Raphaelite Brotherhood,* 2 vols. (London, 1905).
Hunt, Violet, *The Wife of Rossetti* (1932).
"International Copyright in America," *Athenæum* (July, 1881).
Ironsides, Robin, *Pre-Raphaelite Painters* (1948).
James, William, *The Varieties of Religious Experience* (1902).
Knight, Joseph, *Life of Dante Gabriel Rossetti* (1887).
Lafourcade, Georges, *La Jeunesse de Swinburne, 1837–67,* 2 vols. (Oxford, 1928).
———, *Swinburne: A Literary Biography* (1932).
Lang, Cecil Y., *The Swinburne Letters,* 6 vols. (New Haven, Conn., 1959–1961).
Lidden, H. P., *The Life of Edward Bouverie Pusey,* 4 vols. (1893–1897).
Mackail, H. W., *The Life of William Morris,* 2 vols. (1899).
Macmillan, George A., ed., *The Letters of Alexander Macmillan,* printed for private circulation (Glasgow, 1908).
Marillier, H. C., *Dante Gabriel Rossetti* (1899).
Megroz, R. L., *Dante Gabriel Rossetti* (1928).
Mills, Ernestine, *The Life and Letters of Frederick Shields* (1912).

Newman, John Henry, "Prospects of the Anglican Church," in *Essays Critical and Historical* (1895).

Newspaper History 1785–1935, reprinted from 150th anniversary number of the *Times,* Jan. 1, 1935 (1935).

Packer, Lona Mosk, "'The Gospel of Intensity': William Rossetti and the Quilter Controversy," *Victorian Studies* (Dec., 1963).

Parliamentary Debates on Copyright Act: evidence taken before the Copyright Commission of 1876, and Report of the Commission on Home, Colonial, and International Copyrights (1878), Vol. 24 [of official publication of laws], p. 163.

Purves, John, "Dante Gabriel Rossetti: Letters to Miss Alice Boyd," *Fortnightly Review,* Vol. CXXIX, N.S. Vol. CXXIII (May 1, 1928), pp. 577–605.

Quilter, Harry, *Preferences in Art, Life, and Literature* (1892).

Rossetti, Dante Gabriel, *Collected Works,* ed. W. M. Rossetti, 2 vols. (1887–1888).

———, *The Works of Dante Gabriel Rossetti,* ed. W. M. Rossetti (1911). (For correspondence see above under Baum, Doughty, Hill, and Purves, and in Part II, A, 3 of the "Published Sources" in this Bibliography under Packer, W. M. Rossetti, and Troxell.)

Rossetti, Maria, *A Shadow of Dante* (1871).

Rossetti, William Michael, *Swinburne's Poems and Ballads, A Criticism* (1866).

———, *Fine Art, Chiefly Contemporary* (1867).

———, "William Bell Scott and Modern British Poetry," *Macmillan's Magazine,* Vol. XXXIII (March, 1876), pp. 418–429.

———, *Dante Gabriel Rossetti as Designer and Writer* (1889).

———, *Gabriele Rossetti, a Versified Autobiography* (1901). (For additional works edited by W. M. Rossetti see above under Dante Gabriel Rossetti, and under Christina Rossetti, Part II, A, 1 and 3 of the "Published Sources" of this bibliography.)

Ruskin, John, *Pre-Raphaelitism* (1851). Reprinted in *The Complete Works of John Ruskin,* ed. E. T. Cook and A. Wedderburn, 39 vols. (1903–1912), Vol. XII, pp. 338–393.

———, "The Pre-Raphaelite Artists," Letters to the *Times* (1851, 1854), in Vol. XII, pp. 318–335.

Scott, William Bell, *Hades, or the Transit: and the Progress of Mind* (1838).

———, *The Year of the World* (1846).

———, *Memoir of David Scott* (Edinburgh, 1850).

———, *Poems* (1854).

———, *Albert Dürer, His Life and Works* (1869).

———, *Poems* (1875).

———, *Poet's Harvest Home, Being One Hundred Short Poems* (1882).

———, *Illustrations to the King's Quair of King James I of Scotland.* Painted on the Staircase of Penkill Castle, Ayrshire, June 1865 to August 1868. Privately printed (1887).

———, *Autobiographical Notes of the Life of William Bell Scott,* ed. W. Minto, 2 vols. (1892).

"Mr. William Bell Scott, Painter and Poet," in "Public Men of the North" Series, *Northern Examiner,* No. XII (Nov. 25, 1854).

"William Bell Scott, Poet and Painter," *London Quarterly Review,* Vol. XLV (Oct., 1875), pp. 149–167.

(For more articles about Scott see this section above, under W. M. Rossetti, and below, under A. C. Swinburne.)

Sedgewick, Arthur G., "The Copyright Negotiations," *Century,* Vol. XXIII (March, 1882), pp. 667–671.

Sharp, William, *Dante Gabriel Rossetti* (1882).

Skelton, J., *The Table Talk of Shirley* (1895).

Smith, Cecil W., *Florence Nightingale* (1950).

Swinburne, Algernon Charles, *The Complete Works of Algernon Charles Swinburne,* eds. Sir Edmund Gosse and Thomas J. Wise, 20 vols. (1925–1927). The Bonchurch Edition.

———, "The New Terror" [an attack on Scott], *Fortnightly Review,* Vol. LVIII, N.S. Vol. LII (Dec., 1892), pp. 830–833. Reprinted in Bonchurch ed., Vol. VI, pp. 11–17.

(See also this section below, under Edmund Wilson, and under Swinburne in Part II B of the "Published Sources" in this Bibliography.)

Thale, Jerome, "The Third Rossetti," *Western Humanities Review,* Vol. X, No. 3 (Summer, 1956), pp. 277–284.

Trombley, Albert E., "Rossetti the Poet," *University of Texas Bulletin 2060* (Oct. 25, 1920).

Viets, Henry R., "John William Polidori, M. D., and Lord Byron—a Brief Interlude in 1816," *New England Journal of Medicine,* Vol. 264 (March 16, 1961), pp. 553–557.

Vincent, F. R., *Gabriele Rossetti in England* (Oxford, Eng., 1936).

Warren, Austin, "Gerard Manley Hopkins" in *Gerard Manley Hopkins* by the Kenyon Critics (New York, 1945). Reprint of articles in *The Kenyon Review,* Vol. VI (1944) with additional studies by A. Warren and F. R. Leavis.

Waugh, Evelyn, *Rossetti, His Life and Works* (1928).

Welby, T. W., *The Victorian Romantics* (1929).

Welland, D. S. R., *The Pre-Raphaelites in Literature and Art* (1953).

Wilenski, Reginald H., *John Ruskin: An Introduction to Further Study of His Life and Works* (1933).

Williams, Thomas Jay, *Priscilla Lydia Sellon* (New York, 1950).

———, "A Lost Treasure," *Holy Cross Magazine,* Vol. 67, No. 4 (April, 1956), pp. 100–104.

Wilson, Edmund, "Swinburne of Capheaton and Eton," *New Yorker,* Vol. XXXVIII, No. 3 (Oct. 6, 1962), pp. 165–200.

Worksworth, F., *The Life of Burrows* (1894).

(For periodical reviews of Christina Rossetti's published books, see T. G. Ehrsam and R. H. Deily, *Bibliographies of Twelve Victorian Authors* [New York, 1936], p. 196; and for additional reviews, short notices, eulogies, and obituaries, see J. P. Anderson's bibliography in Mackenzie Bell, *Christina Rossetti* [1898].)

INDEX

D1274500

FEB 5 - 1964